CURRENT RESEARCH IN PSYCHOLOGY:
A Book of Readings

CURRENT RESEARCH IN PSYCHOLOGY:
A Book of Readings

EDITED BY

HENRY CLAY LINDGREN
DONN BYRNE
FREDRICA LINDGREN

JOHN WILEY AND SONS, INC.

New York   London   Sydney   Toronto

Library of Congress Catalog Card Number: 73-130430
ISBN 0-471-53668-7 (cloth) ISBN 0-471-53669-5 (paper)

Printed in the United States of America

10 9 8 7 6 5 4 3 2 1

PREFACE

Textbooks for introductory courses in psychology are inevitably open to the criticism of superficiality. The chief problem is that such textbooks must, of necessity, cover a vast range of material in order to provide any decent coverage of the field. Unfortunately, psychology includes an infinite number of topics that are intriguing, provocative, and controversial, and that call for further exploration, but the authors must arbitrarily cut their discussions short and hurry on to the next topic, leaving the reader dissatisfied and unfulfilled, for an extended treatment of any one topic means that other topics, equally important, must be slighted.

Under these circumstances a book of readings can be of considerable help to the student, for it offers opportunities to explore at greater depth those areas of interest that are touched on lightly or glossed over in the main text. A selection of readings can, furthermore, fill out the picture of the psychological field by presenting papers that further discuss in detail issues presented in the main text.

There are two major routes for selecting and assembling papers for a book of readings. One is to assemble a sampling of classic statements and studies made by early and eminent leaders in the field, which can then serve as background material for an examination, through class discussion, of current trends and issues in psychology. A number of excellent readers have used that approach. A second approach is to select studies and papers that emphasize current research and that reflect what psychologists are doing and discussing today. It is this second method that has guided the efforts of the editors of this book of readings.

The editors have adopted this more topical approach also because psychology is a rapidly changing science, both as to emphases and methodology, and classical statements seem less and less relevant to the current scene as trends change and events move swiftly along. For example, who could have predicted twenty years ago that clinical psychologists would become so deeply involved in community psychology? The emphasis in this book of readings on the current and topical also has the added advantage of enabling students to see the relevance between their own life experiences and the concerns of psychologists today. Not only clinical psychologists, but also psychologists in a variety of specialties are studying and interpreting to an increasing extent the problems that face the world today. This emphasis on recent developments does not mean that we have ignored the historical roots of psychology. A number of papers we have included do in fact trace the background of their research problems through a series of studies that may go back to the beginning of the century. We have also included papers that serve as a bridge between psychology as it was and psychology as it is today. The paper by Allan Davisson on William James in the first section is one; the forty-year follow-up of Terman's "gifted group" by Melita H. Oden in Section 7 is another.

We have for the most part made use of brief papers. This decision enabled us to give maximum coverage within the space available to us and at the same time to present a greater sampling of research strategies, viewpoints, and findings. Most of the selections are from psychological journals rather than from published textbooks because it is in the journals that the forefront of scientific advance appears. This is as true of psychology as it is of other sciences.

Although the readings are organized according to the sections and chapters of Lindgren and Byrne's *Psychology: An Introduction to a Behavioral Science,* the areas covered and the papers selected are such that *Current Research in Psychology* could stand alone and should thus be useful for any instructor wishing to organize his course around contemporary psychological issues. By the same token, the book could also be used in conjunction with any standard introductory textbook in psychology, in view of the fact that such books cover many of the same general topics.

The first section in this book consists of papers dealing with the general theme of science as it applies to the study of human behavior. It is also unique in that it includes one example of a research study where findings contradict common sense psychology. The succeeding sections deal, in turn, with developmental psychology, learning, physiological psychology, perception, motivation and emotion, measurement and individual differences, psychopathology and its treatment, social behavior, organizational and industrial psychology, and community psychology.

The editors would like to express their appreciation to the scientists who permitted their work to be reproduced here, to the journals and professional associations that permitted articles to be reprinted, and to Daniel Katz, of the University of Michigan, who advised the editors on selections to be included.

HENRY CLAY LINDGREN
DONN BYRNE
FREDRICA LINDGREN

San Francisco, California
May, 1970

CONTENTS

CURRENT RESEARCH IN PSYCHOLOGY:
A Book of Readings

SECTION 1

INTRODUCTION

The first selection consists of an address given by the late Lord Brain at a meeting of the American Association for the Advancement of Science concerning the attitudes the general public has toward science and scientific endeavor. In it, he deals with some of the perplexing problems that scientists have as they attempt to explain human behavior in general terms. The second article, by William C. Hitt of the Battelle Memorial Institute in Columbus, Ohio, analyzes the problems posed by the two major approaches psychologists use in studying human behavior: the behavioristic model that is used primarily, but not exclusively, by experimental psychologists, and the phenomenological model that is used by personality theorists, as well as by psychotherapists and other applied psychologists. Hitt finds that both approaches have strengths and shortcomings and that each has something to offer psychologists who are attempting to develop explanations of human behavior that are as complete as possible.

The two remaining papers in this section deal with more specific topics. The article by Allan Davisson, of the University of Minnesota, is concerned with the historical background of modern behavioral science. Specifically, it focuses on the psychology of William James and its relationship to the "American mind"—the attitudes, values, and ways of thinking that are characteristically American.

The final selection consists of a research study by Barbara R. Slater of the Pelham Public Schools in Pelham, New York. It is included in this section as an example of an experiment that is both relevant and practical. Her findings are, furthermore, contrary to common sense and the conventional wisdom. Although almost everyone would expect that noise would have an adverse effect on classroom performance, Slater's results showed that its effect on performance was nil. One of the roles of the behavioral scientist is that of putting commonly held assumptions to the experimental test and of determining their validity. Often the assumptions are verified, but sometimes they are not, as Slater's study shows. In other words, although common sense and the conventional wisdom may be useful in many everyday situations, they are not a dependable guide when it comes to understanding and predicting human behavior.

1

1.1 Science and Antiscience

WALTER RUSSELL BRAIN

I very much appreciate the privilege of addressing you and of attending this meeting as the representative of the Council of the British Association for the Advancement of Science. A few months ago, as president of that Association, I delivered an address on "Science and Behaviour." That is a large subject, and I did not attempt to do more than deal with it in outline. I realized that I left many important questions unanswered, and some, indeed, unasked. This, together with some reactions to my address in the English press and elsewhere, made me welcome this opportunity of carrying some of my ideas further.

In my presidential address I drew attention to our collective failure to foresee the consequences of much recent and current scientific work, and I stressed the need for more education in science. Tonight, however, I am concerned with more subtle, and therefore less obvious, obstacles to the acceptance of scientific ideas, for I want to inquire into the nature of current prejudices against science and scientists. By prejudices I mean emotional attitudes more positive and active than mere ignorance, even though, as I hope to show, some of them are the outcome of ignorance. No doubt these prejudices vary in force from one country to another, and in individual countries from one stratum of society to another. They need to be taken seriously, because scientists constitute a minority of all populations, and in democratic societies the practical uses of their achievements depend to a considerable extent upon their acceptance by the majority. And in that majority there are intelligent people whose education has given them little or no knowledge of science. Some of these are suspicious of a culture which they do not understand. Since these intelligent people are often also influential, they tend to propagate their suspicions among those who listen to what they say. My object in this address is, first, to try to remove some at least of the unreasonable suspicions which the nonscientists may harbor about science, and to make scientists themselves aware of them.

But it would be a mistake to suppose that all the hostility to science is due to either ignorance or prejudice. Science seems to many to present a complex challenge to other ways of thought, which, though not perhaps actually older, were well established for centuries before science grew out of its infancy. Part of this challenge, however, comes, not from science itself, but from philosophical ideas which science is thought to support; but part of it is more fundamental because it is the challenge of new facts about man and the world, which science is revealing, and of novel situations which call for decisions about action.

MISUNDERSTANDING ABOUT SCIENTISTS

Let me begin by dealing with the misunderstandings about the nature of science itself. What is science? The first definition given by Webster's *Dictionary* is "knowledge." I suggest that those who ask anxious questions about the influence of science, or the supposed conflict between science and some established system of belief, should try the effect of replacing the word *science* by the word *knowledge*. Knowledge surely can conflict only with ignorance.

Science, of course, is knowledge obtained in a particular way—by the use of scientific methods. But because the term is used collectively for all knowledge of this kind, there is a tendency to project the general concept of science on to a collective group of scientists who are supposed to be responsible, in some way not always understood or defined by the nonscientist, for various of our current problems.

This is a complex misapprehension. In the first place scientists often have no more in common with each other than that they are all seeking knowledge by means of scientific methods. Professor A uses these methods to investigate the light from receding nebulae, while Professor B is interested in the physiological clock which regulates the habits of shore-inhabiting crustaceans in relation to the tides. Dr. C is investigating the atomic nucleus and antimatter, and so on through to Professor Z, who is studying the virus-carrying capacity of mosquitoes in a tropical forest. These scientists have probably never met one another. They may differ in age, sex, race, language, religion, and their general mode of life, and none of them may be interested in what the others are doing. As for the remote effects of their scientific activities, what Professor A does may be of importance for our ideas about the origin of the universe, while Professor B's work may have some implications for the storage of information in the brain, and possibly for our understanding of the relationship between the brain and the mind. Dr. C deals with a subject which has already had profound importance in relation to the development of nuclear energy and today is likely to interest the philosophers of physics who are concerned with the ultimate nature of matter and the relationship between the observer and what he observes. And Professor Z's investigation of viruses concerns a scientific topic of great importance for our understanding of cell behavior, information at the molecular level, the nature of the gene, and the cancer cell. The immediate social effects of his work may well be the elimination of a particular group of diseases in tropical areas, and a resulting increase in the local population, which is already too great for its food supplies. Unless they are rather exceptional men in their particular field of work, none of these scientists may be much interested in its more remote implications. At any rate, they can all be first-class scientists without such an interest.

I chose these examples at random, but I could well have chosen any other of the varieties of scientific work being practiced by the hundreds of thousands of scientists in the world. Scientists, of course, meet one another to exchange ideas, to promote their own particular branch of science, or science in general, or because they are aware of its social implications. Nevertheless, such collective activities, important though they may be in themselves, play a small part in their lives. Scientists, though they must always be aware of the work of their fellows in their own fields, are essentially individualists; and the body of knowledge to which they are contributing is an impersonal one. Apart from contributing to it, they have no collective consciousness, interest, or aim.

The next misconception with which I want to deal is the idea that scientists are responsible for the applications of science. This is true only in the sense that without science there would be no scientific technology. But, as I have just pointed out, many scientists, perhaps most, are not concerned with the applications of their work. The question of scientific responsibility was raised in its most urgent form by the development of nuclear weapons. Here surely we must distinguish between science and technology. Whether the scientific knowledge which made possible the release of atomic energy should be applied to the production of nuclear weapons is a difficult ethical question, but it is a different question from that of whether scientific knowledge is good or bad in itself. All scientists appear to take for granted that it *is* good in itself, whatever may be the case with the uses to which it is put. To argue otherwise would be in any case a waste of time, since the impulse to know is evidently an inherent part of human nature. I pointed out earlier that man does not sufficiently foresee the consequences of scientific discoveries. It follows that he certainly has not the capacity to decide that some particular line of scientific research ought to be abandoned because of its supposed evil consequences for mankind.

This brings me to the point that the idea of the scientist which we have been discussing is clearly an abstraction. The scientist is a member of society, and it is society which educates him, pays him for his work, and neglects to foresee its consequences. And society is responsible for what it does or fails to do with the scientist's discoveries, though he has a special responsibility as a member of society, as we shall see.

Nuclear weapons present a problem of urgency and immediacy, but there are other problems of applied science almost equally urgent and important. I spoke to the British Association about the world population crisis. This of course has come about as a result of the pursuit by scientists of immediate ends which seemed obviously good in themselves—for what could seem more clearly desirable than the abolition of malaria or smallpox? Neither of these scourges is by any means abolished yet, but the incidence of malaria in many countries has been greatly reduced by public health measures utilizing the recently introduced insecticides, and the incidence of smallpox, of course, by vaccination. But the scientists who invented the insecticides and the antimalarial drugs, and the devoted field workers who distribute them in and around villages in malarious regions, do not think about the effects of their actions on population growth in relation to food supplies. They cannot be blamed for this, for it was not their job to do so, and if they had thought about it there was little they could have done.

I have just mentioned insecticides in connection with the war on malaria, but their use in agriculture has also had unforeseen results in their deleterious effect upon wild life. On the other hand, agriculturalists, in particular those concerned with food supplies in developing countries, say that, by increasing crops, insecticides are saving many human lives. We do not know at present whether the consumption of minute amounts of these substances in our food has any long-term ill effects upon human beings. Moreover, we must also remember that substances introduced by scientists, who are accustomed to accurate measurements, have to be used and distributed by workers most of whom have no knowledge of science, and who may not adequately appreciate the importance of accuracy in calculating the amounts of these powerful substances to be used. This illustrates the fact that a scientific culture demands some scientific virtues in a large part of the population.

There are those who try to minimize the population crisis. It may well be true that, with a better organization of its resources, the world could support a much larger population than it does now. But the organization is not at present there, and even assuming the utmost cooperation among all the countries concerned, it must take a considerable time to set up. Such an organization, moreover, could operate only through individual countries, in many of which progress is hampered by reluctance to abandon ancient traditions, lack of education, and inadequate means of communication. Whatever may be the theoretical possibilities, a large part of the world's population is now undernourished, and population growth seems at present likely to outstrip the growth of food supplies.

Looked at from the evolutionary standpoint, man has achieved his present dominant position because his intelligence has been of survival value to him. This may no longer be the case. As a recent writer in the *New Scientist* put it (1), ". . . it is essential to remember what we mean by evolution. There is a strong danger of thinking of it as a process which runs on a predetermined course like a clockwork motor with its spring unwinding (or, since the complexity is increasing, a better analogy would be a motor that wound its spring *up*). According to this attitude, once life has begun it automatically ends up producing intelligent beings, or something more 'advanced.' It is a completely fallacious view of evolution and the antithesis of what Darwin meant and common sense dictates. Evolution is primarily a fortuitous process based on the random mutations that occur in genetic material and the effects of environmental selection upon these mutations. What one ends up with at any given stage is the life-form best adapted to the prevailing conditions, whether its attributes include memory and associated intelligence or not. It is arguable, for example, that with man's invention of the H-bomb and his growing influence over his own environment, intelligence has become a factor threatening, rather than enhancing, his chances of survival."

To look at the matter in a different way, survival of the individual depends upon the development of a nervous system in which differentiation (that is, specialization of function) is balanced by integration (that is, the control of partial activities by the organism as a whole). The evolution of the human race is now threatened by a failure of integration. That integration is a social function, necessary both within individual national societies and, in the interests of our common humanity, between those societies. Our present crises have been partly produced by the activities of scientists. Scientists therefore must seize every opportunity to bring home to those who make the practical decisions about social organization the urgency of the problems with which they are faced and their true nature; and they can themselves contribute to their solution.

Sir Howard Florey said in his presidential address to the Royal Society this year (2): "Ought we as a society to be considering how science and scientists can contribute to the great problem of bringing the human population into satisfactory, even if dynamic, equilibrium with its surroundings? Or should we wait for these matters to be tackled by people who may have little connection with us? I have no doubt myself that we should try to lead scientific advances by positive action." But positive action does not mean dictation. I say this because of a strange idea which sometimes finds expression—that scientists seek to control human beings, and regulate their behavior in pursuit of some supposed aims of their own, in the same spirit in which they may organize the lives of, and perform experiments upon, animals in the laboratory. An example of this occurred in a comment on my own presidential address to the British Association. Pleading for more foresight in respect of the population problem, I said that animal breeders looked further ahead, and showed more concern for the future of the race with which they dealt, than the average human being does. This provoked a comment in an English newspaper about the chilling attitude of scientists who wish to breed human beings like animals. Similar criticism is familiar to those geneticists who think that a knowledge of genetics may be of some value for improving the human race. The truth is, as I have already suggested, that scientists, far from wanting to impose their ideas upon other people, are often too little interested in the social implications of their work, and in any case too much occupied with it to have time for political activities. On the other hand, as the recent history of Germany has shown, politicians may, if they get the power, try to impose their own pseudo-scientific ideas upon the people they rule.

A variant of this fear, which perhaps needs rather more serious consideration, is that the computer may put some unforeseen powers of controlling mankind into the hands of the scientists. In their more fantastic forms these ideas verge upon science fiction, and contemplate machines which, it is supposed, will ultimately develop a life of their own and control the men who constructed them. More seriously it may be argued that computers, together with modern means of communication linked to knowledge of the psychology of persuasion, may be used to create a tyranny more complete and unbreakable than any which has dominated human beings in the past.

As I said earlier, science is knowledge. All computers can do is to provide knowledge, in the form of information, more rapidly, and over a wider range of data, than has ever been possible before. This knowledge can be used to influence man's minds on a scale and with an effectiveness that are unprecedented. But though computers are a product of science, such uses are not scientific but social. It is not scientists who are likely to want to control human beings in this way, though they may be faced with the ethical decision of whether and how far they should lend their aid to politicians who may. We must be alert to these dangers, and remember that if the price of liberty is eternal vigilance, vigilance without knowledge is blindfold.

Let me now sum up what I have said so far. I have suggested that some popular misconceptions about science and the aims of scientists spring from ignorance, and I believe it is important that scientists should be aware of them, and that it should be part of the task of the public relations of science to try to disabuse the minds of nonscientists of these ideas.

I went on to say that, far from its being true that scientists were endeavoring to impose their ideas upon society as a whole, there is a great danger that society, including the scientists themselves, may not sufficiently foresee the technological and social consequences of much scientific work. This idea is today possibly in danger of becoming so much a platitude that people will accept its truth and do nothing further about it. What should be done is a difficult problem, and a good deal of the responsibility for finding an answer to it must, I would suggest, rest with the scientists, since they alone know what is happening in science. But it must often be extremely hard, and sometimes impossible, to foresee far ahead the social and technological consequences of particular scientific discoveries. Nevertheless, I believe we have to try to do it. If scientists are to be enabled to attempt it, society as a whole must recognize the need and provide the facilities; and may we not hope that the social scientists, in particular, will in this matter provide a bridge between society as a whole and scientists working in other fields? Even now such machinery for extrapolation in the field of the population crisis exists in a relatively embryonic form in the activities of some agencies of the United Nations Organization; this is a promising beginning, but these activities need to be developed with a much more wholehearted cooperation of all countries and a much greater readiness to look at all aspects of the problem if they are to be really successful.

Both the world population crisis and the dangers of nuclear warfare can be regarded, as in the passage I quoted, as challenging the evolutionary value of human intelligence. Is man too intelligent, or perhaps not intelligent enough? The world population crisis, as I suggested, may illustrate a lack of social integration of the intelligence of individuals. When we turn to consider international tensions, however, it may be said that individual societies are fully aware of their dangers, but that the tensions are the emotional reactions to a state of affairs which is the product of highly complex social, political, and historical causes. Many people would agree that there is a lack of integration between the individual national units which compose the world society; but what, it may be asked, can human intelligence be expected to do about that, more than it is doing? Has science any contribution to make to the solution of this problem? Any such claim must, I am sure, be extremely modest, for the social and psychological sciences are much younger than physics and physiology. Nevertheless, science can do two things which, though modest, may be important. It can challenge the emotional reactions, which political leaders take for granted, by saying that these, too, are the appropriate subjects of scientific study and may therefore be capable of modification. Secondly, as science is international, it can bring together scientists of many nations who are prepared to try not to take for granted the emotional attitudes of their own societies, but to look beyond

them in search of the common interests of all nations. And perhaps the two approaches have something in common. International cooperation, or even competition, in coping with the population crisis might be a constructive antidote to international tension leading to competitive armaments.

CAN SCIENCE EXPLAIN MAN?

Now I turn to my second theme, the impact of science on man's ideas about himself. Can science explain man?

During the last quarter of a century we have learned a great deal about the part played by the brain in the life of the mind. Much of this knowledge has been gained from observations made on animals, and there are very great differences between the highest nonhuman animals and man. But these differences are related to the functions of those parts of the brain which have developed much further in human beings than in animals. Basically, those parts which are concerned with the emotional reactions and instinctive drives are similar in animals and man. As well as studying the results of experiments on animals, we can investigate in man how disease of the brain, and drugs, affect the mental life. From all these observations we have come to recognize that emotional reactions have their neurological basis in certain parts of the brain, and that other areas are particularly concerned with memory, others again with speech, and so on. We know too that the complex activities of the nervous system are influenced profoundly by biochemical factors, among others the secretions of the endocrine glands carried to the brain by the blood. There are still, however, many details of which we are ignorant. We do not know in detail how nerve cells behave when we think, nor how memories are stored and made available again. Nevertheless, the progress made so far suggests that these are not inherently insoluble problems, even though we do not yet possess the detailed knowledge to solve them.

All this leads to the conclusion that it is likely that we shall find some activity of the brain correlated with every recognizable activity of the mind, and therefore that ultimately we shall possess explanations of those mental activities in physicochemical terms.

For perhaps half a century now we have been offered explanations of mental activity at a different level, as it were— namely, psychological interpretations. Psychology is now a vast and varied field of knowledge. In his laboratory the psychologist studies many aspects of normal mental activities such as perception, learning, memory, and language. In the hospital he applies these methods to the investigation of the effects of brain disease on these functions, and in the school he tests intelligence and specific capacities. He studies animal behavior, too, in intact animals and animals with experimental brain damage. Then there is analytical psychology, which includes not only psychoanalysis but other schools of psychological thought which claim to provide explanations of human behavior in terms of mental factors, some of which are held to be unconscious.

While analytical psychology developed as a method of medical treatment (that is, it was concerned with people who went to a doctor because they had symptoms which troubled them), it soon became clear that unconscious mental processes play an important part in the lives of normal people too. Parallel with the development of analytical psychology, anthropology and social psychology have been demonstrating the profound influence of social forces of various kinds upon our mental attitudes and beliefs.

All these trends of thought in their different ways have tended to change man's ideas about himself. If his thoughts and feelings are the products of a nervous system behaving in accordance with physical laws, what becomes of the freedom of the will, or indeed, of the dignity of the personality? If man is influenced by factors of which he is unconscious, how can he be regarded as a rational being? If he is largely molded from infancy by his social environment, what remains of his individuality? Moreover, the concept of personality has been undermined in a more subtle way by the fact that all these modes of thought seem to be concerned less with the individual man than with the psychological features or nervous structures which he has in common either with everyone else or with particular groups of people who share his characteristics.

Such ideas tend to lead to what I may describe as a reductionist view of human nature. Man is regarded as reducible in physical terms to the activity of nerve cells, and in psychological terms to conflicting mental elements.

PUBLIC DESCRIPTIONS AND PRIVATE EXPERIENCES

Such views as these seem to me to involve several misapprehensions. Although they are apt to be regarded as scientific, they are not scientific but philosophical. To investigate what activity of the neurons in the brain is involved in thought, speech, memory, or feeling is a scientific activity, but, as science, it does not logically involve any particular view of the nature of the mind, or of the relationship between mind and brain. Sherrington, one of the greatest neurophysiologists, was himself a dualist, who did not identify the mind and the brain; Jung, for all his lifetime of contributions to analytical psychology, did not believe that the psyche could be finally reduced to the interaction of the psychological components revealed by analysis.

But even though it is a misunderstanding to believe that such views have a scientific basis, they dwell on the borderland between science and philosophy, and since scientists have frequently donned the gown of the philosopher (sometimes without acknowledging it) to discuss them, and since they are for various reasons of great importance today, I shall venture to say a little about them.

I shall begin by questioning the idea that current physical concepts of causation, which are valid at the molecular level, necessarily completely explain the interrelated activities of the millions of nerve cells which must be involved in all our higher mental activities. There are already hints that this may not be so. I have myself recently pointed out that the time of physical events in the nervous system is not identical with the time of conscious experience (3). What the psychologists call the specious present, or the mental present, must itself have some duration in time. And I quoted from some recent work in phonetics

which showed that "in the mental present there is not only overlapping, but mutual modification of the representations of events, which in physical time are successive." Thus the naive physical determinism, which appealed particularly to some 19th-century writers, may not be applicable to present-day interpretation of the brain-mind relationship. Then one may question whether there is not a logical fallacy in the idea that the mind is capable of explaining itself in terms of its own ideas. Indeed, the brain is not describable as a machine, MacKay has recently argued (3), for no machine could embody within itself a complete description of itself. That, he maintains, is logically self-contradictory, and he adds that Gödel's theorem can be regarded as a formal demonstration of this proposition as a special case.

Aldous Huxley in *Literature and Science*, a book written just before he died (5), drew a distinction which has important implications for our present purposes. "All our experiences," he wrote, "are strictly private; but some experiences are less private than others. They are less private in the sense that, under similar conditions, most normal people will have similar experiences and, having had them, can be relied upon to interpret the spoken or written reports of such experiences in much the same way. . . . Science may be defined as a device for investigating, ordering and communicating the more public of human experiences. Less systematically, literature also deals with such public experiences. Its main concern, however, is with man's more private experiences, and with the interactions between the private worlds of sentient, self-conscious individuals and the public universes of 'objective reality,' logic, social conventions and the accumulated information currently available."

It follows that when a scientist describes what is happening in the brain of a human being he is describing some part of that individual's private world, but he can do so only in public terms. Indeed, if one person's nerve impulses did not behave like another's there could be no scientific description of them at all. But the gulf between these private and public descriptions is so great that the scientist cannot correlate the nervous impulses with thoughts, feelings, or memories unless the subject of his investigation gives access to his private world by saying what his experiences are. Science in its descriptions of man must inevitably concentrate on the generic at the expense of the individual, but it is our private individual experiences which are the essence of our lives. To quote Aldous Huxley again, "the world with which literature deals is the world into which human beings are born and live and finally die; the world in which they love and hate; in which they experience triumph and humiliation, hope and despair; the world of sufferings and enjoyments, of madness and commonsense, of silliness, cunning and wisdom; the world of social pressures and individual impulses, of reason against passion, of instincts and conventions, of shared language and unshareable feeling and sensation; of innate differences and the rules, the roles, the solemn or absurd rituals imposed by the prevailing culture. . . . As a private individual, the scientist inhabits the many-faceted world in

which the rest of the human race does its living and dying. But as a professional chemist, say, a professional physicist or physiologist, he is the inhabitant of a radically different universe—not the universe of given appearances but the world of inferred fine structures, not the experienced world of unique events and diverse qualities, but the world of quantified regularities. Knowledge is power, and, by a seeming paradox, it is through their knowledge of what happens in this unexperienced world of abstractions and inferences that scientists and technologists have acquired their enormous and growing power to control, direct and modify the world of manifold appearances in which human beings are privileged and condemned to live."

In all the talk and disputation about the two cultures the important thing, it seems to me, is not whether there are two or more cultures, or whether those who are said to belong to one understand the other. The important thing is that there is not *one* culture in the world today, in the sense in which Hellenism, for example, was the dominating and unifying culture in the Mediterranean for centuries. The reason why we have to speak of two or more cultures is that we have not yet achieved a similar unifying world view which can integrate the public knowledge of science with the private experiences of persons, and on which we can base a comprehensive conception of the nature of man.

I suggest that one of the essential ingredients of such a view should be the primacy of the private, personal, subjective, individual experience over any public account which science can give. This means that persons are to be regarded as values in themselves, and not as reducible to either physicochemical systems or bundles of psychological trends or impulses. The social and political implications of this are important. One of them is that science, though an end in itself to the scientist, is only a means to an end where other people are concerned, that end being the possibility of their greater fulfilment as persons.

But this does not mean that the explanations which neurophysiology and psychology give of human behavior are not important. Here we meet again the old philosophical conundrum about the relationship between the parts and the whole. A knowledge of the parts is none the less valuable because there is a sense in which the whole is more than the sum of its parts; and yet a knowledge of the whole alone may leave us without the power to influence it which we possess if we know how it is made up of its parts, and how they work. Though *body* and *mind* are convenient, indeed essential, terms, they are abstractions, and all abstractions leave something out. Each partially describes a person. But what we think about the nature of persons and their status in the universe is not a question for science, though it must take account of any facts which science can provide about either. Ultimately, it must depend upon our personal view of the nature of things.

VALUES

Since this concerns values, let me end with some reflections on the relations between science and values. It is yet another illustration of our failure to attain to a unified world view that many,

perhaps most, people find it difficult to reconcile two views about the nature and origin of human values. Bronowski, in a recent book called *Science and Human Values,* says (6): "There have always been two ways of looking for truth. One is to find concepts which are beyond challenge, because they are held by faith or by authority or the conviction that they are self-evident. This is the mystic submission to truth which the East has chosen, and which dominated the axiomatic thought of the scholars of the Middle Ages. So St. Thomas Aquinas holds that faith is a higher guide to truth than knowledge is: the master of medieval science puts science firmly into second place. But long before Aquinas wrote, Peter Abelard had already challenged the whole notion that there are concepts which can only be felt by faith or authority. All truth, even the highest, is accessible to test, said Abelard: 'By doubting we are led to enquire, and by enquiry we perceive the truth.' . . . The habit of testing and correcting the concept by its consequences in experience has been the spring within the movement of our civilisation ever since."

Science, then, has a morality of its own, the foundation of which is respect for truth, and which, therefore, is bound to come into conflict with all attempts to curb freedom of thought and speech by any form of authoritarianism. Moreover, scientific thought and its devotion to truth are themselves a product of the evolutionary process, and must therefore have proved themselves, hitherto at any rate, to have survival value.

But the idea that all ethical considerations can be derived from the evolutionary process has not gone unchallenged. If, it is said, survival is what counts in evolution, on what grounds is man to be preferred to the tiger, the tapeworm, or the tetanus bacillus, all of which have up to now survived? (It may be noted that man alone of these organisms asks this question.) But just as mind cannot explain itself except by taking some mental activity for granted, so we cannot explain values without assuming some value, if only the value of truth. In the course, and as the result, of the evolutionary process man has developed systems of values. In the individual these, as we now know, are the products of numerous and complex factors, including his family life, social circumstances, cultural traditions, education, and many others. Since man is a social animal his values arise in society and interpenetrate his social and personal relationships. Some maintain that the nature of life is such as to produce ever-increasing complexity in the individual and society, and with it a progressive enrichment of the individual consciousness. The test of our values, they claim, is whether they promote, or conflict with, those tendencies, which are held to be of the essence of life itself. General ethical principles are to be laid down on this basis, but individual actions must often be empirical, and ethical views may well change in the light of changing knowledge, and as fresh problems have to be faced.

Others, whose values and ethics are derived from other sources, may differ from these views. But we cannot indefinitely disregard what science teaches us about human nature, and if we believe the universe to be rational, it would seem unreasonable to treat ethics as beyond the criticism of reason. On the other hand, I suspect that at the foundation of an evolutionary theory of values there lies an act of faith, which cannot altogether be justified by reason.

But ought we to—can we—leave the matter there? Man seems to have a strong disposition to fit his beliefs into some unified system, so already we find the systematizers at work. And this is not merely a matter of abstract thought, for what we believe about the nature of man is likely to influence the way in which we behave toward him.

Aldous Huxley, whose words I quoted earlier, defined science as "a device for investigating, ordering and communicating the more public of human experiences," while the main concern of literature, he said, "is with man's more private experiences" and with the interactions between these private worlds and the public universes of "objective reality." Have we here a basis of distinction between the "two cultures"? But, as Huxley points out, both science and literature describe man, and the same man, and his identical activities. How, if at all, are these descriptions to be reconciled? How are we to harmonize "our private and unshareable experiences with the scientific hypotheses in terms in which they are explained"? I said earlier that science concentrates on the generic at the expense of the individual. Let me in conclusion carry this idea a little further. Science is not primarily concerned with the uniqueness of events but with what they have in common with other events, so that it can explain their uniqueness in terms of general principles. Literature, art, and history, on the other hand, are chiefly concerned with unique human experiences and events, and even though they use public terms in their attempts to communicate those experiences, or general principles to try to explain them, there is always a unique element in their subject matter which is irreducible and inescapable. It is when science studies man himself that the tension between these two modes of understanding becomes acute.

Perhaps we cannot at present escape from the polarity between the public scientific description and the private world. Perhaps, indeed, at our present stage of knowledge the tension between them is itself a condition of development; as William Blake said, "without contrar-

ies is no progression"—an intuitive anticipation of Darwin. But if we *are* to progress toward a unified culture it must be through a mutual understanding, to which scientists have much to contribute.

REFERENCES

1. P. Stubbs, *New Scientist*, 1964, **24,** 448.
2. H. Florey, *ibid.*, p. 639.
3. Lord Brain, *Brain*, 1963, **86,** 381.
4. D. M. MacKay, in *Man and His Future*, G. Wolstenholme, Ed., London: Churchill, 1963, p. 181.
5. A. Huxley, *Literature and Science*, New York: Harper, 1963.
6. J. Bronowski, *Science and Human Values*, London: Hutchinson, 1961, p. 55.

1.2 Two Models of Man

WILLIAM D. HITT

A symposium sponsored by the Division of Philosophical Psychology of the American Psychological Association clearly pointed up the cleavage in contemporary theoretical and philosophical psychology. The symposium was held at Rice University to mark the inception of the Division of Philosophical Psychology as a new division of the APA. Participants included Sigmund Koch, R. B. MacLeod, B. F. Skinner, Carl R. Rogers, Norman Malcolm, and Michael Scriven. The presentations and associated discussions were organized in the book: *Behaviorism and Phenomenology: Contrasting Bases for Modern Psychology* (Edited by T. W. Wann, 1964).

THE ARGUMENT

As indicated in the title of the book, the main argument of the symposium dealt with phenomenology versus behaviorism. This argument also could be described as one between existential psychology and behavioristic psychology. The presentations dealt with two distinct models of man and the scientific methodology associated with each model. The discussions following each presentation may be described as aggressive, hostile, and rather emotional; they would suggest that there is little likelihood of a reconciliation between the two schools of thought represented at the symposium.

To illustrate the nature of the argument, some of the statements made by the participants are presented below.

In Support of Behaviorism

Skinner (1964). An adequate science of behavior must consider events taking place within the skin of the organism, not as physiological mediators of behavior, but as part of behavior itself. It can deal

Reprinted from the *American Psychologist*, 1969, **24**, 651–658, with permission of the author and the American Psychological Association, Inc.

with these events without assuming that they have any special nature or must be known in any special way. . . . Public and private events have the same kinds of physical dimensions [p. 84].

Malcolm (1964). Behaviorism is right in insisting that there must be some sort of conceptual tie between the language of mental phenomena and outward circumstances and behavior. If there were not, we could not understand other people, nor could we understand ourselves [p. 152].

Attacks on Behaviorism

Koch (1964). Behaviorism has been given a hearing for fifty years. I think this generous. I shall urge that it is essentially a role-playing position which has outlived whatever usefulness its role might once have had [p. 6].

Rogers (1964). It is quite unfortunate that we have permitted the world of psychological science to be narrowed to behavior observed, sounds emitted, marks scratched on paper, and the like [p. 118].

In Support of Phenomenology

MacLeod (1964). I am . . . insisting that what, in the old, prescientific days, we used to call "consciousness" still can and should be studied. Whether or not this kind of study may be called a science depends on our definition of the term. To be a scientist, in my opinion, is to have boundless curiosity tempered by discipline [p. 71].

Rogers (1964). The inner world of the individual appears to have more signifi-

cant influence upon his behavior than does the external environmental stimulus [p. 125].

Attacks on Phenomenology

Malcolm (1964). I believe that Wittgenstein has proved this line of thinking (introspectionism) to be disastrous. It leads to the conclusion that we do not and cannot understand each other's psychological language, which is a form of solipsism[1] [p. 148].

Skinner (1964). Mentalistic or psychic explanations of human behavior almost certainly originated in primitive animism [p. 79]. . . . I am a radical behaviorist simply in the sense that I find no place in the formulation for anything which is mental [p. 106].

This appears to be the heart of the argument:

The behaviorist views man as a passive organism governed by external stimuli. Man can be manipulated through proper control of these stimuli. Moreover, the laws that govern man are essentially the same as the laws that govern all natural phenomena of the world; hence, it is assumed that the scientific method used by the physical scientist is equally appropriate to the study of man.

The phenomenologist views man as the *source* of acts; he is free to choose in each situation. The essence of man is *inside* of man; he is controlled by his own consciousness. The most appropriate methodology for the study of man is phe-

[1]Solipsism is defined as the theory that only the self exists, or can be proven to exist.

nomenology, which begins with the world of experience.

These two models of man have been proposed and discussed for many years by philosophers and psychologists alike. Versions of these models may be seen in the contrasting views of Locke and Leibnitz (see Allport, 1955), Marx and Kierkegaard, Wittgenstein and Sartre, and, currently, Skinner and Rogers. Were he living today, William James probably would characterize Locke, Marx, Wittgenstein, and Skinner as "tough-minded," while Leibnitz, Kierkegaard, Sartre, and Rogers would be viewed as "tender-minded." Traditionally, the argument has been one model versus the other. It essentially has been a black-and-white argument.

The purpose of this article is to analyze the argument between the behaviorist and the phenomenologist. This analysis is carried out by presenting and discussing two different models of man.

CONTRASTING VIEWS OF MAN

The two models of man are presented in terms of these contrasting views:

1. Man can be described meaningfully in terms of his behavior; or man can be described meaningfully in terms of his consciousness.
2. Man is predictable; or man is unpredictable.
3. Man is an information transmitter; or man is an information generator.
4. Man lives in an objective world; or man lives in a subjective world.
5. Man is a rational being; or man is an arational being.
6. One man is like other men; or each man is unique.

7. Man can be described meaningfully in absolute terms; or man can be described meaningfully in relative terms.
8. Human characteristics can be investigated independently of one another; or man must be studied as a whole.
9. Man is a reality; or man is a potentiality.
10. Man is knowable in scientific terms; or man is more than we can ever know about him.

Each of these attributes is discussed below.

SUPPORT FOR BOTH MODELS

The evidence offered below in support of each of the two models of man is both empirical and analytical. Perhaps some of the evidence is intuitive, but it at least seems logical to the author of this article.

Man Can Be Described Meaningfully in Terms of His Behavior; or Man Can Be Described Meaningfully in Terms of His Consciousness

According to John B. Watson, the founder of American behaviorism, the behavior of man and animals was the only proper study for psychology. Watson strongly advocated that

Psychology is to be the science, not of consciousness, but of behavior. . . . It is to cover both human and animal behavior, the simpler animal behavior being indeed more fundamental than the more complex behavior of man. . . . It is to rely wholly on objective data, introspection being discarded [Woodworth & Sheehan, 1964, p. 113].

Behaviorism has had an interesting, and indeed productive, development since the time of Watson's original manifesto. Tolman, Hull, and a number of other psychologists have been important figures in this development. Today, Skinner is the leading behaviorist in the field of psychology. Skinner (1957) deals with both overt and covert behavior; for example, he states that "thought is simply *behavior*—verbal or nonverbal, covert or overt [p. 449]."

As a counterargument to placing all emphasis on behavior, Karl Jaspers, an existential psychologist and philosopher, points up the importance of consciousness or self-awareness. According to Jaspers (1963), consciousness has four formal characteristics: (*a*) the feeling of activity—an awareness of being active; (*b*) an awareness of unity; (*c*) awareness of identity; and (*d*) awareness of the self as distinct from an outer world and all that is not the self (p. 121). Jaspers (1957) stresses that "Man not only exists but knows that he exists [p. 4]."

It is apparent from this argument that psychologists over the years have been dealing with two different aspects of man—on the one hand, his actions, and on the other, his self-awareness. It seems reasonable that man could be described in terms of either his behavior *or* his consciousness or both. Indeed, behavior is more accessible to scientific treatment, but the systematic study of consciousness might well give the psychologist additional understanding of man.

Man Is Predictable; or Man Is Unpredictable

Understanding, prediction, and control are considered to be the three objectives of science. Prediction and control are sometimes viewed as evidence of the scientist's understanding of the phenomenon under study. The objective of prediction rests on the assumption of determinism, the doctrine that all events have sufficient causes. Psychological science has traditionally accepted the objective of predicting human behavior and the associated doctrine of determinism.

Indeed, there have been some notable successes in predicting human behavior. Recent predictions of the number of fatalities resulting from automobile accidents on a given weekend, for example, have been within 5–10% of the actual fatalities. College administrators can predict fairly accurately the number of dropouts between the freshman and sophomore years. Further, a psychometrician can readily predict with a high degree of accuracy the distribution of scores resulting from an achievement test administered to a large sample of high school students. As another example, the mean reaction time to an auditory stimulus can be predicted rather accurately for a large group of subjects. All of these examples lend support to the doctrine of determinism.

There also have been some notable failures in attempts to predict human behavior. For example, the therapist has had little success in predicting the effectiveness of a given form of therapy applied to a given patient. Similarly, the guidance counselor has had relatively little success in predicting the occupation to be chosen by individual high school students. Such failures in predicting human behavior sometimes prompt one to question the basic assumption of determinism.

To illustrate the complexity associated with predicting the behavior of man—as contrasted with that of other complex systems—consider the following illustration. Suppose that a research psychologist has made a detailed study of a given human subject. He now tells the subject that he predicts that he will choose Alternative A rather than Alternative B under such and such conditions at some future point in time. Now, with this limited amount of information, what do you predict the subject will do?

The evidence suggests that there is support for both sides of this issue. It is difficult to argue with the deterministic doctrine that there are sufficient causes for human actions. Yet these causes may be unknown to either the observer or the subject himself. Thus, we must conclude that man is both predictable and unpredictable.

Man Is an Information Transmitter; or Man Is an Information Generator

The information theorists and cyberneticists have formulated a model of man as an information transmitter. W. Ross Ashby (1961), the cyberneticist, has proposed a basic postulate that says that man is just as intelligent as the amount of information fed into him.

Intelligence, whether of man or machine, is absolutely bounded. And what we can build into our machine is similarly bounded. The amount of intelligence we can get into a machine is absolutely bounded by the quantity of information that is put into it. We can get out of a machine as much intelligence as we like, if and only if we insure that at least the corresponding quantity of information gets into it [p. 280].

Ashby believes that we could be much more scientific in our study of man if we would accept this basic postulate and give up the idea that man, in some mysterious manner, generates or creates new information over and above that which is fed into him.

The information-transmitting model of man is indeed very compelling. It promises considerable rigor and precision; it is compatible with both empiricism and stimulus–response theory; and it allows the behavioral scientist to build on past accomplishments in the fields of cybernetics, systems science, and mechanics.

But, alas, man does not want to be hemmed in by the information-transmitting model. Man asks questions that were never before asked; he identifies problems that were never before mentioned; he generates new ideas and theories; he formulates new courses of action; and he even formulates new models of man. Now to say that all of these human activities are merely a regrouping or recombining of existing elements is an oversimplification, a trivialization of human activity. Further, the assumption that all information has actually been in existence but hidden since the days of prehistoric man is not intuitively satisfying.

Considering the evidence in support of man both as an information transmitter and as an information generator, would it be reasonable to view man as both a *dependent* variable and an *independent* variable?

Man Lives in an Objective World; or Man Lives in a Subjective World

Man lives in an objective world. This is the world of facts and data. This is a reliable world; we agree that this or that event actually occurred. This is a tangible world; we agree that this or that object is actually present. This is the general world that is common to all.

But man also lives in a subjective world. This is the individual's private world. The individual's feelings, emotions, and perceptions are very personal; he attempts to describe them in words but feels that he can never do complete justice to them.

In making this comparison between the objective world and subjective world, it is important to distinguish between two types of knowledge. We can know *about* something, or we can personally *experience* something. These two forms of knowledge are not the same.

We conclude that man is both object and subject. He is visible and tangible to others, yet he is that which thinks, feels, and perceives. The world looks at man, and he looks out at the world.

Are both the objective world and the subjective world available to the methods of science? Empiricism in general and the experimental method in particular can be applied to the objective world; phenomenology can be applied to the subjective world. In his efforts to understand man, perhaps the psychologist should attempt to understand both worlds.

Man Is a Rational Being; or Man Is an Arational Being

Man is sometimes referred to as a rational animal. He is intelligent; he ex-

ercises reason; he uses logic; and he argues from a scientific standpoint. Indeed, man is considered by man to be the *only* rational animal.

An individual's action or behavior, of course, is sometimes considered irrational. This is the opposite of rational. The irrational person defies the laws of reason; he contradicts that which is considered rational by some particular community of people.

But man also is arational. This characteristic transcends the rational-irrational continuum; it essentially constitutes another dimension of man's life. As an example of man being arational in his life, he makes a total commitment for a way of life. This commitment may be for a given faith, a religion, a philosophy, a vocation, or something else. It may be that any analysis of this decision would reveal that it was neither rational nor irrational—it merely was.

Man's actions are guided by both empirical knowledge and value judgment. Empirical knowledge belongs to the rational world, whereas value judgment often belongs to the arational world. According to Jaspers (1967): "An empirical science cannot teach anybody what he ought to do, but only what he can do to reach his ends by statable means [p. 60]."

To achieve greater understanding of man, it would seem essential that the psychologist investigate man's arational world as well as his rational world.

One Man Is Like Other Men; or Each Man Is Unique

A major goal of science is to develop general laws to describe, explain, and predict phenomena of the world. These laws are frequently based upon the study of one sample of objects or events and are then expected to be valid for a different sample of objects or events. It then follows that a major goal of psychology is to formulate general laws of man. In fact, without the possibility of developing general laws of human behavior, can psychology even be considered a science?

There is a considerable amount of evidence to support the possibility of developing general laws of human behavior. For example, the results of the reaction-time experiments have held up very well over the decades. Moreover, the many conditioning experiments conducted over the past several decades—either classical or operant—certainly suggest that man is governed by general laws applicable to all. Further, the cultural anthropologist and social psychologist have clearly pointed up the similarity of people in a given culture, suggesting that they might be taken from the same mold.

On the other hand, there is considerable evidence to support the concept of individual uniqueness. For example, there are thousands of possible gene combinations and thousands of different environmental determinants, all of which bring about millions of different personalities. Further, it is apparent that no two people ever live in exactly the same environment. As someone once said about two brothers living in the same house, with the same parents, and with the same diet: "Only one of the boys has an older brother." Then, too, we might reflect on a statement made by William James (1925): "An unlearned carpenter of my acquaintance once said in my hearing:

'There is very little difference between one man and another; but what little there is, *is very important*' [pp. 242–243]."

Our conclusion from this brief analysis is that the evidence appears to support both models of man: (*a*) that he is governed by general laws that apply to all of mankind, and (*b*) that each individual is unique in a nontrivial way.

Man Can Be Described Meaningfully in Absolute Terms; or Man Can Be Described Meaningfully in Relative Terms

If we believe that man can be described in absolute terms, we view such descriptions as being free from restriction or limitation. They are independent of arbitrary standards. Contrariwise, if we believe that man can be described in relative terms, we see him as existing or having his specific nature only by relation to something else. His actions are not absolute or independent.

If the concept of absoluteness is supported, we must accept the idea of general laws for all of mankind, and we also must accept the related idea that man is governed by irrefutable natural laws. On the other hand, if the concept of relativism is supported, we probably can have no general laws of man; we must realize that everything is contingent upon something else; and we can be certain of nothing.

It would appear that there is evidence to support the concept of absoluteness in psychology. The basic psychophysical laws, for example, might be characterized as irrefutable natural laws. Similarly, the basic laws of conditioning seem to be free from restriction or limitation. This evidence might lead us to conclude that man can be described in absolute terms.

But before we can become smug with this false sense of security, the relativist poses some challenging questions. For example: What is considered intelligent behavior? What is normal behavior? What is an aggressive personality? What is an overachiever? At best, it would seem that we could answer such questions only in relative terms. The answers would be contingent on some set of arbitrary standards.

What can we conclude? Perhaps man can be described meaningfully in either absolute terms or relative terms, depending on what aspect of man is being described.

Human Characteristics Can Be Investigated Independently of One Another; or Must Be Studied as a Whole

The question here is: Can man be understood by analyzing each attribute independently of the rest, or must man be studied as a whole in order to be understood? Another way of phrasing the question is: Can we take an additive approach to the study of man, or is a holistic or Gestalt approach required?

There is some evidence to support an additive approach to the study of man. Consider the following areas of research: psychophysics, physiological psychology, motor skills, classical and operant conditioning, and sensation. All of these areas have produced useful results from experimentation involving the manipulation of a single independent variable and measuring the concomitant effects on a single dependent variable. Useful results have been produced by investigating a single characteristic independently of other characteristics.

Other areas of research, however, point up the value of a holistic point of view. Research in the area of perception, for example, has demonstrated the effect of individual motivation on perception. Similarly, studies of human learning have shown the great importance of motivation and intelligence on learning behavior. Further, as one more example, research in the area of psychotherapy has revealed that the relation between the personality of the therapist and that of the patient has a significant influence on the effectiveness of the therapy. All of these examples illustrate the importance of the interactions and interdependencies of the many variables operating in any given situation.

Support for a holistic view of man is seen in the works of Polanyi and Tielhard de Chardin, to mention only two. Polanyi (1963) gives this example: "Take a watch to pieces and examine, however carefully, its separate parts in turn, and you will never come across the principles by which a watch keeps time [p. 47]." Tielhard de Chardin (1961) says:

In its construction, it is true, every organism is always and inevitably reducible into its component parts. But it by no means follows that the sum of the parts is the same as the whole, or that, in the whole, some specifically new value may not emerge [p. 110].

What can be concluded from this discussion? First, it would seem that a detailed analysis of man is essential for a systematic understanding. Yet, synthesis also is required in order to understand the many interactions and interdependencies. We can conclude that the most effective strategy for the behavioral scientist might be that used by the systems analyst—a working back and forth between analysis and synthesis.

Man Is a Reality; or Man Is a Potentiality

Is man a reality? If so, he exists as fact; he is actual; he has objective existence. Or is man a potentiality? If so, he represents possibility rather than actuality; he is capable of being or becoming. The question here is: Can we study man as an actually existing entity—as we would study any other complex system—or must we view man as a completely dynamic entity, one that is constantly emerging or becoming?

There is support for the view of man as an actuality. The numerous results from the many years of research in the area of experimental psychology, for example, suggest that man is definable and measurable, and is capable of being investigated as an actually existing complex system. Further, the many current studies in the area of cybernetics, which point up similarities between man and machine, lend credence to the concept of man as an existing system.

There also is evidence to support the view of man as a potentiality. For example, case studies have revealed that long-term criminals have experienced religious conversions and then completely changed their way of life. Further, complete personality transformations have resulted from psychoanalysis and electroshock therapy. Indeed, man is changeable, and any given individual can become something quite different from what he was in the past.

Maslow (1961) has stressed the importance of human potentiality:

I think it fair to say that no theory of psychology will ever be complete that does not centrally incorporate the concept that man has his future within him, dynamically active at this present moment [p. 59].

What can be conclude? Only that man is both a reality and a potentiality. He represents objective existence, yet he can move toward any one of many different future states that are essentially unpredictable.

Man Is Knowable in Scientific Terms; or Man Is More Than We Can Ever Know about Him

This final issue is basic to the entire study of man, and is closely tied to all the previous issues discussed. Is man knowable in scientific terms, or is man more than we can ever know about him?

There are many centuries of evidence to support the idea that man is scientifically knowable. Aristotle, for example, applied the same logic to his study of man as he did to other phenomena in the world. Further, volumes of data resulting from psychological experiments since the time of Wundt's founding of the first experimental psychology laboratory in 1879 indicate that man is scientifically knowable. Then, too, the many laboratory experiments and field studies recently conducted by the different disciplines included in the behavioral and social sciences certainly suggest that man is scientifically knowable.

Yet, there also is support for the idea that man is more than we can ever know about him. Man has continued to transcend himself over the past million or so years, as demonstrated by the theory of evolution. Further, on logical grounds, it can be demonstrated that man becomes something different every time he gains new knowledge about himself, which would suggest that man is truly an "open system."

It is apparent that we know very little about man. William James (1956) says: "Our science is a drop, our ignorance a sea [p. 54]." Erich Fromm (1956) believes that "Even if we knew a thousand times more of ourselves, we would never reach bottom [p. 31]."

What can we conclude? We must conclude that man is scientifically knowable—at least to a point. Yet there is no evidence to support the idea that man is—or ever will be—*completely* knowable.

CONCLUSIONS

This paper has presented two models of man:

The behavioristic model: Man can be described meaningfully in terms of his behavior; he is predictable; he is an information transmitter; he lives in an objective world; he is rational; he has traits in common with other men; he may be described in absolute terms; his characteristics can be studied independently of one another; he is a reality; and he is knowable in scientific terms.

The phenomenological model: Man can be described meaningfully in terms of his consciousness; he is unpredictable; he is an information generator; he lives in a subjective world; he is arational; he is unique alongside millions of

other unique personalities; he can be described in relative terms; he must be studied in a holistic manner; he is a potentiality; and he is more than we can ever know about him.

This analysis of behaviorism and phenomenology leads to these conclusions:

1. The acceptance of either the behavioristic model or a phenomenological model has important implications in the everyday world. The choice of one versus the other could greatly influence human activities (either behavior or awareness) in such areas as education, psychiatry, theology, behavioral science, law, politics, marketing, advertising, and even parenthood. Thus, this ongoing debate is not just an academic exercise.

2. There appears to be truth in both views of man. The evidence that has been presented lends credence to both the behavioristic model and the phenomenological model. Indeed, it would be premature for psychology to accept either model as the final model.

3. A given behavioral scientist may find that both models are useful, depending upon the problem under study. The phenomenological model, for example, might be quite appropriate for the investigation of the creative process in scientists. On the other hand, the behavioristic model might be very useful in the study of environmental factors that motivate a given population of subjects to behave in a certain manner.

4. Finally, we must conclude that the behaviorist and the phenomenologist should listen to each other. Both, as scientists, should be willing to listen to opposing points of view. Each should

endeavor to understand what the other is trying to say. It would appear that a dialogue is in order.

REFERENCES

Allport, G. W. *Becoming: Basic Considerations for a Psychology of Personality.* New Haven: Yale University Press, 1955.

Ashby, W. R. "What is an intelligent machine?" *Proceedings of the Western Joint Computer Conference*, 1961, **19**, 275–280.

de Chardin, P. T. *The Phenomenon of Man.* New York: Harper & Row, 1961 (Harper Torchback Edition).

Fromm, E. *The Art of Loving.* New York: Harper & Row, 1956.

James, W. *The Will to Believe and Other Essays on Popular Philosophy.* New York: Dover, 1956 (Orig. publ. 1896).

James, W. "The individual and society," in, *The Philosophy of William James.* New York: Modern Library, 1925 (Orig. publ. 1897).

Jaspers, K. *Man in the Modern Age.* New York: Doubleday, 1957 (Orig. publ. in Germany, 1931).

Jaspers, K. *General Psychopathology.* Manchester, England: Manchester University Press, 1963 (Published in the United States by the University of Chicago Press).

Jaspers, K. *Philosophy Is for Everyman.* New York: Harcourt, Brace & World, 1967.

Koch, S. "Psychology and emerging conceptions of knowledge as unitary," in T. W. Wann (Ed.), *Behaviorism and Phenomenology: Contrasting Bases for Modern Psychology.* Chicago: University of Chicago Press, 1964.

MacLeod, R. B. "Phenomenology: A challenge to experimental psychology," in T. W. Wann (Ed.), *Behaviorism and Phenomenology: Contrasting Bases for Modern Psychology.* Chicago: University of Chicago Press, 1964.

Malcolm, N. "Behaviorism as a philosophy of psychology," in T. W. Wann (Ed.), *Behaviorism and Phenomenology: Contrasting Bases for Modern Psychology.* Chicago: University of Chicago Press, 1964.

Maslow, A. H. "Existential psychology—What's in it for us?" in R. May (Ed.), *Existential Psychology.* New York: Random House, 1961.

Polanyi, M. *The Study of Man.* Chicago: University of Chicago Press, 1963 (First Phoenix Edition).

Rogers, C. R. "Toward a science of the person," in T. W. Wann (Ed.), *Behaviorism and Phenomenology: Contrasting Bases for Modern Psychology.* Chicago: University of Chicago Press, 1964.

Skinner, B. F. *Verbal Behavior.* New York: Appleton-Century-Crofts, 1957.

Skinner, B. F. "Behaviorism at fifty," in T. W. Wann (Ed.), *Behaviorism and Phenomenology: Contrasting Bases for Modern Psychology.* Chicago: University of Chicago Press, 1964.

Wann, T. W. (Ed.), *Behaviorism and Phenomenology: Contrasting Bases for Modern Psychology.* Chicago: University of Chicago Press, 1964.

Woodworth, R. S., and Sheehan, M. R. *Contemporary Schools of Psychology.* New York: Ronald Press, 1964.

1.3 American Mind and the Psychology of William James

ALLAN DAVISSON

Boring (1950) points out that scientific advancement must contend with two limitations: "ignorance, for one discovery waits upon that other which opens the way to it," and the *Zeitgeist*, which restricts because of "the habits of thought that pertain to the culture of any region and period." But Boring also notes that the *Zeitgeist* guides and contributes to scientific development. The interaction between the intellectual and cultural currents of a nation or an era and the course that science takes deserves even more attention than historians usually give it.

An unfortunate result of lack of understanding of the cultural environment of the psychologist is summarized in Watson's (1967) indictment of psychology. He decries the lack of agreement about the nature of the contentual model for psychology and then observes: "An even more telling illustration . . . is the presence of national differences in psychology to such an extent that in the United States there is an all too common dismissal of work in psychology in other countries as quaint, odd, or irrelevant. . . . A provincialism in psychology in the United States is the consequence [p. 436]."

The hypothesis, then, is that intellectual history in a general sense can be applied more fruitfully to the history of psychology. Support for this hypothesis is offered via consideration of the American intellectual climate of the late nineteenth century and its effect on the thinking of William James—the man generally recognized as the father of American psychology. Individualism, personal freedom, naturalness, spontaneity, supernaturalism, utilitarianism, deductivism—these are terms and attitudes which describe the intellectual climate of late nineteenth century America and

Reprinted from the *Proceedings of the 77th Annual Convention of the American Psychological Association*, 1969, **4**, 847–848, with permission of the author and the American Psychological Association, Inc.

which can be related to the psychology of that day.

First, a brief look at the American mind of the late nineteenth century from the perspective of American intellectual historians David Noble (1965) and Richard Hofstadter (1955)—two of the historians exploring the underlying cultural paradigms in American history—will establish the setting within which James worked. The next concern is with William James, an essayist, philosopher, moralist, and man of letters, but "not a psychologist" as he once declared anxiously. To conclude the discussion some suggestions about what a psychology reflecting these late nineteenth century American intellectual currents would be expected to consider are compared with some of the key aspects of James' psychology.

A critical view of the American mind and its guiding principles is summarized by Noble (1965).

"Americans live not as members of a historical community with its inevitable structure of institutions and traditions, but as the children of nature who are given earthly definition by the virgin land that had redeemed their ancestors when they stepped out of the shifting sands of European history. Our historians, until World War II, proclaimed that Europe was history and America was nature because the Old World had institutions and traditions and the New World had none." Spontaneity, individuality, heroic salvation figures, a return to a sacred and eternal pattern of existence—these are but a few of the central themes in the American Puritan–Protestant tradition.

The populism of the 1890s that Hofstadter (1955) described "expressed the discontents of a great many farmers and businessmen with the economic challenges of the late nineteenth century." Populist spokesmen and the subsequent progressive movement were dedicated to restoring (Hofstadter, 1955) "a type of economic individualism and political democracy that was widely believed to have existed earlier in America and to have been destroyed by the great corporation and the corrupt political machine; and with that restoration to bring back a kind of morality and civic purity that was also believed to have been lost." The emphasis on the worth of the individual and the right of men to own property found its voice in nineteenth century Social Darwinism (McCloskey, 1951). Darwin had shown how nature improved by "the survival of the fittest" and it was but a short step to assert that the "fittest" could be epitomized by the industrial magnate. At the same time, a group of men that Hofstadter depicts as "a small imperialist elite representing, in general, the same type that had once been Mugwumps" developed in the eastern United States. "Disinherited farmers" and "ambitious gentlemen"— they felt that the "*arriviste* manufacturers and railroaders and the all-too-potent banking houses" had disrupted the American dream.

Despite the disagreements and antipathies of the groups discussed above, there was a common core of ideas that they all shared. The free individual living in harmony with the natural order can bring to fruition the dream of sacredness without its antithesis—profane human institutions. While this was their basic paradigm, the disharmony resulting from discrepant definitions of the terms of this paradigm seemed on the verge of shattering the American dream. A visible result of this disagreement was the needless Spanish–American War which seemed momentarily to unite the American populace against an outside enemy. After the war, the problems America faced were altered, but, as Hofstadter (1955) shows, the paradigm remained the same.

This, in brief, was the American intellectual climate reflected in a number of William James' articles and letters. The area around Linville, North Carolina, prompted him to exclaim: "The serpent has not yet made his appearance in this Eden around which stand the hills covered with primeval forests of the most beautiful description . . . [H. James, 1920, I, p. 316]." His observations while in Florence, Italy, describe an opposite feeling: "I have a sort of organic protestation against certain things here, the toneless air in the streets, which feels like used-up indoor air, the 'general debility' which pervades all ways and institutions . . . [H. James, 1920, I, p. 329]." So "American" was William James in his viewpoint that his brother Henry James embodied William's "Americanism" in the character of Mr. Babcock in his novel *The American*. One of his students, George Santayana (1921), said of James that "he was one of those elder Americans still disquieted by the ghost of tyranny, social and ecclesiastical. Even the beauties of the past troubled him; he had a puritan feeling that they were tainted." Ralph Barton Perry, James' major biographer, concurs with this view of James' Americanism. Perry (1935) quotes James in terms of two fundamental moral attitudes: "Elaborating the charge that Eu-

rope was relatively corrupt, [James] said: '[American] millionaires and syndicates have their immediate cash to pay, but they have no entrenched prestige to work with. . . . We "intellectuals" in America must all work to keep our precious birthright of individualism, and freedom from these institutions.' . . . The other attitude which strongly reinforced James' Americanism was his repugnance to the decadent and effete—his preference of the simple, the natural, the vigorous, the forward looking. . . . 'Still, one loves America above all things, for her youth, her greenness, her plasticity, innocence, good intentions, friends, everything' [II, p. 316]."

Even though James was American in his perspective, his distaste for the Spanish–American War and for war in general shows that his thinking was not restricted by a pro-American parochialism. Neither was his work in psychology restricted in its range. Heidbreder (1933) discusses his "democratic" acceptance of all ideas, and the range of topics which he considered in his texts included most of the work in psychology at the time. But the issues to which he devoted the most space as well as some of the points he covered in the development of his topics show an emphasis that can be described as "American." To better understand James' psychology in terms of the influences of the American *Zeitgeist*, the general question "What would a turn-of-the-century 'American' psychology be like?" needs to be discussed first.

Boring's brief answer to the question provides some insight: "By 1900 the characteristics of American psychology had become well defined. It had inherited its physical body from German experimentalism, but it had got its mind from Darwin. America's psychology was to deal with the mind in use [p. 506]." Boring goes on to contrast American and German psychology and the impact of the theory of evolution.

America was ready for evolutionism —readier than Germany, than England even. America was a new pioneer country. Land was free—to the strong pioneer who was ready to take it and wrest a living from nature. Survival by adaptation to environment was the key to the culture of the New World. America's success philosophy, based on individual opportunity and ambition, is responsible for shirt-sleeves democracy, for pragmatism and functionalism of all kinds, within psychology and without.

But "Americanism" was more than an attitude or frame of mind—it was a conviction about and participation in the American experiment that required an almost religious dedication. The elements of this "faith"—the Protestant work ethic, individualism, personal responsibility, natural spontaneity, heroic action, the profanity of institutions, the decadence of Europe—form the American "sacred and profane" intellectual network of the late nineteenth century. A psychology that partook of this spirit might well include the following perspectives found in Watson's (1967) list of themes: indeterminism, functionalism, deductivism, dualism, idiographicism, utilitarianism, staticism. Each of these themes has its counterpart in the rhetoric of the American *Zeitgeist:* "indeterminism" and the ethic of individual responsibility; "functionalism" and the "practical" pioneer spirit that Boring describes; "utilitarianism," and puritan practicality; and "staticism" and the ahistorical view of America that Noble describes.

Those elements show themselves frequently in James' psychology. James' lengthy moral-philosophical discourse on the reasonableness of free will rather than determinism places him squarely in line with the American view of the free individual. The moral overtones in his chapter on instinct, his elaborations on the "self," his recurring interest in religion, even his "democratic" acceptance of all ideas—the subject matter and development of James' psychology include many of the elements that one could expect of an "American psychology." His orientation is a practical one with a focus on the individual. A natural morality, a somewhat dualistic view of the self, elements of a supernatural standard by which people guide their individual action, a lack of anything more than incidental discussion of a concept of institutional creation and social interaction processes—these are elements of the American mind that William James considers.

Though it is possible to typify James in the general terms of his time, it would be as unjustified to view him as a stereotypical "American" in his psychology as it would have been to call him "parochial" when discussing his general letters and writings. More important is whether American psychology today is restricted by national and cultural parameters to such an extent that Watson's charge of "provincialism" serves as an accurate diagnosis of American psychology. If deviations from an implied set of scientific norms are dismissed as error variance, and nothing more, American psychology must be the poorer for it. The general parameters of American psychology and the important factors in the variance from its real or implied norms can be better accounted for and dealt with when there exists an understanding of the intellectual surround within which American psychology operates.

REFERENCES

Boring, E. *A History of Experimental Psychology.* New York: Appleton-Century-Crofts, 1950.

Heidbreder, E. *Seven Psychologies.* New York: Century, 1933.

Hofstadter, R. *The Age of Reform.* New York: Random House, 1955.

James, H. *The Letters of William James.* Boston: Atlantic Monthly Press, 1920, 2 vols.

McCloskey, R. *American Conservatism in the Age of Enterprise 1865–1910.* New York: Harper & Row, 1951.

Noble, D. *Historians against History.* Minneapolis: University of Minnesota Press, 1965.

Perry, R. *The Thought and Character of William James.* Boston: Little, Brown, 1935, 2 vols.

Santayana, G. *Character and Opinion in the United States.* New York: Scribner, 1921.

Watson, R. "Psychology, a prescriptive science," *American Psychologist,* 1967, **22,** 435–443.

1.4 Effects of Noise on Pupil Performance

BARBARA R. SLATER

Within the past several decades interest in improving educational facilities has seen a steady increase. One of the areas around which much controversy has arisen is that of acoustical environment in the schools. In order to delineate a clear-cut area for investigation, only the specific category of the effect of noise upon written task performance of children was treated in the present study.

PROBLEM

The effects of noise upon human performance has been an area of conflicting reports and research studies for over four decades. Researchers such as Broadbent (1953, 1954, 1958a, 1958b), Grimaldi (1958), Jerison (1959), Kitamura (1964), Lehmann, Creswell, and Huffman (1965), and Weston and Adams (1935) have reported detrimental effects of noise upon performance. Other researchers, such as Super, Braasch, and Shay (1947), Park and Payne (1963), Sanders (1961), Teichner, Arees, and Reilly (1963), and Tinker (1925), have reported either equivocal results or no evidence of a detrimental noise effect.

Much of the existing research has used adult subjects (Ss), artificial conditions, and/or noise levels exceeding those encountered in any but extreme situations. Planning of educational facilities based upon these studies, without evidence of comparability of Ss or conditions may be somewhat misleading. The conflicting results of studies pertinent to educational application further indicate the need for additional research to assist in determining the need for and value of acoustical treatment in schools.

The major objective of this study was to investigate the effects of noise upon written performance in a realistic environmental setting while meeting as many of the requirements of noise research as possible. Such an application

Reprinted with slight abridgment from the *Journal of Educational Psychology,* 1968, **59,** 239–243, with permission of the author and the American Psychological Association, Inc.

necessitated the use of an actual class-room environment, tasks pertinent to school routine, and noise comparable to that encountered by children during school activities. While it might be interesting to prove that noise of approximately 100 decibels transmitted, via earphones, to children working in isolation chambers caused a deterioration in performance, it would be rather difficult to generalize to children who are not subjected to this level of noise, who are not equipped with earphones, and who do not work in isolation chambers. It was also necessary to control for or to take into account physical variables, differences in set caused by instructions and task perceptions, individual differences, the so-called Hawthorne effect of a positive change resulting from any alteration of conditions, and the carry-over effect from one condition to another. The noise characteristics and instrumentation used had to be described for purposes of analysis and possible replication.

A secondary objective was to investigate individual differences under conditions of noise. According to Goodenough (1954, pp. 482–483), girls achieve slightly better in school, possibly because of girls' greater docility and better application to studies. Terman and Tyler (1954, pp. 1064–1114) cited studies indicating that boys may be more physically active and restless than girls. Considering this, it was expected that boys would be less motivated to work than girls and would be more prone to distraction under conditions of noise.

In line with Sarason's (Sarason, Davidson, Lighthall, Waite, and Ruebush, 1960; Sarason and Gordon, 1953) work on anxiety in children, it was decided to investigate the relationship between anxiety and the effects of noise. The Ss' perceptions of noise and the effects of set toward noise and toward the experiment were also considered as possible secondary factors.

Noise was defined, consistent with Peterson and Gross (1963), as undesired sound. Since the normal noise encountered by children in school is intermittent or irregular-interval noise, the study used this type of noise.

Hypotheses

Hypothesis 1. Under conditions of irregular-interval noise varying approximately 75–90 decibels, children's task performance will be lower than under conditions of relative quiet of approximately 45–55 decibels.

Hypothesis 2. Under conditions of irregular-interval noise at levels of 75–90 decibels, children's task performance will be lower than under conditions of normal or average classroom noise of approximately 55–70 decibels.

Hypothesis 3. Under conditions of relative quiet, children's task performance will be higher than under conditions of normal classroom noise.

Hypothesis 4. Performance levels of boys will be lower than performance levels of girls under conditions of irregular-interval noise of 75–90 decibels.

METHOD

Subjects

The Ss were 129 male and 134 female seventh-grade children from a centralized suburban school on the outskirts of a small urban complex, consisting of three cities, in south-central New York state. No children with hearing deficiencies were included.

Task

The STEP Reading Test, Form 3 was used as the written task. The *S*s were permitted to answer as many of the 70 questions as they were able during the 30 minute testing period in order to prevent a ceiling effect. Two experimental sets were assumed; the tension of a test situation and the more relaxed atmosphere of a homework situation. These assumed sets were induced through differences in answer sheets, instructions, and examiner behavior. Measures of speed, as the total number of questions attempted, and of accuracy, as the percentage correct of the number attempted, were obtained.

Grouping

Eight equated groups were used and each *S* was tested only once. Four days prior to the experiment, Part 1 of an alternate form of the STEP Reading Test was given to each *S*. The total number of correct answers on this pretest was used as the essential basis of equating the eight groups. Scores were arranged from high to low and a matching process ensured that the groups were comparable.

The groups were also roughly equated, by matching, on the basis of IQ, socioeconomic status and achievement to ensure that no systematic differences among groups on these variables occurred and to permit examination of individual differences. Each group consisted of approximately equal numbers of males and females.

table 1

Testing Conditions by Group

Group	N	Condition Situation	Noise	Task
1	31	Classroom	Quiet	Homework
2	37	Classroom	Quiet	Test
3	31	Classroom	Average	Test
4	32	Classroom	Average	Homework
5	31	Classroom	Noisy	Test
6	32	Classroom	Noisy	Homework
7	33	Experimental	Quiet	Test
8	36	Experimental	Noisy	Test

After completion of the matching process, a testing condition was assigned randomly to each of the eight groups. The composition of these groups is presented in Table 1.

Noise Conditions

A study was conducted of possible methods of producing suitable noise conditions, as determined by past research and by surveys of typical noise levels found in schools, and of methods of measuring and analyzing such noise. Sound-pressure levels in decibels were used throughout the study. Typical noise levels from the sample school are presented in Table 2. These levels are comparable to levels reported by Fitzroy and Reid (1963) in an extensive survey of 37 schools.

The hypothesized levels for the quiet (45–55 decibels), average (55–70 decibels), and noisy (75–90 decibels) conditions were selected so as to avoid exceeding the minimum and maximum limits which might be anticipated to occur within a school environment. Noise characteristics of the experiment were as follows:

Part 1: Classroom. The classroom section was divided into quiet, average, and noisy conditions. Only noise familiar in some degree to Ss was used and testing was done in classrooms with the usual row type seating.

For the quiet condition (45–55 decibels) the test room was maintained in an isolated situation. The surrounding classrooms were empty; the corridors were kept free from passage; and bells, buzzers, and intercom systems were temporarily eliminated.

For the average noise condition (55–70 decibels), testing was done while classes were being conducted in both adjacent rooms and with normal corridor

table 2
Typical Noise Ranges of the Sample School

Location	Decibel Range[a]
Classroom	
Occupied—class silent	54–62
Occupied—normal speech	60–72
Unoccupied—school unoccupied	46–55
Unoccupied—adjacent to band	72–86
Unoccupied—adjacent to chorus	72–78
Unoccupied—classes in adjacent rooms	52–58
Art room—class in session	56–84
Corridor	
During classes	49–58
Between classes	68–89
Study hall (small)	54–65
Cafeteria during a lunch block	76–94

Note.—Readings were taken over 10-minute time intervals and repeated at least once for each range given. A Model SS-375 Sound Spectrometer from the Industrial Acoustics Company set on Scale C (flat from 37.5–9600 cps) on fast speed was used.

[a] Decibels re .0002 microbar.

traffic including student passage, voices, and the noises of locker usage.

For the noisy condition (75–90 decibels) three kinds of noise were used. The first was an external machinery noise created by having a tractor-run power mower pass back and forth outside of the open and curtained windows. The second was a tape recording of *The Blitzkrieg* played in rooms on both sides of the testing room, with the speakers touching the walls. The third kind of noise was human in nature and was created by four male assistants working in the corridors and in adjacent rooms. This noise consisted of running with metal tapped shoes, banging on and slamming wall lockers, talking, whistling, and laughing, banging on walls and blackboards, dragging chairs and desks across the floors, and moving audio-visual equipment through the corridors.

Part 2: Experimental. The experimental section was divided into quiet and noisy conditions. The Ss were tested on the stage, which was draped to shield against extraneous noise. Prerecorded white noise issued from a central speaker with Ss seated around and equidistant from it. The quiet condition consisted of steady white noise of approximately 50 decibels. The noisy condition consisted of phases of quiet white noise of approximately 50 decibels alternated with phases of loud white noise of approximately 80 decibels. The quiet and noisy periods each consisted of a total of 15 minutes with intervals ranging 30–180 seconds and with a mean interval of 75 seconds.

Tape recordings were made of each entire testing session, and measurements

table 3

Noise Characteristics of the Actual Experiment

Group	Condition	Decibel Range	M	SD
	Classroom			
1	Quiet—Homework	49–58	54.8	1.8
2	Quiet—Test	50–57	54.5	2.2
3	Average—Test	54–72	62.7	5.4
4	Average—Home-work	56–72	64.7	4.7
5	Noisy—Test	74–91	82.6	4.7
6	Noisy—Homework	74–90	82.0	4.6
7	Experimental Quiet—Test	50–55	52.6	1.1
8	Experimental Noisy—Test			
	Phase 1—Quiet	52–56	53.2	1.3
	Phase 2—Noisy	79–82	79.9	.9

of the actual sound-pressure levels present during the testing sessions were taken every 60 seconds, providing 30 measurements for each condition. Measurements were made with an Industrial Acoustics Company Model SS 375 Sound Spectrometer set on Scale C at fast speed and an H. H. Scott Type 450 Sound Survey Meter set on C weighting. The noise characteristics for each condition are presented in Table 3.

Supplemental Data

Following testing, the Sarason Test Anxiety Scale for Children (Sarason, et al., 1960) and two questionnaires designed to assess Ss' perceptions of noise and their awareness of the purpose of the experiment were administered to each S. The data from these instruments were used to determine the relationship between individual differences and the effects of noise.

Testing Procedure

The experiment was carried out during the first three periods of two consecutive days to avoid the contamination of fatigue, which might have increased during the latter part of the day. Quiet and average classroom conditions were run on the first day to avoid feedback of information from Ss tested to those to be tested. This might have occurred, resulting in a noise set, had the conditions more obviously connected with noise been run first. The Ss were instructed that they were taking part in a reading project and that the instruments were a means of timing the tests and later checking on the accuracy of timing and instructions.

Treatment of Data

The major body of data was treated in three steps. The means and standard deviations for both speed and accuracy on the reading comprehension test were computed. An F maximum test was then used to determine the feasibility of performing analyses of variance. The observed F_{max} numbers were not within the critical regions. Therefore, analyses of variances were carried out as the best method of answering the questions raised by the hypotheses.

Data pertaining to the secondary questions were treated descriptively. The secondary questions were those pertaining to individual differences, such as the relationships between pupil perceptions and the effect of noise, or between anxiety and the effects of noise, and were not included in the hypotheses.

RESULTS

Although there was a slight tendency for boys to work faster and to perform less accurately than girls under both of the unfamiliar conditions of white noise, this tendency was of too small a magnitude to be of any practical value. There was no other trend indicating any effect of noise upon performance.

The results of two-way analyses of variance performed on the data for speed and for accuracy indicated that there were no significant differences for condition, sex, or interaction for either speed or accuracy. None of the hypotheses was supported in any degree by the data. Not only were there no significant differences, but there were no trends indicative of any noise effect, detrimental or otherwise.

While there were some minor individual differences, these were not consistent enough or of enough magnitude

for practical consideration. The Ss' perceptions of the effects of noise upon their performance, the degree of noise which was present during the experiment, and the annoyance value of noise had little relationship to actual performance under the noise conditions used. Similarly, measured anxiety had little relationship to actual performance.

DISCUSSION

The major body of data, as treated by analysis of variance, was strong evidence against any effect of noise under the specifications of the experiment and upon the population used. According to existing literature, if a noise effect had been demonstrated, it could have occurred in either the hypothesized detrimental direction or in the opposite direction of assisting performance. Neither effect was demonstrated.

Consideration of the representativeness of the sample, the pertinence of the task to typical school behavior, and the applicability of the conditions used to actual school conditions appeared to warrant generalization outward from the experiment to the public school population in general. At the junior high school level, and possibly at other grade levels, children's tested performance on written tasks, requiring reading comprehension, of the limited duration of a class period in length, is not affected either positively or negatively by the peaks of noise which are typical of a normal school environment.

The effects of noise over time, the effects of noise upon learning, the effects of noise upon tasks of a different nature, and the effects of noise at levels above and below those found in schools were not investigated in the present study.

The major portion of the present study was designed to examine the differences between equated groups of children, rather than the interactions between individual Ss and particular noise conditions. The reason for this choice was that practical school planning must consider children in groups. Since the data indicated that school children, as a whole, are not affected detrimentally by noise, it might now be of value to examine individual Ss tested under a variety of conditions. While summary inspection of data did not indicate that the results were brought about by extremes of performance cancelling each other out, this does not preclude the possibility that certain individuals might show test-retest changes. An experiment designed to examine this factor, if differences are demonstrated, might provide further insight into possible means of best handling particular children to facilitate the learning process.

SUMMARY

263 7th-grade public school children were tested to determine whether quiet (45–55 db.), average (55–70 db.), and noisy (75–90 db.) classroom and experimental conditions had a relationship to written task performance of relatively short duration. It was hypothesized that Ss would perform better under quiet than under average and noisy conditions and that boys would be more detrimentally affected by noise than girls. Noise typical of that experienced in schools and white noise were both used. Means and standard deviations were compared across the conditions used and analyses of variance were performed on the data. No noise effect, either detrimental or facilitating, was demonstrated on speed or on accuracy of performance. Ss' perceptions of the effects of noise and measured anxiety had little relationship to actual performance.

REFERENCES

Broadbent, D. E. "Noise, paced performance and vigilance tasks," *British Journal of Psychology*, 1953, **44**, 295–303.

Broadbent, D. E. "Some effects of noise on visual performance," *Quarterly Journal of Experimental Psychology*, 1954, **6**, 1–5.

Broadbent, D. E. "Effects of noise on an 'intellectual task,'" *Journal of the Acoustical Society of America*, 1958, **30**, 824–827 (a).

Broadbent, D. E. "Effects of noise on behavior," in C. M. Harris (Ed.), *Handbook of Noise Control.* New York: McGraw-Hill, 1958, pp. 10-1–10-34 (b).

Fitzroy, D., and Reid, J. L. *Acoustical Environment of School Buildings: Technical Report 1.* New York: Educational Facilities Laboratories, 1963.

Goodenough, F. L. "The measurement of mental growth in children," in L. Carmichael (Ed.), *Manual of Child Psychology.* (2nd ed.) New York: Wiley, 1954, pp. 459–491.

Grimaldi, J. V. "Sensori-motor performance under varying noise conditions," *Ergonomics*, 1958, **2**, 34–43.

Jerison, H. J. "Effects of noise on human performance," *Journal of Applied Psychology*, 1959, **43**, 96–101.

Kitamura, S. "Study of influences of train noise upon schoolchildren: I," *Tohoku Psychologica Folia*, 1964, **23**, 1–2.

Lehmann, D. W., Creswell, W. H., and Huffman, W. J. "An investigation of the effects of various noise levels as measured by psychological performance and energy expenditure," *Journal of School Health*, 1965, **35**, 212–214.

Park, J. F., and Payne, M. C., Jr. "Effects of noise level and difficulty of task in performing division," *Journal of Applied Psychology*, 1963, **47**, 367–368.

Peterson, A. P. G., and Gross, E. E., Jr. *Handbook of Noise Measurement*. West Concord, Mass.: General Radio Company, 1963.

Sanders, A. F. "The influence of noise on two discrimination tasks," *Ergonomics*, 1961, **4**, 253–258.

Sarason, S. B., Davidson, K. S., Lighthall, F. F., Waite, R. R., and Ruebush, B. K. *Anxiety in Elementary School Children*. New York: Wiley, 1960.

Sarason, S. B., and Gordon, E. M. "The test anxiety questionnaire: Scoring norms," *Journal of Abnormal Psychology*, 1953, **48**, 447–448.

Super, D. E., Braasch, W. F., and Shay, J. B. "The effect of distraction on test results," *Journal of Educational Psychology*, 1947, **38**, 373–377.

Teichner, W. H., Arees, E., and Reilly, R. "Noise and human performance. A psychophysiological approach," *Ergonomics*, 1963, **6**, 83–97.

Terman, L. M., and Tyler, L. E. "Psychological sex differences," in L. Carmichael (Ed.), *Manual of Child Psychology*. (2nd ed.) New York: Wiley, 1954, pp. 1064–1114.

Tinker, M. A. "Intelligence in an intelligence test with an auditory distractor," *American Journal of Psychology*, 1925, **36**, 467–468.

Weston, H. C., and Adams, S. The performance of weavers under varying conditions of noise: Industrial Health Research Board, Report Number 70. London: H. M. Stationary Office, 1935.

SECTION 2

DEVELOPMENTAL PSYCHOLOGY

Genetic factors are the initial determinants of form and behavior. The first paper in this section is concerned with genetics and was read at the 1967 convention of the American Association for the Advancement of Science by Michael Polyani, former Fellow of Merton College, Oxford University, and Emeritus Professor of Social Studies at the University of Manchester, England, where he had previously occupied the Chair of Physical Chemistry. Polyani's paper deals with the way in which the information and mechanisms present in DNA molecules function as genetic codes and set what he terms "boundary conditions" that are not reducible to physical and chemical terms.

A number of theories place the need for love or attention among the basic developmental needs. The research of I. Charles Kaufman and Leonard A. Rosenblum, of the Department of Psychiatry of the Downstate Medical Center, Brooklyn, N. Y., shows what happens when infant monkeys are separated from their mothers for four weeks. Like human infants, the infant monkeys reacted first with agitation, followed by depression. When mothers and infants were reunited, there was a marked intensification of mutual contact, as though they were "making up for lost time." The observations of the researchers appear to support the idea that infants, whether human or monkey, have needs to be fondled, attended to, and cared for. In everyday terms, they have a "need to be loved."

The ideas regarding the development of cognitive functioning in children that have been expressed by Jean Piaget over the last fifty years have had a considerable impact on developmental psychology, particularly in very recent years. The study by Irwin Silverman and Dale S. Schneider of the State University of New York at Buffalo, is an attempt to validate some of Piaget's observations. Piaget has at times been criticized because he tends to accept the oral reports of children at face value, and the question has been raised as to whether the child actually means what the experimenter (Piaget) thinks he means. The study by Silverman and Schneider made use of a nonverbal approach, and results supported the conclusions reached by Piaget.

One of the problems faced by adults who deal with children concerns the efficacy of punishment. The long-range purpose of punishment is of course that of getting children to refrain from future wrong-doing, yet common experience shows that it often fails to achieve this aim. Justin Aronfreed and Arthur Reber of the University of Pennsylvania, in the fourth paper, examine the mechanisms whereby children "internalize" forms of behavior. The results of their research show that punishment administered at the initiation of an act is more effective in getting children to internalize the suppression of the act than is punishment administered when the action has been completed.

The final paper in this section deals with the relationship between situational variables present during the childhood years and behavior during late adolescence and early adulthood—the college years, in other words. The study, as carried out by Richard E. Nisbett of Yale University, shows that college students who were first-born in their families are less likely to engage in dangerous sports, such as football, than are those who were later-born. This finding is consistent with other research that shows that first-born individuals are more likely to express fear and to behave cautiously. The study is included in this section as demonstrating the way in which childhood experiences influence behavior during the later years of an individual's life.

2.1 Life's Irreducible Structure

MICHAEL POLYANI

If all men were exterminated, this would not affect the laws of inanimate nature. But the production of machines would stop, and not until men arose again could machines be formed once more. Some animals can produce tools, but only men can construct machines; machines are human artifacts, made of inanimate material.

The *Oxford Dictionary* describes a machine as "an apparatus for applying mechanical power, consisting of a number of interrelated parts, each having a definite function." It might be, for example, a machine for sewing or printing. Let us assume that the power driving the machine is built in, and disregard the fact that it has to be renewed from time to time. We can say, then, that the manufacture of a machine consists in cutting suitably shaped parts and fitting them together so that their joint mechanical action should serve a possible human purpose.

The structure of machines and the working of their structure are thus shaped by man, even while their material and the forces that operate them obey the laws of inanimate nature. In constructing a machine and supplying it with power, we harness the laws of nature at work in its material and in its driving force and make them serve our purpose.

This harness is not unbreakable; the structure of the machine, and thus its working, can break down. But this will not affect the forces of inanimate nature on which the operation of the machine relied; it merely releases them from the restriction the machine imposed on them before it broke down.

So the machine as a whole works under the control of two distinct principles. The higher one is the principle of

---

Reprinted from *Science*, 1968, **160**, 1308–1312, by permission of the author and *Science*. Copyright 1968 by the American Association for the Advancement of Science.

the machine's design, and this harnesses the lower one, which consists in the physical-chemical processes on which the machine relies. We commonly form such a two-leveled structure in conducting an experiment; but there is a difference between constructing a machine and rigging up an experiment. The experimenter imposes restrictions on nature in order to observe its behavior under these restrictions, while the constructor of a machine restricts nature in order to harness its workings. But we may borrow a term from physics and describe both these useful restrictions of nature as the imposing of *boundary conditions* on the laws of physics and chemistry.

Let me enlarge on this. I have exemplified two types of boundaries. In the machine our principal interest lay in the effects of the boundary conditions, while in an experimental setting we are interested in the natural processes controlled by the boundaries. There are many common examples of both types of boundaries. When a saucepan bounds a soup that we are cooking, we are interested in the soup; and, likewise, when we observe a reaction in a test tube, we are studying the reaction, not the test tube. The reverse is true for a game of chess. The strategy of the player imposes boundaries on the several moves, which follow the laws of chess, but our interest lies in the boundaries—that is, in the strategy, not in the several moves as exemplifications of the laws. And similarly, when a sculptor shapes a stone or a painter composes a painting, our interest lies in the boundaries imposed on a material, and not in the material itself.

We can distinguish these two types of boundaries by saying that the first represents a test-tube type of boundary whereas the second is of the machine type. By shifting our attention, we may sometimes change a boundary from one type to another.

All communications form a machine type of boundary, and these boundaries form a whole hierarchy of consecutive levels of action. A vocabulary sets boundary conditions on the utterance of the spoken voice; a grammar harnesses words to form sentences, and the sentences are shaped into a text which conveys a communication. At all these stages we are interested in the boundaries imposed by a comprehensive restrictive power, rather than in the principles harnessed by them.

LIVING MECHANISMS ARE CLASSED WITH MACHINES

From machines we pass to living beings, by remembering that animals move about mechanically and that they have internal organs which perform functions as parts of a machine do—functions which sustain the life of the organism, much as the proper functioning of parts of a machine keeps the machine going. For centuries past, the workings of life have been likened to the working of machines and physiology has been seeking to interpret the organism as a complex network of mechanisms. Organs are, accordingly, defined by their life-preserving functions.

Any coherent part of the organism is indeed puzzling to physiology—and also meaningless to pathology—until the way it benefits the organism is discovered. And I may add that any description of such a system in terms of its physical-chemical topography is meaningless, except for the fact that the description covertly may recall the system's physiological interpretation—much as the topography of a machine is meaningless until we guess how the device works, and for what purpose.

In this light the organism is shown to be, like a machine, a system which works according to two different principles: its structure serves as a boundary condition harnessing the physical-chemical processes by which its organs perform their functions. Thus, this system may be called a system under dual control. Morphogenesis, the process by which the structure of living beings develops, can then be likened to the shaping of a machine which will act as a boundary for the laws of inanimate nature. For just as these laws serve the machine, so they serve also the developed organism.

A boundary condition is always extraneous to the process which it delimits. In Galileo's experiments on balls rolling down a slope, the angle of the slope was not derived from the laws of mechanics, but was chosen by Galileo. And as this choice of slopes was extraneous to the laws of mechanics, so is the shape and manufacture of test tubes extraneous to the laws of chemistry.

The same thing holds for machine-like boundaries; their structure cannot be defined in terms of the laws which they harness. Nor can a vocabulary determine the content of a text, and so on. Therefore, if the structure of living things is a set of boundary conditions, this structure is extraneous to the laws of physics and chemistry which the or-

ganism is harnessing. Thus the morphology of living things transcends the laws of physics and chemistry.

DNA INFORMATION GENERATES MECHANISMS

But the analogy between machine components and live functioning organs is weakened by the fact that the organs are not shaped artificially as the parts of a machine are. It is an advantage, therefore, to find that the morphogenetic process is explained in principle by the transmission of information stored in DNA, interpreted in this sense by Watson and Crick.

A DNA molecule is said to represent a code—that is, a linear sequence of items, the arrangement of which is the information conveyed by the code. In the case of DNA, each item of the series consists of one out of four alternative organic bases.[1] Such a code will convey the maximum amount of information if the four organic bases have equal probability of forming any particular item of the series. Any difference in the binding of the four alternative bases, whether at the same point of the series or between two points of the series, will cause the information conveyed by the series to fall below the ideal maximum. The information content of DNA is in fact known to be reduced to some extent by redundancy, but I accept here the assumption of Watson and Crick that this redundancy does not prevent DNA from effectively functioning as a code. I accordingly disregard, for the sake of

[1]More precisely, each item consists of one out of four alternatives consisting in two positions of two different compound organic bases.

brevity, the redundancy in the DNA code and talk of it as if it were functioning optimally, with all of its alternative basic bindings having the same probability of occurrence.

Let us be clear what would happen in the opposite case. Suppose that the actual structure of a DNA molecule were due to the fact that the bindings of its bases were much stronger than the bindings would be for any other distribution of bases, then such a DNA molecule would have no information content. Its codelike character would be effaced by an overwhelming redundancy.

We may note that such is actually the case for an ordinary chemical molecule. Since its orderly structure is due to a maximum of stability, corresponding to a minimum of potential energy, its orderliness lacks the capacity to function as a code. The pattern of atoms forming a crystal is another instance of complex order without appreciable information content.

There is a kind of stability which often opposes the stabilizing force of a potential energy. When a liquid evaporates, this can be understood as the increase of entropy accompanying the dispersion of its particles. One takes this dispersive tendency into account by adding its powers to those of potential energy, but the correction is negligible for cases of deep drops in potential energy or for low temperatures, or for both. We can disregard it, to simplify matters, and say that chemical structures established by the stabilizing powers of chemical bonding have no appreciable information content.

In the light of the current theory of evolution, the codelike structure of DNA must be assumed to have come about by a sequence of chance variations established by natural selection. But this evolutionary aspect is irrelevant here; whatever may be the origin of a DNA configuration, it can function as a code only if its order is not due to the forces of potential energy. It must be as physically indeterminate as the sequence of words is on a printed page. As the arrangement of a printed page is extraneous to the chemistry of the printed page, so is the base sequence in a DNA molecule extraneous to the chemical forces at work in the DNA molecule. It is this physical indeterminacy of the sequence that produces the improbability of occurrence of any particular sequence and thereby enables it to have a meaning—a meaning that has a mathematically determinate information content equal to the numerical improbability of the arrangement.

DNA ACTS AS A BLUEPRINT

But there remains a fundamental point to be considered. A printed page may be a mere jumble of words, and it has then no information content. So the improbability count gives the *possible,* rather than the *actual,* information content of a page. And this applies also to the information content attributed to a DNA molecule; the sequence of the bases is deemed meaningful only because we assume with Watson and Crick that this arrangement generates the structure of the offspring by endowing it with its own information content.

This brings us at last to the point that I aimed at when I undertook to analyze the information content of DNA: Can the control of morphogenesis by

DNA be likened to the designing and shaping of a machine by the engineer? We have seen that physiology interprets the organism as a complex network of mechanisms, and that an organism is—like a machine—a system under dual control. Its structure is that of a boundary condition harnessing the physical-chemical substances within the organism in the service of physiological functions. Thus, in generating an organism, DNA initiates and controls the growth of a mechanism that will work as a boundary condition within a system under dual control.

And I may add that DNA itself is such a system, since every system conveying information is under dual control, for every such system restricts and orders, in the service of conveying its information, extensive resources of particulars that would otherwise be left at random, and thereby acts as a boundary condition. In the case of DNA this boundary condition is a blueprint of the growing organism.[2]

We can conclude that in each embryonic cell there is present the duplicate of a DNA molecule having a linear arrangement of its bases—an arrangement which, being independent of the chemical forces within the DNA molecules, conveys a rich amount of meaningful information. And we see that when this information is shaping the growing embryo, it produces in it boundary conditions which, themselves being independent of the physical chemical forces

in which they are rooted, control the mechanism of life in the developed organism.

To elucidate this transmission is a major task of biologists today, to which I shall return.

SOME ACCESSORY PROBLEMS ARISE HERE

We have seen boundary conditions introducing principles not capable of formulation in terms of physics or chemistry into inanimate artifacts and living things; we have seen them as necessary to an information content in a printed page or in DNA, and as introducing mechanical principles into machines as well as into the mechanisms of life.

Let me add now that boundary conditions of inanimate systems established by the history of the universe are found in the domains of geology, geography, and astronomy, but that these do not form systems of dual control. They resemble in this respect the test-tube type of boundaries of which I spoke above. Hence the existence of dual control in machines and living mechanisms represents a discontinuity between machines and living things on the one hand and inanimate nature on the other hand, so that both machines and living mechanisms are irreducible to the laws of physics and chemistry.

Irreducibility must not be identified with the mere fact that the joining of parts may produce features which are not observed in the separate parts. The sun is a sphere, and its parts are not spheres, nor does the law of gravitation speak of spheres; but mutual gravitational interaction causes the parts of the sun to form

[2]The blueprint carried by the DNA molecule of a particular zygote also prescribes individual features of this organism, which contribute to the sources of selective evolution, but I shall set these features aside here.

a sphere. Such cases of holism are common in physics and chemistry. They are often said to represent a transition to living things, but this is not the case, for they are reducible to the laws of inanimate matter, while living things are not.

But there does exist a rather different continuity between life and inanimate nature. For the beginnings of life do not sharply differ from their purely physical-chemical antecedents. One can reconcile this continuity with the irreducibility of living things by recalling the analogous case of inanimate artifacts. Take the irreducibility of machines; no animal can produce a machine, but some animals can make primitive tools, and their use of these tools may be hardly distinguishable from the mere use of the animal's limbs. Or take a set of sounds conveying information; the set of sounds can be so obscured by noise that its presence is no longer clearly identifiable. We can say, then, that the control exercised by the boundary conditions of a system can be reduced gradually to a vanishing point. The fact that the effect of a higher principle over a system under dual control can have any value down to zero may allow us also to conceive of the continuous emergence of irreducible principles within the origin of life.

WE CAN NOW RECOGNIZE ADDITIONAL IRREDUCIBLE PRINCIPLES

The irreducibility of machines and printed communications teaches us, also, that the control of a system by irreducible boundary conditions does not *interfere* with the laws of physics and chemistry. A system under dual control relies, in fact, for the operations of its higher prin-

ciple, on the working of principles of a lower level, such as the laws of physics and chemistry. Irreducible higher principles are *additional* to the laws of physics and chemistry. The principles of mechanical engineering and of communication of information, and the equivalent biological principles, are all additional to the laws of physics and chemistry.

But to assign the rise of such additional controlling principles to a selective process of evolution leaves serious difficulties. The production of boundary conditions in the growing fetus by transmitting to it the information contained in DNA presents a problem. Growth of a blueprint into the complex machinery that it describes seems to require a system of causes not specifiable in terms of physics and chemistry, such causes being additional both to the boundary conditions of DNA and to the morphological structure brought about by DNA.

This missing principle which builds a bodily structure on the lines of an instruction given by DNA may be exemplified by the far-reaching regenerative powers of the embryonic sea urchin, discovered by Driesch, and by Paul Weiss's discovery that completely dispersed embryonic cells will grow, when lumped together, into a fragment of the organ from which they were isolated.[3] We see an integrative power at work here, characterized by Spemann and by Paul Weiss as a "field,"[4] which guides

[3] See P. Weiss, *Proc. Nat. Acad. Sci. U.S.*, **42**, 819 (1956).

[4] The "field" concept was first used by Spemann (1921) in describing the organizer; Paul Weiss (1923) introduced it for the study of regeneration and extended it (1926) to include ontogeny. See P. Weiss, *Principles of Development.* New York: Holt, 1939, p. 290.

the growth of embryonic fragments to form the morphological features to which they embryologically belong. These guides of morphogenesis are given a formal expression in Waddington's "epigenetic landscapes."[5] They say graphically that the growth of the embryo is controlled by the gradient of potential shapes, much as the motion of a heavy body is controlled by the gradient of potential energy.

Remember how Driesch and his supporters fought for recognition that life transcends physics and chemistry, by arguing that the powers of regeneration in the sea urchin embryo were not explicable by a machinelike structure, and how the controversy has continued, along similar lines, between those who insisted that regulative ("equipotential" or "organismic") integration was irreducible to any machinelike mechanism and was therefore irreducible also to the laws of inanimate nature. Now if, as I claim, machines and mechanical processes in living beings are themselves irreducible to physics and chemistry, the situation is changed. If mechanistic and organismic explanations are both equally irreducible to physics and chemistry, the recognition of organismic processes no longer bears the burden of standing alone as evidence for the irreducibility of living things. Once the "field"-like powers guiding regeneration and morphogenesis can be recognized without involving this major issue, I think the evidence for them will be found to be convincing.

There is evidence of irreducible principles, additional to those of mor-

phological mechanisms, in the sentience that we ourselves experience and that we observe indirectly in higher animals. Most biologists set aside these matters as unprofitable considerations. But again, once it is recognized, on other grounds, that life transcends physics and chemistry, there is no reason for suspending recognition of the obvious fact that consciousness is a principle that fundamentally transcends not only physics and chemistry but also the mechanistic principles of living beings.

BIOLOGICAL HIERARCHIES CONSIST OF A SERIES OF BOUNDARY CONDITIONS

The theory of boundary conditions recognizes the higher levels of life as forming a hierarchy, each level of which relies for its workings on the principles of the levels below it, even while it itself is irreducible to these lower principles. I shall illustrate the structure of such a hierarchy by showing the way five levels make up a spoken literary composition.

The lowest level is the production of a voice; the second, the utterance of words; the third, the joining of words to make sentences; the fourth, the working of sentences into a style; the fifth, and highest, the composition of the text.

The principles of each level operate under the control of the next-higher level. The voice you produce is shaped into words by a vocabulary; a given vocabulary is shaped into sentences in accordance with a grammar; and the sentences are fitted into a style, which in turn is made to convey the ideas of the composition. Thus each level is subject to dual control: (i) control in accordance with the laws that apply to its

[5]See, for example, C. H. Waddington, *The Strategy of the Genes.* London: Allen & Unwin, 1957, particularly the graphic explanation of "genetic assimilation" on page 167.

elements in themselves, and (ii) control in accordance with the laws of the powers that control the comprehensive entity formed by these elements.

Such multiple control is made possible by the fact that the principles governing the isolated particulars of a lower level leave indeterminate conditions to be controlled by a higher principle. Voice production leaves largely open the combination of sounds into words, which is controlled by a vocabulary. Next, a vocabulary leaves largely open the combination of words to form sentences, which is controlled by grammar, and so on. Consequently, the operations of a higher level cannot be accounted for by the laws governing its particulars on the next-lower level. You cannot derive a vocabulary from phonetics; you cannot derive grammar from a vocabulary; a correct use of grammar does not account for good style; and a good style does not supply the content of a piece of prose.

Living beings comprise a whole sequence of levels forming such a hierarchy. Processes at the lowest level are caused by the forces of inanimate nature, and the higher levels control, throughout, the boundary conditions left open by the laws of inanimate nature. The lowest functions of life are those called vegetative. These vegetative functions, sustaining life at its lowest level, leave open— both in plants and in animals—the higher functions of growth and in animals also leave open the operations of muscular actions. Next, in turn, the principles governing muscular actions in animals leave open the integration of such actions to innate patterns of behavior; and, again, such patterns are open in their turn to be shaped by intelligence, while intelli-

gence itself can be made to serve in man the still higher principles of a responsible choice.

Each level relies for its operations on all the levels below it. Each reduces the scope of the one immediately below it by imposing on it a boundary that harnesses it to the service of the next-higher level, and this control is transmitted stage by stage, down to the basic inanimate level.

The principles additional to the domain of inanimate nature are the product of an evolution the most primitive stages of which show only vegetative functions. This evolutionary progression is usually described as an increasing complexity and increasing capacity for keeping the state of the body independent of its surroundings. But if we accept, as I do, the view that living beings form a hierarchy in which each higher level represents a distinctive principle that harnesses the level below it (while being itself irreducible to its lower principles), then the evolutionary sequence gains a new and deeper significance. We can recognize then a strictly defined progression, rising from the inanimate level to ever higher additional principles of life.

This is not to say that the higher levels of life are altogether absent in earlier stages of evolution. They may be present in traces long before they become prominent. Evolution may be seen, then, as a progressive intensification of the higher principles of life. This is what we witness in the development of the embryo and of the growing child—processes akin to evolution.

But this hierarchy of principles raises once more a serious difficulty. It seems impossible to imagine that the sequence of higher principles, transcending further at each stage the laws of inanimate nature, is incipiently present in DNA and ready to be transmitted by it to the offspring. The conception of a blue-print fails to account for the transmission of faculties, like consciousness, which no mechanical device can possess. It is as if the faculty of vision were to be made intelligible to a person born blind by a chapter of sense physiology. It appears, then, that DNA *evokes* the ontogenesis of higher levels, rather than *determining* these levels. And it would follow that the emergence of the kind of hierarchy I have defined here can be only evoked, and not determined, by atomic or molecular accidents. However, this question cannot be argued here.

UNDERSTANDING A HIERARCHY NEEDS "FROM-AT" CONCEPTIONS

I said above that the transcendence of atomism by mechanism is reflected in the fact that the presence of a mechanism is not revealed by its physical-chemical topography. We can say the same thing of all higher levels: their description in terms of any lower level does not tell us of their presence. We can generally descend to the components of a lower level by analyzing a higher level, but the opposite process involves an integration of the principles of the lower level, and this integration may be beyond our powers.

In practice this difficulty may be avoided. To take a common example, suppose that we have repeated a particular word, closely attending to the sound we are making, until these sounds have lost their meaning for us; we can recover this meaning promptly by evoking the context in which the word is commonly used. Consecutive acts of analyzing and integrating are in fact generally used for deepening our understanding of complex entities comprising two or more levels.

Yet the strictly logical difference between two consecutive levels remains. You can look at a text in a language you do not understand and see the letters that form it without being aware of their meaning, but you cannot read a text without seeing the letters that convey its meaning. This shows us two different and mutually exclusive ways of being aware of the text. When we look at words without understanding them we are focusing our attention on them, whereas, when we read the words, our attention is directed to their meaning as part of a language. We are aware then of the words only subsidiarily, as we attend to their meaning. So in the first case we are looking at the words, while in the second we are looking *from* them *at their meaning*: the reader of a text has a *front-at* knowledge of the words' meaning, while he has only a *from* awareness of the words he is reading. Should he be able to shift his attention fully toward the words, these would lose their linguistic meaning for him.

Thus a boundary condition which harnesses the principles of a lower level in the service of a new, higher level establishes a semantic relation between the two levels. The higher comprehends the workings of the lower and thus forms the meaning of the lower. And as we ascend a hierarchy of boundaries, we reach to ever higher levels of meaning. Our understanding of the whole hierarchic edifice keeps deepening as we move upward from stage to stage.

THE SEQUENCE OF BOUNDARIES BEARS ON OUR SCIENTIFIC OUTLOOK

The recognition of a whole sequence of irreducible principles transforms the logical steps for understanding the universe of living beings. The idea, which comes to us from Galileo and Gassendi, that all manner of things must ultimately be understood in terms of matter in motion is refuted. The spectacle of physical matter forming the basic tangible ground of the universe is found to be almost empty of meaning. The universal topography of atomic particles (with their velocities and forces) which, according to Laplace, offers us a universal knowledge of all things is seen to contain hardly any knowledge that is of interest. The claims made, following the discovery of DNA, to the effect that all study of life could be reduced eventually to molecular biology, have shown once more that the Laplacean idea of universal knowledge is still the theoretical ideal of the natural sciences; current opposition to these declarations has often seemed to confirm this ideal, by defending the study of the whole organism as being only a temporary approach. But now the analysis of the hierarchy of living things shows that to reduce this hierarchy to ultimate particulars is to wipe out our very sight of it. Such analysis proves this ideal to be both false and destructive.

Each separate level of existence is of course interesting in itself and can be studied in itself. Phenomenology has taught this, by showing how to save higher, less tangible levels of experience by not trying to interpret them in terms of the more tangible things in which their existence is rooted. This method was intended to prevent the reduction of man's mental existence to mechanical structures. The results of the method were abundant and are still flowing, but phenomenology left the ideal of exact science untouched and thus failed to secure the exclusion of its claims. Thus, phenomenological studies remained suspended over an abyss of reductionism. Moreover, the relation of the higher principles to the workings of the lowest levels in which they are rooted was lost from sight altogether.

I have mentioned how a hierarchy controlled by a series of boundary principles should be studied. When examining any higher level, we must remain subsidiarily aware of its grounds in lower levels and, turning our attention to the latter, we must continue to see them as bearing on the levels above them. Such alternation of detailing and integrating admittedly leaves open many dangers. Detailing may lead to pedantic excesses, while too-broad integrations may present us with a meandering impressionism. But the principle of stratified relations does offer at least a rational framework for an inquiry into living things and the products of human thought.

I have said that the analytic descent from higher levels to their subsidiaries is usually feasible to some degree, while the integration of items of a lower level so as to predict their possible meaning in a higher context may be beyond the range of our integrative powers. I may add now that the same things may be seen to have a joint meaning when viewed from one point, but to lack this connection when seen from another point. From an airplane we can see the traces of prehistoric sites which, over the centuries, have been unnoticed by people walking over them; indeed, once he has landed, the pilot himself may no longer see these traces.

The relation of mind to body has a similar structure. The mind–body problem arises from the disparity between the experience of a person observing an external object—for example, a cat—and a neurophysiologist observing the bodily mechanism by means of which the person sees the cat. The difference arises from the fact that the person observing the cat has a *from*-knowledge of the bodily responses evoked by the light in his sensory organs, and this *from*-knowledge integrates the joint meaning of these responses to form the sight of the cat, whereas the neurophysiologist, looking at these responses from outside, has only an *at*-knowledge of them, which, as such, is not integrated to form the sight of the cat. This is the same duality that exists between the airman and the pedestrian in interpreting the same traces, and the same that exists between a person who, when reading a written sentence, sees its meaning and another person who, being ignorant of the language, sees only the writing.

Awareness of mind and body confront us, therefore, with two different things. The mind harnesses neurophysiological mechanisms and is not determined by them. Owing to the existence of two kinds of awareness—the focal and the subsidiary—we can now distinguish sharply between the mind as a "from-at" experience and the subsidiaries of this experience, seen focally as a bodily mechanism. We can see then that, though rooted in the body, the mind is free in

its actions—exactly as our common sense knows it to be free.

The mind itself includes an ascending sequence of principles. Its appetitive and intellectual workings are transcended by principles of responsibility. Thus the growth of man to his highest levels is seen to take place along a sequence of rising principles. And we see this evolutionary hierarchy built as a sequence of boundaries, each opening the way to higher achievements by harnessing the strata below them, to which they themselves are not reducible. These boundaries control a rising series of relations which we can understand only by being aware of their constituent parts subsidiarily, as bearing on the upper level which they serve.

The recognition of certain basic impossibilities has laid the foundations of some major principles of physics and chemistry; similarly, recognition of the impossibility of understanding living things in terms of physics and chemistry, far from setting limits to our understanding of life, will guide it in the right direction. And even if the demonstration of this impossibility should prove of no great advantage in the pursuit of discovery, such a demonstration would help to draw a truer image of life and man than that given us by the present basic concepts of biology.

SUMMARY

Mechanisms, whether man-made or morphological, are boundary conditions harnessing the laws of inanimate nature, being themselves irreducible to those laws. The pattern of organic bases in DNA which functions as a genetic code is a boundary condition irreducible to physics and chemistry. Further controlling principles of life may be represented as a hierarchy of boundary conditions extending, in the case of man, to consciousness and responsibility.

REFERENCES

Polanyi, M. *American Psychologist,* Jan. 1968, **23,** 27–43. *The Tacit Dimension.* New York: Doubleday, 1967.

2.2 Depression in Infant Monkeys Separated from Their Mothers

CHARLES KAUFMAN AND LEONARD ROSENBLUM

In children severe and serious effects are known to follow separation from mother for more than a brief period (1, 2). Higher organisms, who are not precocial, require parental care to develop normally. The relationship between infant and mother is thus crucial and the consequences of its disruption are momentous (3).

In our study of infant pigtail monkeys (*Macaca nemestrina*) we found two striking effects of a 1-month separation: (i) three of four infants developed a severe depression, and (ii) in all four there was a marked and long-lasting intensification of the mother–infant relationship after the mother and infant were reunited.

The subjects were four infant monkeys, 4.8 to 6.1 months of age at separation, who were born in the laboratory and raised from birth by their feral mothers in a group which also included their sire and an infantless adult female.

The group, which had been together for over 2 years at the start of the study, was housed in a pen 2.4 m wide, 4 m deep, and 2.1 m high (4). Observations, made through one-way vision windows, began 1 to 2 months before separation and continued for 3 months after reunion. They were spread over 3 to 5 days per week, for a total of about 2 hours per week for each dyad in the month before and after separation, and for each infant alone during separation. Observation time was reduced by half in the second and third months after reunion. With a keyboard-clock-counter device the observer recorded the total duration and frequency of a wide variety of behaviors by the mother and the infant; they included, for the infant, both filial and nonfilial behaviors and, for the mother, both maternal and nonmaternal behaviors (5).

The physical separation of mother

Reprinted with slight abridgment from *Science*, 1967, **155**, 1030–1031, with permission of the authors and *Science*. Copyright 1967 by the American Association for the Advancement of Science.

and infant was done outside the pen with a minimum of handling and trauma. The mother was placed in a separate location, and the infant was returned to the group. After 4 weeks the mother was returned to the group. There was a 3-week overlap in the separations of the first two infants, and again in the separations of the second two, approximately 10 weeks later.

The reaction during separation, in three infants, fell into three phases: agitation, depression, and recovery.† The fourth infant showed only the first and third phases. During the first phase pacing, searching head movements, frequent trips to the door and windows, sporadic and short-lived bursts of erratic play, and brief movements towards other members of the group seemed constant. Cooing, the rather plaintive distress call of the young macaque, was frequent. There was an increased amount of self-directed behavior, such as sucking of digits, and mouthing and handling of other parts of the body, including the genitals (Fig. 1). This reaction persisted throughout the first day, during which time the infant did not sleep.

After 24 to 36 hours the pattern in three infants changed strikingly. Each infant sat hunched over, almost rolled into a ball, with his head often down between his legs. Movement was rare except when the infant was actively displaced. The movement that did occur

appeared to be in slow motion, except at feeding time or in response to aggression. The infant rarely responded to social invitation or made a social gesture, and play behavior virtually ceased (Fig. 1). The infant appeared disinterested in and disengaged from the environment (Fig. 2). Occasionally he would look up and coo.‡

After persisting unchanged for 5 or 6 days the depression gradually began to lift. The recovery started with a resumption of a more upright posture and a resurgence of interest in the inanimate environment. Slow tentative exploration appeared with increasing frequency. Gradually, the motherless infant also began to interact with his social environment, primarily with his peers, and then he began to play once again. The depression continued, but in an abated form. Periods of depression alternated with periods of inanimate-object exploration and play. Movement increased in amount and tempo. Toward the end of the month the infant appeared alert and active a great deal of the time; yet he still did not behave like a typical infant of that age.

The fourth infant, the offspring of the dominant female, did not show the phase of depression. During the agitation phase, unlike the other infants, she spent a great deal of her time with the adult females in the group. As she recovered she became actively involved in exercise play and in exploration of the inanimate environment, followed later in the month

†Seay and Harlow (3) have described an initial "violent protest" in separated rhesus infants followed by a stage "characterized by low activity, little or no play, and occasional crying." Hinde, et al. (3) in their study of separated rhesus infants also noted increased crying and a reduction in play and locomotor behavior, and described "a characteristic hunched posture."

‡The facial expression had an appearance similar to that which Darwin [*The Expression of the Emotions in Man and Animals* (1872) (New York: Philosophical Library, 1955)] described and believed "to be universally and instantly recognized as that of grief."

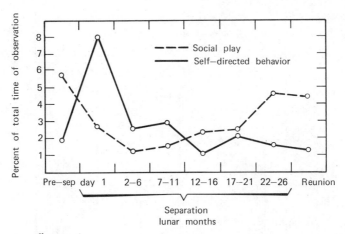

figure 1
Mean duration of self-directed behaviors and of social play for all four infants during the month before separation, successive periods of the month of separation, and the month after reunion.

by social play. However, the non-depressed infant showed many of the same behavioral changes as the other infants.

During the separation month all four showed a significant increase in self-directed behavior ($P < .05$) and explo-

ration of inanimate objects ($P < .01$), and a significant decrease in play ($P < .01$), both social and nonsocial. The early reaction to separation included a drastic fall in social play and a great rise in self-directed behavior, whereas recovery was accompanied by a gradual

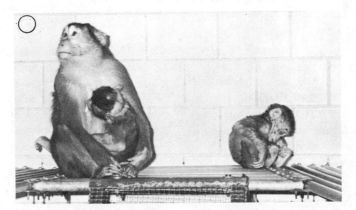

figure 2
A depressed motherless pigtail infant showing the characteristic posture. He is completely disengaged from the mother (not his) and her infant sitting nearby in close ventral–ventral contact.

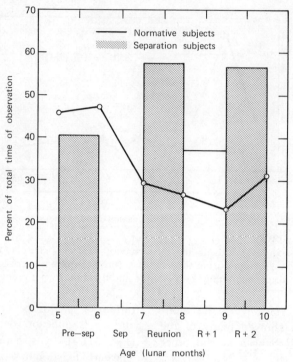

figure 3

Mean duration of ventral–ventral contact between mother and infant for four pigtail dyads over the course of the separation study (represented by the columns) and for nine pigtail dyads that were not separated over the same age period (represented by the line of points).

rise in social play and normal levels of self-directed behavior (Fig. 1).

When the mother was reintroduced to the group another dramatic change occurred. There was a tremendous reassertion of the dyadic relationship with marked increases in various measures of closeness in all four pairs. Clinging by the infant (Fig. 3), protective enclosure by the mother, and nipple contact all rose significantly ($P < .01$) in the month after the reunion as compared to the frequency of these actions in the month before separation. Even in the third month after

the reunion this trend was evident. This significant rise in measures of dyadic closeness is particularly striking in view of the fact that ordinarily for the age periods involved (6) these particular behaviors fall considerably.

The increased closeness was manifest in other ways as well. A measure of mother–infant physical separation that we have found valuable in our normative studies concerns departures (usually by the infant) to another level of the pen. The frequency of such departures during the month after the reunion fell to 20 percent of the departures in the month before the separation. Furthermore, the mean duration of these departures fell from 60.5 seconds to 34.4 seconds. Finally, maternal behavior which normally discourages dyadic cohesiveness at this age, such as punitive deterrence and nipple withdrawal, appeared very rarely.†

The individual differences in the reaction to separation may in part be explained in terms of the ontogenetic influence of the regulation of monkey behavior by the dominance hierarchy (7). The offspring of dominant females may develop greater coping ability and thus have a greater likelihood of survival if the mother is lost. This is consistent with selective advantage of dominance.

The stages of the reaction appear to be successive efforts at adaptation. The first two stages are comparable to the two basic response systems proposed by Engel (8) as available to the organism for dealing with mounting stress. The agitated phase, which appears to coincide with Engel's "flight-fight" response pattern, is likely to effect reunion with mother, if she is available. The second stage is strikingly similar to the syndrome of "anaclitic depression," reported by Spitz (2), in human infants separated from their mothers, an example of the

response pattern described by Engel as "conservation-withdrawal, [which] involves inactivity . . . and withdrawal from the environment," and which appears to conserve energy and avoid injury. The striking similarity between the early stages of the reaction to separation of pigtail infants and children suggests that the mediating central nervous response systems may be common to both species. The third stage, recovery in the continued absence of the mother, which was not reported in the human infants, may in the monkey infant be attributed to his greater locomotor ability, which enables him to reengage the environment actively on his own.

SUMMARY

The mothers of four pigtail (*Macaca nemestrina*) infants living in a group were removed for 4 weeks. All infants reacted initially with agitation. Three of the four infants then became severely depressed. The depression lasted about a week and was strikingly similar to the "anaclitic depression" of human infants who lost their mothers. When they were reunited, all four dyads showed a marked and prolonged intensification of the mother–infant relationship.

†Hinde, *et al.* (3) reported that after reunion only one pair showed a long-lasting increase in closeness. Seay and Harlow (3) found that despite an increase of mother–infant contact on the first reunion day the increase disappeared within 2 weeks. They concluded that "the result of mother–infant separation on the mother–infant relationship of these animals was transient and apparently unimportant." In this regard our results differ dramatically from theirs, since we found a marked and long-lasting intensification of the relationship in all our dyads.

REFERENCES

1. H. Bakwin, *Amer. J. Diseases Children,* 1942, **63,** 30; A. Freud and D. Burlingham, *Infants Without Families.* New York: International Universities Press, 1944; C. M. Heinicke and I. J. Westheimer, *Brief Separations.* New York: International Universities Press, 1965; J. Robertson and J. Bowlby, *Courr. Centre Intern. Enfance,* 1952, **2,** 131;

H. R. Schaffer and W. M. Callender, *Pediatrics*, 1959, **24**, 5; R. A. Spitz, *Psychoanal. Stud. Child*, 1945, **1**, 53.

2. R. A. Spitz, *Psychoanal. Stud. Child*, 1946, **2**, 313.

3. R. A. Hinde, Y. Spencer-Booth, M. Bruce, *Nature*, 1966, **210**, 1021; G. D. Jensen and C. W. Tolman, *J. Comp. Physiol. Psychol.*, 1962, **55**, 131; B. Seay, E. Hansen, H. F. Harlow, *J. Child Psychol. Psych.*, 1962, **3**, 123; B. Seay and H. F. Harlow, *J. Nervous Mental Disease*, 1965, **140**, 434; K. W. Spence, *J. Psychol. Norm. Pathol.*, 1937, **34**, 445.

4. The characteristics of the pen are detailed in L. A. Rosenblum, I. C. Kaufman, A. J. Stynes, *Animal Behav.*, 1964, **12**, 338.

5. I. C. Kaufman and L. A. Rosenblum, *Primates*, 1966, **7**, 205. All scores were transformed into percentages of total time of observation to equate for variations in the length of observation. Repeated measures analyses of variance were utilized throughout to assess the statistical significance of the data.

6. L. A. Rosenblum and I. C. Kaufman, in *Social Interaction Among Primates*. Chicago: Univ. of Chicago Press (in press); I. C. Kaufman and L. A. Rosenblum, in *Determinants of Infant Behavior IV*. London: Methuen (in press).

7. I. C. Kaufman and L. A. Rosenblum, *Psychosomat. Med.*, in press.

8. G. L. Engel and F. Reichsman, *J. Amer. Psychoanal. Ass.*, 1956, **4**, 428; G. L. Engel, *Psychological Development in Health and Disease*. Philadelphia: Saunders, 1962; _____ , *Intern. J. Psychoanal.*, 1962, **43**, 89.

A Study of the Development of Conservation by a Nonverbal Method

IRWIN SILVERMAN AND
DALE S. SCHNEIDER

A. INTRODUCTION

Basic to the much cited theory of cognitive development by Piaget and his colleagues (6) is the acquisition of conservation. In Piaget's laboratory, conservation of quantity was studied by presenting the child with equal and equal-appearing amounts of some substance (e.g., liquid or plasticine), then altering the appearance of one of the quantities (e.g., by pouring the liquid into a different shaped container or stretching the plasticine) and asking the child, in simple language, whether the amount had changed as well (9). One of the major findings was that children do not typically show the conservation of quantity until the age of about 7. Although the original reports were based on very small Ns, there have been several larger scale replications (3, 4, 5, 7, 8, 10, 11, 12) which

have generally corroborated this conclusion.

Piaget's methods, however, have been criticized for their dependence on the verbal report of the child. Braine has commented that "the child presumably responds to the 'meanings' he attributes to the experimenter's words. What these 'meanings' are we do not know . . ." (2, p. 46). With specific reference to the studies of conservation, Berko and Brown (1, pp. 536–537) have suggested that the child may equate the words "more" and "less" to dimensions of height or length, the implication being that children may have the concept of conservation before they have the capacity for semantic distinctions necessary to demonstrate it in Piaget's paradigm.

In the present study, the development of conservation of quantity was investigated by a procedure adapted from

Reprinted with slight abridgment from *Journal of Genetic Psychology*, 1968, **112**, 287–291, with permission of the senior author and The Journal Press.

Piaget's, but with a criterion other than verbal report.

B. METHOD

1. Subjects

These were 147 children, 66 males and 81 females, ranging in age from 4 to 10. Subjects came in approximately equal numbers from four sources, three of these with a predominantly lower socioeconomic class population and the other predominantly middle class.

2. Procedure

Each child was administered the test of conservation individually by the second author. The child was shown two identical glass jars containing differential amounts of candies (see Figure 1) and was asked, "Which jar has more candy?" The experimenter then told the child, "Watch me. I am going to pour the candy from this jar into this one," and she poured the lesser amount of candy into a third jar, which was longer and nar-rower (Figure 1), and placed it next to the jar containing the greater amount. Then she said to the child, "You can have all of the candy in one of these jars, whichever one you choose. Which one would you like?" After the child made his choice, the experimenter asked, "Why did you pick that one?" The quantity of candy chosen by the child was put into another container and given to him.

The child was considered to have conservation if he responded correctly to the question of which of the original jars had more candy, selected that amount rather than the lesser amount in the longer, narrower jar, and indicated in his explanation that he chose it because it was more. The child was considered not to have conservation if he answered the first question correctly and chose the lesser amount with the same explanation. It was not expected that many children would deliberately choose the lesser amount, but it was assumed that this would be detected, if it occurred, in the responses to the post-test question.

figure 1

From left to right, the lesser and greater amounts of candy in the standard jars, and the lesser amount in the longer, narrower jar.

C. RESULTS AND DISCUSSION

All of the subjects correctly reported which of the original two jars contained more candy. All but two subjects, a male and a female, indicated in their post-selection explanations that they thought they had chosen the jar with the greater amount of candy. The two exceptions actually chose the lesser amount and indicated that they were aware of this and did so because they wanted less. Although it may be assumed that these two children had conservation, they were

table 1

Percentages of Children Showing Conservation at One-Year Age Levels Between 4 and 10, Separately by Sex and Combined

	Male		Female		Combined	
Age	N	% Conserved	N	% Conserved	N	% Conserved
4–5	6	0	8	0	14	0
5–6	13	0	24	21	37	14
6–7	7	57	17	47	24	50
7–8	8	38	12	75	20	60
8–9	18	61	12	92	30	73
9–10	13	85	7	71	20	80

excluded from the sample for the sake of keeping the criterion measure homogeneous.

There were no apparent differences between the lower and middle class samples in the percentages of children showing conservation at the various age levels; hence these groups were combined in the presentation of the data. The Ns within each age group for the middle class sample were quite small, however (the total N was 44), and not enough to warrant a generalization about the absence of social class differences in the development of conservation.

Table 1 presents the percentages of children at each age level who showed conservation, separately by sex and combined. It may be seen that these percentages conform very closely to Piaget's and subsequent observations that a majority of children do not possess conservation prior to age 7, and that the age at which approximately 75 per cent of children can conserve is about 8 (6, p. 383). Our conclusion, then, is that Piaget's criteria are valid measures of conservation, independent of the child's capacity for verbal distinctions.

There appear in the present data to be trends for three age groups which suggest earlier development of conservation in females, though none of the sex differences achieved the 10 per cent confidence level by Fisher's Exact Test. Again, Ns for sexes within age levels were too small to permit a valid generalization. It is noted, however, that the data of Pratoomraj and Johnson (10) showed an identical nonsignificant trend of sex differences, and this may be a question worthy of further investigation.

D. SUMMARY

One hundred and forty-seven children, ranging in age from 4 to 10, were tested for conservation of quantity by a method which did not depend upon the child's statements of "more" or "less." The percentages of children at one-year age levels showing conservation conformed closely to Piaget's reports and subsequent replications which used verbal methods. Though sex differences within age groups did not achieve significance, there was a trend which suggested that females may develop conservation earlier than males.

REFERENCES

1. Berko, J., and Brown, R. "Psycholinguistic research methods," in P. H. Mussen (Ed.), *Handbook of Research Methods in Child Development.* New York: Wiley, 1960. pp. 517–557.

2. Braine, M. D. S. "Piaget on reasoning: A methodological critique and alternative proposals," in W. Kessen and C. Kuhlman, *Thought in the Young Child. Monog. Soc. Res. Child Devel.,* 1962, **27,** 41–60.

3. Bruner, J. S. "On the conservation of liquids," in J. S. Bruner, *et al., Studies in Cognitive Growth.* New York: Wiley, 1966. pp. 183–207.

4. Elkind, D. "The development of quantitative thinking: A systematic replication of Piaget's studies," *J. Genet. Psychol.,* 1961, **98,** 37–46.

5. ———. "Children's discovery of the conservation of mass, weight and volume: Piaget replication. Study II," *J. Genet. Psychol.,* 1961, **93,** 219–227.

6. Flavell, J. H. *The Developmental Psychology of Jean Piaget.* New York: Van Nostrand, 1963.

7. Greenfield, P. M. "On culture and conservation," in J. S. Bruner, *et al., Studies in Cognitive Growth.* New York: Wiley, 1966. pp. 225–256.

8. Lovell, K., and Ogilvie, E. "A study of the concept of conservation of substance in the junior school child," *Brit. J. Educ. Psychol.,* 1960, **30,** 109–118.

9. Piaget, J., and Inhelder, B. *Le Developpement des Quantités chez l'Enfant.* Neuchatel: Delachaux et Niesthe, 1941.

10. Pratoomraj, S., and Johnson, R. C. "Kinds of questions and types of conservation tasks as related to children's conservation responses," *Child Devel.,* 1966, **37,** 343–353.

11. Soenstroem, A. M. "On the conservation of solids," in J. S. Bruner, *et al., Studies in Cognitive Growth.* New York: Wiley, 1966. pp. 208–224.

12. Uzgiris, I. C. "Situational generality of conservation," *Child Devel.,* 1964, **35,** 831–842.

2.4 Internalized Behavioral Suppression and the Timing of Social Punishment

JUSTIN ARONFREED AND ARTHUR REBER

Many forms of conduct tend to become internalized as they are acquired in the course of social learning. They can then be elicited, and maintained to some extent, in the absence of surveillance or reinforcement. Developmental conceptions of conscience (Bronfenbrenner, 1960; Miller and Swanson, 1960, Ch. 5; Sears, Maccoby, and Levin, 1957, Ch. 10) and theoretical approaches to the social psychology of conformity (Kelman, 1958; Thibaut and Kelley, 1959, Ch. 13) commonly appear to assume that this kind of intrinsic control over behavior requires the individual's adoption of the values or standards of others. It seems very doubtful, however, that either moral or other kinds of evaluative processes are indispensable to the stability of conduct in the absence of external monitors. Preverbal children and even animals are capable of suppressing previously punished behavior, for example, over sig-nificant periods of time during which punishment contingencies are no longer present. Recent studies of older children (Aronfreed, 1961, 1964) indicate that their internalized reactions to already committed transgressions also can be established and maintained with little evidence that they are applying evaluative standards to their own behavior. And common observation suggests that adults likewise have many durable patterns of social behavior which are remarkably independent of external outcomes and yet do not call upon their evaluative resources.

Much of the intrinsic control of behavior which human beings show is, of course, mediated by evaluative cognition. But the experimental socialization paradigms which will be described in this paper are designed to provide a relatively simple context for examining the motivational and reinforcement mechanisms

Reprinted with slight abridgment from *Journal of Personality and Social Psychology*, 1965, **1**, 3–16, with permission of the authors and the American Psychological Association, Inc.

through which internalized behavioral suppression is established. These mechanisms are presumed to be fundamentally constant, regardless of the complexity of the cognitive structures which may intervene between a stimulus situation and the individual's ultimate behavior. Accordingly, the paradigms minimize the place of cognitive structure in the internalization process and emphasize the role of intrinsic cues which are closely tied to behavior itself. Even under these conditions, there is a problem in specifying the operational criteria for internalization. The degree to which conduct is internalized may be indeterminate even though it is maintained without direct social observation. For example, its maintenance may be controlled by the individual's expectations of rewards or punishments which will be eventually contingent on his alternative actions. Whiting's (1959) cross-cultural observations illustrate that control over behavior in the absence of socializing agents remains dependent, in many societies, on perceived external surveillance and sanctions. The rationales which children of different ages offer as justification for specific acts of conduct (Kohlberg, 1963; Piaget, 1948) also reveal how the evaluative processes which support internalization may vary in the extent of their reference to external outcomes.

A proper criterion of internalization might specify that an act is internalized to the extent that it can be maintained in the absence of external outcomes which have directly reinforcing consequences for the actor (and, one might wish to add, in the absence of the actor's anticipation of such outcomes). A more pragmatic extension of this criterion, to be used in the present study, is that conduct be considered internalized if it can be reliably elicited in the absence of socializing agents, after having been acquired under the control of either direct response outcomes which were mediated by the agents or the display of similar conduct by the agents. Whatever the precise meaning to be assigned to internalization, its demonstration clearly requires evidence that the maintenance of conduct has shown some movement from external to intrinsic control. We may conceive of the intrinsic control as being mediated by changes of affective state which have become partially contingent on the stimulus properties of behavior itself (response-produced cues) or on the cognitive representations of the behavior. In the case of internalized suppression, the relevant affective changes are the induction and attenuation of anxiety, which were originally controlled by the aversive social outcomes of particular forms of behavior. These aversive outcomes can be roughly assumed under the heading of social punishment, since they usually occur in a context where they are perceived as being transmitted by an agent who specifically intends to introduce them in response to one's actions. It is unlikely that any substantial repertoire of behavior becomes independent of external outcomes, in the course of naturalistic socialization, through interaction that is exclusively punitive. But the distinct contribution that response-contingent punishment makes to internalization can be examined in experimental situations where the effects of positive reinforcement have been reduced to a minimum.

The experiment to be reported here attempts to test a conception of internalized behavioral suppression that specifies a two-step acquisition process. It can be most conveniently illustrated in terms of the socialization of the child. The first acquisition mechanism is the attachment of anxiety to stimuli which are intrinsically produced. The most general common effect of all types of socially mediated punishment is their induction of an aversive affective state in the child. This state may have a number of qualitative variations (such as fear, guilt, or shame) which are dependent on the cognitive setting in which it is embedded. But its invariant motivational properties may be broadly designated as anxiety. Once the child has had some experience with a punished act, the role of punishment in eliciting anxiety can be easily displaced to social cues which have acquired secondary aversive value through their previous association with punishment. The incipient and even ongoing actions of children are frequently brought under the control of warning signals which are provided by their socializing agents.

Although the aversive social consequences of a child's behavior do not always reflect the violation of recognized norms of conduct, they do always imply some form of behavioral constraint between the child and the agent of punishment. It is therefore convenient to refer to any act as a transgression, when it is followed by social punishment of sufficient consistency and intensity to pro-

duce suppression of the act. If the punishment does have some minimally consistent relationship to the child's act, then a component of anxiety will necessarily become attached to the intrinsic stimulus correlates of the act. These intrinsic stimuli may be cues directly produced by the performance of the act itself. They also may be the cue properties of cognitive or verbal representations of the act—in the form, for example, of intentions or evaluative processes. Thus, certain kinds of actions, and their intrinsic representations, become capable of eliciting anxiety both during their performance and before they are even carried out, without the benefit of any external surveillance or objective threat of punishment.

The second mechanism in the internalization of behavioral suppression follows from the motivating properties of anxiety. Children quickly discover that they can avoid or attenuate social punishment and aversive warning stimuli by terminating an ongoing transgression or by arresting a transgression while it is still in an incipient stage. A variety of alternative nonpunished behaviors, including simple suppression of the transgression, consequently acquire instrumental value for them in reducing the anxiety elicited by aversive external events. At the same time, these suppressive behavioral modifications (and their representative cognitive processes) eliminate the intrinsic stimulus correlates of transgression and attenuate whatever anxiety may have been already independently attached to such correlates. Anxiety reduction will then gradually become attached directly to the intrinsic response-produced and cognitive correlates of suppression. And it will serve to reinforce the suppression, regardless of whether or not there are external consequences of the kind associated with surveillance and punishment. This entire two-step formulation is consistent with phenomena which are readily observable in naturalistic socialization, and also with the findings of extensive experimentation on the effects of punishment learning in animals (Estes, 1944; Mowrer, 1960a, Ch. 2; Solomon and Brush, 1956). It can also be extended to the learning of internalized reactions to transgressions which have already been committed (Aronfreed, 1963, 1964; Hill, 1960).[1]

Temporal Locus of Internalized Anxiety

Most of the acts which are defined by social punishment as transgressions are not punished indiscriminately without reference to the conditions of their occurrence. Ordinarily, an act has been punished in some situations, but not in others. The suppression of a transgression therefore cannot be viewed as being entirely mediated by intrinsic cues merely because it occurs in the absence of surveillance. The changes of affective state which motivate and reinforce suppression must rather be dependent on stimulus complexes which consist of both intrinsic and external cues, even though the external cues may not include the presence of a socializing agent. In order to examine the function of intrinsic cues in the mediation of suppression, it is

necessary to have an experimental method in which these cues are given a variable relationship to the course of anxiety, while the role of external situational cues remains constant. One such method is to observe the effects of variation in the timing of punishment with respect to the initiation and completion of a punished act. The rationale for this procedure is implicit in the common finding that punishment is less effective in suppressing the behavior of animals when it follows an act only after a relatively long temporal interval (Bixenstine, 1956; Kamin, 1959; Mowrer, 1960a, Ch. 2). The particular variant of the procedure used here was suggested by an informal report on work in progress with dogs by R. L. Solomon (see Mowrer, 1960b, pp. 399–404). Solomon's observations of 6-month-old puppies tentatively indicated that punishment upon approach to a forbidden food resulted in more prolonged suppression, during a test in which the experimenter was absent, than did punishment after a considerable portion of the food had been eaten. There was also some indication that puppies who did trangress during the test were more likely to show reactive signs of distress if they had been punished originally after having eaten part of the food.

Any act may be regarded as having a number of distinguishable components. In addition to intentions or other implicit precursors of the act, there are intrinsic cues which occur as the act is initiated. When the act is fully committed, there will be other intrinsic stimulus correlates which have some duration in time, and they may actually extend beyond the point of its completion. If we assume that

---

[1] The anxiety induced by punishment may disrupt punished responses not only because it motivates alternative responses, but also because it serves in itself as a competing response.

internalized suppression requires some mediation of anxiety by the sequence of intrinsic cues associated with a punished act, then we would expect the temporal locus of the original social punishment to have a significant impact on the effective motivation for subsequent suppression when the child is no longer under surveillance. Punishment used at initiation of a transgression would attach maximal anxiety to the intrinsic cues which occur at that point. In contrast, punishment administered only when a transgression has been already committed would tend to produce greater intensity of internalized anxiety at the point where subsequent transgressions have also been completed.

The difference in the effects of these two temporal loci of punishment would be limited by generalization or spread of anxiety to elements of the act other than those immediately present at the point of punishment. But to the extent that responses alternative to transgression (including its suppression) are motivated by anxiety and reinforced by anxiety reduction, they should have a greater probability of being elicited by the incipient cues of transgression—before the transgression is actually carried out—if punishment originally occurred at its initiation. If punishment occurred only after the commission of a transgression, the anxiety generalized to the point of onset might not be intense enough to motivate subsequent suppression when the child has been removed from the external presence of the punitive agent. Moreover, if punishment were to occur consistently after a transgression was socially perceived as having been already committed, suppression would not acquire much anxiety-reducing value at the point where maximal internalized anxiety would eventually be concentrated. When a child has completed a transgression, suppression is ordinarily no longer instrumental to the avoidance or attenuation of punishment.

METHOD

Two experimental socialization paradigms were constructed to require children to choose, on each of nine training trials, between a punished class of responses and a nonpunished class of active alternative responses (rather than between punished responses and passive suppression). This technique insured that there would be some opportunity for punishment training among all of the children, since they could not reduce their anxiety about the entire situation by resorting to a generalized suppression of all active responses. Consequently, the suppression to become evident during training appeared not simply as absence of the punished response, but rather as the positive choice of a nonpunished alternative. The children were confronted with a relatively simple discrimination. They were asked to choose between two small toy replicas of real objects commonly found in their social environment, to pick up the chosen toy, and to describe its function if they were asked to do so. The pair of toys varied from trial to trial, but one was always quite attractive, while the other was relatively unattractive. Punishment was consistently administered for choice of the attractive toy, and the child was not permitted to describe its function. Choice of the unattractive toy was not punished, but was also not rewarded, except for the minimal social reinforcement inherent in being permitted to describe its function and in the experimenter's noncommittal recognition of the child's verbal statement (in the form of a casual "uh-huh").

The experimenter's role as a socializing agent was predominantly punitive and provided in itself no model for the behavioral changes which the child was to acquire. A very limited cognitive context for punishment was provided by telling the children that certain of the toys were supposed to be chosen only by older children. This restriction was imparted during instructions and was repeated each time that the child was punished. In one training condition, punishment was administered as soon as the child's hand approached the attractive toy, and before the child picked it up. In the other training condition, the child was permitted to pick up the attractive toy and hold it for a few seconds (but not to handle it), and then punishment was given and the toy was removed from the child's hand. A control condition without explicit punishment was also devised, primarily to control for any possible effects of the difference between the two punishment conditions in habituation to picking up the toys during punished choices.

Following the nine trials used under each of these conditions, the children were tested for internalized suppression of the punished behavior. The experimenter set out a tenth pair of toys, one of which was highly attractive, and then left the room on a pretext. When he returned, he was able to discern whether the attractive toy had been picked up or even moved. The experiment was not designed to assess the effects of timing of punishment upon internalized reactions to completed transgressions, because of the difficulty of eliciting overt evidence of such reactions without disclosing the hidden monitoring of the children's behavior during the test for internalization. However, an attempt was made to get a tentative index of responses which the children might have used to reduce their anxiety following transgressions in the test situation.

Subjects

The subjects used in the experiment were 88 boys from the fourth and fifth grades of two public schools in a large urban school system.[2] The subjects were divided as follows among the three conditions: Punishment at Initiation, 34; Punishment at Completion, 34; Control, 20.

Procedure

Each child was taken individually from his classroom to the experimental room by the experimenter, who was a male. The child was asked to sit at a small table, and the experimenter seated himself across from the child. A rectangular wooden presentation board, roughly 12 × 18 inches in size, lay centered on the table. At the experimenter's right was a second table, upon which lay a black compartmentalized box and the experimenter's recording materials. The box had 24 compartments, each of which held a pair of toy replicas. Only the first 10 pairs were actually used for the nine training trials and the test trial. The toys

[2] The experiment was made possible through the cooperation of a number of administrators and teachers in the Philadelphia public school system.

were all quite small, and varied in their outer dimensions from roughly .5 inch to 2.5 inches. The attractive member of each pair was always somewhat larger, had more detailed fidelity to its realistic prototype, and had a higher relevance to masculine interests (for example, a tiny electric motor, a camera with moving parts, etc.). The unattractive items were, in contrast, smaller, shabbily designed, and more generally associated with feminine interests (for example, a barrette, a thimble, etc.). The pairs of items were used in a fixed order under all conditions.

Punishment at Initiation. The experimenter's instructions were given as follows:

I'm going to put some toys down here on this board. Each time I'll put down two toys. Here's what you do— pick up the one you want to tell about, hold it over the board [the experimenter indicated appropriate action with hand, using his fingers to show that the item was to be easily visible when held], look at it for a while, and just think about what you're going to say. Then, if I ask you, tell me what it's for or what you do with it. Do you understand?

Following the child's indication of understanding, the experimenter continued:

Now some of the toys here are only supposed to be for older boys, so you're not supposed to pick them. When you pick something that's only for older boys, I'll tell you.

The experimenter then began the first trial by placing the initial pair of toys on the board and saying: "All right, now pick up the one you want to tell about, look at it for a while, and just think about what you're going to say." To indicate subsequent trials, the experimenter said: "All right, pick up the one you want to tell about," or simply "All right." The position of the attractive toy was consistently alternated over the nine training trials, so that it appeared at the child's left on odd-numbered trials and at his right on even-numbered trials (thus providing another cue, in addition to attractiveness, to simplify the discrimination).

After the experimenter initiated each trial by placing a pair of toys, he dropped his hands lightly to an apparently casual resting position just behind the toys. When the child reached for the unattractive toy, he was permitted to pick it up and hold it over the board, in accordance with the instructions. After 2 or 3 seconds, the experimenter said: "All right, tell me about it." Following the subject's description of the toy's function (usually rather brief), the experimenter simply said "uh-huh" (quite flatly) and removed both toys from the board after the child had put down the toy he had chosen. When the child reached for the attractive toy, the experimenter said: "No—that's for the older boys" (firmly, though not very sharply), and raised the fingers of his hand behind the toy as though to slightly cover it. The experimenter's verbal disapproval was always given before the child actually touched the toy, but when the child's hand was rather close to it. The disapproval was almost always immediately effective in causing the child to withdraw his hand without even touching the toy. The experimenter then first removed the attractive toy, leaving the unattractive one for a few seconds, in the event that the child would want to pick it up and thus correct its original transgression. But very few children ever used the opportunity to pick up an unattractive toy, once they had already been punished for their choice of the attractive one.

Punishment at Completion. The instructions and general procedure for the training condition, and the experimenter's behavior when the child chose an unattractive toy, were identical with those described above for the Punishment at Initiation condition. The only difference was in the timing of punishment when the child chose an attractive toy. Here, the child was permitted to pick up the attractive toy and hold it over the board, just as in the case of an unattractive toy. Then, after 2 or 3 seconds, the experimenter said: "No—that's for the older boys," and gently but firmly removed the toy from the child's hand (the position in which the children had been instructed to hold the toys was such that the toy was never actually handled and was readily removable). As in the first condition, the unattractive toy was removed from the board a few seconds later, so as to give the child an opportunity to correct himself.

Control. The Control condition was constructed to observe the effects of lack of opportunity to pick up the attractive toys, during training in which there was no response-contingent punishment. Instructions and procedure were similar to those used for the punishment conditions, but had to be slightly modified to define a situation in which the child would never actually pick up the toys,

without the necessity of using explicit punishment. A statement was also added to specifically indicate which of the toys were intended only for older boys, since the general prohibition on choosing such toys, imparted in the instructions, was concretized in the other training conditions by the information conveyed on punishment trials.

The experimenter's modified instructions were as follows:

I'm going to put some toys down here on this board. Each time I'll put down two toys. Here's what you do—you just point to the one you want to tell about [the experimenter demonstrated with his hand], look at it for a while, and just think about what you're going to say. Then, if I ask you, tell me what it's for or what you do with it. Do you understand?

Following the child's indication of understanding, the experimenter continued:

Now some of the toys here are only supposed to be for older boys, so you're not supposed to pick them up. The nicer-looking, more interesting toys are for the older boys.

The experimenter then initiated the training trials. On each trial, the child was asked to indicate his choice by pointing. When the child pointed to an unattractive toy, the experimenter said: "All right, tell me about it." After the child had finished describing the toy's function, the experimenter said "uh-huh" and removed both toys. When the child pointed to the attractive toy, the experimenter simply removed both toys without saying anything (a procedure which, while it was not explicitly punitive, may well have been frustrating or otherwise aversive to the child).

Test Situation. The two objects used on the tenth (test) were related to one another in the same way as were the members of previous pairs used during training. But they were somewhat less toylike. There was visible action within the attractive object, whereas the other object was not only unattractive but also relatively difficult to identify. Consequently, some generalization had to be exercised by the child in carrying his response tendencies to the test situation. The attractive object was a two-chambered glass timer in which an enclosed quantity of salt ran down from the upper to the lower chamber in a period of 1 minute (previous pilot work had suggested that the tendency to turn the timer, or at least to handle it, was difficult to resist). The unattractive object was a dingy, yellow, 2-inch square of terry cloth, folded into an approximation of a piece of toweling. As the tenth trial began, the experimenter was about to place these objects, but then turned hesitatingly to his folder of papers, in which he had been recording the child's choices, and said (in a halting and distracted fashion, while looking into the folder):

> It looks like I forgot some of the papers I need . . . I must have left them in my car . . . I'll have to go outside on the street and get them.

The experimenter then placed the pair of toys. The presentation board was unfinished and had on its surface a number of scratches. One of these was actually a faint marker inserted for the test situation, a straight line about .5 inch in length. A barely visible scratch line had also been made on each of the timer's two hexagonal rubber bases, running from their edges along their upper surfaces. The experimenter placed the timer so that the scratch line on one of its bases was exactly orthogonal to the faint line on the board. As the experimenter placed the item, he also rose and said:

> I'll be gone for about 5 or 10 minutes . . . while I'm gone, you can be deciding which one of these toys you want to tell about.

The experimenter then took his folder and left the room, closing the door firmly behind him. The experimenter remained out of the room for 5 minutes, and then reentered, first rattling the doorknob, so as to give the child time to replace either of the toys which he might have picked up. While the experimenter was walking over to the table where the child was sitting, he asked: "While I was gone, were you thinking about the toys?" Then the experimenter continued, after sitting down and opening his folder to his recording sheet: "Well, I don't want you to choose yet, but tell me what you were thinking while I was gone." Following the child's response to this inquiry, the experimenter asked: "While I was gone, did you decide on which one you want to tell about?" The child's responses to each of these questions were recorded verbatim. The experimenter also noted whether the timer had been moved during his absence.

After the inquiry described above was completed, the experimenter closed

table 1

Frequency of Test Transgression and Nontransgression Following
Each of Three Training Paradigms

| | Training Paradigms | | |
Behavior during Test Situation	Punishment at Initiation ($N = 34$)	Punishment at Completion ($N = 34$)	Control ($N = 20$)
Transgression	9	24	16
Nontransgression	25	10	4

the procedure on the pretext that the remaining toys in the box could not be used because he could not find his misplaced papers. A further statement was added to put the child at ease about his performance and to invoke his cooperation in not discussing his experience with other children.

RESULTS

The primary observations were of whether or not the children picked up or handled the attractive minute-glass in the experimenter's absence, an index of the internalized effectiveness of the suppression acquired during training. Table 1 shows, for each of the training conditions, the numbers of children who did and did not transgress. Chi-square values for the 2×2 contingency tables which compare each two of the three training conditions, with respect to frequencies of transgression and nontransgression during the test, are as follows: Punishment at Initiation versus Punishment at Completion: $\chi^2 = 11.54$, $p < .001$; Punishment at Initiation versus Control:

table 2

Frequency of Transgression and Punishment during Training among Test Transgressors and
Nontransgressors Trained under Each of Two Variations in Timing of Punishment

| Experimental Group | Frequency of Punishment during Training | | | | | | | |
	0	1	2	3	4	5	6	7
Punishment at Initiation								
Transgressors	1	3	2	2		1		
Nontransgressors	1	11	7	5		1		
Both test groups	2	14	9	7		2		
Punishment at Completion								
Transgressors	1	5	10	4	1	2		1
Nontransgressors		2	3	3		1	1	
Both test groups	1	7	13	7	1	3	1	1

$\chi^2 = 12.44$, $p < .001$; Punishment at Completion versus Control: $\chi^2 = .19$, ns.[3]

These differences in the effectiveness of internalized suppression, during the test situation, were complemented by the behavior of the children during training. Despite the mild prohibition conveyed in the instructions, the children in the Control condition persistently pointed to the attractive toys, even though this behavior resulted in no opportunity to describe the function of the toys. The great majority of these children chose the attractive toy on six to eight of the nine trials. More than a few chose it on all nine trials. The discriminability of the toys within each pair, and the consistent difference in their attractiveness, was also apparent in the responses of children in the punishment training conditions, but in a very different way that clearly showed the effects of the punishment. Under punishment training, the typical sequence of behavior was to choose the attractive toy on the first one, two, or three trials, and then to fairly consistently choose the unattractive toy thereafter. A single punishment was sufficient, for 21 of the children, to inhibit further choices of the attractive toys. Occasionally, a child would revert once, near the middle of the series of trials, to choosing an attractive toy, but would then return immediately to choosing the unattractive ones.

It is particularly interesting to note that children punished at initiation of transgression exposed themselves to punishment *less* frequently than did those punished at completion. Table 2 shows the distribution of frequencies of punishment in the two punishment training paradigms, separately for those children who transgressed and those who did not transgress in the test situation. The two total training groups are significantly different from one another ($\chi^2 = 3.16$, $p < .05$), if we compare the number of children who received less than two punishments with those who received two or more punishments.[4] Clearly, it is not the number of punishments during training that makes punishment at initiation more effective as a paradigm for inducing internalized suppression. A comparison of all transgressors with all nontransgressors also indicates that behavior in the test situation is not attributable to frequency of punishment during training.

For reasons already set forth, it might be expected that children trained under punishment at completion and would experience more anxiety *following* a transgression in the test situation than would children trained under punish-

---

[3] All values shown here are for one-tailed tests and incorporate a correction for continuity.

[4] The value shown is for a one-tailed test and incorporates a correction for continuity. The comparison given results in the least disproportionate division possible along the frequency scale. Separate analogous comparisons of the two punishment conditions, within the transgressor and nontransgressor groups, would not be meaningful because of the extremely small samples which would appear in some cells of the relevant frequency tables.

The effects of differential timing of punishment are also visible in the occurrence of reversals. Seventeen of the children punished at completion reverted momentarily to choosing an attractive toy after suppression had begun to be established during training, but this behavior was shown by only nine of the children punished at initiation.

ment at initiation. Since the anxiety was not likely to be so intense as to overflow into an overt display of affect, the only evidence of its presence would be in certain responses which might be instrumental to its reduction. In the present experiment, it was important that the experimenter's knowledge of the child's transgression not be revealed, and consequently it was not possible to employ techniques which would directly elicit observable responses such as confession and reparation. It appeared, however, that some of the children might be using a quasi-confessional response, predispositionally available from past experience, to reduce their anxiety following a transgression in the experimenter's absence. When the experimenter returned to the room, there were virtually no spontaneous responses from the children which could be easily classified as internalized reactions to transgression. But there were some interesting variations of response to the inquiry about their thoughts during the test situation. Children who had been in the Control condition almost invariably indicated that they had been "thinking" about the attractive test object, a verbal response that agreed with their behavior during the test. In contrast, a substantial majority of the children exposed to the two punishment conditions reported that they had thought about the unattractive object (a few indicated that they had not thought about either one). However, roughly one third of the punished children did admit thinking about the attractive object. Closer inspection of the data, shown in Table 3, revealed that these latter children were predominantly those trained under punishment at completion, and

table 3

Frequency of Admission and Nonadmission Reactions Following Test Situation among Transgressors and Nontransgressors Trained under Each of Two Variations in Timing of Punishment

Experimental Group	Reaction Following Test Situation	
	Admission	Non-admission
Punishment at Initiation		
Transgressors	4	5
Nontransgressors	1	24
Both test groups	5	29
Punishment at Completion		
Transgressors	16	8
Nontransgressors	2	8
Both test groups	18	16

that they were almost entirely transgressors. In view of the overall contrast between the Control and punishment groups, it seemed that their response to the inquiry might be regarded as a reaction of "admission."[5]

Comparison of the total numbers of transgressors and nontransgressors who showed admission and nonadmission reactions shows a highly significant difference ($\chi^2 = 18.29$, $p < .001$). The same difference appears when the comparison is made only among children

[5] The term guilt is unwarranted in reference to the effects of this kind of experimental situation, if one regards guilt as a phenomenon of rather specific cognitive properties interwoven with an affective base of anxiety (Aronfreed, 1964). The situation does not provide the kind of evaluative processes through which the perception of transgression can properly be said to arouse a moral affect (for example, cognitive focus on intentions or on the consequences of action for others).

trained under punishment at completion ($\chi^2 = 4.44$, $p < .05$; $p < .02$ for the Fisher exact test). And a similar tendency is apparent among children punished at initiation (though it does not attain statistical significance in the latter case). If the admission of having thought about the attractive test object did serve to reduce the anxiety that followed transgression, then we would expect to find it more commonly among transgressors trained under punishment at completion than among transgressors trained under punishment at initiation. Inspection of Table 3 does reveal a tendency in this direction, but it does not attain statistical significance, in part because of the restricted number of children who transgress following punishment at initiation.[6]

DISCUSSION

The difference between the effects of the Punishment at Initiation and the Punishment at Completion paradigms indicates that timing of punishment is a very significant determinant of internalized behavioral suppression, at least when the punishment is accompanied by only minimal cognitive structure. This finding strongly supports the view that the suppression is some positive function of the intensity of the anxiety which is mobilized at the onset of a transgression, and that the anxiety is in turn a function of the original temporal relationship between this locus and the occurrence of punishment. It also supports the broader conception of the internalization of social control through punishment as resting

[6]The values shown are for one-tailed tests and incorporate a correction for continuity.

first on the attachment of anxiety to intrinsic cues associated with transgression, and secondly on the attachment of anxiety reduction to intrinsic cues associated with alternative nonpunished behavior.

The great majority of the children who were exposed to the Control paradigm picked up the attractive toy during the test, even though they were never permitted to pick up any toys during training. This last observation clearly indicates that transgressions had to be specifically punished in order to induce internalized suppression, and that the differential effects of the two punishment paradigms cannot be attributed to lack of opportunity to pick up attractive toys during training with punishment at initiation. Effects which are similar to those of the Control paradigm are commonly observed in naturalistic socialization. In the absence of external surveillance, previous mild injunctions and prophylactic restrictions of opportunity to transgress are often insufficient, without the addition of punishment, to suppress behavior which may have other highly reinforcing consequences for the child.

It will be observed that the experimentally induced suppression, during the test for internalization, cannot be attributed simply to "generalized" anxiety that might have become attached to the external cues which remain when the socializing agent has left the situation. Nor is it reasonable to suppose that the suppression is mediated by variable expectations about the risk of punishment. The difference in the effects of the two variations in the timing of punishment was apparent not only during the test, but also while the socializing agent was still present during training. And during both training and test, external cues and conditions of risk were identical for children who were exposed to either of the two punishment paradigms. It is likewise implausible to attribute the experimental findings to differences between the two paradigms in whatever positive reinforcement may have been associated with the act of choosing (but never being able to tell about) an attractive toy. The children who were trained under punishment at completion were permitted to pick up attractive toys, but they were required to do so in such a way that they could not handle them. They were also subjected to an additional period of uncertainty while they awaited the experimenter's punitive response (particularly during the early training trials), and to the possibly enhanced frustration entailed in having the toys removed from their hands. Moreover, it should be noted that children trained under the Control paradigm transgressed even more freely during the test than did children trained under punishment at completion, even though they were prevented from picking up any toys during training.

There may well have been some cognitive mediation of the experimental effects, despite the attempt to minimize cognitive structure. If the two variations in timing of punishment induced different temporal patterns of arousal and reduction of anxiety, these patterns might have become intrinsically mediated by intentions or other cognitive representations of the sequential elements in the acts of choice. Such cognitive interventions would tend to restrict the mediational role of cues which were directly produced by the punished and

nonpunished acts. But they would not require any change in the more general view that behavioral suppression becomes internalized when the course of anxiety begins to be monitored by intrinsic stimuli. If one were to assume that the primary difference between the two experimental groups, at the point of decision between transgression and nontransgression, was cognitive rather than motivational—for example, that the perceived determinant of punishment was reaching for the attractive toy in one group, but was picking it up in the other group—it would be difficult to account for the observed effects. Such an assumption would make no reference to the variable intensity of anxiety which might precede or accompany a punished act. It would lead us to expect that children in the Punishment at Completion group would be more likely than those in the Punishment at Initiation group to *reach for* the attractive test toy. It would also lead, however, to the prediction that the Punishment at Completion group would not go so far as to *pick up* the attractive toy. But the observations during both training and the test for internalization indicate that children in this group do pick up the attractive test toys more frequently than do children trained under punishment at initiation.[7]

The acquisition and maintenance of internalized suppression are not determined only by the intensity of the anxiety that becomes attached to the intrinsic

[7] The assumption that the experimental groups differ in their cognition of the determinants of punishment is perhaps not very credible in any case. The common general instructions to the children clearly convey the idea that "picking" a toy (i.e., the act of choice) is the relevant determinant.

cues associated with an incipient transgression. They are also affected by the reinforcement of behavioral alternatives to the punished act (including suppression). When the timing of social punishment is predictable to a child, as it is in the experimental paradigms, it may result in a delay-of-reinforcement effect upon suppression. The direction of this reinforcement effect would be parallel to the direction of the motivational effect that timing of punishment exercises upon suppression through its impact on the intrinsic temporal locus of anxiety. When children are confronted with choices between punished and nonpunished acts, they will experience some anxiety in connection with any choice, particularly early in the learning process before discriminant cues are firmly established. And the temporal relationship between nonpunished behavior and the reinforcement inherent in anxiety reduction will tend to be a direct function of the timing with which punishment predictably occurs for transgressions. In the Punishment at Initiation paradigm, for example, the external cues which signal that the child will not be punished begin to become apparent to him as soon as his hand reaches an unattractive toy without a punitive interruption. The anxiety reduction that reinforces the suppression of attractive choices thus soon becomes virtually immediate. In the Punishment at Completion condition, however, the anxiety reduction that follows nonpunished behavior is considerably more delayed, since the external safety signals do not occur until the child has been asked to tell about the toy. A possible implication of this analysis for naturalistic socialization is that children who are closely supervised by their parents may tend to experience more immediate reinforcement for their suppression of transgressions. It is also interesting to note that children may be forced to rely too heavily on the external outcomes of their behavior, if anxiety reduction cannot easily become discriminately attached to the intrinsic correlates of nonpunished behavior. This difficulty might arise if they were faced with complex discriminations in which they could not distinguish between punished and nonpunished responses, or if the anxiety induced by punishment were so intense as to disrupt the discrimination of relevant cues.

Some Further Theoretical Implications

The Punishment at Completion paradigm seems to be hardly more effective than the Control paradigm in producing internalized suppression. This finding suggests that the anxiety mobilized by an incipient transgression during the test situation was not sufficient to motivate suppression, when its intensity was attenuated across a gradient of generalization from the total complex of cues which were originally present at punishment of a completed transgression during training. The relative lack of effectiveness of the Punishment at Completion paradigm presents an instructive contrast to the observations made in a similar experiment conducted by Walters and Demkow (1963). These investigators used reaching for attractive toys versus touching the toys as their two temporal positions of punishment, and found that these training conditions produced only a tenuous difference in the subsequent effectiveness of the child's behavioral suppression in the experimenter's absence. The limitation on the effect which they observed was very probably due to the fact that their variation in timing cut a rather fine difference into the topography of the punished act and into the generalization gradients of the anxiety induced at the two points of punishment. A comparison of their findings with the findings of the present study indicates that the anxiety induced by the social punishment of an act does generalize from the intrinsic stimuli which are immediately present at the point of punishment to closely surrounding stimulus components of the punished act.

It may appear to be somewhat surprising that so many transgressions occur in the test situation following the Punishment at Completion paradigm, since naturalistic socialization commonly produces effective internalized suppression, even though it is very dependent on the punishment of already committed transgressions. Although the punishment of parents and socializing agents may be extremely variable in its timing, the ecology of socialization does not present too many opportunities to introduce punishment when a child is only on the threshold of transgressions. Part of this apparent discrepancy between naturalistic and experimental socialization may be an artifact of the use of a gross index of suppression in the test situation—the occurrence or nonoccurrence of transgression in a limited time period. A more sensitive index, such as elapsed time before the occurrence of transgression, might have revealed differences in the strength of the internalized suppression induced by the two punishment training

conditions, without implying that the small variation in timing was so powerful as to determine whether a transgression could be elicited at all. The use of an elapsed time measure might have disclosed, for example, that transgressions following the Punishment at Completion paradigm occurred later in the test period than transgressions following the Control paradigm. Conversely, a longer test period might have raised the attractiveness of the forbidden toy, or might have resulted in extinction of some of the anxiety attached to intrinsic cues of incipient transgression, so that transgression would have been more common following training under punishment at initiation.

Variation of the precise timing of punishment, within the microstructure of a punished act, may be a convenient method for teasing out the specific mechanisms through which behavioral suppression becomes acquired and internalized. But naturalistic socialization has a number of other features which would tend to dilute the significance of timing, and to facilitate internalization even when punishments typically follow transgressions at temporal intervals well beyond these used in the experimental paradigms. The anxiety aroused by the punishment of agents to whom the child has strong positive attachments (particularly the parents) may be substantially greater than the anxiety aroused by an experimenter's verbal disapproval. And even if punishment follows a committed transgression, a greater intensity of anxiety at its point of application will be more likely to insure enough generalization to motivate suppression at the point of subsequent incipient transgressions. The punishment and warning signals emitted by parents are also often patterned in accordance with the continuous or intermittent character of many of a child's transgressions. Parents sometimes punish in the midst of a committed but sustained transgression, or after a discrete repeatable act that the child has completed but is about to initiate again. Under these conditions, substantial anxiety can become directly attached to the intrinsic cues associated with an incipient transgression, even though punishment is originally contingent on visible commission of the transgression. Moreover, the child may be given the opportunity to avoid or escape punishment by introducing its own behavioral control in the course of an ongoing transgression—a corrective option that is not available in the experimental paradigms—with the result that suppression may acquire instrumental, anxiety-reducing value even when it does not initially prevent the occurrence of transgression.

In the social interaction between parents and children, the reinforcement of behavioral suppression is not entirely defined, of course, by the presence or absence of aversive outcomes. Parents often react with affection, praise, or other forms of positive reinforcement, when they are aware of evidence of suppression in their children's behavior. A significant component of the intrinsic reinforcement that supports internalized suppression may consequently be derived from positive affect which was originally induced by social rewards, rather than from the reduction of the anxiety which is elicited by incipient transgression. It is for this reason that situational assessments of children's al-

ready acquired dispositions to suppress socially prohibited behavior are ambiguous with respect to the motivational antecedents and reinforcing consequences of the suppression. Such dispositions will be the resultants of a complex history of interaction of the effects of direct punishments and rewards (and also, perhaps, of the effects of modeling). Two well-designed surveys (Burton, Maccoby, and Allinsmith, 1961; Grinder, 1962) have, in fact, uncovered only tenuous and inconsistent relationships between children's internalized suppression of social transgressions and the discrete practices of punishment or reward which are used by their parents.

Probably the feature of naturalistic socialization that most effectively insures internalized suppression, regardless of the temporal locus of punishment, is the extensive verbal mediation used by parents. A verbal medium of punishment makes it possible for the child's anxiety to become monitored by intentions, conceptual labels, and other cognitive processes. Such cognitive processes may act as common mediators of anxiety. They can become attached to any of the concrete patterns of proprioceptive and external cues which emerge sequentially in the performance and aftereffects of a transgression. And they can consequently bridge the microstructure and temporal separation of these concrete cues, so that the cues retain only a negligible function in governing the course of anxiety. The intensity of the anxiety that is elicited at the point of an incipient transgression would thus become independent of the original temporal relationship between the cues which are immediately present at that point and the occurrence of punishment. When a child is enabled to represent its intentions to itself, for example, in close conjunction with punishment that occurs long after a transgression has taken place, then its intentions may elicit sufficient anxiety to motivate suppression when they subsequently intercede before a transgression is carried out.

A number of surveys (Bandura and Walters, 1959; Maccoby, 1961; Sears, 1961; Sears, *et al.*, 1957, Ch. 7) have reported some evidence that children's internalized control over socially prohibited actions is positively associated with the closeness of supervision exercised by their parents. As was pointed out earlier, it is unlikely that close supervision affects suppression merely through the opportunity that it affords to punish the child's incipient transgressions. The association is more probably generated by the tendency of parents who closely control their children's behavior to also use verbal mediation and to be more attentive to the intrinsic cognitive and motivational precursors of transgression. Support for this observation can be found in the correlates of the different disciplinary methods to which parents in our society are disposed (Aronfreed, 1961; Bronfenbrenner, 1958; Davis and Havighurst, 1946; Kohn, 1959; Maccoby and Gibbs, 1954). Middle-class parents tend to be more oriented toward their children's intentions. They are likely to use reasoning and explanation to induce an internal governor in their children, and not merely to sensitize them to the punitive external consequences of transgression. They also often actively induce their children to initiate

their own self-corrective processes. Working-class parents are more prone to react to the concretely visible consequences of their children's transgressions, and to sensitize their children to the threat of punishment. Their methods of punishment are more direct and occur in a less verbal medium. And they are less oriented toward reinforcing signs of internally mediated control in their children. Middle-class children do show more of a corresponding orientation toward internal monitors in the control of behavior, while working-class children show more of an external orientation (Aronfreed, 1961; Boehm, 1962; Kohlberg, 1963). Some surveys (Allinsmith, 1960; Bandura and Walters, 1959; MacKinnon, 1938; Sears, *et al.*, 1957, Ch. 7) have found direct relationships between the internal versus external orientation of parental discipline and parallel differences of orientation in children's suppression of socially prohibited behavior.

Children do acquire highly general and integrative evaluative systems for some areas of social behavior. Such value systems may affect internalized control over behavior in ways which are not apparent from the effects of direct response outcomes in a simple discrimination situation. It is possible, for example, that more massive and cognitive forms of internalization can occur through acquisition processes of the kind implied in theories of identification. Certainly, stable behavioral changes can be induced in children through their tendency to reproduce the behavior of models (Bandura and Walters, 1963) without the initial support of direct external reinforcement. But the experimental findings reported in this paper show that internalized suppression can be acquired through a form of aversive learning that is highly sensitive to the timing of punishment, a parameter of social learning that is not readily translatable into the child's disposition to adopt the role of a model. A general conception of mechanisms of internalization must take into account, then, that some forms of internalized control over behavior can be established through the direct reinforcement and punishment of the child's overtly emitted responses.

SUMMARY

This paper reports an experiment which demonstrates that punishment of an act at its initiation is more effective than punishment at its completion in producing internalized suppression of the act. The experiment, which is carried out with 9- and 10-year-old children, is used to support a theoretical analysis of internalized suppression in terms of two sequential acquisition processes. The first process is the attachment of anxiety to the intrinsic cues provided by either the behavioral or cognitive stimulus correlates of an incipient transgression. The second is the attachment of anxiety reduction to the intrinsic correlates of suppression. The experimental findings are also extended to suggest that a number of features of naturalistic socialization, other than timing of punishment, affect internalized suppression through their impact on: (a) the temporal locus and intensity of the anxiety that motivates suppression and (b) the rein-

forcement of the suppression itself. The verbal mediation of socializing agents is singled out as the most significant of these features.

REFERENCES

Allinsmith, W. "The learning of moral standards," in D. R. Miller and G. E. Swanson (Eds.), *Inner Conflict and Defense*. New York: Holt, 1960, pp. 141–176.

Aronfreed, J. "The nature, variety, and social patterning of moral responses to transgression," *Journal of Abnormal and Social Psychology*, 1961, **63**, 223–240.

Aronfreed, J. "The effects of experimental socialization paradigms upon two moral responses to transgression," *Journal of Abnormal and Social Psychology*, 1963, **66**, 437–448.

Aronfreed, J. "The origin of self-criticism," *Psychological Review*, 1964, **71**, 193–218.

Bandura, A., and Walters, R. H. *Adolescent Aggression*. New York: Ronald Press, 1959.

Bandura, A., and Walters, R. H. *Social Learning and Personality Development*. New York: Holt, Rinehart, and Winston, 1963.

Bixenstine, V. E. "Secondary drive as a neutralizer of time in integrative problem-solving," *Journal of Comparative and Physiological Psychology*, 1956, **49**, 161–166.

Boehm, Leonore. "The development of conscience: A comparison of American children of different mental and socioeconomic levels," *Child Development*, 1962, **33**, 575–590.

Bronfenbrenner, U. "Socialization and social class through time and space," in Eleanor E. Maccoby, T. M. Newcomb, and E. L. Hartley (Eds.), *Readings in Social Psychology*. (3rd ed.) New York: Holt, 1958, pp. 400–425.

Bronfenbrenner, U. "Freudian theories of identification and their derivatives," *Child Development*, 1960, **31**, 15–40.

Burton, R. V., Maccoby, Eleanor E., and Allinsmith, W. "Antecedents of resistance to temptation in four-year-old children," *Child Development*, 1961, **32**, 689–710.

Davis, A., and Havighurst, R. J. "Social class and color differences in child-rearing," *American Sociological Review,* 1946, **11,** 698–710.

Estes, W. K. "An experimental study of punishment," *Psychological Monographs,* 1944, **57,** (3, Whole No. 263).

Grinder, R. E. "Parental childrearing practices, conscience, and resistance to temptation of sixth-grade children," *Child Development,* 1962, **33,** 803–820.

Hill, W. F. "Learning theory and the acquisition of values," *Psychological Review,* 1960, **67,** 317–331.

Kamin, L. J. "The delay-of-punishment gradient," *Journal of Comparative and Physiological Psychology,* 1959, **52,** 434–437.

Kelman, H. C. "Compliance, identification, and internalization: Three processes of attitude change." *Journal of Conflict Resolution,* 1958, **2,** 51–60.

Kohlberg, L. "Moral development and identification," in H. W. Stevenson (Ed.), *Yearbook of the National Society for the Study of Education. Part I. Child psychology.* Chicago: Univer. Chicago Press, 1963, pp. 277–332.

Kohn, M. L. "Social class and the exercise of parental authority," *American Sociological Review,* 1959, **24,** 352–366.

Maccoby, Eleanor E. "The taking of adult roles in middle childhood," *Journal of Abnormal and Social Psychology,* 1961, **63,** 493–503.

Maccoby, Eleanor E., and Gibbs, Patricia K. "Methods of child-rearing in two social classes," in W. E. Martin and Celia B. Stendler (Eds.), *Readings in Child Development.* New York: Harcourt, Brace, 1954, pp. 380–396.

MacKinnon, D. W. "Violation of prohibi-

tions," in H. A. Murray (Eds.), *Explorations in Personality: A Clinical and Experimental Study of Fifty Men of College Age.* New York: Oxford Univer. Press, 1938, pp. 491–501.

Miller, D. R., and Swanson, G. E. (Eds.) *Inner Conflict and Defense.* New York: Holt, 1960.

Mowrer, O. H. *Learning Theory and Behavior.* New York: Wiley, 1960 (a).

Mowrer, O. H. *Learning Theory and the Symbolic Processes.* New York: Wiley, 1960 (b).

Piaget, J. *The Moral Judgment of the Child.* Glencoe, Ill.: Free Press, 1948.

Sears, R. R. "Relation of early socialization experiences to aggression in middle childhood," *Journal of Abnormal and Social Psychology,* 1961, **63,** 466–492.

Sears, R. R., Maccoby, Eleanor E., and Levin, H. *Patterns of Child Rearing.* Evanston, Ill.: Row, Peterson, 1957.

Solomon, R. L., and Brush, Elinor S. "Experimentally derived conceptions of anxiety and aversion," in M. R. Jones (Ed.), *Nebraska Symposium on Motivation: 1956.* Lincoln: Univer. Nebraska Press, 1956, pp. 212–305.

Thibaut, J. W., and Kelley, H. H. *The Social Psychology of Groups.* New York: Wiley, 1959.

Walters, R. H., and Demkow, Lillian. "Timing of punishment as a determinant of response inhibition," *Child Development,* 1963, **34,** 207–214.

Whiting, J. W. M. "Sorcery, sin, and the superego: Some cross-cultural mechanisms of social control," in M. R. Jones (Ed.), *Nebraska Symposium on Motivation: 1959.* Lincoln: Univer. Nebraska Press, 1959, pp. 174–195.

2.5 Birth Order and Participation in Dangerous Sports

RICHARD E. NISBETT

Several findings reported by Schachter (1959) in *The Psychology of Affiliation* indicate that firstborns find physical pain more aversive or the prospect of it more frightening than do later-born individuals. When told that they were to receive severe electric shock, firstborn females reported more fear than did later-born females. In an experiment on toleration of electric shock, firstborn females asked the experimenter to terminate the shock earlier in the series than did later-born females. And an analysis of data obtained by Torrance (1954) indicated that in a situation involving considerable physical danger—piloting a fighter plane in combat—firstborns were less effective than later borns.

If it is true that firstborns find pain or the prospect of it more aversive than do later borns, one would expect them to avoid activities where the risk of physical injury is high. This paper ex-amines the proportion of first- and later-born individuals who participate in one such activity—dangerous sports.

METHOD

Birth-order information was obtained from four samples: (*a*) A complete record of the intercollegiate athletic participation of the 2,432 undergraduates enrolled at Columbia in 1963 was obtained from the college files. Data on athletics or birth order were missing for fewer than 1% of the population; (*b*) reports of interscholastic participation in high school sports and birth-order information were obtained by questionnaire from 110 Pennsylvania State University freshmen enrolled in introductory psychology in 1964; (*c*) similar reports were obtained from 384 Yale University students enrolled in introductory psychology in 1967; (*d*) birth-order reports were obtained by mailed questionnaire in 1964

Reprinted with slight abridgment from *Journal of Personality and Social Psychology*, 1968, **8**, 351–353, with permission of the author and the American Psychological Association, Inc.

from a professional football team—the New York Giants—and a professional baseball team—the New York Mets. Response to the mailed questionnaire was a little less than 50% in each club.

RESULTS

The proportion of Columbia students who participated in a dangerous intercollegiate sport at some point in their college career is presented in Table 1 as a function of birth order and family size. Dangerous sports were defined as those which a sample of 35 students rated as the three most dangerous played at Columbia. These were football, soccer, and rugby.

Two striking effects in Table 1 should be observed in passing: (a) Firstborns are markedly overrepresented in the sample. At every family size, the number of firstborns is greater than the number of children at every other position. This is consistent with Schachter's (1963) finding that firstborns are more likely to attend college; (b) the probability that an individual will play a dangerous sport increases with family size. This fact is consistent with Schachter's (1959) finding that large-family children were less frightened by the prospect of electric shock than small-family children, but since the family-size effect was observed only in the Columbia and Yale samples, it may be due to an idiosyncrasy of the Ivy League population.

Table 1 clearly shows the predicted birth order effect. At all but the very largest family sizes, firstborns are less likely to play a dangerous sport than later borns.[1] Students from large families are

[1] The reversal for families of six or more children is not significant.

table 1

Proportion of Columbia Undergraduates Who Play Dangerous Sports as a Function of Birth Order and Number of Children in Family

| Birth Order | Family Size | | | | | | |
	1	2	3	4	5	6 or More	Total
First	.088	.072	.096	.129	.206	.438	.091
N	(443)	(639)	(272)	(93)	(34)	(16)	(1497)
Second		.106	.130	.280	.400	.167	.130
N		(473)	(177)	(50)	(15)	(6)	(721)
Third			.121	.278	.111	.000	.150
N			(99)	(29)	(9)	(3)	(140)
Fourth				.250	.375	.000	.250
N				(20)	(8)	(4)	(32)
Fifth					.182	1.00	.308
N					(11)	(2)	(13)
Sixth						.143	.143
N						(7)	(7)
Total proportion	.088	.086	.111	.203	.247	.143	.110
N	(443)	(1112)	(548)	(192)	(77)	(7)	(2410)

table 2

Ratio of Firstborns to Second Borns as a Function of Athletic Participation

	Columbia		Pennsylvania State		Yale		Professional Teams	
	Students Who Play Danger-ous Sports (College)	Students Who Do Not Play Danger-ous Sports	Students Who Play Danger-ous Sports (in High School)	Students Who Do Not Play Danger-ous Sports	Students Who Play Danger-ous Sports (in High School)	Students Who Do Not Play Danger-ous Sports	Football	Baseball
Ratio of first borns to second borns	.510	.603	.560	.660	.508	.581	.600	.727
N	(192)	(1583)	(25)	(53)	(124)	(260)	(15)	(11)

more likely to play a dangerous sport than those from small families, and, on the average, later borns are members of larger families than are first-borns. Thus, to examine the birth order effect it is necessary to control for family size. Of a variety of ways to do this, one of the more conservative is simply to compare players and nonplayers on the ratio of first- to *second* borns from families with two or more children. This throws away much of the data, but completely circumvents the confounding effects of family size. The resulting χ^2 is 6.15, which for $df = 1$ is significant at the .02 level. The data on which this test is based are presented in Table 2.

Also presented in Table 2 are the comparable proportions for players and nonplayers for the Pennsylvania State and the Yale samples, and the proportions for the professional football and baseball teams. These differences are of the same magnitude and direction as that for the larger sample of Columbia students.

It may have occurred to the reader that football, rugby, and soccer are not only dangerous sports but team sports and that this latter similarity might account for the differential participation of firstborns and later borns. A comparison of the participation of firstborns in nondangerous team[2] sports with their participation in nondangerous individual[3] sports renders this alternative unlikely. For the Columbia group, where the sample was large enough to perform the appropriate analysis, firstborns were nonsignificantly *more* likely to play a nondangerous individual sport: The ratio of first- to second borns from families of two or more children among students playing team sports was .62, while the ratio for those playing only individual sports was .55. Finally, the underrepresentation of firstborns in the dangerous sports is not due to an avoidance of sports in general. At all three schools the proportion of firstborns among players of nondangerous sports was entirely similar to the proportion of firstborns among students who played no sports at all.

[2] Baseball, basketball, crew.
[3] Wrestling, track, swimming, tennis, fencing, golf.

DISCUSSION

In summary, the evidence is in complete accord with the expectation that firstborns would avoid dangerous activity. Firstborns are as likely to play sports with low risk of injury as later borns, but less likely to play those involving high risk. The underrepresentation of firstborns in the dangerous sports is not a pronounced effect but it is a consistent one. In high school, college, and professional athletics, firstborns are less likely to play the high-risk sports.

This type of evidence is of course subject to all the ills that correlational data are heir to. A variety of explanations could be marshalled to explain the finding that firstborns avoid dangerous sports. The fact that they do not avoid the safer sports eliminates many of the contending alternative explanations, however. In addition, the only empirically demonstrated birth order difference which can comfortably explain the finding is the observation that firstborns react with more anxiety to the prospect of physical harm than do later borns.

Since Sampson, in his review of the birth-order literature (1965), gives the impression that there are no consistent birth order differences with respect to anxiety, a re-review of the evidence on this point is in order. It is correct to conclude that the evidence is contradictory and confused regarding chronic anxiety and situational anxiety where the threat is not physical. However, the evidence concerning reaction to physical danger is virtually uncontradicted. In addition to the studies cited in the introduction, Helmreich and Collins (1967) have replicated with a male population the finding that firstborns respond with more fear to the prospect of physical harm than do later borns; and Helmreich (1966) has shown that firstborns express more fear than later borns in a hazardous diving situation, and, as Torrance (1954) found with fighter pilots, perform more poorly. A reanalysis of data reported by Nisbett and Schachter (1966) again replicates the finding that firstborns respond with more fear to the prospect of physical harm than do later borns. Following the fear manipulation, subjects in that experiment were given a jarring and unpleasant electric shock. Firstborns were judged by observers to react more strongly to it than later borns ($p < .06$). The firstborn subjects also reported the shock to be more painful than did later-born subjects ($p < .05$). While it is possible that firstborns are in some way more sensitive to pain (and this conclusion was reached by Carman in 1899), a more cautious interpretation is to say that the reaction to the electric shock provides behavioral evidence that firstborns were more fearful than later borns.

Only one study reviewed by Sampson failed to report significantly greater fear on the part of firstborns in response to physical danger (Weller, 1962). The writer is not aware of any other contradictory evidence. It seems safe to conclude that firstborns are more frightened by the prospect of physical harm than are later borns, and it is plausible to infer that they avoid dangerous sports for this reason.

SUMMARY

It was found that firstborns are less likely than later borns to participate in dangerous sports. The finding is consistent with evidence showing firstborns to be more frightened by the prospect of physical injury than later borns.

REFERENCES

Carman, A. "Pain and strength measurements of 1,507 school children in Saginaw, Michigan," *American Journal of Psychology,* 1899, **10,** 392–398.

Helmreich, R. L. Prolonged stress in Sealab II: A field study of individual and group reactions. Unpublished doctoral dissertation, Yale University, 1966.

Helmreich, R. L., and Collins, B. E. "Situational determinants of affiliative preference under stress," *Journal of Personality and Social Psychology,* 1967, **6,** 79–85.

Nisbett, R. E., and Schachter, S. "Cognitive manipulation of pain," *Journal of Experimental Social Psychology,* 1966, **2,** 227–236.

Sampson, E. E. "The study of ordinal position: Antecedents and outcomes," in B. A. Maher (Ed.), *Progress in Experimental Personality Research.* Vol. 2. New York: Academic Press, 1965.

Schachter, S. "Birth order, eminence, and higher education," *American Sociological Review,* 1963, **28,** 757–768.

Schachter, S. *The Psychology of Affiliation.* Stanford: Stanford University Press, 1959.

Torrance, E. B. A psychological study of American jet aces. Paper presented at the meeting of the Western Psychological Association, Long Beach, California, 1954.

Weller, L. "The relationship of birth order to anxiety," *Sociometry,* 1962, **25,** 415–417.

SECTION 3

LEARNING

The laboratory animal that has figured extensively in many of the operant conditioning experiments conducted by B. F. Skinner has been the pigeon. One of the advantages that the pigeon has over the rat is that it works harder and longer for less food. This characteristic has made it particularly useful for research in learning concerned with the "shaping" of behavior. The first paper in this section, by Thom Verhave of Queens College, Flushing, New York, describes how pigeons may be trained to do simple, repetitive tasks calling for accuracy in stimulus discrimination.

Although teaching machines were first developed by Sidney Pressey in the 1920s, models adapted for the use of "programs," or organized presentations of learning sequences, did not receive general attention until B. F. Skinner adapted them for use with operant learning techniques. The more recent development in this field, however, has been computer-assisted instruction. Richard C. Atkinson of Stanford University discusses some of the more sophisticated approaches to this method of teaching and learning.

The final paper in this section has been contributed by Neal E. Miller of the Rockefeller University, New York City. In it he analyzes a considerable amount of animal research showing how visceral and glandular responses can be modified by operant or instrumental learning and points up the fallacy of assuming that the autonomic nervous system is of a somewhat "lower order" than the central nervous system.

3.1 The Pigeon as a Quality-Control Inspector[1]

THOM VERHAVE

Many of the operations involved in the quality-control inspection of commercial products consist of monotonous checking jobs performed by human operators. In addition to monotony, these (usually visual) inspection jobs have several other characteristics in common: (a) They require little if any manual skill or dexterity, (b) they require good visual acuity, (c) they require a capacity for color vision, and (d) they are extremely difficult to automate. There is, however, an organic device which has the following favorable properties: (a) an average life span of approximately 10–15 years (Levi, 1963), (b) an extreme flexibility in adjusting to its environment as well as an enormous learning ability (Ferster and Skinner, 1957; Smee, 1850), (c) a visual acuity as good as the human eye (Reese, 1964), (d) color vision (Reese, 1964). The price for one such device is only (approximately) $1.50; its name: *Columba livia domestica* or the pigeon.

Because of the characteristics listed above it is quite feasible to train pigeons to do all the visual checking operations involved in commercial manufacture. What follows is a brief account of an exploratory attempt to put the above suggestion into actual practice (Verhave, 1959). This paper is written partially in self-defense: Stories about the pill-inspecting pigeons have circulated for many years—many versions containing gross inaccuracies.

In July of 1955 I was employed as a "psychopharmacologist" at one of the larger pharmaceutical companies. The main purpose of the laboratory was to develop and evaluate techniques for the

[1]Opinions and conclusions contained in this article are those of the author. They are not to be construed as necessarily reflecting the views or the endorsement of either the pharmaceutical industry or any pigeon.

Reprinted with slight abridgment from the *American Psychologist*, 1966, **21**, 109–115, with permission of the author and the American Psychological Association, Inc.

experimental analysis of the effects of drugs on the behavior of animals.

Sometime, probably early in 1958, I finally took the tour of the plant, which is mandatory for all new employees. During the all-day tour of the extensive research and manufacturing facilities, I ran into the (gelatin) drug-capsule facilities. The capsules are manufactured by several very large and extremely complex machines, which together have a maximum production capacity of approximately 20,000,000 capsules per day. All of the capsules, which are made in a large number of sizes, and colors, are visually inspected. This job was done by a contingent of about 70 women. After inspection the capsules go to other machines which fill them automatically with the appropriate pharmaceuticals. The capsules are inspected in batches. The number of caps in a batch depends on the volume or size of the capsule: the larger the capsule size the smaller the number in a batch to be inspected. All of the capsules in a particular batch are of the same shape, size, and color. A big reservoir with a funnel drops the capsules at a fixed rate on an endless moving belt. The inspector, or "capsule sorter" as she is called, is located in front of the moving belt which is illuminated from underneath. She "pattern scans" the capsules as they move by and picks up and throws out all "skags." A skag is a discard capsule because it is off-color, has a piece of gelatin sticking out, or has a dent in it. This also includes all double-cap capsules. When the capsule comes to the capsule sorter, it is already closed by putting two halves, a cap and a body, together. This step was already performed by the production machine.

Sometimes, however, during transportation or in storage a second cap (the larger half of a capsule) is put on top of an already capped capsule (a cap and body may vibrate apart and a loose cap may then slide over the body of another already capped capsule). Such a "double-cap skag" produces problems later on in the filling machine. After inquiry, I was told that the double-cap skag is also one of the more difficult types to spot.

The sorters (all female) are paid off on a group-bonus schedule employing "error cost." After the inspection of a batch is completed, a supervisor (usually also female) scoops a ladleful of inspected capsules out of the barrel in which they were collected. The types of skag defects are categorized and the inspector can allow up to three or four of the more minor imperfections per sample before a batch is rejected. If she finds more than the allowed number of skags in the sample ladled from the batch, the inspector has to reinspect the entire batch of capsules. She is thus likely to reduce her bonus pay for the day since it depends partially on her own inspection output.

To come back to the main story: On seeing those women and their simple monotonous task, and knowing about Skinner's "Pigeons in a Pelican" (1960, 1965), I said to myself, "Hell, a pigeon can do that!" Sometime later, I mentioned my birdbrain idea to a friend and fellow scientist in the physiochemistry department who also supervised the electronics shop which supported the research division. He almost fell out of his chair and choked in a fit of laughter. However, after the joke had worn off, we talked more seriously about my odd notion, especially after I told him about Project orcon (organic control—Skinner, 1960, 1965). Eventually the director of research and I talked about it. It so happened that I had come up with my suggestion at an opportune time. The company had recently spent a considerable sum of money on a machine constructed by an outside engineering firm designed to inspect automatically for double caps. It did not work. After some deliberation the director of research gave me the go-ahead to build a demonstration and tryout setup. With the able help and splendid cooperation of the instrument-shop people, under the direction of my friend of the physiochemistry department, a demonstration apparatus was built. The result of our labors is shown in Figures 1, 2, 3, and 4. Figure 1 provides a general overview of the entire apparatus except the endless belt-driving mechanism, a close-up of which is given in Figure 2. Figure 3 gives a top view of the "business end" of the pigeon's work space, and Figure 4 shows one of the birds in action.

While the apparatus was being designed and built, I had plenty of opportunity to consider varying aspects of the discrimination-training problems I would be faced with. The first decision to be made was which particular "skag" problem to tackle first. I obtained samples of various sized capsules of different colors. It was tempting to tackle the most troublesome problem first: the double-cap skag, especially those involving small

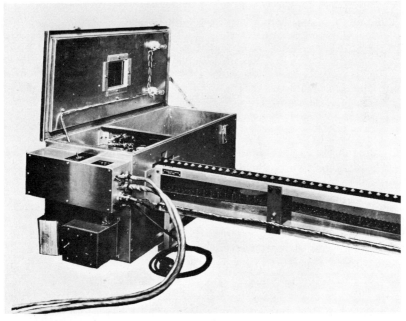

figure 1

General overview of pill-inspection apparatus (except endless belt-driving mechanism).

figure 2
Close-up of endless belt-driving mechanism of pill-inspection apparatus.

capsules of colorless and transparent gelatin. On the actual inspection line these were the most difficult to spot. After playing around with different ways of presenting these capsules to a pigeon behind a modified pigeon key, a simple solution to the double-cap problem was discovered by accident. One of the minor problems to be solved was the lighting of the capsules presented behind the key. I discovered that by shining a narrow beam of light at the proper angle on a three-dimensional transparent curved surface, one obtains a focal point inside the object. (The tops and bottoms of all capsules are either round or oval.) In the case of a double-cap skag, one gets two clearly distinct focal points in slightly different positions. So, even in the case of the transparent double-cap capsule, all

a pigeon had to do was to discriminate between one versus two bright spots of light inside the curious objects behind his key: no problem![2]

For the purpose of working out the details of the actual training and work procedure, however, I decided to take the simplest discrimination problem possible. I chose a simple color discrimination: white versus red capsules. Two naive birds were selected for inspection duty. For one bird the red capsules were arbitrarily defined as skag (S^{Δ}). For the other bird, the white capsules were given the same status.

As is clear from Figure 4, there were two pigeon keys. One key was actually

[2]The opaque, single-color double cap may still be a difficult discrimination problem, even for a pigeon.

a small transparent window, the other was opaque. The capsules could be brought into view behind the transparent key one by one at a maximum rate of about two per second. After a preliminary training phase, the birds were run as follows: A single peck on the weakly illuminated opaque key would (*a*) momentarily (.5 second) turn off the light behind the transparent key, and (*b*) weakly illuminate the window key to an extent insufficient to see much of the capsule in place behind it.

Next, a single peck on the now weakly lit window key would turn on a bright and narrow beam of light which clearly illuminated the capsule. The capsules were individually mounted in small and hollow bottlestops glued onto the

metal plates of the endless belt (see Figures 2, 3, 4). If the bird now pecked three more times on the window key with the new illuminated capsule exposed to view, a brief tone would sound. Next came the moment of decision. If the capsule exposed to view was judged to be a skag, the bird was required to make two more pecks on the window key. This would (*a*) turn off the beam of light illuminating the capsule, (*b*) move up the next capsule, and (*c*) produce food by way of the automatic hopper on a fixed-percentage basis (usually 100%). However, if the capsule was considered to be acceptable, the bird indicated this by changing over to the opaque key. A peck on this key would also (*a*) turn off the beam of light behind the other key

figure 3
Pill-inspection apparatus: top view of work space.

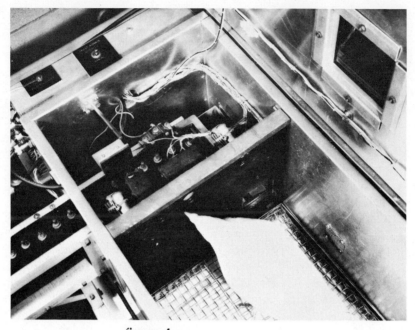

figure 4
Pill-inspection apparatus: pigeon at work.

(window), and (*b*) move up the next capsule. It would not, however, produce reinforcement.

A bird, then, determined his own inspection rate. A peck on the opaque key would initiate an inspection cycle. However, reinforcement came only after making the appropriate number of pecks on the window key in case of a true skag only. Skags occurred rarely; they made up 10% of all the capsules on the belt. Wrong pecks, either false alarms or misses, did not get reinforced, and produced a blackout (Ferster, 1954) of 30 seconds. The results were very encouraging: Both birds inspected on a 99% correct basis within 1 week of daily discrimination training. The director of the pharmacology division, my immediate superior, who had watched the entire project with serious misgiving since its inception (he was sincerely afraid I was making a fool of myself), was delighted. In his immediate enthusiasm he called the director of research, who came over for a look. One week later the vice presidents as well as the president of the company had been given a demonstration. Everybody, including my immediate associates and co-workers, was greatly excited. The situation, as Skinner had previously discovered in a similar situation (Skinner, 1960), was a great source for jokes. There was talk about a new company subsidiary: "Inspection, Inc.!" (Company slogan: "It's for the birds!")

There were some sobering thoughts, however. One of them concerned the staggering problem of the logistics involved in getting pigeons to inspect as many as 20,000,000 separate objects each day. Although this problem did not seem insoluble to me, the details of the various possible approaches to a solution were never worked out.

After the company president had watched my feathered pupils perform, he congratulated me on my achievement. I was subsequently informed that serious consideration would be given to the further use and development of the method. I was also told that I could expect a visit from the chairman of the board and his brother, both elder statesmen of the company, who made all final policy decisions of importance. During their brief visit to the laboratory, one of them raised the question of possible adverse publicity. What about the Humane Society, and more important, suppose salesmen from other pharmaceutical houses would tell doctors not to buy any of our company's products: "Who would trust medicine inspected by pigeons?!" I suggested that the use of pigeons was incidental, and that, for example, one could use hawks just as well; after all, what is better than a hawk's eye? This suggestion produced a wan smile.

One other problem that was brought up raised the question of the pigeons coming in contact with what was being inspected. The competition could well choose to ignore the mechanical details of the situation and exploit the more distasteful but imaginary possibilities. Even though the birds would only see the capsules at a distance through a window, the first mental picture[3] is usually

one of a pigeon "manually" (proboscically?) sorting capsules, a thought no doubt repulsive to many people, especially to those who already have an aversion to birds as such.

After a brief stay, and a polite pat on the back, my distinguished visitors left.

Three weeks went by without any further word from HUM (Higher-Up-Management—Verhave, 1961). I concluded that probably meant that my pigeons were finished. I was right. Sometime later I was so informed. Through the grapevine I learned that the board of directors had voted 13 to 1 not to continue to explore the use of animals for quality-control inspection. The one "yes" vote presumably came from the director of research who initially had given me the green light for the preliminary demonstration.

There is one further amusing tale to the story: The company did try to patent my inspection method. The poor lawyer assigned to the case almost developed a nervous breakdown. It turned out to be "unpatentable" because, as the lawyers of the patent office put it (so succinctly), the method involved "a mental process" which is unpatentable in principle.[4] I tried to pin my lawyer friends down on what they meant by a "mental process." I suggested that the pigeon was merely an organic computor. However, I got nowhere. Lawyers apparently want no part of either physicalism or behaviorism.

So much as far as my own story is concerned. My efforts stimulated another exploratory attempt by my friend Wil-

---

[3]If a behaviorist may be excused for using such illegitimate terms . . .

[4]On this point, I may refer the reader to a recent article in *Science* by J. H. Munster, Jr., and Justin C. Smith (1965).

liam Cumming, of Columbia University, who trained pigeons to inspect diodes. Brief descriptions of his work can be found in an article by Ferster and Ferster (1962), an anonymous (1959) article in *Factory*, and a recent article in *The Atlantic Monthly* by R. J. Herrnstein (1965).

One problem not yet touched on deserves some discussion. In the demonstration apparatus the capsules were coded as to whether they were acceptable or skags. In this way the automatic programing (relay) circuit could set up and enforce the appropriate discriminatory behavior of the birds. However, on an actual inspection line, this aspect of the training procedure could no longer be maintained. There would be no way of knowing which capsules are skags except by actual inspection. Consequently on a real inspection line there would be no way of knowing when to reward or not to reward the animal inspector! As a result, due to the lack of differential reward, the animal's discriminations would rapidly deteriorate.[5] There are two solutions. I discarded the first and most obvious one because it seemed mechanically cumbersome and not as interesting as the other solution.

The first solution would involve the use of known skags. A certain percentage of the capsules inspected would consist of such labeled duds, and be used to check up on the discriminatory behavior of the birds. This is similar to the use of catch tests in human psychophysical experiments. This solution to the

problem of guaranteeing that the animal inspector conforms to the values of his human employers makes it necessary to determine what minimum percentage of the objects inspected have to be planted skags in order to keep the inspecting behavior at an acceptable level of reliability.

As a solution to the conformity-enforcement problem, however, this general solution is expensive and awkward. The on-line inspection equipment would need special machinery to insert in a random manner a fixed percentage of "stool-pigeon skags" and after inspection remove them again automatically for later reuse. The slightest observable difference between the "planted" objects and the other ones would lead to the development of a conditional discrimination (Lashley, 1938), and reintroduce the problem one set out to solve initially.

The second solution is simpler from a purely mechanical point of view. It also is of more theoretical or philosophical interest.

Briefly, it would involve the use of a minimum to two animals to simultaneously inspect each object. Initially, each animal would be trained to inspect capsules by using a training apparatus such as the one I had already constructed. In this apparatus all the capsules would be labeled as to whether they were skags or not and thus control the reward circuit.

After the desired discriminatory performance was well established the two birds would be removed to the on-line inspection situation. From then on the birds would only be rewarded if they *both* agreed on whether a particular object was a skag or not. Such an agreement-

[5]Skinner, in his World War II project to train pigeons to home missiles, did not face this problem. His birds were meant to "extinguish" after a brief period of duty.

contingency setup would most likely be quite adequate to maintain the desired behavior. There is, of course, the possibility that both birds would indeed, once in a while, agree to treat a skag as an acceptable object. However, the probability of this happening for any particular object on a particular inspection trial is the product of the error frequencies (the probability of such an error) of each bird. If, therefore, each bird independently has an error frequency as high as 1 out of 100, the probability of both birds being wrong but still rewarded would be 1 out of 10,000! Hooking additional animals into the agreement-contingency circuit would make the possibility of the development of a "multiple folly" very unlikely.

The solution is of some philosophical interest because it makes the pigeon observers act according to Charles Pierce's (1923, orig. publ. 1878) pragmatic theory of truth: "The opinion which is fated to be ultimately agreed to by all who investigate, is what is meant by the truth, and the object represented in this opinion is real [pp. 56–57]." It also appears to me that the agreement-contingency type of arrangement provides a basic paradigm for the experimental analysis of social behavior, a terra incognita so far hardly even explored by a systematic experimental investigation (Verhave, 1966).

In conclusion, let me point out that the idea of using trained animals for the dubious purposes of Homo sapiens is very old indeed. Since antiquity man has domesticated many animals. It seems an obvious development to apply our modern knowledge of behavior theory to the task of training some of our animal companions for the performance of various sophisticated tasks (Clarke, 1958; Herrnstein, 1965).

The obstacle in the way of such developments is not our ignorance of behavior, though it is still large, but mainly, it seems, the obstinate belief of man in his intellectual superiority over other creatures as well as a generalized fear of the imagined consequences of novel developments.

REFERENCES

Anonymous. "This inspector is a bird," *Factory*, 1959 (Dec.), 219–221.

Clarke, A. C. "Our dumb colleagues," *Harper's Magazine*, 1958, **216**, 32–33.

Ferster, C. B. "Use of the blackout in the investigation of temporal discrimination in fixed-interval reinforcement," *Journal of Experimental Psychology*, 1954, **47**, 69–74.

Ferster, C. B., and Skinner, B. F. *Schedules of Reinforcement*. New York: Appleton-Century-Crofts, 1957.

Ferster, Marilyn B., and Ferster, C. B. "Animals as workers," *New Scientist*, 1962, **15**, 497–499.

Herrnstein, R. J. "In defense of bird brains," *Atlantic Monthly*, 1965 (Sept.), **216**, 101–104.

Lashley, K. S. "Conditional reactions in the rat," *Journal of Psychology*, 1938, **6**, 311–324.

Levi, W. M. *The Pigeon*. (Rev. ed.) Sumter, S. C.: Levi Publishing Company, 1963.

Munster, J. H., Jr., and Smith, J. C. "The care and feeding of intellectual property," *Science*, 1965, **148**, 739–743.

Peirce, C. "How to make our ideas clear," (Orig. publ. 1878), in M. R. Cohen (Ed.), *Chance, Love and Logic*. New York: Harcourt Brace, 1923.

Reese, E. P. *Experiments in Operant Behavior*. New York: Appleton-Century-Crofts, 1964.

Skinner, B. F. "Pigeons in a pelican," *American Psychologist*, 1960, **15**, 28–37.

Skinner, B. F. "Stimulus generalization in an operant: A historical note," in D. I. Mostofsky (Ed.), *Stimulus Generalization.* Stanford: Stanford Univer. Press, 1965.

Smee, A. *Instinct and Reason.* London: Reeve, Benham and Reeve, 1850.

Verhave, T. "Recent developments in the experimental analysis of behavior," *Proceedings of the Eleventh Research Conference, American Meat Institute Foundation,* 1959, Mar., 113–116.

Verhave, T. "Is the system approach of engineering psychology applicable to social organizations?" *Psychological Record,* 1961, **11,** 69–86.

Verhave, T. *The Experimental Analysis of Behavior: Selected Readings.* New York: Appleton-Century-Crofts, 1966, in press.

3.2 Computerized Instruction and the Learning Process

RICHARD C. ATKINSON

In recent years there has been a tremendous number of articles and news releases dealing with computer-assisted instruction, or as it has been abbreviated, CAI. One might conjecture that this proliferation is an indicant of rapid progress in the field. Unfortunately, I doubt that it is. A few of the reports about CAI are based on substantial experience and research, but the majority are vague speculations and conjectures with little if any data or real experience to back them up. I do not want to denigrate the role of speculation and conjecture in a newly developing area like CAI. However, of late it seems to have produced little more than a repetition of ideas that were exciting in the 1950s but, in the absence of new research, are simply well-worn cliches in the late 1960s.

These remarks should not be misinterpreted. Important and significant research on CAI is being carried on in many laboratories around the country, but certainly not as much as one is led to believe by the attendant publicity. The problem for someone trying to evaluate developments in the field is to distinguish between those reports that are based on fact and those that are disguised forms of science fiction. In my paper, I shall try to stay very close to data and actual experience. My claims will be less grand than many that have been made for CAI, but they will be based on a substantial research effort.

In 1964 Patrick Suppes and I initiated a project under a grant from the Office of Education to develop and implement a CAI program in initial reading and mathematics. Because of our particular research interests, Suppes has taken responsibility for the mathematics curriculum and I have been responsible for

Reprinted with some abridgment from the *American Psychologist*, 1968, **23**, 225–239, with permission of the author and the American Psychological Association, Inc.

the initial reading program. At the beginning of the project, two major hurdles had to be overcome. There was no lesson material in either mathematics or reading suitable for CAI, and an integrated CAI system had not yet been designed and produced by a single manufacturer. The development of the curricula and the development of the system have been carried out as a parallel effort over the last 3 years with each having a decided influence on the other.

Today I would like to report on the progress of the reading program with particular reference to the past school year when for the first time a sizable group of students received a major portion of their daily reading instruction under computer control. The first year's operation must be considered essentially as an extended debugging of both the computer system and the curriculum materials. Nevertheless, some interesting comments can be made on the basis of this experience regarding both the feasibility of CAI and the impact of such instruction on the overall learning process.

Before describing the Stanford Project, a few general remarks may help place it in perspective. Three levels of CAI can be defined. Discrimination between levels is based not on hardware considerations, but principally on the complexity and sophistication of the student–system interaction. An advanced student–system interaction may be achieved with a simple teletype terminal, and the most primitive interaction may require some highly sophisticated computer programming and elaborate student terminal devices.

At the simplest interactional level are those systems that present a fixed, linear sequence of problems. Student errors may be corrected in a variety of ways, but no real-time decisions are made for modifying the flow of instructional material as a function of the student's response history. Such systems have been termed "drill-and-practice" systems and at Stanford University are exemplified by a series of fourth-, fifth-, and sixth-grade programs in arithmetic and language arts that are designed to supplement classroom instruction. These particular programs are being used in several different areas of California and also in Kentucky and Mississippi, all under control of one central computer located at Stanford University. Currently as many as 2,000 students are being run per day; it requires little imagination to see how such a system could be extended to cover the entire country. Unfortunately, I do not have time to discuss these drill-and-practice programs in this paper, but there are several recent reports describing the research (Fishman, Keller, and Atkinson, 1968; Suppes, 1966; Suppes, Jerman, and Groen, 1966).

At the other extreme of our scale characterizing student–system interactions are "dialogue" programs. Such programs are under investigation at several universities and industrial concerns, but to date progress has been extremely limited. The goal of the dialogue approach is to provide the richest possible student–system interaction where the student is free to construct natural-language responses, ask questions in an unrestricted mode, and in general exercise almost complete control over the sequence of learning events.

"Tutorial" programs lie between the

above extremes of student-system inter-action. Tutorial programs have the capa-bility for real-time decision making and instructional branching contingent on a single response or on some subset of the student's response history. Such pro-grams allow students to follow separate and diverse paths through the curriculum based on their particular performance records. The probability is high in a tutorial program that no two students will encounter exactly the same sequence of lesson materials. However, student responses are greatly restricted since they must be chosen from a prescribed set of responses, or constructed in such a man-ner that a relatively simple text analysis will be sufficient for their evaluation. The CAI Reading Program is tutorial in na-ture, and it is this level of student inter-action that will be discussed today.

THE STANFORD CAI SYSTEM

The Stanford Tutorial System was de-veloped under a contract between the University and the IBM Corporation. Subsequent developments by IBM of the basic system have led to what has been designated the IBM-1500 Instructional System which should soon be commer-cially available. The basic system consists of a central process computer with ac-companying disc-storage units, proctor stations, and an interphase to 16 student terminals. The central process computer acts as an intermediary between each student and his particular course material which is stored in one of the disc-storage units. A student terminal consists of a picture projector, a cathode ray tube (CRT), a light pen, a modified typewriter keyboard, and an audio system which

can play prerecorded messages (see Figure 1).

The CRT is essentially a television screen on which alpha-numeric charac-ters and a limited set of graphics (i.e., simple line drawings) can be generated under computer control. The film pro-jector is a rear-view projection device which permits us to display still pictures in black and white or color. Each film strip is stored in a self-threading cartridge and contains over 1,000 images which may be accessed very quickly under computer control. The student receives audio messages via a high-speed device capable of selecting any number of mes-sages varying in length from a few sec-onds to over 15 minutes. The audio mes-sages are stored in tape cartridges which contain approximately 2 hours of mes-sages and, like the film cartridge, may be changed very quickly. To gain the student's attention, an arrow can be placed at any point on the CRT and moved in synchronization with an audio message to emphasize given words or phrases, much like the "bouncing ball" in a singing cartoon.

The major response device used in the reading program is the light pen, which is simply a light-sensitive probe. When the light pen is placed on the CRT, coordinates of the position touched are sensed as a response and recorded by the computer. Responses may also be entered into the system through the typewriter keyboard. However, only limited use has been made of this re-sponse mode in the reading program. This is not to minimize the value of key-board responses, but rather to admit that we have not as yet addressed ourselves to the problem of teaching· first-grade

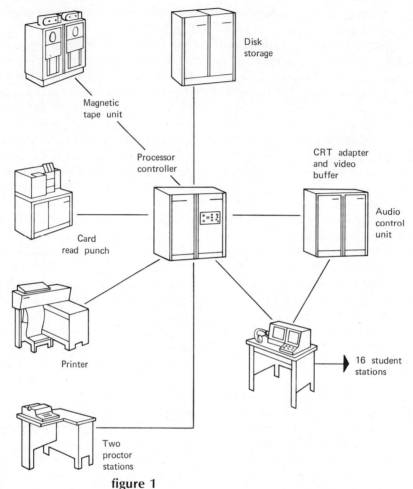

figure 1

System configuration for Stanford CAI System.

children to handle a typewriter keyboard.

The CAI System controls the flow of information and the input of student responses according to the instructional logic built into the curriculum materials. The sequence of events is roughly as follows: The computer assembles the necessary commands for a given instructional sequence from a disc-storage unit. The commands involve directions to the terminal device to display a given sequence of symbols on the CRT, to present a particular image on the film projector, and to play a specific audio message. After the appropriate visual and auditory materials have been presented, a "ready" signal indicates to the student that a response is expected. Once a response has been entered, it is evaluated and, on the basis of this evaluation and the student's past history, the computer makes a decision as to what materials will subsequently be presented. The time-sharing nature of the system allows us to handle 16 students simultaneously and to cycle through these evaluative steps so rapidly that from a student's viewpoint it appears that he is getting immediate attention from the computer whenever he inputs a response.

THE CAI READING CURRICULUM

The flexibility offered by this computer system is of value only if the curriculum materials make sense both in terms of the logical organization of the subject matter and the psychology of the learning processes involved. Time does not permit a detailed discussion of the rationale behind the curriculum that we have developed. Let me simply say that our approach to initial reading can be characterized as applied psycholinguistics. Hypotheses about the reading process and the nature of learning to read have been formulated on the basis of linguistic information, observations of language use, and an analysis of the function of the written code. These hypotheses have been tested in a series of pilot studies structured to simulate actual teaching situations. On the basis of these experimental findings, the hypotheses have been modified, retested, and ultimately incorporated into the curriculum as principles dictating the format and flow of the instructional sequence. Of course, this statement is somewhat of an idealization, since very little curriculum material can be said to have been the perfect end product of rigorous empirical evaluation. We would claim, however,

that the fundamental tenets of the Stanford reading program have been formulated and modified on the basis of considerable empirical evidence. It seems probable that these will be further modified as more data accumulate.

The introduction of new words from one level of the curriculum to the next is dictated by a number of principles (Rodgers, 1967). These principles are specified in terms of a basic unit that we have called the vocalic center group (VCG). The VCG in English is defined as a vowel nucleus with zero to three preceding and zero to four following consonants. The sequencing of new vocabulary is determined by the length of the VCG units, and the regularity of the orthographic and phonological correspondences. Typical of the principles are the following:

1. VCT sets containing single consonant elements are introduced before those containing consonant clusters (*tap* and *rap* before *trap*).
2. VCG sets containing initial consonant clusters are introduced before those containing final consonant clusters (*stop* before *post*).
3. VCG sets containing check (short) vowels are introduced before those containing letter name (long) vowels (*met* and *mat* before *meat* or *mate*).
4. Single VCG sequences are introduced before multiple VCG sequences (*mat* before *matter*, *stut* before *stutter*).

More detailed rules are required to determine the order for introducing specific vowels and consonants within a VCG pattern, and for introducing specific VCG patterns in polysyllabic words. These rules frequently represented a compromise between linguistic factors, pattern productivity, item frequency, and textual "usefulness," in that order of significance.

The instructional materials are divided into eight levels each composed of about 32 lessons.[2] The lessons are designed so that the average student will complete one in approximately 30 minutes, but this can vary greatly with the fast student finishing much sooner and the slow student sometimes taking 2 hours or more if he hits most of the remedial material. Within a lesson, the various instructional tasks can be divided into three broad areas: (*a*) decoding skills, (*b*) comprehension skills, (*c*) games and other motivational devices. Decoding skills involve such tasks as letter and letter-string identification, word list learning, phonic drills, and related types of activities. Comprehension involves such tasks as having the computer read to the child or having the child himself read sentences, paragraphs, or complete stories about which he is then asked a series of questions. The questions deal with the direct recall of facts, generalizations about main ideas in the story, and inferential questions which require the child to relate information presented in the story to his own experience. Finally, many different types of games are sequenced into the lessons primarily to encourage continued attention to the materials. The games are similar to those played in the classroom and are structured to evaluate the developing reading skills of the child.

[2]For a detailed account of the curriculum materials see Wilson and Atkinson (1967) and Rodgers (1967). See also Atkinson and Hansen (1966) and Hansen and Rodgers (1965).

Matrix Construction. To illustrate the instructional materials focusing on decoding skills let me describe a task that we have called matrix "construction." This task provides practice in learning to associate orthographically similar sequences with appropriate rhyme and alliteration patterns. Rhyming patterns are presented in the columns of the matrix, and alliteration patterns are presented in the rows of the matrix as indicated in Figure 4.

The matrix is constructed one cell at a time. The initial consonant of a CVC word is termed the initial unit, and the vowel and the final consonant are termed the final unit. The intersection of an initial unit row and a final unit column determines the entry in any cell.

The problem format for the construction of each cell is divided into four parts: Parts A and D are standard instructional sections and Parts B and C are remedial sections. The flow diagram in Figure 2 indicates that remedial Parts B and C are branches from Part A and may be presented independently or in combination.

To see how this goes, let us consider the example illustrated in Figure 3. The student first sees on the CRT the empty cell with its associated initial and final units and an array of response choices. He hears the audio message indicated by response request 1 (RR 1) in Part A of Figure 3. If the student makes the correct response (CA) (i.e., touches *ran* with his light pen), he proceeds to Part D where he sees the word written in the cell and receives one additional practice trial.

In the initial presentation in Part A, the array of multiple-choice responses is designed to identify three possible types of errors:

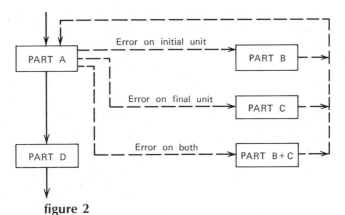

figure 2

Flow chart for the construction of a cell in the matrix construction task.

1. The initial unit is correct, but the final unit is not.

2. The final unit is correct, but the initial unit is not.

3. Neither the initial unit nor the final unit is correctly identified.

If, in Part A, the student responds with *fan* he is branched to remedial Part B where attention is focused on the initial unit of the cell. If a correct response in made in Part B, the student is returned to Part A for a second attempt. If an

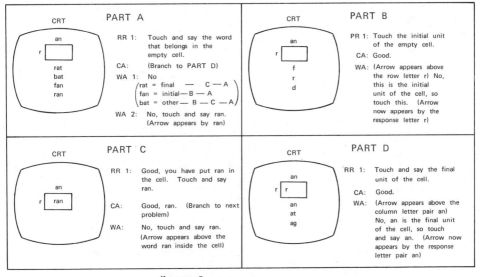

figure 3

First cell of the matrix construction task.

incorrect response (WA) is made in Part B, an arrow is displayed on the CRT to indicate the correct response, which the student is then asked to touch.

If, in Part A, the student responds with *rat,* he is branched to remedial Part C where additional instruction is given on the final unit of the cell. The procedure in Part C is similar to Part B. However, it should be noted that in the remedial instruction the initial letter is never pronounced (Part B), whereas the final unit is always pronounced (Part C). If, in Part A, the student responds with *bat,* then he has made an error on both the initial and final unit and is branched through both Part B and Part C.

When the student returns to Part A after completing a remedial section, a correct response will advance him to Part D as indicated. If a wrong answer response is made on the second pass, an arrow is placed beside the correct response area and held there until a correct response is made. If the next response is still an error, a message is sent to the proctor and the sequence is repeated from the beginning.

When a student has made a correct response on Parts A and D, he is advanced to the next word cell of the matrix which has a problem format and sequence identical with that just described. The individual cell building is continued block by block until the matrix is complete. The upper left-hand panel of Figure 4 indicates the CRT display for adding the next cell in our example. The order in which row and column cells are added is essentially random.

When the matrix is complete, the entries are reordered and a criterion test is given over all cell entries. The test involves displaying the full matrix with

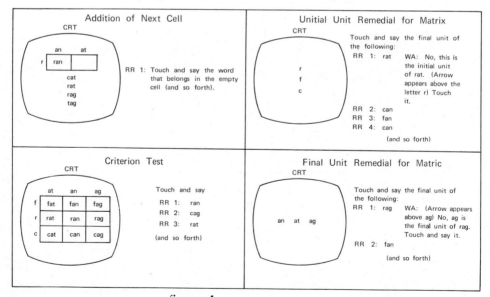

figure 4
Continuation of matrix construction task.

complete cell entries as indicated in the lower left-hand panel of Figure 4. Randomized requests are made to the student to identify cell entries. Since the first pass through the full matrix is viewed as a criterion test, no reinforcement is given. Errors are categorized as initial, final, and other; if the percentage of total errors on the criterion test exceeds a predetermined value, then remedial exercises are provided of the type shown in the two right-hand panels of Figure 4. If all the errors are recorded in one category (initial or final), only the remedial material appropriate to that category is presented. If the errors are distributed over both categories, then both types of remedial material are presented. After working through one or both of the remedial sections, the student is branched back for a second pass through the criterion matrix. The second pass is a teaching trial as opposed to the initial test cycle; the student proceeds with the standard correction and optimization routines.

An analysis of performance on the matrix task is still incomplete, but some preliminary results are available. On the initial pass (Part A) our students were correct about 45% of the time; however, when an error did occur, 21% of the time it involved only the final unit, 53% of the time only the initial unit, and 26% of the time both initial and final units. The pattern of performances changed markedly on the first pass through the criterion test. Here the subject was correct about 65% of the time; when an error occurred, 32% of the time it involved only the final unit, 33% of the time only the initial unit, and 35% of the time both units. Thus performance showed a sig-

nificant improvement from Part A to the criterion test; equally important, initial errors were more than twice as frequent as final errors in Part A, but were virtually equal on the criterion test.

The matrix exercise is a good example of the material used in the curriculum to teaching decoding skills. We now consider two examples ("form class" and "inquiries") of tasks that are designed to teach comprehension skills.

Form Class. Comprehension of a sentence involves an understanding of English syntax. One behavioral manifestation of a child's syntactic sophistication is his ability to group words into appropriate form classes. This task provides lesson materials that teach the form-class characteristics of the words just presented in the matrix section of a lesson. The following type of problem is presented to the student (the material in the box is displayed on the CRT and below are audio messages; the child answers by appropriately placing his light pen on the CRT):

	tan	
	fat	
Dan saw the	man	hat.
	run	

Only one of the words in the column will make sense in the sentence. Touch and say the word that belongs in the sentence.

CA: Yes, Dan saw the tan hat. Do the next one.

WA: No, tan is the word that makes sense. Dan saw the tan hat. Touch and say tan. (An arrow then appears above tan.)

The sentence is composed of words that are in the reading vocabulary of the student (i.e., they have been presented in previous or current lessons). The response set includes a word which is of the correct form class but is semantically inappropriate, two words that are of the wrong form class, and the correct word. A controlled variety of sentence types is employed, and the answer sets are distributed over all syntactic slots within each sentence type. Responses are categorized in rather broad terms as *nouns, verbs, modifiers,* and *other.* The response data can be examined for systematic errors over a large number of items. Examples of the kinds of questions that can be asked are: (*a*) Are errors for various form classes in various sentence positions similarly distributed? (*b*) How are response latencies affected by the syntactic and serial position of the response set within the sentence? Answers to these and other questions should provide information that will permit more systematic study of the relationship of sentence structure to reading instruction.

Inquiries.   Individual words in sentences may constitute unique and conversationally correct answers to questions. These questions take the interrogative "Who ....? What ....? How ....?" etc. The ability to select the word in a sentence that uniquely answers one of these questions demonstrates one form of reading comprehension. The inquiry exercises constitute an assessment of this reading comprehension ability. In the following example, the sentence "John hit the ball" is displayed on the CRT accompanied by these audio messages:

Touch and say the word that answers the question.
RR 1   Who hit the ball?
CA: Yes, the word "John" tells us who hit the ball.
WA: No, John tells us who hit the ball. Touch and say John. (An arrow then appears on the CRT above John.)
RR 2   What did John hit?
CA: Yes, the word "ball" tells us what John hit.
WA: No, ball tells us what John hit. Touch and say ball. (An arrow then appears above ball.)

As in the form-class section, each sentence is composed of words from the student's reading vocabulary. A wide variety of sentence structures is utilized, beginning with simple subject-verb-object sentences and progressing to structures of increasing complexity. Data from this task bear on several hypotheses about comprehension. If comprehension is equated with a correct response to an inquiry question, then the following statements are verified by our data: (*a*) Items for which the correct answer is in the medial position of the sentence are more difficult to comprehend than items in the initial or final positions; final position items are easier to comprehend than items in the initial position. (*b*) Items for which the correct answer is an adjective are more difficult to comprehend than items in which the correct answer is a noun or verb; similarly nouns are more difficult than verbs. (*c*) Longer sentences, measured by word length, are more difficult to comprehend than shorter sentences.

These are only a few examples of the types of tasks used in the reading curriculum, but they indicate the nature of the student–system interaction. What is not illustrated by these examples is the potential for long-term optimization policies based on an extended response history from the subject. . . .

SOME RESULTS FROM THE FIRST YEAR OF OPERATION

The Stanford CAI Project is being conducted at the Brentwood School in the Ravenswood School District (East Palo Alto, California). There were several reasons for selecting this school. It had sufficient population to provide a sample of well over 100 first-grade students. The students were primarily from "culturally disadvantaged" homes. And the past performance of the school's principal and faculty had demonstrated a willingness to undertake educational innovations.

Computerized instruction began in November of 1966 with half of the first-grade students taking reading via CAI and the other half, which functioned as a control group, being taught reading by a teacher in the classroom. The children in the control group were not left out of the project, for they took mathematics from the CAI system instead. The full analysis of the student data is a tremendous task which is still underway. However, a few general results have already been tabulated that provide some measure of the program's success.

Within the lesson material there is a central core of problems which we have termed main-line problems. These are problems over which each student must exhibit mastery in one form or another.

Main-line problems may be branched around by successfully passing certain screening tests, or they may be met and successfully solved; they may be met with incorrect responses, in which case the student is branched to remedial material. The first year of the project ended with a difference between the fastest and slowest student of over 4,000 main-line problems completed. The cumulative response curves for the fastest, median, and slowest students are given in Figure 5. Also of interest is the rate of progress during the course of the year. Figure 6 presents the cumulative number of problems completed per hour on a month-by-month basis again for the fastest, median, and slowest student. It is interesting to note that the rate measure was essentially constant over time for increase for the fast student.

From the standpoint of both the total number of problems completed during the year and rate of progress, it appears that the CAI curriculum is responsive to individual differences. The differences noted above must not be confused with a variation in rate of response. The difference in response rate among students was very small. The average response rate was approximately four per minute and was not correlated with a student's rate of progress through the curriculum. The differences in total number of main-line problems completed can be accounted for by the amount of remedial material, the optimization routines, and the number of accelerations for the different students.

It has been a common finding that girls generally acquire reading skills more rapidly than boys. The sex differences in reading performance have been

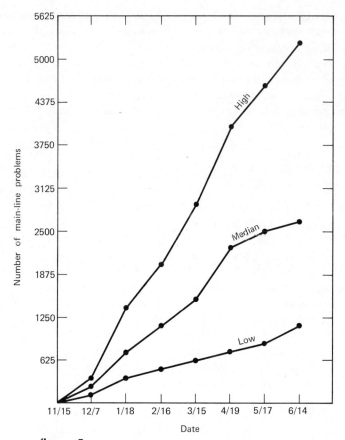

figure 5

Cumulative number of mail-line problems for fastest, median, and slowest student.

attributed, at least in part, to the social organization of the classroom and to the value and reward structures of the predominantly female primary grade teachers. It has also been argued on developmental grounds that first-grade girls are more facile in visual memorization than boys of the same age, and that this facility aids the girls in the sight-word method of vocabulary acquisition commonly used in basal readers. If these two arguments are correct, then one would expect that placing students in a CAI environment and using a curriculum which emphasizes analytic skills, as opposed to rote memorization, would minimize sex differences in reading. In order to test this hypothesis, the rate of progress scores were statistically evaluated for sex effects. The result, which was rather surprising, is that there was no difference between male and female students in rate of progress through the CAI curriculum.

Sex differences however might be a factor in accuracy of performance. To test this notion the final accuracy scores on four standard problem types were examined. The four problem types, which are representative of the entire curriculum, were Letter Identification, Word List Learning, Matrix Construction, and Sentence Comprehension. On these four tasks, the only difference between boys and girls that was statistically significant at the .05 level was for word-list learning. These results, while by no means definitive, do lend support to the notion that when students are removed from the normal classroom environment and placed on a CAI program, boys perform as well as girls in overall rate of progress. The results also suggest that in a CAI environment the sex difference is minimized in proportion to the emphasis on analysis rather than rote memorization in the learning task. The one problem type where the girls achieved significantly higher scores than the boys, word-list

learning, is essentially a paired-associate learning task.

As noted earlier, the first graders in our school were divided into two groups. Half of them received reading instruction from the CAI system; the other half did not (they received mathematics instruction instead). Both groups were tested extensively using conventional instruments before the project began and again near the end of the school year. The two groups were not significantly different at the start of the year. Table 1 presents the results for some of the tests that were administered at the end of the year. As inspection of the table will show, the group that received reading instruction via CAI performed significantly better on all of the post-tests except for the comprehension subtest of the California Achievement Test. These results are most encouraging. Further, it should be noted that at least some of the factors that might result in a "Hawthorne phenomenon" are not present here; the "control"

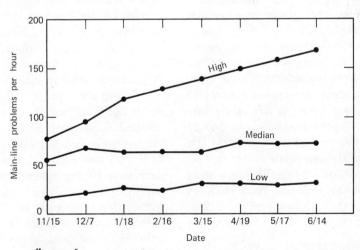

figure 6
Cumulative rate of progress for fastest, median, and slowest student.

table 1

Post-test Results for Experimental and Control Groups

Test	Experimental	Control	p value
California Achievement Test			
Vocabulary	45.91	38.10	<.01
Comprehension	41.45	40.62	—
Total	45.63	39.61	<.01
Hartley Reading Test			
Form class	11.22	9.00	<.05
Vocabulary	19.38	17.05	<.01
Phonetic discrimination	30.88	25.15	<.01
Pronunciation			
Nonsense word	6.03	2.30	<.01
Word	9.95	5.95	<.01
Recognition			
Nonsense word	18.43	15.25	<.01
Word	19.61	16.60	<.01

group was exposed to CAI experience in their mathematics instruction. While that may leave room for some effects in their reading, it does remove the chief objection, since these students also had reason to feel that special attention was being given to them. It is of interest to note that the average Stanford-Binet IQ score for these students (both experimental and control) is 89.[3]

Owing to systems and hardware difficulties, our program was not in full operation until late in November of 1966. Initially, students were given a relatively brief period of time per day on the terminals. This period was increased to 20 minutes after the first 6 weeks; in the last month we allowed students to stay on the terminal 30 to 35 minutes. We wished to find out how well first-grade students would adapt to such long periods of time. They adapt quite well, and next year we

[3]More details on these and other analyses may be found in Atkinson (1967) and Wilson and Atkinson (1967).

plan to use 30-minute periods for all students throughout the year. This may seem like a long session for a first-grader, but our observations suggest that their span of attention is well over a half hour if the instructional sequence is truly responsive to their response inputs. This year's students had a relatively small number of total hours on the system. We hope that by beginning in the early fall and using half-hour periods, we will be able to give each student at least 80 to 90 hours on the terminals next year.

In my view, the development of a viable theory of instruction and the corresponding learning theory will be an interactive enterprise, with advances in each area influencing the concepts and data base in the other. For too long, psychologists studying learning have shown little interest in instructional problems, whereas educators have made only primitive and superficial applications of learning theory. Both fields would have advanced more rapidly if an appropriate interchange of ideas and problems had existed. It is my hope that prospects for CAI, as both a tool for research and a mode of instruction, will act as a catalyst for a rapid evolution of new concepts in learning theory as well as a corresponding theory of instruction.

REFERENCES

Atkinson, R. C., and Hansen, D. N. "Computer-assisted instruction in initial reading: The Stanford Project," *Reading Research Quarterly*, 1966, **2**, 5–25.

Atkinson, R. C., and Shiffrin, R. M. "Human memory: A proposed system and its control processes," in K. W. Spence and J. T. Spence (Eds.), *The Psychology of Learning and Motivation: Advances in Research and Theory.* Vol. 2. New York: Academic Press, 1968, in press.

Fishman, E. J., Keller, L., and Atkinson, R. C. "Massed vs. distributed practice in computerized spelling drills," *Journal of Educational Psychology*, 1968, **59**, in press.

Groen, G. J., and Atkinson, R. C. "Models for optimizing the learning process," *Psychological Bulletin*, 1966, **66**, 309–320.

Hansen, D. N., and Rogers, T. S. An exploration of psycholinguistic units in initial reading. Technical Report 74, 1965, Stanford University, Institute for Mathematical Studies in the Social Sciences.

Rodgers, T. S. Linguistic considerations in the design of the Stanford computer-based curriculum in initial reading. Technical Report 111, 1967, Stanford University, Institute for Mathematical Studies in the Social Sciences.

Suppes, P. "The uses of computers in education," *Scientific American*, 1966, **215**, 206–221.

Suppes, P., Jerman, M., and Groen, G. J. "Arithmetic drills and review on a computer-based teletype," *Arithmetic Teacher*, 1966, April, 303–308.

Wilson, H. A., and Atkinson, R. C. Computer-based instruction in initial reading: A progress report on the Stanford project. Technical Report 119, 1967, Stanford University, Institute for Mathematical Studies in the Social Sciences. (To be published in H. Levin and J. Williams, Eds., *Basic Studies in Reading.* New York: Harper and Row.)

3.3 Learning of Visceral and Glandular Responses

NEAL E. MILLER

There is a strong traditional belief in the inferiority of the autonomic nervous system and the visceral responses that it controls. The recent experiments disproving this belief have deep implications for theories of learning, for individual differences in autonomic responses, for the cause and the cure of abnormal psychosomatic symptoms, and possibly also for the understanding of normal homeostasis. Their success encourages investigators to try other unconventional types of training. Before describing these experiments, let me briefly sketch some elements in the history of the deeply entrenched, false belief in the gross inferiority of one major part of the nervous system.

HISTORICAL ROOTS AND MODERN RAMIFICATIONS

Since ancient times, reason and the voluntary responses of the skeletal muscles have been considered to be superior, while emotions and the presumably involuntary glandular and visceral responses have been considered to be inferior. This invidious dichotomy appears in the philosophy of Plato (1), with his superior rational soul in the head above and inferior souls in the body below. Much later, the great French neuroanatomist Bichat (2) distinguished between the cerebrospinal nervous system of the great brain and spinal cord, controlling skeletal responses, and the dual chain of ganglia (which he called "little brains") running down on either side of the spinal cord in the body below and controlling emotional and visceral responses. He indicated his low opinion of the ganglionic system by calling it "vegetative"; he also believed it to be largely independent of the cerebrospinal system, an opinion which is still reflected in our modern name for it, the autonomic nervous system. Considerably later, Cannon (3) studied the sympathetic part of the autonomic nervous system and concluded that the different nerves in it all fire simultaneously and are incapable of the finely differentiated individual responses possible for the cerebrospinal system, a conclusion which is enshrined in modern textbooks.

Many, though not all, psychiatrists have made an invidious distinction between the hysterical and other symptoms that are mediated by the cerebrospinal nervous system and the psychosomatic symptoms that are mediated by the autonomic nervous system. Whereas the former are supposed to be subject to a higher type of control that is symbolic, the latter are presumed to be only the direct physiological consequences of the type and intensity of the patient's emotions (see, for example, 4).

Similarly, students of learning have made a distinction between a lower form, called classical conditioning and thought to be involuntary, and a superior form variously called trial-and-error learning, operant conditioning, type II conditioning, or instrumental learning and believed to be responsible for voluntary behavior. In classical conditioning, the reinforcement must be by an unconditioned stimulus that already elicits the specific response to be learned; therefore, the possibilities are quite limited. In instrumental learning, the reinforcement, called a reward, has the property of strengthening any immediately preceding response. Therefore, the possibilities for reinforcement are much greater; a given reward may reinforce any one of a number of different responses, and a given response may be reinforced by any one of a number of different rewards.

Finally, the foregoing invidious distinctions have coalesced into the strong traditional belief that the superior type

of instrumental learning involved in the superior voluntary behavior is possible only for skeletal responses mediated by the superior cerebrospinal nervous system, while, conversely, the inferior classical conditioning is the only kind possible for the inferior, presumably involuntary, visceral and emotional responses mediated by the inferior autonomic nervous system. Thus, in a recent summary generally considered authoritative, Kimble (5) states the almost universal belief that "for autonomically mediated behavior, the evidence points unequivocally to the conclusion that such responses can be modified by classical, but not instrumental, training methods." Upon examining the evidence, however, one finds that it consists only of failure to secure instrumental learning in two incompletely reported exploratory experiments and a vague allusion to the Russian literature (6). It is only against a cultural background of great prejudice that such weak evidence could lead to such a strong conviction.

The belief that instrumental learning is possible only for the cerebrospinal system and, conversely, that the autonomic nervous system can be modified only by classical conditioning has been used as one of the strongest arguments for the notion that instrumental learning and classical conditioning are two basically different phenomena rather than different manifestations of the same phenomenon under different conditions. But for many years I have been impressed with the similarity between the laws of classical conditioning and those of instrumental learning, and with the fact that, in each of these two situations, some of the specific details of learning vary with the specific conditions of

learning. Failing to see any clear-cut dichotomy, I have assumed that there is
only one kind of learning (7). This assumption has logically demanded that
instrumental training procedures be able
to produce the learning of any visceral
responses that could be acquired through
classical conditioning procedures. Yet it
was only a little over a dozen years ago
that I began some experimental work on
this problem and a somewhat shorter
time ago that I first, in published articles
(8), made specific sharp challenges to the
traditional view that the instrumental
learning of visceral responses is impossible.

SOME DIFFICULTIES

One of the difficulties of investigating
the instrumental learning of visceral
responses stems from the fact that the
responses that are the easiest to measure—namely, heart rate, vasomotor responses, and the galvanic skin response—are known to be affected by
skeletal responses, such as exercise,
breathing, and even tensing of certain
muscles, such as those in the diaphragm.
Thus, it is hard to rule out the possibility
that, instead of directly learning a visceral
response, the subject has learned a skeletal response the performance of which
causes the visceral change being recorded.

One of the controls I planned to use
was the paralysis of all skeletal responses
through administration of curare, a drug
which selectively blocks the motor end
plates of skeletal muscles without eliminating consciousness in human subjects
or the neural control of visceral responses, such as the beating of the heart.

The muscles involved in breathing are
paralyzed, so the subject's breathing
must be maintained through artificial
respiration. Since it seemed unlikely that
curarization and other rigorous control
techniques would be easy to use with
human subjects, I decided to concentrate
first on experiments with animals.

Originally I thought that learning
would be more difficult when the animal
was paralyzed, under the influence of
curare, and therefore I decided to post-
pone such experiments until ones on
nonparalyzed animals had yielded some
definitely promising results. This turned
out to be a mistake because, as I found
out much later, paralyzing the animal
with curare not only greatly simplifies the
problem of recording visceral responses
without artifacts introduced by movement but also apparently makes it easier
for the animal to learn, perhaps because
paralysis of the skeletal muscles removes
sources of variability and distraction.
Also, in certain experiments I made the
mistake of using rewards that induced
strong unconditioned responses that interfered with instrumental learning.

One of the greatest difficulties,
however, was the strength of the belief
that instrumental learning of glandular
and visceral responses is impossible. It
was extremely difficult to get students to
work on this problem, and when paid
assistants were assigned to it, their attempts were so half-hearted that it soon
became more economical to let them
work on some other problem which they
could attack with greater faith and enthusiasm. These difficulties and a few
preliminary encouraging but inconclu-
sive early results have been described
elsewhere (9).

SUCCESS WITH SALIVATION

The first clear-cut results were secured by Alfredo Carmona and me in an experiment on the salivation of dogs. Initial attempts to use food as a reward for hungry dogs were unsuccessful, partly because of strong and persistent unconditioned salivation elicited by the food. Therefore, we decided to use water as a reward for thirsty dogs. Preliminary observations showed that the water had no appreciable effects one way or the other on the bursts of spontaneous salivation. As an additional precaution, however, we used the experimental design of rewarding dogs in one group whenever they showed a burst of spontaneous salivation, so that they would be trained to increase salivation, and rewarding dogs in another group whenever there was a long interval between spontaneous bursts, so that they would be trained to decrease salivation. If the reward had any unconditioned effect, this effect might be classically conditioned to the experimental situation and therefore produce a change in salivation that was not a true instance of instrumental learning. But in classical conditioning the reinforcement must elicit the response that is to be acquired. Therefore, conditioning of a response elicited by the reward could produce either an increase or a decrease in salivation, depending upon the direction of the unconditioned response elicited by the reward, but it could not produce a change in one direction for one group and in the opposite direction for the other group. The same type of logic applies for any unlearned cumulative

aftereffects of the reward; they could not be in opposite directions for the two groups. With instrumental learning, however, the reward can reinforce any response that immediately precedes it; therefore, the same reward can be used to produce either increases or decreases.

The results are presented in Fig. 1, which summarizes the effects of 40 days of training with one 45-minute training session per day. It may be seen that in this experiment the learning proceeded slowly. However, statistical analysis showed that each of the trends in the predicted rewarded direction was highly reliable (10).

Since the changes in salivation for the two groups were in opposite directions, they cannot be attributed to classical conditioning. It was noted, however, that the group rewarded for increases seemed to be more aroused and active than the one rewarded for decreases. Conceivably, all we were doing was to change the level of activation of the dogs, and this change was, in turn, affecting the salivation. Although we did not observe any specific skeletal responses, such as chewing movements or panting, which might be expected to elicit salivation, it was difficult to be absolutely certain that such movements did not occur. Therefore, we decided to rule out such movements by paralyzing the dogs with curare, but we immediately found that curare had two effects which were disastrous for this experiment: it elicited such copious and continuous salivation that there were no changes in salivation to reward, and the salivation was so viscous that it almost immediately gummed up the recording apparatus.

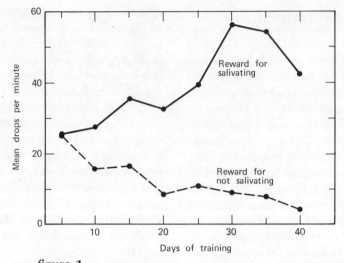

figure 1

Learning curves for groups of thirsty dogs rewarded with water for either increases or decreases in spontaneous salivation. (From Miller and Carmona (*10*).)

HEART RATE

In the meantime, Jay Trowill, working with me on this problem, was displaying great ingenuity, courage, and persistence in trying to produce instrumental learning of heart rate in rats that had been paralyzed by curare to prevent them from "cheating" by muscular exertion to speed up the heart or by relaxation to slow it down. As a result of preliminary testing, he selected a dose of curare (3.6 milligrams of *d*-tubocurarine chloride per kilogram, injected intraperitoneally) which produced deep paralysis for at least 3 hours, and a rate of artificial respiration (inspiration–expiration ratio 1 : 1; 70 breaths per minute; peak pressure reading, 20 cm-H_2O) which maintained the heart at a constant and normal rate throughout this time.

In subsequent experiments, DiCara and I have obtained similar effects by starting with a smaller dose (1.2 milligrams per kilogram) and constantly infusing additional amounts of the drug, through intraperitoneal injection, at the rate of 1.2 milligrams per kilogram per hour, for the duration of the experiment. We have recorded, electromyographically, the response of the muscles, to determine that this dose does indeed produce a complete block of the action potentials, lasting for at least an hour after the end of infusion. We have found that if parameters of respiration and the face mask are adjusted carefully, the procedure not only maintains the heart rate of a 500-gram control animal constant but also maintains the vital signs of temperature, peripheral vasomotor responses, and the pCO_2 of the blood constant.

Since there are not very many ways to reward an animal completely paralyzed by curare, Trowill and I decided to use direct electrical stimulation of re-warding areas of the brain. There were other technical difficulties to overcome, such as devising the automatic system for rewarding small changes in heart rate as recorded by the electrocardiogram. Nevertheless, Trowill at last succeeded in training his rats (11). Those rewarded for an increase in heart rate showed a statistically reliable increase, and those rewarded for a decrease in heart rate showed a statistically reliable decrease. The changes, however, were disap-pointingly small, averaging only 5 per-cent in each direction.

The next question was whether larger changes could be achieved by im-proving the technique of training. DiCara and I used the technique of shaping—in other words, of immediately rewarding first very small, and hence frequently occurring, changes in the correct direc-tion and, as soon as these had been learned, requiring progressively larger changes as the criterion for reward. In this way, we were able to produce in 90 minutes of training changes averaging 20 percent in either direction (12).

KEY PROPERTIES OF LEARNING: DISCRIMINATION AND RETENTION

Does the learning of visceral responses have the same properties as the learning of skeletal responses? One of the im-portant characteristics of the instru-mental learning of skeletal responses is that a discrimination can be learned, so that the responses are more likely to be made in the stimulus situations in which they are rewarded than in those in which they are not. After the training of the first

few rats had convinced us that we could produce large changes in heart rate, DiCara and I gave all the rest of the rats in the experiment described above 45 minutes of additional training with the most difficult criterion. We did this in order to see whether they could learn to give a greater response during a "time-in" stimulus (the presence of a flashing light and a tone) which indicated that a response in the proper direction would be rewarded than during a "time-out" stimulus (absence of light and tone) which indicated that a correct response would not be rewarded.

Figure 2 shows the record of one of the rats given such training. Before the beginning of the special discrimination training it had slowed its heart from an initial rate of 350 beats per minute to a rate of 230 beats per minute. From the top record of Fig. 2 one can see that, at the beginning of the special discrim-ination training, there was no appreciable reduction in heart rate that was specifi-cally associated with the time-in stimu-lus. Thus it took the rat considerable time after the onset of this stimulus to meet the criterion and get the reward. At the end of the discrimination training the heart rate during time-out remained ap-proximately the same, but when the time-in light and tone came on, the heart slowed down and the criterion was promptly met. Although the other rats showed less change than this, by the end of the relatively short period of discrim-ination training their heart rate did change reliably ($P < .001$) in the pre-dicted direction when the time-in stimu-lus came on. Thus, it is clear that instru-mental visceral learning has at least one of the important properties of instru-

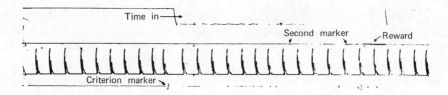

Beginning of Discrimination Training

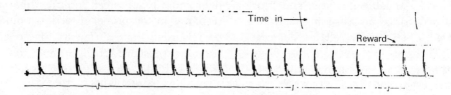

After 45 Minutes of Discrimination Training

figure 2

Electrocardiograms at the beginning and at the end of discrimination training of curarized rat rewarded for slow heart rate. Slowing of heart rate is rewarded only during a "time-in" stimulus (tone and light). (From Miller and DiCara (12).)

mental skeletal learning—namely, the ability to be brought under the control of a discriminative stimulus.

Another of the important properties of the instrumental learning of skeletal responses is that it is remembered. DiCara and I performed a special experiment to test the retention of learned changes in heart rate (13). Rats that had been given a single training session were returned to their home cages for 3 months without further training. When curarized again and returned to the experimental situation for nonreinforced test trials, rats in both the "increase" and the "decrease" groups showed good retention by exhibiting reliable changes in the direction rewarded in the earlier training.

ESCAPE AND AVOIDANCE LEARNING

Is visceral learning by any chance peculiarly limited to reinforcement by the unusual reward of direct electrical stimulation of the brain, or can it be reinforced by other rewards in the same way that skeletal learning can be? In order to answer this question, DiCara and I (14) performed an experiment using the other of the two forms of thoroughly studied reward that can be conveniently used with rats which are paralyzed by curare—namely, the chance to avoid, or escape from, mild electric shock. A shock signal was turned on; after it had been on for 10 seconds it was accompanied by brief pulses of mild electric shock delivered to the rat's tail. During the first 10 seconds the rat could turn off the shock signal and avoid the shock by making the correct response of changing its heart rate in the required direction by the required amount. If it did not make the correct response in time, the shocks continued to be delivered until the rat escaped them by making the correct response, which immediately turned off both the shock and the shock signal.

For one group of curarized rats, the correct response was an increase in heart rate; for the other group it was a decrease. After the rats had learned to make small responses in the proper direction, they were required to make larger ones. During this training the shock signals were randomly interspersed with an equal number of "safe" signals that were not followed by shock; the heart rate was also recorded during so-called blank trials—trials without any signals or shocks. For half of the rats the shock signal was a tone and the "safe" signal was a flashing light; for the other half the roles of these cues were reversed.

The results are shown in Fig. 3. Each of the 12 rats in this experiment changed its heart rate in the rewarded direction. As training progressed, the shock signal began to elicit a progressively greater change in the rewarded direction than the change recorded during the blank trials; this was a statistically reliable trend. Conversely, as training progressed, the "safe" signal came to elicit a statistically reliable change in the opposite direction, toward the initial base line. These results show learning when escape and avoidance are the rewards; this means that visceral responses in curarized rats can be reinforced by rewards other than direct electrical stimulation of the brain. These

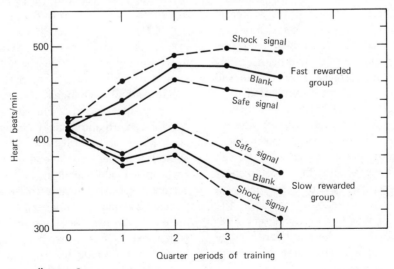

figure 3

Changes in heart rate during avoidance training. (From DiCara and Miller (14).)

rats also discriminate between the shock and the "safe" signals. You will remember that, with noncurarized thirsty dogs, we were able to use yet another kind of reward, water, to produce learned changes in salivation.

TRANSFER TO NONCURARIZED STATE: MORE EVIDENCE AGAINST MEDIATION

In the experiments discussed above, paralysis of the skeletal muscles by curare ruled out the possibility that the subjects were learning the overt performance of skeletal responses which were indirectly eliciting the changes in the heart rate. It is barely conceivable, however, that the rats were learning to send out from the motor cortex central impulses which would have activated the muscles had they not been paralyzed. And it is barely conceivable that these central impulses affected heart rate by means either of inborn connections or of classically conditioned ones that had been acquired when previous exercise had been accompanied by an increase in heart rate and relaxation had been accompanied by a decrease. But, if the changes in heart rate were produced in this indirect way, we would expect that, during a subsequent test without curare, any rat that showed learned changes in heart rate would show the movements in the muscles that were no longer paralyzed. Furthermore, the problem of whether or not visceral responses learned under curarization carry over to the noncurarized state is of interest in its own right.

In order to answer this question, DiCara and I (15) trained two groups of curarized rats to increase or decrease, respectively, their heart rate in order to avoid, or escape from, brief pulses of mild electric shock. When these rats were tested 2 weeks later in the noncurarized state, the habit was remembered. Statistically reliable increases in heart rate averaging 5 percent and decreases averaging 16 percent occurred. Immediately subsequent retraining without curare produced additional significant changes of heart rate in the rewarded direction, bringing the total overall increase to 11 percent and the decrease to 22 percent. While, at the beginning of the test in the noncurarized state, the two groups showed some differences in respiration and activity, these differences decreased until, by the end of the retraining, they were small and far from statistically reliable ($t = 0.3$ and 1.3, respectively). At the same time, the difference between the two groups with respect to heart rate was increasing, until it became large and thus extremely reliable ($t = 8.6$, $df = 12$, $P < .001$).

In short, while greater changes in heart rate were being learned, the response was becoming more specific, involving smaller changes in respiration and muscular activity. This increase in specificity with additional training is another point of similarity with the instrumental learning of skeletal responses. Early in skeletal learning, the rewarded correct response is likely to be accompanied by many unnecessary movements. With additional training during which extraneous movements are not rewarded, they tend to drop out.

It is difficult to reconcile the foregoing results with the hypothesis that the differences in heart rate were mediated primarily by a difference in either respiration or amount of general activity. This is especially true in view of the research, summarized by Ehrlich and Malmo (16), which shows that muscular activity, to affect heart rate in the rat, must be rather vigorous.

While it is difficult to rule out completely the possibility that changes in heart rate are mediated by central impulses to skeletal muscles, the possibility of such mediation is much less attractive for other responses, such as intestinal contractions and the formation of urine by the kidney. Furthermore, if the learning of these different responses can be shown to be specific in enough visceral responses, one runs out of different skeletal movements each eliciting a specific different visceral response†. Therefore, experiments were performed on the learning of a variety of different visceral responses and on the specificity of that learning. Each of these experiments was, of course, interesting in its own right, quite apart from any bearing on the problem of mediation.

SPECIFICITY: INTESTINAL VERSUS CARDIAC

The purpose of our next experiment was to determine the specificity of visceral learning. If such learning has the same properties as the instrumental learning

† "It even becomes difficult to postulate enough different thoughts each arousing a different emotion, each of which in turn innately elicits a specific visceral response. And if one assumes a more direct specific connection between different thoughts and different visceral responses, the notion becomes indistinguishable from the ideo-motor hypothesis of the voluntary movement of skeletal muscles." (W. James, *Principles of Psychology:* New York: Dover, new ed., 1950, vol. 2, chap. 26.)

of skeletal responses, it should be possible to learn a specific visceral response independently of other ones. Furthermore, as we have just seen, we might expect to find that, the better the rewarded response is learned, the more specific is the learning. Banuazizi and I worked on this problem (17). First we had to discover another visceral response that could be conveniently recorded and rewarded. We decided on intestinal contractions, and recorded them in the curarized rat with a little balloon filled with water thrust approximately 4 centimeters beyond the anal sphincter. Changes of pressure in the balloon were transduced into electric voltages which produced a record on a polygraph and also activated an automatic mechanism for delivering the reward, which was electrical stimulation of the brain.

The results for the first rat trained, which was a typical one, are shown in Fig. 4. From the top record it may be seen that, during habituation, there were some spontaneous contractions. When the rat was rewarded by brain stimulation for keeping contractions below a certain amplitude for a certain time, the number of contractions was reduced and the base line was lowered. After the record showed a highly reliable change indicating that relaxation had been learned (Fig. 4, second record from the top), the conditions of training were reversed and the reward was delivered whenever the amplitude of contractions rose above a certain level. From the next record (Fig. 4, middle) it may be seen that this type of training increased the number of contractions and raised the base line. Finally (Fig. 4, two bottom records) the reward was discontinued and, as would be ex-

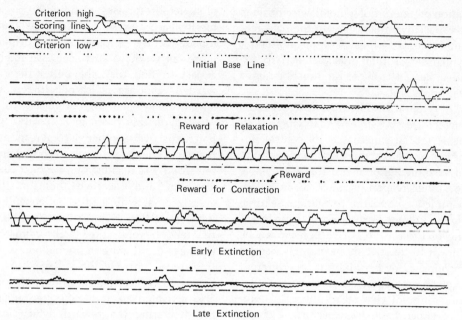

Criterion high
Scoring line
Criterion low

Initial Base Line

Reward for Relaxation

Reward

Reward for Contraction

Early Extinction

Late Extinction

figure 4

Typical samples of a record of instrumental learning of an intestinal response by a curarized rat. From top to bottom: Record of spontaneous contraction before training; record after training with reward for relaxation; record after training with reward for contractions; record during nonrewarded extinction trials. (From Miller and Banua-zizi (17).)

pected, the response continued for a while but gradually became extinguished, so that the activity eventually returned to approximately its original base-line level.

After studying a number of other rats in this way and convincing ourselves that the instrumental learning of intestinal responses was a possibility, we designed an experiment to test specificity. For all the rats of the experiment, both intestinal contractions and heart rate were recorded, but half the rats were rewarded for one of these responses and half were rewarded for the other response. Each of these two groups of rats was divided into two subgroups, rewarded, respectively, for increased and

decreased response. The rats were completely paralyzed by curare, maintained on artificial respiration, and rewarded by electrical stimulation of the brain.

The results are shown in Figs. 5 and 6. In Fig. 5 it may be seen that the group rewarded for increases in intestinal contractions learned an increase, the group rewarded for decreases learned a decrease, but neither of these groups showed an appreciable change in heart rate. Conversely (Fig. 6), the group rewarded for increases in heart rate showed an increase, the group rewarded for decreases showed a decrease, but neither of these groups showed a change in intestinal contractions.

The fact that each type of response

changed when it was rewarded rules out the interpretation that the failure to secure a change when that change was not rewarded could have been due to either a strong and stable homeostatic regulation of that response or an inability of our techniques to measure changes reliably under the particular conditions of our experiment.

Each of the 12 rats in the experiment showed statistically reliable changes in the rewarded direction; for 11 the changes were reliable beyond the $P <$ .001 level, while for the 12th the changes were reliable only beyond the .05 level. A statistically reliable negative correlation showed that the better the rewarded visceral response was learned, the less change occurred in the other, nonrewarded response. This greater specificity with better learning is what we

had expected. The results showed that visceral learning can be specific to an organ system, and they clearly ruled out the possibility of mediation by any single general factor, such as level of activation or central commands for either general activity or relaxation.

In an additional experiment, Banuazizi (18) showed that either increases or decreases in intestinal contractions can be rewarded by avoidance of, or escape from, mild electric shocks, and that the intestinal responses can be discriminatively elicited by a specific stimulus associated with reinforcement.

KIDNEY FUNCTION

Encouraged by these successes, DiCara and I decided to see whether or not the rate of urine formation by the kidney

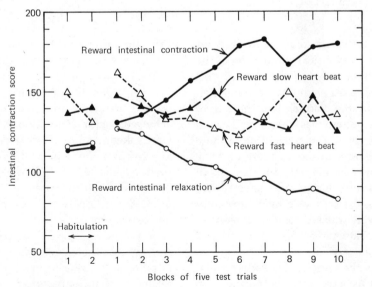

figure 5

Graph showing that the intestinal contraction score is changed by rewarding either increases or decreases in intestinal contractions but is unaffected by rewarding changes in heart rate. (From Miller and Banuazizi (17).)

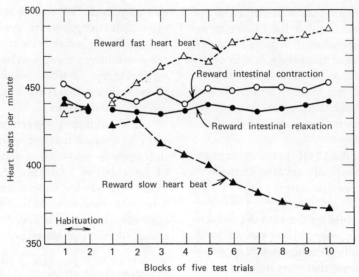

figure 6

Graph showing that the heart rate is changed by rewarding either increases or decreases in heart rate but is unaffected by rewarding changes in intestinal contractions. Comparison with Figure 5 demonstrates the specificity of visceral learning. (From Miller and Banauazizi (*17*).)

could be changed in the curarized rat rewarded by electrical stimulation of the brain (*19*). A catheter, permanently inserted, was used to prevent accumulation of urine by the bladder, and the rate of urine formation was measured by an electronic device for counting minute drops. In order to secure a rate of urine formation fast enough so that small changes could be promptly detected and rewarded, the rats were kept constantly loaded with water through infusion by way of a catheter permanently inserted in the jugular vein.

All of the seven rats rewarded when the intervals between times of urine-drop formation lengthened showed decreases in the rate of urine formation, and all of the seven rats rewarded when these intervals shortened showed increases in

the rate of urine formation. For both groups the changes were highly reliable ($P < .001$).

In order to determine how the change in rate of urine formation was achieved, certain additional measures were taken. As the set of bars at left in Fig. 7 shows, the rate of filtration, measured by means of ^{14}C-labeled inulin, increased when increases in the rate of urine formation were rewarded and decreased when decreases in the rate were rewarded. Plots of the correlations showed that the changes in the rates of filtration and urine formation were not related to changes in either blood pressure or heart rate.

The middle set of bars in Fig. 7 shows that the rats rewarded for increases in the rate of urine formation had an increased rate of renal blood flow, as measured by ^{3}H-p-aminohippuric acid, and that those rewarded for decreases had a decreased rate of renal blood flow. Since these changes in blood flow were not accompanied by changes in general blood pressure or in heart rate, they must have been achieved by vasomotor changes of the renal arteries. That these vasomotor changes were at least somewhat specific is shown by the fact that vasomotor responses of the tail, as measured by a photoelectric plethysmograph, did not differ for the two groups of rats.

The set of bars at right in Fig. 7 shows that when decreases in rate of urine formation were rewarded, a more concentrated urine, having higher osmolarity, was formed. Since the slower passage of urine through the tubules would afford more opportunity for reabsorption of water, this higher concentration does not necessarily mean an in-

crease in the secretion of antidiuretic hormone. When an increased rate of urine formation was rewarded, the urine did not become more diluted—that is, it showed no decrease in osmolarity; therefore, the increase in rate of urine formation observed in this experiment cannot be accounted for in terms of an inhibition of the secretion of antidiuretic hormone.

From the foregoing results it appears that the learned changes in urine formation in this experiment were produced primarily by changes in the rate of filtration, which, in turn, were produced primarily by changes in the rate of blood flow through the kidneys.

GASTRIC CHANGES

In the next experiment, Carmona, Demierre, and I used a photoelectric plethysmograph to measure changes, presumably in the amount of blood, in

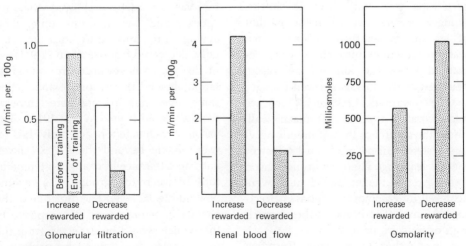

figure 7

Effects of rewarding increased rate of urine formation in one group and decreased rate in another on measures of glomerular filtration, renal blood flow, and osmolarity. (From data in Miller and DiCara (*19*).)

the stomach wall (20). In an operation performed under anesthesia, a small glass tube, painted black except for a small spot, was inserted into the rat's stomach. The same tube was used to hold the stomach wall against a small glass window inserted through the body wall. The tube was left in that position. After the animal had recovered, a bundle of optical fibers could be slipped snugly into the glass tube so that the light beamed through it would shine out through the unpainted spot in the tube inside the stomach, pass through the stomach wall, and be recorded by a photocell on the other side of the glass window. Preliminary tests indicated that, as would be expected, when the amount of blood in the stomach wall increased, less light would pass through. Other tests showed that stomach contractions elicited by injections of insulin did not affect the amount of light transmitted.

In the main experiment we rewarded curarized rats by enabling them to avoid or escape from mild electric shocks. Some were rewarded when the amount of light that passed through the stomach wall increased, while others were rewarded when the amount decreased. Fourteen of the 15 rats showed changes in the rewarded direction. Thus, we demonstrated that the stomach wall, under the control of the autonomic nervous system, can be modified by instrumental learning. There is strong reason to believe that the learned changes were achieved by vasomotor responses affecting the amount of blood in the stomach wall or mucosa, or in both.

In another experiment, Carmona (21) showed that stomach contractions can be either increased or decreased by instrumental learning.

It is obvious that learned changes in the blood supply of internal organs can affect their functioning—as, for example, the rate at which urine was formed by the kidneys was affected by changes in the amount of blood that flowed through them. Thus, such changes can produce psychosomatic symptoms. And if the learned changes in blood supply can be specific to a given organ, the symptom will occur in that organ rather than in another one.

PERIPHERAL VASOMOTOR RESPONSES

Having investigated the instrumental learning of internal vasomotor responses, we next studied the learning of peripheral ones. In the first experiment, the amount of blood in the tail of a curarized rat was measured by a photoelectric plethysmograph, and changes were rewarded by electrical stimulation of the brain (22). All of the four rats rewarded for vasoconstriction showed that response, and, at the same time, their average core temperature, measured rectally, decreased from 98.9° to 97.9°F. All of the four rats rewarded for vasodilatation showed that response and, at the same time, their average core temperature increased from 99.9° to 101°F. The vasomotor change for each individual rat was reliable beyond the $P < .01$ level, and the difference in change in temperature between the groups was reliable beyond the .01 level. The direction of the change in temperature was opposite to that which would be expected from the heat conservation caused by peripheral vasoconstriction or the heat loss caused by peripheral vasodilatation. The changes are in the direction which would be expected if the training had altered the rate of heat production, causing a change in temperature which, in turn, elicited the vasomotor response.

The next experiment was designed to try to determine the limits of the specificity of vasomotor learning. The pinnae of the rat's ears were chosen because the blood vessels in them are believed to be innervated primarily, and perhaps exclusively, by the sympathetic branch of the autonomic nervous system, the branch that Cannon believed always fired nonspecifically as a unit (3). But Cannon's experiments involved exposing cats to extremely strong emotion-evoking stimuli, such as barking dogs, and such stimuli will also evoke generalized activity throughout the skeletal musculature. Perhaps his results reflected the way in which sympathetic activity was elicited, rather than demonstrating any inherent inferiority of the sympathetic nervous system.

In order to test this interpretation, DiCara and I (23) put photocells on both ears of the curarized rat and connected them to a bridge circuit so that only differences in the vasomotor responses of the two ears were rewarded by brain stimulation. We were somewhat surprised and greatly delighted to find that this experiment actually worked. The results are summarized in Fig. 8. Each of the six rats rewarded for relative vasodilatation of the left ear showed that response, while each of the six rats rewarded for relative vasodilatation of the right ear showed that response. Recordings from the right and left forepaws showed little if any change in vasomotor response.

It is clear that these results cannot be by-products of changes in either heart rate or blood pressure, as these would be expected to affect both ears equally. They show either that vasomotor responses mediated by the sympathetic

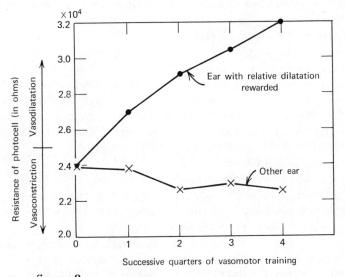

figure 8

Learning a difference in the vasomotor responses of the two ears in the curarized rat. (From data in DiCara and Miller (23).)

nervous system are capable of much greater specificity than has previously been believed, or that the innervation of the blood vessels in the pinnae of the ears is not restricted almost exclusively to sympathetic-nervous-system components, as has been believed, and involves functionally significant parasympathetic components. In any event, the changes in the blood flow certainly were surprisingly specific. Such changes in blood flow could account for specific psychosomatic symptoms.

BLOOD PRESSURE INDEPENDENT OF HEART RATE

Although changes in blood pressure were not induced as by-products of rewarded changes in the rate of urine formation, another experiment on curarized rats showed that, when changes in systolic blood pressure are specifically reinforced, they can be learned (24). Blood pressure was recorded by means of a catheter permanently inserted into the aorta, and the reward was avoidance of, or escape from, mild electric shock. All seven rats rewarded for increases in blood pressure showed further increases, while all seven rewarded for decreases showed decreases, each of the changes, which were in opposite directions, being reliable beyond the $P < .01$ level. The increase was from 139 mm-Hg, which happens to be roughly comparable to the normal systolic blood pressure of an adult man, to 170 mm-Hg, which is on the borderline of abnormally high blood pressure in man.

Each experimental animal was "yoked" with a curarized partner, maintained on artificial respiration and having shock electrodes on its tail wired in series with electrodes on the tail of the experimental animal, so that it received exactly the same electric shocks and could do nothing to escape or avoid them. The yoked controls for both the increase-rewarded and the decrease-rewarded groups showed some elevation in blood pressure as an unconditioned effect of the shocks. By the end of training, in contrast to the large difference in the blood pressures of the two groups specifically rewarded for changes in opposite directions, there was no difference in blood pressure between the yoked control partners for these two groups. Furthermore, the increase in blood pressure in these control groups was reliably less ($P < .01$) than that in the group specifically rewarded for increases. Thus, it is clear that the reward for an increase in blood pressure produced an additional increase over and above the effects of the shocks per se, while the reward for a decrease was able to overcome the unconditioned increase elicited by the shocks.

For none of the four groups was there a significant change in heart rate or in temperature during training; there were no significant differences in these measures among the groups. Thus, the learned change was relatively specific to blood pressure.

TRANSFER FROM HEART RATE TO SKELETAL AVOIDANCE

Although visceral learning can be quite specific, especially if only a specific response is rewarded, as was the case in the experiment on the two ears, under some circumstances it can involve a more generalized effect.

In handling the rats that had just recovered from curarization, DiCara noticed that those that had been trained, through the avoidance or escape reward, to increase their heart rate were more likely to squirm, squeal, defecate, and show other responses indicating emotionality than were those that had been trained to reduce their heart rate. Could instrumental learning of heart-rate changes have some generalized effects, perhaps on the level of emotionality, which might affect the behavior in a different avoidance-learning situation? In order to look for such an effect, DiCara and Weiss (26) used a modified shuttle avoidance apparatus. In this apparatus, when a danger signal is given, the rat must run from compartment A to compartment B. If he runs fast enough, he avoids the shock; if not, he must run to escape it. The next time the danger signal is given, the rat must run in the opposite direction, from B to A.

Other work had shown that learning in this apparatus is an inverted U-shaped function of the strength of the shocks, with shocks that are too strong eliciting emotional behavior instead of running. DiCara and Weiss trained their rats in this apparatus with a level of shock that is approximately optimum for naive rats of this strain. They found that the rats that had been rewarded for decreasing their heart rate learned well, but that those that had been rewarded for increasing their heart rate learned less well, as if their emotionality had been increased. The difference was statistically reliable $(P < .001)$. This experiment clearly demonstrates that training a visceral response can affect the subsequent learning of a skeletal one, but additional work will be required to prove the hypothesis that training to increase heart rate increases emotionality.

VISCERAL LEARNING WITHOUT CURARE

Thus far, in all of the experiments except the one on teaching thirsty dogs to salivate, the initial training was given when the animal was under the influence of curare. All of the experiments, except the one on salivation, have produced surprisingly rapid learning—definitive results within 1 or 2 hours. Will learning in the normal, noncurarized state be easier, as we originally thought it should be, or will it be harder, as the experiment on the noncurarized dogs suggests? DiCara and I have started to get additional evidence on this problem. We have obtained clear-cut evidence that rewarding (with the avoidance or escape reward) one group of freely moving rats for reducing heart rate and rewarding another group for increasing heart rate produces a difference between the two groups (27). That this difference was not due to the indirect effects of the overt performance of skeletal responses is shown by the fact that it persisted in subsequent tests during which the rats were paralyzed by curare. And, on subsequent retraining without curare, such differences in activity and respiration as were present earlier in training continued to decrease, while the differences in heart rate continued to increase. It seems extremely unlikely that, at the end of training, the highly reliable differences in heart rate $(t = 7.2; P < .0001)$ can be explained by the highly unreliable differences in activity and respiration ($t = .07$ and 0.2, respectively).

Although the rats in this experiment showed some learning when they were trained initially in the noncurarized state, this learning was much poorer than that which we have seen in our other experiments on curarized rats. This is exactly the opposite of my original expectation, but seems plausible in the light of hindsight. My hunch is that paralysis by curare improved learning by eliminating sources of distraction and variability. The stimulus situation was kept more constant, and confusing visceral fluctuations induced indirectly by skeletal movements were eliminated.

LEARNED CHANGES IN BRAIN WAVES

Encouraged by success in the experiments on the instrumental learning of visceral responses, my colleagues and I have attempted to produce other unconventional types of learning. Electrodes placed on the skull or, better yet, touching the surface of the brain record summative effects of electrical activity over a considerable area of the brain. Such electrical effects are called brain waves, and the record of them is called an electroencephalogram. When the animal is aroused, the electroencephalogram consists of fast, low-voltage activity; when the animal is drowsy or sleeping normally, the electroencephalogram consists of considerably slower, higher-voltage activity. Carmona attempted to see whether this type of brain activity, and the state of arousal accompanying it, can be modified by direct reward of changes in the brain activity (27, 28).

The subjects of the first experiment were freely moving cats. In order to have a reward that was under complete control and that did not require the cat to move, Carmona used direct electrical stimulation of the medial forebrain bundle, which is a rewarding area of the brain. Such stimulation produced a slight lowering in the average voltage of the electroencephalogram and an increase in behavioral arousal. In order to provide a control for these and any other unlearned effects, he rewarded one group for changes in the direction of high-voltage activity and another group for changes in the direction of low-voltage activity.

Both groups learned. The cats rewarded for high-voltage activity showed more high-voltage slow waves and tended to sit like sphinxes, staring out into space. The cats rewarded for low-voltage activity showed much more low-voltage fast activity, and appeared to be aroused, pacing restlessly about, sniffing, and looking here and there. It was clear that this type of training had modified both the character of the electrical brain waves and the general level of the behavioral activity. It was not clear, however, whether the level of arousal of the brain was directly modified and hence modified the behavior; whether the animals learned specific items of behavior which, in turn, modified the arousal of the brain as reflected in the electroencephalogram; or whether both types of learning were occurring simultaneously.

In order to rule out the direct sensory consequences of changes in muscular tension, movement, and posture. Carmona performed the next experiment on rats that had been paralyzed by means of curare. The results, given in Fig. 9,

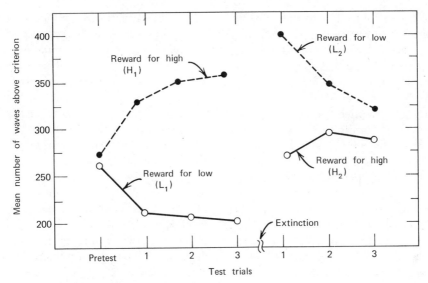

figure 9

Instrumental learning by curarized rats rewarded for high-voltage or for low-voltage electroencephalograms recorded from the cerebral cortex. After a period of nonrewarded extinction, which produced some drowsiness, as indicated by an increase in voltage, the rats in the two groups were then rewarded for voltage changes opposite in direction to the changes for which they were rewarded earlier. (From Carmona (28).)

show that both rewarded groups showed changes in the rewarded direction; that a subsequent nonrewarded rest increased the number of high-voltage responses in both groups; and that, when the conditions of reward were reversed, the direction of change in voltage was reversed.

At present we are trying to use similar techniques to modify the functions of a specific part of the vagal nucleus, by recording and specifically rewarding changes in the electrical activity there. Preliminary results suggest that this is possible. The next step is to investigate the visceral consequences of such modification. This kind of work may open up possibilities for modifying the activity of specific parts of the brain and the functions that they control. In some cases, directly rewarding brain activity may be a more convenient or more powerful technique than rewarding skeletal or visceral behavior. It also may be a new way to throw light on the functions of specific parts of the brain (29).

HUMAN VISCERAL LEARNING

Another question is that of whether people are capable of instrumental learning of visceral responses. I believe that in this respect they are as smart as rats. But, as a recent critical review by Katkin and Murray (30) points out, this has not yet been completely proved. These authors have comprehensively summarized the recent studies reporting successful use of instrumental training to modify human heart rate, vasomotor responses, and the galvanic skin response. Because of the difficulties in subjecting human subjects to the same rigorous controls, including deep paralysis by means of curare, that can be used with animal subjects, one of the most serious questions about the results of the human studies is whether the changes recorded represent the true instrumental learning of visceral responses or the unconscious learning of those skeletal responses that can produce visceral reactions. However, the able investigators who have courageously challenged the strong traditional belief in the inferiority of the autonomic nervous system with experiments at the more difficult but especially significant human level are developing ingenious controls, including demonstrations of the specificity of the visceral change, so that their cumulative results are becoming increasingly impressive.

POSSIBLE ROLE IN HOMEOSTASIS

The functional utility of instrumental learning by the cerebrospinal nervous system under the conditions that existed during mammalian evolution is obvious. The skeletal responses mediated by the cerebrospinal nervous system operate on the external environment, so that there is survival value in the ability to learn responses that bring rewards such as food, water, or escape from pain. The fact that the responses mediated by the autonomic nervous system do not have such direct action on the external environment was one of the reasons for believing that they are not subject to instrumental learning. Is the learning ability of the autonomic nervous system something that has no normal function other than that of providing my students

with subject matter for publications? Is it a mere accidental by-product of the survival value of cerebrospinal learning, or does the instrumental learning of autonomically mediated responses have some adaptive function, such as helping to maintain that constancy of the internal environment called homeostasis?

In order for instrumental learning to function homeostatically, a deviation away from the optimum level will have to function as a drive to motivate learning, and a change toward the optimum level will have to function as a reward to reinforce the learning of the particular visceral response that produced the corrective change.

When a mammal has less than the optimum amount of water in his body, this deficiency serves as a drive of thirst to motivate learning; the overt consummatory response of drinking functions as a reward to reinforce the learning of the particular skeletal responses that were successful in securing the water that restored the optimum level. But is the consummatory response essential? Can restoration of an optimum level by a glandular response function as a reward?

In order to test for the possible rewarding effects of a glandular response, DiCara, Wolf, and I (31) injected albino rats with antidiuretic hormone (ADH) if they chose one arm of a T-maze and with the isotonic saline vehicle if they chose the other, distinctively different, arm. The ADH permitted water to be reabsorbed in the kidney, so that a smaller volume of more concentrated urine was formed. Thus, for normal rats loaded in advance with H_2O, the ADH interfered with the excess-water excretion required for the restoration of homeostasis, while the control injection of isotonic saline allowed the excess water to be excreted. And, indeed, such rats learned to select the side of the maze that assured them an injection of saline so that their glandular response could restore homeostasis.

Conversely, for rats with diabetes insipidus, loaded in advance with hypertonic NaCl, the homeostatic effects of the same two injections were reversed; the ADH, causing the urine to be more concentrated, helped the rats to get rid of the excess NaCl, while the isotonic saline vehicle did not. And, indeed, a group of rats of this kind learned the opposite choice of selecting the ADH side of the maze. As a further control on the effects of the ADH per se, normal rats which had not been given H_2O or NaCl exhibited no learning. This experiment showed that an excess of either H_2O or NaCl functions as a drive and that the return to the normal concentration produced by the appropriate response of a gland, the kidney, functions as a reward.

When we consider the results of this experiment together with those of our experiments showing that glandular and visceral responses can be instrumentally learned, we will expect the animal to learn those glandular and visceral responses mediated by the central nervous system that promptly restore homeostasis after any considerable deviation. Whether or not this theoretically possible learning has any practical significance will depend on whether or not the innate homeostatic mechanisms control the levels closely enough to prevent any deviations large enough to function as a drive from occurring. Even if the innate control should be accurate enough to preclude

learning in most cases, there remains the intriguing possibility that, when pathology interferes with innate control, visceral learning is available as a supplementary mechanism.

IMPLICATIONS AND SPECULATIONS

We have seen how the instrumental learning of visceral responses suggests a new possible homeostatic mechanism worthy of further investigation. Such learning also shows that the autonomic nervous system is not as inferior as has been so widely and firmly believed. It removes one of the strongest arguments for the hypothesis that there are two fundamentally different mechanisms of learning, involving different parts of the nervous system.

Cause of Psychosomatic Symptoms. Similarly, evidence of the instrumental learning of visceral responses removes the main basis for assuming that the psychosomatic symptoms that involve the autonomic nervous system are fundamentally different from those functional symptoms, such as hysterical ones, that involve the cerebrospinal nervous system. Such evidence allows us to extend to psychosomatic symptoms the type of learning-theory analysis that Dollard and I (7, 32) have applied to other symptoms.

For example, suppose a child is terror-stricken at the thought of going to school in the morning because he is completely unprepared for an important examination. The strong fear elicits a variety of fluctuating autonomic symptoms, such as a queasy stomach at one time and pallor and faintness at another; at this point his mother, who is particularly concerned about cardiovascular symptoms, says, "You are sick and must stay home." The child feels a great relief from fear, and this reward should reinforce the cardiovascular responses producing pallor and faintness. If such experiences are repeated frequently enough, the child, theoretically, should learn to respond with that kind of symptom. Similarly, another child whose mother ignored the vasomotor responses but was particularly concerned by signs of gastric distress would learn the latter type of symptom. I want to emphasize, however, that we need careful clinical research to determine how frequently, if at all, the social conditions sufficient for such theoretically possible learning of visceral symptoms actually occur. Since a given instrumental response can be reinforced by a considerable variety of rewards, and by one reward on one occasion and a different reward on another, the fact that glandular and visceral responses can be instrumentally learned opens up many new theoretical possibilities for the reinforcement of psychosomatic symptoms.

Furthermore, we do not yet know how severe a psychosomatic effect can be produced by learning. While none of the 40 rats rewarded for speeding up their heart rates have died in the course of training under curarization, 7 of the 40 rats rewarded for slowing down their heart rates have died. This statistically reliable difference ($\chi^2 = 5.6$, $P < .02$) is highly suggestive, but it could mean that training to speed up the heart helped the rats resist the stress of curare rather than that the reward for slowing down the heart was strong enough to overcome innate regulatory mechanisms and induce sudden death. In either event the visceral learning had a vital effect. At present, DiCara and I are trying to see whether or not the learning of visceral responses can be carried far enough in the noncurarized animal to produce physical damage. We are also investigating the possibility that there may be a critical period in early infancy during which visceral learning has particularly intense and long-lasting effects.

Individual and Cultural Differences. It is possible that, in addition to producing psychosomatic symptoms in extreme cases, visceral learning can account for certain more benign individual and cultural differences. Lacey and Lacey (33) have shown that a given individual may have a tendency, which is stable over a number of years, to respond to a variety of different stresses with the same profile of autonomic responses, while other individuals may have statistically reliable tendencies to respond with different profiles. It now seems possible that differential conditions of learning may account for at least some of these individual differences in patterns of autonomic response.

Conversely, such learning may account also for certain instances in which the same individual responds to the same stress in different ways. For example, a small boy who receives a severe bump in rough-and-tumble play may learn to inhibit the secretion of tears in this situation since his peer group will punish crying by calling it "sissy." But the same small boy may burst into tears when he gets home to his mother, who will not punish weeping and may even reward tears with sympathy.

Similarly, it seems conceivable that different conditions of reward by a culture different from our own may be responsible for the fact that Homer's adult heroes so often "let the big tears fall." Indeed, a former colleague of mine, Herbert Barry III, has analyzed cross-cultural data and found that the amount of crying reported for children seems to be related to the way in which the society reacts to their tears (34).

I have emphasized the possible role of learning in producing the observed individual differences in visceral responses to stress, which in extreme cases may result in one type of psychosomatic symptom in one person and a different type in another. Such learning does not, of course, exclude innate individual differences in the susceptibility of different organs. In fact, given social conditions under which any form of illness will be rewarded, the symptoms of the most susceptible organ will be the most likely ones to be learned. Furthermore, some types of stress may be so strong that the innate reactions to them produce damage without any learning. My colleagues and I are currently investigating the psychological variables involved in such types of stress (35).

Therapeutic Training. The experimental work on animals has developed a powerful technique for using instrumental learning to modify glandular and visceral responses. The improved training technique consists of moment-to-moment recording of the visceral function and immediate reward, at first, of very small changes in the desired direction and then of progressively larger ones. The success of this technique suggests that it should be able to produce therapeutic changes. If the patient who is highly motivated to get rid of a symptom understands that a signal, such as a tone, indicates a change in the desired direction, that tone could serve as a powerful reward. Instruction to try to turn the tone on as often as possible and praise for success should increase the reward. As patients find that they can secure some control of the symptom, their motivation should be strengthened. Such a procedure should be well worth trying on any symptom, functional or organic, that is under neural control, that can be continuously monitored by modern instrumentation, and for which a given direction of change is clearly indicated medically—for example, cardiac arrhythmias, spastic colitis, asthma, and those cases of high blood pressure that are not essential compensation for kidney damage†.The obvious cases to begin with are those in which drugs are ineffective or contraindicated. In the light of the fact that our animals learned so much better when under the influence of curare and transferred their training so well to the normal, nondrugged state, it should be worth while to try to use hypnotic suggestion to achieve similar results by enhancing the reward effect of the signal indicating a change in the desired direction, by producing relaxation and regular breathing, and by removing interference from skeletal responses and distraction by irrelevant cues.

†Objective recording of such symptoms might be useful also in monitoring the effects of quite different types of psychotherapy.

Engel and Melmon (*36*) have reported encouraging results in the use of instrumental training to treat cardiac arrhythmias of organic origin. Randt, Korein, Carmona, and I have had some success in using the method described above to train epileptic patients in the laboratory to suppress, in one way or another, the abnormal paroxysmal spikes in their electroencephalogram. My colleagues and I are hoping to try learning therapy for other symptoms—for example, the rewarding of high-voltage electroencephalograms as a treatment for insomnia. While it is far too early to promise any cures, it certainly will be worth while to investigate thoroughly the therapeutic possibilities of improved instrumental training techniques.

REFERENCES

1. *The Dialogues of Plato*, B. Jowett, Transl. London: Univ. of Oxford Press, ed. 2, 1875, vol. 3, "Timaeus."

2. X. Bichat, *Recherches Physiologiques sur la Vie et le Mort.* Paris: Brosson, Gabon, 1800.

3. W. B. Cannon, *The Wisdom of the Body.* New York: Norton, 1932.

4. F. Alexander, *Psychosomatic Medicine: Its Principles and Applications.* New York: Norton, 1950, pp. 40–41.

5. G. A. Kimble, *Hilgard and Marquis' Conditioning and Learning.* New York: Appleton-Century-Crofts, ed. 2, 1961, p. 100.

6. B. F. Skinner, *The Behavior of Organisms.* New York: Appleton-Century, 1938; O. H. Mowrer, *Harvard Educ. Rev.*, **17**, 102 (1947).

7. N. E. Miller and J. Dollard, *Social Learning and Imitation.* New Haven: Yale Univ. Press, 1941, J. Dollard and N. E. Miller, *Personality and Psychotherapy.* New York: McGraw-Hill, 1950; N. E. Miller, *Psychol. Rev.*, **58**, 375 (1951).

8. N. E. Miller, *Ann. N.Y. Acad. Sci.* **92**, 830 (1961); ———, in *Nebraska Symposium on Motivation,* M. R. Jones, Ed. Lincoln: Univ. of Nebraska Press, 1963; ———, in *Proc. 3rd World Congr. Psychiat., Montreal, 1961,* 1963, **3**, p. 213.

9. ———, in "Proceedings, 18th International Congress of Psychology, Moscow, 1966," in press.

10. ——— and A. Carmona, *J. Comp. Physiol. Psychol.,* 1967, **63**, 1.

11. J. A. Trowill, *ibid.,* p. 7.

12. N. E. Miller and L. V. DiCara, *ibid.,* p. 12.

13. L. V. DiCara and N. E. Miller, *Commun. Behav. Biol.,* 1968, **2**, 19.

14. ———, *J. Comp. Physiol. Psychol.,* 1968, **65**, 8.

15. ———, *ibid.,* in press.

16. D. J. Ehrlich and R. B. Malmo, *Neuropsychologia,* 1967, **5**, 219.

17. N. E. Miller and A. Banuazizi, *J. Comp. Physiol. Psychol.,* 1968, **65**, 1.

18. A. Banuazizi, thesis, Yale University (1968).

19. N. E. Miller and L. V. DiCara, *Amer. J. Physiol.,* 1968, **215**, 677.

20. A. Carmona, N. E. Miller, T. Demierre, in preparation.

21. A. Carmona, in preparation.

22. L. V. DiCara and N. E. Miller, *Commun. Behav. Biol.,* 1968, **1**, 209.

23. ———, *Science,* 1968, **159**, 1485.

24. ———, *Psychosom. Med.,* 1968, **30**, 489.

25. L. V. DiCara and J. M. Weiss, *J. Comp. Physiol. Psychol.,* in press.

26. L. V. DiCara and N. E. Miller, *Physiol. Behav.,* in press.

27. N. E. Miller, *Science,* 1966, **152**, 676.

28. A. Carmona, thesis, Yale University (1967).

29. For somewhat similar work on the single-cell level, see J. Olds and M. E. Olds, in *Brain Mechanisms and Learning,* J. Delafresnaye, A. Fessard, J. Konorski, Eds. London: Blackwell, 1961.

30. E. S. Katkin and N. E. Murray, *Psychol.*

Bull., 1968, **70**, 52; for a reply to their criticisms, see A. Crider, G. Schwartz, S. Shnidman, *ibid.*, in press.

31. N. E. Miller, L. V. DiCara, G. Wolf, *Amer. J. Physiol.*, 1968, **215**, 684.

32. N. E. Miller, in *Personality Change*, D. Byrne and P. Worchel, Eds. New York: Wiley, 1964, p. 149.

33. J. I. Lacey and B. C. Lacey, *Amer. J. Psychol.*, 1958, **71**, 50; *Ann. N.Y. Acad. Sci.*, 1962, **98**, 1257.

34. H. Barry III, personal communication.

35. N. E. Miller, *Proc. N.Y. Acad. Sci.*, in press.

36. B. T. Engel and K. T. Melmon, personal communication.

SECTION 4

NEUROPHYSIOLOGY AND THE SENSES

The author of the first paper in this section, Walter R. Hess, is emeritus professor of physiology, University of Zurich, Switzerland. Hess's work helps to bridge the gap between neurophysiology and psychology and is concerned with the physiological processes involved in consciousness.

D. E. Broadbent, the author of the second paper, is the director of the Applied Psychology Unit of the Medical Research Council in Cambridge, England. Like Hess, Broadbent takes an interdisciplinary view of the nervous system. He attacks the outmoded idea that the nervous system functions like an old-fashioned telephone exchange. Instead, it operates in a far more complex way, selecting from among the many messages it receives, processing information in ways that are affected by the prevailing motivational state of the organism. He notes that there is a great deal of uncertainty and unreliability about the way in which the nervous systems of individuals process and respond to messages, a problem that calls for sophisticated research on the part of physiologists and psychologists.

The third paper describes some research dealing with the functioning of brain tissue, specifically, the connection between the two halves of the cerebrum. The author of the paper, R. W. Sperry of the California Institute of Technology in Pasadena, cites data to show that the two hemispheres perform somewhat different specialized functions. When tissue connecting the hemispheres has been severed, individuals can still perform highly complex operations, but are unable to match verbal instructions with appropriate actions in certain instances. Sperry's paper is included here as an example of the kind of research being conducted today by interdisciplinary teams of physiologists, neurologists, and psychologists.

4.1 Causality, Consciousness, and Cerebral Organization

WALTER R. HESS

Psychology has been largely, if not exclusively, regarded as being in the domain of philosophy, and, until recently, reference to the brain as the substrate of psychological function was infrequent. It should be admitted that regional differences of approach exist; for example, in the United States psychological concepts are influenced more by the natural sciences than they are in tradition-bound Europe. The works of Herrick (1), Lashley (2), and Hebb (3), the publications of the experimentally oriented Canadian neurosurgeon Wilder Penfield (4), and more recent noteworthy works of Klüver (5), Ploog (6), Delgado (7), MacLean (8), and others are significant in this connection. On the other hand, it is surprising that the physiologists show some reluctance to teach psychological concepts. More than a minimum knowledge of the relationship between brain and psychological function is essential for students in biology and medicine, both because this function plays a role in the biology of men and the other higher mammals and because such knowledge is necessary for an understanding of mental illness. For all these reasons, an effort to survey psychological problems in biological perspective seems justified.

If a series of events relating to our past experience comes to our attention, we feel compelled to look for a causal link. In other words, it seems that an innate tendency to integrate simultaneous and successively induced perceptions leads us to an awareness of a causal relationship. The achievement of insight into cause and effect brings a feeling of satisfaction and relieves psychic tension. A simple example may illustrate this psychophysiological assertion. From my

Reprinted from *Science,* 1967, **158,** 1279–1283, with permission of the author and *Science.* Copyright 1967 by the American Association for the Advancement of Science.

desk I see on the horizon a dark bank of clouds coming nearer and nearer. Suddenly lightning from the cloud strikes the earth. A little later I hear the thunder. Momentarily ignoring earlier experiences of this nature, I am confronted with a visual, followed by an auditory, experience. The two phenomena manifest themselves independently of one another. Continuing to watch, out of curiosity, I see after some time another flash of lightning and hear again, later, a clap of thunder. Repetitions of these essentially identical sensory experiences lead inescapably to the interpretation that the optical and the subsequent acoustical phenomena are somehow related.

With increasing frequency of repetition analogous successions are established as associative links, so that the conjecture of a causal relationship ultimately assumes the character of a certainty. Strictly speaking, no certainty exists but, at best, a high degree of probability. In everyday life one is, to be sure, surprisingly ready to assume a causal relationship. Obviously such a "short circuit" ordinarily suffices as a basis for adaptive behavior. In the case of a scientific investigation, one requires a higher number of identical successions before being ready to accept the intuitively conceived causal relationship as an established reality. Even then, in the area of biology at least, the causal relationship remains basically conjectural as long as the number of repetitions is not infinite. Nevertheless, we have to admit that, even in the pursuit of scientific interest, the number of repetitions required before the impression of pure coincidence is eliminated is relatively soon reached.

After all, the willingness to think *post hoc, propter hoc* depends to a considerable degree on the personality of the observer. Irrespective of the number of repetitions, the persuasive power of the repetitions, depends on conditional factors. There are men, for example, with a strong inclination to associate a comparatively short series of successive similar data with one another in the sense of a causal relationship. On the other hand, one knows laymen and researchers of outspoken skepticism who will not integrate successive similar data into an inferred causal chain even when the probability of an accidental succession is low. In the tendency to integrate or not to integrate, the individual's temperament, his previous experiences, his physical health, and his biological constitution play a not unimportant role. When the probable causal relationship offers a reward, he may be more likely to accept it. Further, mental age is a factor—as is seen, for example, when the child experiences a fairy tale as reality. The young, still inexperienced observer instinctively attempts to find a causal relationship, while the mature person is critical and does not exclude accidental succession so quickly. In the end, none of these arguments alters the fact that reality provides no objective criteria for arriving at a construct of causal relationships.

THE PHYSIOLOGICAL BASIS OF CONSCIOUSNESS

The waking human being or higher animal has a large number of sense organs for making contact with the internal and external environment. The sensory cells function as receptors of organ-specific stimuli. Light flashes, for example, stimulate the rods and cones of the retina of the eye. Thereby the order of optic phenomena generated by the visual system is transformed into patterns of excitation of the visual pathways whose morphological organization is relatively well known (9)—for example, the projection of circumscribed retinal areas to corresponding elements of the visual areas in the occipital lobes of the brain. Far less advanced is exploration of the functional laws of the living brain. Actually, research in this sector of physiology is only now in process of development. The school of Jung (10) and the team of Hubel and Wiesel (11) have made significant contributions, particularly with respect to visual perception. Basic information is derived from observations concerning electrical stimulation of the visual cortex in man (4). Patients subjected to such stimulation in an effort to localize pathological foci in that area reported visual phenomena arising with the onset of stimulation. The sense of hearing was similarly involved when the stimulating electrode was applied to a certain region of the temporal lobe. Further, it has been experimentally established that the visual and auditory sensations experienced are associated with one another in the sense of a "causal" connection on the basis of temporal coincidence or spatial contiguity. In such cases consistent relationships between brain stimulation and subjective sensations (4) are as evident as those existing between natural stimuli and a determined flow of consciousness.

Findings such as the foregoing raise the question, How may the "causal" relationship between excitatory patterns of the nervous system and the development of conscious perceptions come about? Before we pose this problem, we must acknowledge that it is not now possible, and may not be possible in the future, to obtain such information. The subjective experience may be a direct expression of the condition of excitation of those centers which receive and integrate the sensory signals. In this case it would be only another aspect of the same process which one can objectify in the form of evoked potentials. An alternative explanation would be that of transmission of the integrated excitation pattern to a *specific system* whose principal activity is one of implementing release of the contents of consciousness. However, no criteria which would allow us to define such a process of transmission are, as yet, known. For the entire process which leads from the sensory stimulation pattern to the content of consciousness results exclusively in the mediating of relevant information. The process of transmission itself lies in an area into which we have no insight. Obviously reference to a reflex mechanism leads no further, so that physiology must give up the attempt to submit a comprehensive explanation. This is not to deny that there is a correlation between patterns of neural excitation and the release of corresponding contents of consciousness.

This situation is not unlike that existing with respect to verbal communication. The listener is unaware of the pressure changes acting upon his eardrum, and he does not perceive their transmission upon the sensory surface within the organ of Corti. Nor is he aware of the nervous impulses which are sent from the organ of Corti to the auditory centers of the brain. Yet he can understand the meaning of a spoken message. This achievement is based upon associations which were developed between sensory stimulation and central patterns of nerve excitation at an early stage in the learning process. Whenever similar patterns of verbal stimuli are presented, the old memories and the corresponding contents of consciousness become reactivated and comprehended. Thus, there is no trace of a causal evolution of understanding of verbal stimuli by way of an uninterrupted chain of conscious correlates of the sensory mechanisms. Instead, central patterns of excitation are elicited as though by resonance when specific sensory messages arrive. However logical this may sound it does not explain the process of transformation itself, which seems to be a separate biological faculty. No road to its understanding seems open at present.

SUBJECTIVE EXPERIENCE AND NEURAL EVENTS

It has been known for a long time that light surface elements in the neighborhood of a dark field appear lighter than elements that lie away from the light-dark border. This difference in brightness is felt explicitly although objective checking shows that all the light fields are identical in tone. Therefore, until a short while ago the so-called simultaneous contrast had been interpreted as a subjective phenomenon. Recently this contrast effect was shown to be already manifest in the neural plane of the visual system (12). This was something of a surprise. The evidence discloses that contrast phenomena are basically produced by collateral inhibition involving neighboring elements at retinal as well as central levels. The physiological effect of this mechanism is the sharpening of the border between light and dark areas in the visual field. Thus the correspondence between subjective impressions and patterns of neural activity in the visual system is documented.

A second example of the close inter-relationship between function of brain systems and mental processes is the well-known fact that consciousness is lost when critical areas of the brainstem are damaged (13). In contrast, consciousness remains unaffected when only parts of the cerebral cortex are damaged. At most, a limited defect may result, such as a scotoma of perceptive integration. In spite of this defect, the patient remains conscious of the situation and is capable of answering questions intelligently. His self-awareness and his orientation in space and time are undisturbed. With this, proof exists that specific psychic functions are bound to specific nervous structures. Still, the intervening process between stimulation of nervous elements and the formation of a conscious perception remains beyond our grasp.

A third example concerns the release of definite sensations through artificially induced stimulation of the brain. One recalls the activation of a characteristic behavior pattern in experimental animals (goats) after intradiencephalic injection of hypertonic saline. Their response was a massive intake of water (14). This behavioral reaction is identical with that induced by long-term deprivation of water. The electrolyte concentration in the tissue is increased, and the thirsty animal is impelled, as the human is under similar conditions, to quench its thirst by drinking. The observation implies that the stimulated area of the brain contains receptors which control osmotic pressure by regulating the water balance. The immediate impulse is normally given by the specific sensation of thirst in association with the positively conditioned satisfaction of removing the thirst sensation.

Another example of drive behavior elicited by stimulation of the diencephalon concerns food intake (15). Here, extreme voracity may develop under the influence of central excitation, resembling that seen after prolonged fasting or as a consequence of insulin-induced fall of the blood sugar level. Such increased intake of food (bulimia) is also seen in some psychically disturbed human subjects. Thus, physiological hunger, experimentally induced hyperphagia, and pathological bulimia appear interrelated inasmuch as they may be subserved by identical cerebral systems.

Another set of observations refers to manifestation of rage and fear elicited by stimulation of the hypothalamus in cats (15). With the onset of artificial stimulation the cat begins to snarl, hiss, and spit. It arches its back or crouches, it bristles, and it lashes its tail. Thus, the typical defense reaction develops, as in an animal threatened by an enemy—for example, a cat threatened by an attacking dog. The question is raised. Are these effects due to the direct stimulation of efferent pathways? This is obviously not the explanation. For, if the experimenter reaches toward the cat at the climax of excitement, it strikes at him angrily in a well-directed attack. At the onset of stimulation the animal may inspect the environment and, in its search for a refuge, may suddenly jump off the laboratory table and flee to a hiding place. These observations indicate strongly that the stimulation, induced attack, and flight reactions are not purely motor effects; rather, they represent interactions between highly integrated central patterns of motivational behavior and conscious visual perceptions of the environment.

The experiment with goats mentioned above is even more convincing (16). In the standard experimental procedure the animals are first acquainted with a well-defined source of water. After being deprived of water for a period they begin to seek water at this source. To reach it, they must surmount an obstruction and climb a ladder. After many trials the second part of the experiment begins—namely, electrical stimulation of specific structures of the diencephalon when the animal is hydrated. The trained animal uses the ladder promptly, goes directly to the familiar water vessel, and drains it. The short time between the beginning of stimulation and the action described leads to one conclusion: the effect of electrical stimulation of specific diencephalic structures manifests itself in the subjective sphere as a drive, thirst. This drive gives inducement and direction to the behavior, through which the tension of drive is relieved. Thus, it seems appropriate to conclude that, under the influence of brain stimulation, experiences stored in the memory are actively integrated with instant perceptions and released as behavioral responses.

EFFECTS OF PSYCHOTROPIC DRUGS

Electrical brain stimulation is not the only means whereby subjective experiences may be elicited or modified; they may be influenced considerably by the action of chemical agents. One of the best-known examples is the effect of ethyl alcohol. With moderate doses, the individual's mood is usually improved; he experiences an increased desire for adventure, including an urge for verbal communication. His euphoria is accompanied by a suppression of inhibition. For this reason the ventures of the inebriate lead all too often to catastrophe. Another group of substances, the amphetamine compounds, also increase initiative and give the individual the courage for risky undertakings. Certain drugs which influence mental disturbances are particularly interesting from the medical point of view. The effect of stronger doses of ethyl alcohol is revealing; such doses lead to a dimming of consciousness, even to total loss of consciousness. This observation indicates an important sensitivity of consciousness to chemical influences (17), which is further revealed in the action of anesthetics upon basic properties of cerebral elements. Such modifications show that chemically defined receptors, as constituents of nerve cells, are in play at the molecular level. Little is known about this field today; however, the means for further investigation are at hand—for example, through study of the effect of drugs on explants of clinical biopsy material.

In addition to drugs which suppress consciousness there are drugs whose action manifests itself in the psychic sphere in other ways. One of these, lysergic acid diethylamide (LSD), is an appropriate "research instrument." Even minimum doses produce very striking psychic effects—for example, primitive visual perceptions such as colored clouds and changes in brightness of visual patterns, like scintillations or flickerings. One psychiatrist (18) has described more complex visual impressions, such as spirals, ornaments, fern branchings, and wood carvings, which he experienced in a self-trial. Such imagery arises from latent memory traces. Even more impressive is the case where fragments of acquired knowledge appear in the visual field—for instance, images of benzene rings or chromosomes. Experiences of this nature are noteworthy because similar visual phenomena, such as stars, wheels, colored balls, and disks, are reported by the patient when the brain surgeon applies electrical current to the occipital cortex for purposes of diagnosis (4). Artificially elicited perception of the contents of consciousness, on the one hand through electrical stimulation and on the other hand through the administration of a chemically defined substance, is all the more arresting because this activity is based on excitation of elements that lie in the visual-projection areas of the brain. Thus the actions of LSD may be considered a modification of discharge of nervous elements of the visual system. As mentioned above, fragments of stored experience are often part of the activated pattern of excitation. An example is one subject's identification of a wall with a railway embankment. A hallucination was joined to this illusion; the subject believed that he saw an overhead electric line, which in reality was not there but which belonged to the full picture of the electrified Swiss train system. From this, it appears that the mechanism of hallucination may eventually become understood through a biologically oriented approach.

CAUSALITY AND MOTIVATION OF BEHAVIOR

The behavior of a cat in an open field on the lookout for an enemy seems to be motivated by the imminent threat. The cat's watchfulness and active search for a refuge confirm this interpretation. While emotions may be the impelling force, the *waking consciousness* determines the organization of a flight reaction. For successful avoidance, coordinated muscular action is called upon. Such action occurs through excitation of precisely defined central mechanisms. To me it is clear that such an explanation can be deduced only from one's own experience. From the objective point of view one might take exception to this interpretation. On the other hand, scientific observers can be expected to be guided in their view by their specialized knowledge concerning the organization of brain and behavior—knowledge which has led to the recognition of principles applicable in both man and other higher animals. Such is the problem of motive and execution of acts controlled by the conscious will. Therefore, the question is, Where do the activating impulses originate?

One may say that this category of phenomena cannot be compared with the category discussed above. On the other hand, no one can deny that the display of behavior presupposes the action of forces, for, without them, nothing would be set in motion and there would be no resistance to be overcome. Voluntary acts are no exception. What is difficult is to determine the type of activating force. As the matter stands, one can only argue by exclusion. Certainly, conditions required for the release of nuclear forces are not present; gravitational forces also are excluded, for today it has been shown that psychic processes take place normally under conditions of weightlessness. The activating forces could be molecular or electromagnetic. Possibly, as yet undiscovered forces may be active which belong to none of the known categories, forces inherent in the living neuronal system of man and other higher animals. Such a concept may mean, to be sure, a revival of the long-departed vitalistic theory. This suggestion is not so absurd, since the experiments which seem to have ruled out vitalistic processes have concerned only somatic or organic functions. However, psychic functions are a reality for the living individual even though they cannot be objectified by outsiders.

CAUSALITY AND COMMUNICATION

The substitution of verbal symbols for perceptions of reality plays an important role in causal thinking. An example of such substitution is the reporting of a conference, with mention of the names of the participants. To this conference report only a few details need be added to convey meaningful information concerning the course of the transactions and the conclusions reached.

Acoustical and optical symbols are also used, moreover, and not only for communication between man and man. A dog reacts to the call of its name as a consequence of its education. It looks about, comes to its master, and responds when asked, through word and sign, to perform tricks it has learned.

In the human, basically complex information can be reduced to symbols of fixed, brief design which denote, nevertheless, wide-reaching conclusions. The highest development is found in the symbols of mathematics. Here, data can be expressed through ciphers and other signs which denote qualitative as well as quantitative aspects, and new insights can be developed.

Sense stimulations which are integrated into a pattern of neural excitation are transferred automatically to the environment by the receiving and perceiving subject. This transfer corresponds to the long-known rule of excentric projection. The consequence of this is that no clue concerning localization and organization of the nervous system comes to us from the cerebral process, which is induced through sense organs. On the other hand we receive through the resolving power of receptive systems information about the environmental source of stimulation. In visual perceptions derived from both eyes, for example, paralactic shift is utilized in composing an integrated stereo image. The impression that the sensory stimulation originates in the environment is confirmed through the directed motor reaction—for example, through the grasping of a visually localized object. The successful attempt to grasp the object confirms the correlation between perception and reality. Involved are consistent temporal and spatial relationships which produce the impression of causality (*19*).

Simple mechanisms for the preservation of life are genetically controlled and subject to phylogenetic selection. Important individual behavioral patterns are determined prenatally. Complex reactions, on the other hand, are learned postnatally, and their release is under the control of conscious will. Through frequent repetition, psychic functions become partially or totally automated. As a result, the desired success is achieved with more speed and more precision, and mechanisms of great complexity are mastered.

SUMMARY

This article is based upon data which are suitable for the correlation of behavioral research and experimental neurophysiology. Causal thinking manifests a sort of integrative activity which brings simultaneous and successive patterns of nervous excitation into a subjectively meaningful frame of reference. While neuronal patterns determine the content of consciousness, they fail to provide clues concerning the transformation of such patterns into subjective experience.

REFERENCES

1. C. J. Herrick, *The Evolution of Human Nature*. Austin: Univ. of Texas Press, 1956.

2. *The Neuropsychology of Lashley* (selected papers of K. S. Lashley), F. A. Beach, D. O. Hebb, C. T. Morgan, H. W. Nissen, Eds. New York: McGraw-Hill, 1960.

3. D. O. Hebb, *The Organization of Behavior*. New York: Wiley, 1949.

4. W. Penfield and T. Rasmussen, *The Cer-*

ebral Cortex of Man. New York: Macmillan, 1950.

5. H. Klüver, *J. Lancet,* 1952, **72**, 567; ————, in *Ciba Foundation Symposium on the Neurological Basis of Behavior,* G. E. W. Wolstenholme and C. M. O'Connor, Eds. Boston: Little, Brown, 1958, p. 175.

6. D. W. Ploog, *Jahrb, Max-Planck-Ges.,* 1963, p. 130; P. D. MacLean, *Animal Behavior,* 1963, 11, 32.

7. J. M. R. Delgado, *Intern. Rev. Neurobiol.,* 1964, **6**, 349.

8. P. D. MacLean, *Psychosomat. Med.,* 1949, **11**, 338; *A.M.A. Arch. Neurol. Psychiat.,* 1957, **78**, 113.

9. S. L. Polyak, *The Vertebrate Visual System.* Chicago: Univ. of Chicago Press, 1957.

10. R. Jung, in *The Visual System,* R. Jung and H. Kornhuber, Eds. Berlin: Springer, 1961, p. 410.

11. D. H. Hubel and T. N. Wiesel, *J. Neurophysiol.,* 1965, **28**, 229.

12. G. Baumgartner, in *The Visual System,* R. Jung and H. Kornhuber, Eds. Berlin: Springer, 1961, p. 296.

13. B. J. Alpers, *Res. Pub. Ass. Nervous Mental Diseases,* 1940, **20**, 725.

14. B. Andersson, *Acta Physiol. Scand.,* 1953, **28**, 188; ————, P. A. Jewell, S. Larsson, *Ciba Foundation Symposium on the Neurological Basis of Behavior.* Boston: Little, Brown, 1958, p. 76; B. K. Anand and J. R. Brobeck, *Yale J. Biol.,* 1951, **24**, 123.

15. W. R. Hess, *Diencephalon, Autonomic and Extrapyramidal Functions,* O. Krayer, Trans. New York: Grune & Stratton, *Helv. Physiol. Pharmacol. Acta,* 1943, **1**, 33; R. W. Hunsperger, *ibid.,* 1956, **14**, 70.

16. B. Andersson and W. Wyrwicka, *Acta Physiol. Scand.,* 1957, **41**, 194.

17. W. R. Hess, *The Biology of Mind.* Chicago: Univ. of Chicago Press, 1964.

18. W. A. Stoll, *Schweiz. Arch. Neurol. Neurochir. Psychiat.,* 1947, **60**, 1.

19. W. R. Hess, *Psychologie in Biologischer Sicht.* Stuttgart: Thieme, ed. 2, 1967.

4.2 Information Processing in the Nervous System

D. E. BROADBENT

The study of the nervous system can be carried out in at least three major ways. First, one may examine the *physiological* mechanisms by detecting the electrical and chemical events that go on in the system while it is operating. Second, one may examine the *behavior* of a man or animal from outside, either by observing what occurs spontaneously or by devising experimental situations which will throw certain functions into relief. Third, one can devise mechanical or mathematical analogies and *models* for processes similar to those performed by nervous systems; this type of study can be carried out as an end in itself, in order to produce effective machines, or it may be deliberately pursued as shedding light on the processes in nervous systems which are found in nature. All these three approaches are of value, and no one of them should be neglected.

Although such statements may seem trite, there is undoubedly a tendency for specialists in any one field to undervalue the other two. This tendency should always be resisted: it is idle to devise theoretical mechanisms to explain the brain without considering the actual functions which real nervous systems perform and the mechanisms that they have available to do so. It is equally useless to consider behavior alone without reference to mechanisms which are known to exist from physiology, or to those which can be logically devised to perform a certain function. Finally, it is unprofitable simply to consider the physiology of the nervous system and the various things which such components might conceivably do without examining the behavior of animals or men to see what they really can do. It should therefore be borne in mind that the following

Reprinted from *Science*, 1965, **150**, 457–461, with permission of the author and *Science*. Copyright 1965 by the American Association for the Advancement of Science.

remarks are written from the point of view of a student of behavior and that the physiologist or automaton theorist could add a great deal to each of the topics mentioned.

It now goes almost without saying that these three approaches find a common language for discussing the nervous system by using the language of information processing. If we discuss only the electrical and chemical changes in nerves produced by certain disturbances at the sense organs, there may seem little in common with any statement in the language of traditional psychology. There may seem no point of contact between, on the one hand, the occurrence of light of a certain wavelength followed by a particular distribution of nervous impulses and, on the other hand, the experience of seeing red. In informational language, however, we can take a unified view of the nervous system.

We think, then, of a set of different possible environments, one of which is actually confronting a particular nervous system at a particular time; and there is a set of possible outputs which the system might make, one of which it actually does make on a particular occasion. If there is a perfect correspondence between the set of outputs and the set of possible input situations, so that the animal or man always produces a response which is unique to the situation in which he finds himself, then a similar correspondence must equally apply at every stage within the nervous system. It will of course be more usual for events within the nervous system to correspond to the particular input only up to a certain point, and for rather complex changes

and transformations to take place before the output occurs, just as the output of a computer will be the result of a series of complicated operations performed upon the input that is delivered to it. However, by considering sets of alternatives at each point of the system and the way in which one element out of the set is selected when a particular element occurs at a previous stage, we can pass easily from physiological to psychological problems, and to mechanical analogies.

LIMITS OF CAPACITY

Such a description of the functioning of nervous systems immediately raises the point that there is a very large variety of different possible situations in which an animal or man may be placed. Since most nervous systems are reasonably small, there is almost bound to be a problem of providing a set of different possible states of the brain which will correspond to a sufficiently large number of different possible states of the environment. It is not sufficient, say, simply to take each sensory cell in the retina of the eye and to make some further cell in the brain active or inactive depending upon the state of the retinal cell. As has been a problem for many previous approaches, patterns of stimulation can be consistently recognized, so that an environment containing a triangle can consistently produce a different reaction from an environment containing a square, even though the shape falls on a quite different part of the eye on each occasion it is seen. It is possible to devise mechanical systems which would perform such a discrimination, and even to produce hypothetical systems which might in principle learn to make the discrimination from an original randomly connected state. Such, for example, is the perceptron, in which each of a set of sensory elements is connected randomly with several association elements later in the system (1). Some of these association elements will receive information from combinations of sensory elements, so that there might well be some association element which would become active whenever a triangle was presented in one location, another when a rather different location was used, and so on. With some suitable modification of the interconnections, following "right" and "wrong" outputs, such a system might well discriminate triangles and squares anywhere on the sensory surface; but it would need a very large number of association elements to do so.

The problem of *capacity*, the size of the set of available states within the nervous system, thus becomes very serious, and this is true of most systems of pattern recognition that have been suggested. Indeed, I have minimized the problem by supposing simply that the retina receives a square or triangular set of stimuli; whereas in fact the sides of a square or triangular pattern will probably be distorted more or less severely before they reach the sense organs on the retina. This will happen because the eye will probably not view the pattern directly at right angles, and even in the exceptional cases when it is seen straight on, the optical characteristics of the eye will introduce some distortion of their own. A complete set of mechanisms for

calculating back from the pattern of stimulation on the retina, to the original pattern of events in the outside world which must have produced this distorted pattern on the retina, must therefore be supposed.

Although visual examples have been taken because of their familiarity, similar difficulties arise in other senses as well. Thus in the perception of speech, the identification of different vowel sounds depends upon the detection of the relative position of resonant frequencies in different parts of the spectrum, so that the problem is very similar to that of discriminating squares from triangles; and, furthermore, there are compensatory mechanisms which take account of the fact that one may be listening to a person with a large or small head, so that the sounds which one speaker produces may be shifted up or down the range of audible frequencies, as compared with those which another speaker produces. The machinery necessary to recognize patterns must therefore be multiplied even further so as to cope with all the senses; and indeed some experiments have shown that the understanding of speech is less efficient if the listener cannot see the lips of the talker, even for ordinary listeners who do not realize that they are lip reading. Thus the mechanisms of analysis must be capable of dealing with combinations of stimulation by different senses, in addition to patterns of stimulation, within a sense. On general principles, therefore, it seems that a major feature of information processing in the nervous system should be procedures for economizing in mechanism.

INPUT SELECTION AND INTERFERENCE

Purely a priori arguments such as those I have been advancing are by themselves rather unconvincing. Fortunately, however, there are certain areas of behavior in which one can show experimentally phenomena which seem reasonable if limits of capacity are a problem for the nervous system. One device which might be expected, for example, is the use of the same components to serve different functions at different times. This would mean that the system would be capable of carrying a variety of tasks, but not of doing them simultaneously. Although there are indeed some cases in which information is processed in parallel and simultaneously, there are a number of experiments in which one can show that two tasks performed at the same time create difficulty for one another. To take an initial example from outside the laboratory, it has been shown that the ability of a pilot to fly a prescribed maneuver on instruments is better when the radio communication system to which he also has to listen is arranged so as to be more easily intelligible (2). Listening to speech sounds interferes in some way with viewing instruments and making control movements. This kind of effect is sufficiently widespread for applied psychologists to have made considerable use of it in recent years as a method of measuring the difficulty of tasks (3). While the man is doing some job, such as driving an automobile in particular traffic conditions, he is also asked to carry out some other task which does not use the same senses or limbs, and the efficiency with which he does the second task is taken as a measure of the difficulty of the first one.

An overall score of the efficiency of instrument flying, or of the number of questions answered while simultaneously driving a car, does not give us a really detailed picture of what is going on in the nervous system. Laboratory tasks can be made more analytic: as a step in the direction of abstraction, consider somebody who is asked to call out letters of the alphabet in random order while simultaneously sorting a deck of playing cards into separate red and black piles (4). He will not, of course, be successful in calling out the letters quite randomly, but rather will show a disproportionate tendency to produce such habitual responses as following one letter by the letter immediately preceding it in the alphabet. We can measure the percentage of such stereotyped responses, or indeed calculate the information transmitted overall by his calling of letters, and if we do so we find that the departure from randomness depends upon the nature of the other simultaneous task. If the deck of cards has to be sorted into the four suits rather than into two colors, then the man is less able to call out letters at random: while if the deck had to be sorted into eight categories, the calling of letters would be still more stereotyped. Thus the extent to which task A interferes with task B depends upon the number of different alternative states of the environment that may be involved in task A, the number of such states in turn presumably affecting the number of different possible states of the nervous system that have to be reserved for that task in order to allow efficient performance.

Therefore when some task involving a good deal of information has to be performed, such as listening to a rather unpredictable speech, or indeed reading a paper such as the present one, successful performance requires the elimination of other activities. One technique to achieve this end is of course adjustment of the sense organs, such as wearing ear plugs when one is reading or closing the eyes when listening. It is not therefore too surprising to find experimentally that performance of a complex task is easier when all the relevant information arrives by some particular channel, while other irrelevant information does not arrive by the same channel. For example, if one has to answer a series of questions which are accompanied by other quite irrelevant speech, it is easier to do so when the questions are delivered to one ear and the irrelevant speech to the other ear than when both are mixed into the same ear (2, pp. 11–35).

There has been much interest on the part of physiologists in the past decade in the possibility that the sensitivity of sense organs may be controlled directly by outgoing messages proceeding from the brain to the sense organ, in the opposite direction to the more familiar messages traveling from the sense organs into the brain. It is somewhat difficult to distinguish direct effects on the senses produced in this way from indirect effects such as change in the size of the pupil of the eye and in the tension of the muscles which adjust the eardrum. However, in the case of the ear there does seem satisfactory evidence that the sensitivity of the sense organ itself can be changed

(5). Thus it is conceivable that the nervous system actually switches off one ear in order to listen to the other and thus preserves the central mechanisms of limited capacity from the interference which would otherwise arise. Such change in sensitivity of the sense organs themselves is undoubtedly not the whole story, since, for example, a man will find it easier to listen to one message and ignore another if the two messages are made to appear to come from different directions by altering the time relations between stimulation of the two ears (6). In this case, each ear is in fact receiving both messages, and turning off one ear would not help. The signals reaching the two ears must be admitted to the nervous system, combined in such a way as to detect the two apparently separated sources of sound, and only then is the information from one voice passed on for further processing while that from the other voice is not. As yet the physiological basis of this more central filtering process is not understood.

There seems evidence in behavior, therefore, that indeed the nervous system admits only part of the information reaching the sensory organs, and much of the remainder is lost. A most important part of the learning which goes on during life is the selection of the particular information which is going to be of the greatest use at any particular time, and it is at least logically possible that the principles governing such learning will be rather different from those which govern the learning of one action rather than another. Sutherland and Mackintosh have recently conducted a major series of experiments on animal learning, which do indeed suggest that this is so

(7). One kind of experiment which has long aroused interest, for example, is to train an animal until it is performing perfectly to go through a black rather than a white door when given a choice, and then to teach it the exactly opposite action, to go to white and avoid black. Additional training on the original discrimination, after performance is perfect, may increase the speed with which the opposite learning takes place. This only happens, however, if the two doors differ in a large number of other ways, such as being of different shapes, although these other qualities tell the animal nothing about whether the particular door is the correct one or not. Thus the extra training seems to be affecting the ability to select the right information, to notice the color of the door rather than its shape, and it seems to be having a much larger effect upon the selection than it is upon the actual response of approach or avoidance which is made to a particular color.

I have somewhat oversimplified the situation by talking as if the nervous system shut off information coming from certain sources and let through only that from other sources: because there is a rather different selective process, which also has the effect of economizing in the capacity necessary, and this reveals itself in the fact that a listener will hear his own name even when the name occurs in speech which he is ignoring in order to concentrate on some other message (8). Thus a nervous system which is admitting information from one source is not completely indifferent to what is going on elsewhere in its surroundings, but seems able to make some responses even to information from other sources.

These responses can be regarded as those towards which the system is for one reason or another biased, and this can perhaps be best understood in the light of certain other features of information processing which should now be considered.

COMBATING RANDOM DISTURBANCE

An actual nervous system differs from many machines in the degree of reliability of its components. The parts of which it is made are not turned out to a standardized pattern, like pieces of an automobile, but rather may show a range of variability like the range of different bodily sizes which we are accustomed to encountering in our everyday dealings with people. Biological components may also change in state from time to time, depending upon the general chemical condition of the body, and also on momentary factors. Thus for example a nerve fiber has to recover after the passage of each impulse, and on a larger time scale a number of cells in our brain die each day as we get older. One cannot therefore rely on any particular component's performing as it should on any particular occasion, and processing must take a form which is resistant to this kind of random interference. A technique which machines may use for this purpose is to send any message through a system several times by different routes, so that there are several different components involved and the failure of any one of them will not ruin the whole operation. This principle is of course employed in important man-made devices, such as automatic blind-landing systems for aircraft, but it does involve a large increase in the number of components necessary to carry out any particular operation. Theoretical analysis of the most economical way of combating unreliability of components has shown that it can be done most efficiently by making the activity of any component at one stage in the process depend upon the activity of several different components at an earlier stage, rather than by making each component at one stage depend upon one component at an earlier stage (9). This means that, if we have an array of sensory cells as in the retina of the eye, we ought to expect that stimulation of any one point would not merely produce activity in a single fiber leading into the brain from that point, but also should produce modifications in other adjacent fibers, which are also affected by other points on the retina. Such lateral interconnection has of course long been evident both anatomically and from physiological observation, and it represents an economical method of combating random disturbances in transmission.

Even with such devices in play, however, the message reaching some point deep in the nervous system may not be a completely reliable indicator of the presence or absence of some particular event at the senses. This has long been recognized, since a man will not always hear a sound that is presented in the region of the faintest sounds he can hear, although he will sometimes do so. Until recently it has usually been supposed in such cases that the event inside the nervous system corresponding to "hearing the sound" only occurred when the sound was really there, although sometimes it might not occur even then. Ad-

mittedly, people who are asked to listen for faint sounds do sometimes report hearing something even when nothing is presented, but this has usually been regarded as a reprehensible tendency to guess and has been discouraged in careful experiments on the limits of the senses. This interpretation might be regarded as supported by the fact that such "false positives" become more frequent if the man has reason to believe that a sound is probable, or if he is given a financial reward for hearing sounds and only fined some smaller amount for reporting something which is not there. However, if this interpretation were correct, then if we change the amount of reward and so change the number of false positives, the corresponding change in the number of correct reports of a sound should be proportional to the change in false positives. It should also be rather less than that change. In a large number of cases, neither of these expectations is fulfilled; the change in the number of correct detections is at first much larger than in that of false positives, and then becomes less when the false-positive rate is high (10).

There are various possible interpretations of this experimental result, but it is clear that the traditional view is completely out of court. The possible explanations which have been put forward usually involve the idea that the report of hearing a sound is based on events inside the nervous system which are inherently rather unreliable indications of what is going on at the senses. This evidence then produces the response "I hear a sound" on principles which minimize the ill effects of the randomness. One particularly widely held view, for example, is that the output occurs whenever the evidence within the nervous system exceeds a critical value C such that the ratio of the probability of C given a signal to the probability of C given no signal is sufficiently high. This critical value is supposed to decrease when signals are more likely and when detecting them secures a larger reward. It would be rational for it to do so, according to statistical decision theory. A critical level moving in this way would secure the greatest possible advantage given the degree of unreliability in the system that is present.

On this view, there are two quite independent ways in which the frequency of detection of signals may be changed. One of them is by changes in the critical value already mentioned, and the other is by changes in the reliability of the evidence delivered by the senses to the central mechanisms. If the changes are due to the first of these causes, an increase in detections will usually be accompanied by an increase in false positives, while if they are due to the second, it may not, and may even be accompanied by a decrease. Experiment shows, as already mentioned, that changes in the probability of a signal or in the payoffs for being right and wrong will produce the first kind of change; while it is also found that changes in the physical strength of a stimulus will produce the second kind of change (11). Even if the mechanism which produces these changes is not analogous to a statistical decision process, it certainly has these two modes of operation.

At this stage, we can return to the selective processes which allow only certain information entering the nervous system to be analyzed. By presenting a rather inconspicuous signal to one ear of the listener, and asking him to report when he hears it, we can measure the correct detections and false positives and so obtain a measure of his performance when he is concentrating upon the signal. We can also deliver speech to his other ear and compare his performance on the one hand when he is told to ignore this speech, and on the other hand when he is told to reproduce the speech as well as to report the presence or absence of tone. In looking at the results, we can then ask whether division of attention has changed the critical level, or the reliability of the evidence, in terms of the statistical theory of perception mentioned a little earlier. In other words, does division of attention produce a change like that produced by a change in the probability of a signal, or like that produced by a change in the strength of the signal? In fact, experiment shows that the latter is the case, and therefore that the paying of attention to one ear apparently has an effect comparable to increasing or decreasing the sensitivity of the sense organ (12).

On the other hand, it has already been pointed out that a man does hear his own name even in a conversation to which he is not listening, or more generally, will hear words which are at that moment very probable, even if his attention is not directed toward the sense organ to which they are delivered (8, 13). It is tempting to suppose that this is because there has been a change in the critical level for some words as opposed to others, which means that they will be perceived even when the evidence in their favor is relatively slight. Indeed, some direct experimental evidence has been produced to support such a view, by an analysis of the proportions of correct perceptions and of different kinds of error when words of different probability are presented through a noise which makes them difficult to hear (14).

In general, therefore, it can be accepted that the unreliability of the nervous system causes a certain number of false perceptions, but that the ill effects of this are minimized by the nature of the mechanism which translates the evidence provided by the senses into a percept.

CHOICE OF APPROPRIATE ACTIONS

If we ask a man not simply to perceive what happens in some situation, but to take an action about it, we can measure how long his decision takes. In simple cases, we may tell him that we are going to light one of a number of lamps and that he is to press one of a number of corresponding buttons. Such a process might seem too simple to deserve the name of decision, since the correct action appears almost unconsciously, and one might almost suppose that the time taken between stimulation and response is taken up in neural transmission processes of no great psychological interest. However, there are some features of choice-reaction time which are related to the problem of limited capacity of the nervous system and to the means of economy which one must therefore expect the system to employ. In a variety of situations, reaction time increases as the number of alternative possible actions increases, but does so as a loga-rithmic function of the number of alternatives. If we want to send one of a fixed set of messages along a telegraph wire, using a small or fixed vocabulary of symbols, the length of the coded message proceeding along the telegraph wire will increase logarithmically with the number of different possible messages from which we chose the one we actually sent. Thus the similar relationship found in choice-reaction time has caused many investigators to regard it as evidence that the nervous system is limited in capacity, just as the fixed set of symbols limits the capacity of the telegraph channel, and that the code is adjusted efficiently to fit the particular situation in which the man is reacting at any given time. There are, however, certain detailed features of the experimental results which are not covered by such a view.

For example, if the man is pressed to react to a series of signals delivered to him at a fixed speed regardless of his own response, he seems to reach maximum efficiency at a response rate of two or three actions per second, even when the number of alternative actions among which he is choosing is varied (15). Perhaps most important, however, are the results of a number of recent experiments which have shown that a highly practiced task gives less increase in reaction time as the number of alternative possible actions is doubled than does an unpracticed task. This applies even if the particular job has never been performed by the man before, but nevertheless seems natural to him because the reaction required bears a relationship to the stimulus that he has often met previously. For example, if we flash a series of numbers on a screen, and the man has a row of keys in front of him, it will be easy and natural for him if the correct response to the number 4 is the fourth key from the left, and so on, rather than having keys numbered randomly. Such "compatible" relationships between stimulus and response show much less effect on reaction time when the number of possible responses is increased (16).

This kind of result has caused some investigators to put forward theories of the choice between different actions which are closely similar mathematically to the theories of detection of signals mentioned in the last section. It is a familiar general principle that, when one is collecting rather unreliable evidence, one can increase its reliability by taking the average of a number of observations over a longer period of time. If we look at two highways in order to see which is carrying the more traffic, one day's observation may conceivably give us the wrong answer; at the opposite extreme, a full year's observation is very likely indeed to give us the correct answer. In such a situation there are in fact statistical techniques which will allow us to go on watching for a number of days until the difference in the average traffic we have observed becomes sufficiently great to exceed a critical level of confidence, so that we may safely conclude that any further observations would not change the conclusion we have reached.

If we now think of a nervous system faced with two possible stimuli and two reaction keys, we may suppose that the application of a stimulus does not produce a completely determinate and reliable chain of events leading automatically to the correct reaction, but rather that there is a certain amount of uncer-

tainty and unreliability about the messages traveling from the senses to the centers controlling action. The less practiced or compatible the situation, the greater this uncertainty might reasonably be supposed to be. If the nervous system delays before action, a higher degree of reliability can be obtained by averaging successive messages in any particular pathway. There are two ways in which this can be done. On the one hand, a fixed time could be set in advance, before any stimulus is received. On the other hand, the mechanism could conceivably work by accumulating evidence until there is sufficient in favor of one alternative rather than the other. The first of these possibilities is mathematically the most tractable, when there are more than two alternatives; and it has been shown that it will predict the general logarithmic relationship between reaction time and the number of alternative reactions (17).

Unfortunately, this is almost certainly not the mechanism which the nervous system actually employs, because we can, in one and the same experiment, use probable and improbable signals, and we then find that the reaction time to the probable signal is considerably faster than that to the improbable one. If the time taken for the decision was laid down in advance of any signal's arriving, this could hardly be the case. The second type of mechanism, unhappily, is much harder to analyze mathematically, for cases in which there are more than two possible signals: but there are certain features which such a mechanism would have and which human performance seems to show. For example, the mistakes made by such a mechanism would usually take the form of making probable responses to improbable stimuli, rather than vice versa, and this is indeed what people usually do (*18*). A good deal of research effort is at present going into finding ways of checking whether this hypothetical mechanism is really the way in which the nervous system operates in performing choice reactions.

CONCLUSIONS

The foregoing discussion has left out of account a large number of features of information processing which are of much current interest. These include, for example, the possible distinction between short-term and long-term memory processes, or the extent and fashion in which changes in general physiological state due to drugs or other stresses may modify the processes. The particular problems discussed have been chosen to emphasize the ways in which the nervous system is forced to economize on mechanism and to compensate for unreliability. Both these principles have modified our attitude toward the brain: for it was once easy and natural to think of the nervous system as resembling an old-fashioned manual telephone exchange, in which each incoming message is connected to an outgoing pathway, completely determinately and by its own private cord, quite independent of any other connections that might exist. Such an analogy has now been out of date for many years, and we must think rather of a mechanism which cannot deal with all the incoming messages and which therefore selects among them.

Above all it is becoming increasingly likely that central processes inside the nervous system contain an appreciable amount of unreliability, and that this is taken into account in the way the nervous system operates. This latter development is particularly significant, because it suggests a parallel with statistical decisions, which take into account gains and losses. Thus it may afford a place in the study of information processing for motivational factors of a sort which have traditionally been considered more by intuitive and clinical psychology than by those abstract and instrumental investigators concerned with reaction time and with sensory thresholds. As yet, even the bonds between physiology, artificial intelligence, and experimental psychology are regrettably weak; and connections with clinical psychology are not yet on the horizon. Nevertheless, those connections will ultimately need to be made, and it is gratifying that recent studies of information processing are beginning to find a place for motivational variables such as gain and loss.

REFERENCES

1. F. Rosenblatt, *Psychol. Rev.*, 1958, **65,** 386.
2. D. E. Broadbent, *Perception and Communication.* New York: Pergamon, 1958, pp. 76–77.
3. I. D. Brown, *Trans. Assoc. Ind. Med. Officers,* 1964, **14,** 44; W. B. Knowles, *Human Factors,* 1963, **5,** 155.
4. A. D. Baddeley, Ph.D. thesis, University of Cambridge, England (1962).
5. J. E. Desmedt, in *Neural Mechanisms and Vestibular Systems,* G. L. Rasmussen and W. Wendle, Eds. Springfield, Ill.: Thomas, 1960, pp. 152–164.
6. D. E. Broadbent, *J. Exp. Psychol.,* 1954, **47,** 191.
7. N. S. Sutherland, N. J. Mackintosh, J. B. Wolfe, *ibid.,* 1965, **69,** 56; N. J. Mackintosh,

Quart. J. Exp. Psychol., 1965, **17,** 26. See also earlier references in these papers.

8. N. Moray, *Quart. J. Exp. Psychol.*, **11,** 56 (1959).

9. S. Winograd and J. D. Cowan, *Reliable Computation in the Presence of Noise.* Cambridge: Massachusetts Institute of Technology Press, 1963.

10. J. A. Swets, *Science,* **134,** 168 (1961); see also D. E. Broadbent and M. Gregory, *Brit. J. Psychol.*, 1963, **54,** 309.

11. *Signal Detection and Recognition by Human Observers,* J. A. Swets, Ed. New York: Wiley, 1964.

12. D. E. Broadbent and M. Gregory, *Proc. Roy. Soc. London Ser. B*, 1963, **158,** 222.

13. A. Treisman, *Quart. J. Exp. Psychol.*, 1960, **12,** 242.

14. D. E. Broadbent, *Bull. Brit. Psychol. Soc.*, 1965, **18,** No. 60.

15. E. A. Alluisi, P. F. Miller, P. M. Fitts, *J. Exp. Psychol.*, 1957, **53,** 153.

16. D. E. Broadbent and M. Gregory, *Brit. J. Psychol.*, 1965, **56,** 61.

17. M. Stone, *Psychometrika,* 1960, **25,** 251.

18. D. R. J. Laming, Ph.D. thesis, University of Cambridge, England (1963).

4.3 Hemisphere Deconnection and Unity in Conscious Awareness

R. W. SPERRY

The following article is a result of studies my colleagues and I have been conducting with some neurosurgical patients of Philip J. Vogel of Los Angeles. These patients were all advanced epileptics in whom an extensive midline section of the cerebral commissures had been carried out in an effort to contain severe epileptic convulsions not controlled by medication. In all these people the surgical sections included division of the corpus callosum in its entirety, plus division also of the smaller anterior and hippocampal commissures, plus in some instances the massa intermedia. So far as I know, this is the most radical disconnection of the cerebral hemispheres attempted thus far in human surgery. The full array of sections was carried out in a single operation.

No major collapse of mentality or personality was anticipated as a result of this extreme surgery: earlier clinical observations on surgical section of the corpus callosum in man, as well as the results from dozens of monkeys on which I had carried out this exact same surgery, suggested that the functional deficits might very likely be less damaging than some of the more common forms of cerebral surgery, such as frontal lobotomy, or even some of the unilateral lobotomies performed more routinely for epilepsy.

The first patient on whom this surgery was tried had been having seizures for more than 10 years with generalized convulsions that continued to worsen despite treatment that had included a sojourn in Bethesda at the National Institutes of Health. At the time of the surgery, he had been averaging two major attacks per week, each of which left him debilitated for another day or

Reprinted with slight abridgment from the *American Psychologist*, 1968, **23**, 723–733, with permission of the author and the American Psychological Association, Inc.

so. Episodes of *status epilepticus* (recurring seizures that fail to stop and represent a medical emergency with a fairly high mortality risk) had also begun to occur at 2- to 3-month intervals. Since leaving the hospital following his surgery over $5\frac{1}{2}$ years ago, this man has not had, according to last reports, a single generalized convulsion. It has further been possible to reduce the level of medication and to obtain an overall improvement in his behavior and well being (see Bogen and Vogel, 1962).

The second patient, a housewife and mother in her 30s, also has been seizure-free since recovering from her surgery, which was more than 4 years ago (Bogen, Fisher, and Vogel, 1965). Bogen related that even the EEG has regained a normal pattern in this patient. The excellent outcome in the initial, apparently hopeless, last-resort cases led to further application of the surgery to some nine more individuals to date, the majority of whom are too recent for therapeutic evaluation. Although the alleviation of the epilepsy has not held up 100% throughout the series (two patients are still having seizures, although their convulsions are much reduced in severity and frequency and tend to be confined to one side), the results on the whole continue to be predominantly beneficial, and the overall outlook at this time remains promising for selected severe cases.

The therapeutic success, however, and all other medical aspects are matters for our medical colleagues, Philip J. Vogel and Joseph E. Bogen. Our own work has been confined entirely to an examination of the functional outcome, that is, the behavioral, neurological, and psycho-logical effects of this surgical disruption of all direct cross-talk between the hemispheres. Initially we were concerned as to whether we would be able to find in these patients any of the numerous symptoms of hemisphere deconnection that had been demonstrated in the so-called "split-brain" animal studies of the 1950s (Myers, 1961; Sperry, 1967a, 1967b). The outcome in man remained an open question in view of the historic Akelaitis (1944) studies that had set the prevailing doctrine of the 1940s and 1950s. This doctrine maintained that no important functional symptoms are found in man following even complete surgical section of the corpus callosum and anterior commissure, provided that other brain damage is excluded.

These earlier observations on the absence of behavioral symptoms in man have been confirmed in a general way to the extent that it remains fair to say today that the most remarkable effect of sectioning the neocortical commissures is the apparent lack of effect so far as ordinary behavior is concerned. This has been true in our animal studies throughout, and it seems now to be true for man also, with certain qualifications that we will come to later. At the same time, however—and this is in contradiction to the earlier doctrine set by the Akelaitis studies—we know today that with appropriate tests one can indeed demonstrate a large number of behavioral symptoms that correlate directly with the loss of the neocortical commissures in man as well as in animals (Gazzaniga, 1967; Sperry, 1967a, 1967b; Sperry, Gazzaniga, and Bogen, 1968). Taken collectively, these symptoms may be referred to as the syndrome of the neocortical commissures or the syndrome of the forebrain commissures or, less specifically, as the syndrome of hemisphere deconnection.

One of the more general and also more interesting and striking features of this syndrome may be summarized as an apparent doubling in most of the realms of conscious awareness. Instead of the normally unified single stream of consciousness, these patients behave in many ways as if they have two independent streams of conscious awareness, one in each hemisphere, each of which is cut off from and out of contact with the mental experiences of the other. In other words, each hemisphere seems to have its own separate and private sensations; its own perceptions; its own concepts; and its own impulses to act, with related volitional, cognitive, and learning experiences. Following the surgery, each hemisphere also has thereafter its own separate chain of memories that are rendered inaccessible to the recall processes of the other.

This presence of two minds in one body, as it were, is manifested in a large number and variety of test responses which, for the present purposes, I will try to review very briefly and in a somewhat streamlined and simplified form. First, however, let me take time to emphasize that the work reported here has been very much a team project. The surgery was performed by Vogel at the White Memorial Medical Center in Los Angeles. He has been assisted in the surgery and in the medical treatment throughout by Joseph Bogen. Bogen has also been collaborating in our behavioral testing program, along with a number of graduate students and postdoctoral fellows, among whom M. S. Gazzaniga, in particular, worked closely with us during the first several years and managed much of the testing during that period. The patients and their families have been most cooperative, and the whole project gets its primary funding from the National Institute of Mental Health.

Most of the main symptoms seen after hemisphere deconnection can be described for convenience with reference to a single testing setup—shown in Figure 1. Principally, it allows for the lateralized testing of the right and left halves of the visual field, separately or together, and the right and left hands and legs with vision excluded. The tests can be arranged in different combinations and in association with visual, auditory, and other input, with provisions for eliminating unwanted stimuli. In testing vision, the subject with one eye covered centers his gaze on a designated fixation point on the upright translucent screen. The visual stimuli on 35-millimeter

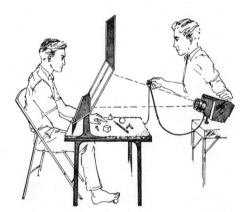

figure 1

Apparatus for studying lateralization of visual, tactual, lingual, and associated functions in the surgically separated hemispheres.

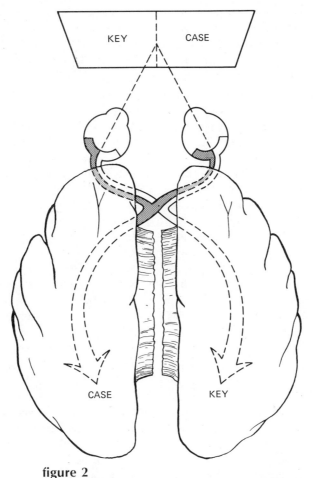

figure 2

Things seen to the left of a central fixation point with either
eye are projected to the right hemisphere and vice-versa.

transparencies are arranged in a standard
projector equipped with a shutter and are
then back-projected at $\frac{1}{10}$ of a second
or less—too fast for eye movements to
get the material into the wrong half of
the visual field. Figure 2 is merely a re-
minder that everything seen to the left
of the vertical meridian through either
eye is projected to the right hemisphere
and vice versa. The midline division

along the vertical meridian is found to
be quite precise without significant gap
or overlap (Sperry, 1968).

When the visual perception of these
patients is tested under these conditions
the results indicate that these people
have not one inner visual world any
longer, but rather two separate visual inner worlds, one serving the right half of
the field of vision and the other the left

half—each, of course, in its respective hemisphere. This doubling in the visual sphere shows up in many ways: For example, after a projected picture of an object has been identified and responded to in one half field, we find that it is recognized again only if it reappears in the same half of the field of vision. If the given visual stimulus reappears in the opposite half of the visual field, the subject responds as if he had no recollection of the previous exposure. In other words, things seen through the right half of the visual field (i.e., through the left hemisphere) are registered in mental experience and remembered quite separately from things seen in the other half of the field. Each half of the field of vision in the commissurotomized patient has its own train of visual images and memories.

This separate existence of two visual inner worlds is further illustrated in reference to speech and writing, the cortical mechanisms for which are centered in the dominant hemisphere. Visual material projected to the right half of the field—left-hemisphere system of the typical right-handed patient—can be described in speech and writing in an essentially normal manner. However, when the same visual material is projected into the left half of the field, and hence to the right hemisphere, the subject consistently insists that he did not see anything or that there was only a flash of light on the left side. The subject acts as if he were blind or agnostic for the left half of the visual field. If, however, instead of asking the subject to tell you what he saw, you instruct him to use his left hand to point to a matching picture or object presented among a collection of other pictures or objects, the subject has no

trouble as a rule in pointing out consistently the very item that he has just insisted he did not see.

We do not think the subjects are trying to be difficult or to dupe the examiner in such tests. Everything indicates that the hemisphere that is talking to the examiner did in fact not see the left-field stimulus and truly had no experience with, nor recollection of, the given stimulus. The other, the right or nonlingual hemisphere, however, did see the projected stimulus in this situation and is able to remember and recognize the object and can demonstrate this by pointing out selectively the corresponding or matching item. This other hemisphere, like a deaf mute or like some aphasics, cannot talk about the perceived object and, worse still, cannot write about it either.

If two different figures are flashed simultaneously to the right and left visual fields, as for example a "dollar sign" on the left and a "question mark" on the right and the subject is asked to draw what he saw using the left hand out of sight, he regularly reproduces the figure seen on the left half of the field, that is, the dollar sign. If we now ask him what he has just drawn, he tells us without hesitation that the figure he drew was the question mark, or whatever appeared in the right half of the field. In other words, the one hemisphere does not know what the other hemisphere has been doing. The left and the right halves of the visual field seem to be perceived quite separately in each hemisphere with little or no cross-influence.

When words are flashed partly in the left field and partly in the right, the letters on each side of the midline are perceived and responded to separately. In the "key case" example shown in Figure 2 the subject might first reach for and select with the left hand a key from among a collection of objects indicating perception through the minor hemisphere. With the right hand he might then spell out the word "case" or he might speak the word if verbal response is in order. When asked what kind of "case" he was thinking of here, the answer coming from the left hemisphere might be something like "in *case* of fire" or "the *case* of the missing corpse" or "a *case* of beer," etc., depending upon the particular mental set of the left hemisphere at the moment. Any reference to "key case" under these conditions would be purely fortuitous, assuming that visual, auditory, and other cues have been properly controlled.

A similar separation in mental awareness is evident in tests that deal with stereognostic or other somesthetic discriminations made by the right and left hands, which are projected separately to the left and right hemispheres, respectively. Objects put in the right hand for identification by touch are readily described or named in speech or writing, whereas, if the same objects are placed in the left hand, the subject can only make wild guesses and may often seem unaware that anything at all is present. As with vision in the left field, however, good perception, comprehension, and memory can be demonstrated for these objects in the left hand when the tests are so designed that the subject can express himself through nonverbal responses. For example, if one of these objects which the subject tells you he cannot feel or does not recognize is taken

from the left hand and placed in a grab bag or scrambled among a dozen other test items, the subject is then able to search out and retrieve the initial object even after a delay of several minutes is deliberately interposed. Unlike the normal subject, however, these people are obliged to retrieve such an object with the same hand with which it was initially identified. They fail at cross-retrieval. That is, they cannot recognize with one hand something identified only moments before with the other hand. Again, the second hemisphere does not know what the first hemisphere has been doing.

When the subjects are first asked to use the left hand for these stereognostic tests they commonly complain that they cannot "work with that hand," that the hand "is numb," that they "just can't feel anything or can't do anything with it," or that they "don't get the message from that hand." If the subjects perform a series of successful trials and correctly retrieve a group of objects which they previously stated they could not feel, and if this contradiction is then pointed out to them, we get comments like "Well, I was just guessing," or "Well, I must have done it unconsciously."

With other simple tests a further lack of cross-integration can be demonstrated in the sensory and motor control of the hands. In a "symmetric handpose" test the subject holds both hands out of sight symmetrically positioned and not in contact. One hand is then passively placed by the examiner into a given posture, such as a closed fist, or one, two, or more fingers extended or crossed or folded into various positions. The subject is then instructed verbally or by demonstration to form the same pose with the other hand, also excluded from vision. The normal subject does this quite accurately, but the commissurotomy patient generally fails on all but the very simplest hand postures, like the closed fist or the fully extended hand.

In a test for crossed topognosis in the hands, the subject holds both hands out of sight, forward and palm up with the fingers held apart and extended. The examiner then touches lightly a point on one of the fingers or at the base of the fingers. The subject responds by touching the same target point with the tip of the thumb of the same hand. Cross-integration is tested by requiring the patient to use the opposite thumb to find the corresponding mirror point on the opposite hand. The commissurotomy patients typically perform well within either hand, but fail when they attempt to cross-locate the corresponding point on the opposite hand. A crude cross-performance with abnormally long latency may be achieved in some cases after practice, depending on the degree of ipsilateral motor control and the development of certain strategies. The latter breaks down easily under stress and is readily distinguished from the natural performance of the normal subject with intact callosum.

In a related test the target point is presented visually as a black spot on an outline drawing of the hand. The picture is flashed to the right or left half of the visual field, and the subject then attempts as above to touch the target spot with the tip of the thumb. The response again is performed on the same side with normal facility but is impaired in the commissurotomy patient when the left visual field is paired with a right-hand response

and vice versa. Thus the duality of both manual stereognosis and visuognosis is further illustrated; each hemisphere perceives as a separate unit unaware of the perceptual experience of the partner.

If two objects are placed simultaneously, one in each hand, and then are removed and hidden for retrieval in a scrambled pile of test items, each hand will hunt through the pile and search out selectively its own object. In the process each hand may explore, identify, and reject the item for which the other hand is searching. It is like two separate individuals working over the collection of test items with no cooperation between them. We find the interpretation of this and of many similar performances to be less confusing if we do not try to think of the behavior of the commissurotomy patient as that of a single individual, but try to think instead in terms of the mental faculties and performance capacities of the left and the right hemispheres separately. Most of the time it appears that the major, that is, the left, hemisphere is in control. But in some tasks, particularly when these are forced in testing procedures, the minor hemisphere seems able to take over temporarily.

It is worth remembering that when you split the brain in half anatomically you do not divide in half, in quite the same sense, its functional properties. In some respects cerebral functions may be doubled as much as they are halved because of the extensive bilateral redundancy in brain organization, wherein most functions, particularly in sub-human species, are separately and rather fully organized on both sides. Consider for example the visual inner world of either of the disconnected hemispheres in these patients. Probably neither of the separated visual systems senses or perceives itself to be cut in half or even incomplete. One may compare it to the visual sphere of the hemianopic patient who, following accidental destruction of an entire visual cortex of one hemisphere, may not even notice the loss of the whole half sphere of vision until this has been pointed out to him in specific optometric tests. These commissurotomy patients continue to watch television and to read the paper and books with no complaints about peculiarities in the perceptual appearance of the visual field.

At the same time, I want to caution against any impression that these patients are better off mentally without their cerebral commissures. It is true that if you carefully select two simple tasks, each of which is easily handled by a single hemisphere, and then have the two performed simultaneously, there is a good chance of getting better than normal scores. The normal interference effects that come from trying to attend to two separate right and left tasks at the same time are largely eliminated in the commissurotomized patient. However, in most activities that are at all complex the normally unified cooperating hemispheres still appear to do better than the two disconnected hemispheres. Although it is true that the intelligence, as measured on IQ tests, is not much affected and that the personality comes through with little change, one gets the impression in working with these people that their intellect is nevertheless handicapped in ways that are probably not revealed in the ordinary tests. All the patients have marked short-term memory deficits, which are especially pronounced during the first year, and it is open to question whether this memory impairment ever clears completely. They also have orientation problems, fatigue more quickly in reading and in other tasks requiring mental concentration, and presumably have various other impairments that reduce the upper limits of performance in functions that have yet to be investigated. The patient that has shown the best recovery, a boy of 14, was able to return to public school and was doing passing work with B to D grades, except for an F in math, which he had to repeat. He was, however, a D student before the surgery, in part, it would seem, for lack of motivation. In general, our tests to date have been concerned mostly with basic cross-integrational deficits in these patients and the kind of mental capacities preserved in the subordinate hemisphere. Studied comparisons of the upper limits of performance before and after surgery are still needed.

Much of the foregoing is summarized schematically in Figure 3. The left hemisphere in the right-handed patients is equipped with the expressive mechanisms for speech and writing and with the main centers for the comprehension and organization of language. This "major" hemisphere can communicate its experiences verbally and in an essentially normal manner. It can communicate, that is, about the visual experiences of the right half of the optic field and about the somesthetic and volitional experiences of the right hand and leg and right half of the body generally. In addition, and not indicated in the figure, the major hemisphere also communicates, of course, about all of the more general, less later-

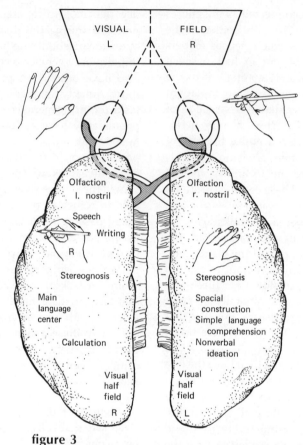

figure 3

Schematic outline of the functional lateralization evident in behavioral tests of patients with forebrain commissurotomy.

alized cerebral activity that is bilaterally represented and common to both hemispheres. On the other side we have the mute aphasic and agraphic right hemisphere, which cannot express itself verbally, but which through the use of nonverbal responses can show that it is not agnostic; that mental processes are indeed present centered around the left visual field, left hand, left leg, and left half of the body; along with the auditory, vestibular, axial somatic, and all other cerebral activities that are less lateralized and for which the mental experiences of the right and left hemispheres may be characterized as being similar but separate.

It may be noted that nearly all of the symptoms of cross-integrational impairment that I have been describing are easily hidden or compensated under the conditions or ordinary behavior. For example, the visual material has to be flashed at $\frac{1}{10}$ of a second or less to one half of the field in order to prevent compensation by eye movements. The defects in manual stereognosis are not apparent unless vision is excluded; nor is doubling in olfactory perception evident without sequential occlusion of right and left nostril and elimination of visual cues. In many tests the major hemisphere must be prevented from talking to the minor hemisphere and thus giving away the answer through auditory channels. And, similarly, the minor hemisphere must be prevented from giving nonverbal signals of various sorts to the major hemisphere. There is a great diversity of indirect strategies and response signals, implicit as well as overt, by which the informed hemisphere can be used to cue-in the uninformed hemisphere (Levy-Agresti, 1968).

Normal behavior under ordinary conditions is favored also by many other unifying factors. Some of these are very obvious, like the fact that these two separate mental spheres have only one body, so they always get dragged to the same places, meet the same people, and see and do the same things all the time and thus are bound to have a great overlap of common, almost identical, experience. Just the unity of the optic image—and even after chiasm section in animal experiments, the conjugate movements of the eyes—means that both hemispheres automatically center on, focus on, and hence probably attend to, the same items in the visual field all the time. Through sensory feedback a unifying body schema is imposed in each hemisphere with common components that similarly condition in parallel many processes of perception and motor action onto a common base. To get different activities going and different experiences and different

memory chains built up in the separated hemispheres of the bisected mammalian brain, as we do in the animal work, requires a considerable amount of experimental planning and effort.

In motor control we have another important unifying factor, in that either hemisphere can direct the movement of both sides of the body, including to some extent the movements of the ipsilateral hand (Hamilton, 1967). Insofar as a response involves mainly the axial parts and proximal limb segments, these patients have little problem in directing overall response from sensory information restricted to either single hemisphere. Control of the distal limb segments and especially of the finer finger movements of the hand ipsilateral to the governing hemisphere, however, are borderline functions and subject to considerable variation. Impairments are most conspicuous when the subject is given a verbal command to respond with the fingers of the left hand. The absence of the callosum, which normally would connect the language processing centers in the left hemisphere to the main left-hand motor controls in the opposite hemisphere, is clearly a handicap, especially in the early months after surgery. Cursive writing with the left hand presents a similar problem. It may be accomplished in time by some patients using shoulder and elbow rather than finger movement. At best, however, writing with the left hand is not as good after as before the surgery. The problem is not in motor coordination per se, because the subject can often copy with the left hand a word already written by the examiner when the same word cannot be written to verbal command.

In a test used for more direct deter-

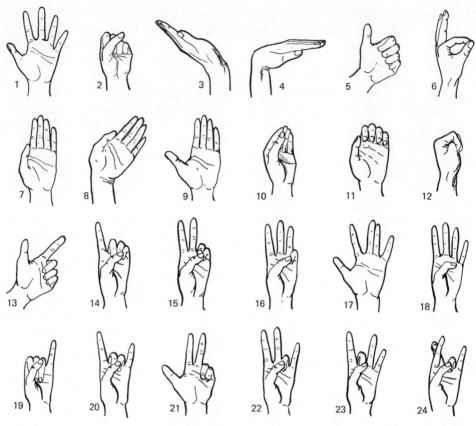

figure 4

In tests for ipsilateral motor control, different hand postures in outline drawing are projected one at a time to left or right bisual field (see Figure 1). Subject attempts to copy the sample hand pose with the homolateral and the contralateral hand.

mination of the upper limits of this ipsilateral motor control, a simple outline sketch of a finger posture (see Figure 4) is flashed to a single hemisphere, and the subject then tries to mimic the posture with the same or the opposite hand. The sample posture can usually be copied on the same side (i.e., through the main, contralateral control system) without difficulty, but the performance does not go so easily and often breaks down completely when the subject is obliged to use the opposite hand. The closed fist and the open hand with all fingers extended seem to be the two simplest responses, in that these can most often be copied with the ipsilateral hand by the more adept patients.

The results are in accord with the thesis (Gazzaniga, Bogen, and Sperry, 1967) that the ipsilateral control systems are delicate and marginal and easily disrupted by associated cerebral damage and other complicating factors. Preservation of the ipsilateral control system in varying degree in some patients and not in others would appear to account for many of the discrepancies that exist in the literature on the symptoms of hemisphere deconnection, and also for a number of changes between the present picture and that described until 2 years ago. Those acquainted with the literature will notice that the present findings on dyspraxia come much closer to the earlier Akelaitis observations than they do to those of Liepmann or of others expounded more recently (see Geschwind, 1965).

To try to find out what goes on in that speechless agraphic minor hemisphere has always been one of the main challenges in our testing program. Does the minor hemisphere really possess a true stream of conscious awareness or is it just an agnostic automaton that is carried along in a reflex or trancelike state? What is the nature, the quality, and the level of the mental life of this isolated subordinate unknown half of the human brain—which, like the animal mind, cannot communicate its experiences? Closely tied in here are many problems that relate to lateral dominance and specialization in the human brain, to the functional roles mediated by the neocortical commissures, and to related aspects of cerebral organization.

With such in mind, I will try to review briefly some of the evidence obtained to date that pertains to the level and nature of the inner mental life of the disconnected minor hemisphere. First, it is clear that the minor hemisphere can perform intermodal or cross-modal transfer of perceptual and mnemonic information at a characteristically human level. For example, after a picture of some object, such as a cigarette, has been flashed to the minor hemisphere through the left visual field, the subject can retrieve the item pictured from a collection of objects using blind touch with the left hand, which is mediated through the right hemisphere. Unlike the normal person, however, the commissurotomy patient is obliged to use the corresponding hand (i.e., the left hand, in this case) for retrieval and fails when he is required to search out the same object with the right hand (see Figure 5). Using the right hand the subject recognizes and can call off the names of each object that he comes to if he is allowed to do so, but the right hand or its hemisphere does not know what it is looking for, and the hemisphere that can recognize the correct answer gets no feedback from the right hand. Hence, the two never get together, and the performance fails. Speech and other auditory cues must be controlled.

It also works the other way around: that is, if the subject is holding an object in the left hand, he can then point out a picture of this object or the printed name of the object when these appear in a series presented visually. But again, these latter must be seen through the corresponding half of the visual field; an object identified by the left hand is not recognized when seen in the right half of the visual field. Intermodal associations of this sort have been found to work between vision, hearing and touch, and, more recently, olfaction in various combinations within either hemisphere but not across from one hemisphere to the other. This perceptual or mnemonic transfer from one sense modality to another has special theoretical interest in

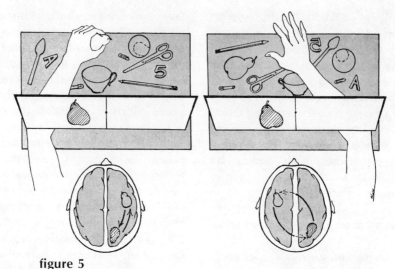

figure 5

Visuo-tactile associations succeed between each half of the visual field and the corresponding hand. They fail with crossed combinations in which visual and tactual stimuli are projected into opposite hemispheres.

that it is something that is extremely difficult or impossible for the monkey brain. The right hemisphere, in other words, may be animallike in not being able to talk or write, but in performances like the foregoing and in a number of other respects it shows mental capacities that are definitely human.

Other responses from the minor hemisphere in this same testing situation suggest the presence of ideas and a capacity for mental association and at least some simple logic and reasoning. In the same visuo-tactual test described above, the minor hemisphere, instead of selecting objects that match exactly the pictured item, seems able also to select related items or items that "go with" the particular visual stimulus, if the subject is so instructed. For example, if we flash a picture of a wall clock to the minor side and the nearest item that can be found tactually by the left hand is a toy wrist

watch, the subjects significantly select the watch. It is as if the minor hemisphere has an idea of a timepiece here and is not just matching sensory outlines. Or, if the picture of a dollar sign is flashed to the minor side, the subject searches through the list of items with the left hand and finally selects a coin such as a quarter or a 50¢ piece. If a picture of a hammer is presented, the subject may come up with a nail or a spike after checking out and rejecting all other items.

The capacity to think abstractly with symbols is further indicated in the ability of the minor hemisphere to perform simple arithmetical problems. When confronted with two numerals each less than 10, the minor hemisphere was able in four of six subjects so tested to respond with the correct sum or product up to 20 or so. The numbers were flashed to the left half of the visual field or presented as plastic block numerals to the left hand for identification. The answer was expressed by pointing to the correct number in columns of seen figures, or by left-hand signals in which the fingers were extended out of the subject's sight, or by writing the numerals with the left hand out of sight. After a correct left-hand response had been made by pointing or by writing the numeral, the major hemisphere could then report the same answer verbally, but the verbal report could not be made prior to the left-hand response. If an error was made with the left hand, the verbal report contained the same error. Two different pairs of numerals may be flashed to right and left fields simultaneously and the correct sum or products signaled separately by right and left hands. When verbal confirmation of correct left-hand signals is required under these conditions, the speaking hemisphere can only guess fortuitously, showing again that the answer must have been obtained from the minor and not from the major hemisphere. This has been demonstrated recently in a study still in progress by Biersner and the present writer. The findings correct an earlier impression (Gazzaniga and Sperry, 1967) in which we underestimated the capacity for calculation on the minor side. Normal subjects and also a subject with agenesis of the callosum (Saul and Sperry, 1968) were able to add or to multiply numerals shown one in the left and one in the right field under these conditions. The commissurotomy subjects, however, were able to perform such calculations only when both numerals appeared in the same half of the visual field.

According to a doctrine of long standing in the clinical writings on aphasia, it is believed that the minor hemisphere, when it has been disconnected by commissural or other lesions from the language centers on the opposite side, becomes then "word blind," "word deaf," and "tactually alexic." In contradiction to this, we find that the disconnected minor hemisphere in these commissurotomy patients is able to comprehend both written and spoken words to some extent, although this comprehension cannot be expressed verbally (Gazzaniga and Sperry, 1967; Sperry, 1966; Sperry and Gazzaniga, 1967). If the name of some object is flashed to the left visual field, like the word "eraser," for example, the subject is able then to search out an eraser from among a collection of objects using only touch with the left hand. If the subject is then asked what the item is after it has been selected correctly, his replies show that he does not know what he is holding in his left hand—as is the general rule for left-hand stereognosis. This means of course that the *talking* hemisphere does not know the correct answer, and we concluded accordingly that the minor hemisphere must, in this situation, have read and understood the test world.

These patients also demonstrate comprehension of language in the minor hemisphere by being able to find by blind touch with the left hand an object that has been named aloud by the examiner. For example, if asked to find a "piece of silverware," the subject may explore the array of test items and pick up a fork. If the subject is then asked what it is that he has chosen, he is just as likely in this case to reply "spoon" or "knife" as fork. Both hemispheres have heard and understood the word "silverware," but only the minor hemisphere knows what the left hand has actually found and picked up. In similar tests for comprehension of the spoken word, we find that the minor hemisphere seems able to understand even moderately advanced definitions like "shaving instrument" for razor or "dirt remover" for soap and "inserted in slot machines" for quarter.

Work in progress shows that the minor hemisphere can also sort objects into groups by touch on the basis of shape, size, and texture. In some tests the minor hemisphere is found to be superior to the major, for example, in tasks that involve drawing spatial relationships and performing block design tests. Perceptive mental performance in the minor hemisphere is also indicated in other situations in which the two hemispheres function concurrently in parallel at different tasks. It has been found, for example, that the divided hemispheres are capable of perceiving different things occupying the same position in space at the same time, and of learning mutually conflicting discrimination habits, something of which the normal brain is not capable. This was shown in the monkey work done some years ago by Trevarthen (1962) using a system of polarized light filters. It also required section of the optic chiasm, which of course is not included in the human surgery. The human patients, unlike normal subjects, are able to carry out a double voluntary reaction-time task as fast as they carry out a single task (Gazzaniga and Sperry, 1966). Each hemisphere in this situation has to perform a separate and different visual discrimination in order to push with the corresponding hand the correct one of a right and left pair of panels.

Whereas interference and extra delay are seen in normal subjects with the introduction of the second task, these patients with the two hemispheres working in parallel simultaneously perform the double task as rapidly as the single task.

The minor hemisphere is also observed to demonstrate appropriate emotional reactions as, for example, when a pinup shot of a nude is interjected by surprise among a series of neutral geometric figures being flashed to the right and left fields at random. When the surprise nude appears on the left side the subject characteristically says that he or she saw nothing or just a flash of light. However, the appearance of a sneaky grin and perhaps blushing and giggling on the next couple of trials or so belies the verbal contention of the speaking hemisphere. If asked what all the grinning is about, the subject's replies indicate that the conversant hemisphere has no idea at this stage what it was that had turned him on. Apparently, only the emotional effect gets across, as if the cognitive component of the process cannot be articulated through the brainstem.

Emotion is also evident on the minor side in a current study by Gordon and Sperry (1968) involving olfaction. When odors are presented through the right nostril to the minor hemisphere the subject is unable to name the odor but can frequently tell whether it is pleasant or unpleasant. The subject may even grunt, make aversive reactions or exclamations like "phew!" to a strong unpleasant smell, but not be able to state verbally whether it is garlic, cheese, or some decayed matter. Again it appears that the affective component gets across to the speaking hemisphere, but not the more specific information. The presence of the specific information within the minor hemisphere is demonstrated by the subject's correct selection through left-hand stereognosis of corresponding objects associated with the given odor. The minor hemisphere also commonly triggers emotional reactions of displeasure in the course of ordinary testing. This is evidenced in the frowning, wincing, and negative head shaking in test situations where the minor hemisphere, knowing the correct answer but unable to speak, hears the major hemisphere making obvious verbal mistakes. The minor hemisphere seems to express genuine annoyance at the erroneous vocal responses of its better half.

Observations like the foregoing lead us to favor the view that in the minor hemisphere we deal with a second conscious entity that is characteristically human and runs along in parallel with the more dominant stream of consciousness in the major hemisphere (Sperry, 1966). The quality of mental awareness present in the minor hemisphere may be comparable perhaps to that which survives in some types of aphasic patients following losses in the motor and main language centers. There is no indication that the dominant mental system of the left hemisphere is concerned about or even aware of the presence of the minor system under most ordinary conditions except quite indirectly as, for example, through occasional responses triggered from the minor side. As one patient remarked immediately after seeing herself make a left-hand response of this kind, "Now I know it wasn't me did that!"

Let me emphasize again in closing that the foregoing represents a somewhat abbreviated and streamlined account of the syndrome of hemisphere deconnection as we understand it at the present time. The more we see of these patients and the more of these patients we see, the more we become impressed with their individual differences, and with the consequent qualifications that must be taken into account. Although the general picture has continued to hold up in the main as described, it is important to note that, with respect to many of the deconnection symptoms mentioned, striking modifications and even outright exceptions can be found among the small group of patients examined to date. Where the accumulating evidence will settle out with respect to the extreme limits of such individual variations and with respect to a possible average "type" syndrome remains to be seen.

REFERENCES

Akelaitis, A. J. "A study of gnosis, praxis, and language following section of the corpus callosum and anterior commissure," *Journal of Neurosurgery*, 1944, **1**, 94–102.

Bogen, J. E., Fisher, E. D., and Vogel, P. J. "Cerebral commissurotomy: A second case report," *Journal of the American Medical Association*, 1965, **194**, 1328–1329.

Bogen, J. E., and Vogel, P. J. "Cerebral commissurotomy: A case report," *Bulletin of the Los Angeles Neurological Society*, 1962, **27**, 169.

Gazzaniga, M. S. "The split brain in man," *Scientific American*, 1967, **217**, 24–29.

Gazzaniga, M. S., Bogen, J. E., and Sperry, R. W. "Dyspraxia following division of the cerebral commissures," *Archives of Neurology*, 1967, **16**, 606–612.

Gazzaniga, M. S., and Sperry, R. W. "Simultaneous double discrimination following brain bisection," *Psychonomic Science,* 1966, **4,** 262–263.

Gazzaniga, M. S., and Sperry, R. W. "Language after section of the cerebral commissures," *Brain,* 1967, **90,** 131–148.

Geschwind, N. "Disconnexion syndromes in animals and man," *Brain,* 1965, **88,** 237–294, 584–644.

Gordon, H. W., and Sperry, R. W. "Olfaction following surgical disconnection of the hemispheres in man," in, *Proceedings of the Psychonomic Society* (1968), in press.

Hamilton, C. R. "Effects of brain bisection on eye-hand coordination in monkeys wearing prisms," *Journal of Comparative and Physiological Psychology,* 1967, **64,** 434–443.

Levy-Agresti, J. "Ipsilateral projection systems and minor hemisphere function in man after neocommissurotomy," *Anatomical Record,* 1968, **160,** 384.

Myers, R. E. "Corpus callosum and visual gnosis," in J. F. Delafresnaye (Ed.), *Brain Mechanisms and Learning.* Oxford: Blackwell, 1961.

Saul, R., and Sperry, R. W. "Absence of commissurotomy symptoms with agenesis of the corpus callosum." *Neurology,* 1968, **17,** in press.

Sperry, R. W. "Brain bisection and mecha-nisms of consciousness," in J. C. Eccles (Ed.), *Brain and Conscious Experience.* New York: Springer-Verlag, 1966.

Sperry, R. W. "Mental unity following surgical disconnection of the hemispheres," *The Harvey Lectures.* Series 62. New York: Academic Press, 1967 (a).

Sperry, R. W. "Split-brain approach to learning problems," in G. C. Quarton, T. Melnechuk, and F. O. Schmitt (Eds.), *The Neurosciences: A Study Program.* New York: Rockefeller University Press, 1967 (b).

Sperry, R. W. "Apposition of visual half-fields after section of neocortical commissures," *Anatomical Record,* 1968, **160,** 498–499.

Sperry, R. W., and Gazzaniga, M. S. "Language following surgical disconnection of the hemispheres," in C. H. Milikan (Ed.), *Brain Mechanisms Underlying Speech and Language.* New York: Grune & Stratton, 1967.

Sperry, R. W., Gazzaniga, M. S., and Bogen, J. E. "Function of neocortical commissures: Syndrome of hemisphere deconnection," in P. J. Vinken and G. W. Bruyn (Eds.), *Handbook of Neurology.* Amsterdam: North Holland, 1968, in press.

Trevarthen, C. B. "Double visual learning in split-brain monkeys," *Science,* 1962, **136,** 258–259.

SECTION 5

PERCEPTION

The initial selection in this section is an investigation by B. R. Bugelski of the State University of New York at Buffalo of a common perceptual phenomenon: the apparent tendency at night of the taillights of automobiles to pass through and go beyond the traffic light at an intersection, even though the cars have actually stopped short of the entrance to the intersection. Bugelski hypothesized that the phenomenon is due to the fact that the taillights and the traffic lights are at different angles from the line of vision and conducted an experiment with lights arranged at various angles. Results confirmed his hypothesis.

Psychologists are frequently asked to explain this or that seemingly miraculous cognitive feat. One of the more intriguing is that of the individual who can "see" with his finger tips. Martin Gardner, editor of the Mathematical Games Department of the *Scientific American,* turns a skeptical eye on such seemingly inexplicable feats and explains them in terms of performers' ability to hoodwink observers by a very simple technique: peeking down the side of the nose.

The pupil of the eye is highly responsive not only to light but also to the amount of interesting information available in the immediate environment. Stimuli that hold promise of additional information cause an enlargement of the pupil; uninteresting stimuli cause it to contract. Much of the work in this field has been conducted by Eckhard H. Hess of the University of Chicago. The third paper in this section consists of a study by Hess, Seltzer, and Shlien of the differences in the effect that pictures of men and women have on the pupillary responses of hetero- and homosexual males.

The fourth contribution in this section consists of a research report by Marianne W. Kristofferson of McMaster University, Hamilton, Ontario, who studied the effect of alcohol on perceptual field dependence. Field dependence in her research was measured by subjects' ability to bring the rod in Witkin's rod-and-frame test to a vertical position. Results showed that the ingestion of alcohol increased field dependence—that is, subjects taking the test after drinking made more errors in the rod-and-frame test than they did before drinking. Persons showing a high degree of field independence before the experiment were affected as much as those who were more field dependent—in other words, alcohol increased the field dependence of all subjects to approximately the same degree.

185

5.1 Traffic Signals and Depth Perception

B. R. BUGELSKI

An amusing illusion can be experienced by any motorist driving at night in city traffic whenever he finds himself following an automobile that is approaching a traffic signal. From a viewing distance of about a city block away, the taillights of the lead car will appear to "go through" a red stoplight and the car will appear to stop someplace beyond the intersection. As the follower closes the gap he sees the lead vehicle standing discretely well in front of the signal light. What the observation amounts to is this: at a certain low angle of elevation, a stimulus will look closer to the observer than a stimulus at or below eye level. In the traffic signal illusion the lower lights (taillights) appear to be beyond the upper (traffic signal) light. To make the lower lights appear to be just under the signal the automobile would have to be backed up, closer to the observer.

This illusion, which is readily experienced by anyone looking for it, does not appear to have been reported hitherto. The closest reference to such a phenomenon is a casual remark by Adelbert Ames (in 1) in his description of unusual perceptual experiences to the effect that in an otherwise dark room a light on a wall below another light will appear more distant if both are above eye level and that the reverse effect appears if the lights are below eye level. Kilpatrick (2) cites the same perceptual effects.

In a laboratory study by Epstein (3) subjects judged two lights vertically separated by from $3\frac{1}{2}$ to $7\frac{1}{2}$ deg of visual angle and reported no differences in depth between the lights when no textural cues were present. It may be that the visual angles employed by Epstein were too large for the illusory or any other effect

Reprinted from *Science*, 1967, **157**, 1464–1465, with permission of the author and *Science*. Copyright 1967 by the American Association for the Advancement of Science.

to appear in the absence of texture. He did find that when texture was supplied the upper light appeared more distant.

The illusion reported here is then doubly illusory in that, as Epstein reports, "the higher of two objects will generally appear more distant." The latter statement stems from Gibson's (4) descriptions of depth perception as a function of optical gradients of texture. It should be noted that in the illusion described here, textural cues are at a minimum, as the illusion is experienced best at night.

Because of the contradiction of reality and presumed common phenomenal experience, the illusion appeared worthy of some study, and the traffic situation was brought into the laboratory via a procedure that lends itself to numerous parametric investigations.

To reproduce the street situation, a box 8 by 2 by 1 foot (2.4 by 0.6 by 0.3 m) was constructed, open at the front end. The inside of the box was painted flat black. Ten inches (25 cm) above the floor of the box a small ($\frac{1}{2}$ inch) radio unfaceted ruby-light was mounted in a fixed position. On the floor of the box a small wooden block was arranged with strings leading from the front end and rear over pulleys so that a continuous loop of string could be manipulated to draw the block back and forth. On the block a duplicate ruby light was mounted. Both lights were powered by a 6-volt transformer. A stylus fitted to the block projected through a slit in the side of the box and ran along a meter stick mounted on the side. The box was fitted so that it could be placed on one side to provide a horizontal displacement. In principle, except for substituting

lights for dowels, the box resembles the rather unreliable Howard-Dolman apparatus as discussed by Weymouth and Hirsch (5).

College student subjects ($N = 23$) from an elementary psychology class were seated so that the lower light was at eye level, 20 feet away. The upper light was seen at an angle of approximately 2 deg (head position was not fixed). In a darkened hallway the subjects could see nothing of importance but the two lights. The experimenter gave the endless loop of string to the subject and asked him to pull one way or another to bring the lower light precisely under the upper light (vertical condition) or to bring the right light next to the left light (horizontal condition). Half the subjects went through the vertical condition first; the other subjects began with the horizontal condition. The experimenter moved the comparison stimulus well ahead or well beyond the standard before each trial. Each subject made 15 settings in each condition. The method of average error was followed and deviations from the correct setting were scored $+$ or $-$, depending on whether the comparison stimulus was set at a greater or lesser (closer to the subject) distance.

The average error score of the 23 subjects in the vertical condition was -4.73 inches (standard deviation, 3.81 inches). In general, then, the subjects drew the lower light ahead of the upper light when they attempted to equalize the positions. Their average error score in the horizontal condition was -0.86 inch (standard deviation, 2.17 inches). With 44 degrees of freedom the t of 4.23 between vertical and horizontal settings is significant at better than the .01 level.

Only two of the 23 subjects tended to be satisfied with settings that resulted in the lower light being set beyond the upper one. In the horizontal condition seven of the subjects had such positive constant errors.

It is evident that a negative constant error was markedly and predominantly present when the subject tried to locate a lower light below an upper light. This tendency was also present (significantly greater than 0.0) in the horizontal condition but to a far less degree.

From the results it is clear that the street scene was successfully reproduced in the laboratory in a miniature model. The illusion is open to further exploration of such variables as intensity and color of lights, visual angle, location with respect to eye level, and so forth. The present limited objective was to demonstrate the illusion per se.

Under the conditions that were established it appears that an illuminated stimulus that is in fact slightly farther away (the upper light) appears closer to the observer than a similar light at eye level. Although the present experiment did not explore the variable of degree of elevation, it is clear from street observations that the illusion disappears as the visual angle is increased. The present conclusions apply only to the angle employed, that is, 2 deg, and to the unstructured or untextured conditions. Whether "the higher of two objects will generally appear more distant" may depend on how much higher it is in the absence of other cues.

SUMMARY

Automobiles approaching red traffic signals at night appear to go beyond them when viewed from some distance to the rear. The phenomenon is doubly illusory because the higher of two objects has been presumed to appear more distant. The illusion is probably limited to small visual angles (about 2 degrees).

REFERENCES

1. W. H. Ittelson, *The Ames Demonstration in Perception*. Princeton, N.J.: Princeton University Press, 1952.

2. F. P. Kilpatrick, *Human Behavior from the Transactional Point of View*. Hanover, N.H.: Institute of Associate Research, 1952.

3. W. Epstein, *J. Exp. Psychol.*, 1966, **72,** 335.

4. J. J. Gibson, *The Perception of the Visual World*. Boston: Houghton Mifflin, 1950.

5. F. W. Weymouth and M. J. Hirsch, *Amer. J. Psychol.*, 1945, **58,** 379.

5.2 Dermo-optical Perception: A Peek Down the Nose

MARTIN GARDNER

Science reporting in United States newspapers and mass-circulation magazines is more accurate and freer of sensationalism than ever before, with pseudoscience confined largely to books. A reverse situation holds in the Soviet Union. Except for the books that defended Lysenko's theories, Soviet books are singularly free of pseudoscience, and now that Lysenko is out of power, Western genetics is rapidly entering the new Russian biology textbooks. Meanwhile, Russian newspapers and popular magazines are sensationalizing science much as our Sunday supplements did in the 1920s. The Soviet citizen has recently been presented with accounts of fish brought back to life after having been frozen 5000 years, of deep-sea monsters that leave giant tracks across the ocean floor, of absurd perpetual-motion devices, of extraterrestrial scientists who

have used a laser beam to blast an enormous crater in Siberia, and scores of similar stories.

By and large, the press in the United States has not taken this genre of Soviet science writing seriously. But in 1963 and 1964 it gave serious attention to a sudden revival, in Russia's popular press, of ancient claims that certain persons are gifted with the ability to "see" with their fingers.

The revival began with a report, in the summer of 1962, in the Sverdlovsk newspaper *Uralsky Rabochy*. Isaac Goldberg, of First City Hospital in Lower Tagil, had discovered that an epileptic patient, a 22-year-old girl named Rosa Kuleshova, could read print simply by moving a fingertip over the lines. Rosa went to Moscow for more testing, and sensational articles about her abilities appeared in *Izvestia* and other newspapers

Reprinted from *Science*, 1966, **151**, 654–657, with permission of the author and *Science*. Copyright 1966 by the American Association for the Advancement of Science.

and popular magazines. The first report in the United States was in *Time*, January 25, 1963.

When I first saw *Time*'s photograph of Goldberg watching Rosa, who was blindfolded, glide her middle finger over a newspaper page, I broke into a loud guffaw. To explain that laugh, I must back up a bit. For 30 years my principal hobby has been magic. I contribute to conjuring journals, write treatises on card manipulation, invent tricks, and, in brief, am conversant with all branches of this curious art of deception, including a branch called "mentalism."

For half a century professional mentalists—performers, such as Joseph Dunninger, who claim unusual mental powers—have been entertaining audiences with "eyeless vision" acts. Usually the mentalist first has a committee from the audience seal his eyes shut with adhesive tape. Over each eye is taped something opaque, such as a powder puff or a silver dollar. Then a large black cloth is pulled around the eyes to form a tight blindfold. Kuda Bux, a Mohammedan who comes from Kashmir, is perhaps the best known of today's entertainers who feature such an act. He has both eyes covered with large globs of dough, then many yards of cloth are wound like a turban to cover his entire face from the top of his forehead to the tip of his chin. Yet Kuda Bux is able to read books, solve mathematical problems on a blackboard, and describe objects held in front of him.

Now I do not wish to endanger my standing in the magic fraternity by revealing too much, but let me say that Kuda Bux and other mentalists who feature eyeless vision do obtain, by trickery, a way of seeing. Many ingenious methods have been devised, but the oldest and simplest, surprisingly little understood except by magicians, is known in the trade as the "nose peek." If the reader will pause at this point and ask someone to blindfold him, he may be surprised to discover that it is impossible, without injury to his eyes, to prepare a blindfold that does not permit a tiny aperture, on each side of the nose, through which light can enter each eye. By turning the eyes downward one can see, with either eye, a small area beneath the nose and extending forward at an angle of 30 to 40 degrees from the vertical. A sleep-mask blindfold is no better; it does not fit snugly enough around the nose. Besides, slight pressure on the top of the mask, under the pretense of rubbing the forehead, levers out the lower edge to permit even wider peeks. The great French magician Robert-Houdin (from whom Houdini took his name), in his memoirs (1), tells of watching another conjuror perform a certain card trick while blindfolded. The blindfold, Robert-Houdin writes, "was a useless precaution . . . for whatever care may be taken to deprive a person of sight in this way, the projection of the nose always leaves a vacuum sufficient to see clearly." Pushing wads of cotton or cloth into the two apertures accomplishes nothing. One can always, while pretending to adjust the blindfold, secretly insert his thumb and form a tiny space under the wadding. The wadding can actually be an asset in maintaining a wider aperture than there would be without it. I will not go into more subtle methods used by mentalists for overcoming such apparent obstacles as adhesive tape criss-crossed over the eyelids, balls of dough, and so on.

If the mentalist is obtaining information by a nose peek (there are other methods), he must carefully guard against what has been called the "sniff" posture. When the head of a blindfolded person is in a normal position, the view down the nose covers anything placed on the near edge of a table at which the person is seated. But to extend the peek farther forward it is necessary to raise the nose slightly, as though one is sniffing. Practiced performers avoid the sniff posture by tilting the head slightly under cover of some gesture, such as nodding in reply to a question, scratching the neck, and other common gestures.

One of the great secrets of successful blindfold work is to obtain a peek in advance, covered by a gesture, quickly memorize whatever information is in view, then later—perhaps many minutes later—to exploit this information under the pretense that it is just then being obtained. Who could expect observers to remember exactly what happened 5 minutes earlier? Indeed, only a trained mentalist, serving as an observer, would know exactly what to look for.

Concealing the "sniff" demands much cleverness and experience. In 1964, on a television show in the United States, a girl who claimed powers of eyeless vision was asked to describe, while blindfolded, the appearance of a stranger standing before her. She began with his shoes, then went on to his trousers, shirt, and necktie. As her description moved upward, so did her nose. The photograph in *Time* showed Rosa wearing a conventional blindfold. She is seated, one hand on a newspaper, and sniffing. The entire newspaper page is comfortably within the range of a simple nose peek.

OTHER DOP CLAIMANTS

After the publicity about Rosa, Russian women of all sorts turned up, performing even more sensational feats of eyeless vision. The most publicized of these was Ninel Sergyeyevna Kulagina. The Leningrad newspaper *Smena*, January 16, 1964, reported on her remarkable platform demonstration at the Psychoneurological Department of the Lenin-Kirovsk District. The committee who examined Ninel's blindfold included S. G. Fajnberg (Ninel's discoverer), A. T. Alexandrov, rector of the University of Leningrad, and Leonid Vasiliev, whose laboratory at the University is the center of parapsychology research in Russia. No magicians were present, of course. While "securely blindfolded," Ninel read from a magazine and performed other sensational feats. Vasiliev was reported as having described her demonstration as "a great scientific event."

There were dozens of other DOP claimants. The magazine *USSR* (now *Soviet Life*), published here in English, devoted four pages to some of them in its February 1964 issue (2). Experiments on Rosa, this article said, made it unmistakably clear that her fingers were reacting to ordinary light and not to infrared heat rays. Filters were used which could block either light or heat. Rosa was unable to "see" when the light (but not heat) was blocked off. She "saw" clearly when the heat rays (but not light) were blocked off. "The fingers have a retina," biophysicist Mikhail Smirnov is quoted as saying. "The fingers 'see' light."

Accounts of the women also appeared in scientific publications. Goldberg contributed a report on his work with Rosa to *Voprossy Psikhologii* in 1963 (3). Biophysicist N. D. Nyuberg wrote an article about Rosa for *Priroda,* May 1963 (4). Nyuberg reports that Rosa's fingers, just like the human eye, are sensitive to three color modes, and that, after special training at the neurological institute, she "succeeded in training her toes to distinguish between black and white." Other discussions of Rosa's exploits appeared in Soviet journals of philosophy and psychology.

Not only did Rosa read print with her fingers, she also described pictures in magazines, on cigarette packages, and on postage stamps. A *Life* correspondent reported that she read his business card by touching it with her elbow. She read print placed under glass and cellophane. In one test, when she was "securely blindfolded," scientists placed a green book in front of her, then flooded it with red light. Exclaimed Rosa: "The book has changed color!" The professors were dumbfounded. Rosa's appearance on a TV program called "Relay" flushed out new rivals. *Nedelya,* the supplement of *Izvestia,* found a 9-year-old Kharkov girl, Lena Bliznova, who staggered a group of scientists by reading print ("securely blindfolded") with fingers held a few inches *off* the page. Moreover, Lena read print just as easily with her toes and shoulders. She separated the black from the white chess pieces without a single error. She described a picture covered by a thick stack of books (see my remarks above about exploiting previously memorized information).

In the United States, *Life* (June 12, 1964) published a long uncritical article by Albert Rosenfeld (5), the writer whose card Rosa had read with her elbow. The Russian work is summarized and hailed as a major scientific breakthrough. Colored symbols are printed on one page so the reader can give himself a DOP test. Gregory Razran, who heads the psychology department at Queens College, New York, is quoted as saying that perhaps "some entirely new kind of force or radiation" has been detected. Razran expected to see "an explosive outburst of research in this field. . . . To see without the eyes—imagine what that can mean to a blind man!"

Let us hope that Razran, in his research, will seek the aid of knowledgeable mentalists. In a photograph of one of his DOP tests, shown in the *Life* article, the subject wears a conventional sleepmask, with the usual apertures. She is reaching through a cloth hole in the center of an opaque partition to feel one of two differently colored plates. But there is nothing to prevent her from reaching out with her other hand, opening the cloth a bit around her wrist, then taking a nose peek through the opening.

The most amusing thing about such experimental designs is that there is a simple, but never used, way to make sure all visual clues are eliminated. A blindfold, in any form, is totally useless, but one can build a light-weight aluminum box that fits over the subject's head and rests on padded shoulders. It can have holes at the top and back for breathing, but the solid metal must cover the face and sides, and go completely under the chin to fit snugly around the front of the neck. Such a box eliminates at one stroke the need for a blindfold, the cumbersome screen with arm holes, various bib devices that go under the chin, and other clumsy pieces of apparatus designed by psychologists unfamiliar with the methods of mentalism. No test made without such a box over the head is worth taking seriously. It is the only way known to me by which all visual clues can be ruled out. There remain, of course, other methods of cheating, but they are more complicated and not likely to be known outside the circles of professional mentalism.

In its 1964 story *Life* did not remind its readers of the three pages it had devoted, in 1937, to Pat Marquis, "the boy with the X-ray eyes" (6). Pat was then 13 and living in Glendale, California. A local physician, Cecil Reynolds, discovered that Pat could "see" after his eyes had been taped shut and covered with a blindfold. Pat was carefully tested by reporters and professors, said *Life*, who could find no trickery. There are photographs of Pat, "securely blindfolded," playing ping-pong, pool, and performing similar feats. Naturally he could read. Reynolds is quoted as saying that he believed that the boy "saw" with light receptors in his forehead. Pat's powers were widely publicized at the time by other magazines and by the wire services. He finally agreed to being tested by J. B. Rhine, of Duke University, who caught him nose peeking (7).

The truth is that claims of eyeless vision turn up with about the same regularity as tales of sea serpents. In 1898 A. N. Khovrin, a Russian psychiatrist, published a paper on "A rare form of hyperaesthesia of the higher sense organs" (8), in which he described the DOP feats of a Russian woman named Sophia. There are many earlier reports of blind persons who could tell colors with their fingers, but "blindness" is a relative term,

and there is no way now to be sure how blind those claimants really were. It is significant that there are no recent cases of persons known to be totally blind who claim the power to read ordinary print, or even to detect colors, with their fingers, although it would seem that the blind would be the first to discover and develop such talents if they were possible.

JULES ROMAINS' WORK

Shortly after World War I the French novelist Jules Romains, interested in what he called "paroptic vision," made an extensive series of tests with French women who could read while blindfolded. His book, *Vision Extra-Rétinienne* (9) should be read carefully by every psychologist tempted to take the Russian claims seriously, for it describes test after test exactly like those that have been given to today's Russians. There are the same lack of controls, the same ignorance of the methods of mentalism, the same speculations about the opening of new scientific frontiers, the same unguarded predictions about how the blind may someday learn to "see," the same scorn for those who remain skeptical. Romains found that DOP was strongest in the fingers, but also present in the skin at any part of the body. Like today's Russian defenders of DOP, Romains is convinced that the human skin contains organs sensitive to ordinary light. His subjects performed poorly in dim light and could not see at all in total darkness. Romains thought that the mucous lining of the nose is especially sensitive to colors, because in dim light, when colors were hard to see, his subjects had a

marked tendency to "sniff spontaneously."

The blindfolding techniques Romains used are similar to those used by
the more recent investigators. Adhesive
tape is crossed over the closed eyes, then
folded rectangles of black silk, then the
blindfold. At times cotton wool is pushed
into the space alongside the nose, at
times a projecting bib is placed under the
chin. (Never a box over the head.)
Anatole France witnessed and commented favorably on some of Romains'
work. One can sympathize with the
novelist when he complained to a U.S.
reporter (10) that both Russian and
American psychologists had ignored his
findings and had simply "repeated one
twentieth of the discoveries I made and
reported."

It was Romains' book that probably
aroused magicians in the United States
to devise acts of eyeless vision. Harlan
Tarbell, of Chicago, worked out a remarkable act of this type which he performed frequently (11). Stanley Jaks, a
professional mentalist from Switzerland,
later developed his method of copying
a stranger's signature, upside down and
backward, after powder puffs had been
taped over his eyes and a blindfold added
(12). Kuda Bux uses still other techniques
(13). At the moment, amateurs every-
where are capitalizing on the new wave
of interest in DOP. In my files is a report
on Ronald Coyne, a 12-year-old Okla-
homa boy who lost his right eye in an
accident. When his left eye is "securely
blindfolded," his empty right eye socket
reads print without hesitation. Young
Coyne has been appearing at revival
meetings to demonstrate his miraculous
power. "For thirteen years he has had

continuous vision where there is no eye,"
reads an advertisement in a Miami
newspaper for an Assembly of God
meeting. "Truly you must say 'Mine eyes
have seen the glory of God.'"

TESTS IN THE UNITED STATES

The most publicized DOP claimant in the
United States is Patricia Stanley. Richard
P. Youtz, of the psychology department
at Barnard College, was discussing the
Soviet DOP work at a faculty lunch one
day. Someone who had taught high
school in Owensboro, Kentucky, recalled that Patricia, then a student, had as-
tounded everyone by her ability to identify objects and colors while blindfolded.
Youtz traced Patricia to Flint, Michigan,
and in 1963 he made several visits to
Flint, tested her for about 60 hours, and
obtained sensational results. These results were widely reported by the press
and by such magazines of the occult as
Fate (14). The soberest account, by science writer Robert K. Plumb, appeared
in the *New York Times,* January 8, 1964
(15). Mrs. Stanley did not read print, but
she seemed able to identify the colors of
test cards and pieces of cloth by rubbing
them with her fingers. Youtz's work, together with the Russian, provided the
springboard for Leonard Wallace Robinson's article "We have more than five
senses" in the *New York Times Magazine,*
Sunday, March 15.

Youtz's first round of tests, in my
opinion, were so poorly designed to
eliminate visual clues that they cannot
be taken seriously. Mrs. Stanley wore a
conventional sleep-mask. No attempt
was made to plug the inevitable apertures. Her hands were placed through

black velvet sleeves, with elastic around the wrists, into a lightproof box constructed of plywood and painted black. The box could be opened at the other side to permit test material to be inserted. There was nothing to prevent Mrs. Stanley from picking up a test card or piece of colored cloth, pushing a corner under the elastic of one sleeve, and viewing the exposed corner with a simple nose peek. Youtz did have a double sleeve arrangement that might have made this difficult, but his account (16) of his first round of tests, on which Mrs. Stanley performed best, indicate that it was attached only on the rare occasions when a photomultiplier tube was used. Such precautions as the double sleeve, or continuous and careful observation from behind, seemed unnecessary because Mrs. Stanley was securely blindfolded. Moreover, there was nothing to prevent Mrs. Stanley from observing, by nose peeks, the test material as it was being placed into the light-tight box.

Here is a description of Mrs. Stanley's performance by the *New York Times* reporter who observed her: "Mrs. Stanley concentrates hard during the experiments. . . . Sometimes she takes three minutes to make up her mind. . . . She rests her forehead under the blindfold against the black box as though she were studying intently. Her jaw muscles work as she concentrates" (17). While concentrating, she keeps up a steady flow of conversation with the observers, asking for hints on how she is doing.

Youtz returned to Flint in late January 1964 for a second round of tests, armed with more knowledge of how blindfolds can be evaded (we exchanged several letters about it) (18) and plans for tighter controls. I had been unsuccessful in persuading him to adopt a box over the head, but even without this precaution, results of the second round were not above chance expectation. These negative results were reported by the *New York Times* (17), but not by any other newspaper or news magazine that had publicized the positive results of the first round of tests. Youtz was disappointed, but he attributed the failure to cold weather (19).

A third series of tests was made on 20 April for an observing committee of four scientists. Results were again negative. In the warm weather of June, Youtz tested Mrs. Stanley a fourth time, over a 3-day period. Again, performance was at chance level. Youtz attributes this last failure to Mrs. Stanley's fatigue (19). He remains convinced that she does have the ability to detect colors with her fingers and suspects that she does this by sensing delicate differences in temperature (20). Although Russian investigators had eliminated this as an explanation of Rosa's powers, Youtz believes that his work with Mrs. Stanley, and later with less skillful Barnard students, will eventually confirm this hypothesis. He strongly objects to calling the phenomenon "vision." None of his subjects has displayed the slightest ability to read with the fingers.

NINEL IS CAUGHT CHEATING

In Russia, better-controlled testing of Rosa has strongly indicated nose peeking. Several articles have suggested this, notably those by L. Teplov, author of a well-known book on cybernetics, in the March 1–7, 1964 issue of *Nedelya*, and in the 25 May issue of the Moscow *Litera-turnaya Gazeta*. Ninel Kulagina, Rosa's chief rival, was carefully tested at the Bekhterev Psychoneurological Scientific Research Institute in Leningrad. B. Lebe-dev, the institute's head, and his associates summarize their findings as follows (*21*):

> In essence, Kulagina was given the same tasks as before, but under conditions of stricter control and in accordance with a plan prepared beforehand. And this was the plan: to alternate experiments in which the woman could possibly peek and eavesdrop with experiments where peeking would be impossible. The woman of course did not know this. As was to be expected, phenomenal ability was shown in the first instance only. In the second instance [under controls] Kulagina could distinguish neither the color nor the form. . . .

Thus the careful checking fully exposed the sensational "miracle." There were no miracles whatever. There was ordinary hoax.

In a letter to *Science* (*22*), Joseph Zubin, a biometrics researcher at the New York State Department of Mental Hygiene, reported the negative results of his testing of an adolescent who "read fluently" after blindfolds had been secured around the edges with adhesive tape. Previous testing by several scientists had shown no evidence of visual clues. It became apparent, however, that the subject tensed muscles in the blindfolded area until "a very tiny, inconspicuous chink appeared at the edge. Placing an opaque disk in front of the chink prevented reading, but not immediately.

The subject had excellent memory and usually continued for a sentence or two after blocking of the reading material." Applying zinc ointment to the edges of the adhesive proved only temporarily effective, because muscle tensing produced new chinks (made easier to detect by the white ointment). A professional magician, Zubin reports, participated in the investigations.

The majority of psychologists, both here and in the Soviet Union, have remained unimpressed by the latest revival of interest in DOP. In view of the failures of subjects to demonstrate DOP when careful precautions were taken to rule out peeks through minute apertures, and in view of the lack of adequate precautions in tests that yielded positive results, this prevailing scepticism appears to be strongly justified.

REFERENCES

1. J. E. Robert-Houdin, *Confidences d'un Prestidigitateur*, Blois, 1858, chap. 5; English translation, *Memoirs of Robert-Houdin: Ambassador, Author, and Conjuror*, London, 1859; reprinted as *Memoirs of Robert-Houdin: King of the Conjurers*. New York: Dover, 1964.

2. *USSR*, 1964, **89**, 32.

3. For English translation, see I. Goldberg, *Soviet Psychol. Psychiat.*, 1963, **2**, 19.

4. For English translation, see N. D. Nyuberg, *Federation Proc.*, 1964, **22**, T701.

5. A. Rosenfeld, "Seeing color with the fingers," *Life*, June 12, 1964, **1964**, 102–113.

6. "Pat Marquis of California can see without his eyes," *Life*, April 19, 1937, **1937**, 57–59.

7. J. B. Rhine, *Parapsychol. Bull.*, Aug. 1963, **66**, 2–4.

8. A. N. Khovrin, in *Contributions to Neuropsychic Medicine*, Moscow, 1898.

9. J. Romains, *Vision Extra-Rétinienne,* Paris, 1919; English translation. *Eyeless Vision,* C. K. Ogden, transl. New York: Putnam, 1924.

10. J. Davy, *Observer,* Feb. 2, 1964.

11. See H. Tarbell, "X-ray eyes and blindfold effects," in *The Tarbell Course in Magic* New York: Tannen, 1954, vol. 6, pp. 251-261. Tarbell speaks of his own work in this field as a direct result of his interest in Romains' work, and briefly describes an eyeless vision act by a woman who performed under the stage name of Shireen in the early 1920's.

12. See M. Gardner, *Sphinx,* Feb. 1949, **12,** 334-337; *Linking Ring,* Oct. 1964, **34,** 23-25; also, G. Groth, "He writes with your hand," in *Fate,* Oct. 1952, **5,** 39-43.

13. A description of an early eyeless vision act by Kuda Bux will be found in H. Price; *Confessions of a Ghost-Hunter.* New York: Putnam, 1936, chap. 19.

14. P. Saltzman, *Fate,* May 1964, **17,** 38-48.

15. R. K. Plumb, "Woman who tells color by touch mystifies psychologist," in *New York Times,* Jan. 8, 1964; see also Plumb's followup article, "6th Sense is hinted in ability to 'see' with fingers," *ibid.,* Jan. 26, 1964. The *Times* also published an editorial, "Can fingers 'see'?" Feb. 6, 1964.

16. R. P. Youtz, "Aphotic Digital Color Sensing: A Case under Study," photocopied for the Bryn Mawr meeting of the Psychonomic Society, Aug. 29, 1963.

17. "Housewife is unable to repeat color 'readings' with fingers," *New York Times,* Feb. 2, 1964.

18. For an exchange of published letters, see M. Gardner, *New York Times Magazine,* April 5, 1964, and R. P. Youtz, *ibid.,* April 26, 1964.

19. R. P. Youtz, "The Case for Skin Sensitivity to Color; with a Testable Explanatory Hypothesis," photocopied for the Psychonomic Society, Niagara Falls, Ontario, Oct. 9, 1964.

20. See R. P. Youtz, letter, *Sci. Amer.,* June 1965, **212,** 8-10.

21. B. Lebedev, *Leningradskaya Pravda,* March 15, 1964; translated for me by Albert Parry, department of Russian studies, Colgate University.

22. J. Zubin, *Science,* 1965, **147,** 985.

5.3 Pupil Response of Hetero- and Homosexual Males to Pictures of Men and Women: A Pilot Study

ECKHARD H. HESS, ALLAN L. SELTZER, AND JOHN M. SHLIEN

Change in the size of the pupil of the human eye has been reported to vary with a subject's interest in various pictorial stimuli (Hess and Polt, 1960). Male subjects had a larger pupil while looking at pictures of women than when looking at pictures of men. The reverse was true for female subjects: they had larger pupils looking at men. Unpublished work with a large number of subjects has continued to substantiate the finding of this difference between the sexes.

If this difference in pupil response is truly a reflection of interest in the male or female figure as a sexual object then homosexuals would be expected to show a larger pupil response to pictures of their own sex. In the course of our work a few subjects have given a larger response to pictures of their own sex; as measured by pupil size, same-sex pictures seemed more interesting to them.

Review of these anomalous cases increased the plausibility of the idea that this same-sex response might be typical of homosexuals. The present report, a pilot study of a small group of overt male homosexuals, strongly supports that hypothesis.

METHOD

Subjects

Ten young adult male subjects were tested. Five of these, students or workers in our laboratory—the heterosexual group—were well known to us over a period of several years. Their sexual outlet was judged to be exclusively heterosexual. The other five were known, through observation, interview, and in every case by their own voluntary admission to one of the authors who had gained their trust, to have overt homo-

Reprinted with minor abridgment from *Journal of Abnormal Psychology,* 1965, **70**, 165–168, with permission of the authors and the American Psychological Association, Inc.

sexuality as their sole or primary sexual outlet. All 10 were of roughly the same age (between 24 and 34 years), same education (all but one were graduate students), and same social level. None was hospitalized or in therapy.

Procedure and Apparatus

In a dimly-lit room, a subject was seated before a viewing aperture, fitted with a headrest, which was inserted in a large plywood panel. The panel concealed the working of the apparatus from the subject. Resting his head against the aperture, the subject faced a rear-projection screen, set in an otherwise black box, at a distance of $2\frac{1}{2}$ feet from his eyes. A 35-millimeter slide projector behind this screen projected a 9×12-inch picture onto it. Changing of slides was controlled by the experimenter from his position behind the panel where he also operated a concealed 16-millimeter camera fitted with a frame counter. As the slides were being viewed a half-silvered mirror placed at a 45-degree angle across the subject's line of vision permitted unobtrusive filming of the eye, at the rate of two frames per second. Illumination for this photography was furnished by a 100-watt bulb on rheostat control.

Fifteen picture slides, representations of the human figure, were shown in the order indicated in Table 1. The presentation of each of these stimulus pictures was preceded by the presentation of a medium gray "control" slide. The total sequence was 30 slides in this order: Control A, Stimulus A, Control B, Stimulus B, etc., each shown for 10 seconds, with a total viewing time of 5 minutes for the entire sequence.

table 1

Order of Presenting Slides of Human Figures

Slide Content	Scoring Category
A. Painting, cubist, five figures	Art
B. Painting, realistic, crucifixion	Art
C. Painting, two nude males	Male
D. Painting, reclining female nude	Female
E. Photograph, nude man, head and upper torso	Male
F. Painting, seated nude female, rear view	Female
G. Painting, sailor, nude upper torso	Male
H. Painting, nude male and nude female	Art
I. Photograph, nude female torso	Female
J. Photograph, nude man, rear view	Male
K. Painting, nude female, head and upper torso	Female
L. Painting, two partly clothed males	Male
M. Painting, nude female, head and torso	Female
N. Painting, abstract, three figures	Art
O. Painting, cubist, three figures	Art

From the list of slides it can be seen that five were scored as being pictures of females and five were scored as pictures of males. The "male" pictures (C, E, G, J, and L), considered to be the homosexual equivalent of pinups, were culled from physique magazines and were generally more crude artistically than the pictures of females. These latter (D, F, I, K, and M) represented a rather lush concept of the female figure: for example, "D" was a Titian "Venus," "K" an Ingres "Odalisque."

The five "art" slides (A, B, H, N, and O) ranged in style and period from a Michelangelo to a Picasso. None of these was a clearly male or clearly "female" picture; the abstracts (A, N, and O) were ambiguous sexually, "H" showed both sexes, "B" had a strong religious connotation. This group of slides was included in the series for several reasons. Firstly, it was deemed desirable to place the sexual pictures in an artistic setting to reduce the threat to some subjects that might inhere in the obviously sexual material. Secondly, an abnormally high response is frequently given to the first stimulus shown to a subject. By placing art slides "A" and "B" first in the sequence, the male and the female slides, which were of major interest, were protected from this artifact. Thirdly, homosexuals are often thought to have artistic interests and, indeed, most of the homosexuals in this study did verbally indicate such interests. It was useful, therefore, to include a group of slides which would permit appraisal of response to the artistic quality of pictures separate from their representation of sexual objects. Such a separation of pictorial content from its artistic mode of expression appears feasible since (a) the homosexuals, as a group, showed a high response to the artistically good but sexually ambiguous art slides but (b) they also showed a high response to the artistically crude male pictures yet (c) they showed a low response to the artistically good female pictures. Thus, in addition to the use made of it in this report, the data point also to the potential value of the pupil technique in esthetics research.

Measurement and Scoring

The processed 16-millimeter film was projected, frame by frame, onto the underside of an opal-glass insert in a table, to a magnification of approximately 20 times. The diameter of the pupil in each frame was measured with a millimeter rule and recorded, giving a set of 20 measurements for each control presentation and a set of 20 for each stimulus. Averages were then computed for each stimulus set and for each preceding control set. In order to compare average pupil size during viewing of a picture to the pupil size during the preceding control this method was used: for each control-stimulus pair the percentage of increase or decrease in average pupil size was computed by dividing the difference between stimulus average and control average by the control average. A positive percentage indicated a larger pupil size when the subject was viewing the stimulus than when he viewed the preceding control. A negative percentage meant a smaller average pupil size during stimulus viewing. For each subject, the five percentages of his response to each of the male pictures (C, E, G, J, and L) were added together to give his "response to 'male' picture" score (Table 2, first column). The total of percentages of his response to the female pictures (D, F, I, K, and M) gave his "response to 'female' picture" score (Table 2, second column). The algebraic subtraction of each subject's male picture total from his female picture total (column two minus column one) gave each subject's relative male-female response measure (Table 2, third column). Using this order of procedure for the table, a positive figure in the

table 2

Pupil Size Increase or Decrease when Comparing Stimuli to Controls
Expressed in Percentage Totals

Subject	Total Response to "Male" Pictures	Total Response to "Female" Pictures	Relative "Male-Female" Response Score
Heterosexuals			
1	−00.4	+05.9	+06.3
2	−54.5	−22.4	+32.1
3	+12.5	+19.2	+06.7
4	+06.3	+39.0	+32.7
5	−01.5	+23.1	+24.6
Homosexuals			
6	+18.8	+11.2	−07.6
7	−04.6	−38.0	−33.4
8	+18.9	+18.1	−00.8
9	+18.2	−05.6	−23.8
10	+15.8	+21.5	+05.7

third column indicates that the subject had a greater total response to pictures of females than to pictures of males; a negative figure indicates lesser response to pictures of females but greater response to pictures of males.

RESULTS

These male-female response measures clearly discriminate between the subject groups, as is shown in the last column of Table 2. There is no overlap between the groups in that the lowest heterosexual response is +06.3 while the highest homosexual response is no higher than +05.7. All heterosexual males show a larger response to pictures of women than to pictures of men (positive scores). Four of the homosexuals show a larger response to pictures of men (negative scores).

DISCUSSION

Some of the female pictures drew a high-positive response from some of the homosexuals and some of the male pictures drew a high-positive response from some of the heterosexuals. Therefore, response to any single stimulus did not serve to categorize individuals. The total response of a group of subjects to any single stimulus, however, usually served to categorize that stimulus. Total heterosexual response to three of the five female pictures was positive. Total homosexual response to each of the five male pictures was positive. The pictures used in this pilot study were chosen on an a priori basis. The information they have given us and more recent advances in our technique—especially in the matter of brightness matching of pictures—may now permit the formulation of a test battery of pictorial stimuli designed to give a more absolute reflection of a single subject's sex-object interest. It should be emphasized, however, that since *all* subjects in this study saw identical stimuli, the brightness factor could not in any way account for the reported difference between individuals and the resultant groups.

The cooperation of the homosexual subjects, it should be noted, was an unusual relaxation of their customary defense against identification as homosexuals. They were all effectively operating in a normal living environment, in school, at work, with friends. Their sexual preferences were not obvious, and they were ordinarily most reluctant to talk about or reveal them, yet the pupil technique, using a response that is nonverbal and beyond voluntary control, was able to differentiate them from the heterosexual subjects. This is not to say that the pupil response as an index of preference is a predictive substitute for the ultimate criterion of the behavior itself. It does mean that where both preference and behavior are homosexual, even though socially concealed, the pupil response has been shown in this sample to have discriminating power.

Pupil response has already seen application in the area of studies of cognition (Hess and Polt, 1964). In the study of some aspects of personality, compared with projective tests and other instruments and techniques that have been used, this technique appears to us to open up entirely new dimensions.

SUMMARY

The pupil response of each individual in a group of heterosexual males was greater when looking at pictures of women than when looking at pictures of men. Homosexual male S_s responded in the opposite direction. Measurement of changes in pupil size permitted clear-cut discrimination between the 2 groups.

REFERENCES

Hess, E. H., and Polt, J. M. "Pupil size as related to interest value of visual stimuli," *Science*, 1960, **132**, 349–350.

Hess, E. H., and Polt, J. M. "Pupil size in relation to mental activity during simple problem-solving," *Science*, 1964, **143**, 1190–1192.

5.4 Effect of Alcohol on Perceptual Field Dependence

MARIANNE W. KRISTOFFERSON

The association between alcoholism and field-dependent perceptual performance has been established in several studies (Bailey, Hustmeyer, and Kristofferson, 1961; Karp, Poster, and Goodman, 1963; Witkin, Karp, and Goodenough, 1959). Using a special series of perceptual tests, these studies have shown that the performance of alcoholics is strongly dominated by the organization of the prevailing field; that is, their perception is extremely field dependent. This relationship has been interpreted in two ways: (a) prolonged ingestion of alcohol results in the development of a high level of perceptual field dependence; that is, perceptual field dependence is a consequence of drinking, and (b) field dependence, which has been shown to be associated with a whole constellation of personality characteristics (Witkin, Dyk, Faterson, Goodenough, and Karp, 1962; Witkin, Lewis, Hertzman, Machover, Meissner, and Wapner, 1954), is a state which is present prior to the development of alcoholism, and may contribute to the development of that condition.

Investigators who favor the latter interpretation have recently reported on a series of studies of stability of perceptual field dependence during the alcoholic cycle, which were undertaken to provide evidence about the plausibility of the "predisposing" versus the "consequence" hypothesis.

In the first study of this series (Karp, Witkin, and Goodenough, 1965), the effects of acute intoxication of male alcoholic Ss on three tests of field dependence were investigated: (a) the rod-and-frame test (RFT), (b) the body-adjustment test (BAT), and (c) the embedded-figures test (EFT). For two of the tests, the RFT and the BAT, there was found to be no significant effect of alcohol on performance. For the EFT, time required to locate

Reprinted with slight abridgment from the *Journal of Abnormal Psychology*, 1968, **73**, 387–391, with permission of the author and the American Psychological Association, Inc.

a simple figure in the complex design was significantly increased under the influence of alcohol, or, that is, level of field dependence was significantly increased. The authors point out that, unlike the other two tests, the EFT is a speed test in which lapses of concentration or interest result in a more-field-dependent score. They attribute this change to these factors rather than to a change in perception as such.

In the second study, Karp and Konstadt (1965) compared performance of groups of alcoholics differing markedly in length of alcoholic history, in an attempt to determine the effect of length of heavy drinking on field dependence. Length of drinking was found not to affect performance on three tests of field dependence: the BAT, RFT, and EFT. It was noted, however, that field dependence increased with age, and was greater among alcoholics than matched controls at any age.

In the third study of the series, Karp, Witkin, and Goodenough (1966) examined the effect of cessation of drinking upon field dependence. Again using the RFT, BAT, and EFT as tests of dependence, currently drinking alcoholics were compared with alcoholics who had maintained sobriety for a minimum of 15 mo. The drinking and abstaining alcoholics were found not to differ significantly in extent of field dependence.

The results of these studies, together with evidence from studies with non-alcoholic Ss which show measures of field dependence to be highly stable over time (Witkin, et al., 1962) and with changes in psychological state induced by various kinds of drugs (Witkin, et al., 1962), led Karp, et al. (1966) to conclude that:

This evidence of stability of field dependence over various phases of the alcoholismic cycle makes less likely the hypothesis that field dependence is a consequence of alcoholism and to that extent makes the alternative hypothesis of predisposition more plausible. A long-range prediction study in which level of field dependence, determined during early adolescence, is evaluated as a predictor of later alcoholism, thereby becomes more reasonable [p. 584].

Consistent with the interpretation that a high level of field dependence is a consequence of alcoholism is a study by Bailey, Hustmeyer, and Kristofferson (1961). Using RFT performance as a measure of level of field dependence, the following groups were compared in Experiment I: (*a*) hospitalized patients with chronic brain syndromes with psychotic reaction associated with alcoholism, (*b*) members of Alcoholics Anonymous who had abstained for a minimum period of 1 yr., (*c*) a group of college student controls, and (*d*) a group of older controls who were volunteers from the community. The control groups were found not to differ from each other. Both the AA group and the hospitalized alcoholic group were found to be significantly more field dependent than the combined control groups. The hospitalized alcoholics showed greater, but not significantly greater, dependence than the AA group. Three additional groups were run in Experiment II: (*a*) hospitalized patients with diffuse brain damage without a history of alcoholism, (*b*) hospitalized patients diagnosed as psychopathic personality with alcoholism, and (*c*) hospitalized patients diagnosed as paranoid schizophrenics without a history of alcoholism. Brain-damaged patients were found to have a significantly higher level of dependence than the controls, indicating that brain damage without alcoholism is associated with perceptual dependence. The performance of the psychopathic alcoholics was very similar to that of the AA group, and neither of these groups showed a level of field dependence as extreme as the brain-damaged men. The idea that an increase in dependence might be the result of prolonged hospitalization or psychopathology was not supported since the paranoid schizophrenic group did not differ from the control group.

Bailey, et al. (1961) interpreted the results of this study as suggesting that ". . . alcoholism is associated with dependence not because alcoholics are dependent perceivers prior to becoming alcoholics but, rather, that dependence may be the result of an organic impairment produced by drinking [p. 392]."

While most attempts to bring about a change in level of field dependence through the use of various direct experimental means have failed, not all have. Of particular interest is a study by Jacobson (1966) who tried to determine whether brief sensory deprivation would act to decrease perceptual field dependence. Using college students as Ss, the experimental group was given the RFT, followed by 1 hr. of sensory deprivation, and then a repeated test. There was a significant decrease ($p < .01$) in errors (absolute degrees deviation from the true vertical) on the posttest. For the control group, 1 hr. of controlled activity was inserted between the pretest and posttest RFTs. There was no significant change

in performance from the first to the second RFT testing. The difference between the experimental and control groups' mean error reduction was significant at $p < .05$. In the same paper, Jacobson (1966) reported on a preliminary study using alcoholic Ss. Fifteen male alcoholics underwent 1 hr. of modified sensory deprivation following a pretest RFT. A matched control group was allowed an hour of normal activity following the pretest. On posttest measures the experimental group showed a significant ($p < .01$) reduction in RFT errors, while the controls showed a nonsignificant change. The difference between the two groups' change was significant at $p < .05$.

The present study investigated the stability of field dependence, as determined from RFT performance, when alcohol was ingested by nonalcoholic Ss, and was also concerned with the question of whether Ss classified as high and low in level of field dependence on the basis of performance prior to ingestion of alcohol are differentially affected by alcohol.

Witkin, et al. (1962), have reviewed a number of studies in which unsuccessful attempts were made to alter level of field dependence (mainly based on RFT scores) through the use of such drugs as barbiturates, amphetamines, tranquilizers, and antidepressants. While no relationship has been reported between prolonged use of any of the above-mentioned drugs and level of field dependence, it is known that prolonged and heavy ingestion of alcohol is associated with a high level of field dependence, and thus it seems possible that alcohol might have an effect even though other drugs do not.

The "consequence" hypothesis remains tenable, if it can be shown that for nonalcoholic Ss an increase in field dependence follows ingestion of alcohol, and, further, that this increase is maintained in the sober as well as in the inebriated state by the time the individual can be designated as an alcoholic. This study dealt with the first requirement of the "consequence" hypothesis.

METHOD

Subjects

The S group was composed of 48 volunteer male McMaster University students, 21 or more yr. old. All Ss had had some drinking experience and none were chronic heavy drinkers. They were paid for participating in the experiment. The Ss were asked not to consume any alcohol for a 24-hr. period preceding their appointment, and to fast for the 9 hr. immediately before the testing period, which began at approximately 9:00 A.M.

Test and Apparatus

The rod-and-frame test (RFT) is conducted in a totally darkened room. The S, sitting upright or tilted, can see only a luminous frame. The rod and frame are in tilted positions. The S must adjust the rod to a position he perceives as upright while the frame remains tilted. The S's score is the total, for the 24 trials comprising the test, of the absolute degrees of deviation of the rod from the true vertical. Larger scores reflect greater field dependence.

The physical aspects of the experimental situation, the instructions to Ss, the order of administration of the test trials, and the testing procedure, were in all essential respects like those described

by Witkin (1948). A commercially produced rod-and-frame apparatus (Polymetric Company, Model V-1260) was modified to allow for remote control by S of the movement of the rod in three degree steps.

Blood alcohol levels were measured using a Breathalyzer, Model 900, Stephenson Corporation.

All Ss were tested individually by the same E. An equal number of Ss were randomly assigned to the experimental (Alcohol) and the control (No Alcohol) groups. The S was given a pretest RFT. Immediately after the completion of the pretest, S was instructed on the use of the Breathalyzer, and a breath sample was taken and analyzed to rule out the possibility of the presence of alcohol in the blood before administration of the drink. The S was then asked to leave the room while his drink was being prepared. The bottle labeled "absolute alcohol" was left in plain view when S returned. No information was given S about the quantity of alcohol administered and he was not allowed to see the subsequent Breathalyzer readings. The 24 Ss assigned to the experimental group were given a drink consisting of 1 cc of absolute alcohol per kg. of body weight, mixed with 3 cc of grapefruit and orange juice per kg. of body weight. For the control group the drink consisted of 3 cc of grapefruit and orange juice per kg. of body weight, and the rim of the glass was rubbed with alcohol.[1] One hour after initiation of drinking, S was again given the RFT. Blood alcohol level readings were taken immediately before and after

---

[1] This technique was employed in an attempt to minimize the differences between experimental and control groups; however, it is not suggested that a complete placebo condition was obtained.

the second RFT administration. The average blood alcohol level obtained from these two measures for the Alcohol group was .08, and varied from .062 to .097 among Ss. For the No Alcohol group, Breathalyzer readings of .00 blood alcohol were always obtained from every S.

RESULTS

The Alcohol and No Alcohol groups were compared on pretest RFT performance and were found not to differ significantly in means ($t = .30, p > .10$) or variances ($F = 1.06, p > .10$) of total degrees deviation from the vertical. The Alcohol group had a mean of 234.75° deviation and an SD of 98.51; for the No Alcohol group these values were 243.42 and 95.59°, respectively.

On post-test measures, the Alcohol group showed a mean increase in total degrees of deviation from the vertical of 45.13°, which was significantly different from pretest performance at $p < .01$ ($t = 3.43$). The No Alcohol group showed a mean reduction of 4.83°, a nonsignificant change ($t = .39, p > .70$). The difference between the two groups' change scores was significant at $p < .01$ ($t = 2.79$). The SDs on the post-test were only slightly larger than on the pretest, the increase being 11.6° for the No Alcohol group, and 11.7° for the Alcohol group. The interaction between level of field dependence on the pretest and degree of change on the post-test following ingestion of alcohol was found not to be significant ($F = .0153$). A high degree of correlation was found between pretest and post-test performance. For the Alcohol group, $r = .82$; for the No Alcohol group, $r = .84$.

DISCUSSION AND CONCLUSIONS

The significant difference in RFT change scores when the Alcohol and No Alcohol groups were compared; the significant increase in total degrees deviation by the Alcohol group on the RFT post-test; and the finding that the No Alcohol group showed no significant change in RFT performance on the post-test, lead to the conclusion that, for nonalcoholic Ss, ingestion of a moderate amount of alcohol results in significantly increasing field-dependent performance. Further, the lack of a significant interaction between pretest level of field dependence and change scores for the Alcohol group suggests that the increase in field dependence following alcohol ingestion does not differentially affect Ss classified prior to the administration of alcohol as high and low in field dependence.

The results of this study make the "consequence" hypothesis a more feasible interpretation of the known relationship between alcoholism and field dependence than previous research has indicated, in that they demonstrate one crucial step required by the "consequence" hypothesis to show the development of this relationship.

Nor do the results of the Karp, *et al.* (1965, 1966), and Karp and Konstadt (1965) studies with alcoholics seem incompatible with the "consequence" hypothesis. Assuming that the high level of dependence found in alcoholics is a consequence of alcoholism, it seems not unreasonable that the effects of prolonged ingestion of alcohol become stabilized over a period of time, and that the level of field dependence would be both high and invariant by the time an individual can be classified as an alcoholic whether alcohol was or was not ingested prior to measurement and whether S was an active alcoholic or one who had maintained sobriety for some period of time.

On the other hand, the present study shows that field dependence is unstable in the sense that it can be changed by alcohol. This does not rule out the possibility that a high level of field dependence predisposes one to alcoholism. This study suggests that if persons with various levels of field dependence prior to drinking were to become alcoholics, they would attain a high level of field dependence as a consequence of alcoholism. However, it may be that only, or mainly, individuals with a high prealcoholic level of field dependence and the personality characteristics associated with it become alcoholic.

These differing interpretations of the present experiment and those reported previously can only remain speculative until a definitive longitudinal study is carried out.

SUMMARY

The stability of perceptual field dependence, as determined from rod-and-frame test (RFT) performance, when alcohol is ingested by nonalcoholic Ss was investigated. Ss randomly assigned to the experimental (Alcohol) and the control (No Alcohol) groups were found not to differ significantly on pretest RFT scores. A significant increase in perceptual field dependence occurred on the post-test for the Alcohol group, while the No Alcohol group showed no significant change. The difference between the change scores for the two groups was significant at $p < .01$. Further analysis revealed that the noted increase in field dependence following alcohol ingestion does not differentially affect Ss classified prior to the administration of alcohol as high or low in field dependence. The relevance of these results to the "consequence" and "predisposition" interpretations of the known relationship between alcoholism and field dependence is discussed.

REFERENCES

Bailey, W., Hustmeyer, F., and Kristofferson, A. B. "Alcoholism, brain damage and perceptual dependence," *Quarterly Journal of Studies in Alcoholism*, 1961, **22**, 387–393.

Jacobson, G. R. "Effect of brief sensory deprivation on field dependence," *Journal of Abnormal Psychology*, 1966, **71**, 115–118.

Karp, S. A., and Konstadt, N. L. "Alcoholism and psychological differentiation: Long-range effect of heavy drinking on field dependence," *Journal of Nervous and Mental Disease*, 1965, **140**, 412–416.

Karp, S. A., Poster, D. C., and Goodman, A. "Differentiation in alcoholic women," *Journal of Personality*, 1963, **31**, 386–393.

Karp, S. A., Witkin, H. A., and Goodenough, D. R. "Alcoholism and psychological differentiation: Effect of alcohol on field dependence," *Journal of Abnormal Psychology*, 1965, **70**, 262–265.

Karp, S. A., Witkin, H. A., and Goodenough, D. R. "Alcoholism and psychological differentiation: Effect of achievement of sobriety on field dependence," *Quarterly Journal of Studies in Alcoholism*, 1966, **27**, 580–585.

Witkin, H. A. The effect of training and of structural aids on performance in three tests of space orientation. Civil Aeronautics Administration, Division of Research, Report No. 80, Washington, D. C., 1948.

Witkin, H. A., Dyk, R. B., Faterson, H. F., Goodenough, D. R., and Karp, S. A. *Psychological Differentiation*. New York: Wiley, 1962.

Witkin, H. A., Karp, S. A., and Goodenough, D. R. "Dependence in alcoholics." *Quarterly Journal of Studies in Alcoholism*, 1959, **20**, 493–504.

Witkin, H. A., Lewis, H. B., Hertzman, M., Machover, K., Meissner, P. B., and Wapner, S. *Personality through Perception*. New York: Harper, 1954.

SECTION 6

MOTIVATION AND EMOTION

This section begins with a discussion of the hunger drive in man, a survey that draws upon research with both human and animal subjects, with particular reference to the findings of recent studies. The author, Eliot Stellar of the University of Pennsylvania, approaches the topic primarily from the standpoint of the physiological mechanisms involved.

The topic of motivation in psychology has almost from the beginning been concerned with the physiological aspects of such drives as hunger, thirst, and sex, but in recent years personality psychologists have been active in the field as well, focusing their efforts primarily on what are termed secondary drives or motives. David C. McClelland of Harvard University has become particularly well known for his work with the need for achievement, although his initial research in the field of motivation was concerned with the hunger drive as reflected in projective techniques. Although projective tests of personality have been used extensively in psychodiagnostics, McClelland and his coworkers have shown that these tests can be used to measure both primary and secondary drives as well. In the second paper in this section, McClelland discusses the way in which motives are acquired, with particular reference to n Achievement, or the motive to achieve.

In the third selection, P. O. Davidson of the University of Calgary describes an experiment in which subjects who had knowledge of a simulated crime were tested on a polygraph, an instrument used to record changes in changes in body state in stress situations. The dependent variable used in this study was galvanic skin response (GSR), a measure of the electrical conductivity of the skin. Results showed that all of the subjects classified by the GSR index as "innocent" were in fact innocent, while 92 percent of those classified as "guilty" were in fact guilty. The research shows how affective or emotional states, which are usually thought of as being primarily "psychological," also have their physiological components. The human organism functions as a whole and not as a separate "mind" and "body."

6.1 Hunger in Man: Comparative and Physiological Studies

ELIOT STELLAR

The great pleasure in having to give the Eastern Psychological Association Presidential Address is that it makes you look back over your work and see where you started, where you have gotten, and where you are going. As many of you know, the main work in our laboratory over the years has been the study of the neurological and physiological basis of feeding and drinking in animals. Out of this work, we have gained a conception of how the many factors controlling these behaviors go together in a regulatory mechanism. And now in a true comparative psychology, we have gone on to the study of man, armed with the concepts and techniques derived from the animal investigations.

Historically, our scientific conceptions of hunger, food intake, and food motivation were derived from questions arising in the experiences and introspections of man. Yet it is a surprising thing that in the many, many investigations of hunger in man, no one has bothered to measure his food intake objectively in an experimental situation. This is all the more striking in view of the great behavioristic tradition of psychology and in view of the fact that the study of food intake in animals has made such great headway.

First, I want to tell you about the animal studies done in our laboratory. Then I want to tell you about our recent experiments on man.

Figure 1 shows, in schematic form, the mechanism we envisioned in 1954 (Stellar), as the controlling mechanism of hunger and other kinds of motivated behaviors. It is gratifying that it still serves us well today. There are two main points to be derived from this diagram. First, hunger and feeding are under multifactor control. Many sensory factors, both learned and unlearned, contribute,

Reprinted with slight abridgment from the *American Psychologist*, 1967, **22**, 105–117, with permission of the author and the American Psychological Association, Inc.

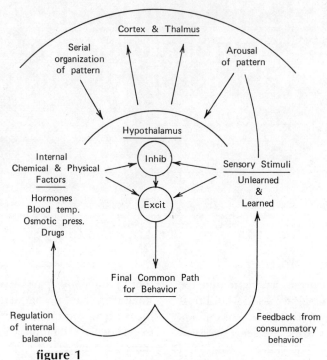

figure 1

Schematic diagram of the physiological factors controlling motivated behavior (Stellar, 1954).

in an additive way, to the arousal of hunger and to the development of satiation: taste, smell, gastric contractions, and gastric distension, to name some major ones. Added to these are powerful influences from the internal environment, including both osmotic and specific chemical changes. The second main point is that all of these factors are integrated in the central nervous system, particularly in the hypothalamus, where there are both excitatory and inhibitory mechanisms controlling food intake and hunger motivation.

Many of the investigations in our laboratory have been concerned with verifying the existence of these excitatory and inhibitory mechanisms and we have tried to specify their characteristics by appropriate lesions and brain stimulation techniques. But I do not want to talk about these today. Rather, I want to describe to you our attempts to uncover the major factors controlling feeding and drinking and to learn how they work together to yield the behavior we can measure in the laboratory. The design of these investigations is shown in Figure 2. The heavy, solid arrows show the normal sequence of ingestion and indicate the controlling factors that are brought into play at the oropharyngeal, gastric, postabsorptive, and central-nervous-system levels. The other arrows, entering the sequence at various levels, show the spirit of the experiments we have undertaken in our efforts to separate the contribution of different factors, operating at different levels in the sequence.

But first, let me show you the basic ingestion behavior we are measuring. This is illustrated in Figure 3 where the drinking of the rat is shown as a function of different degrees of deprivation (Stellar and Hill, 1952). The story is much the same with feeding behavior, but we can record drinking much more sensitively by use of the drinkometer. With this device, the rat's tongue completes an electronic circuit with each lap of the water and chalks up a count. Calibration shows that the rat gets .003 cubic centimeter of water with each lap and that its tongue laps at a constant rate of 6–7

per second whenever it drinks. Inspection of the record shows that the rat drinks in bursts and rests. When the animal is thirsty, the bursts of drinking are long and the rests are short, and as the animal satiates, the bursts are very brief and the rests very long.

With this type of measurement situation, one of the first things we did was to determine the effects of putting various pure foods in solution at different concentrations. We thought we were varying primarily taste, but it turned out to be more complicated than that. The response of rats to different concentrations of sodium chloride solutions is seen in the preference-aversion function shown in Figure 4 (Weiner and Stellar, 1951). These values are based on 1-hour drinking tests, following 15 hours of thirst, where the animals have access to

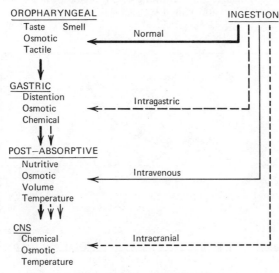

figure 2

The plan of investigations, designed to analyze the contribution to feeding behavior of different factors operating at various levels of the ingestion pathway.

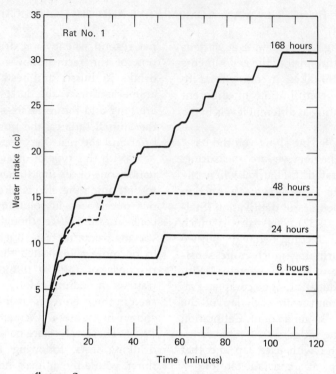

figure 3

The pattern of ingestion; drinking as a function of deprivation in the rat (Stellar and Hill, 1952).

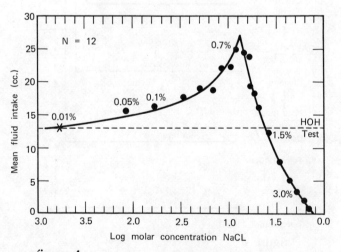

figure 4

Preference-aversion function for NaCl in the rat (Stellar, Hyman, and Samet, 1954).

just one solution a day. Peak intake or peak preference is around isotonic concentration (.9%). The same data are plotted as cumulative intake curves in Figure 5, and show that the rats commit themselves to higher or lower rates of drinking within the first few minutes of the 1-hour test. Because the effect of concentration on drinking was so rapid, we felt confident that it was all a matter of positive and negative tastes.

We were wrong, as data from Robert McCleary's thesis on sugar preference illustrate. In Figure 6, we see the same type of preference-aversion curve for glucose and fructose, with peak intake around the isotonic concentration (McCleary, 1953). The aversion limb of the curve, over the hypertonic solutions, is hard to explain as just negative taste since rats will work hard for hypertonic sugars. It turns out that there is a nega-

tive postingestional factor as Figure 7 demonstrates. Here the rats are intubated with 3 cubic centimeters of isotonic and hypertonic glucose solutions before the test and it makes a big difference in their drinking. Gastric loads of hypertonic glucose increase water drinking and decrease the drinking of hypertonic glucose, and these effects are also produced within the first few minutes of drinking. This is an osmotic effect and is independent of the stomach itself as Figure 8 shows. These data are on the rabbit, given intravenous loads of 3% NaCl just before drinking, and quite clearly the same effects are produced. So there is a prompt postingestional effect of drinking hypertonic solutions which inhibits further drinking of hypertonic solutions. This is an osmotic effect caused by pulling water into the stomach from other tissues or by adding electrolyte to

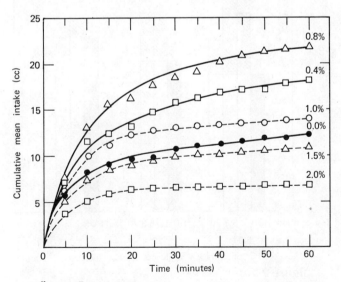

figure 5

Cumulative intake of different concentrations of NaCl (Weiner and Stellar, 1951).

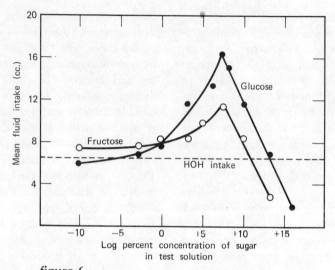

figure 6

Preference–aversion functions for glucose and fructose in the rat (McCleary, 1953).

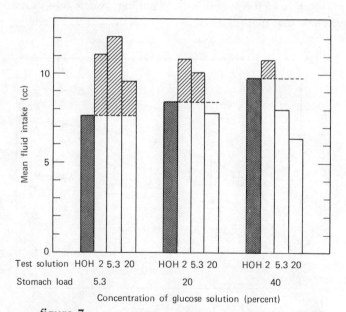

figure 7

Effect of isotonic and hypertonic gastric loads on the drinking of different concentrations of glucose in the rat (McCleary, 1953).

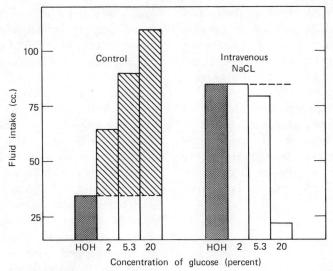

figure 8

Effect of intravenous injections of NaCl on the glucose ingestion of the rabbit (McCleary, 1953).

the blood. Similar dehydration by simple water deprivation will produce the same effects.

Yet preference-aversion functions can be a matter of taste as Figure 9 shows is the case with saccharine drinking (Stellar, 1960). Here is the same rising and falling function, but isotonic con-

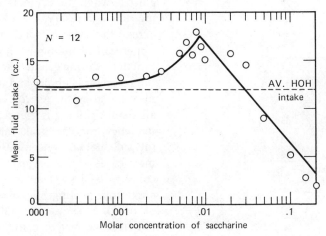

figure 9

Preference–aversion function for saccharine in the rat (Stellar, 1960).

centration is way out at the bottom of the aversion limb (arrow). In keeping with this notion, operant conditioning studies show that the low concentrations are positively reinforcing and the higher concentrations are aversive.

By far the clearest separation of the roles of oral and postingestional factors comes from the work of Douglas Mook (1963) who investigated the rat with the esophageal fistula (Figure 10). In this preparation, the esophagus is severed

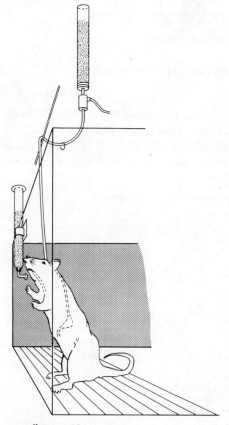

figure 10
Arrangement for testing ingestion in the rat with an esophageal fistula (Mook, 1963).

and brought out at the neck so that everything the animal takes from the drinking tube flows out of the fistula. A polyethylene tube is inserted into the stomach through the lower end of the esophagus and the other end is mounted on the skull so that it can be attached to a polyvinylchloride tube connected through a solenoid valve to another overhead reservoir. Every time the rat laps from the drinking tube, it completes a drinkometer circuit and the set-up is arranged so that the solenoid valve opens every 20 laps and delivers to the stomach an equivalent volume of water. Thus the rat is equipped with an "electronic esophagus" and can drink normally in the sense that fluid enters the stomach in perfect synchrony with the animal's drinking. By varying the contents of the drinking tube and the reservoir independently, some beautiful experiments can be done.

The lower part of Figure 11 shows normal preference-aversion curves for glucose when the contents of the drinking tube and reservoir are kept the same across the various concentrations. The upper part of the figure shows the same functions during "sham" drinking, when the reservoir is empty and nothing flows into the stomach. As you might expect, all sham drinking is elevated; there is a tendency for the peak intake to shift toward higher concentrations, and in most cases, for the aversion limb of the curve to be less steep than when there are normal postingestional consequences of drinking. The same results have been obtained with sucrose and sodium chloride preference-aversion functions.

In another experiment, the system is set up so that the animal drinks the

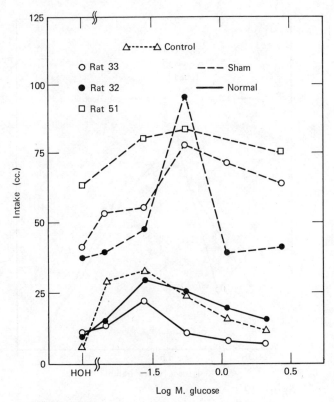

figure 11

Normal and sham drinking of glucose solutions by the rat with an esophageal fistula (Mook, 1963).

various concentrations of sodium chloride, but obtains in the stomach osmotically matched concentrations of glucose. The results show that the fistulated rat drinks the same amount of sodium chloride as it does when it is receiving the same concentration of sodium chloride in its stomach (Figure 12). Thus, under these experimental conditions, the rat is indifferent to specific chemical effects in the stomach, but rather regulates its drinking in terms of postingestional osmotic effects. The reverse experiment, where the animal drinks glucose and is loaded with sodium chloride solutions, works equally well.

Perhaps the most potent experiment of all is the one in which the fistulated rat is allowed to drink the various concentrations of sodium chloride, glucose, and sucrose, and in each case, receives plain water in its stomach. In this way, it is possible to determine the animal's oral responses to the various concentrations of these substances when there are no unfavorable, osmotic postingestional effects and its hydrational needs are cared for during the drinking test.

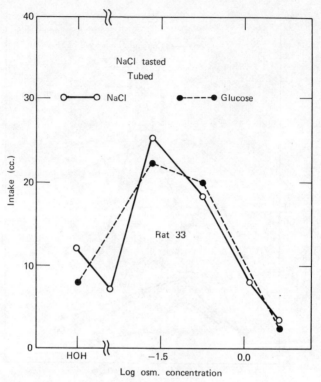

figure 12

The fistulated rat drinking NaCl solution and getting either the same NaCl or osmotically matched glucose in the stomach (Mook, 1963).

The results are amazing (Figure 13). The preference for sodium chloride completely disappears and only the aversion limb remains. The preference for hypotonic glucose solutions also essentially disappears, but in this case, there is an increasing intake of the hypertonic solutions. Under these conditions, sucrose drinking is a positive, negatively accelerated function of concentration.

The implication of these findings is that, once hydrational needs are cared for by letting water flow into the stomach, drinking of the various concentrations is almost completely regulated by oral fac-

tors, particularly taste. In fact, it is quite striking that Hagstrom and Pfaffmann (1959), recording from the chorda tympani nerve of the rat, found essentially the same kind of positively accelerated function for glucose and negatively accelerated function for sucrose over the same range of concentrations.

In the light of these findings, how do we account for the preference for hypotonic sodium chloride and glucose solutions in the normal rat? Here we can borrow the concept of "dilute water" from Deutsch (Deutsch and Jones, 1960). As the thirsty rat encounters these hypotonic solutions in increasing concentration, it has to take more and more solute with its fluid and thus adds to its hydrational needs as it tries to solve them. So it must drink more and more, the more solute there is. Hence the rising preference limb. It is clearly not a matter of taste. It is an osmotic matter, clearly postingestional. But there may also be an oral osmotic mechanism as the presence of the preference limb during sham drinking suggests (Figure 11). Yet the postingestional mechanism must be the

stronger of the two, witness the elimination of the preference limb when hydrational needs are met by letting water flow into the stomach.

Thus it appears that the simple preference-aversion function is complicated indeed. It may be a matter of positive and negative taste as in the case of saccharine; or positive taste as in the preference limb of sucrose; or negative taste as in the aversion limb of sodium chloride. Clearly, the preference limbs for sodium chloride and glucose repre-

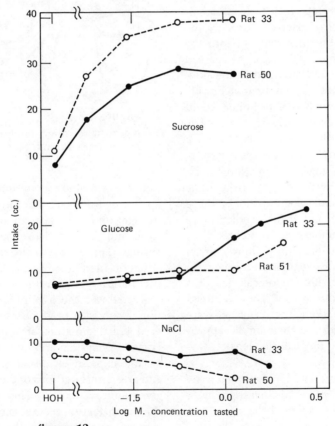

figure 13
The fistulated rat drinking NaCl, glucose, and sucrose solutions when only water reaches the stomach (Mook, 1963).

sent the operation of an osmotic mechanism, probably a "dilute water" mechanism, partly oral, but mostly postingestional. The aversion limbs of sodium chloride, glucose, and sucrose all have a major osmotic mechanism, related to the effects of hypertonic solutions in the stomach, presumably their property of pulling water into the stomach and thus transiently dehydrating the animal.

Similar approaches have been taken by Alan Epstein and Philip Teitelbaum (1962) in the effort to separate oral and postingestional factors. In this case, they prepared their rats with indwelling intragastric tubes, inserted through the nares, down the pharynx and into the stomach. The other end was passed under the skin and mounted on the skull for attachment by polyvinylchloride tubing to a pump which the animal could operate by pressing a lever (Figure 14). So equipped, the rat could feed itself a liquid diet intragastrically, thus bypassing all oropharyngeal stimulation and all chewing and swallowing. On the basis of postingestional factors alone, these rats could eat and drink, taking more when motivation was high and less when it was low. In fact, they showed even more remarkable regulation by their response to the dilution of calories of a liquid diet with water. They doubled their intake when the calories were halved and reduced their intake appropriately when the caloric density was restored.

A still further step was taken by John Corbit (1965) in his investigation of the drinking behavior of the rat with a chronic intravenous catheter. In this preparation, a fine polyethylene or silastic tube was passed into the external

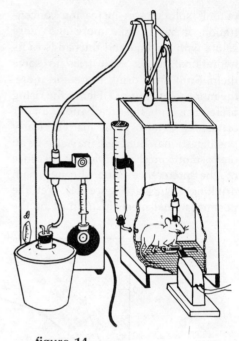

figure 14

Arrangement for direct intragastric feeding in the rat (Epstein and Teitelbaum, 1962).

jugular vein and down into the right atrium of the heart. The other end was brought under the skin, mounted on the skull and connected to a motor-driven syringe (Figure 15). In the experimental situation the animal was first trained to press a lever to activate a syringe which delivered water into a cup for oral ingestion. Then each press of the lever delivered equal amounts of water into the circulatory system and into the cup, and as the experiment progressed, greater and greater proportions of the water were given intravenously. The results are shown in Figure 16. As long as it was getting some oral water, the animal regulated perfectly. Without oral water, it extinguished. That this was not simply

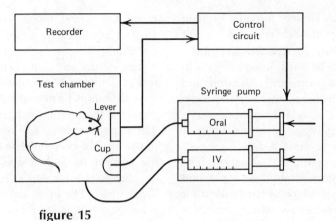

figure 15

Arrangement for intravenous and oral feeding in the rat (Corbit, 1965).

a volume effect was seen in the remarkable result obtained when isotonic saline was used for intravenous injection. Even at unfavorable ratios, the animal took its regular amount of water orally, thereby loading its circulatory system with several times the rat's blood volume in a 1-hour period.

That is an outline of our major findings with animals. Now I would like to tell you about comparable experiments in man. These were done with the col-

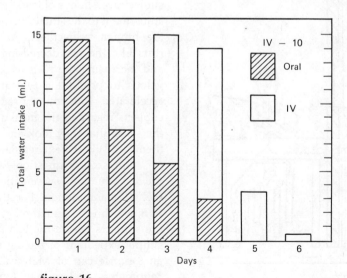

figure 16

Regulation of water intake when more and more of it is "ingested" intravenously (Corbit, 1965).

laboration of Henry Jordan, William Wieland, Susan Zebley, and Albert Stunkard (1966). As I said at the outset, our effort was to put human subjects in a rat-style experimental situation and measure their food intake objectively. This means a standard environment, a standard, single-food diet, and a standard, single, test meal a day. Figure 17 shows the experimental situation. The subject sits comfortably in a pleasant room at a table which is bare except for a stainless steel straw which protrudes at a 50° angle. The straw is connected by Tygon tubing beneath the table to a 1,000-cubic centimeter graduated burette which is out of sight of the subject. With the burette at the right height the liquid diet fills the straw and may be sucked as anyone would suck a milkshake. Be-

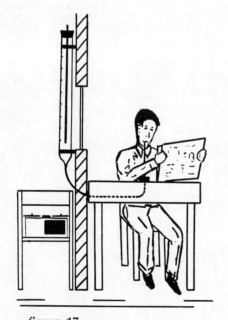

figure 17

Arrangement for objective measurement of food intake in man.

cause it is so well quality controlled and so well specified, we used Metrecal as our diet, giving the subject a choice between vanilla and Dutch chocolate. The test meals were 20 minutes long, and we gave the subject a newspaper to read and provided him with background music. The experimenter read the level of diet in the burette every minute and watched the subject through a one-way screen.

Subjects were run at breakfast and lunch times. The breakfast subjects were asked not to eat after midnight and to refrain from eating after the test meal until their normal lunchtime. The lunch subjects ate a normal breakfast, fasted until the test meal and then did not eat again until their regular dinnertime. Our first question was whether we could obtain reliable day-to-day ingestion patterns from human subjects. The answer, a clear "yes," is shown in Figure 18. Here are plotted the cumulative intakes of one subject over 4 days of testing, after initial adjustment to the situation. Quite clearly, the human subject eats in bursts and rests like the rat, decreasing the bursts and increasing the rests as satiation develops to produce a typical negatively accelerated function. In addition, the subjects regarded the meal as a meal in the sense that they took enough to hold them until their next regular meal.

Our second question was whether the test situation was sensitive to experimental manipulation. For this exploration, we chose the method of preloading the subjects before the test meal by the simple expedient of having them down an 8-ounce can of Metrecal (235 cubic centimeters) in less than 1 minute. The experiment then consisted of making them wait from 1 minute to 1 hour before

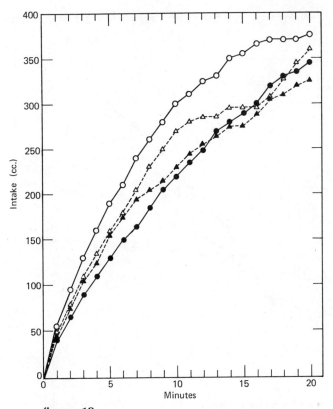

figure 18
Reliability of ingestion patterns of man, shown in 4 successive days of drinking Metrecal.

taking the test meal through the straw. As Figure 19 indicates, the experiment was a success, for the interval made a big difference, and not in any simple pattern the subjects might have figured out.

In all of our tests, we always asked the subject to estimate how much he had eaten. We did this by simply showing him an 8-ounce glass and asking him to say how many glasses he had drunk. With no visual cues or cues from hefting a glass, the subjects were very poor at this. Some consistently overestimated

and some underestimated (Figure 20) and none correlated well with their actual intake on a day-to-day basis, provided we did not give them knowledge of results. If we told the subject how much he drank each day, his estimates became very accurate (Figure 21). But even so, if we then withheld this information, the subject lost his anchor points, lost his confidence, and lost his accuracy.

On the other hand, the subjects were quite good at rating their hunger reduction during the test meal. Before the test and at 5-minute intervals throughout the

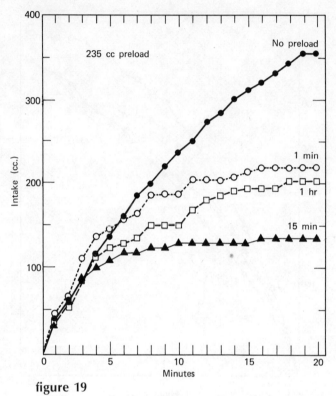

figure 19

Effect of 8-ounce preloads of Metrecal at different times before eating.

test, we asked the subjects to mark a "hunger-rating" scale which ranged from "not hungry" to "the hungriest ever," with "moderately hungry" in the middle and "slightly hungry" and "very hungry" on either side of the middle. The results are plotted in Figure 22, along with the subject's minute-to-minute intake. With a preload, the subject's initial rating was greatly reduced, and the hunger rating appropriately fell to the bottom of the scale when eating stopped after 10 minutes. We ran the correlation between hunger rating and eating in the next 5 minutes and obtained values in the 80s

in all our subjects, a very gratifying validation of our hunger rating scale against the meaningful, objective criterion of eating behavior.

With confidence in our experimental method, we then ran a group of 10 subjects on the preloading experiment and found that most of them showed maximal depression when made to wait somewhere between 15 and 30 minutes between the loading and the testing. Two subjects showed maximal depression at 1 minute and 1 remained depressed out to an hour. Water preloads had minimal effects, which were usually over with by

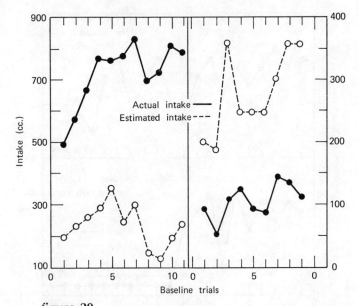

figure 20

Inability of subjects to estimate their intake in the experimental eating tests without knowledge of results.

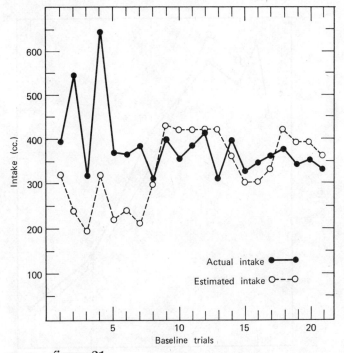

figure 21

Development of ability to estimate intake when knowledge of results is given.

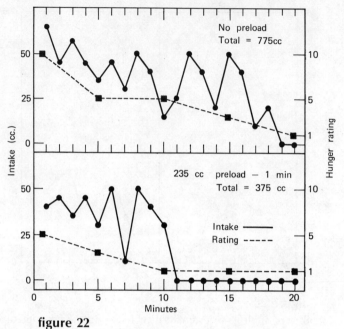

figure 22

Hunger ratings and food intake during a 20-minute test meal.

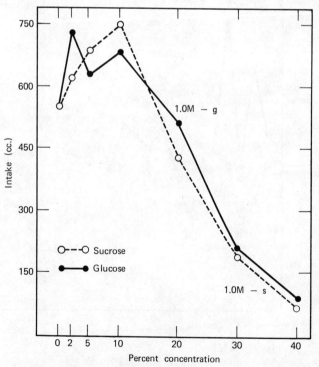

figure 23

Preference–aversion functions for glucose and sucrose in man.

15 minutes. Distension per se, thus, does not seem to be a major factor; undoubtedly gastric emptying time is. Perhaps the most striking thing about the preloading experiment is the fact that all subjects overate and thus did not take the preload fully into account in their regulation. This finding suggests the idea that the regulatory mechanism may not be able to meter adequately the rapid ingestion involved in preloading.

A second main area in our investigations was to explore the preference-aversion functions that have served us so well in the study of the rat. For this purpose, we used a 10-minute test period in the middle and late morning, asking the subjects to neither eat nor drink after breakfast. The familiar rising and falling preference-aversion functions for glucose and sucrose may be seen in Figure 23. Here the human subject's report of his experience is of interest, particularly at the higher concentrations. By 20% concentration, the sugars became too sweet, sticky, and dehydrating. By 40%, they were almost sickening, producing a burning sensation in the mouth, and made the subjects want water. Here also the phylogenetic comparisons are of great interest, for not only do the human curves look like those of the rat and

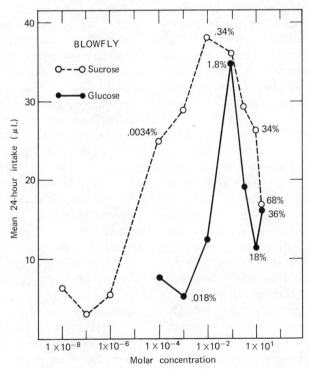

figure 24

Preference–aversion functions for glucose and sucrose in the blowfly (Dethier and Rhoades, 1954).

rabbit, but they have the same shape as in the blowfly, although the magnitudes are quite different (Figure 24, Dethier and Rhoades, 1954).

Data collected thus far on sucrose, saccharine, and sucaryl are plotted in Figures 25, 26, and 27 as cumulative curves. They bear a striking resemblence to the same plots for the rat, particularly in the fact that the human subject also commits himself in the first few minutes of drinking to a high rate of drinking for preferred concentrations and a low rate for aversive concentrations. Unlike the rat, the human subject does not seem to prefer saccharine in water to plain water, for the saccharine has a bitter as well as a sweet component even at the lowest discriminable concentrations. Sucaryl has no noticeable bitter component and yields an excellent preference-aversion function. The aversive concentrations are simply too sweet. Thus sucaryl appears to be the ideal nonnutritive substance to use with man.

The final study I want to talk about is the most exciting to date, for it represents the first successful attempt to investigate direct intragastric feeding in man. The technique is simple. A gastric tube is passed through the nose of a well-paid, volunteer subject, down the pharynx and into the stomach. Then the subject simply presses a button to operate a pump that will deliver Metrecal directly into the stomach.

Our first pilot subject had been in the previous preloading experiment, sucking through the straw. Then we trained him to use the pump to deliver food into his mouth through a curved adaptor placed on the end of the stainless steel straw. The pump delivered Metrecal at 100 cubic centimeters per minute which approximated the subject's maximal rate of extended sucking. The system was set so that the pump delivered as long as the button was held down. Figure 28 shows the comparison of the three methods of ingestion. The curve for oral sucking is the lowest and the steadiest, probably because the subject was limited in his rate of ingestion because of the effort factor. The oral ingestion with the pump and the intragastric ingestion are remarkably similar, not only in the amount ingested but in the shape of the curve.

Despite this marked similarity in ingestion, the effects of oral and intragastric feeding on the hunger ratings were quite different (Figure 29). Understandably, the hunger rating was somewhat lowered with the gastric tube in place before the start of the test. But what is remarkable is that the hunger rating was not reduced as much with intragastric ingestion as with oral ingestion. The oral factor clearly plays an important role in subjective satiation and the suggestion is that the regulation of food intake and the experience of hunger or satiation may be partially dissociated in intragastric feeding. In the same vein, it is interesting to note that the subject was willing to make estimates of his intake after oral ingestion, but felt completely at a loss after intragastric ingestion.

The experiment is summarized in Figure 30. After 6 days of steady baseline oral intake with the pump delivering 100 cubic centimeters per minute, the subject is switched to intragastric feeding. Intake is depressed for 2 days of adjustment, but then reaches the same steady baseline that was obtained with oral feeding.

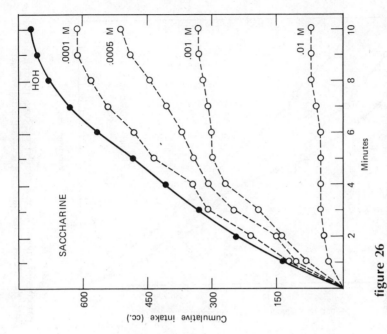

figure 26

Cumulative intake of different concentrations of saccharine in man.

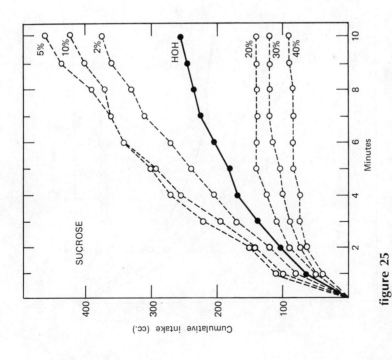

figure 25

Cumulative intake of different concentrations of sucrose in man.

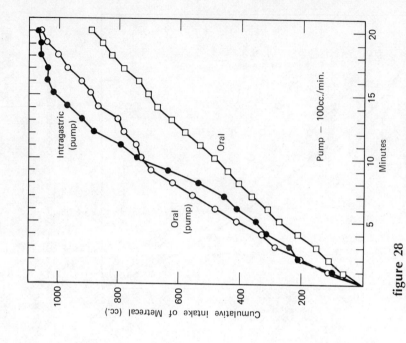

figure 28

Patterns of ingestion of a subject sucking, pumping food into the mouth, and pumping food into the stomach.

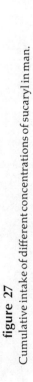

figure 27

Cumulative intake of different concentrations of sucaryl in man.

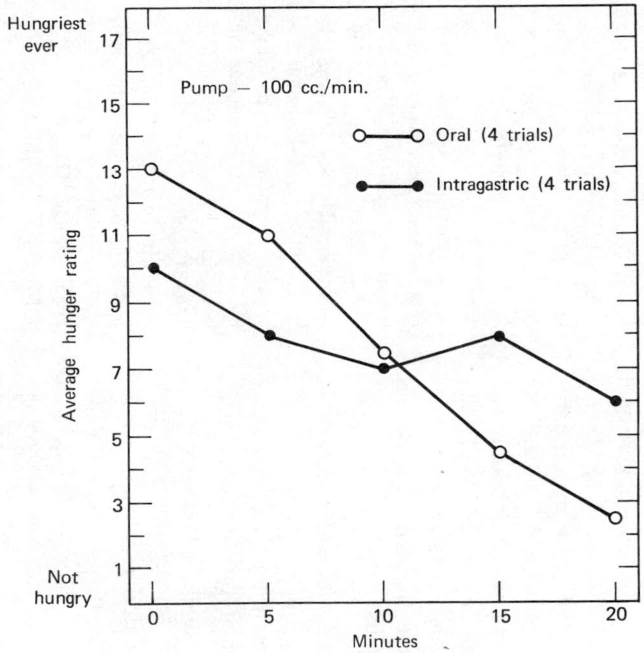

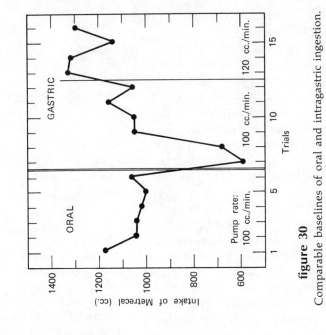

figure 30

Comparable baselines of oral and intragastric ingestion.

figure 29

Hunger ratings during oral and intragastric ingestion.

At this point, by accident the delivery of the pump rose to 120 cubic centimeters per minute, and the subject's intragastric intake went up still further. So again, rate of ingestion seems to be a factor in determining the amount of ingestion.

We want to test more subjects in intragastric feeding. More than that, we want to take advantage of the fact that the human subject, like the rat, can ingest orally with the intragastric tube in place. This then allows us to do some powerful experiments with two pumps, delivering orally and intragastrically synchronously. Will the subject regulate food intake orally when some or most of the Metrecal is delivered intragastrically? What will happen to regulation if water or diluted Metrecal is delivered intragastrically while the subject is drinking full-strength Metrecal orally? Can we do the same experiments with the preference-aversion functions as we have done with the rat and separate oral and postingestional factors, taste, and osmotic factors?

Can we do the same experiments with intravenous infusion? Probably we should begin with water drinking and water and saline injections. Will man regulate as well as the rat?

Let me leave these questions and draw some conclusions.

1. We can study feeding behavior in man objectively.

2. In our experimental situation, we can reduce human feeding to a basic, physiological, regulatory response.

3. Man is a superb physiological preparation, and under the right conditions permits the use of experimental manipulations.

4. The study of man also gives us access to the whole subjective side of hunger, with validation in actual food intake.

5. Finally, hunger and thirst are under the control of a number of physiological factors, contributing to a central neural integrating mechanism that yields the physiological regulation, the motivational control, and perhaps also the subjective experience.

REFERENCES

Corbit, J. D. "Effect of intravenous sodium chloride on drinking in the rat," *Journal of Comparative and Physiological Psychology*, 1965, **60**, 397–406.

Dethier, V. G., and Rhoades, M. V. "Sugar preference-aversion functions for the blowfly," *Journal of Experimental Zoology*, 1954, **126**, 177–204.

Deutsch, J. A., and Jones, A. D. "Diluted water: An explanation of the rat's preference for saline," *Journal of Comparative and Physiological Psychology*, 1960, **53**, 122–127.

Epstein, A. N., and Teitelbaum, P. "Regulation of food intake in the absence of taste, smell, and other oropharyngeal sensations," *Journal of Comparative and Physiological Psychology*, 1962, **55**, 753–759.

Hagstrom, E. C., and Pfaffman, C. "The relative taste effectiveness of different sugars for the rat," *Journal of Comparative and Physiological Psychology*, 1959, **52**, 259–262.

Jordan, H. A., Weiland, W. F., Zebley, S. P., Stellar, E., and Stunkard, A. J. "The direct measurement of food intake in man: A method for the objective study of eating behavior," *Psychosomatic Medicine*, 1966, **28**, 836–842.

McCleary, R. A. "Taste and postingestion factors in specific-hunger behavior," *Journal of Comparative and Physiological Psychology*, 1953, **46**, 411–421.

Mook, D. "Oral and postingestional determinants of the intake of various solutions in rats with esophageal fistulas," *Journal of Comparative and Physiological Psychology*, 1963, **56**, 645–659.

Stellar, E. "The physiology of motivation," *Psychological Review*, 1954, **61**, 5–22.

Stellar, E. "Drive and motivation," in J. Field (Ed.), *Handbook of Physiology*. Vol. 3. Baltimore: Williams and Wilkins, 1960, pp. 1501–1527.

Stellar, E., and Hill, J. H. "The rat's rate of drinking as a function of water deprivation," *Journal of Comparative and Physiological Psychology*, 1952, **45**, 96–102.

Stellar. E., Hyman, R., and Samet, S. "Gastric factors controlling water and salt solution drinking." *Journal of Comparative and Physiological Psychology*, 1954, **47**, 220–226.

Weiner, I. H., and Stellar, E. "Salt preference of the rat determined by a single-stimulus method," *Journal of Comparative and Physiological Psychology*, 1951, **44**, 391–401.

6.2 Toward a Theory of Motive Acquisition

DAVID C. McCLELLAND

Too little is known about the processes of personality change at relatively complex levels. The empirical study of the problem has been hampered by both practical and theoretical difficulties. On the practical side it is very expensive both in time and effort to set up systematically controlled educational programs designed to develop some complex personality characteristic like a motive, and to follow the effects of the education over a number of years. It also presents ethical problems since it is not always clear that it is as proper to teach a person a new motive as it is a new skill like learning to play the piano. For both reasons, most of what we know about personality change has come from studying psychotherapy where both ethical and practical difficulties are overcome by the pressing need to help someone in real trouble. Yet, this source of information leaves much to be desired: It has so far proven difficult to identify and systematically vary the "inputs" in psychotherapy and to measure their specific effects on subsequent behavior, except in very general ways (cf. Rogers and Dymond, 1954).

On the theoretical side, the dominant views of personality formation suggest anyway that acquisition or change of any complex characteristic like a motive in adulthood would be extremely difficult. Both behavior theory and psychoanalysis agree that stable personality characteristics like motives are laid down in childhood. Behavior theory arrives at this conclusion by arguing that social motives are learned by close association with reduction in certain basic biological drives like hunger, thirst, and physical discomfort which loom much larger in childhood than adulthood. Psychoanalysis, for its part, pictures adult motives as stable resolutions of basic conflicts occurring in early childhood.

Reprinted with slight abridgment from the *American Psychologist*, 1965, **20**, 321–333, with permission of the author and the American Psychological Association, Inc.

Neither theory would provide much support for the notion that motives could be developed in adulthood without somehow recreating the childhood conditions under which they were originally formed. Furthermore, psychologists have been hard put to it to find objective evidence that even prolonged, serious, and expensive attempts to introduce personality change through psychotherapy have really proven successful (Eysenck, 1952). What hope is there that a program to introduce personality change would end up producing a big enough effect to study?

Despite these difficulties a program of research has been under way for some time which is attempting to develop the achievement motive in adults. It was undertaken in an attempt to fill some of the gaps in our knowledge about personality change or the acquisition of complex human characteristics. Working with [the need to achieve (n Achievement)] has proved to have some important advantages for this type of research: The practical and ethical problems do not loom especially large because previous research (McClelland, 1961) has demonstrated the importance of high n Achievement for entrepreneurial behavior and it is easy to find businessmen, particularly in underdeveloped countries, who are interested in trying any means of improving their entrepreneurial performance. Furthermore, a great deal is known about the origins of n Achievement in childhood and its specific effects on behavior so that educational programs can be systematically planned and their effects evaluated in terms of this knowledge. Pilot attempts to develop n Achievement have gradually led to the formulation of some theoretical notions of what motive acquisition involves and how it can be effectively promoted in adults. These notions have been summarized in the form of 12 propositions which it is the ultimate purpose of the research program to test. The propositions are anchored so far as possible in experiences with pilot courses, in supporting research findings from other studies, and in theory.

Before the propositions are presented, it is necessary to explain more of the theoretical and practical background on which they are based. To begin with, some basis for believing that motives could be acquired in adulthood had to be found in view of the widespread pessimism on the subject among theoretically oriented psychologists. Oddly enough we were encouraged by the successful efforts of two quite different groups of "change agents"—operant conditioners and missionaries. Both groups have been "naive" in the sense of being unimpressed by or ignorant of the state of psychological knowledge in the field. The operant conditioners have not been encumbered by any elaborate theoretical apparatus; they do not believe motives exist anyway, and continue demonstrating vigorously that if you want a person to make a response, all you have to do is elicit it and reward it (cf. Bandura and Walters, 1963, pp. 238 ff.). They retain a simple faith in the infinite plasticity of human behavior in which one response is just like any other and any one can be "shaped up" (strengthened by reward)—presumably even an "achievement" response as produced by a subject in a fantasy test. In fact, it was the naive optimism of one such researcher (Burris, 1958) that had a lot to do with getting the present research under way. He undertook a counseling program in which an attempt to elicit and reinforce achievement-related fantasies proved to be successful in motivating college students to get better grades. Like operant conditioners, the missionaries have gone ahead changing people because they have believed it possible. While the evidence is not scientifically impeccable, common-sense observation yields dozens of cases of adults whose motivational structure has seemed to be quite radically and permanently altered by the educational efforts of Communist Party, Mormon, or other devout missionaries.

A man from Mars might be led to observe that personality change appears to be very difficult for those who think it is very difficult, if not impossible, and much easier for those who think it can be done. He would certainly be oversimplifying the picture, but at the very least his observation suggests that some theoretical revision is desirable in the prevailing views of social motives which link them so decisively to early childhood. Such a revision has been attempted in connection with the research on n Achievement (McClelland, Atkinson, Clark, and Lowell, 1953) and while it has not been widely accepted (cf. Berelson and Steiner, 1964), it needs to be briefly summarized here to provide a theoretical underpinning for the attempts at motive change to be described. It starts with the proposition that all motives are learned, that not even biological discomforts (as from hunger) or pleasures (as from sexual stimulation) are "urges" or "drives" until they are linked to cues that can

signify their presence or absence. In time clusters of expectancies or associations grow up around affective experiences, not all of which are connected by any means with biological needs (McClelland, et al., 1953, Ch. 2), which we label motives. More formally, motives are "affectively toned associative networks" arranged in a hierarchy of strength or importance within a given individual. Obviously, the definition closely fits the operations used to measure a motive: "an affectively toned associative cluster" is exactly what is coded in a subject's fantasies to obtain an n Achievement score. The strength of the motive (its position in the individual's hierarchy of motives) is measured essentially by counting the number of associations belonging to this cluster as compared to others that an individual produces in a given number of opportunities. If one thinks of a motive as an associative network, it is easier to imagine how one might go about changing it: The problem becomes one of moving its position up on the hierarchy by increasing its salience compared to other clusters. It should be possible to accomplish this end by such tactics as: (a) setting up the network—discovering what associations, for example, exist in the achievement area and then extending, strengthening, or otherwise "improving" the network they form; (b) conceptualizing the network—forming a clear and conscious construct that labels the network; (c) tying the network to as many cues as possible in everyday life, especially those preceding and following action, to insure that the network will be regularly rearoused once formed; and (d) working out the relation of the network to superordinate associative clusters, like the self-concept, so that these dominant schemata do not block the train of achievement thoughts—for example, through a chain of interfering associations (e.g., "I am not really the achieving type").

This very brief summary is not intended as a full exposition of the theoretical viewpoint underlying the research, but it should suffice to give a rough idea of how the motive was conceived that we set out to change. This concept helped define the goals of the techniques of change, such as reducing the effects of associative interference from superordinate associate clusters. But what about the techniques themselves? What could we do that would produce effective learning of this sort? Broadly speaking, there are four types of empirical information to draw on. From the animal learning experiments, we know that such factors as repetition, optimal time intervals between stimulus, response, and reward, and the schedule of rewards are very important for effective learning. From human learning experiments, we know that such factors as distribution of practice, repetitions, meaningfulness, and recitation are important. From experiences with psychotherapy (cf. Rogers, 1961), we learn that warmth, honesty, nondirectiveness, and the ability to recode associations in line with psychoanalytic or other personality theories are important. And, from the attitude-change research literature, we learn that such variables as presenting one side or two, using reason or prestige to support an argument, or affiliating with a new reference group are crucial for developing new attitudes (cf. Hovland, Janis, and Kelley, 1953). Despite the fact that many

of these variables seem limited in application to the learning situation in which they were studied, we have tried to make use of information from all these sources in designing our "motive acquisition" program and in finding support for the general propositions that have emerged from our study so far. For our purpose has been above all to produce an effect large enough to be measured. Thus we have tried to profit by all that is known about how to facilitate learning or produce personality or attitude change. For, if we could not obtain a substantial effect with all factors working to produce it, there would be no point to studying the effects of each factor taken one at a time. Such a strategy also has the practical advantage that we are in the position of doing our best to "deliver the goods" to our course participants since they were giving us their time and attention to take part in a largely untried educational experience.[1]

Our overall research strategy, therefore, is "subtractive" rather than "additive." After we have demonstrated a substantial effect with some 10–12 factors working to produce it, our plan is to subtract that part of the program that deals with each of the factors to discover if there is a significant decline in the effect. It should also be possible to omit several factors in various combinations to get at interactional effects. This will

[1] Parenthetically, we have found several times that our stated desire to evaluate the effectiveness of our course created doubts in the minds of our sponsors that they did not feel about many popular courses for managers that no one has ever evaluated or plans to evaluate. An attitude of inquiry is not always an asset in education. It suggests one is not sure of his ground.

obviously require giving a fairly large number of courses in a standard institutional setting for the same kinds of businessmen with follow-up evaluation of their performance extending over a number of years. So obviously it will be some time before each of the factors incorporated into the propositions which follow can be properly evaluated so far as its effect on producing motive change is concerned.

The overall research strategy also determined the way the attempts to develop the achievement motive have been organized. That is to say, in order to process enough subjects to permit testing the effectiveness of various "inputs" in a reasonable number of years, the training had to be both of *short duration* (lasting 1–3 weeks) and *designed for groups* rather than for individuals as in person-to-person counseling. Fortunately these requirements coincide with normal practice in providing short courses for business executives. To conform further with that practice, the training has usually also been *residential* and *voluntary*. The design problems introduced by the last characteristic we have tried to handle in the usual ways by putting half the volunteers on a waiting list or giving them a different, technique-oriented course, etc. So far we have given the course to develop n Achievement in some form or another some eight times to over 140 managers or teachers of management in groups of 9–25 in the United States, Mexico and India. For the most part the course has been offered by a group of 2–4 consultant psychologists either to executives in a single company as a company training program, or to executives from several different companies as a self-improvement program, or as part of the program of an institute or school devoted to training managers. The theoretical propositions which follow have evolved gradually from these pilot attempts to be effective in developing n Achievement among businessmen of various cultural backgrounds.

The first step in a motive development program is to create confidence that it will work. Our initial efforts in this area were dictated by the simple practical consideration that we had to "sell" our course or nobody would take it. We were not in the position of an animal psychologist who can order a dozen rats, or an academic psychologist who has captive subjects in his classes, or even a psychotherapist who has sick people knocking at his door every day. So we explained to all who would listen that we had every reason to believe from previous research that high n Achievement is related to effective entrepreneurship and that therefore business executives could expect to profit from taking a course designed to understand and develop this important human characteristic. What started as a necessity led to the first proposition dealing with how to bring about motive change.

Proposition 1. The more reasons an individual has in advance to believe that he can, will, or should develop a motive, the more educational attempts designed to develop that motive are likely to succeed. The empirical support for this proposition from other studies is quite impressive. It consists of (*a*) the prestige-suggestion studies showing that people will believe or do what prestigeful sources suggest (cf. Hovland, *et al.*, 1953); (*b*) the so-called "Hawthorne effect" showing that people who feel they are especially selected to show an effect will tend to show it (Roethlisberger and Dickson, 1947); (c) the "Hello-Goodbye" effect in psychotherapy showing that patients who merely have contact with a prestigeful medical authority improve significantly over waiting list controls and almost as much as those who get prolonged therapy (Frank, 1961); (d) the "experimenter bias" studies which show that subjects will often do what an experimenter wants them to do, even though neither he nor they know he is trying to influence them (Rosenthal, 1963); (e) the goal-setting studies which show that setting goals for a person particularly in the name of prestigeful authorities like "science" or "research" improves performance (Kausler, 1959; Mierke, 1955); (f) the parent-child interaction studies which show that parents who set higher standards of excellence for their sons are more likely to have sons with high n Achievement (Rosen and D'Andrade, 1959). The common factor in all these studies seems to be that goals are being set for the individual by sources he respects—goals which imply that his behavior should change for a variety of reasons and that it can change. In common-sense terms, belief in the possibility and desirability of change are tremendously influential in changing a person.

So we have used a variety of means to create this belief: the authority of research findings on the relationship of n Achievement to entrepreneurial success, the suggestive power of membership in an experimental group designed to show an effect, the prestige of a great university, our own genuine enthusiasm for the course and our conviction that it would work, as expressed privately and in public speeches. In short, we were trying to make every use possible of what is sometimes regarded as an "error" in such research—namely, the Hawthorne effect, experimenter bias, etc., because we believe it to be one of the most powerful sources of change.

Why? What is the effect on the person, theoretically speaking, of all this goal setting for him? Its primary function is probably to arouse what exists of an associative network in the achievement area for each person affected. That is, many studies have shown that talk of achievement or affiliation or power tends to increase the frequency with which individuals think about achievement or affiliation or power (cf. Atkinson, 1958). And the stronger the talk, the more the relevant associative networks are aroused (McClelland, et al., 1953). Such an arousal has several possible effects which would facilitate learning: (a) It elicits what exists in the person of a "response" thus making it easier to strengthen that response in subsequent learning. (b) It creates a discrepancy between a goal . . . and a present state . . . which represents a cognitive dissonance the person tries to reduce (cf. Festinger, 1957); in common-sense terms he has an image clearly presented to him of something he is not but should be. (c) It tends to block out by simple interference other associations which would inhibit change—such as, "I'm too old to learn," "I never learned much from going to school anyway," "What do these academics know about everyday life?" or "I hope they don't get personal about all this."

After the course has been "sold" sufficiently to get a group together for training, the first step in the course itself is to present the research findings in some detail on exactly how n Achievement is related to certain types of successful entrepreneurial performance. That is, the argument of *The Achieving Society* (McClelland, 1961) is presented carefully with tables, charts, and diagrams, usually in lecture form at the outset and with the help of an educational TV film entitled the *Need to Achieve*. This is followed by discussion to clear up any ambiguities that remain in their minds as far as the central argument is concerned. It is especially necessary to stress that not all high achievement is caused by high n Achievement—that we have no evidence that high n Achievement is an essential ingredient in success as a research scientist, professional, accountant, office or personnel manager, etc.; that, on the contrary, it seems rather narrowly related to entrepreneurial, sales, or promotional success, and therefore should be of particular interest to them because they hold jobs which either have or could have an entrepreneurial component. We rationalize this activity in terms of the following proposition.

Proposition 2. The more an individual perceives that developing a motive is consistent with the demands of reality (and reason), the more educational attempts designed to develop that motive are likely to succeed. In a century in which psychologists and social theorists have been impressed by the power of unreason, it is well to remember that research has shown that rational arguments do sway opinions, particularly among the doubtful or the uncommitted (cf. Hovland, *et al.*, 1953). Reality in the form of legal, military, or housing rules does modify white prejudice against

Negroes (cf. Berelson and Steiner, 1964, p. 512). In being surprised at Asch's discovery that many people will go along with a group in calling a shorter line longer than it is, we sometimes forget that under most conditions their judgments conform with reality. The associative network which organizes "reality"—which places the person correctly in time, place, space, family, job, etc.—is one of the most dominant in the personality. It is the last to go in psychosis. It should be of great assistance to tie any proposed change in an associative network in with this dominant schema in such a way as to make the change consistent with reality demands or *"reasonable"* extensions of them. The word "reasonable" here simply means extensions arrived at by the thought processes of proof, logic, etc., which in adults have achieved a certain dominance of their own.

The next step in the course is to teach the participants the n Achievement coding system. By this time, they are a little confused anyway as to exactly what we mean by the term. So we tell them they can find out for themselves by learning to code stories written by others or by themselves. They take the test for n Achievement before this session and then find out what their own score is by scoring this record. However, we point out that if they think their score is too low, that can be easily remedied, since we teach them how to code and how to write stories saturated with n Achievement; in fact, that is one of the basic purposes of the course: to teach them to think constantly in n Achievement terms. Another aspect of the learning is discriminating achievement thinking from thinking in terms of power or affiliation. So usually the elements of these other two coding schemes are also taught.

Proposition 3. The more thoroughly an individual develops and clearly conceptualizes the associative network defining the motive, the more likely he is to develop the motive. The original empirical support for this proposition came from the radical behaviorist Skinnerian viewpoint: If the associative responses are the motive (by definition), to strengthen them one should elicit them and reinforce them, as one would shape up any response by reinforcement (cf. Skinner, 1953). But, support for this proposition also derives from other sources, particularly the "set" experiments. For decades laboratory psychologists have known that one of the easiest and most effective ways to change behavior is to change the subject's set. If he is responding to stimulus words with the names of animals, tell him to respond with the names of vegetables, or with words meaning the opposite, and he changes his behavior immediately and efficiently without a mistake. At a more complex level Orne (1962) had pointed out how powerful a set like "This is an experiment" can be. He points out that if you were to go up to a stranger and say something like "Lie down!" he would in all probability either laugh or escape as soon as possible. But, if you say "This is an experiment! Lie down!" more often than not, if there are other supporting cues, the person will do so. Orne has demonstrated how subjects will perform nonsensical and fatiguing tasks for very long periods of time under the set that "This is an experiment." At an even more complex level, sociologists have demonstrated often how quickly a person will

change his behavior as he adopts a new role set (as a parent, a teacher, a public official, etc.). In all these cases an associative network exists usually with a label conveniently attached which we call set and which, when it is aroused or becomes salient, proceeds to control behavior very effectively. The purpose of this part of our course is to give the subjects a set or a carefully worked out associative network with appropriate words or labels to describe all its various aspects (the coding labels for parts of the n Achievement scoring system like Ga^+, I^+, etc.; cf. Atkinson, 1958). The power of words on controlling behavior has also been well documented (cf. Brown, 1958).

It is important to stress that it is not just the label (n Achievement) which is taught. The person must be able to produce easily and often the new associative network itself. It is here that our research comes closest to traditional therapy which could be understood as the prolonged and laborious formation of new associative networks to replace anxiety-laden ones. That is, the person over time comes to form a new associative network covering his relations, for example, to his father and mother, which still later he may label an "unresolved Oedipus complex." When cues arise that formerly would have produced anxiety-laden associations, they now evoke this new complex instead, blocking out the "bad" associations by associative interference. But all therapists, whether Freudian or Rogerian, insist that the person must learn to produce these associations in their new form, that teaching the label is not enough. In fact, this is probably why so-called directive therapy is ineffective: It tries to substitute new constructs ("You should become an achiever") for old neurotic or ineffective ones ("rather than being such a slob") without changing the associative networks which underlie these surface labels. A change in set such as "Respond with names of vegetables" will not work unless the person has a whole associative network which defines the meaning of the set. The relation of this argument is obvious both to Kelly's (1955) insistence on the importance of personal constructs and to the general semanticists' complaints about the neurotic effects of mislabeling or overabstraction (Korzybski, 1941).

But, theoretically speaking, why should a change in set as an associative network be so influential in controlling thought and action? The explanation lies in part in its symbolic character. Learned acts have limited influence because they often depend on reality supports (as in typewriting), but learned thoughts (symbolic acts) can occur any time, and place, in any connection, and be applied to whatever the person is doing. They are more generalizable. Acts can also be inhibited more easily than thoughts. Isak Dinesen tells the story of the oracle who told the king he would get his wish so long as he never thought of the left eye of a camel. Needless to say, the king did not get his wish, but he could easily have obeyed her prohibition if it had been to avoid *looking* at the left eye of a camel. Thoughts once acquired gain more control over thoughts and actions than acquired acts do because they are harder to inhibit. But why do they gain control over actions? Are not thoughts substitutes for actions? Cannot a man learn to think achievement thoughts and still not

act like an achiever in any way? The question is taken up again under the next proposition, but it is well to remember here that thoughts are symbolic acts and that practice of symbolic acts facilitates performing the real acts (cf. Hovland, 1951, p. 644).

The next step in the course is to tie thought to action. Research has shown that individuals high in n Achievement tend to act in certain ways. For example, they prefer work situations where there is a challenge (moderate risk), concrete feedback on how well they are doing, and opportunity to take personal responsibility for achieving the work goals. The participants in the course are therefore introduced to a "work" situation in the form of a business game in which they will have an opportunity to show these characteristics in action or more specifically to develop them through practice and through observing others play it. The game is designed to mimic real life: They must order parts to make certain objects (e.g., a Tinker Toy model bridge) after having estimated how many they think they can construct in the time allotted. They have a real chance to take over, plan the whole game, learn from how well they are doing (use of feedback), and show a paper profit or loss at the end. While they are surprised often that they should have to display their real action characteristics in this way in public, they usually get emotionally involved in observing how they behave under pressure of a more or less "real" work situation.

Proposition 4. The more an individual can link the newly developed network to related actions, the more the change in both thought and action is likely to occur and endure. The evidence for the importance of action for producing change consists of such diverse findings as (a) the importance of recitation for human learning, (b) the repeated finding that overt commitment and participation in action changes attitudes effectively (cf. Berelson and Steiner, 1964, p. 576), and (c) early studies by Carr (cf. McGeoch and Irion, 1952) showing that simply to expose an organism to what is to be learned (e. g., trundling a rat through a maze) is nowhere near as effective as letting him explore it for himself in action.

Theoretically, the action is represented in the associative network by what associations precede, accompany, and follow it. So including the acts in what is learned *enlarges* the associative network or the achievement construct to include action. Thus, the number of cues likely to trip off the n Achievement network is increased. In commonsense terms, whenever he works he now evaluates what he is doing in achievement terms, and whenever he thinks about achievement he tends to think of its action consequences.

So far the course instruction has remained fairly abstract and removed from the everyday experiences of businessmen. So, the next step is to apply what has been learned to everyday business activities through the medium of the well-known case-study method popularized by the Harvard Business School. Actual examples of the development of the careers or firms of business leaders or entrepreneurs are written up in disguised form and assigned for discussion to the participants. Ordinarily, the instructor is not interested in illustrating "good" or "bad" managerial behavior— that is left to participants to discuss—

but in our use of the material, we do try to label the various types of behavior as illustrating either n Achievement and various aspects of the achievement sequence (instrumental activity, blocks, etc.), or n Power, n Affiliation, etc. The participants are also encouraged to bring in examples of managerial behavior from their own experience to evaluate in motivational terms.

Proposition 5. The more an individual can link the newly conceptualized association-action complex (or motive) to events in his everyday life, the more likely the motive complex is to influence his thoughts and actions in situations outside the training experience. The transfer-of-training research literature is not very explicit on this point, though it seems self-evident. Certainly, this is the proposition that underlies the practice of most therapy when it involves working through or clarifying, usually in terms of a new, partially formed construct system, old memories, events from the last 24 hours, dreams, and hopes of the future. Again, theoretically, this should serve to enlarge and clarify the associative network and increase the number of cues in everyday life which will rearouse it. The principle of symbolic practice can also be invoked to support its effectiveness in promoting transfer outside the learning experience.

For some time most course participants have been wondering what all this has to do with them personally. That is to say, the material is introduced originally on a "take it or leave it" objective basis as something that ought to be of interest to them. But, sooner or later, they must confront the issue as to what meaning n Achievement has in their own personal lives. We do not force this choice on them nor do we think we are brainwashing them to believe in n Achievement. We believe and we tell them we believe in the "obstinate audience" (cf. Bauer, 1964), in the ultimate capacity of people to resist persuasion or to do in the end what they really want to do. In fact, we had one case in an early session of a man who at this point decided he was not an achievement-minded person and did not want to become one. He subsequently retired and became a chicken farmer to the relief of the business in which he had been an ineffective manager. We respected that decision and mention it in the course as a good example of honest self-evaluation. Nevertheless, we do provide them will all kinds of information as to their own achievement-related behavior in the fantasy tests, in the business game, in occasional group dynamics session—and ample opportunity and encouragement to think through what this information implies so far as their self-concept is concerned and their responsibilities to their jobs. Various devices such as the "Who am I?" test, silent group meditation, or individual counseling have been introduced to facilitate this self-confrontation.

Proposition 6. The more an individual can perceive and experience the newly conceptualized motive as an improvement in the self-image, the more the motive is likely to influence his future thoughts and actions. Evidence on the importance of the ego or the self-image on controlling behavior has been summarized by Allport (1943). In recent years, Rogers and his group (Rogers, 1961; Rogers and Dymond, 1954) have measured improvement in psychotherapy largely in terms of improvement of the self-concept in relation to the ideal self. Indirect evidence of the importance of the self-schema comes from the discussion over whether a person can be made to do things under hypnosis that are inconsistent with his self-concept or values. All investigators agree that the hypnotist can be most successful in getting the subject to do what might normally be a disapproved action if he makes the subject perceive the action as consistent with his self-image or values (cf. Berelson and Steiner, 1963, p. 124).

The same logic supports this proposition. It seems unlikely that a newly formed associative network like n Achievement could persist and influence behavior much unless it had somehow "come to terms" with the pervasive superordinate network of associations defining the self. The logic is the same as for Proposition 2 dealing with the reality construct system. The n Achievement associations must come to be experienced as related to or consistent with the ideal self-image; otherwise associations from the self-system will constantly block thoughts of achievement. The person might be thinking, for example: "I am not that kind of person; achievement means judging people in terms of how well they perform and I don't like to hurt people's feelings."

Closely allied to the self-system is a whole series of networks only half conscious (i.e., correctly labeled) summarizing the values by which the person lives which derive from his culture and social milieu. These values can also interfere if they are inconsistent with n Achievement as a newly acquired way of thinking. Therefore, it has been customary at this point in the course to introduce a value analysis of the participants' culture based on an analysis of children's stories, myths, popular religion, comparative attitude surveys, customs, etc., more or less in line with traditional, cultural anthropological practice (cf. Benedict, 1946; McClelland, 1964). For example, in America we have to work through the problem of how being achievement oriented seems to interfere with being popular or liked by others which is highly valued by Americans. In Mexico a central issue is the highly valued "male dominance" pattern reflected in the patriarchal family and in the *macho* complex (being extremely masculine). Since data show that dominant fathers have sons with low n Achievement and authoritarian bosses do not encourage n Achievement in their top executives (Andrews, 1965), there is obviously a problem here to be worked through if n Achievement is to survive among thoughts centered on dominance. The problem is not only rationally discussed. It is acted out in role-playing sessions where Mexicans try, and often to their own surprise fail, to act like the democratic father with high standards in the classic Rosen and D'Andrade (1959) study on parental behavior which develops high n Achievement. Any technique is used which will serve to draw attention to possible conflicts between n Achievement and popular or traditional cultural values. In the end it may come to discussing parts of the *Bhagavad Gita* in India, or the *Koran* in Arab countries, that seem to oppose achievement striving or entrepreneurial behavior.

Proposition 7. The more an individual can perceive and experience the newly conceptualized motive as an improvement on prevailing cultural values, the more the motive is likely to influence his future thoughts and actions. The cultural anthropologists for years have argued how important it is to understand one's own cultural values to overcome prejudices, adopt more flexible attitudes, etc., but there is little hard evidence that doing so changes a person's behavior. What exists comes indirectly from studies that show prejudice can be decreased a little by information about ethnic groups (Berelson and Steiner, 1963, p. 517), or that repeatedly show an unconscious link between attitudes and the reference group (or subculture to which one belongs—a link which presumably can be broken more easily by full information about it, especially when coupled with role-playing new attitudes (cf. Berelson and Steiner, 1963, pp. 566 ff).

The theoretical explanation of this presumed effect is the same as for Propositions 2 and 6. The newly learned associative complex to influence thought and action effectively must somehow be adjusted to three superordinate networks that may set off regularly interfering associations—namely, the networks associated with reality, the self, and the social reference group or subculture.

The course normally ends with each participant preparing a written document outlining his goals and life plans for the next 2 years. These plans may or may not include references to the achievement motive; they can be very tentative, but they are supposed to be quite specific and realistic; that is to say, they should represent moderate levels of aspiration following the practice established in learning about n Achievement of choosing the moderately risky or challenging alternative. The purpose of this document is in part to formulate for oneself the practical implications of the course before leaving it, but even more to provide a basis for the evaluation of their progress in the months after the course. For it is explained to the participants that they are to regard themselves as "in training" for the next 2 years, that 10–14 days is obviously too short a time to do more than conceive a new way of life: It represents the residential portion of the training only. Our role over the next 2 years will be to remind them every 6 months of the tasks they have set themselves by sending them a questionnaire to fill out which will serve to rearouse many of the issues discussed in the course and to give them information on how far they have progressed toward achieving their goals.

Proposition 8. The more an individual commits himself to achieving concrete goals in life related to the newly formed motive, the more the motive is likely to influence his future thoughts and actions.

Proposition 9. The more an individual keeps a record of his progress toward achieving goals to which he is committed, the more the newly formed motive is likely to influence his future thoughts and actions. These propositions are both related to what was called "pacing" in early studies of the psychology of work. That is, committing oneself to a specific goal and then comparing one's performance to that goal has been found to facilitate learning (cf. Kausler, 1959), though most studies of levels of aspiration have dealt with goal setting as a result rather than as a "cause" of performance. At any rate, the beneficial effect of concrete feedback on learning has been amply demonstrated by psychologists from Thorndike to Skinner. Among humans the feedback on per-

formance is especially effective if they have high n Achievement (French, 1958), a fact which makes the relevance of our request for feedback obvious to the course participants.

The theoretical justification for these propositions is that in this way we are managing to keep the newly acquired associative network salient over the next 2 years. We are providing cues that will regularly rearouse it since he knows he is still part of an experimental training group which is supposed to show a certain type of behavior (Proposition 1 again). If the complex is rearoused sufficiently often back in the real world, we believe it is more likely to influence thought and action than if it is not aroused.

As described so far the course appears to be devoted almost wholly to cognitive learning. Yet this is only part of the story. The "teachers" are all clinically oriented psychologists who also try to practice whatever has been learned about the type of human relationship that most facilitates emotional learning. Both for practical and theoretical reasons this relationship is structured as warm, honest, and nonevaluative, somewhat in the manner described by Rogers (1961) and recommended by distinguished therapists from St. Ignatius[2] to Freud.

[2] In his famous spiritual exercises which have played a key role in producing and sustaining personality change in the Jesuit Order, St. Ignatius states: "The director of the Exercizes ought not to urge the exercitant more to poverty or any promise than to the contrary, nor to one state of life or way of living more than another . . . [while it is proper to urge people outside the Exercizes] the director of the Exercizes . . . without leaning to one side or the other, should permit the Creator to deal directly with the creature, and the creature directly with his Creator and Lord."

That is to say, we insist that the only kind of change that can last or mean anything is what the person decides on and works out by himself, that we are there not to criticize his past behavior or direct his future choices, but to provide him with all sorts of information and emotional support that will help him in his self-confrontation. Since we recognize that self-study may be quite difficult and unsettling, we try to create an optimistic relaxed atmosphere in which the person is warmly encouraged in his efforts and given the opportunity for personal counseling if he asks for it.

Proposition 10. Changes in motives are more likely to occur in an interpersonal atmosphere in which the individual feels warmly but honestly supported and respected by others as a person capable of guiding and directing his own future behavior. Despite the widespread belief in this proposition among therapists (except for operant conditioners), one of the few studies that directly supports it has been conducted by Ends and Page (1957) who found that an objective learning-theory approach was less successful in treating chronic alcoholics than a person-oriented, client-centered approach. Rogers (1961) also summarizes other evidence that therapists who are warmer, more empathic, and genuine are more successful in their work. Hovland, *et al.* (1953), report that the less manipulative the intent of a communicator, the greater the tendency to accept his conclusions. There is also the direct evidence that parents of boys with high n Achievement are warmer, more encouraging and less directive (fathers only) than parents of boys with low n Achievement (Rosen and D'Andrade, 1959). We tried to model ourselves after those parents on the theory that what is associated with high n Achievement in children might be most likely to encourage its development in adulthood. This does not mean permissiveness or promiscuous reinforcement of all kinds of behavior; it also means setting high standards as the parents of the boys with high n Achievement did but having the relaxed faith that the participants can achieve them.

The theoretical justification for this proposition can take two lines: Either one argues that this degree of challenge to the self-schema produces anxiety which needs to be reduced by warm support of the person for effective learning to take place, or one interprets the warmth as a form of direct reinforcement for change following the operant-conditioning model. Perhaps both factors are operating. Certainly there is ample evidence to support the view that anxiety interferes with learning (cf. Sarason, 1960) and that reward shapes behavior (cf. Bandura and Walters, 1963, pp. 283 ff).

One other characteristic of the course leads to two further propositions. Efforts are made so far as possible to define it as an "experience apart," "an opportunity for self-study," or even a "spiritual retreat" (though that term can be used more acceptably in India than in the United States). So far as possible it is held in an isolated resort hotel or a hostel where there will be few distractions from the outside world and few other guests. This permits an atmosphere of total concentration on the objectives of the course including much informal talk outside the sessions about Ga^+, Ga^-, I^+, and other categories in the coding definition. It still comes as a surprise to us to hear these terms suddenly in an informal group of participants talking away in Spanish or Telugu. The effect of this retreat from everyday life into a special and specially labeled experience appears to be twofold: It dramatizes or increases the salience of the new associative network and it tends to create a new reference group.

Proposition 11. Changes in motives are more likely to occur the more the setting dramatizes the importance of self-study and lifts it out of the routine of everyday life. So far as we know there is no scientific evidence to support this proposition, though again if one regards Jesuits as successful examples of personality change, the Order has frequently followed the advice of St. Ignatius to the effect that "the progress made in the Exercizes will be greater, the more the exercitant withdraws from all friends and acquaintances, and from all worldly cares." Theory supports the proposition in two respects: Removing the person from everyday routine (*a*) should decrease interfering associations (to say nothing of interfering appointments and social obligations), and (*b*) should heighten the salience of the experience by contrast with everyday life and make it harder to handle with the usual defenses ("just one more course," etc.). This is to say, the network of achievement-related associations can be more strongly and distinctly aroused in contrast to everyday life, making cognitive dissonance greater and therefore more in need of reduction by new learning. By the same token we have found that the dramatic quality of the experience cannot be sustained very long in a 12–18-hour-a-day schedule without a new routine attitude developing. Thus, we have found that a period somewhere

between 6 to 14 days is optimal for this kind of "spiritual retreat." St. Ignatius sets an outside limit of 30 days, but this is when the schedule is less intensive (as ours has sometimes been), consisting of only a few hours a day over a longer period.

Proposition 12. Changes in motives are more likely to occur and persist if the new motive is a sign of membership in a new reference group. No principle of change has stronger empirical or historical support than this one. Endless studies have shown that people's opinions, attitudes, and beliefs are a function of their reference group and that different attitudes are likely to arise and be sustained primarily when the person moves into or affiliates with a new reference group (cf. Berelson and Steiner, 1963, pp. 580 ff). Many theorists argue that the success of groups like Alcoholics Anonymous depends on the effectiveness with which the group is organized so that each person demonstrates his membership in it by "saving" another alcoholic. Political experience has demonstrated that membership in small groups like Communist or Nazi Party cells is one of the most effective ways to sustain changed attitudes and behavior.

Our course attempts to achieve this result (*a*) by the group experience in isolation—creating the feeling of alumni who all went through it together; (*b*) by certain signs of identification with the group, particularly the language of the coding system, but also including a certificate of membership; and (*c*) by arranging where possible to have participants come from the same community so that they can form a "cell" when they return that will serve as an immediate reference group to prevent gradual undermining of the new network by other pressures.

In theoretical terms a reference group should be effective because its members constantly provide cues to each other to rearouse the associative network, because they will also reward each other for achievement-related thoughts and acts, and because this constant mutual stimulation, and reinforcement, plus the labeling of the group, will prevent assimilation of the network to bigger, older, and stronger networks (such as those associated with traditional cultural values).

In summary, we have described an influence process which may be conceived in terms of "input," "intervening," and "output" variables as in Table 1. The propositions relate variables in Column A via their effect on the intervening variables in Column B to as yet loosely specified behavior in Column C, which may be taken as evidence that "development" of n Achievement has "really" taken place. The problems involved in evaluation of effects are as great and as complicated as those involved in designing the treatment, but they cannot be spelled out here, partly for lack of space, partly because we are in an even earlier stage of examining and classifying the effects of our training 1 and 2 years later preparatory to conceptualizing more clearly what happens. It will have to suffice to point out that we plan extensive comparisons over a 2-year period of the behaviors of our trained subjects compared with matched controls along the lines suggested in Column C.

What the table does is to give a brief

table 1

Variables Conceived as Entering into the Motive Change Process

A Input or Independent Variables	B Intervening Variables	C Output or Dependent Variables
1. Goal setting for the person (P1, P11)	Arousal of associative network (salience)	Duration and/or extensiveness of changes in:
2. Acquisition of n Achievement associative network (P2, P3, P4, P5)	Experiencing and labeling the associative network	1. n Achievement associative network
3. Relating new network to superordinate networks reality (P2) the self (P6) cultural values (P7)	Variety of cues to which network is linked Interfering associations assimilated or bypassed by reproductive interference	2. Related actions: use of feedback, moderate risk taking, etc. 3. Innovations (job improvements) 4. Use of time and money
4. Personal goal setting (P8)		5. Entrepreneurial success as defined by nature of job held and its rewards
5. Knowledge of progress (P3, P4, P9)		
6. Personal warmth and support (P10)	Positive affect associated with network	
7. Support of reference group (P11, P12)		

Note.—P1, P11, etc., refer to the numbered propositions in the text.

overall view of how we conceptualize the educational or treatment process. What is particularly important is that the propositions refer to *operationally defined* and *separable* treatment variables. Thus, after having demonstrated hopefully a large effect of the total program, we can subtract a variable and see how much that decreases the impact of the course. That is to say, the course is designed so that it could go ahead perfectly reasonably with very little advanced goal setting (P1), with an objective rather than a warm personal atmosphere (P11), without the business game tying thought to action (P9), without learning to code n Achievement and write achievement-related stories (P3), without cultural value analysis (P7), or an isolated residential setting (P1, P11, P12). The study units are designed in a way that they can be omitted without destroying the viability of the treatment which has never been true of other studies of the psychotherapeutic process (cf. Rogers and Dymond, 1954).

But is there any basis for thinking the program works in practice? As yet, not enough time has elapsed to enable us to collect much data on long-term changes in personality and business activity. However, we do know that businessmen can learn to write stories scoring high in n Achievement, that they retain this skill over 1 year or 2, and that they like the course—but the same kinds of things can be said about many unevaluated management training courses. In two instances we have more objective data. Three courses were given to some 34 men from the Bombay area in early 1963. It proved possible to develop a crude but objective and reliable coding

system to record whether each one had shown *unusual* entrepreneurial activity in the 2 years prior to the course or in the 2 years after course. "Unusual" here means essentially an unusual promotion or salary raise or starting a new business venture of some kind. Of the 30 on whom information was available in 1965, 27% had been unusually active before the course, 67% after the course ($\chi^2 = 11.2$, $p < .01$). In a control group chosen at random from those who applied for the course in 1963, out of 11 on whom information has so far been obtained, 18% were active before 1963, 27% since 1963.

In a second case, four courses were given throughout 1964 to a total of 52 small businessmen from the small city of Kakinada in Andhra Pradesh, India. Of these men, 25% had been unusually active in the 2-year period before the course, and 65% were unusually active immediately afterwards ($\chi^2 = 17.1$, $p < .01$). More control data and more refined measures are needed, but it looks very much as if, in India at least, we will be dealing with a spontaneous "activation" rate of only 25%–35% among entrepreneurs. Thus we have a distinct advantage over psychotherapists who are trying to demonstrate an improvement over a two-thirds spontaneous recovery rate. Our own data suggest that we will be unlikely to get an improvement or "activation" rate much above the two-thirds level commonly reported in therapy studies. That is, about one-third of the people in our courses have remained relatively unaffected. Nevertheless the two-thirds activated after the course represent a doubling of the normal rate of unusual entrepreneurial activity—no mean achievement in the light of the current pessimism among psychologists as to their ability to induce lasting personality change among adults.

One case will illustrate how the course seems to affect people in practice. A short time after participating in one of our courses in India, a 47-year-old businessman rather suddenly and dramatically decided to quit his excellent job and go into the construction business on his own in a big way. A man with some means of his own, he had had a very successful career as employee-relations manager for a large oil firm. His job involved adjusting management-employee difficulties, negotiating union contracts, etc. He was well-to-do, well thought of in his company, and admired in the community, but he was restless because he found his job increasingly boring. At the time of the course his original n Achievement score was not very high and he was thinking of retiring and living in England where his son was studying. In an interview, 8 months later, he said the course had served not so much to "motivate" him but to "crystallize" a lot of ideas he had vaguely or half consciously picked up about work and achievement all through his life. It provided him with a new language (he still talked in terms of standards of excellence, blocks, moderate risk, goal anticipation, etc.), a new construct which served to organize those ideas and explain to him why he was bored with his job, despite his obvious success. He decided he wanted to be an n-Achievement-oriented person, that he would be unhappy in retirement, and that he should take a risk, quit his job, and start in business on his own. He acted on his decision and in 6 months had drawn plans and raised over $1,000,000 to build the tallest building in his large city to be called the "Everest Apartments." He is extremely happy in his new activity because it means selling, promoting, trying to wangle scarce materials, etc. His first building is partway up and he is planning two more.

Even a case as dramatic as this one does not prove that the course produced the effect, despite his repeated use of the constructs he had learned, but what is especially interesting about it is that he described what had happened to him in exactly the terms the theory requires. He spoke not about a new motive force but about how existing ideas had been crystallized into a new associative network, and it is this new network which *is* the new "motivating" force according to the theory.

How generalizable are the propositions? They have purposely been stated generally so that some term like "attitude" or "personality characteristic" could be substituted for the term "motive" throughout, because we believe the propositions will hold for other personality variables. In fact, most of the supporting experimental evidence cited comes from attempts to change other characteristics. Nevertheless, the propositions should hold best more narrowly for motives and especially the achievement motive. One of the biggest difficulties in the way of testing them more generally is that not nearly as much is known about other human characteristics or their specific relevance for success in a certain type of work. For example, next to nothing is known about the need for power, its relation to success, let us say, in politics or bargaining situations, and its origins and course of development in the life history of individuals. It is precisely the knowledge we have about such matters for the achievement motive that puts us in a position to shape it for limited, socially and individually desirable ends. In the future, it seems to us, research in psychotherapy ought to follow a similar course. That is to say, rather than developing "all purpose" treatments, good for any person and any purpose, it should aim to develop specific treatments or educational programs built on laboriously accumulated detailed knowledge of the characteristic to be changed. It is in this spirit that the present research program in motive acquisition has been designed and is being tested out.

REFERENCES

Allport, G. W. "The ego in contemporary psychology," *Psychological Review*, 1943, **50**, 451–478.

Andrews, J. D. W. "The achievement motive in two types of organizations," *Journal of Personality and Social Psychology*, 1965, in press.

Atkinson, J. W. (Ed.) *Motives in Fantasy, Action and Society*. Princeton, N.J.: Van Nostrand, 1958.

Bandura, A., and Walters, R. H. *Social Learning and Personality Development*. New York: Holt, Rinehart and Winston, 1963.

Bauer, R. A. "The obstinate audience: The influence process from the point of view of social communication," *American Psychologist*, 1964, **19**, 319–329.

Benedict, Ruth. *The Chrysanthemum and the Sword*. Boston: Houghton Mifflin, 1946.

Berelson, B., and Steiner, G. A. *Human Behavior: An Inventory of Scientific Findings*. New York: Harcourt, Brace, 1964.

Brown, R. W. *Words and Things*. Glencoe, Ill.: Free Press, 1958.

Burris, R. W. The effect of counseling on achievement motivation. Unpublished doctoral dissertation, University of Indiana, 1958.

Ends, E. J., and Page, C. W. "A study of three types of group psychotherapy with hospitalized male inebriates," *Quarterly Journal on Alcohol*, 1957, **18**, 263–277.

Eysenck, H. J. "The effects of psychotherapy: An evaluation," *Journal of Consulting Psychology*, 1952, **16**, 319–324.

Festinger, L. *A Theory of Cognitive Dissonance*. New York: Harper & Row, 1957.

Frank, J. *Persuasion and Healing*. Baltimore: Johns Hopkins Press, 1961.

French, E. G. "Effects of the interaction of motivation and feedback on task performance," in J. W. Atkinson (Ed.), *Motives in Fantasy, Action and Society*. Princeton, N. J.: Van Nostrand, 1958, pp. 400–408.

Hovland, C. I. "Human learning and retention," in S. S. Stevens (Ed.), *Handbook of Experimental Psychology*. New York: Wiley, 1951.

Hovland, C. I., Janis, I. L., and Kelley, H. H. *Communication and Persuasion: Psychological Studies of Opinion Change*. New Haven: Yale Univer. Press, 1953.

Kausler, D. H. "Aspiration level as a determinant of performance," *Journal of Personality*, 1959, **27**, 346–351.

Kelley, G. A. *The Psychology of Personal Constructs*. New York: Norton, 1955.

Korzybski, A. *Science and Sanity*. Lancaster, Pa.: Science Press, 1941.

McClelland, D. C. *The Achieving Society*. Princeton, N. J.: Van Nostrand, 1961.

McClelland, D. C. *The Roots of Consciousness*. Princeton, N. J.: Van Nostrand, 1964.

McClelland, D. C., Atkinson, J. W., Clark, R. A., and Lowell, E. L. *The Achievement Motive*. New York: Appleton-Century, 1953.

McGeoch, J. A., and Irion, A. L. *The Psychology of Human Learning*. (2nd ed.) New York: Longmans, Green, 1952.

Mierke, K. *Wille und Leistung.* Göttingen: Verlag für Psychologie, 1955.

Orne, M. "On the social psychology of the psychological experiment: With particular reference to demand characteristics and their implications," *American Psychologist,* 1962, **17,** 776–783.

Roethlisberger, F. J., and Dickson, W. J. *Management and the Worker.* Cambridge: Harvard Univer. Press, 1947.

Rogers, C. R. *On Becoming a Person.* Boston: Houghton Mifflin, 1961.

Rogers, C. R., and Dymond, R. F. (Eds.) *Psychotherapy and Personality Change.* Chicago: Univer. Chicago Press, 1954.

Rosen, B. C., and D'Andrade, R. G. "The psychosocial origins of achievement motivation," *Sociometry,* 1959, **22,** 185–218.

Rosenthal, R. On the social psychology of the psychological experiment: The experimenter's hypothesis as unintended determinant of experimental results," *American Scientist,* 1963, **51,** 268–283.

Sarason, I. Empirical findings and theoretical problems in the use of anxiety scales," *Psychological Bulletin,* 1960, **57,** 403–415.

Skinner, B. F. *Science and Human Behavior.* New York: Macmillan, 1953.

6.3 Validity of the Guilty-Knowledge Technique: The Effects of Motivation

P. O. DAVIDSON

The first recommendation arising out of Orlansky's (1962) review on lie-detection capability was for further investigation of the validity of lie-detection techniques. This view has been reiterated recently in investigations by the Committee on Government Operations (1965, 1966) of the United States House of Representatives concerning the use of polygraphs as "lie detectors" by the Federal Government. A common problem in studying the validity of lie detection, although not commonly recognized by many lie-detector operators, is that the polygraph merely indicates that a physiological response has occurred. The operator must *infer* the lie on the basis of the observed physiological response. In spite of some extravagant claims (cf. Lee, 1953), the inference that autonomic responses can indicate lying must be viewed with extreme skepticism since the physiological responses measured by

polygraphs can be produced by a wide variety of stimuli quite incidental to any process of lying. Lykken (1959) has suggested that the detection of guilt by using physiological measurements involves a more reasonable inference than the detection of lying. If a guilty individual is presented with some relevant details about his crime interspersed among similar but irrelevant items, he would be expected to respond differently than an innocent individual who had no "guilty knowledge" about which items were relevant. The assumption here is not that the subject (*S*) will respond in a particular, recognizable way when he is lying, but merely that he will respond differently to relevant details of his crime than to irrelevant details.

Lykken found that he could correctly identify, using a simple objective scoring procedure, all innocent *S*s and 93.9% of his guilty *S*s against a chance expectancy

Reprinted with slight abridgment from the *Journal of Applied Psychology*, 1968, **52**, 62–65, with permission of the author and the American Psychological Association, Inc.

of 50%. He noted, however, that his Ss were not particularly emotionally involved in their crime, nor were they strongly motivated to try and defeat the test. In a later study he found this guilty-knowledge technique highly resistant to faking (Lykken, 1960). The present study was designed to evaluate the validity of the guilty-knowledge technique under more ego-involving circumstances and varying amounts of motivation.

METHOD

The Ss used in this experiment were 48 volunteer college students assigned at random to 12 groups. Three Ss chosen at random from each group took part in the crime as "hunters"; the fourth S did not and he had no knowledge of the nature of the experiment. The "hunter" game was used for enacting each crime since it seemed to be a highly egoinvolving game for university students. The three hunters from each group were seen individually by the experimenter (E) and shown a photograph of a student who was to be their intended victim (the 12 victims were all collaborating psychology students). Basic information concerning the name of the victim, his faculty, and his lecture schedule was supplied. Each hunter was told that the victim would be carrying a sealed envelope which the hunter was to take and examine if he could successfully hunt down the victim and enact his murder. The hunter was informed that the envelopes contained vouchers for prizes ranging in value up to $50 and that he would be permitted to cash the voucher if he was not detected as the criminal after a polygraph examination. The hunter would not know the

value of the voucher unless he was successful in enacting the crime. Although the hunters were not aware of it, half of the 12 victims had envelopes with vouchers ranging in value from $25 to $50, while the other half ranged in value from 10¢ to $1. Each hunter was informed that there were other hunters after the same victim and that the first successful hunter would be the one to get the envelope. Each hunter was free to choose his own method, time, and place for enacting the crime; the only restrictions were that he must work alone and tell no one of his plans or success. As an additional incentive to the hunters, prizes were awarded upon completion of the experiment for the most ingeniously devised crimes, whether the hunter was successful in getting the envelope or not.

The hunters were told that in order to add some uncertainty to the success of the crime the victim had been given a random timetable with specified time intervals on it when any crime attempted would not be successful. If an attempt was made during one of these "safe periods" the crime was said to have failed, the envelope was not surrendered, and the hunter was barred from trying again for 24 hr. The hunter would not know until he made an attempt whether it would succeed or not. In fact, no such timetable existed and the first hunter to make an attempt was always told that his victim was in a "safe period" and the attempt had failed. The second hunter to make an attempt was always judged successful and took the envelope.

Each victim had a code number which was posted on a central campus bulletin. This number was to be checked before making any attempt and to be removed as soon as any hunter was successful in obtaining the envelope by enacting the murder of his victim. Thus, if the number was gone, the other hunters would know the game was over and would not make any further attempts on the victim.

In this way, for every victim there were four suspects: one who had committed the crime, one who had tried and failed, one who was motivated to attempt the crime but had no opportunity, and a fourth "suspect" who in fact knew nothing about the crime or the victim and was in no way involved or motivated.

As soon as the second hunter had succeeded in obtaining the envelope the victim supplied E with answers to some questions relevant to the crime (e.g., where it occurred, murder weapon used, etc.). Six multiple-choice questions about the crime and the content of the envelope were made up with five alternatives for each question (cf. Lykken, 1959). The first alternate on every question was always a foil and not scored. This was done in order to reduce the possibility of incorrectly scoring orienting responses. The four suspects were then brought in for interrogation by another E who had no knowledge about who the criminal was, or which answers to the multiple-choice questions were correct. The S was seated in the interrogation room, GSR electrodes were attached to his dominant hand, and a pair of headphones adjusted to his ears. The E was located with a Grass Model 7 polygraph in an adjoining room and spoke to S via a microphone. Each S was told he was to be questioned in relation to a crime. He

was to listen to each question consisting of several parts but to make no answer. The standardized list of six questions was then read to S and his GSR responses to each of the five alternates were recorded. Heart rate and respiration rate were monitored but not scored.

Scoring of the GSR response after the recording was completed was simple and objective (Lykken, 1959). Scoring was done without prior knowledge of the correct answers in order to prevent any criterion contamination. An S's GSR's to the several alternatives in a given question were ranked in order of amplitude. If his largest response was found to be a relevant alternative he was given a score of 2 on that question. If his second largest response was to the relevant alternative he was given a score of 1. Thus a perfect innocent score was 0 and a perfect guilty score was 12.

RESULTS

Following Lykken's (1959) criteria, all scores of 6 or less were classified "innocent" and all scores over 6 "guilty." All six of the guilty Ss who were highly motivated to deception because of the high value of their vouchers were correctly classified. Five of the six guilty Ss who were under low motivation to deception (negligible value of vouchers) were correctly identified. The difference in classification between these two groups was not significant (Fisher exact probability $p = .50$ [Siegel, 1956]). Combining the two groups, 11 of the 12 guilty Ss were correctly classified as guilty (92%). All 36 of the innocent Ss (100%) were correctly classified as not guilty.

There was a total of 48 interrogations and 47 of these were correctly classified—giving an overall 98% correct classification against a chance level of 25%.

DISCUSSION

There were several reasons for the fairly involved procedure used in this study. Primarily it was designed to simulate, a little closer, actual situations involving real crimes, but at the same time maintain rigorous experimental control. By allowing S to choose his own time, place, and method, plus the incentive for ingenious crimes, S became much more actively and personally involved than if he merely walked through the motions of a staged crime. Some of the uncertainties involved in real crimes were introduced. Not every crime attempted is automatically successful and there is usually no way of knowing in advance. A criminal usually does not know exactly what his gains will be (if any) until he successfully completes the crime. Furthermore, in order to keep the rewards of his crime he must be able to escape detection. The motivation for escaping detection may be a complex one involving some combination of fear of punishment and hope of reward. Most experimental studies have increased this motivation by threat of punishment (usually electric shock). In the present study, the hope of reward was experimentally varied to see if this had any effect on ability to escape detection in a polygraph examination. It has sometimes been suggested that successful detection rates in actual crimes would be significantly higher than in experimental studies since the tremendous motivation involved in the former would increase the amount of autonomic responsiveness to questions relevant to the crime. While the differences in this study are in this direction, they do not support this hypothesis. They do not clearly refute it either. The small samples of guilty Ss and the limited rewards combined with no real threats of punishment in the present study require caution in interpreting these results.

One observation did occur which merits further study. A common attitude in the lie-detection field (cf. Lee, 1953) is that the GSR is not useful because it is "too sensitive." Lykken (1960) discounted this objection to the GSR on the basis of his experimental studies with essentially fairly low levels of motivation to deception. In the present study it was observed, particularly in guilty Ss who possessed $50 vouchers, that there seemed to be a great many spontaneous fluctuations in base-line GSR. Scoring GSR responses to relevant questions must be done very carefully in such cases to prevent the confusion of spontaneous base-line fluctuations from being counted as GSRs. While this was not too difficult in the present experiment, it does indicate caution in uncritical adoption of Lykken's scoring criteria for criminal investigations. Malmo (1957) has suggested that base-line fluctuations can be a useful index of drive level and, consequently, a very high drive level produced in a suspect for any reason (e.g., merely being suspected of a crime) would reduce the reliability of scoring GSR responses. In this sense the "extraordinary sensitivity of the GSR" may not be a "clear virtue" as Lykken (1960) suggests that it is.

Some experimental studies stack the odds for correct detection very much in favor of the polygraph examiner by merely requiring him to separate one guilty suspect from several innocent controls. In criminal investigations the odds are not always so nice. Often there are several suspects who had good motives for committing the crime, some may have been planning it and some may have even attempted it unsuccessfully. But to the extent that these experimental results can be generalized, the guilty-knowledge technique seems to work as well in either situation. The 92% correct classification of guilty Ss and 100% correct classification of innocent Ss is essentially the same using the present procedure as the 93.9% correct classification of guilty Ss and 100% correct classification of innocent Ss using Lykken's (1959) procedure.

SUMMARY

48 Ss divided into 12 groups took part in an experimental investigation of detection of a simulated crime. For each of 12 crimes, 3 Ss were highly motivated to commit the crime; 1 succeeded, 1 attempted but failed, and 1 did not make an attempt. The 4th S interrogated for each crime was an innocent control. Motivation for deception (hope of reward) was high ($25–$50) for half of the crimes and low (< $1) for the other half. Detection of deception using a polygraph recording of GSR and the guilty-knowl-edge technique resulted in correct classification of 92% of "guilty" Ss and 100% of "innocent" Ss. No significant differences were found due to level of motivation for deception. Results were discussed in terms of their relationship to similar studies and actual criminal investigations.

REFERENCES

Committee on Government Operations. (10th report) *Use of Polygraphs as "Lie Detectors" by the Federal Government.* 89th Congress, 1st Session, House Report No. 198. Washington, D.C., 1965.

Committee on Government Operations. (39th report) *Use of Polygraphs as "Lie Detectors" by the Federal Government (Part 2).* 89th Congress, 2nd Session, House Report No. 2081. Washington, D.C.: 1966.

Lee, C. D. *The Instrumental Detection of Deception.* Springfield, Ill.: Charles C Thomas, 1953.

Lykken, D. T. "The GSR in the detection of guilt." *Journal of Applied Psychology,* 1959, **43,** 385–388.

Lykken, D. T. "The validity of the guilty knowledge technique: The effects of faking." *Journal of Applied Psychology,* 1960, **44,** 258–262.

Malmo, R. B. "Anxiety and behavioral arousal." *Psychological Review,* 1957, **64,** 276–287.

Orlansky, J. *An Assessment of Lie Detection Capability.* Institute of Defence Analyses, Research and Engineering Support Division. Technical Report No. 62–16. Washington, D.C., 1962.

Siegel, S. *Nonparametric Statistics for the Behavioral Sciences.* New York: McGraw-Hill, 1960.

SECTION 7

MEASUREMENT AND INDIVIDUAL DIFFERENCES

The first article in this section consists of a brief statement by C. West Churchman of the School of Business Administration, University of California in Berkeley. Churchman is interested in the use of computers in social research, but also addresses himself to the larger problem of the role that behavioral scientists should play in "building a better world."

Alexander C. Wesman of the Psychological Corporation, New York, is the author of the second paper. He discusses problems and issues in intelligence testing, including the use and misuse of tests.

Intelligence testing is also the concern of Melita H. Oden, who was for many years a co-researcher with Lewis Madison Terman in a longitudinal study of 1528 individuals who had IQs of over 140 when tested as school children in the 1920s. The selection included here consists of excerpts from her most recent (1960) survey of the members of this group, who at that time were approximately 50 years of age. Among other things, her results show how intelligence tends to be associated with other personality and experiential characteristics. Those subjects who were the most successful not only were better adjusted even as children, but also had more intellectually oriented parents who encouraged them to succeed.

Tests are not the only means of measuring personality characteristics. The fourth paper consists of a study by Anne Anastasi and Charles E. Schaefer of Fordham University, a study that correlates biographical information with indications of artistic and literary creativity of high school students. Although the present study is concerned with the creativity of adolescent girls, the authors also compare their results with those obtained in an earlier, similar study of adolescent boys. One of their interesting findings is that the parent of the opposite sex to that of the child appears to have the greater influence in stimulating or facilitating the development of creativity.

7.1 The Prospects for Social Experimentation

C. WEST CHURCHMAN

Each culture seems to have to go through its own muddle concerning the planning of social systems. One age is concerned with the role of reason, another with the democratic base. What seems to characterize the muddle of 20th-century American culture is the use of science in the design of societies. Although the invention of pure science seems to have had little to do with how men should seek the good life, the invention of applied science is altogether concerned with this matter. Applied science tries to adapt the procedures of observation, reason, test, and verification—that is, "experiment"—to the real problems of human society.

The philosophy indigenous to America called pragmatism attempted to create a sound basis for applied experimentation. Charles S. Peirce, William James, John Dewey, and Edgar Singer are four outstanding philosophers who tried to clear up the muddle. For muddle it was. It is all very well to speak generally of the need to "experiment" with educational processes, but when we come down to the specifics, what do we mean? The pure scientist insists on experimental controls, a strict calibration of instruments, the exclusion of the interplay of unwanted variables, a well-designed manipulation of the wanted variables, a precise statistical test, and so on. But in a democratic social system we simply can't control the variables in the manner required by pure science, for reasons too obvious to mention. Two choices seem apparent. One is to say that the method of experiment is not appropriate in the planning of society because its demands are too rigorous, and the other is to say that the method of experiment is broader than a specific technique and that the

Reprinted from *Science*, 1968, **159**, 965–966, with permission of the author and *Science*. Copyright 1968 by the American Association for the Advancement of Science. This selection consists of portions of a review of Harold Sackman, *Computers, System Science, and Evolving Society*. New York: Wiley, 1967.

method is applicable to social systems. Pragmatism took the second choice, and tried to provide a comprehensive view of the nature of experiment, a view which encompasses both the rigorous, precise technique of pure science and the less rigorous, more purpose-oriented technique of applied social science.

The advent of the large digital computer came decades after the fundamental philosophical work of pragmatism had been accomplished. But the computer, in principle at least, seems to provide an opportunity for social-system experiment that no earlier pragmatist could dream of. Before 1950 we could only watch a few variables in very circumscribed situations. Now it is possible, by means of this new extension of our brains, to watch millions of variables and to perform meaningful analyses on huge clusters of data.

The missing item in the pragmatist's theory is who shall design the experiment, who shall run it, who shall draw the conclusions, who shall implement the results. Does the pragmatist dare say that the answer is "those who are qualified"? Then who decides on qualifications? Scientists? Why should the rest of society trust the scientist? Because he knows more? But knowledge can be turned to evil as well as good.

The muddle of our age is implementation. There are those who believe that people of quality should study social problems and implement their findings in order to provide the "best" environment for all to live in. They want the experts to educate the uneducated, develop underdeveloped countries, employ the unemployed. The ultimate aim of the experts is to bring the underprivileged into a society where eventually all persons are qualified, all will share in designing better systems. Unfortunately, none of these modern do-gooders can tell us why he is especially qualified to do the job he has set out to do. Surely the privileged people outside of Watts need "retraining" as much as the people inside, because they have a distorted view of social reality.

It is not altogether ridiculous to say that social experimentation requires that there be no experts—or, if you wish, that everyone is an expert on some relevant aspect of planning. Indeed, one measure of performance of social planning might very well be the extent of contribution of all members of society. One of the most frustrating aspects of society today is the very little that most of us can contribute to the planning of social change; at best we have an occasional vote (often on undesirable alternatives) or an occasional letter to a representative. It would be a tragedy if all the good work of the earlier pragmatists produced a society ruled by "scientific" experts, no matter how elegant their experiments might be.

I'd feel a lot happier about the coming age of man-machine digital systems if I could more clearly understand a theory of implementation of the results of social experiment.

7.2 Intelligent Testing

ALEXANDER G. WESMAN

The nature of intelligence has been a favorite subject for contemplation and disputation for centuries—perhaps from the dawn of man as Homo sapiens. The topic is being studied and debated today by educators, sociologists, geneticists, neurophysiologists, and biochemists, and by psychologists specializing in various branches of the discipline. Despite this attention and effort, however—or perhaps *because* of it—there appears to be no more general agreement as to the nature of intelligence or the most valid means of measuring intelligence than was the case 50 years ago. Concepts of intelligence and the definitions constructed to enunciate these concepts abound by the dozens, if not indeed by the hundreds.

With so many diverse definitions of intelligence, it is perhaps not surprising that we cannot agree on how to measure intelligence. It is my conviction that much of the confusion which plagued us in the past, and continues to plague us today, is attributable to our ignoring two propositions which should be obvious:

1. Intelligence is an attribute, not an entity.
2. Intelligence is the summation of the learning experiences of the individual.

We have all too often behaved as though intelligence is a physical substance, like a house or an egg crate composed of rooms or cells; we might better remember that it is no more to be reified than attributes like beauty, or speed, or honesty. There are objects which are classifiable as beautiful; there are performances which may be characterized as speedy; there are behaviors which display honesty. Each of these is measurable, with greater or lesser objectivity. Because they can be measured, however, does not mean they are substances. We

Reprinted with slight abridgment from the *American Psychologist*, 1968, **23**, 267–274, with permission of the author and the American Psychological Association, Inc.

may agree with E. L. Thorndike that if something exists it can be measured; we need not accept the converse notion that if we can measure something it has existence as a substance.

Intelligence as here defined is a summation of learning experiences. The instances in which intelligent behavior is observed may be classified in various ways that appear to be logical or homogeneous, but they are individual instances all the same. Each instance represents a response the organism has learned; each learned response in turn predisposes the organism for learning additional responses which permit the organism to display new acts of intelligent behavior.

For our present purposes, it matters little whether we are more comfortable with stimulus-response bonds, with experience-producing drives, with imprinting, or with neuropsychological explanations of *how* or *why* learning occurs; whatever the learning theory, the fundamental principle is universal. We start with an organism which is subject to modification by interaction with the environment; as a product of that interaction, the organism has been modified. Further interaction involves a changed organism—one which is ready to interact with its environment in a new way.

Organisms may differ from one another in their susceptibility to modification. One organism may need a more potent stimulus to trigger reaction to the environment than does another. A particular organism may respond to a given class of stimuli more readily than it does to other kinds of stimuli. Organisms may differ from one another in their readiness to respond to different classes of stimuli. There may be important differences in the ability of organisms to modify their behavior in effective ways as a result of experience.

We may develop and investigate hypotheses as to whether such differences in response as are displayed arise from variations in neurological endowment or in conducive environment. All that we can be sure of, at least as of now, is that what we are dealing with is a response-capable organism which has been exposed to environmental stimuli, has interacted in some way with those stimuli, and has been modified thereby.

The bits or modules which constitute intelligence may be information or may be skill; i.e., they may be content or process. Furthermore, they are multidimensional, and some modules may have more dimensions than do others. Each module is subject to essential change as the individual is exposed to further learning experiences. Each act of learning serves to create new modules, change the existing ones, or both. Modules are not independent; rather, they may overlap with several or many other modules; thus, they are complex both in their number of dimensions and in their interrelationships. Even early percepts are rarely if ever simple. A toy ball when first seen has at least size, shape, and color; if it is touched, it has texture and hardness as well. Accordingly, few if any modules of learning are truly simple.

The whole of a person's intelligence at any given moment may well be thought of as an amorphous mass—not a regular geometric figure. Within this mass, modules may cluster with greater or lesser permanence, and may be organized along principles of relatedness. Thus, word knowledge may form a cluster—but the words of which one has knowledge will be components of other clusters as well. A pencil is an object one writes with; it has shape in common with other objects, it has function in common with pens and crayons, it produces color of varying intensity, it has a number property, it is usually associated with paper. The learned module "pencil" may thus be part of many clusters.

One need not posit that a learning module is permanent. It could, presumably, disappear entirely, although far more often we would expect it to undergo essential change by taking on a more complex character. This model does assume that higher learning depends so intimately and essentially on certain previous learnings that the more complex modules cannot exist without the antecedent modules from which they grew. For example, if the ability to subtract numbers should disappear, the ability to do long division could not remain unaffected. Thus, retention of learning is integral to the concept here proposed.

The simple-minded conceptualization outlined above may have horrified those of my colleagues who are even moderately sophisticated with respect to modern learning theories. To those colleagues I apologize, but I also beg their indulgence. Oversimplified as the conceptualization undoubtedly is, I believe it does no *essential* violence to any current theory; it has, I hope, the virtue of permitting a view of the organization of intelligence, and of the nature of the

testing of intelligence, which may prove illuminating for several issues which confront us.

ISSUE I: THE CLASSIFICATION OF ABILITY TESTS INTO APTITUDE, ACHIEVEMENT, AND INTELLIGENCE MEASURES

As soon as we have agreed that what we know and what we can do intellectually is learned, the artificiality of the above classification becomes self-evident. Historically, we have recognized that what achievement tests measure is what the examinee has learned. We have been less ready to accord similar recognition to intelligence tests. In their case, we have too often behaved as though what these tests measure is somehow independent of the learning phenomenon. We have played the role of Aladdin seeking a magical lamp, complete with a genie ready to spring forth with full power to accomplish all sorts of wondrous things. We have pondered wistfully on the number of critical issues that would be resolved if we could only somehow measure "intelligence" separately from "achievement."

We have been similarly unrealistic in treating the concept of "aptitude." Our textbooks enunciate the distinction that aptitude tests measure what the individual *can* learn, while achievement tests measure what he *has* learned. Some of our leading theorists aggravate the confusion by ignoring the implications of their special use of the term. "Aptitude" is typically used in laboratory learning experiments as a matching or otherwise controlling variable; it is employed to assure that groups to be compared start the experiment as equal in initial ability. One gets a strong impression that the aptitude instrument is perceived as measuring the innate potential of the individual as distinguished from what is to be achieved (i.e., learned) in the experimental process. If learning theorists recognize that what they are calling "aptitude" (or, for that matter, "intelligence") is "previously learned" (as, clearly, at least some of them do), the artificiality of the distinction between "aptitude" or "intelligence" and "achievement" should be eminently apparent.

I wish that at least a few of my psychometric colleagues would leave off searching for *the* structure of intelligence, and devote their wisdom and energy to learning more about the learning process, and to teaching learning theorists about testing. I am convinced that both specialties would profit immeasurably from the cooperative enterprise. It is my strong impression that the inattention of the psychometrician to the facts of learning is matched fully by the unsophisticated treatment accorded to testing by many learning theorists.

All ability tests—intelligence, aptitude, and achievement—measure what the individual *has* learned—and they often measure with similar content and similar process. Let us take, for example, an item[1] such as this: A square and a rectangle have the same perimeter. The square has an area of 10,000 square feet. The rectangle has an area of 9,324 square

[1]This item was proposed by G. K. Bennett in another context as an example of an arithmetic problem which might be correctly answered by any of several methods.

feet. What are the dimensions of the rectangle?

This item would clearly be deemed appropriate whether it appeared in an achievement test in high school mathematics, a test of aptitude for mathematics, or the numerical portion of an "intelligence" test. I submit that a great many items can equally readily fit any of the three categories.

Such justification as we have for our labeling system resides entirely in the *purpose* for which the test is used, not in the test document itself. If our intent is to discover how much the examinee has learned in a particular area, such as a school course, we may select items which probe for the distinctive learnings the schooling was intended to stimulate. We label the test an "achievement" test. If our intent is to predict what success an individual is likely to attain in learning a new language, or a new job, we seek those specific previous learnings the possession of which bodes favorably for that future learning, and we label the test an "aptitude" test or a "special aptitude test." If our intent is to predict future acquisition of learning over broad areas of environmental exposure, we seek those previous learnings the possession of which will be relevant to as many, and as important, future learning situations as we can anticipate. This test we label an "intelligence" test. The selection of test items or sample tasks for the three purposes may or may not differ; but in each instance what is measured is what was previously learned. We are not measuring different abilities; we are merely attending to different criteria. It is the *relevance* of the learnings we select for investigation that largely determines how we name our test, and whether we will succeed in our purpose.

ISSUE II: THE UTILITY OF CULTURE-FREE AND CULTURE-FAIR TESTS

The notion of relevance of previous learnings leads naturally to a consideration of some follies we have committed in the search for culture-free or culture-fair instruments. I do not wish to impugn the high social motives which stimulate the search for such devices; I do wish to question that such a search, in its usual setting, is sensible. A culture-free test would presumably probe learnings which had not been affected by environment; this is sheer nonsense. A culture-fair test attempts to select those learnings which are common to many cultures. In the search for experiences which are common to several different cultures or subcultures, the vital matter of relevance of the learning for our purpose is subordinated or ignored.

The implicit intent in the attempt to create culture-free or culture-fair tests is somehow to measure intelligence without permitting the effects of differential exposure to learning to influence scores. This contains the tacit assumption that "native intelligence" lies buried in pure form deep in the individual, and needs only to be uncovered by ingenious mining methods. If we recognize that intelligence comprises learning experiences, it becomes clear that our attempts are not ingenious, but ingenuous.

It is true that we can probe learnings that have occurred in nonverbal, non-numerical domains. This means only that we can test selected aspects of intelligence. The question immediately arises of the relevance of these special domains to the kinds of learnings we will want to predict. The measurement purpose for which culture-fair tests are ordinarily developed is that of predicting academic or industrial performance. Most academic courses and most industrial jobs involve some use of verbal abilities. Since further learning is conditioned by relevant past learning, the individual who has developed more of the prerequisite ability inevitably has an advantage over the individual with less of the prerequisite ability. If we wish to predict whether an individual will profit appreciably from additional exposure to learning, our best predictor must be a measure which appraises what prerequisite learning he has acquired heretofore. Appropriate verbal abilities are more relevant to the largely verbal learning we usually wish to predict than other abilities are.

It has on occasion been suggested that tests be developed which sample the verbal skills or factual information which are peculiar to a given subculture. Such tests are proposed as a "fairer" measure of the "intelligence," or readiness to learn, of the members of that subculture. The response to this proposal is "readiness to learn *what?*" If our purpose is to distinguish members of that subculture from their peers with respect to how much of that special culture they have assimilated, such a test might well be useful. If, as is more likely the case, we wish to predict future learnings of the content of the more general culture (e.g., the so-called white, middle-class culture which typifies what the majority of our schools are organized to transmit), tests designed for the subculture will be less relevant than those which sample from the general culture. This is not intended to imply that the members of the subculture *could* not learn what the schools as constituted are offering. It does emphasize that, at the moment at which we make our appraisal, what the individual has already learned from the general culture domain is the most significant information as to what he is then ready to learn. The less relevant the previous learnings we appraise, the more hazardous must be our predictions of future learnings.

As long as our educational system and our general culture are dependent on conventional verbal abilities, those who aspire to progress in that system and that culture will need to command those abilities. In a verbal society, verbal competence cannot sensibly be ignored.

ISSUE III: IS "VERBAL ABILITY" SYNONYMOUS WITH "INTELLIGENCE"?

To say that we cannot afford to ignore learnings in relevant verbal areas when we are appraising "intelligence" does not imply that *only* the verbal domain is important. The development of tests of "general mental ability" which sample only the verbal domain implies that since verbal tests predict school criteria best, it is unnecessary to attend to other cognitive abilities the student has developed; in other words, that, in effect, "verbal ability" is synonymous with "intelligence." It would be most unfortunate

if, consciously or unconsciously, we adopted this too narrow perspective.

That verbal tests are typically good predictors of grades in many academic courses is undeniable. *Why* this is the case warrants some thought. Is it because all, or even most, of what constitutes "intelligence" is represented by verbal ability? Certainly the chief symbol system of our society is verbal. Even when we deal with numerical, spatial, or figural problems we often transform them to verbal expressions. It is one thing, however, to recognize the involvement of verbal abilities in all kinds of learning experiences and quite another to grant them exclusive sovereignty over learning domains. Many domains require the possession of other abilities as well, but our appraisal methods are often inadequate to reveal that need. Because it is easier to employ verbal criteria, or more convenient—or because we have given insufficient thought to criterion validity—we predetermine the finding that verbal abilities dominate the scene.

A particularly revealing demonstration of this phenomenon came to the attention of the authors of the Differential Aptitude Tests some years ago. Grades in an auto mechanics course were found to be better predicted by the Verbal Reasoning test of the DAT than by the Mechanical Reasoning test. We had the unusual good fortune of having access to further information about the course. We discovered that early in the course the teacher had been called from the room for almost a half-hour. In his absence, the students had disobeyed his instructions not to fool around with the automobile motors. To let the punishment fit the crime, he conducted the rest of the course almost entirely by lecturing, giving the students minimum opportunity for actually working with the engines. That grades in a course taught by lecture and evaluated by a written test should be best predicted by a verbal test is not too surprising!

An illustration such as the above should force us to stop and think. As we study tables replete with validity coefficients, how many of those coefficients represent similar instances? As we develop hypotheses as to the importance of particular aspects of intelligence, how well do we understand the *criteria* which gave rise to the coefficients on which our hypotheses are based? Would the use of more valid criteria in courses for which curricular goals transcend verbal skills, have produced similar data, or different? Would the admittedly broad pervasiveness of verbal skills seem quite so broad if more appropriate measures of learning were employed? If we remain complacent about criteria composed largely of behaviors from the verbal domain, we are unlikely to see the relevance of other abilities.

In his APA presidential address in 1964, McNemar paid flattering attention to the Differential Aptitude Tests; he quite accurately reported that the verbal tests were most frequently the best predictors of course grades. The data he cited certainly supported the point he was making: Verbal tests predict grades in many academic courses. What might well have been added was recognition that the nature of our educational criteria exaggerates the real importance of verbal skills. If (and it is hoped *when*) grades or other criterion statements become more content-valid, the relevance of a number of other skills will be more demonstrable.

Industry has perforce learned this lesson. Few mechanical apprentices are selected solely, or even primarily, because they can describe a process, rather than perform it. The military has learned that the ability to diagnose a malfunctioning torpedo is poorly demonstrated by verbal exposition, but well demonstrated by a work sample requiring actual mechanical repairs. It is to be hoped that education will increasingly become more realistic with respect to what *its* criteria *should* be.

ISSUE IV: THE GROWTH AND DECLINE OF "INTELLIGENCE"

So preoccupied have we been with reifying intelligence as some mystical substance that we have too often neglected to take a common-sense look at what intelligence tests measure. We find ourselves distressed at our failure to predict with satisfactory accuracy the intelligence test scores of a teenager from his intelligence test scores as an infant. Why should this occasion surprise, let alone distress? If we look inside the tests, it should be obvious that the kinds of learnings we typically appraise at the earlier ages bear little resemblance, and may have little relevance, to the kinds of learnings we appraise later.

At the earlier age levels, we have typically tested for such characteristics as motor dexterity, perception, and similar features of physical development. When intellectual concepts become available for testing as baby grows to infant, to child, to teenager, we change the focus of our testing from the physical domains to the cognitive—we appraise knowledge, concept formation, and reasoning.

It is possible that future research will disclose that possession of certain physical abilities or tendencies is prerequisite to the development of concept formation, and that earlier possession of these characteristics will foretell the future intellectual development of the individual. Interesting and promising research now being conducted is directed toward this goal. It is my opinion that, because learning experiences vary so from one child to another, there is some practical limit beyond which we will be unable to predict, however penetrating our research. In any event, we would do well at this moment to recognize that since we are measuring in different ability domains at infant and school-age levels, we should not expect good prediction from one level to the other—and we should certainly not behave as though the data permitted confident prediction.

At the other end of the age spectrum we have, with similar lack of insight, proceeded to corollary errors. We have accepted the gloomy dictum that once we have passed the age of 18, or 25, or 35, we have passed our peak; from that age, our ability to learn declines. Our texts are peppered with charts showing that depressing downhill slide. What is the basis for this widely accepted conclusion? The principal basis is that when we apply our conventional measures of intelligence to older people, we find that average scores decrease. We have implicitly accepted the idea that intelligence is defined by what is measured by these particular intelligence tests. If, however, we

return to our previous formulation of intelligence as what we know in a wide variety of domains, and hence as a base for what we can learn at a given moment, our perspective changes. We then proceed to compare what the intelligence tests measure with the kinds of learning individuals have engaged in from age 30 or 40 on. The relevance of the tests, except perhaps as measures of retention, is seen as increasingly remote with each passing year. Most individuals have not failed to learn more with added years of life. Their learnings have occurred in areas (science, business, politics, psychology, psychometrics), often relatively specialized, which are not measured by conventional intelligence tests.

It is true that new learnings of adults occur in such a variety of endeavors that it would be virtually impossible to find a common core on which all could be examined. We should not, however, pretend we do not suffer this psychometric disability; we should not continue to use less relevant measures to support deceptive graphs and curves of the decline of "intelligence." We might better recognize the limitations of our measure, until such time as we can devise relevant measures of the significant learnings which do occur. For the present, we can conclude only that with each passing decade older people do less well on tests designed for younger adults.

ISSUE V: THE SEARCH FOR PURITY

A discussion of the nature of intelligence, and of intelligent testing, should not ignore the topic of factor analysis. It is a method which has influenced test construction and test selection. It is a technique which has stimulated the promulgation of theories of the structure of intellect.

The history of psychometrics gives evidence that each new major technique has attained a heyday of popularity, during which unrealistic hopes led to unbridled use. In the 1920s and 1930s, Pearson product-moment coefficients held the stage; everybody seemed to be correlating everything with everything else with wild abandon. We appear, in more recent times, to have been engaging in factor analyses with almost equal fenzy. With so much activity going on, it is perhaps to be expected that some studies, and some conclusions, would be characterized more by enthusiasm than by wisdom.

To criticize factor analysis as a procedure because individuals have misled themselves through its use would be very silly indeed. Among the benefits it has provided are the ability to summarize vast masses of data, and to facilitate the organization of information in a way that inspires, and then leads to investigation of interesting and often fruitful research hypotheses. At the same time, we need not believe that the power of the tool assures the validity of the product. Some of the conclusions which have been drawn, some attitudes which have been adopted, and some theories which have occasionally been treated as though they were established fact might well be exposed to scrutiny.

There have been instances in which a test battery was chosen for practical use *because* it had its origins in a program of factorial research. Presumably, the rationale was that such a battery consists

of relatively "pure"tests, and would show near-zero intercorrelation among the tests; it would therefore be more efficient than a battery of similar measures not derived from factorial studies. If this rationale survived empirical study, it would still not of itself be adequate justification for selecting one set of tests rather than another. Efficiency is certainly desirable—but *validity* is *crucial*. How tests were constructed is interesting and even germane; how they *work* is the critical issue.

Let us return, however, to the rationale. Is the leap from "factorial origin" to "purity" defensible? The "pure" tests developed in psychometric laboratories often do correlate very little with one another. To some degree, at least, this low correlation is frequently ascribable to the unreliability of short, experimental tests, or to restriction in range of the various abilities of the subject, or both. For exploratory and research purposes, these conditions represent a reasonable situation. Practical test use situations are something else again.

When batteries of reliable tests with factorial ancestry, and batteries testing in similar domains but not factor oriented, are given to the same students, the within-battery intercorrelation of scores is ordinarily of about the same order. For example, with one ninth-grade group of boys, the average inter-r among the Differential Aptitude Tests was .37; for the same group, the average inter-r of the Primary Mental Abilities Tests was .36. Similar results were obtained in a comparison of the DAT and the General Aptitude Test Battery scores for a twelfth-grade group. Thus, there was little evidence of greater "purity" in the factorially derived batteries than in the

DAT, which were not so derived. (In the everyday world, it appears, "purity" is all too likely to be an illusion.) Accordingly, we would be well advised when choosing tests for practical use to concentrate on how they work, not on how they were built.

Let us now turn briefly to the role of factor analysis as a stimulator of hypotheses concerning the structure of intellect. Its influence has often seemed to be not so much mathematicodeductive as mathematico*seductive*! The power of the method as a way of manipulating great masses of data appears all too often to have led us astray. Even our more eminent protagonists of the technique have not always appeared immune. When expounding on the theory of factor analysis, experts almost invariably agree that factors are merely descriptive categories; they are not functional entities. But when engaged in interpreting the factors which have emerged from their studies, some analysts apparently succumb to the mystic charm of rotating axes and perceive entities which, they have told us, do not exist. The lure of the temptation to discover a psychological structure analogous to the periodic table of the elements is too powerful to resist. We then hear of "primary mental abilities" or are shown "the three faces of intellect." Though the authors of such creations have sometimes demonstrated in other writings that they well understand the difference between the reality of descriptive categories and the illusion of underlying entities, some of their disciples and many of their readers seem less clear in their perception.

If we accept the thesis that the modules or bits which constitute intelli-gence are themselves complex, a combination of such modules can hardly be expected to be simple or "pure." A 6-year-old who assembles three alphabet blocks to spell out "cat" has employed, at a minimum, verbal and spatial skills; if he is aware that there are three blocks or letters, he has engaged in numerical perception as well. The ability to perform the task has required cognition, memory, convergent thinking, and evaluation. The product is figural, symbolic, and semantic. All this, and we have not yet taken into account such considerations as the motor-manipulative activity, the perception of color, the earlier learning experiences which enabled him to perform the task successfully, or the imagery which the concept "cat" induces in him. We, as analysts, may choose to attend to only a single aspect of the behavior—but the behavior itself remains multifaceted and complex. To assume that we can abstract from a host of such activities a pure and simple entity is to ignore the psychological meaning of intelligent behavior.

Let us continue to explore, by all means available to us (including factor analysis) the nature of man's abilities. Let us *not* assume that the results of research obtained under closely managed conditions in the laboratory will hold true as realities in day-to-day situations. Let us not unwittingly forget that the descriptive categories we adopt for convenience in communication do not have real existence as ultimate psychological entities.

CONCLUSION

To what view of a structure of intellect am I led by the ideas I have enunciated here? Essentially, I believe intelligence is *un*structured. I believe that it is differently comprised in every individual—the sum total of all the learning experiences he has uniquely had up to any moment in time. Such structure as we perceive is structure which we have imposed. We can so select samples of previous learnings to examine as to reveal a general factor, or group factors, or specifics. We can sample from domains that are relatively homogeneous and apply labels such as verbal, numerical, spatial; we can sample from a wider variety of learnings, and apply labels such as "general mental ability" or, simply, "intelligence."

There are many bases on which we may choose which kinds of learnings we will sample. The most reasonable basis, I believe, is that of predictive purpose. Those previous learnings should be probed which are most relevant to the particular future learnings we wish to predict. In addition to criterion—or, more likely, *criteria*—relevance, the principles of band width and fidelity (as enunciated by Cronbach and Gleser) might well serve as guides. If we are interested in forecasting narrow-band criteria, selection of highly homogeneous, directly relevant behaviors is indicated. If we are interested in a wide range of criteria, we have at least two options: we may choose to select small samples from widely scattered domains—as in a Binet, a Wechsler, or a broader gauge instrument still to be devised—or examine more intensively with several narrower gauge tests, as in the Differential Aptitude Tests. The broader gauge instruments will offer economy, but lesser fidelity for selected

criteria. The narrower gauge instruments will be longer and more time consuming—but the possibility of more direct relevance to one or more particular criteria should permit higher fidelity.

The critical issue, then, is not which approach measures intelligence—each of them does, in its own fashion. No approach save sampling from every domain in which learnings have occurred—an impossible task—fully measures intelligence. The question is rather which approach provides the most useful information for the various purposes we wish the test to serve. Recognition that what we are measuring is what the individual has learned, and composing our tests to appraise *relevant* previous learnings, will yield the most useful information. We, and those who utilize the results of our work—educators, personnel men, social planners—face problems for which intelligence test data are relevant, and sometimes crucial. We must remember, and we must teach, what our test scores really reflect. The measurement of intelligence is not, and has not been, a matter of concern only to psychology. It has always been, and continues to be, an influence on educational and social programs. If we are to avert uninformed pressures from government agencies, from school administrators, from the courts, and indeed from psychologist colleagues, we must understand and we must broadly communicate what these scores truly represent. Only then can we who build tests and they who use them properly claim that we are indeed engaged in intelligent testing.

7.3 The Fulfillment of Promise: 40-Year Follow-up of the Terman Gifted Group

MELITA H. ODEN

I. HISTORY AND BACKGROUND, 1921-1960

It was more than 40 years ago that Dr. Lewis M. Terman undertook his monumental study of gifted children, and scattered rather widely throughout the world today are close to 1400 more or less middle-aged people who have one thing in common: in 1921-1922 they were selected as subjects in the Terman Study of the Gifted. The only requisite for inclusion in this group was an intelligence rating that placed the student in the top 1 per cent of the school population as measured by a standardized test of intelligence. The purpose of the study was to discover what gifted children are like as children, what sort of adults they become, and what some of the factors are that influence their development.

The search for subjects was confined chiefly to the public schools of the larger and medium-sized urban areas of California. A total of 1528 subjects (857 boys and 671 girls) were selected. For children below high school age the requirement was a Stanford-Binet IQ of 140 or higher. This group who made up 70 per cent of the total had a mean IQ of 151 with 77 subjects testing at IQ 170 or higher. Because of the lack of top in the 1916 Stanford-Binet, students of high school age were given the Terman Group Test of Mental Ability. The requirement for this test was a score within the top 1 per cent of the general school population on which the norms were established. Later follow-up tests indicated that the older subjects were as highly selected for mental ability as the Binet-tested group. The subjects averaged about 11 years of age (boys, 11.5 years; girls, 10.8 years) when originally tested and ranged in age from 3 to 19 years. The range of age by year of birth, however, is more than 20

Reprinted from *Genetic Psychology Monographs*, 1968, **77**, 3–93, with permission of the author and The Journal Press. This selection consists of brief portions of the original article, and readers are referred to it for more complete details.

years; this is accounted for by the inclusion of a small number who had been tested in a preliminary study (1917–1920) and a group of 58 siblings added as a result of the testing program in the 1927–1928 follow-up study of the original group. No subjects except siblings of the original group were added after 1923 and none at all after 1928.

At the time of the original investigation, in addition to the intelligence score on which the selection of the subjects was based, a large amount of case data was collected including developmental record, health history and medical examinations, home and family background, school history, trait ratings and personality evaluations by parents and teachers, tests of interests, character and personality, and a battery of school achievement tests. In the 40 years that the group has been under observation, their development has been followed closely through follow-up surveys at fairly regular intervals. Three of these surveys have been field studies in which the subjects and their families were interviewed, tests of both intelligence and personality administered, and questionnaire data of various kinds secured. The field follow-ups were made in 1927–1928, 1939–1940, and 1950–1952. Surveys by mail were made in 1936, 1945, 1955, and, most recently, in 1960.

The extent to which contact with the subjects has been maintained is unequalled for longitudinal studies. In the course of the investigation only 26 subjects (10 men and 16 women) have been lost track of entirely. For these persons no information has been obtained at least since 1928 and in some cases not since 1922. Although the subjects have not all been equally cooperative, in the field

studies approximately 95 per cent have participated actively and for another 3 per cent some, though often fragmentary, information has been obtained. As might be expected, in the follow-ups by mail the proportion of cooperating subjects dropped slightly to about 90 per cent in 1936, 1945, and 1955. However, except for the 26 lost cases, some information, even if only a confirmation of address, has been obtained in every survey for all but a very few members of the group. The findings to 1955 of this long-term research program have been presented in detail in the following four volumes published by the Stanford University Press: *Mental and Physical Traits of a Thousand Gifted Children* (5), *The Promise of Youth* (1), *The Gifted Child Grows Up* (6), and *The Gifted Group at Mid-Life* (7).

The present report is in two parts. The first part gives the findings of the 1960 follow-up for the total group with the data reported separately for men and women. The second part is a study of success among gifted men based on an analysis of the total case history data in order to identify the correlates of vocational achievement. . . .†

1960 FOLLOW-UP OF TOTAL GROUP: SUMMARY AND CONCLUSIONS

The Terman Study of the Gifted was undertaken with two purposes: (*a*) to discover the physical, mental, and personality traits that are characteristic of intellectually superior children, and (*b*)

†Editor's Note: Space limitations do not permit reprinting of the rather extensive data reported by Dr. Oden, and only her summaries will be reported here. Interested readers are referred to her original article for the details of her findings.

to observe the development of these children to maturity (and beyond, as it turned out) in order to learn what sort of adult the typical gifted child becomes. The first question was answered in the original investigation of 1922 which, in brief, showed that children of IQ 140 or higher are, in general, appreciably superior to unselected children in physique, health, and social adjustment; markedly superior in moral attitudes as measured by either character tests or trait ratings; and vastly superior in mastery of school subjects. The typical gifted child is characterized by many and varied interests with an interest maturity level two or three years above the age norm. His ability as shown by tests is so general as to refute completely the traditional belief that gifted children are one-sided. There is, however, a wide range of variability within the gifted group, and emphasis on central tendencies should not obscure the fact that gifted children, far from falling into a single pattern, represent a variety of patterns (7).

The most recent follow-up brings the records up to 1960 when the subjects averaged approximately 50 years of age. Thus it is now possible after close to 40 years of continuous follow-up to give a definitive answer to the question: "What sort of adults do they become?" All the evidence indicates that with few exceptions the superior child becomes the superior adult. He maintains his intellectual ability, as measured by the Concept Mastery tests of 1940 and 1950; his mortality rate is lower than that of the general white population of like age; his physical health, according to his own opinion and substantiated by the field worker reports and other sources of in-

formation, is good or very good (so rated by approximately 90 per cent of subjects). The incidence of serious mental illness and personality problems appears to be no greater, and perhaps less, than that found in the general population; and crime is practically nonexistent.

In educational and vocational achievements persons of superior intelligence should be expected to rank considerably above the general population, and the gifted subjects, both men and women, more than fulfill this expectation. Approximately 87 per cent of men are engaged in occupations at the professional and higher business and semiprofessional levels. Additional evidence of the superior vocational record of the majority of the gifted men is found in a long list of publications, patents, and other professional and business output, as well as in the many recognitions and honors accorded them.

Women are far less interested in vocational careers and achievements than are men. Some 42 per cent of the women are employed full-time, with three-fifths of the employed women doubling as housewives. The two most frequent occupations are school teaching in first place and secretarial and related office work in second place. A number of the relatively small group of women who have seriously and wholeheartedly pursued a professional or business career have enjoyed marked success, shown in the importance and prestige of their positions, their scientific and literary contributions, and the distinctions won. Being a housewife and homemaker is an important and satisfying career in the opinion of most gifted women, but few housewives in the Terman group limit their activities to the home. The majority of the women, both the housewives and those who are employed, are active participants in the promotion of community welfare and civic betterment.

Civic and community activities, however, are not limited to women, either the housewives or those employed. The majority of men also find time to make important contributions in time and effort to the promotion of the common good. Both men and women have shown their interest in and obligation to our democratic society in their voting record; approximately 95 per cent say they vote "always" or "usually." In political and social viewpoint the subjects tend, on the average, to consider themselves about midway between "extremely radical" and "extremely conservative." Men, however, somewhat more often than women rate themselves to the right of center. Both sexes moved to the right in the 20-year period between 1940 and 1960. The trend to conservatism may be a function of age or may be due to the changing socioeconomic milieu; probably both factors play a part.

Two-thirds of the men and almost as large a proportion of the women consider that they have lived up to their intellectual abilities fully or reasonably well. Opinion on the extent to which intellectual abilities have been realized is related both to education and to occupational status. Those with college degrees, both men and women, more often feel that they have lived up to their abilities. Men on the upper rungs of the vocational ladder are also more likely to express satisfaction with their accomplishments. More of the women who are employed full-time than of housewives consider

that they have lived up to their abilities; however, close to three-fifths of housewives rate themselves as living up to their intellectual abilities fully or reasonably well.

In selecting those aspects of life from which the greatest satisfaction is derived, more than 80 per cent of men check "work itself." Only 53 per cent of all women check this aspect of life, but of the employed women 84 per cent check "work itself" as a source of satisfaction, a slightly larger figure than that for men. "Marriage" and "children" are in second and third place with both men and women as sources of satisfaction. When the percentages who name these two aspects of life are computed for married subjects only, "marriage" ranks slightly ahead of "work itself" as the aspect of life from which the greatest satisfaction is derived.

An earlier volume in the series of publications on the Terman study was *The Promise of Youth* (1). Now after 40 years of careful investigation there can be no doubt that for the overwhelming majority of subjects the promise of youth has been more than fulfilled. The Terman study has shown that the great majority of gifted children do indeed live up to their abilities. . . .

COMPARATIVE STUDY OF MOST AND LEAST SUCCESSFUL MEN IN THE TERMAN GIFTED GROUP: SUMMARY AND CONCLUSIONS

Because of its longitudinal nature, the Terman Study of the Gifted offers a unique opportunity to study the correlates of vocational achievement among a group of men, all of whom in childhood were in the top 1 per cent of the school population in mental ability. In the present study, the achievements to 1960 of approximately 750 men in the Terman group were evaluated by two judges, and two contrasting groups selected: the 100 most successful (A group) and the 100 least successful (C group). The groups were compared on all aspects of the voluminous data collected between 1921 and 1960 in order to identify the factors that make for outstanding achievement.

Only a few of the many variables in the family background discriminate to a significant extent between the two groups. Outstanding among these are the superior socioeconomic status of the parents of the A group shown in higher educational attainments, and greater frequency of professional occupations. Also important was the stability of the home; the parental divorce rate was markedly lower among the A group than among the C group.

In the autobiographical report made at about 40 years of age, the variables that most distinguished the A and C men in their childhood and youth were the greater extent to which the A parents encouraged initiative and independence on the part of the subjects, and their encouragement as well as their expectation of school success and of college attendance. Reporting in retrospect, the A's reliably more often than the C's indicate above average interest, in their youth and early adulthood, in school success, in leadership, and in having friends. The A's also more often report above average energy, vocational planning at an earlier age, and greater satisfaction in their work.

A comparison of the interests, abili-ties, and personality characteristics in childhood and youth yielded only a few items that differed reliably. Chief among these were the trait ratings of the subjects made by the parents and teachers in 1922, and again in 1928. In 1922, although the ratings on all traits favored the A's, the difference was significant only for the volitional traits. In 1928, however, when the subjects were adolescent, the A's were rated significantly higher not only on the volitional but also in the intellectual and, to a less marked degree, on the moral and social traits.

The early scholastic records showed little difference between the groups; however, the A's were more accelerated in grade placement than were the C's, finishing both eighth grade and high school at reliably younger ages. The groups began to pull apart in achievement in high school with the A's excelling not only in school marks but also in extent of participation in extracurricular activities. The trend toward scholastic achievement continued and more than twice as many A's as C's graduated from college. The A's were younger at receiving their degrees, earned better grades, won more honors, and more often held positions of leadership in college activities.

Other distinguishing characteristics in the early years were the greater interest of the A's in collections, their greater liking for school, and their greater tractability in regard to discipline.

Ratings made on 13 traits of personality by the parents, the wives (if married), and the subjects themselves in 1940 when the men averaged close to age 30 brought out significant differences in personality between the A and C groups.

The traits in which they differed the most were self-confidence, perseverance, and integration toward goals. The three sets of ratings, each made independently, agreed in rating the A's as possessing these traits to a reliably greater degree than the C's. The A's also suffered less often from feelings of inferiority than the C's, but the difference on this trait was not quite so marked. The subjects as adults were rated by the field workers on 12 characteristics at two follow-up dates: 20 years and 10 years (1940 and 1950, respectively) before their selection for the A and C groups. The ratings all favored the A group; especially notable were the significantly higher ratings for the A's on appearance, attractiveness, poise, attentiveness, curiosity, and originality.

Since in childhood all subjects ranked within the 99th percentile in intellectual abilities, no great difference could be expected in early test scores. Although the mean childhood Binet IQ for the A's was 157, the mean IQ of 150 for the C's was also well within the top one per cent of the norms and about the same as the mean for the total group of gifted subjects. The scores on the Terman Group Test given to high school age subjects in 1922 and in 1928 were practically the same for the two groups. The Concept Mastery Test given in 1940 and again in 1950 yielded a higher mean score at both dates for the A's than for the C's, but at least some of this difference can be accounted for by the difference in education of the groups. Even though scoring about half a standard deviation below the A's, the C men score well above the norms for various college graduate and graduate student popula-

tions. Thus it would appear that the intellectual superiority of the C's as well as that of the A's has, to a large part, been maintained.

By the time the subjects reached adulthood, the differences in a number of variables which, though favoring the A's, had not been marked in the earlier years, became significant. Chief among these were health and general adjustment. In physical health the A men more often than the C men report their condition as good or very good. Even more marked is the difference in general adjustment; according to psychological evaluations, more than four-fifths of the men of the A group are "satisfactory" in adjustment as compared with less than one-half of the C men; in other words, the men of the C group are much more prone to difficulties in social and emotional adjustment.

Related to the poor adjustment on the part of the C men is the fact that they are more often single; and, of those who marry, significantly more C's than A's become divorced.

Other distinguishing variables appeared in the reports made by the subjects in 1960 at average age of 50. Prominent among these are the self-ratings on ambition for excellence in work, recognition for accomplishments, and vocational advancement in all of which the A's far surpass the C's.

In the total picture, the variables most closely associated with vocational success are a home background in which the parents place a high value on education, encourage independence and initiative, and expect a high level of accomplishment; good mental health and all-round social and emotional adjustment; and the possession of certain traits and characteristics of personality. Most important among these traits are perseverance, integration in working toward goals, and self-confidence; interest in being a leader, in having friends, and in academic success; and above average ambition, as compared with their friends and colleagues, for excellence in work, for recognition of accomplishments, and for vocational advancement. How these traits are acquired or developed is not fully answered in these data, but they are fundamental to achievement. These are the traits that provide the motivation, the drive, and the implementation of ambition that lead to the realization of potential.

The correlates of success are not possessed exclusively by the A's, for there are no factors favorable to achievement that are not also found among some, albeit a minority, of the C men, but the magic combination is lacking. It should not be overlooked that a few of the C men have deliberately chosen not to seek "success," expressing a preference for a less competitive way of life with greater opportunity for personal happiness and freedom to pursue their avocational interests.

In any case one must conclude, as was done in the 1940 study of success, that intellect and achievement are far from perfectly correlated, and that emotional stability and a composite of the personality traits that generate a drive to achieve are also necessary for outstanding achievement among intellectually gifted men.

REFERENCES

1. Burks, B. S., Jensen, D. W., and Terman, L. M. *Genetic Studies of Genius: III. The Promise of Youth.* Stanford, Calif.: Stanford Univ. Press, 1930.

2. Dublin, L. I. *Facts of Life.* New York: Macmillan, 1951.

3. Dublin, L. I., Lotka, A. J., and Spiegelman, M. *Length of Life.* New York: Ronald Press, 1949.

4. Strong, E. K., Jr. *Vocational Interests 18 Years After College.* Minneapolis, Minn.: Univ. Minnesota Press, 1955.

5. Terman, L. M. *Genetic Studies of Genius: I. Mental and Physical Traits of a Thousand Gifted Children.* Stanford, Calif.: Stanford Univ. Press, 1925.

6. Terman, L. M., and Oden, M. H. *Genetic Studies of Genius: IV. The Gifted Child Grows Up.* Stanford, Calif.: Stanford Univ. Press, 1947.

7. ———. *Genetic Studies of Genius: V. The Gifted Group at Mid-Life.* Stanford, Calif.: Stanford Univ. Press, 1959.

7.4 Biographical Correlates of Artistic and Literary Creativity in Adolescent Girls

ANNE ANASTASI AND CHARLES E. SCHAEFER

Research on the nature and correlates of creativity has been accumulating at an increasing rate. Golann (1963) classified the various approaches with reference to their emphasis on products, process, measurement, or personality. Methodologically, investigations differ in their use of evaluated achievement (which focuses on products) or test performance as *criteria of creativity*. The test criterion is open to criticism because of limitations of test coverage and inadequate or inconsistent validation data. For these reasons, the criterion employed in this study was evaluated achievement. More specifically, the present criterion reflected the essential conditions of creativeness proposed by MacKinnon (1962), which include (*a*) novelty, originality, or statistical infrequency; (*b*) adaptiveness to reality, involving the achievement of some reality-oriented goal, such as the solution of a scientific or aesthetic problem; and (*c*) sustained activity leading to the development, evaluation, and elaboration of the original idea. It is apparent that tests concentrate on the first of these conditions, largely neglecting the last two.

In the effort to identify the *correlates of creativity*, different investigators have employed aptitude and personality tests, interviews, and biographical inventories. The biographical inventory provides a standardized group procedure for gathering information about the individual's experiential history and about relevant aspects of the psychological environment in which he developed. Insofar as environment may play a significant role in the development of creativity, the biographical inventory technique should serve a dual function: (*a*) prediction of subsequent creative achievement in individuals, (*b*) identification of environmental variables conducive to the development of creative behavior.

Reprinted with slight abridgment from the *Journal of Applied Psychology,* 1969, **53**, 267–273, with permission of the authors and the American Psychological Association, Inc.

As predictive instruments, biographical inventories have repeatedly demonstrated satisfactory validity against complex industrial, military, and educational criteria (Freeberg, 1967; Henry, 1966). With regard to creative achievement, they have proved effective in differentiating between levels of creativity in several groups of scientific research workers. Such results have been obtained with petroleum research scientists (Morrison, Owens, Glennon, and Albright, 1962; Smith, Albright, Glennon, and Owens, 1961), with a variety of research personnel in a pharmaceutical company (Buel, 1965; Tucker, Cline, and Schmitt, 1967), with engineers (McDermid, 1965), and with psychologists and chemists (Chambers, 1964). In a series of studies of scientists in the National Aeronautics and Space Administration (NASA), Taylor, Ellison, and Tucker (1966) obtained validity coefficients in the .40s and .50s when biographical inventory keys were cross-validated against several criteria of creative achievement. It is also noteworthy that such biographical inventory keys have shown substantial validity generalization when applied to research scientists in other fields (Buel, Albright, and Glennon, 1966; Cline, Tucker, and Anderson, 1966).

Investigations at the high school and college level have usually employed tests as criteria, predictors, or both. Few studies have utilized biographical inventories and still fewer have done so against a criterion of evaluated achievement. Taylor, Cooley, and Nielson (1963) applied a modified version of the biographical inventory developed on NASA scientists to high school students participating in a summer science program supported by the National Science Foundation. This biographical inventory proved to be the best overall predictor of creative research performance in these students, its validity being as high as .47 in one of the groups. Parloff and Datta (1965) compared contrasted groups of participants in the Westinghouse Science Talent Search, selected on the basis of judges' ratings of their research projects. However, these groups were compared chiefly in personality test scores, the only background items reported being father's occupation, socioeconomic level, and intactness of family. Dauw (1966) successfully differentiated between highly creative and less creative adolescents by means of a biographical inventory, but his Ss were chosen on the basis of creativity tests only.

A series of studies conducted for the National Merit Scholarship Corporation report significant relationships between biographical data and subsequent creative achievement in college (Holland and Nichols, 1964; Nichols and Holland, 1963). That the obtained relationships are often low may result in part from the highly selected nature of the samples. It is of particular interest that among the many predictors investigated—including aptitude and personality tests—the best predictor of creative achievement in college was creative achievement in the same area in high school (Holland and Astin, 1962; Nichols and Holland, 1964). Even more striking is the finding that, in a large and representative sample of college freshmen, it was the students with superior high school grades who had most often won distinction for creative achievement in high school extracurricular activities (Werts, 1966). Contrary to a prevalent view, academic aptitude was closely related to creativity, especially in scientific and literary fields.

Relevant biographical data have also been obtained in studies employing interviewing or other intensive individual assessment procedures with adults who have made creative contributions in the arts or sciences (MacKinnon, 1962; Roe, 1951a, 1951b, 1953). Similar assessment techniques were utilized by Helson (1967) with college women identified through faculty nominations and ratings of creative achievement in college. In the same series of studies, Helson (1965, 1966, 1967) gathered questionnaire data regarding childhood interests and activities as recalled by her Ss. Finally, parental characteristics have been investigated in relation to children's creativity as determined by either creativity tests or evaluated achievement (Domino, 1969; Dreyer and Wells, 1966; Helson, 1966, 1967; Weisberg and Springer, 1961). The Ss of these studies included school children, high school students, and college women.

In an earlier study by the present writers (Schaefer and Anastasi, 1968), biographical inventory keys were developed in a group of 400 high school boys against criteria of creative achievement in (a) science and (b) art or creative writing. Cross-validation yielded validity coefficients of .35 and .64 for the science and art-writing keys, respectively, both significant at the .001 level. In the present study, the same basic procedures were followed in developing biographical inventory keys for high school girls in creative art and creative writing. These two fields were chosen for further exploration because in the earlier study differ-

entiation between creative and control groups was greater in the combined art and writing group than in the science group. Among high school girls, moreover, outstanding creative achievement in art or writing is more frequent than it is in science. As in the earlier study, a second major objective of the present investigation was to utilize the differentiating biographical inventory items in formulating a description of the antecedents and correlates of creativity in this population.

METHOD

Subjects

The Ss employed in the principal data analyses were 400 female students from seven public high schools in greater New York. These schools were chosen, first, because they offer courses or programs providing opportunities for creative activities and, second, because they have outstanding records of awards, prizes, and other indications of creative student achievement in art or writing. Of the 400 Ss, 246 were seniors, 128 juniors, and 26 sophomores. The group as a whole was superior with regard to educational level of parents, slightly more than one-half of the fathers and one-third of the mothers having attended college for one or more years. While over half of the parents were born in New York City, nearly one-third were foreign-born. The most frequent national ancestries were Russian, Polish, and German, in that order; 24 Ss were Negro.

The total sample comprises four criterion groups of 100 students each, designated as follows: Creative-Art (CrA), Control-Art (CoA), Creative-Writing (CrW), and Control-Writing (CoW). For inclusion in a *creative* group, S had to meet two criteria: (*a*) teacher nomination on the basis of one or more creative products to be listed on a teacher nomination form—any type of visual art or creative writing was acceptable for this purpose; (*b*) score above a minimum cutoff on Guilford Alternate Uses and Consequences tests. The *control* Ss were enrolled in the same courses from which the creative Ss were selected and were nominated by the same teachers as having provided no evidence of creative achievement. They also scored below a maximum cutoff on the two Guilford screening tests. Within each field, creative and control groups were matched in school attended, class, and grade-point average. The 400 Ss in the four criterion groups were selected from an initial pool of 1,114 nominees in the seven schools.

It should be noted that the Guilford tests were employed only as a check on irrelevant factors that might have influenced the nomination of creative or control Ss. The scores on these tests were employed only to exclude cases, never to admit them. Moreover, the two cutoff scores were sufficiently extreme as to exclude only those students whose test performance was highly discordant with their reported achievement. In terms of available published norms, the mean scores of the creative students on the two Guilford tests are approximately equal to those of college students, while the mean scores of the control groups fall close to the ninth grade mean.

Biographical Inventory

Except for minor changes, the biographical inventory employed in this study was the same as that prepared in the earlier study of high school boys (Schaefer and Anastasi, 1968). The questions were originally formulated on the basis of hypotheses and published research findings regarding the correlates of creativity. The 166 questions of this inventory are grouped into five sections designated as physical characteristics, family history, educational history, leisure-time activities, and miscellaneous. Most of the questions cover objective facts regarding present or past activities and experiences; some call for expressions of preference and others pertain to plans and goals.

The inventory contains some multiple-choice and checklist items; but many questions are open-ended. Even with the objective items, moreover, there is usually provision for additional unlisted responses. Although scoring and data analysis are more difficult under these conditions, these types of items yield a richer return of information and are especially appropriate in an exploratory study. All responses were coded prior to tabulation. For each question, there were several possible responses, the number being quite large for some questions. In addition, several questions yielded responses that could be classified from different viewpoints to test different hypotheses. For example, a response to "List your present hobbies" could be scored with reference to number of hobbies or type of hobbies; and hobbies could be sorted into types according to several different schemas. As a result, the 166 questions yielded a total of 3,962 "scorable items" or individual response alternatives employed in the item analysis.

Procedure

The biographical inventory, together with three tests employed in another part of the project, was administered by the same E to groups of 110–256 students during a 2-hr. session held in the school buildings outside of school hours. The Ss were paid for participating in this testing session. Identification numbers were assigned to provide anonymity, and students were assured of the confidentiality of their responses.

In the analysis of biographical inventory data, each of the four criterion groups was subdivided into two subgroups of 50, employed for development of scoring keys and cross-validation, respectively. Each pair of subgroups was equated in number of students from each school, class distribution, grade-point average, and mean score on the screening tests. For each of the 3,962 scorable items, classified as present or absent, a phi coefficient was computed against the dichotomous criterion of creative versus control. These coefficients were computed separately in art and writing criterion groups. All items with phi coefficients at the significance level of $p < .20$ or better were considered for inclusion in the *initial CrA and CrW scoring keys*. Some of these items were excluded because they duplicated other items, were checked by fewer than four Ss in either subgroup, or were inconsistent with other responses or with hypotheses and hence likely to have yielded isolated chance correlations.

In the initial scoring keys, a weight of 1 was assigned to items discriminating between the $p < .20$ and $p < .05$ levels, and a weight of 2 to items discriminating

at the $p < .05$ level or better. Items with higher frequencies in the creative group received positive weights; those with higher frequencies in the control group received negative weights. The initial CrA and CrW scoring keys were used in scoring the biographical inventories of the corresponding creative and control Ss in the cross-validation samples. The scorers were unaware of the criterion status of Ss. The scores thus obtained were correlated with the dichotomous criterion to provide an estimate of the validity of the scoring keys.

In order to utilize all the data in the selection of items for *final scoring keys*, item analyses were carried out independently in initial and cross-validation samples and those items were selected that differentiated between creative and control groups with a compound probability of .05 or better (Baker, 1952).

RESULTS

Application of the initial CrA and CrW biographical inventory keys to the appropriate cross-validation samples yielded the data summarized in Table 1. Although there is considerable overlapping between the scores of creative and control groups, the means of both creative groups are significantly higher than those of the corresponding control groups at the .001 level. Point-biserial correlations between biographical inventory scores and the dichotomous criterion are .34 in the art group and .55 in the writing group.

At least two conditions imposed upon the selection of Ss tend to reduce the differences between creative and control groups. First, creative and control

table 1

Biographical Inventory Scores of Criterion Groups in Cross-validation Samples

Score	Creative Art Key		Creative Writing Key	
	Creative Art	Control Art	Creative Writing	Control Writing
141–150	0	0	1	0
131–140	0	0	6	1
121–130	0	0	6	1
111–120	0	0	5	2
101–110	0	0	11	4
91–100	1	0	10	1
81–90	7	1	4	10
71–80	3	5	3	8
61–70	12	7	3	11
51–60	19	11	1	8
41–50	4	13	0	3
31–40	1	8	0	1
21–30	3	5	0	0
N	50	50	50	50
M	61.26	50.00	104.40	76.24
σ	15.65	15.04	21.57	20.87
Range	24–94	23–89	54–149	39–136
z	3.67*		6.63*	
r_{pbis}	.34*		.55*	

Note.—In order to eliminate negative scores, 50 was added to each raw score. This adjustment, however, does not exclude negative scores from the total possible range, which is −87 to 248 for the CrA key and −60 to 370 for the CrW key.

$^*p < .001$.

Ss were equated in grade-point average, although there is evidence that high school grades are in fact related to creative achievement (e.g., Werts, 1966). Second, the creative and control Ss were enrolled in the same courses in art or writing and attended high schools noted for the creative achievement of their students.

The second condition applies more strongly to the art than to the writing group, since a large proportion of Ss in the art sample were in special high schools whose students are selected on the basis of superior artistic talents. This fact is consistent with the finding that differentiation between creatives and controls was less sharp in the art than in the writing group. Not only were the mean difference and the criterion correlation higher in the writing than in the art group, but the number of significantly differentiating items was also larger in the CrW key than in the CrA key—a difference that is reflected in the higher scores obtained with this key. In the light of these sample characteristics, it should be noted that the present study is concerned with the differentiating biographical characteristics of the more highly creative Ss within an academically superior and talented population.

After the cross-validation of the initial biographical inventory keys, final keys were constructed with items whose compound probability was derived from both initial and cross-validation samples. The CrA key thus developed contains 40 items, the CrW key 82 items. An examination of these items provides a description of the biographical correlates of creativity as revealed within the conditions of this study.

DISCUSSION

Correlates of Creativity across Both Fields

The most conspicuous characteristic of the creatives in both fields is a *pervasive and continuing interest* in their chosen field and absorption in its pursuit. Items in this category include those dealing with favorite subjects in elementary school and high school; subjects found easy and those found difficult; nature of extracurricular activities in elementary school and high school, as well as anticipated extracurricular activities in college; concentration of hobbies in one's field of interest, as well as hobbies bearing a close relation to vocational goal; and reported career plans. Strength of interest is also indicated by the significantly greater number of creatives than controls in both fields reporting that they frequently became so absorbed in a project that they missed a meal or stayed up late.

Typically, the highly creative adolescent girl in this study had manifested an absorbing interest in her field since childhood and her creative activities had received recognition through exhibitions, publication, prizes, or awards. Her initial interest was thus rewarded and reinforced early in life by persons in authority, such as parents and elementary school teachers. The continuity of creative achievement over time is corroborated by the findings of other investigations, notably Helson's (1965, 1967) research with college women, the surveys of National Merit Scholarship finalists (Holland and Astin, 1962; Nichols and Holland, 1964), and our own earlier study of creative high school boys (Schaefer and Anastasi, 1968).

Several significantly differentiating items suggest a predominance of *unusual experiences* in the backgrounds of the creatives as contrasted with the controls. Thus the creatives were more likely than the controls to have had a variety of unusual experiences, to daydream about unusual things, to have collections of an unusual nature (such as ant pictures, mushrooms, and mobiles), and to have experienced eidetic imagery or had imaginary companions in childhood. To some extent, these differences may indicate greater readiness to acknowledge unusual experiences on the part of the creatives and less reluctance to report them. It is also interesting to note that more creatives than controls in both fields reported unusual types of paternal discipline, other than those listed on the inventory form. One could speculate that the prevalence of atypical experiences in their early life may contribute to the low level of conformity and conventionality generally found to characterize creative persons at all ages.

Because of the selection procedures employed, both creative and control groups tended to come from intellectually superior homes. Nevertheless, certain significant differences were found in the *familial backgrounds* of creatives and controls. In both creative groups, significantly more fathers had attended college, graduate school, or professional schools than was true in the corresponding control groups. More controls than creatives reported that no musical instrument was played in the family. Since Ss were not selected for this study on the basis of musical achievement, this difference probably reflects the general cultural level of the home. Also relevant to general home conditions may be the fact that significantly more creatives that controls reported having two or more collections.

Earlier investigations have repeatedly found creativity to be related to parental educational and occupational level and to socioeconomic level of the home, whether Ss be distinguished scientists (Chambers, 1964) or creative high school students (Schaefer and Anastasi, 1968). Nor is the relationship limited to full-fledged creative achievement. Using performance on the Minnesota Tests of Creative Thinking as a criterion, Dauw (1966) found that high-scoring high school seniors had parents with better educational backgrounds and more professional and managerial occupations than did the low scorers. Similarly, in a study of seventh grade children subdivided on the basis of scores on an originality battery, socioeconomic status yielded the largest group difference of all variables investigated (Anderson and Cropley, 1966). In explaining this finding, the authors refer first to typical lower-class parental attitudes that tend to evoke anxiety toward school learning and hence encourage convergent rather than divergent thinking. As a second reason, they cite the more varied and stimulating environment provided by homes at higher socioeconomic levels. In Parloff and Datta's (1965) study of highly selected participants in the Westinghouse Science Talent Search, the entire sample excelled above the general population in socioeconomic level and in parental educational and occupational level, although these variables were unrelated to the rated creativity of projects within the sample.

With regard to parental influence on the creative high school girls in our study, the majority of items differentiating between creatives and controls refer to the *father* rather than to the mother. In our earlier study of high school boys, the reverse was true, more of the differentiating items pertaining to the mother. These findings are consistent with those reported by Dauw (1966) for high school seniors, by MacKinnon (1962) for creative male architects, and by Helson (1966, 1967) for creative women mathematicians and creative college women. In the study of women mathematicians, moreover, Helson (1966, p. 21) reports that "the creative women were judged by interviewers to have had more identification with their fathers than comparison subjects." If such results truly indicate a greater influence of the opposite-sex parent on creative children, they may help to explain the finding that in their attitudes, interests, and problem-solving styles creative individuals show more traits of the opposite sex than do controls and generally conform less closely to sex stereotypes (see e.g., MacKinnon, 1962).

Differences between Creativity Correlates in Art and Writing Groups

The CrA and CrW groups are not directly comparable because of differences in school and class distribution and grade-point average. As might be anticipated, the grades in the CrW group average significantly higher than those in the CrA group. In the present experimental design, each creative group was equated with its own control group in these variables. The question now to be considered is whether the characteristics that significantly differentiate CrA Ss from their own controls differ in any systematic way from those that significantly differentiate the CrW Ss from their controls. This question can be answered by examining the items in the final CrA and CrW keys.

As previously noted, the CrW key contains about twice as many items as the CrA key. With few exceptions, these additional items fall into a cluster indicative of strong intellectual and "cultural" orientation and breadth of interest, both in the student herself and in her home background. The fathers of the CrW girls, as compared with those of the controls, are more likely to have one or more hobbies, frequently of an artistic or literary nature. Magazines regularly available at home are more likely to be of the cultural–intellectual types. The student herself is more likely to own classical records, attend concerts, and read more than 10 books a year, prefera-

bly in science, science fiction, philosophy, languages, or history. She regularly reads more than two sections of a newspaper, including editorials. She frequently visits art museums and galleries, has received lessons in arts or crafts, and has a large number of hobbies, beginning in childhood, to which he now devotes over 5 hr. a week. She reports owning a microscope more often than do the controls. In high school, she participates more extensively in extracurricular activities and anticipates more participation in college. Her college plans are more fully developed and ambitious. In comparison to the controls, the CrW student is more often considering two or more colleges, usually including an Ivy League or small private college, and is less often considering a public city college.

It is noteworthy that the breadth of interests and intellectual orientation characterizing the CrW girls was found in *both* creative groups of boys in our earlier study (Schaefer and Anastasi, 1968). One of these groups was selected because of creative achievement in science, the other because of creative achievement in art or writing. The latter group, however, included 76 boys in creative writing and only 24 in art. It is thus likely that the similarity of this group to the CrW girls resulted from the predominance of creative writing cases within it.

When the results of the two studies are considered together, they indicate that the biographical correlates of creativity are closely similar for boys and girls, with the possible exception of the reversal of role model and the greater influence of the opposite-sex parent upon the creative offspring. With regard to field of creative achievement, certain characteristic differences emerge among science, writing, and art. Cutting across both sex and field, however, are certain common characteristics of creative adolescents: continuity and pervasiveness of interest in chosen field; prevalence of unusual, novel, and diverse experiences; and educational superiority of familial background.

SUMMARY

Biographical inventory keys were developed and cross-validated in a total sample of 400 public high school girls, subdivided into creative and matched control groups in art and writing. Creative Ss were selected principally through teachers' nominations supported by creative products. Cross-validation yielded criterion correlations of .34 and .55 for art and writing keys (each $p < .001$). Final keys, comprising items that differentiated in both initial and cross-validation samples (compound $p < .05$), were used to describe the biographical correlates of creativity. Comparisons were also made with the results of a similar, earlier study of creative boys.

REFERENCES

Anderson, C. C., and Cropley, A. J. "Some correlates of originality," *Australian Journal of Psychology*, 1966, **18**, 218–227.

Baker, P. C. "Combining tests of significance in cross-validation," *Educational and Psychological Measurement*, 1952, **12**, 300–306.

Buel, W. D. "Biographical data and the identification of creative research personnel," *Journal of Applied Psychology*, 1965, **49**, 318–321.

Buel, W. D., Albright, L. E., and Glennon, J. R. "A note on the generality and cross-validity of personal history for identifying creative research scientists," *Journal of Applied Psychology*, 1966, **50**, 217–219.

Chambers, J. A. "Relating personality and biographical factors to scientific creativity," *Psychological Monographs*, 1964, **78**, No. 7 (Whole No. 584).

Cline, V. B., Tucker, M. F., and Anderson, D. R. "Psychology of the scientist: XX. Cross-validation of biographical information predictor keys across diverse samples of scientists." *Psychological Reports*, 1966, **19**, 951–954.

Dauw, D. C. "Life experiences of original thinkers and good elaborators," *Exceptional Children*, 1966, **32**, 433–440.

Domino, G. "Maternal personality correlates of sons' creativity," *Journal of Consulting and Clinical Psychology*, 1969, **33**, 180–183.

Dreyer, A., and Wells, M. "Parental values, parental control, and creativity in young children," *Journal of Marriage and the Family*, 1966, **28**, 83–88.

Freeberg, N. E. "The biographical information blank as a predictor of student achievement," *Psychological Reports*, 1967, **20**, 911–925.

Golann, S. E. "Psychological study of creativity," *Psychological Bulletin*, 1963, **60**, 548–565.

Helson, R. "Childhood interest clusters related to creativity in women," *Journal of Consulting Psychology*, 1965, **29**, 352–361.

Helson, R. "Personality of women with imaginative and artistic interests: The role of masculinity, originality, and other characteristics in their creativity," *Journal of Personality*, 1966, **34**, 1–25.

Helson, R. "Personality characteristics and developmental history of creative college women," *Genetic Psychology Monographs*, 1967, **76**, 205–256.

Henry, E. R. "Conference on the use of biographical data in psychology," *American Psychologist*, 1966, **21**, 247–249.

Holland, J. L., and Astin, A. W. "The prediction of the academic, artistic, scientific, and social achievement of undergraduates of superior scholastic aptitude," *Journal of Educational Psychology,* 1962, **53,** 132–143.

Holland, J. L., and Nichols, R. C. "Prediction of academic and extracurricular achievement in college," *Journal of Educational Psychology,* 1964, **55,** 55–65.

MacKinnon, D. W. "The nature and nurture of creative talent," *American Psychologist,* 1962, **17,** 484–495.

McDermid, C. D. "Some correlates of creativity in engineering personnel," *Journal of Applied Psychology,* 1965, **49,** 14–19.

Morrison, R. F., Owens, W. A., Glennon, J. R., and Albright, L. E. "Factored life history antecedents of industrial research performance," *Journal of Applied Psychology,* 1962, **46,** 281–284.

Nichols, R. C., and Holland, J. L. "Prediction of the first year college performance of high aptitude students," *Psychological Monographs,* 1963, **77,** No. 7 (Whole No. 570).

Nichols, R. C., and Holland, J. L. "The selection of high aptitude high school graduates for maximum achievement in college," *Personnel and Guidance Journal,* 1964, **43,** 33–40.

Parloff, M. B., and Datta, L. E. "Personality characteristics of the potentially creative scientist," *Science and Psychoanalysis,* 1965, **8,** 91–106.

Roe, A. "A psychological study of eminent biologists," *Psychological Monographs,* 1951, **65,** No. 14 (Whole No. 331) (a).

Roe, A. "A psychological study of physical scientists," *Genetic Psychology Monographs,* 1951, **43,** 121–235 (b).

Roe, A. "A psychological study of eminent psychologists and anthropologists, and a comparison with biologists and physical scientists," *Psychological Monographs,* 1953, **67,** No. 2 (Whole No. 287).

Schaefer, C. E., and Anastasi, A. "A biographical inventory for identifying creativity in adolescent boys," *Journal of Applied Psychology,* 1968, **52,** 42–48.

Smith, W. J., Albright, L. E., Glennon, J. R., and Owens, W. A. "The prediction of research competence and creativity from personal history," *Journal of Applied Psychology,* 1961, **45,** 59–62.

Taylor, C. W., Cooley, G. N., and Nielsen, E. C. "Identifying high school students with characteristics needed in research work." NSF-G17543, University of Utah, 1963. Mimeograph

Taylor, C. W., Ellison, R. L., and Tucker M. F. *Biographical Information and the Prediction of Multiple Criteria of Success in Science.* Greensboro, N. C.: Richardson Foundation, 1966.

Tucker, M. F., Cline, V. B., and Schmitt, J. R. "Prediction of creativity and other performance measures from biographical information among pharmaceutical scientists," *Journal of Applied Psychology,* 1967, **51,** 131–138.

Weisberg, P. S., and Springer, K. J. "Environmental factors in creative function," *Archives of General Psychiatry,* 1961, **5,** 555–564.

Werts, C. E. "The many faces of intelligence," *National Merit Scholarship Corporation Research Reports,* 1966, **2,** No. 5.

SECTION 8

PSYCHOPATHOLOGY

The mechanisms we use to cope with anxiety may be seen as either sensitizing or repressing in their general effect. When "sensitizing," we tend to react to psychological disturbance by attempting to cope with it directly or symbolically, whereas when we are "repressing," we react by denying that we are disturbed. Most people use various combinations of sensitizing and repressing mechanisms in dealing with everyday problems, but some tend to make greater use of sensitizing mechanisms and are referred to in research as "sensitizers," whereas those that make more pronounced use of repressing mechanisms are termed "repressors." A considerable amount of research shows that these two groups of individuals, who can be placed at the opposite ends of a sensitization–repression scale, behave in essentially different ways in a number of life situations.

The first paper in this section, by Michael Merbaum and Katsushige Kazaoka of Bowling Green State University, demonstrates some of the differences in the ways that sensitizers and repressors behave. Their findings, which are consistent with other research in this area, show that sensitizers tend to react more negatively during an interview than do repressors. The study is included here as one of a number that shows how personality factors identified by paper-and-pencil tests are related to behavior displayed in social situations, and how the behavior of individual subjects can be used as a way of validating the findings of personality tests.

The second selection consists of portions of a much longer research report by Andrew T. Well, Norman E. Zinberg, and Judith M. Nelson of the effects of marihuana on human behavior. Their study is particularly relevant in view of the great amount of attention this drug has received in recent years. In general, they found that habitual users of marihuana are more likely to get more of a "mood" reaction to smoking marihuana than do naïve smokers. On the other hand, naïve subjects showed more impairment than did experienced smokers in their performance on various complex tests involving manipulation of special types of equipment. Although the research study left many significant questions about the effects of marihuana unanswered, it has made a significant contribution in being the first one to assess the effects of the drug in a properly controlled experimental situation.

297

Although psychologists and other mental health workers have suggested for a number of years that certain kinds of illnesses, such as ulcer, are caused by emotional stress, concrete evidence has been difficult to obtain. The fact that symptom and stress appear together is not sufficient evidence that the stress causes the symptom. In recent years, however, data have been accumulating to show that emotional stress can be considered as a causal factor in the so-called "psychosomatic" ailments. The research of Jay M. Weiss of Rockefeller University indicates that rats subjected to electric shock at predictible intervals are more likely to develop stomach ulcers than unshocked rats. However, when shocks are administered randomly, and hence cannot be predicted by the rat, the amount of emotional stress is higher and the ulcers more numerous and more severe.

The paper by E. K. Eric Gunderson and Ransom J. Arthur of the Navy Medical Neuropsychiatric Research Unit in San Diego is concerned with various characteristics of psychiatric patients that might be predictive of their potential for recovery. The factors they were able to isolate as significant are not necessarily those that would be consistent with common sense. For example, their research shows that the amount of medical treatment received by patients is *negatively* correlated with chances for recovery on the part of neurotics, but *positively* correlated for psychotics.

The study by Charles N. Barthell and David S. Holmes of Northwestern University was also concerned with correlations between symptom and patient experience, but in this instance the attempt was to find data that are correlated with later mental illness. The researchers adopted the ingenious technique of surveying high school yearbooks in search of data that might suggest social isolation. Their results show that the students who had the fewest activities during high school (and who could therefore be considered to be the most isolated) were the ones who were most likely to develop schizophrenia in later years. The activity level of those developing psychoneurotic symptoms tended to fall between that of the schizophrenic patients and that of the normal or "nonclinic" population.

8.1 Reports of Emotional Experience by Sensitizers and Repressors during an Interview Transaction

MICHAEL MERBAUM AND KATSUSHIGE KAZAOKA

In recent years numerous studies have employed the clinical interview as a tool for obtaining insight into various dimensions of personality. The use of the interview as a research method has been predicated on the assumption that a systematic analysis of the verbal behavior emitted during the interview can yield a useful index regarding the internal emotional state of the S (Marsden, 1965). While most studies have gauged emotional reactiveness on the basis of an ex post facto analysis of the frequency and intensity of the interviewee's verbal behavior, none have directly dealt with S's momentary personal appraisal of this reactiveness while the interview was in progress. The purpose of the present investigation was to devise a method for obtaining nonverbal reports of emotional experience within an interview inter-

action which would not seriously disrupt the continuity of the verbal exchange. The aim was to obtain ongoing experiential reports of emotional arousal by allowing each S to select from his verbal responses those which met some personal criterion of emotional significance. The focus was therefore not exclusively on the verbal report per se, but rather on the attribution of emotionality impressed or superimposed onto the verbal report.

The procedure developed was utilized to test a hypothesis suggested by Byrne and Sheffield (1965), who stated that, "in describing their own response to threat, repressors tend to deny and sensitizers freely to admit feelings of anxiety [p. 115]." It was hypothesized, therefore, that repressors will attribute greater emotional significance to positive

Reprinted with slight abridgment from the *Journal of Abnormal Psychology*, 1967, **72,** 101–103, with permission of the authors and the American Psychological Association, Inc.

affective verbal material and, conversely, that sensitizers will select negative emotional material as more personally relevant.

PROCEDURE

Subjects

The Repression–Sensitization (R–S) scale (Byrne, 1961; Byrne and Sheffield, 1965) was administered to a group of 200 college sophomore students. From this pool, 20 Ss were selected representing the extremes of the R–S distribution. Of the 10 Ss selected in each of the repressor-sensitizer groups, 5 were female and 5 male. The mean R–S score for the repression group was 16.10; the range from 10 to 21. The mean score for the sensitizer group was 65.30; the range from 52 to 86. These variations compare favorably with data presented by Byrne and Sheffield (1965). However, the mean scores for their repressor group are considerably higher: $M = 41.55$ to $M = 16.10$ for the combined males and females used in the present study. Their sensitizer group was somewhat higher: $M = 77.60$ to $M = 65.30$ in this investigation.

APPARATUS

The basic unit was a modified Concertone stereo tape recorder. Built into this unit was a code oscillator in capsule form. The module consisted of a power transistor, capacitor, and a resistor powered by a six-volt battery. Connected to the module was a small aluminum box with a red button in the center. When depressed, an auditory signal (beep) was activated and recorded simultaneously on the tape. An interview was recorded on one channel of the tape while the auditory signal (beep) was recorded on the other stereo channel. The auditory signal was inaudible to both E and S.

EXPERIMENTAL PROCEDURE

First Session

Approximately a week after taking the R–S scale, Ss were invited to participate in a study entitled "the personality of college students." Once in the experimental situation, Ss were given brief interview instructions to the effect that E was interested in talking with them about their family and school experiences. It was mentioned that the meeting would last for one half-hour and that they would be free to express feelings about a variety of topics. In addition, each S was assured that the tape recordings would be used exclusively for research purposes.

After this introduction, E demonstrated the auditory signal apparatus and the following instructions were given:

As you see, I have here a small box with a red button in the center. When you depress this button [E demonstrates] an auditory signal appears on the tape. Now I'd like you to hold this box comfortably in your lap. While we are talking I want you to press the button whenever you feel what you are saying has emotional significance or importance to you. Now, you can press it when what you are saying has a positive emotional quality; in other words makes you feel good, happy, elated, loving, etc. Or on the other hand, if what you are saying has a negative emotional quality such as unhappiness, sadness, tension, etc. Remember, whenever you experience some emotional feeling, whether it be negative or positive, simply press the button. Now, you can press the button as much as you want and don't worry about repetitions. Are there any questions? [To increase clarity, the instructions were again repeated.]

The interview conducted was semi-structured. Topics such as emotional reactions to family experiences, sexual behavior, academic performance, and miscellaneous topics were covered. The S was allowed to shift topics and generally discuss any issues which happened to be of immediate interest. The E asked questions and pursued topics if they appeared to have some personal importance to S. In order to partially control for interviewer bias, E was unaware of S's R–S score.

At the conclusion of the interview, Ss were invited for another session scheduled 1 week later. No additional information was offered with regard to the second session.

Second Session

In this session Ss were told that they would listen to the previous interview through headphones. This procedure was adopted to investigate whether memory of the original "beeping" behavior would reflect differences with respect to the personality variables under study. In other words, would the hypothesized relationships, based on the negative and positive dimensions, hold when the original conditions were partially repli-

cated by means of a listening rather than a participant situation. To investigate this aspect Ss were instructed to use the auditory signal apparatus by pressing the button once when "you feel that this was where you pressed during the first session." In addition, it was hypothesized that repressors would not report "new" emotionally meaningful material as often as the sensitizer. Thus, Ss were also instructed to press "twice (two short presses) when you feel what you are hearing has emotional significance but don't remember pressing the 'beeper' the first time." In a postinterview, however, Ss indicated uncertainty about their ability to discriminate emotional behavior on this basis. Furthermore, few felt they remembered where they had signaled emotionality in the original interview. As a way of dealing with this ambiguity a majority reported that they simply pressed the "beeper" only once whenever they felt meaningful emotionality was present. Because of the reinterpretation of the task by Ss, as well as the fact that the total number of two presses comprised less than 10% of the total number of "beeps" in the second session, the numbers of one and two "beeps" were summed into a composite score which was then used as an overall measure of emotionality in the final statistical analyses.

CODING PROCEDURES

Following the initial interview session the tapes were processed by taking down the counter number on the tape recorder indicating the place on the tape where the "beep" occurred, and also, for later identification purposes, the complete sentence or group of sentences which contained the "beep." This was necessary because in the second session the original "beep" would be erased in the recording process. All codings were made by listening to the recorded material.

The following dependent variables were employed. For each S the total number of "beeps" were counted for each session.

A second category consisted of coding the verbal context in which the "beep" occurred. Verbal content and voice inflection were considered in the coding judgment. Three general affect categories were employed: negative emotional context, positive emotional context, and ambiguous emotional context. Negative emotional context was scored when the comments containing and surrounding the "beep" indicated despair, anger, dislike, criticism, inadequacy, and general unhappiness. Positive emotional context was scored when liking, closeness, joy, adequacy, and general happiness were observed. The ambiguous category was scored when no clear-cut affect could be determined. In the statistical analyses this latter category was discarded due to its low frequency of judged occurrence.

Finally, the direction of the affect was also scored. If, for example, S mentioned personal anger toward a specific person, the directional aspect of this affect was noted. A variety of directional categories were derived to cover different S responses.

The five directional categories were:

1. Family: S reports feelings toward mother, father, and siblings.
2. Self: S reports feelings regarding self.

3. Social Peer Relationships: S reports feelings toward peers.
4. Others toward Self: A general category in which S reports feelings of all others toward self; family, friends, enemies, etc.
5. Self toward Others: A general category in which S reports his own feelings toward others; family, friends, enemies, etc.

RESULTS

Reliability

To assess the reliability of the coding of the Ss' interview responses, a second judge independently coded six randomly selected interviews on the positive and negative affect dimension, and the five directional categories. Interrater reliability correlations ranged from .92 to .97, indicating a high degree of agreement on all variables.

Positive and Negative Affect Categories

The means and standard deviations for the Total and Coded "beep" reports are presented in Table 1.

table 1

Means and Standard Deviations for Sensitizers and Repressors on Positive and Negative Categories of Sessions 1 and 2

	Session 1		Session 2	
	Positive	Negative	Positive	Negative
Sensitizer				
M	5.90	19.60	15.20	33.50
SD	4.75	5.38	11.66	9.59
Repressor				
M	14.60	6.30	23.70	11.60
SD	5.66	5.64	14.41	6.29

t tests indicated that the overall frequency of (total) "beeps" did not differ significantly between sensitizer and repressor groups in either Session 1 or Session 2. Therefore, both groups used the apparatus at approximately the same rate. However, from Session 1 to Session 2 there was a significant increase in the frequency of emotional indications for both the repressor and sensitizer groups ($t = 3.442, p < .005; t = 4.297, p < .005$), respectively. Apparently, listening to a previously experienced clinical interaction either creates more discriminable emotional cueing, thereby increasing response frequency, or is a reflection of some inhibition in using the apparatus in the initial sessions. In addition, it is likely that participation and listening are qualitatively dissimilar tasks and would influence the "beeping" behavior in a way which has not yet been systematically explored.

Analyses of the negative affect response category showed significantly greater negative affect responses in the sensitizer group than in the repressor group in both Sessions 1 and 2 ($t = 5.406, p < .01; t = 6.326, p < .01$). It is clear that the sensitizer tends to focus more attention on negative affective material than the repressor. With respect to positive affective material the reverse is observed. In the first interview session, the repressors signaled significantly more positive material as emotionally meaningful than the sensitizers ($t = 2.34, p < .05$), while the trend in the second session is in a similar direction though the differences were not significant. Further *t*-test analyses were performed within groups. In the first interview the repressors gave significantly more "beeps" to positive than to negative

emotional material ($t = 3.134, p < .005$), while the sensitizer selected significantly more negative than positive material ($t = 6.040, p < .005$). These same results are replicated in the second listening session.

It should be noted that the "beeping" behavior is not simply a function of the verbal behavior emitted. For example, it could be argued that since the sensitizer tends to describe his life in negative terms, "beeps" would invariably fall in the midst of negative material. In comparing the positive category, "beeps" for the sensitizer group from the first interview session to the second, a *t*-test analysis reveals highly significant differences ($t = 3.868, p < .005$) in the direction of greater positive responses in the second session. This would indicate that positive material was available to the sensitizer, but was seemingly ignored or discounted as emotionally meaningful during the first session. In other words, during the interview the sensitizer could have "beeped" on positive affective material, but chose to emphasize negative material instead. For the repressor group there was an increase in the endorsement of negative material from the first to the second session ($t = 5.325, p < .005$), showing the presence of negative material which could have been signaled in the first session had the repressor been so disposed. Thus, the sensitizer does not always emit negative emotional material, nor does the repressor exclusively verbalize positive emotion. However, given the instructions to report significant emotional material, the sensitizer will characteristically endorse negative emotion while, in the main, excluding reports of positive emotional experience. The repressor will do just the opposite.

A further analysis was performed on the negative and positive categories by defining whether the response was concerned with self, family, or peer relations. Significantly, more sensitizers reported self material in a negative direction than did the repressors ($\chi^2 = 45.49$, $p < .01$) in the first interview session. Similarly, the same findings are found with respect to family ($\chi^2 = 19.281$, $p < .01$) and peer relations ($\chi^2 = 29.229$, $p < .01$). Two additional categories, others toward self and self toward others, were coded. In both instances, sensitizers reported significantly more negative affect than the repressors in the initial interview session ($\chi^2 = 8.601$, $p < .01$; $\chi^2 = 23.612$, $p < .01$). Almost the identical results are observed in the second listening session.

DISCUSSION

Studies investigating the personality characteristics of sensitizers and repressors have usually employed self-rating inventories as the principal source of data (Byrne and Sheffield, 1965; Lucky and Grigg, 1964). In adding to this body of knowledge, the present study has extended this to the self-disclosures of these groups within a free-response interview transaction.

The overall analyses clearly indicate that the sensitizer predictably selects negative material as more emotionally meaningful than does the repressor, while the repressor significantly chooses material in the opposite direction, emphasizing positive over negative affect. When S listens to the same interview material as an observer, almost identical results are obtained. Moreover, while there is significantly more positive material selected by the sensitizer in the second listening session than was reported in the actual interview session, a correspondingly greater proportion of negative material is also endorsed. The repressors, in turn, increased responsiveness in the opposite direction. It should be remembered that S was under no obligation to respond in either the positive or negative direction unless he himself felt the material was personally relevant. With this in mind, these data are remarkably straightforward. For example, in the first interview session every sensitizer selected more negative than positive emotion while the reverse is found for each repressor S. In the second listening session, one S in each group reversed this performance.

In breaking down the negative and positive response categories clear-cut differences were found. Family relationships, as reported by the sensitizer, were replete with stress, unhappiness, anger, criticism, and affective distance. In contrast, the repressor described family relationships in close, affectionate terms. This finding is in agreement with Byrne (1964). The sensitizer tends to view social and peer relationships with suspicion and guardedness. He sees others as adversaries and profound threats to his self-esteem. The repressor perceives peer relationships as satisfying and describes them in cooperative terms. The sensitizer flounders on feelings of inadequacy and helplessness, while the repressor reports high self-esteem and self-regard.

One provocative and closely related finding was that the sensitizer perceived others as inordinately more critical, angry, and demeaning of him than the repressor. A frequency breakdown of these coded data is quite informative.

Feelings of others toward self	Positive	Negative
Sensitizer	5	40
Repressor	5	3

As can be seen, the repressor group gave little attention to this category, suggesting either avoidance or disinterest with evaluations of others. It would be theoretically consistent to speculate that the sensitizer is more prone to paranoid ideation as well as to placing greater emphasis on projective defenses than the repressor.

In a recent paper Byrne and Sheffield (1965) noted that the lack of verbalized anxiety found in repressor groups does not eliminate the possibility that "denial of anxiety by repressors is accompanied by indirect indicators of disturbance [p. 117]." Byrne also aptly remarks that it is necessary to determine whether the repressor is, in fact, strenuously denying or whether he is relatively free from emotional disturbance. At face value, these data, coupled with a subjective appraisal of the repressor's interview behavior, suggest the latter alternative. However, since selective reports of emotional experience provide the basic datum, it is probable that this behavior could also be regarded as a reflection of response style. For example, it was often observed during the interview that even when the sensitizer expressed very emotional positive material, "beep" reports of emotional significance were invariably absent. Similarly, avoidance of "beeping" on negative material was found to be characteristic of the repressor, though not

as pronounced. On this basis, it is reasonable to assume that some denial or selective inhibition was operating, but in both groups. Thus, it is likely that the sensitizer is initially hesitant in endorsing positive feelings while the repressor experiences similar caution with respect to negative material. Although it has been argued that the repressor has difficulty in tolerating negative affective experience (Byrne and Sheffield, 1965), there is no indication in these data that excessive emotional discomfort accompanied this inhibition.

Considering this observation, the meaning of the R–S scale is still open to question. Indeed, it is conceivable that the scale may represent a more general emotional satisfaction–dissatisfaction dimension. For instance, it would appear that in order for the construct of repression to be employed as a defining label, some independent network of data defining the variable would need to be introduced for Ss to be so classified. In view of this, future investigations will be directed toward changing the nonverbal reports of emotional experience of sensitizers and repressors by varying the interview structure. For example, under probing and stress conditions producing negative verbalizations, will the repressor then report negative material as emotionally significant or will he continue to ignore and/or deny the impact of this experience? An attempt will also be made to change the negative report behavior of sensitizers into more positive channels.

SUMMARY

It was hypothesized that sensitizers will report negative emotion more frequently than repressors and repressors more positive material than sensitizers. From an S pool, 10 sensitizers and 10 repressors were selected on the basis of their extreme high and low repression-sensitization (R–S) scores. An experimental procedure was devised in which S indicated emotionality by pressing an auditory signal apparatus while an interview was in progress. The verbal response surrounding the signal was coded, and it was found that sensitizers endorsed significantly more negative affect than the repressors. The repressor indicated significantly more positive material than the sensitizer, supporting the hypothesized relationships.

REFERENCES

Byrne, D. "The Repression-Sensitization scale: Rationale, reliability and validity," *Journal of Personality*, 1961, **29**, 334–349.

Byrne, D. "Childrearing antecedents of repression-sensitization," *Child Development*, 1964, **35**, 1033–1039.

Byrne, D., and Sheffield, J. "Response to sexually arousing stimuli as a function of repressing and sensitizing defenses," *Journal of Abnormal Psychology*, 1965, **70**, 114–118.

Lucky, A. W., and Grigg, A. E. "Repression-sensitization as a variable in deviant responding," *Journal of Clinical Psychology*, 1964, **20**, 92–93.

Marsden, G. "Content-analysis studies of therapeutic interviews: 1954 to 1964," *Psychological Bulletin*, 1965, **63**, 298–321.

8.2 Clinical and Psychological Effects of Marihuana in Man

ANDREW T. WEIL, NORMAN E. ZINBERG, AND JUDITH M. NELSON

In the spring of 1968 we conducted a series of pilot experiments on acute marihuana intoxication in human subjects. The study was not undertaken to prove or disprove popularly held convictions about marihuana as an intoxicant, to compare it with other drugs, or to introduce our own opinions. Our concern was simply to collect some long overdue pharmacological data. In this article we describe the primitive state of knowledge of the drug, the research problems encountered in designing a replicable study, and the results of our investigations.

Marihuana is a crude preparation of flowering tops, leaves, seeds, and stems of female plants of Indian hemp *Cannabis sativa* L.; it is usually smoked. The intoxicating constituents of hemp are found in the sticky resin exuded by the tops of the plants, particularly the females. Male plants produce some resin but are grown mainly for hemp fiber, not for marihuana. The resin itself, when prepared for smoking or eating, is known as "hashish." Various *Cannabis* preparations are used as intoxicants throughout the world; their potency varies directly with the amount of resin present (1). Samples of American marihuana differ greatly in pharmacological activity, depending on their composition (tops contain most resin; stems, seeds, and lower leaves least) and on the conditions under which the plants were grown. In addition, different varieties of *Cannabis* probably produce resins with different proportions of constituents (2). Botanists feel that only one species of hemp exists, but work on the phytochemistry of the varieties of this species is incomplete (3). Chronic users claim that samples of marihuana differ in quality of effects as well as in potency; that some types cause a

Reprinted from *Science*, 1968, **162**, 1234–1242, with permission of the authors and *Science*. Portions of this report have been omitted in the interests of brevity, and readers are referred to the original for full details.

preponderance of physical symptoms, and that other types tend to cause greater distortions of perception or of thought.

Pharmacological studies of *Cannabis* indicate that the tetrahydrocannabinol fraction of the resin is the active portion. In 1965, Mechoulam and Gaoni (4) reported the first total synthesis of $(-)$-Δ^1-*trans*-tetrahydrocannabinol (THC), which they called "the psychotomimetically active constituent of hashish (marihuana)." Synthetic THC is now available for research in very limited supply.

In the United States, the use of *Cannabis* extracts as therapeutics goes back to the 19th century, but it was not until the 1920's that use of marihuana as an intoxicant by migrant Mexican laborers, urban Negroes, and certain Bohemian groups caused public concern (3). Despite increasingly severe legal penalties imposed during the 1930's, use of marihuana continued in these relatively small populations without great public uproar or apparent changes in numbers or types of users until the last few years. The fact that almost none of the studies devoted to the physiological and psychological effects of *Cannabis* in man was based on controlled laboratory experimentation escaped general notice. But with the explosion of use in the 1960's, at first on college campuses followed by a spread downward to secondary schools and upward to a portion of the established middle class, controversy over the dangers of marihuana generated a desire for more objective information about the drug.

Of the three known studies on human subjects performed by Americans, the first (see 5) was done in the Canal Zone with 34 soldiers; the conse-quences reported were hunger and hyperphagia, loss of inhibitions, increased pulse rate with unchanged blood pressure, a tendency to sleep, and unchanged performance of psychological and neurological tests. Doses and type of marihuana were not specified.

The second study, known as the 1944 LaGuardia Report (6), noted that 72 prisoners, 48 of whom were previous *Cannabis* users, showed minimum physiological responses, but suffered impaired intellectual functioning and decreased body steadiness, especially well demonstrated by nonusers after high doses. Basic personality structures remained unchanged as subjects reported feelings of relaxation, disinhibition, and self-confidence. In that study, the drug was administered orally as an extract. No controls were described, and doses and quality of marihuana were unspecified.

Williams, *et al.* in 1946 (7) studied a small number of prisoners who were chronic users; they were chiefly interested in effects of long-term smoking on psychological functioning. They found an initial exhilaration and euphoria which gave way after a few days of smoking to indifference and lassitude that somewhat impaired performance requiring concentration and manual dexterity. Again, no controls were provided. . . . Investigations outside the United States have been scientifically deficient, and for the most part have been limited to anecdotal and sociological approaches (9–12). So far as we know, our study is the first attempt to investigate marihuana in a formal double-blind experiment with the appropriate controls. It is also the first attempt to collect basic clinical and psychological information on the drug by observing its effects on marihuana-naive human subjects in a neutral laboratory setting. . . .

SUBJECTS

The central group of subjects consisted of nine healthy, male volunteers, 21 to 26 years of age, all of whom smoked tobacco cigarettes regularly but had never tried marihuana previously. Eight chronic users of marihuana also participated, both to "assay" the quality of marihuana received from the Federal Bureau of Narcotics and to enable the experimenters to standardize the protocol, using subjects familiar with their responses to the drug. The age range for users was also 21 to 26 years. They all smoked marihuana regularly, most of them every day or every other day.

The nine "naive" subjects were selected after a careful screening process. An initial pool of prospective subjects was obtained by placing advertisements in the student newspapers of a number of universities in the Boston area. These advertisements sought "male volunteers, at least 21 years old, for psychological experiments." After nonsmokers were eliminated from this pool, the remaining volunteers were interviewed individually by a psychiatrist who determined their histories of use of alcohol and other intoxicants as well as their general personality types. In addition to serving as a potential screening technique to eliminate volunteers with evidence of psychosis, or of serious mental or personality disorder, these interviews served as the basis for the psychiatrist's prediction of the type of response an individual subject might have after smoking marihuana. (It

should be noted that no marihuana-naive volunteer had to be disqualified on psychiatric grounds.) Only after a prospective subject passed the interview was he informed that the "psychological experiment" for which he had volunteered was a marihuana study. If he consented to participate, he was asked to sign a release, informing him that he would be "expected to smoke cigarettes containing marihuana or an inert substance." He was also required to agree to a number of conditions, among them that he would "during the course of the experiment take no psychoactive drugs, including alcohol, other than those drugs administered in the course of the experiment. . . ."

EXPERIMENTAL SESSIONS

Chronic users were tested only on high doses of marihuana with no practice sessions. Each naive subject was required to come to four sessions, spaced about a week apart. The first was always a practice session, in which the subject learned the proper smoking technique and during which he became thoroughly acquainted with the tests and the protocol. In the practice session, each subject completed the entire protocol, smoking two hand-rolled tobacco cigarettes. He was instructed to take a long puff, to inhale deeply, and to maintain inspiration for 20 seconds, as timed by an experimenter with a stopwatch. Subjects were allowed 8 to 12 minutes to smoke each of the two cigarettes. One purpose of this practice smoking was to identify and eliminate individuals who were not tolerant to high doses of nicotine, thus reducing the effect of nicotine on the variables measured during subsequent drug sessions (21). A surprising number (five) of volunteers who had described themselves in screening interviews as heavy cigarette smokers, "inhaling" up to two packs of cigarettes a day, developed acute nicotine reactions when they smoked two tobacco cigarettes by the required method. Occurrence of such a reaction disqualified a subject from participation in the experiments. . . .

RESULTS

1. *Safety of marihuana in human volunteers.* In view of the apprehension expressed by many persons over the safety of administering marihuana to research subjects, we wish to emphasize that no adverse marihuana reactions occurred in any of our subjects. In fact, the five acute nicotine reactions mentioned earlier were far more spectacular than any effects produced by marihuana.

In these experiments, observable effects of marihuana were maximum at 15 minutes after smoking. They were diminished between 30 minutes and 1 hour, and they were largely dissipated 3 hours after the end of smoking. No delayed or persistent effects beyond 3 hours were observed or reported.

2. *Intoxicating properties of marihuana in a neutral setting.* With the high dose of marihuana (2.0 grams), all chronic users became "high" (24) by their own accounts and in the judgment of experimenters who had observed many persons under the influence of marihuana. The effect was consistent even though prior to the session some of these subjects expressed anxiety about smoking marihuana and submitting to tests in a laboratory.

On the other hand, only one of the nine naive subjects (No. 3) had a definite "marihuana reaction" on the same high dose. He became markedly euphoric and laughed continuously during his first battery of tests after taking the drug. Interestingly, he was the one subject who had expressed his desire to get high.

3. *Comparison of naive and chronic user subjects.* Throughout the experiments it was apparent that the two groups of subjects reacted differently to identical doses of marihuana. We must caution, however, that our study was designed to allow rigorous statistical analysis of data from the naive group—it was not designed to permit formal comparison between chronic users and naive subjects. The conditions of the experiment were not the same for both groups: the chronic users were tested with the drug on their first visit to the laboratory with no practice and were informed that they were to receive high doses of marihuana. Therefore, differences between the chronic and naive groups reported below—although statistically valid—must be regarded as trends to be confirmed or rejected by additional experiments.

4. *Recognition of marihuana versus placebo.* All nine naive subjects reported that they had not been able to identify the taste or smell of marihuana in the experimental cigarettes. A few subjects remarked that they noticed differences in the taste of the three sets of cigarettes but could not interpret the differences. Most subjects found the pure marihuana cigarettes (high dose) more mild than the low dose or placebo cigarettes, both of which contained tobacco. . . .

5. *Effect of marihuana on heart rate.* In the naive subjects, marihuana in low dose

or high dose was followed by increased heart rate 15 minutes after smoking, but the effect was not demonstrated to be dose-dependent. The high dose caused a statistically greater increase in the heart rates of chronic users than in those of the naive subjects 15 minutes after smoking. . . .

6. *Effect of marihuana on respiratory rate.* In the naive group, there was no change in respiratory rate before and after smoking marihuana. Chronic users showed a small but statistically significant increase in respiratory rate after smoking, but we do not regard the change as clinically significant.

7. *Effect of marihuana on pupil size.* There was no change in pupil size before and after smoking marihuana in either group.

8. *Effect of marihuana on conjunctival appearance.* Significant reddening of conjunctivae due to dilatation of blood vessels occurred in one of nine subjects receiving placebo, three of nine receiving the low dose of marihuana, and eight of nine receiving the high dose. It occurred in all eight of the chronic users receiving the high dose and was rated as more prominent in them. The effect was more pronounced 15 minutes after the smoking period than 90 minutes after it.

9. *Effect of marihuana on blood sugar.* There was no significant change in blood sugar levels after smoking marihuana in either group. . . .

10. *Effect of marihuana on the Digit Symbol Substitution Test.*

The results indicate that: (i) Decrements in performance of naive subjects following low and high doses of marihuana were significant at 15 and 90 minutes after smoking. (ii) The decrement following marihuana was greater after high dose than after low dose at 15 minutes after taking the drug, giving preliminary evidence of a dose-response relationship. (iii) Chronic users started with good base-line performance and improved slightly on the DSST after smoking 2.0 grams of marihuana, whereas performance of the naive subjects was grossly impaired. Experience with the DSST suggests that absence of impairment in chronic users cannot be accounted for solely by a practice effect. Still, because of the different procedures employed, we prefer to report this difference as a trend. . . .

11. *Effect of marihuana on time estimation.* Before smoking, all nine naive subjects estimated the 5-minute verbal sample to be 5 ± 2 minutes. After placebo, no subject changed his guess. After the low dose, three subjects raised their estimates to 10 ± 2 minutes, and after the high dose, four raised their estimates.

12. *Subjective effects of marihuana.* When questioned at the end of their participation in the experiment, persons who had never taken marihuana previously reported minimum subjective effects after smoking the drug, or, more precisely, few effects like those commonly reported by chronic users. Nonusers reported little euphoria, no distortion of visual or auditory perception, and no confusion. However, several subjects mentioned that "things seemed to take longer." Below are examples of comments by naive subjects after high doses.

Subject 1: "It was stronger than the previous time (low dose) but I really didn't think it could be marihuana. Things seemed to go slower."

Subject 2: "I think I realize why they

took our watches. There was a sense of the past disappearing as happens when you're driving too long without sleeping. With a start you wake up to realize you were asleep for an instant; you discover yourself driving along the road. It was the same tonight with eating a sandwich. I'd look down to discover I'd just swallowed a bite but I hadn't noticed it at the time."

Subject 6: "I felt a combination of being almost-drunk and tired, with occasional fits of silliness—not my normal reaction to smoking tobacco.

Subject 8: "I felt faint briefly, but the dizziness went away, and I felt normal or slightly tired. I can't believe I had a high dose of marihuana."

Subject 9: "Time seemed very drawn out. I would keep forgetting what I was doing, especially on the continuous performance test, but somehow every time an "X" (the critical letter) came up, I found myself pushing the button."

After smoking their high dose, chronic users were asked to rate themselves on a scale of 1 to 10, 10 representing "the highest you've ever been." All subjects placed themselves between 7 and 10, most at 8 or 9. Many of these subjects expressed anxiety at the start of their first battery of tests after smoking the drug when they were feeling very high. Then they expressed surprise during and after the tests when they judged (correctly) that their performance was as good as or better than it had been before taking the drug.

13. The effect of marihuana on the self-rating mood scale, the effect of marihuana on a 5-minute verbal sample, and the correlation of personality type with subjective effects of marihuana will be reported separately.

DISCUSSION

Several results from this study raise important questions about the action of marihuana and suggest directions for future research. Our finding that subjects who were naive to marihuana did not become subjectively "high" after a high dose of marihuana in a neutral setting is interesting when contrasted with the response of regular users who consistently reported and exhibited highs. It agrees with the reports of chronic users that many, if not most, people do not become high on their first exposure to marihuana even if they smoke it correctly. This puzzling phenomenon can be discussed from either a physiological or psychosocial point of view. Neither interpretation is entirely satisfactory. The physiological hypothesis suggests that getting high on marihuana occurs only after some sort of pharmacological sensitization takes place. The psychosocial interpretation is that repeated exposure to marihuana reduces psychological inhibition, as part of, or as the result of a learning process.

Indirect evidence makes the psychological hypothesis attractive. Anxiety about drug use in this country is sufficiently great to make worthy of careful consideration the possibility of an unconscious psychological inhibition or block on the part of naive drug takers. The subjective responses of our subjects indicate that they had imagined a marihuana effect to be much more profoundly disorganizing than what they experienced. For example, subject No. 4, who started with a bias against the possibility of becoming high on marihuana, was able to control subjectively the effect of the drug and report that he had received a placebo when he had actually gotten a high dose. As anxiety about the drug is lessened with experience, the block may decrease, and the subject may permit himself to notice the drug's effects.

It is well known that marihuana users, in introducing friends to the drug, do actually "teach" them to notice subtle effects of the drug on consciousness (25). The apparently enormous influence of set and setting on the form of the marihuana response is consistent with this hypothesis, as is the testimony of users that, as use becomes more frequent, the amount of drug required to produce intoxication decreases—a unique example of "reverse tolerance." (Regular use of many intoxicants is accompanied by the need for increasing doses to achieve the same effects.)

On the other hand, the suggestion arising from this study that users and nonusers react differently to the drug, not only subjectively but also physiologically, increases the plausibility of the pharmacological-sensitization hypothesis. Of course, reverse tolerance could equally well be a manifestation of this sensitization.

It would be useful to confirm the suggested differences between users and nonusers and then to test in a systematic manner the hypothetical explanations of the phenomenon. One possible approach would be to continue to administer high doses of marihuana to the naive subjects according to the protocol described. If subjects begin reporting high responses

to the drug only after several exposures, in the absence of psychedelic settings, suggestions, or manipulations of mood, then the likelihood that marihuana induces a true physiological sensitization or that experience reduces psychological inhibitions, permitting real drug effects to appear, would be increased. If subjects fail to become high, we could conclude that learning to respond to marihuana requires some sort of teaching or suggestion.

An investigation of the literature of countries where anxieties over drug use are less prominent would be useful. If this difference between responses of users and nonusers is a uniquely American phenomenon, a psychological explanation would be indicated, although it would not account for greater effects with smaller doses after the initial, anxiety-reducing stage.

One impetus for reporting the finding of differences between chronic and naive subjects on some of the tests, despite the fact that the experimental designs were not the same, is that this finding agrees with the statements of many users. They say that the effects of marihuana are easily suppressed—much more so than those of alcohol. Our observation, that the chronic users after smoking marihuana performed on some tests as well as or better than they did before taking the drug, reinforced the argument advanced by chronic users that maintaining effective levels of performance for many tasks—driving, for example (26)—is much easier under the influence of marihuana than under that of other psychoactive drugs. Certainly the surprise that the chronic users expressed when they found they were performing more effectively on the CPT, DSST, and pursuit rotor tests than they thought they would is remarkable. It is quite the opposite of the false sense of improvement subjects have under some psychoactive drugs that actually impair performance.

What might be the basis of this suppressibility? Possibly, the actions of marihuana are confined to higher cortical functions without any general stimulatory or depressive effect on lower brain centers. The relative absence of neurological—as opposed to psychiatric —symptoms in marihuana intoxication suggests this possibility (7).

Our failure to detect any changes in blood sugar levels of subjects after they had smoked marihuana forces us to look elsewhere for an explanation of the hunger and hyperphagia commonly reported by users. A first step would be careful interviewing of users to determine whether they really become hungry after smoking marihuana or whether they simply find eating more pleasurable. Possibly, the basis of this effect is also central rather than due to some peripheral physiological change.

Lack of any change in pupil size of subjects after they had smoked marihuana is an enlightening finding especially because so many users and law-enforcement agents firmly believe that marihuana dilates pupils. (Since users generally observe each other in dim surroundings, it is not surprising that they see large pupils.) This negative finding emphasizes the need for data from carefully controlled investigations rather than from casual observation or anecdotal reports in the evaluation of marihuana. It also agrees with the findings of others

that synthetic THC does not alter pupil size (8, 27).

Finally, we would like to comment on the fact that marihuana appears to be a relatively mild intoxicant in our studies. If these results seem to differ from those of earlier experiments, it must be remembered that other experimenters have given marihuana orally, have given doses much higher than those commonly smoked by users, have administered potent synthetics, and have not strictly controlled the laboratory setting. As noted in our introduction, more powerful effects are often reported by users who ingest preparations of marihuana. This may mean that some active constituents which enter the body when the drug is ingested are destroyed by combustion, a suggestion that must be investigated in man. Another priority consideration is the extent to which synthetic THC reproduces marihuana intoxication—a problem that must be resolved before marihuana research proceeds with THC instead of the natural resin of the whole plant.

The set, both of subjects and experimenters, and the setting must be recognized as critical variables in studies of marihuana. Drug, set, and setting interact to shape the form of a marihuana reaction. The researcher who sets out with prior conviction that hemp is psychotomimetic or a "mild hallucinogen" is likely to confirm his conviction experimentally (10), but he would probably confirm the opposite hypothesis if his bias were in the opposite direction. Precautions to insure neutrality of set and setting, including use of a doubleblind procedure as an absolute minimum, are vitally important if the object of investigation is to measure real marihuana-induced responses.

CONCLUSIONS

1. It is feasible and safe to study the effects of marihuana on human volunteers who smoke it in a laboratory.

2. In a neutral setting persons who are naive to marihuana do not have strong subjective experiences after smoking low or high doses of the drug, and the effects they do report are not the same as those described by regular users of marihuana who take the drug in the same neutral setting.

3. Marihuana-naive persons do demonstrate impaired performance on simple intellectual and psychomotor tests after smoking marihuana; the impairment is dose-related in some cases.

4. Regular users of marihuana do get high after smoking marihuana in a neutral setting but do not show the same degree of impairment of performance on the tests as do naive subjects. In some cases, their performance even appears to improve slightly after smoking marihuana.

5. Marihuana increases heart rate moderately.

6. No change in respiratory rate follows administration of marihuana by inhalation.

7. No change in pupil size occurs in short term exposure to marihuana.

8. Marihuana administration causes dilatation of conjunctival blood vessels.

9. Marihuana treatment produces no change in blood sugar levels.

10. In a neutral setting the physiological and psychological effects of a single, inhaled dose of marihuana appear to reach maximum intensity within one-half hour of inhalation, to be diminished after 1 hour, and to be completely dissipated by 3 hours.

REFERENCES

1. R. J. Bouquet, *Bull. Narcotics*, **2**, 14 (1950).

2. F. Korte and H. Sieper, in *Hashish: Its Chemistry and Pharmacology*, G. E. W. Wolstenholme and J. Knight, Eds. Boston: Little, Brown, 1965, pp. 15–30.

3. Task Force on Narcotics and Drug Abuse, the President's Commission on Law Enforcement and the Administration of Justice, *Task Force Report: Narcotics and Drug Abuse* 1967, p. 14.

4. R. Mechoulam, and Y. Gaoni, *J. Amer. Chem. Soc.*, 1965, **67**, 3273.

5. J. F. Siler, W. L. Sheep, L. B. Bates, G. F. Clark, G. W. Cook, W. A. Smith, *Mil. Surg.*, 269–280, (November 1933).

6. Mayor's Committee on Marihuana, *The Marihuana Problem in the City of New York*, 1944.

7. E. G. Williams, C. K. Himmelsbach, A. Winkler, D. C. Ruble, and B. J. Lloyd, *Public Health Rep.*, 1946, **61**, 1059.

8. H. Isbell, *Psychopharmacologia*, **11**, 184 (1967).

9. I. C. Chopra and R. N. Chopra, *Bull. Narcotics*, 1957, **9**, 4.

10. F. Ames, *J. Ment. Sci.*, 1958, **104**, 972.

11. C. J. Miras, in *Hashish: Its Chemistry and Pharmacology*, G. E. W. Wolstenholme and J. Knight, Eds. Boston: Little, Brown, 1965, pp. 37–47.

12. J. M. Watt, in *Hashish: Its Chemistry and Pharmacology*, G. E. W. Wolstenholme and J. Knight, Eds. Boston: Little, Brown, 1965, pp. 54–66.

13. AMA Council on Mental Health, *J. Amer. Med. Ass.*, 1968, **204**, 1181.

14. G. Joachimoglu, in *Hashish: Its Chemistry and Pharmacology*, G. E. W. Wolstenholme and J. Knight, Eds. Boston: Little, Brown, 1965, pp. 2–10.

15. We thank M. Lerner and A. Bober of the U.S. Customs Laboratory, Baltimore, for performing this assay.

16. We thank R. H. Pace and E. H. Hall of the Peter J. Schweitzer Division of the Kimberly-Clark Corp. for supplying placebo material.

17. S. Garattini, in *Hashish: Its Chemistry and Pharmacology*, G. E. W. Wolstenholme and J. Knight, Eds. Boston: Little, Brown, 1965, pp. 70–78.

18. J. H. Jaffee, in *The Pharmacological Basis of Therapeutics*, L. S. Goodman and A. Gilman, Eds. New York: Macmillan, ed. 3, 1965, pp. 299–301.

19. We thank E. L. Richardson, Attorney General of the Commonwealth of Massachusetts for permitting these experiments to proceed and N. L. Chayet for legal assistance. We do not consider it appropriate to describe here the opposition we encountered from governmental agents and agencies and from university bureaucracies.

20. We thank D. Miller and M. Seifer of the Federal Bureau of Narcotics (now part of the Bureau of Narcotics and Dangerous Drugs, under the Department of Justice) for help in obtaining marihuana for this research.

21. The doses of tobacco in placebo and low-dose cigarettes were too small to cause physiological changes in subjects who qualified in the practice session.

22. K. E. Rosvold, A. F. Mirsky, I. Sarason, E. D. Bransome, L. H. Beck, *J. Consult. Psychol.*, 1956, **20**, 343; A. F. Mirsky and P. V. Cardon, *Electroencephalogr. Clin. Neurophysiol.*, 1962, **14**, 1; C. Kornetsky and G. Bain, *Psychopharmacologia*, 1965, **8**, 277.

23. G. M. Smith and H. K. Beecher, *J. Pharmacol.*, 1959, **126**, 50.

24. We will attempt to define the complex nature of a marihuana high in a subsequent paper discussing the speech samples and interviews.

25. H. S. Becker, *Outsiders: Studies in the Sociology of Deviance* New York: Macmillan, 1963, chap. 3.

26. Although the motor skills measured by the pursuit rotor are represented in driving ability, they are only components of that ability. The influence of marihuana on driving skill remains an open question of high medico-legal priority.

27. L. E. Hollister, R. K. Richards, H. K. Gillespie, in preparation.

28. Sponsored and supported by Boston University's division of psychiatry, in part through PHS grants MH12568, MH06795–06, MH7753–06, and MH33319, and the Boston University Medical Center. The authors thank Dr. P. H. Knapp and Dr. C. Kornetsky of the Boston University School of Medicine, Department of Psychiatry and Pharmacology, for consistent support and excellent advice, and J. Finkelstein of 650 Madison Avenue, New York City, for his support at a crucial time.

8.3 Effects of Predictable and Unpredictable Shock on Development of Gastrointestinal Lesions in Rats

JAY M. WEISS

If a noxious event occurs predictably as opposed to unpredictably, will this affect psychosomatic consequences of stress? The present experiment studied the development of stomach lesions in rats that could accurately predict when electric shocks would occur in comparison to Ss that received the same shocks but could not predict their occurrence.

Studies by Myers (1958) and Seligman (1967) have shown that rats are less afraid, as measured by suppression of food and water intake (CER), if an electric shock is preceded by a signal than if it is unsignaled. Seligman reported that 6 out of 8 rats in the unsignaled condition developed stomach lesions while none of the Ss in the signaled condition did. However, Brady, Thorton, and deFisher (1962), Friedman and Ader (1965), and Pare (1964), measuring effects on body weight, found that rats and mice receiving signaled shock lost more weight than

Ss receiving unsignaled shock. Since Weiss (1968) has measured body weight, CER, and stomach lesions, and found similar effects for all measures, it appears unlikely that the opposite results cited above are due to differences in measures. Thus, the psychosomatic effects of being able to predict a noxious event do not, as yet, present a consistent overall picture.

One limitation of all the studies except that by Myers is that grid shock was used, so that Ss could perform responses to reduce the discomfort of shock, such as rearing, or even could escape shock entirely by jumping off the grid; thus, the groups not only differed in the predictable-unpredictable nature of shock but may also have received different amounts of shock and/or differentially performed the coping responses mentioned above. In the present study, the psychosomatic effects of predictable vs. unpredictable

Reprinted from the *Proceedings of the 76th Annual Convention of the American Psychological Association*, 1968, **3**, 263–264, with permission of the author and the American Psychological Association, Inc.

317

shock were investigated without this possible confounding, by delivering the shock through fixed tail electrodes.

METHOD

The Ss were 36 male albino rats (12 triplets of 3 Ss each) weighing 150–200 gm. at the time of experimentation. Each day, one triplet with Ss weighing within 10 gm. of one another was drawn from the colony, and housed for 24 hr. in individual cages without food. Each S was then placed in a hardware-cloth tube 8 in. long and 2 in. in diameter, and a tail electrode consisting of two .5 in. lengths of stainless-steel tubing was taped to S's tail after electrode paste had been rubbed onto the locus of contact. The Ss were then placed in individual soundproof, ventilated chambers.

After 1 hr. of habituation, the experimental session was begun. One S was randomly selected as the Nonshock con-

trol, and never received shock. The other two Ss received shock (3.5 ma., 2-sec. duration) on a variable interval schedule with an average interval of 60 sec. The tail electrodes for the two shock Ss were wired *in series*, so that the shock received by those Ss was of exactly the same current intensity and duration. One shock S (Predictable shock group), chosen randomly by the flip of a coin, received a "beeping" 1,000-cps tone signal that began 10 sec. before each shock. The other shock S (Unpredictable shock group) received the same signal but programmed separately so that it occurred with no relation to the shock. Thus, each triplet consisted of one S from each of the three groups: a Nonshock control, and two matched shock Ss that received the same electric shock, signaled for one, unsignaled for the other.

After 19 hr., Ss were removed from the apparatus, placed in individual cages without food, and 6 hr. later were sacri-

table 1

Gastrointestinal Lesions and Abnormality Ranks for All Groups with Significance of Comparisons

Group	Percentage Showing Lesions	Mean Number of Lesions	Mean Total Length of Lesions (in mm)	Frequency of Abnormality Rank[a] 3	2	1
Unpredictable shock (up)	100	6.6	8.9	12	0	0
Predictable shock (ps)	67	1.2	1.5	0	8	4
Nonshock (NS)	25	0.4	0.5	0	4	8
P-UP	$p < .10$	$p < .001$	$p < .01$	$p < .001$		
NS-UP	$p < .001$	$p < .001$	$p < .01$	$p < .001$		
NS-P	$p < .10$	$p < .10$	$p < .05$	$p < .30$		

[a] Rank from 1 to 3 indicates best to worst.

ficed by decapitation. Stomachs were removed and lesions were counted and measured by E (see Weiss, 1968, for details of procedure). During ulcer evaluation, E did not know which group each S had been in.

RESULTS

Gastric lesions, or "stress ulcers," were found in the glandular area of the stomach, and their presence was confirmed by histological examination. Lesions in the upper, or cardiac, area of the stomach were found in one S in the Unpredictable shock group.

Analysis of gastric lesions, shown in Table 1, indicated that Ss which received Unpredictable shock developed considerably more pathology than Ss which received either the same shock preceded by a signal or no shock. When the three stomachs of each triplet were compared with one another without knowledge of group, the Unpredictable shock S was judged in every case to show the most pathology. As expected, Predictable shock Ss showed more pathology than Nonshock Ss, which developed some lesions after 19 hr. in restraint. Figure 1 illustrates one triplet of several which showed a strikingly large difference between the signaled and unsignaled shock Ss.

DISCUSSION

In earlier studies of coping behavior, Weiss found that a psychological variable—the ability to cope with an electric shock—was more important in affecting various psychosomatic symptoms than whether S did or did not receive the

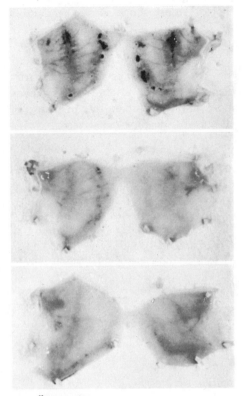

figure 1

The glandular area of the stomachs from one matched triplet showing (top to bottom) animal that received unpredictable shock, predictable shock, and no shock.

physical stressor (shock). The present results again show the great importance of psychological factors in determining physical or psychosomatic reactions to stress. Using a similar procedure of giving matched Ss the same electric shock via fixed tail electrodes wired in series to eliminate possible systematic group differences in shock, the present experiment revealed large differences between Ss that could predict shock and Ss that could not, while the difference between Ss that received predictable shock vs. no shock was considerably smaller. Taken together, the results of these experiments indicate that conceptions of stress must not underestimate the importance of psychological variables, since such variables can be even more important than the presence or absence of the physical stressor.

REFERENCES

Brady, J. P., Thornton, D. R., and deFisher, D. "Deleterious effects of anxiety elicited by conditioned pre-aversive stimuli in the rat," *Psychosomatic Medicine*, 1962, **24**, 590–595.

Friedman, S. B., and Ader, R. Parameters relevant to the experimental production of stress in the mouse," *Psychosomatic Medicine*, 1965, **27**, 27–30.

Myers, A. K. The effects of predictable vs. unpredictable punishment in the albino rat. Unpublished doctoral dissertation, Yale University, 1958.

Pare, W. "The effect of chronic environmental stress on stomach ulceration, adrenal function, and consummatory behavior in the rat," *Journal of Psychology*, 1964, **57**, 143–151.

Seligman, M. E. P. Chronic fear produced by unpredictable electric shock. Unpublished doctoral dissertation, University of Pennsylvania, 1967.

Weiss, J. M. "Effects of coping responses on stress," *Journal of Comparative and Physiological Psychology*, 1968, **65**, 251–260.

8.4 Prognostic Indicators in Psychosis and Neurosis

E. K. ERIC GUNDERSON AND RANSOM J. ARTHUR

A number of clinical and social history factors have repeatedly correlated with outcome of illness in schizophrenia, and findings, although often appearing inconsistent or confusing, have not been altogether discouraging (Huston and Pepernick, 1958). Outcome criteria frequently used in past studies include: (1) time in hospital, readmission to hospital, or a combination of these; (2) assessment of symptomatology on one or more occasions after release from the hospital; and (3) employment record in the community. The first criterion, chronicity versus staying out of the hospital, has been used much more frequently than any other. Hospitalization record alone has limited value as an indicator of the patient's personal and social adjustment; hospitalization may reflect administrative policies, degree of crowding, and so on, as much as the patient's clinical condition. Direct information pertaining to

clinical symptomatology and ability to hold a job would appear important as well in defining outcome of illness.

A wide variety of clinical and social history variables have been studied as prognostic indicators in mental illness. In one study, 200 items of case-history information were related to outcome in schizophrenia with essentially negative results (Schofield, Hathaway, Hastings, and Bell, 1954). In another study, using hospital readmission as a criterion, only 1 of 144 predictor measures, including demographic, psychiatric rating, and test data, was significantly correlated with outcome (Marks, Stauffacher, and Lyle, 1963). In the same study, findings were more frequently positive using adjustment ratings after 1 yr. as a criterion, but only a small number of cases were included in this phase of the study.

In a large-scale study of Veterans Administration schizophrenic patients,

Reprinted with slight abridgment from *Journal of Abnormal Psychology*, 1968, **73**, 468–473, with permission of the authors and the American Psychological Association, Inc.

using time in hospital combined with readmissions as the outcome criterion and selecting the most extreme cases as "successes" or "failures," 9 of 33 predictor variables had low but significant correlations with the success–failure criterion (Sherman, Moseley, Ging, and Bookbinder, 1964). A psychiatric rating of withdrawal was the most important single predictor of success–failure.

The most consistent prognostic indicators in schizophrenia appear to be those identified by Vaillant (1964) and partially confirmed by other investigators (Nameche, Warning, and Ricks, 1964). The seven predictive factors were: acute onset, precipitating factors, depression, nonschizoid premorbid adjustment, confusion, concern with death, and heredity positive for affective psychosis. A simple score based upon the presence of these prognostic factors was reported to be highly related to outcome. A subsequent study found five of the seven prognostic indexes discriminating with respect to extreme cases on a continuum of chronicity (Stephens, Astrup, and Mangrum, 1966).

Relatively little attention has been given to prognosis in disorders other than schizophrenia. In one exploratory study, 44% of those patients diagnosed schizophrenic reaction attained at least a "partial recovery" compared with 57% of psychoneurotic reactions and 83% of cases with periodic depressions (Bucove and Levitt, 1966). In another study, using rehospitalization during 2 yr. as the criterion, nonschizophrenic patients, particularly depressives, had a better prognosis than schizophrenics (Levenstein, Klein, and Pollack, 1966).

The present study is concerned with the prognostic significance of approximately 50 items of clinical and social history information taken from psychiatric and administrative records of Navy and Marine Corps personnel who incurred severe schizophrenic or neurotic disorders in the naval service.

METHOD

Subjects

A sample of 200 Ss for the study was randomly drawn from all Navy and Marine Corps psychiatric cases considered by physical evaluation boards for the Temporary Disability Retired List during 1958. Medical and board data were obtained from the Navy Judge Advocate's Office and from the Federal Personnel Records Center, St. Louis, Missouri, for 173 cases with completed records. Thus, all Ss had been admitted to naval hospitals with diagnosed mental disorders and had been evaluated for presence and degree of psychiatric disability by physical evaluation boards. Composition of the sample by diagnostic subtypes was as follows: 55 paranoid schizophrenics and 30 other schizophrenic types; 29 anxiety neurotics, 34 depressive neurotics, and 25 other neurotic types.

The mean age of the 85 psychotic patients in the sample was 26.2 yr. with a standard deviation of 6.2; the mean length of military service for the psychotic subgroup was 6.9 yr. The mean age of the 88 psychoneurotic patients was 31.8 yr. with a standard deviation of 7.0; the neurotic subgroup had a mean length of service of 12.2 yr. Nine of the psychotic group and eight of the neurotic group were officers; four of the patients were female.

Procedures

Patients had been given thorough physical and psychiatric examinations prior to consideration for retirement, and clinical and social histories were available in the form of narrative summaries by examining psychiatrists. Those patients judged to have a sufficient degree of disability to be placed on the Temporary Disability Retired List were again evaluated by physical evaluation boards after 18 mo., 36 mo., and 54 mo. Before the expiration of 5 yr., the board was required to render a final evaluation of permanent disability. The findings of physical evaluation boards were subject to review and final approval by the Secretary of the Navy; for the purposes of this study, ratings of psychiatric disability recommended by the boards were used for the measure of outcome. Items of information pertaining to demographic and military status, diagnosis, symptomatology, treatment, and postretirement adjustment were coded from clinical records by senior medical students and graduate psychology students. The specific variables included for study are shown in the Results section of the paper.

The diagnostic criteria were those of the *Nomenclature for Recording Psychiatric Conditions,* a Joint Armed Forces publication, which is similar to the diagnostic manual of the American Psychiatric Association.

All of the 85 psychotic patients were followed up for 5 yr. after retirement. A number of the neurotic cases were included only in the analysis of factors related to initial disability rating. Several of these cases had initial disability ratings too low to be placed on the Temporary Disability Retired List, and several were lost to the follow-up study because of death or because of incomplete information; a total of 57 neurotic cases were followed up for the full 5 yr.

RESULTS

As expected, the neurotic and psychotic groups differed on many of the symptom variables. Thought disturbances, ideas of reference, hallucinations, delusions, and flat or inappropriate affect were highly characteristic of psychotic patients; neurotics, on the other hand, more frequently manifested severe anxiety, many physical and psychological complaints, depression, and suicidal attempts or threats. In general, symptom patterns evidenced by the various diagnostic subgroups were highly consistent with widely accepted diagnostic criteria. Analyses of prognostic indicators were conducted separately for psychotic and neurotic groups.

The Outcome Criterion

Before considering correlates of initial disability or significant predictors of improvement, further attention is given to the nature of the criterion and to significant factors affecting it. Outcome or improvement was measured by the amount of change in disability ratings given by physical evaluation boards over a 5-yr. period. The numerical percentages of disability assigned by the boards were given values on a 6-point scale: 100% = 1, 70% = 2, 50% = 3, 30% = 4, 10% = 5, and 0% or severance from the retirement list = 6. The difference between initial and final scale values was the measure of recovery or improvement.

Three types of information concerning adjustment were thought to be important in determining changes in disability ratings: hospitalization record, employment record, and remission of symptoms as shown by clinical examination. Hospitalization record and employment record were obviously related in that patients who remained or became hospitalized could not be employed. Patients who were not hospitalized might be employed all of the time, part of the time, or not at all. Regardless of hospitalization or employment, all patients were reexamined periodically to evaluate symptomatology and social adjustment.

Hospitalization record, employment record, and symptom remission all were found to be related to changes in disability rating over the 5 yr. for both neurotics and psychotics. Employment status alone was moderately related to disability ratings for psychotics in that an employment score, reflecting amount and stability of employment, correlated .46 with the improvement criterion for psychotics. Improvement was less highly correlated with employment or hospitalization in neurotics and appeared to be more dependent upon evaluations of symptomatology in this group.

Correlates of Initial Disability Ratings for Neurotics

Diagnosis obviously was an important factor in the initial evaluation of disability in patients generally: all psychotics were rated 100% disabled while neurotics varied widely in ratings and most were rated 50% or less disabled. Thus, it was possible to examine the correlates of initial disability ratings for neurotics but not for psychotics.

Results for the 88 neurotics who were initially evaluated for disability are presented in Table 1. The most important correlates of initial disability were symptoms of withdrawal and anxiety.

table 1

Correlates of Initial Disability and of Recovery

Variable	Degree of Initial Disability: Neurotics	Degree of Recovery	
		Neurotics	Psychotics
Demographic and social background			
Age	14	-40^a	-21^b
Race (Caucasian)	-11	07	31^a
Religion (Protestant)	06	10	06
Region of birth (South)	-08	09	-20
Education	23^a	-15	05
Hobbies	04	-21	21
Delinquency record	-06	07	17
Military experience			
Years of military service	12	-33^a	-17
Rank/pay grade	02	-28^a	-10
Military status (officer)	-02	-21	-03
Duty station (ship/overseas)	02	01	-12

table 1 (cont.)

Variable	Degree of Initial Disability: Neurotics	Degree of Recovery	
		Neurotics	Psychotics
Family and marital background			
Parents divorced/separated	19	03	−06
Parent deceased	23[a]	18	01
No. siblings	−14	05	−16
Firstborn	09	−26	10
Married	−09	−21	−07
No. dependents	04	02	−10
Unsatisfactory marriage	13	−03	−06
Diagnosis			
Paranoid schizophrenic	—[c]	—	−25[a]
Anxiety neurosis	13	−15	—
Depressive neurosis	04	02	—
Other neurosis	−29[a]	20	—
Symptoms			
Disoriented	—	—	13
Ideas of reference	—	—	−32[a]
Delusions of persecution	—	—	−21[b]
Hallucinations	—	—	07
Flat affect	−18	−07	−19[b]
Inappropriate affect	—	—	07
Depressed affect	10	−05	−02
Thought disturbance	25[a]	10	−20[a]
Hostility (suspicious/irritable)	10	−05	−08
Hostility (menacing)	—	—	10
Disturbed behavior (violent)	—	—	01
Disturbed behavior (excited)	—	—	05
Withdrawn/apathetic	39[a]	−21	04
Social life (inadequate)	37[a]	−28[a]	−14
Suicide (attempt/threat)	11	−11	02
Anxiety	34[a]	19	23[a]
Psychological complaints	14	13	−06
Physical complaints	−09	−26	09
Hypochondriasis	−01	19	−05
Treatment history			
Drugs	16	09	−13
Shock treatment	−01	11	16
Psychotherapy	22[a]	10	06
Medical treatment	09	−28[a]	24[a]
Hospital recommended	13	12	−04
Length of hospitalization	—	−16	−18

Note.—Decimals omitted.

[a] Product-moment correlations significant beyond .05 level of significance, two-tailed test.

[b] Correlations significant beyond .05 level of significance, one-tailed test.

[c] Values are omitted where incidence is zero or near zero.

Neurotic patients described by examining psychiatrists as withdrawn or apathetic, very limited in social life, or high in anxiety tended to be rated high in disability by physical evaluation boards. Other significantly positive correlates of initial disability were diagnostic subtype, education level, parent deceased, history of psychotherapy, and thought disturbances. Thought disturbances referred to poor concentration, preoccupation, confusion, or obsessive thinking; 31% of the neurotic group evidenced one or another form of thought disturbance. Although the incidence of other psychotic-like symptoms, such as disorientation, ideas of reference, etc., was very low in the neurotic group, presence of any of these symptoms tended to be associated with high disability ratings.

The significant correlation between history of psychotherapy and initial disability rating probably can be accounted for by the fact that having received psychotherapy was substantially correlated with anxiety level.

Education level was positively correlated with withdrawal symptoms, the variable most highly correlated with disability rating. A plausible explanation for the relationship between education and withdrawal among the neurotics was not readily apparent.

The relationship of anxiety symptoms to diagnostic subtype apparently accounted for the fact that patients with neuroses other than anxiety or depressive types tended to receive low initial disability ratings.

Prognostic Indicators in Neurosis

Initial disability rating was independent of improvement in disability status for neurotics ($r = .12$). The most important predictor of outcome was age at time of hospitalization (onset). Older patients were less likely to recover than younger patients. Variables highly correlated with age, that is, length of military service and rank or pay grade, similarly correlated negatively with improvement.

Other significant correlates of outcome for neurotics were inadequate social life ($r = -.28$) and a history of medical treatment for other than psychiatric conditions ($r = -.28$). Manifesting physical complaints, which was positively correlated with medical treatment, tended to correlate negatively with recovery, but this relationship was of borderline significance ($r = -.26$, $p < .06$). Receiving medical treatment for physical complaints apparently had an adverse effect upon outcome in certain neurotic cases.

Anxiety level manifested during hospitalization did not correlate significantly with improvement for the neurotic group.

The correlation of birth order (firstborn) with improvement ($r = -.26$, $p < .06$) attained only borderline statistical significance as a single variable. When the oldest child variable was combined with age by the regression technique, however, it made a significant contribution to the prediction of improvement. The multiple correlation attained with these two variables was .48. The addition of other variables did not significantly increase the multiple correlation. The degree of prediction possible with the present set of variables, therefore, is rather low; additional prognostic indicators are needed in order to attain useful prediction with neurotic patients.

Prognostic Indicators in Psychosis

Significant predictors of improvement in the psychotic group were ideas of reference, diagnostic subtype (paranoid), race (Caucasian), medical treatment, and anxiety. The first two factors were negatively related to improvement while the other three were positively related.

One of the most consistent indicators of poor prognosis in previous studies has been paranoid ideation, that is, persecutory delusions and ideas of reference. The present results are highly consistent with the earlier findings.

Non-Caucasion (predominantly Negro) psychotic patients in this study were less likely to show reductions in disability ratings over 5 yr. than were Caucasian psychotic patients. This result was not a function of educational level because education was unrelated to improvement and, in fact, was negatively related to employment during the first 18 mo. after retirement.

Examination of the employment record of the Negro and Caucasian psychotic groups showed that Negroes were at a disadvantage over the first follow-up period; after 18 mo. the percentage of "never employed" since retirement was much higher for non-Caucasians (64%) than for Caucasians (28%). However, at the second and third evaluation periods (36 and 54 mo.) differences in percentages of "never employed" were no longer significant.

A history of medical treatment for conditions other than psychiatric was positively correlated with recovery for psychotics. A relationship in the opposite direction was present for neurotics. In other words, medical treatment for physical complaints among neurotics was related to persistence of illness while medical treatment among psychotics was related to remission.

Based upon previous studies, it was reasonable to hypothesize that age of onset, delusions, thought disturbance, flat affect, and length of hospitalization would have significant relationships with outcome in the present psychotic sample; therefore one-tailed significance tests could be applied. By this standard, all of the obtained correlations for these variables were significant beyond the .05 level except length of hospitalization which was of borderline significance ($r = .18$, $p = .06$). It is noted, however, that these correlations were universally low.

When the regression technique was applied to evaluate independent contributions of each predictor variable, five items contributed significantly to recovery. These variables, listed in order of the magnitude of their beta weights from high to low, were: ideas of reference (negative), number of hobbies, medical treatment, Caucasian, and anxiety. A multiple correlation with the criterion of .54 was obtained with the above combination of predictors. Although the hallucinations item as a single variable had a low correlation with the criterion, in combination with the aforementioned set of five significant predictors this item increased the multiple correlation to .57. This result was of interest in view of previous evidence concerning the presence of hallucinations, confusion, and other evidence of acute onset as positive indicators for recovery in schizophrenia.

DISCUSSION

After 5 yr. a high proportion of the psychiatric patients in this study was employed and only a small number was hospitalized. Both neurotic and psychotic groups showed considerable symptomatic improvement, and many individuals were free of significant psychopathology. As expected, neurotic cases tended to recover more rapidly and completely than did psychotics.

Specific prognostic indicators differed for the two patient groups; only age at onset was a significant predictor for both groups. Outcome, as measured by changes in disability rating, was more predictable for the psychotic group than for the neurotic group.

Disability ratings in psychotics were more dependent upon objective indicators of adjustment, namely, hospitalization and employment, than in neurotics. This fact suggests that the improvement measure for psychotics may have been more reliable than that for neurotics. Studies of prognosis usually neglect to examine determinants of the outcome criterion used. The present study emphasizes the desirability of using a broader and more inclusive adjustment criterion than rehospitalization and of evaluating the relative importance of various components of the criterion where this is possible.

In spite of some justifiable caution and skepticism, the authors feel that the large number of empirical studies conducted in the past two decades have provided many useful guidelines and promising hypotheses for future research. These trends were well summarized earlier by Huston and Pepernick (1958). The present study exemplifies the difficulty of isolating useful prognostic indicators but confirms or supports the prognostic value of a number of demographic, social, and clinical factors for schizophrenics in the military setting. The foremost of these are paranoid diagnostic subtype, ideas of reference, persecutory delusions, and anxiety. The prognostic significance of racial group in the present study perhaps reflects the often observed relationship of socioeconomic status to success of rehabilitative efforts.

Consideration of birth order as a prognostic factor in mental illness has been conspicuously neglected in previous studies. The significance of being firstborn for outcome in severe neuroses merits further study.

SUMMARY

Neurotic and psychotic patients who had been temporarily retired from naval service were reevaluated periodically and rated on degrees of disability by physical evaluation boards. Personal history and symptom variables were correlated with changes in amount of psychiatric disability over a 5-yr. period. Recovery or improvement was more rapid and complete in neurotics, but improvement was more predictable in psychotics. Significant correlates of improvement for neurotics were: age at time of hospitalization, pay grade (rank), inadequate social life, and medical treatment for other than psychiatric condition. Significant prognostic indicators for psychotics included: diagnostic subtype (paranoid), age at the time of hospitalization, racial group, ideas of reference, delusions, thought disturbance, and anxiety level.

REFERENCES

Bucove, A. D., and Levitt, L. I. "A seven-year follow-up study of patients in a general hospital psychiatric service," *American Journal of Psychiatry,* 1966, **122,** 1088–1095.

Huston, P. E., and Pepernick, M. C. "Prognosis in schizophrenia," in L. Bellak (Ed.), *Schizophrenia.* New York: Logos, 1958.

Levenstein, S., Klein, D. F., and Pollack, M. "Follow-up study of formerly hospitalized voluntary psychiatric patients: The first two years," *American Journal of Psychiatry,* 1966, **122,** 1102–1109.

Marks, J., Stauffacher, J. C., and Lyle, C. "Predicting outcome in schizophrenia," *Journal of Abnormal and Social Psychology,* 1963, **66,** 117–127.

Nameche, G., Waring, M., and Ricks, D. "Early indicators of outcome in schizophrenia," *Journal of Nervous and Mental Disease,* 1964, **139,** 232–240.

Schofield, W., Hathaway, S. R., Hastings, D. W., and Bell, D. "Prognostic factors in schizophrenia," *Journal of Consulting Psychology,* 1954, **18,** 155–166.

Sherman, L. J., Moseley, E. C., Ging, R., and Bookbinder, L. J. "Prognosis in schizophrenia," *Archives of General Psychiatry,* 1964, **10,** 123–130.

Stephens, J. H., Astrup, C., and Mangrum, J. C. "Prognostic factors in recovered and deteriorated schizophrenics," *American Journal of Psychiatry,* 1966, **122,** 1116–1121.

Vaillant, G. E. "Prospective prediction of schizophrenic remission," *Archives of General Psychiatry,* 1964, **11,** 509–518.

8.5 High School Yearbooks: A Nonreactive Measure of Social Isolation in Graduates Who Later Became Schizophrenic

CHARLES N. BARTHELL AND DAVID S. HOLMES

Of the numerous hypotheses relating early social experience to the development of schizophrenia, none has been more frequently stated than that of "social isolation" (Faris, 1934; Kohn and Clausen, 1955). This hypothesis suggests that the preschizophrenic personality attempts to avoid painful exposure of his low level of self-esteem by reducing inter-personal contact or by rigidly controlling the nature of the interaction (Auerback, 1959; Sechehaye, 1956; White, 1956; Wolman, 1965). The individual consequently shuts himself off from communicative feedback and thus avails himself of fewer opportunities for reality testing. The avoidance of participation with others makes social participation progressively more difficult, and the individual falls further and further behind his peers in the development of

social skills. It has been specifically suggested that "at adolescence, when various new social skills are required, such individuals are likely to drop fatally out of step and still further restrict their future development [White, 1956, p. 530]."

A number of studies have been conducted to determine the extent of social isolation among preschizophrenics while in high school (i.e., during adolescence). Schofield and Balian (1959) found that preschizophrenics, when compared with a "normal" control group, could be characterized by "higher rates of social withdrawal, lack of social adeptness and poise, and narrow interests [p. 225]." Further support for the social isolation hypothesis was provided by Bower, Shellhamer, and Daily (1960) who found that with few exceptions preschizophrenics could be characterized as "tend-

Reprinted with minor abridgment from *Journal of Abnormal Psychology,* 1968, **73**, 313–316, with permission of the authors and the American Psychological Association, Inc.

ing toward the shut-in, withdrawing kind of personality [p. 728]." Finally, Kohn and Clausen (1955) found that roughly one-third of their schizophrenic sample reported a sufficient lack of activities and friendship patterns to lead the authors to classify them as isolates or partial isolates, whereas only 4% of the normals reported such patterns.

Although these studies support the social isolation hypothesis, an equal number of studies throw some doubt on its tenability. Bellak and Parcell (1946) found that in their study of the prepsychotic personalities of 100 cases diagnosed as dementia praecox,

> . . . 35 had distinctly extrovert prepsychotic personalties, 28 had distinctly introvert prepsychotic personalities, and 37 had to be considered ambivert, or a mixture between extroversion and introversion [p. 630].

Morris, Soroker, and Burrus (1954) evaluated the current adjustment of 54 individuals who, when seen in a clinic from 16 to 27 yr. previously, had been described as "internal reactors." They found that these individuals were "relatively free of overt mental or emotional illness and getting along quite well [p. 749]." Last, in the follow-up study of Michael, Morris, and Soroker (1957), only 1 of the 10 Ss who carried the diagnosis of schizophrenia as an adult had been classed as an introvert from the social history collected at childhood.

It is clear then that there are inconsistencies and points of disagreement in the literature on the relationship between schizophrenia and social withdrawal in the prepsychotic personality. One criticism of the previous studies, and

a possible source of the inconsistencies, lies in the fact that in most studies the patient's social history was compiled by interviewing relatives and acquaintances after the patient had become psychotic, that is, retrospectively. This leaves the studies subject to a number of errors. First of all, inaccuracies may result from the fact that reliable informants may be difficult if not impossible to find, and their reports may have been distorted or changed with the passage of time. Second, if S had been identified as a patient (either as an adult or as a child who was later followed-up), informants may have been influenced in their reporting by what they had heard about mental disorders. Last, those studies in which information was gathered from patients may suffer from the disadvantage of unreliable information due to the patient's disorder and feelings about hospitalization.

Webb, Campbell, Schwartz, and Sechrest (1966) have recently outlined the value of using "nonreactive measures" such as archival material which would not be distorted by the passage of time or by the measurement process. With these measures there is no masking or sensitivity as there may be when the producer of the data knows he is being studied by some social scientist. According to Webb et al. (1966), "this gain by itself makes the use of archives attractive if one wants to compensate for the reactivity which riddles the interview and the questionnaire [p. 53]." In the present study, the activity summaries found in high school yearbooks were used as a means of determining the relative social isolation of the preschizophrenic and prepsychoneurotic individual.

METHOD

Subjects

A group of 20 hospitalized schizophrenics (14 males and 6 females) and a group of 20 hospitalized psychoneurotics (14 males and 6 females) were selected from the medical records of the Illinois State Psychiatric Institute. The criteria applied in S selection were the following: (a) All Ss were born between the years 1934 and 1944; (b) all Ss graduated from Chicago-area high schools between the years 1952 and 1962; (c) no S was selected who had been hospitalized within 2 yr. following the date of his high school graduation; (d) no schizophrenic patient was selected whose hospital stay was less than 3 mo. The 2-yr. period following graduation and prior to hospitalization was thought necessary in order to insure the fact that Ss were not overtly or incapacitatingly schizophrenic or neurotic while attending high school at which time the data were recorded. Schizophrenic Ss hospitalized for less than 3 mo. were excluded on the grounds that their schizophrenic break was more likely to be of a reactive nature, and less likely to be the culmination of a long-term developmental process.

A "normal" control group was selected using the method introduced by Bower, Shellhamer, and Daily (1960). At the time that data were being recorded from the yearbooks of each schizophrenic and psychoneurotic S, data were also collected for the student pictured next to him. This rule was followed unless the student pictured next to the patient S was of a different sex, of a different race, or of the same name indicating the possibility of a family relationship. In such cases, the next student pictured was selected as control S. Thus, for every schizophrenic or psychoneurotic S from a given high school, there was a control S from the same high school who had graduated in the same year and had been free to choose from the same number and types of activities offered by the high school at that time.

Procedure

A list of all of the activities in which each S had participated was taken from the index and/or the senior summary of each S's senior yearbook. Only high school graduates were used in this study since it is only in the senior year of high school that any extensive record is set down of the students' activities in school. At the time of the data collection, the experimenter knew to which group any one S belonged. Therefore, for each S, the entire list of activities was copied verbatim and was later analyzed blindly. Following the collection of the data, each S's activities were classified into one of the following categories: (a) social activities, (b) service activities, (c) performance activities, and (d) athletic activities. Those activities classified as social included all clubs, organizations, and activities whose primary purpose was a social one. Examples of activities classified as such included student-council or student-government organizations; language, academic, or special-interest clubs; and student publications. Those activities classified as service activities included activities in which some service was performed for the high school. Such activities were of the type that necessitated very little social interaction. Examples of activities classified under this heading included hall guard, office helper, library assistant, teacher's aide, and the like. Performance activities included musical or dramatic organizations, while athletic activities included all individual and team sports as well as intramurals and athletic associations. There was a 95% agreement between two independent judges on the classification of all of the activities into the above categories.

RESULTS AND DISCUSSION

Number of Activities

An analysis of variance was performed to test the significance of sex, diagnostic category, type of activity, and the interaction of these variables as related to number of activities participated in by Ss. The results of this analysis are presented in Table 1.[1] Both the variables of diagnostic category and type of activity were significant ($p < .01$). In light of the significant F for diagnostic categories, Kramer's (1956) multiple-range test for means based on unequal Ns was used to test the mean differences over all activities for the three diagnostic groups. The results of this analysis are presented in Table 2. This analysis indicated that the mean number of activities participated in by schizophrenics, as well as psychoneurotics, differed significantly from the mean number of activities for the control group ($p < .01$). There was, however, no significant difference found between the mean number of activities for the schizophrenic and psychoneurotic groups, although the difference was in the expected direction.

While schizophrenic Ss were found

[1] Table 1 has been omitted in the interests of brevity.

table 2

Significant Ranges for Kramer's Extension of Duncan's New Multiple-Range Test

	Schizophrenic	Neurotic	Normal
	Mean no. high school activities		
M	3.75	4.00	6.85
	Mean no. social activities		
M	1.60	1.95	2.83
	Mean no. service activities		
M	.75	.85	1.55
	Mean no. performance activities		
M	.65	.40	1.20
	Mean no. athletic activities		
M	.75	.80	1.28

Note.—Any two means not underlined by the same line are significantly different at the .01 level. Any two means underlined by the same line are not significantly different.

to differ significantly from normals in the mean number of activities in which they had participated, it is of interest to note that the mean number of activities for the schizophrenic group did not differ significantly from that of the psychoneurotic group. On the basis of these findings, one is forced to conclude, then, that *both* hospitalized groups showed a tendency toward withdrawal and isolation when compared to the control group. It is important to remember, however, that the psychoneurotics used in this study were all hospitalized. Since psychoneurotics do not as a general rule require hospitalization, it might be that the psychoneurotics in this sample could be considered more severely disturbed than psychoneurotics in general. This fact might explain the similarity found between the two patient groups.

Type of Activity

A number of analyses on the mean differences between social, service, performance, and athletic activities for the three S groups were performed, again using Kramer's multiple-range test. The results of these analyses are presented in the lower part of Table 2. Significant differences were found between the mean number of social activities for the schizophrenic and normal groups ($p < .01$), while the mean of the psychoneurotic group fell between those of the schizophrenics and normals but did not differ significantly from either. There were no significant differences found between the means of the three groups on any of the other activity classifications: service, performance, or athletic activities.

From this data, it would appear, then, that social activity level forms a continuum, with schizophrenics and normals falling at the extreme ends and psychoneurotics in the middle. It is important to note that there were no significant differences between the groups on any of the other types of activities considered. That is, it was only when social activities per se were considered that schizophrenics were found to fall behind their peers in level of participation. This fact seems an important finding and lends support to those investigators who hypothesize that the individual who becomes schizophrenic is socially withdrawn and introverted during adolescence.

In general the results of this research which employed a nonreactive measure offered support for those studies which have found that individuals who became schizophrenic were less active in the social realm prior to being diagnosed as schizophrenic. Social isolation may not, however, be unique to schizophrenics, for in the present study psychoneurotics evidenced a similar trend.

SUMMARY

The research on "social isolation" as a precipitating factor in the development of schizophrenia was reviewed, and it was pointed out that the previous measures were "reactive" in nature. The present study employed yearbook senior summaries as a nonreactive archival measure of level of high school activity. It was found that high school graduates who were later diagnosed as schizophrenic had participated in significantly fewer activities than did their normal controls. The activity level of psychoneurotics was found to fall between that of the schizophrenics and normals. The difference in overall activity level was found to be a function of the fact that patients engaged in significantly fewer "social activities."

REFERENCES

Auerback, A. (Ed.) *Schizophrenia, an integrated approach.* New York: Ronald Press, 1959.

Bellak, L., and Parcell, B. "The prepsychotic personality in dementia praecox," *Psychiatric Quarterly,* 1946, **20,** 627–637.

Bower, E. M., Shellhamer, T. A., and Daily, J. M. "School characteristics of male adolescents who later became schizophrenic," *American Journal of Orthopsychiatry*, 1960, **30,** 712-729.

Faris, R. "Cultural isolation and the schizophrenic personality," *American Journal of Sociology*, 1934, **40,** 155-169.

Kohn, M. L., and Clausen, J. A. "Social isolation and schizophrenia," *American Sociological Review*, 1955, **20,** 265-273.

Kramer, C. "Extension of multiple range test to group means with unequal numbers of replications," *Biometrics*, 1956, **12,** 307-310.

Michael, C. M., Morris, D. P., and Soroker, E. "Follow-up studies of shy, withdrawn children: II. Relative incidence of schizophrenia," *American Journal of Orthopsychiatry*, 1957, **24,** 331-337.

Morris, D. P., Soroker, E., and Burrus, G. "Follow-up studies of shy, withdrawn children: I. Evaluation of later adjustment," *American Journal of Orthopsychiatry*, 1954, **24,** 743-753.

Schofield, W., and Balian, L. "A comparative study of the personal histories of schizophrenic and nonpsychiatric patients." *Journal of Abnormal and Social Psychology*, 1959, **59,** 216-225.

Sechehaye, M. *A New Psychotherapy for Schizophrenia*. New York: Grune and Stratton, 1956.

Webb, E. J., Campbell, D. T., Schwartz, R. D., and Sechrest, L. *Unobtrusive Measures: Nonreactive Research in the Social Sciences*. Chicago: Rand McNally, 1966.

White, R. W. *The Abnormal Personality*. New York: Ronald Press, 1956.

Wolman, B. B. (Ed.) *Handbook of Clinical Psychology*. New York: McGraw-Hill, 1965.

SECTION 9

TREATMENT OF PSYCHOLOGICAL DISORDERS

It would be impossible to attempt a full discussion of psychological treatment in anything less than a full-size book; hence we have tried, in this section, to give some brief glimpses of some of the more recent developments in the field. Behavior therapy in its various forms is treated in three of the articles, and the use of laymen as therapists is discussed in two. The encounter group, another recent development, is also included in this section.

The first study concerns the use of lay volunteers in working with elementary school children who were encountering adademic difficulties or who were having problems of adjustment in their classrooms. Previous research suggested that therapists rating high on genuineness, warmth, and empathy, and low on dogmatism, would be more successful. The present study found that both warmth and empathy on the part of the volunteer therapists was positively correlated with improvement on the part of the children, but that the other two traits were not. Although the study was conducted on a relatively small scale and had many built-in limitations, the results suggest that volunteer mental health workers can be used effectively, and the author, Dean L. Stoffer of the Ohio State University, suggests a number of ways in which such a program could be made to function more successfully.

The second article, contributed by D. Vincent Biase and George DeLeon, is concerned with attempts to help sociopaths—heroin addicts in this instance—through a group therapy technique: the encounter group. Measures administered before and after participation in the encounter group show a reduction in hostility, depression, and anxiety, an effect that did not occur when the same patients engaged in work and recreational activity. The encounter-group experiment was therefore shown to be effective in bringing about desirable changes in affect on the part of patients of this type.

One of the main controversies today in mental health work is the relative effectiveness of behavior therapy in contrast with the more traditional "relationship therapy," a category that includes psychoanalysis, nondirective therapy, and other forms of therapist–patient interaction in which the chief objective is the insight of the patient into his difficulties. The study by John Marks, Beverly Sonoda, and Robert

337

Shalock, all of the Mental Health Research Institute in Fort Steilacoom, Washington, compares the effect of the two kinds of therapy with chronic schizophrenic patients. Previous research had shown that behavior therapy in the form of reinforcement techniques is dramatically effective in bringing about desirable changes in the behavior of patients. Somewhat to the surprise of the investigators, both types of therapy were found to be effective, and no consistently significant differences between the two emerged. The only advantage to the reinforcement technique appeared in its efficiency: it required the time of one extra person, whereas relationship therapy required six additional people for the 22 patients involved.

One of the commonest forms of psychopathology to be encountered on a college campus is test anxiety: the panic that grips many a student as he faces an examination and finds that he has forgotten everything about the subject that he learned so arduously during the previous days and weeks. Desensitization, a form of behavior therapy that has been used with some success with phobias and other forms of aversive reactions, would seem to be "made to order" for such a problem. In the fourth paper in this section, Robert Cohen and Sanford J. Dean of Syracuse University, report on their experiences in using group methods in order to desensitize students to test situations. The subjects who completed the twelve sessions in the experimental program showed an over-all reduction in test anxiety as well as some improvement in grade-point-average the following semester.

The final paper reports the experiences of Irwin Hirsch and Leopold Walder in training mothers to serve as reinforcement therapists for their own children. Although their study suffers from the limitation of not having independent observations of the mothers' behavior with their children over the period of training (a point which is made by the authors themselves), it does serve as an illustration of the ingenuity of psychologists in attempting to cope with the everpresent problem of lack of sufficient number of trained workers to meet the demand for therapists.

9.1 Investigation of Therapeutic Success as a Function of Genuineness, Nonpossessive Warmth, Empathic Understanding, and Dogmatism in the Helping Person

DEAN L. STOFFER

Review of previous research suggests that there are elements within the therapeutic relationship which cut across theoretical boundaries (Fiedler, 1950; Strupp, Wallach, and Wogan, 1964; Whitehorn and Betz, 1954). Three of these elements (*a*) genuineness, (*b*) communication of nonpossessive warmth, and (*c*) communication of accurate empathy have been defined operationally and investigated (Truax and Carkhuff, 1966; Rogers, Gendlin, Kiesler, and Truax, 1967; Barrett-Lennard, 1962). The evidence suggests that therapeutic outcome is related to these 3 conditions for neurotic and schizophrenic adults. In addition there is evidence which suggests that the less

dogmatic person is more likely to provide these 3 conditions in the helping relationship (Kemp, 1962). This study is an attempt to extend and clarify the evidence concerning the 3 therapeutic conditions in a relationship involving untrained volunteers working with elementary school children who were experiencing behavioral and academic difficulty.

PROCEDURE

The *Ss* of the study were 35 students and 35 adult helpers who participated in the Franklin County Community Helper Program during the 1966–1967 school

Reprinted from the *Proceedings of the 76th Annual Convention of the American Psychological Association*, 1968, **3**, 619–620, with permission of the author and the American Psychological Association, Inc.

year. Community Helpers were volunteers who worked with 1 child twice each week for 3 mo. Interviews varied in length from 30 min. to 1 hr. The purpose of the program was to determine the value of using untrained personnel in the helping relationship with a minimum of professional supervision. Helpers were instructed to establish a good relationship. They were allowed to choose their activities and to structure the relationship in their own way.

Each child was examined before and after treatment. Measures of behavioral change included an individual intelligence test (Stanford-Binet, Form L-M, or WISC); gains in achievement (Wide Range Achievement Test, Gray Oral Reading Test, teacher grades); reduction in teacher-rated behavior problems (Quay-Peterson Behavior Problem Checklist and an Interpersonal Adjective Checklist); and gains in motivation (selected picture projective tests). Resulting indexes of behavioral change were combined to yield a total outcome index.

Three scales developed by Truax and reported by Truax and Carkhuff (1966) were used to rate levels of genuineness, nonpossessive warmth, and accurate empathy provided to the child by the helper. A relationship inventory adapted from the Barrett-Lennard Relationship Inventory (Barrett-Lennard, 1962) attempted to measure the child's and helper's perceptions of the levels of therapeutic conditions offered by the helper. The Rokeach Dogmatism Scale (Rokeach, 1960) was used to measure the relative dogmatism of helpers.

Three judges were trained to listen to and to rate the interpersonal relationship according to the 3 Truax Scales.

From audio tapes taken from one interview early in treatment and one near the end of treatment, judges rated helpers as to the levels of therapeutic conditions which they were providing. Three 3-min. segments from each interview were used for analysis. Each judge rated all segments on one variable before beginning another. Nonpossessive warmth, accurate empathy, and genuineness were rated in that order by the same 3 judges. Combined rated scores were intercorrelated with each other and with each of the 4 individual indexes and combined outcome index.

The relationship inventories were used to determine child and helper perceptions of the levels of conditions offered by the helper. Each helper and each child completed parallel forms of the 24-item true–false relationship inventory near the end of treatment. Four subscale scores each contained 6 items which attempted to measure level of regard, conditionality of regard, accurate empathy, and genuineness on the part of the helper. Inventories were examined for intercorrelations among subscales. Total inventory scores were intercorrelated with rated conditions and with each of the 5 outcome indexes.

The Rokeach Dogmatism scale was administered to each helper near the middle of the treatment program. Scores were intercorrelated with rated conditions, helper and child relationship inventory total scores, and each of the 5 outcome indexes.

In order to account for as much of the outcome variance as possible, multiple correlations were determined between 5 selected conditions measures (rated nonpossessive warmth, rated accurate empathy, helper relationship inventory total score, child relationship inventory total score, and Dogmatism score) and each of the 5 outcome indexes.

RESULTS

Judges agreed on the levels of nonpossessive warmth ($r = .75$) and accurate empathy ($r = .74$) offered by the helper and these ratings were combined for further analysis. They were unable to agree, however, as to the helper's level of genuineness. In general, it can be said that without instruction, the untrained volunteers who were attempting to establish a good one-to-one relationship provided relatively low levels of genuineness, nonpossessive warmth, and accurate empathy as rated by judges. Ratings of nonpossessive warmth correlated highly with ratings of accurate empathy within the same interview ($r = .70$). However, ratings from the early interview are poor predictors of the ratings in a later interview ($r = .12$ between nonpossessive warmth—early to late, $r = .35$ between accurate empathy—early to late).

Helpers tended to preceive themselves in the helping relationship more favorably than did the children. In addition, helper responses tended to differentiate between the 4 conditions while children responded in a global fashion which appears to be most closely related to nonpossessive warmth as rated by judges and perceived by helpers. Children and helpers were in substantial agreement as to the overall level of therapeutic conditions ($p < .01$). Children's relationship inventory total scores were also positively related to rated nonpos-

sessive warmth ($p < .05$). Helper relationship inventory total scores were not significantly related to rated conditions.

Helper Dogmatism scores were not significantly related to any of the rated or perceived levels of therapeutic conditions.

Provision of high levels of rated nonpossessive warmth in the later interview was found to be significantly related to gains in achievement ($p < .01$), reduction in teacher-rated behavior problems ($p < .05$) and gains reflected by the combined outcome index ($p < .01$) on the part of the children. Similarly, high levels of rated accurate empathy in the late interview were significantly related to gains in achievement ($p < .05$) and gains reflected by the combined index ($p < .05$).

Children's overall perceptions of the relationship were significantly related to reduction in teacher-rated behavior problems ($p < .05$) and gains reflected in the combined index ($p < .01$). Helpers' overall perceptions of the relationship neared the .05 level of significance for the combined index only.

Helper dogmatism scores were not significantly related to any of the outcome indexes.

Use of multiple correlations added relatively little to the best single predictor of therapeutic outcome. None of the 5 multiple correlations reached the .05 level of significance.

CONCLUSIONS AND IMPLICATIONS

The evidence presented in this study provides considerable support for the hypotheses that nonpossessive warmth and accurate empathy, both rated and perceived, are important elements of the therapeutic relationship for elementary school children who are experiencing academic and behavioral problems. Discussion of the implications will assume the importance of these variables in the therapeutic relationship.

1. It is well known that there is a scarcity of mental health personnel to work with elementary school children. The possibility of using untrained volunteers in the helping relationship needs further exploration. The present study has shown that some volunteers are warm and understanding and that these persons tended to have a therapeutic effect upon the children with whom they work. Many other helpers, however, did not possess these qualities and the children with whom they worked tended to remain unchanged or to deteriorate. Taking the average of good and poor helpers, the program has little to offer. However, the same can be said for programs utilizing trained counselors (Eysenck, 1961; Levitt, 1957). Certain steps must be taken to improve the average level of therapeutic conditions. One way this might be done is through better selection procedures. This study, however, was able to add little information on how to best select helpers. It may be that a different kind of group such as college students would be better able to provide these conditions. A comprehensive school volunteer program utilizing helpers for various other tasks would give professional personnel a better chance to observe potential helpers before assigning them to a child. Tests other than the one used in this study might prove effective in predicting successful helpers. There is some evidence which suggests that lay personnel can be trained to provide high levels of therapeutic conditions within a relatively short period of time (Truax and Carkhuff, 1966). Attempts need to be made to help the volunteers to raise the level of therapeutic conditions which they offer.

2. Ratings and participant perceptions which contained predictive validity were administered near the end of treatment. While the evidence suggests that nonpossessive warmth and accurate empathy are important elements in therapeutic outcome, their value as predictors will depend upon the earliest interview in which they become significantly related to outcome indexes. Future studies need to record and rate a large number of interviews throughout the treatment program. Relationship inventories also need to be administered earlier and more often.

3. Ratings of the levels of therapeutic conditions are relatively difficult to obtain. By contrast, child perceptions are relatively easily obtained and are significantly related to both rated conditions and outcome. Refinement of the children's relationship inventory should greatly increase its validity.

4. The therapeutic variables used in this study account for a relatively small amount of the total outcome variance. Other variables should be sought which will add to the therapeutic value of the helping relationship.

REFERENCES

Barrett-Lennard, G. T. "Dimensions of the client's experience of his therapist associated with personality change," *Psychological Monographs*, 1962, 76(43, Whole No. 562).

Eysenck, H. J. "The effects of psychotherapy," in H. J. Eysenck (Ed.), *Handbook of Abnormal Psychology*, New York: Basic Books, 1961.

Fiedler, F. E. "The concept of an ideal therapeutic relationship," *Journal of Consulting Psychology*, 1950, **14**, 239–245.

Kemp, C. G. "Influence of dogmatism on the training of counselors," *Journal of Counseling Psychology*, 1962, **9**, 155–157.

Levitt, B. E. "The results of psychotherapy with children: an evaluation," *Journal of Consulting Psychology*, 1957, **21**, 189–196.

Rogers, C. R., Gendlin, E. T., Kiesler, D. J., and Truax, C. B. *The Therapeutic Relationship and Its Impact*. Madison: University of Wisconsin Press, 1967.

Rokeach, Milton. *The Open and Closed Mind*. New York: Basic Books, 1960.

Strupp, H. H., Wallach, M. S., and Wogan, M. "Psychotherapy experience in retrospect: questionnaire survey of former patients and their therapists," *Psychological Monographs*, 1964, **78** (11, Whole No. 588).

Truax, C. B., and Carkhuff, R. R. *Toward Effective Counseling and Psychotherapy*, Chicago: Aldine Publishing, 1966.

Whitehorn, J. C., and Betz, B. J. "A study of psychotherapeutic relationships between physicians and schizophrenic patients, *American Journal of Psychiatry*, 1954, **111**, 321–331.

9.2 The Encounter Group— Measurement of Some Affect Changes

D. VINCENT BIASE AND GEORGE DE LEON

This study investigated mood-affect change occurring in a Synanon-type Encounter group. Within the past 10 yr., this form of Encounter has come to be regarded as an effective therapeutic technique within a residential setting for drug addicts and alcoholics. Moreover, there recently has proliferated a wide variety of forms of the Encounter, as weekend workshops and marathons involving laymen, housewives, specific occupational groups, industrial managers, and professionals. Despite this increased popularity, there has been a conspicuous lag in sound empirical investigation or assessment as to process and/or outcome of the Encounter. In an effort to determine the feasibility of assessing Encounter effects, the present authors carried out a preliminary study involving 30 male heroin addicts, all of whom were residents of New York City's Addiction Services Agency, Phoenix House Induc-

tion Community. Results showed that anxiety scores on an affect check list were significantly lower following a $2\frac{1}{2}$-hr. Encounter group session. The present study, the second in a planned program of research, attempted to clarify the specific influence of the Encounter group on mood-affects (Anxiety–Depression–Hostility) by comparing three forms of activity which are included regularly in the regime of the therapeutic community.

METHOD

Subjects

The Ss were 40 male heroin addicts who were drug-free while being full-time live-in residents in an ASA Phoenix House Induction Community located at the Morris Bernstein Institute in New York City. The Ss ranged in age from 16–44 yr. with a mean age of 24 yr. The mean grade of schooling completed was

Reprinted from the *Proceedings of the 77th Annual Convention of the American Psychological Association*, 1969, **4**, 497–498, with permission of the authors and the American Psychological Association, Inc.

the eleventh, with a standard deviation of 1.6 grades. The median number of days of residence in the therapeutic community was 57, with a range of 6–78. The Ss were essentially from the lower socioeconomic stratem and included Negroes, Puerto Ricans, and whites.

Phoenix House Encounter Groups

The form of the Encounter group at Phoenix House is usually composed of varying numbers of residents in a face-to-face group setting. Each participant is the object of focus by other participants. All overt behaviors and demonstration of attitudes are topics for confrontations and indictments. While there is no formal leader, it is general policy to include older residents to function in a participant–trainer role. A basic view of the Phoenix House program is that drug abuse is symptomatic of an underlying emotional and/or impulse disorder. Thus, an important Encounter goal is to teach residents to be more aware and to verbalize their feeling states. Achievement of this goal is usually manifested in the participants' behavioral styles which range from displays of empathy and concern, to overtly volatile and exaggerated verbal confrontation.

Instrumentation

Two considerations dictated the choice of the Multiple Affect Adjective Check List (MAACL) developed by Zuckerman and Lubin (1965). First, the form of the MAACL is designed to measure three affect states rather than traits—Anxiety, Depression, and Hostility. Second, this instrument satisfied several empirical criteria, in that it is suitable for the test–retest procedure, and

is composed of items which do not require a reading level above the eighth grade.

Procedure

Prior to testing, 24 Ss were assigned randomly to Group 1 (Encounter +) in order to obtain their affect scores before and after each of three regularly scheduled $2\frac{1}{2}$-hr. activities: Wednesday morning Free Activity, followed by Thursday morning Work Activity, and the following Tuesday evening Encounter group session. Group 2 (Encounter only, N = 16) also participated in the three regularly scheduled activities. However, in order to control for possible practice effects of the repeated test taking of Group 1, affect scores were obtained for Group 2 before and after the Tuesday evening Encounter session only. In all instances, the check list was administered in a group setting within 10 min. before and after each activity.

RESULTS

Table 1 shows the mean Pre-Post MAACL scores for both groups in each of the conditions of the study, along with the two-tailed probability values obtained with the correlated t tests of significance. It can be seen that Post-Encounter Anxiety, Depression, and Hostility scores were significantly lower than Pre-Encounter scores for both groups. The t tests revealed no significant Pre-Post changes for Anxiety, Depression, and Hostility in either the Work or Free Activity conditions. Also, there were no differences in Anxiety, Depression, or Hostility scores in either Pre-Encounter, Pre-Work, or Pre-Free Activity. Thus, the

table 1

Mean Pre-Post MAACL Scores for Anxiety–Depression–Hostility of Each Group in All Conditions of the Study

Group	Free Activity			Work			Encounter		
	Pre	Post	Prob.	Pre	Post	Prob.	Pre	Post	Prob.
Encounter Group 1									
Anxiety	9.6	9.1	ns	9.8	10.0	ns	10.8	8.2	*
Depression	16.4	15.1	ns	15.2	16.3	ns	16.5	12.6	*
Hostility	9.4	9.3	ns	10.0	10.9	ns	12.0	8.2	**
Encounter only Group 2									
Anxiety	Participated but not tested			Participated but not tested			12.3	7.0	**
Depression							16.2	12.0	*
Hostility							12.7	8.6	**

Note.—All probability values are two-tailed.
*$p < .05$.
**$p < .01$.

significant Post-score decreases following the Encounter were not attributable to Pre-score levels. Nor were these significant decreases related to the test-taking variable (practice) as evidenced by the data of Group 2. It appears then that of those activities studied in the Phoenix House Therapeutic Community only the Encounter significantly decreased affect scores.

DISCUSSION

The MAACL authors report significant correlations among the three affect scales. In their attempt to reduce these apparent interdependences, they empirically developed briefer scales for all three affect data from which did yield lower intercorrelations. A correlational analysis of the present data also indicated a significant degree of relationship among Ss'

Anxiety, Depression, and Hostility scores in the Encounter condition, a finding which suggested that lack of scale independence might have contributed to the significant Pre-Post drops across all three affects in the Encounter condition. Therefore, the MAACL Encounter data of all Ss in the present study were rescored according to the brief scale. The t tests applied to these Pre-Post differences gave results which partially supported those of the previous analyses based on the full scales. For Group 1 there was a nonsignificant drop in Hostility scores while for Group 2 there was a nonsignificant drop in Depression scores. However, for both groups, a significant decrease in Anxiety-Post scores ($t = 2.395 < .05$, Group 1), ($t = 3.59 < .01$, Group 2), was again obtained along with significant decreases in Depression scores ($t = 2.498 < .05$) for

Group 1 and in Hostility scores ($t = 3.90$ $< .01$) for Group 2. Thus, it may be concluded that with the full and brief MAACL scales, the Encounter group significantly influenced the level of affect scores—particularly those of Anxiety— with less consistent decreases occurring in Depression and Hostility. The duration of the affect score changes obtained with the Encounter activity remains an empirical problem to be investigated along with the elaboration and refinement of instrumentation.

REFERENCE

Zuckerman, M., and Lubin, B. *Multiple Affect Adjective Check List Manual.* San Diego: Educational and Industrial Testing Service, 1965.

9.3 Reinforcement versus Relationship Therapy for Schizophrenics

JOHN MARKS,
BEVERLY SONODA, AND
ROBERT SCHALOCK

There is no doubt that treatment based on reinforcement principles can dramatically change the behavior of chronic mental hospital patients (Atthowe, 1966; Atthowe and Krasner, 1965; Ayllon and Azrin, 1964, 1965; Ayllon and Michael, 1959; Gericke, 1965; Mishler, 1964; Schaefer, 1966). However, to date there has been no attempt to compare systematically the success of reinforcement-based therapy with more conventional forms of treatment with chronic patients. This was the purpose of the present study.

METHOD

The Ss were 22 chronic schizophrenic males assigned to the Research Ward which is jointly administered by Western State Hospital and the Mental Health Research Institute, Fort Steilacoom, Washington. Their mean length of hospitalization was 15 yr. and their ages ranged from 21 to 55 with a mean of 35.6. None had any chronic physical illness or clinically significant brain damage.

Before the study began, attendants on the ward rated each of the patients on the Hospital Adjustment Scale (HAS; McReynolds and Ferguson, 1946). On the basis of total HAS adjustment scores, 11 matched pairs were selected. One member of each pair was randomly placed in the group which started with reinforcement (Group A) and the other member of the pair was assigned to Group B which started with relationship. Each S received both forms of treatment. Both members of each matched pair spent the same amount of time on both treatments (10–13 wk. on each), and both members of the pair had approximately equal numbers of interviews while they were on relationship.

During the present study all other

Reprinted from the *Journal of Abnormal Psychology*, 1968, **73**, 397–402, with permission of the authors and the American Psychological Association, Inc.

treatments for the patients were maintained, so far as possible, at an unchanged level. If it was necessary to adjust medications for some patients, the data for these patients were handled separately in the analyses.

The therapy modes were explicitly defined at the outset.

Reinforcement

While on reinforcement therapy each man received tokens (poker chips) for specified socially desirable behavior and paid 10 poker chips for each meal. Each man's tokens were labeled to prevent confusion or exchange of tokens among the patients. While they were not in the patient's possession, tokens remained in individual containers labeled for each patient in the ward office.

Ward staff carried out payment and collection of chips. To minimize contamination with the relationship program, the staff was asked to dispense the tokens as mechanically and impersonally as possible. Payment of tokens was not on a strict earned basis per unit of behavior, but was, within the limits of the program, left to the discretion of staff, so that patients could not accumulate a large supply of tokens. Thus, a patient was not paid a specified number of tokens each time he combed his hair or conversed with another patient, but was paid according to staff judgment of his compliance with the requirements designed to keep him working toward higher levels of achievement. Not only was this reinforcement schedule administratively most convenient but also it was a schedule of variable ratio reinforcement which might theoretically be expected to

foster persisting behavior (Ferster and Skinner, 1957).

All patients in the reinforcement program met weekly with the administrator who outlined the behavior to be rewarded during that week. During the first few weeks of reinforcement, the goals were set by staff members on the basis of the level at which the individual patient was functioning. In later meetings the patients themselves helped select the behaviors to be reinforced during the following week. After the meeting a list showing what was expected of each patient was posted where both patients and staff could refer to it.

During the first 2 wk. of reinforcement treatment, while patients were becoming accustomed to the program, the staff made sure the men had enough tokens to avoid missing any meals. After this period the program was more strictly enforced, and men without the required 10 tokens at mealtimes were kept from the dining room.

Medical consultation insured that no patient's health was jeopardized by the requirements of the program. Safeguards included the provision that if a patient missed more than two meals in succession an adjustment was made in his program so that he earned enough tokens for the next meal. Two men who repeatedly came up short in their supplies of tokens received a high-protein nutritional supplement (Meritine) at medication time, dispensed as a medication.

It was the aim of the reinforcement program to keep the patient moving toward increasingly complex and responsible levels of functioning. The characteristics of the individual, as known both from the rating scales and from knowledge of the patient, governed the selection of behaviors to be reinforced. While one man was being rewarded for simply going along with the receiving and paying of tokens, another was given tokens for discussing discharge plans with a social worker. While some patients were reinforced for improving personal appearance, others were rewarded for expressing feelings. More than one patient, for example, was reinforced for "griping." Reinforcement therapy, then, involved the systematic and explicit selection of short-term behavioral goals or tasks appropriate to the patient's level of functioning at the time, reinforcement of the attainment of these goals or tasks by poker chips exchangeable for meals, and resetting of goals at increasingly higher levels.

Relationship

Relationship therapy, on the other hand, was conceived as an attempt to enlarge and deepen the patient's self-understanding and to increase his self-acceptance and autonomy. While in this phase, each patient had a therapist who met with him approximately an hour each day, 5 days per week, and attempted to form a relationship in which the patient would feel free to express and examine his feelings. The therapy was clearly not directive, and, as conceived here, was unconcerned with specific items of behavior except for those behaviors necessary to form the relationship and to further self-understanding and self-acceptance.

Although it was hoped that a main vehicle for treatment would be a sort of dialogue, it soon became evident that many of these men were not accustomed to verbal exchange. Some relationships, then, were formed over a Ping-Pong table or during walks on the hospital grounds or during rides in an automobile. In some cases, the relationship was fostered by drawing on skills of the patient, such as piano playing or calligraphy.

Nine therapists worked on the study. Three served as relationship therapists for both Group A and Group B. The other six served during only one phase. The therapists came from a variety of backgrounds. Two ward attendants, two graduate students in psychology, one physician, and four research assistants with varying amounts of graduate or undergraduate work in psychology functioned as relationship therapists. The panel of therapists met once a week to discuss problems experienced in the therapy.

Measures

Measures were used to tap the various functions expected to be affected by the treatments. These functions included both target behaviors such as self-care and sociability and also more subtle aspects of personality. Some key measures were the Hospital Adjustment Scale (HAS) and a series of rating scales devised here at the Institute. The HAS provided four scores: (a) communication and inter-personal relations; (b) self-care; (c) activity participation; and (d) total adjustment which was the sum of these other three. The rating scales provided operationally independent scores on work competence (i.e., the level of self-care and of productive work); social competence (ability to interact meaningfully with others); and conceptual competence (ability to perceive and understand the world in which he is immersed). Each scale had 11–13 steps which were arranged progressively; higher steps involved mastery of the lower ones so that the scales represented levels of human development or of recovery from severe psychosis.

In addition, 11 short tests were given to all *S*s. Several scores were derived for each test, but for the purposes of this presentation one score was selected from each test so that each of the 11 scores represents an independent determination. The 11 tests and the scores derived from them were:

1. Tests of mental efficiency: (*a*) Shipley Institute of Living Scale—total IQ; (*b*) Wechsler Memory Scale—the Verbal Memory tests were used, alternating the forms on successive testings. The total number of memories recalled was the score analyzed.

2. Tests of associative looseness (*a*) Word Association—24 words from the Kent-Rosanoff lists were used, selected to include both neutral and conflict-arousing words. First associations to these words and reaction times were recorded. The communality score was the number of responses which were among the five most common responses to each word according to the Kent-Rosanoff norms. (*b*) Symbolic-Literal Meaning Test (Chapman, 1960)—In this test (which was divided into two alternate forms for successive administrations) *S*s were asked to make such choices as determining whether "Mary gave us a warm welcome" meant that the house was well heated or that Mary was cordial. The score was the total number of correct choices made.

3. Tests of speed and maintenance of work set: (*a*) Cancellation—in this test *S* was presented with a passage of printed meaningful text (all in capitals) and asked to cross out the Es. His score was the number correctly cancelled in 1 min. (*b*) Aiming—this test from the Repetitive Psychological Measures (Moran and Mefferd, 1959) required *S* to place pencil dots in small successively scattered circles. The score was number of circles correctly dotted in 1 min. (*c*) Stroop Color-Word Test (Thurstone and Mellinger, 1953). In this test *S*'s speed at naming the colors of 100 blocks of ink each printed in one of four colors was compared with his speed in naming the same number and succession of ink colors when they were used to print the names of other colors—the word "green," for example, printed in red ink. The score was the ratio of times for the two tasks.

4. Tests tapping language and social skills: (*a*) Social Memory (Moran, Kimble, and Mefferd, 1960). In this test *S* viewed for 30 sec. a sheet containing photographs of 16 different persons. Then he identified those persons on a second sheet of 32 photographs. The score was the number of correct identifications minus the number incorrect. (*b*) Word fluency—this was the number of different words beginning with the letter "S" that *S* could name in 1 min.

5. Tests of self-concept: (*a*) Gough Adjective Check List. The *S* was given 20 min. to check those words which described him. The score was the percentage of checked adjectives which were favorable. (*b*) Draw A Person Test. The *S* was given 3 min. to draw a person. The drawing was scored for conceptual ade-

quacy (presence of body features, etc.) by means of an objective checklist. Two scorers correlated .95 over this group's productions.

Thus there were 11 independent test scores. It was expected that reinforcement therapy would have the most effect upon such rating variables as self-care, activity participation, and work competence and upon such test variables as those of speed and work set. Relationship, by contrast, was expected to induce changes in ratings of communications and conceptual competence and in tests of associative looseness and of self-concept.

All Ss were rated and tested at the beginning and at the end of the study. At the time of switchover between therapies they were rated once at the time the first phase treatment ceased and again before the second phase treatment began. Switchover testing occurred in the interval between therapies.

RESULTS

The two therapies were compared by means of the Wilcoxon matched-pairs signed-rank test (Wilcoxon, 1945). The change within each individual on each of the 18 rating and test scores under reinforcement was compared with the change under relationship. The results are shown in Table 1. It will be seen that there are few consistent differences between the effects of the two methods. Performance on the Stroop was the only variable which showed a difference between the methods, and this difference was, as expected, in favor of the reinforcement method. On the other hand,

the Draw A Person conceptual adequacy score which was expected to show greater improvement under relationship showed a difference of borderline significance and this was in favor of reinforcement rather than of relationship.

The same type of analysis was used to compare the changes within individuals during Phase 1 with the changes during Phase 2. None of the Wilcoxons for these comparisons was significant. There was no detectable difference between the two periods of the study.

Since the order of the therapy phases was not a significant factor and since there were no consistent differences between the types of therapy, an analysis was done to see whether the interaction between order and therapy type was significant. Changes from beginning to end for each S in Group A were compared using the Wilcoxon with the corresponding changes in his matched S in Group B. In terms of overall improvement, it did not seem to matter which came first, reinforcement or relationship. Moreover, social competence scores (Zigler and Phillips, 1961) did not predict individual response to the two modes.

Since the therapies were essentially equivalent, as were the orders, it was possible to assess overall change from the beginning to the end of the project. The results appear in Table 2. Of the 18 scores, 12 show significant improvement from beginning to end. Social competence scores, however, failed to predict which patients would show this improvement.

A more exacting test is shown in Table 3. Here results for only 13 Ss from this study—ones who had no change in

table 1

Differences within Individuals between Changes under Reinforcement and Relationship Therapies

Test or Rating	N	By Wilcoxon Signed-Rank Test Smaller Sum Ranks[a]
Shipley: total	20	−87.0
Wechsler Memory: number	19	+94.0
Word Association: communality	20	+72.5
Symbolic–Literal: correct	18	−59.5
Cancellation: number	20	+76.5
Aiming: correct	22	+83.5*
Stroop: Time II/Time III	19	−49**
Special Memory: correct–incorrect	22	−118
Word Fluency: number	18	+75.5
Adjective Check List: % favorable	19	−69.5
Draw A Person: adequacy	17	−41.5*
Hospital Adjustment Scale		
Communication and interpersonal relations (I)	22	−117.5
Self-care (II)	22	+109.0
Activity participation (III)	22	+118.5
Total adjustment	22	−119.0
Rating Scales		
Work competence	16	−58.0
Social competence	15	+50.5
Conceptual competence	15	−53.5

[a] A negative sign indicates reinforcement superior; positive, relationship superior.
* $p < .20$, two-tailed.
** $p < .05$, two-tailed.

psychotropic medication during the period beginning 2 mo. before the initiation of the study—are compared with the results from a drug study completed just before the present study began. The study covered a span of time similar to that of the present study, was, like it, a switchover study, and included 11 of the patients who were on the present study. Many of the measures used in the present study were also used in the drug study. Since there was no significant change during the drug study, and since drug and placebo did not differ in their effects, change within patients in the course of the drug study is compared with change in the present comparative therapies study. It will be seen that of the nine measures which were common to both studies, eight showed greater improvement under the comparative therapies study than under the drug study. This is particularly true for the crucial ward ratings but it also seems to affect tests of attention and of associative control.

table 2

Overall Changes within Individuals during Entire Project

Test or Rating	N	By Wilcoxon Signed-Rank Test — Smaller Sum Ranks[a]
Shipley: total	16	−38.5
Wechsler Memory: number	17	75.5
Word Association: communality	16	−43
Symbolic–Literal: correct	17	−27.5***
Cancellation: number	21	−22****
Aiming: correct	22	−110
Stroop: Time II/Time III	20	103.5
Social Memory: correct–incorrect	16	−36*
Word Fluency: number	17	−39.5**
Adjective Check List: % favorable	19	−74.5
Draw A Person: adequacy	18	−53.5*
Hospital Adjustment Scale		
Communication and interpersonal relations (I)	21	−18****
Self-care (II)	22	−51***
Activity participation (III)	22	−60***
Total adjustment	22	−29.5****
Rating Scales		
Work competence	22	−43.5****
Social competence	20	−35****
Conceptual competence	22	−67**

[a] A negative sign indicates improvement in the test score or rating.
* $p < .10$, one-tailed.
** $p < .05$, one-tailed.
*** $p < .025$, one-tailed.
**** $p < .005$, one-tailed.

DISCUSSION

The results are a little surprising. Although both types of therapy had observable results—both helped the functioning of these patients—there was no consistent difference in overall effectiveness between the two. Moreover reinforcement showed no consistent differences from relationship in the functions which it facilitated. Thus, both methods seem effective and, in fact, enabled some of these very chronic patients to graduate to rehabilitation programs and leave the hospital.

The lack of difference in end results may be related to the difficulty encountered in keeping the methods separate. Reinforcement staff found it difficult to act like machines even when they wanted to do so, which was not very often. Similarly not all relationship therapists could remain passively understanding. Some, by nature or training, were more directive than others. Most could not help showing their satisfaction when the patient with whom they were working started to display more mature behavior. Nevertheless the two therapy modes did differ along the initially defined reinforcement-relationship dimensions although neither was an "ideal" type.

One finding that emerged was that reinforcement can be used in a "psychodynamic" way: it need not be entirely oriented toward shaping acceptable behavior. Sometimes a patient needed to learn to argue, to assert himself, to be lazy, to flirt, or to dominate. It is not just socially conforming behavior which can be reinforced but almost any kind of behavior the patient currently needs.

Similarly it may be that the relationship therapy opened up some patients to the naturally occurring reinforcement systems surrounding them. Relationship patients changed not only in their thinking and, apparently, in their

self-view but also in their apparent willingness to cooperate and conform. Relationship may have enhanced the patients' sensitivity to the reinforcement contingencies in the hospital.

A number of criticisms can be made of the relationship therapy in this study. One was the difficulty in keeping the two methods separate. A second concerns the duration of the relationship therapy phase. Three months is a short time for a relationship to take effect. Yet it should be remembered that this relationship therapy was intensive. Within 3 mo. or less these patients were seen for 40 or more hr. Certainly in terms of the patient's time alone—to say nothing of the therapist's—one should expect a relationship to develop.

This raises the question of the relative economy of forces. The reinforcement part of the project required

table 3

Changes in Tests and Ratings during Entire Project for 13 Patients with No Medication Changes Compared with Drug Project Changes

Test or Rating	Comparative Therapies Project			Drug Project			
	M	N	s^2	M	N	s^2	t
Wechsler Memory	.27	13	5.6	−.54	13	6.4	.84
Word Association	0	12	2.4	.25	12	4.7	.32
Symbolic Literal	1.09	11	6.5	−1.18	11	19.4	1.48**
Cancellation	5.92	13	80.1	−4.00	14	57.1	3.12****
Stroop	2.42	12	423.4	−6.25	12	239.8	1.17*
Hospital Adjustment Scale							
Communication and interpersonal							
relations	15.23	13	320.8	1.22	18	265.5	2.27***
Self-care	10.62	13	342.1	−6.33	18	358.6	2.49****
Activity participation	9.15	13	350.7	−8.11	18	474.8	2.31***
Total adjustment	13.46	13	348.6	−3.83	18	262.6	2.75****

    * $p < .15$, one-tailed.
    ** $p < .10$, one-tailed.
   *** $p < .02$, one-tailed.
  **** $p < .01$, one-tailed.

one extra staff person, the reinforcement coordinator. He had to spend perhaps one-half day a week working on the project, meeting with reinforcement group of patients, reporting to staff, and making up the week's schedules. The rest of the reinforcement program was handled by the regular ward staff who observed the behaviors and doled out the poker chips. On the relationship program a minimum of six extra persons was needed of whom each put in a day or two a week on the project. In staff time the relationship effort was much more expensive.

SUMMARY

The efficacy of reinforcement versus relationship therapy was evaluated on a group of 22 chronic schizophrenic patients. The groups received both therapies in balanced order. Under reinforcement therapy improved behavior was rewarded with poker chips exchangeable for meals. Under relationship therapy each patient met daily for 10–13 wk. with an individual therapist. Before and after each therapy, Ss were rated for social behavior, work competence, and on conceptual and communication skills. Tests of mental efficiency, associative looseness, work set, social skills, and self-concept were also used. Both therapies improved functioning, but there were no systematic differences between them.

REFERENCES

Atthowe, J. M., Jr. The token economy: Its utility and limitations. Paper presented at the meeting of the Western Psychological Association, Long Beach, California, April 1966.

Atthowe, J. M., Jr., and Krasner, L. The systematic application of contingent reinforcement procedures (token economy) in a large social setting: A psychiatric ward. Paper presented at the meeting of the American Psychological Association, Chicago, September 1965.

Ayllon, T., and Azrin, N. H. "Reinforcement and instructions with mental patients," *Journal of the Experimental Analysis of Behavior*, 1964, **7**, 327–331.

Ayllon, T., and Azrin, N. H. "The measurement and reinforcement of behavior of psychotics," *Journal of the Experimental Analysis of Behavior*, 1965, **8**, 357–383.

Ayllon, T., and Michael, J. "The psychiatric nurse as a behavioral engineer," *Journal of the Experimental Analysis of Behavior*, 1959, **2**, 323–334.

Chapman, L. J. "Confusion of figurative and literal usages of words by schizophrenics and brain damaged patients," *Journal of Abnormal and Social Psychology*, 1960, **60**, 412–416.

Ferster, C. B., and Skinner, B. F. *Schedules of Reinforcement*. New York: Appleton-Century-Crofts, 1957.

Gericke, D. L. "Practical use of operant conditioning procedures in a mental hospital," *Psychiatric Studies and Projects*, 1965, **3**, 5.

McReynolds, P. W., and Ferguson, J. T. *Clinical Manual for the Hospital Adjustment Scale*. Palo Alto, Calif.: Consulting Psychologists Press, 1946.

Mishler, K. B. "Of people and pigeons," *Smith Kline and French Psychiatric Reporter*, 1964, **15**, 9–12.

Moran, L. J., and Mefferd, R. B., Jr. "Repetitive psychological measures," *Psychological Reports*, 1959, **5**, 269–275.

Moran, L. J., Kimble, J. F., Jr., and Mefferd, R. B., Jr. "Repetitive psychological measures: Memory for faces," *Psychological Reports*, 1960, **7**, 407–413.

Schaefer, H. H. "Investigations in operant conditioning procedures in a mental hospital," in J. Fisher and R. E. Harris (Eds.), Reinforcement theory in psychological treatment—A symposium. *California Mental Health Monograph*, No. 8, (1966).

Thurstone, L. L., and Mellinger, J. J. *The Stroop Test*. Chapel Hill: Psychometric Laboratory of the Univ. of North Carolina, 1953.

Wilcoxon, F. "Individual comparisons by ranking methods," *Biometrics Bulletin*, 1945, **1**, 80–83.

Zigler, E., and Phillips, L. "Social competence and outcome in psychiatric disorder." *Journal of Abnormal and Social Psychology*, 1961, **63**, 264–271.

Group Desensitization of Test Anxiety

ROBERT COHEN AND
SANFORD J. DEAN

The purpose of this study was to investigate some of the specific learning and motivational variables involved in desensitization therapy, as well as to add to the body of validity data currently available. Two factors were considered in the present study.

Group Interaction as a Source of Motivation and Discrimination Learning

The most obvious reason for doing desensitization with groups rather than individuals, is economy. Group treatment may provide benefits in addition. Three particularly promising therapeutic sources within group interaction are the opportunity to learn behavioral discriminations, the motivational incentives provided by hearing of other persons' progress, and desensitization derived from discussing anxiety provoking situations in a relaxed atmosphere.

The issue here is whether group desensitization may be considered individual therapy *in* groups, therapy *by* groups. In the current study, desensitization was presented separately or in conjunction with discussion.

The Effect of Using a Progressive Hierarchy

A progressive hierarchy consists of a series of problem-related situations, introduced in ascending order of anxiety arousal. The rationale for beginning with slight anxiety-arousing situations and gradually introducing more intense items is that the relaxation response must be stronger than the anxiety response in order to reciprocally inhibit anxiety. If the anxiety elicited is too strong, relaxation cannot successfully inhibit the anxiety.

What does this mean in practical terms? If displacement does not neces-

---

Reprinted from the *Proceedings of the 76th Annual Convention of the American Psychological Association,* 1968, **3,** 615–616, with permission of the authors and the American Psychological Association, Inc.

sarily facilitate recovery from anxiety reactions, there may be no need to spend time and energy progressively moving from low to high anxiety items on the hierarchy. It may take more trials to master a single strong anxiety item, when it is presented without the benefit of practice on less intense items, but the total number of trials necessary to achieve overall inhibition of anxiety may be fewer.

METHOD

Experimental Design

The basic design of the study involved a 2 × 2 paradigm that includes a no-contact control group. The two dimensions were (a) amount of group interaction, and (b) nature of the desensitization hierarchy. On the group interaction discussion, the Ss were either encouraged to interact with other members of the group about issues related to test anxiety problems and alternative means of handling these problems or Ss were not given an opportunity to interact within the group. The noninteraction Ss were asked to write out their questions which were answered, without specific reference to the question, by the E. The amount of time spent in formal group interaction or noninteraction, and the degree of participation by the group leader, were regulated by the E in order to insure equivalency among groups.

The hierarchy dimension consisted of a conventional progressive hierarchy condition in which Ss were asked to visualize all items in the hierarchy, beginning with the least anxiety-provoking scenes and systematically proceeding up

the scale; and a high anxiety hierarchy condition, in which Ss visualized only the most anxiety-provoking scenes (upper one-third of the hierarchy). Ss constructed their hierarchies by individually ranking a predetermined list of 12 scenes, according to the amount of anxiety the scene evoked. The Ss in the progressive hierarchy groups were asked to visualize all items on the hierarchy, while Ss in the high anxiety groups visualized only their 4 most severe anxiety scenes.

The no-contact control group consisted of Ss selected randomly from the upper 30% of the Test Anxiety Scale (TAS) scores of students in the introductory psychology class. These students were not invited to attend the group sessions, but did participate in an experiment to fulfill a class requirement in which they were given pre- and post-measures during the same weeks the experimental Ss received their measures.

Procedure.   Twenty-five introductory psychology students, in the upper 30% of the TAS distribution, responded affirmatively to an invitation to participate in a course designed for test anxiety reduction. They were randomly assigned to 4 experimental groups. The groups met with the author, who served as instructor, and an assistant who coordinated various measures but did not speak during class sessions. Each group met twice per week for a total of 12 sessions. Thirteen students completed the entire course. Six other students, who completed half of the course, were used on a post-hoc basis to study the effects of minimal desensitization.

The first 2 sessions were spent training students to relax, using shorter instructions as students became more proficient at relaxing.

Explanation and practice of the visualization aspect of desensitization were presented in the third session. Students were told to begin by visualizing the first scene in the hierarchy as vividly as possible. If they experienced any anxiety they were to stop thinking of the scene and attempt to relax themselves until further instructions were given. The Ss were instructed to visualize each scene until no anxiety had been experienced for 2 consecutive trials, before moving to the next scene. Scenes were visualized in ascending order, going from low anxiety to high anxiety scenes, with progressive hierarchy Ss beginning with Scene 1 and high anxiety hierarchy Ss starting at Scene 9. Students who successfully completed the hierarchy were told to repeat their hierarchy.

Five 30 sec. visualization trials were presented after each 6 to 8 min. set of relaxation instructions. Each trial was separated by 1 min. of relaxation instructions. The Ss recorded the items visualized, and indicated whether or not they experienced anxiety immediately after each set of trials.

Sessions were divided into desensitization and discussion or lecture-writing periods, with discussion periods (group interaction) being equivalent in time to the other groups' lecture writing periods (group noninteraction). Topics of discussions and lectures included how to identify maladaptive patterns of behavior related to studying and tests, self-confidence as a learned factor influencing test anxiety, means of coping with test anxiety utilizing relaxation and relearning, as well as problems and progress of formal desensitization and students' reaction to tests.

Pre- and post-measures were obtained for the TAS, and single question multiple choice self-rating scales constructed by the author. Experimental Ss also took a 9-item Attraction to Group Scale after the third session and at the end of the course, and a 5-item multiple choice scale measuring attraction toward various components of treatment at the completion of the course. Grade-point averages were available for the semester during which the course was given and for the previous semester.

RESULTS

Initial TAS scores were used as the subject selection criterion. There were no significant differences between the experimental and control groups on the preexperimental TAS measures, nor were there any significant differences among experimental groups.

Experimental Ss reported significantly greater test anxiety reduction than the no-contact control Ss ($t = 2.21$, $df = 1/19$, $p < .05$). A two-way analysis of variance for the experimental groups revealed a significant main effect for the factor of group interaction, with Ss experiencing group interaction reporting more reduction than those Ss in the noninteraction condition ($F = 12.03$, $df = 1/9$, $PR = .01$).

There were no significant main effects for the hierarchy variable, nor was there a significant interaction.

Since there were no significant differences among the experimental and control groups or among the 4 experimental groups on grade point averages for the semester prior to the desensitization course, it seemed justifiable to compare these groups on grade point changes from the semester prior to desensitization to the semester in which they participated in the course. The mean grade point changes for Experimental Ss was greater than the mean changes of Control Ss ($t = 1.74$, $df = 1/18$, $p < .10$).

Mean anticipation of test anxiety reduction increased significantly from the precourse measurement to the response given after the third session for experimental Ss ($t = -3.40$, $df = 12$, $p < .01$). Although there were no pre-experimental differences in expectancy between the experimental and control groups, the experimental Ss tended to anticipate more test anxiety reduction than the control Ss after taking the course ($t = 1.91$, $df = 1/19$, $p < .10$).

On the attraction measures, there were no significant pre- to post-changes in attractiveness among the experimental Ss. On Goldstein's Attraction to Group Scale, group interaction S had a tendency to rate their group as more attractive than group noninteraction Ss, though this difference did not reach significance ($F = 3.16$, $df = 19$, $p < .15$). The group interaction-high anxious group expressed more attraction toward the components of treatment than the group interaction-progressive group ($F = 11.91$, $df = 3/9$, $p < .05$).

Each 30-sec. visualization exposure was considered a trial. Visualization of a scene with complete absence of anxiety served as a criterion of success, and 2 consecutive successes were required to move to the next scene. In order to compare the efficiency of the progressive and high anxious hierarchy methods, an analysis of variance test was performed on the number of trials required for each S to complete the hierarchy. There was a main effect for hierarchy condition, with the progressive groups requiring significantly more trials than the high anxious hierarchy groups ($F = 22.12$, $df = 1/9$, $p < .001$).

DISCUSSION

The present study indicates that test anxious college students completing a short-term program of group desensitization tend to report more anxiety reduction and achieve a greater increase in grade point average than students with equivalent TAS scores who are not given an opportunity to participate in a desensitization program. It also was found among desensitization Ss that students who were encouraged to interact with each other and the instructor, reported more test anxiety reduction than students in minimal interaction groups, though there were no significant differences between groups in grade point changes from the semester prior to desensitization to the semester in which the course was taken. At least in terms of reported anxiety reduction, variables other than formal desensitization may be operating to produce change.

Motivational variables seem more plausible than discrimination learning variables in this instance, since most of the relevant material was presented by the instructor in the noninteraction condition.

There were no significant differences between progressive and high anxious groups, bringing into question the necessity of using a progressive hierarchy when treating test anxiety and adding to the growing body of evidence against the advantage of utilizing displacement in resolving certain conflict situations.

Visual imagery or mediational stimuli, as it is sometimes labelled, seems to be an important factor in the development, maintenance, and reduction of anxiety responses. Though Wolpe's formal theory and method have been questioned, his utilization of mediational behavior in a controlled setting is an important contribution to the study of maladaptive behavior. For instance, Hogan and Kirchner using implosive therapy, a technique emphasizing visualization with maximal anxiety, report reduction in rat phobic behavior comparable to the results of desensitization advocates. Assuming that factors in addition to placebo are operating, one might attempt to find process elements common to both of these procedures. The most obvious mutual feature is repeated vivid visualization of anxiety-provoking scenes in a realistically non-threatening environment.

9.5 Training Mothers in Groups as Reinforcement Therapists for Their Own Children

IRWIN HIRSCH AND LEOPOLD WALDER

Parents perennially seek advice on how to handle problem behavior in their children from individuals in and out of the mental health professions. The literature on parent education, according to a review by Brim (1961), lacks reports of systematic attempts to teach parents ways of managing problems with their children. There have been virtually no reported studies which spell out the content of the instructions, use control measures, and effectively evaluate the outcome. Mental health professionals rarely give parents concrete operations to perform in their quest for means to deal with children's problem behaviors. The general approach is to subject the parents to self-analysis and to avoid giving advice. At best, through this method, the changes in parent–child interactions take a long time to occur, and, at worst, the parents become convinced that they are the cause of the difficulties and indulge in unproductive self-blame. The approach in this study was to provide mothers with systematized instruction in the application of reinforcement techniques to their own children's disturbed behavior. The principles were taken from the psychological literature on behavior modification (e.g., Krasner and Ullmann, 1965). These principles have successfully been taught to nonprofessionals (Ayllon and Michael, 1959), classmates (Patterson, 1965), teachers (Becker, 1966), and parents (Hawkins, Peterson, Schweid, and Bijou, 1966; Pumroy, 1965; Risley and Wolf, 1966; Walder, Cohen, and Daston, 1967) to aid them in changing deviant behavior in children. There is only one reported study where parents in groups have been instructed in this manner. The purpose of the present investigation was to teach parents and thus extend this work, and to evaluate the effects of the educational treatment.

Reprinted from the *Proceedings of the 77th Annual Convention of the American Psychological Association,* 1969, **4,** 561–562, with permission of the authors and the American Psychological Association, Inc.

SUBJECTS

The Ss were 30 white mothers, primarily from upper-middle-class professional families. All of them except three were living with their husbands. Each mother had at least one child that at one time or another had been diagnosed by a professional as severely disturbed. About eight mothers had a child who was called "autistic"; another eight, "retarded"; and another eight "brain-damaged." The remainder had children who were given functional diagnoses such as "schizophrenia of childhood" or "severe personality disturbance." The Ss were solicited by an advertising campaign consisting of a small article in the major newspaper of Washington, D.C., which described the program, and numerous letters sent to individual mothers and organizations on the mailing list of the National Society for Autistic Children. Each S deposited $50, returnable only upon perfect attendance at all of the meetings in the program. They were assigned to a No Wait group ($N = 15$) which began the treatment immediately, and a Wait group ($N = 15$) which began the treatment when the No Wait group finished. Each of these two groups of 15 were divided into a large group of 10 Ss, and a small group of 5 Ss. All groups received the same treatment, though the method of presentation differed somewhat between the large and small groups. The group meetings lasted for nine ($1\frac{1}{2}$-hr.) sessions over a 5-wk. period. Before the meetings began, each S chose one or two very troublesome child behaviors that they hoped to modify. Changing these behaviors became the focus of treatment for the mother. The meetings consisted of highly organized lectures on the principles of the modification of human behavior (reinforcement theory), along with discussion of each S's individual child, and advice on how to deal with the major problem behaviors of that child. The mothers were asked to apply what they learned to the home interaction with the child, to keep daily records of child behavior, and to complete other (non-reading) homework assignments.

HYPOTHESES

The Ss in the study were the mothers, not the children. It was hypothesized that, as a function of the treatment procedure, Ss' level of depression and anxiety would decrease, their rating of the desirability of their child's behavior would show improvement, and their scores on a test of knowledge and application of behavior modification principles would get better. It was further predicted that the frequency of the child's deviant behavior, as scored by the daily record-keeping procedures, would improve in the direction which S specified before the treatment.

RESULTS

Each S was tested three times. The Wait group was used as a delayed treatment-control group. The No Wait group was given a 5-wk. follow-up series of tests. The measures of outcome used to assess change due to the treatment were: the Depression and Anxiety (Welsh) scales of the MMPI; the Depression and Anxiety scales of the Lorr-Daston Mood Scale; the Present vs. Ideal Rating Scale; the Behavior and Achievement Rating Scale; and the Behavioral Vignettes.

Additional tests used were the Henmon-Nelson Test of Mental Ability; scoring sheets based on home ratings by Ss; and a parent questionnaire to obtain the Ss' stated evaluation of the program.

The most strongly significant improvement was seen on the Behavioral Vignettes (Hirsch and Breiter, 1967), a measure of how well the Ss learned to apply the principles of behavior modification. This held up when examined on a 5-wk. follow-up. One definite conclusion from this result was that the Ss at least had the knowledge and verbal facility to effectively apply behavior modification techniques in their own home.

The Ss' records of deviant child behavior in the home showed a significant improvement in the desired direction from before to after the treatment. The deviant behavior that was excessive (e.g., crying, tantrums, head banging) showed a decline, and the behavior called deviant because it was deficient (e.g., mutism, lack of social responses), showed an increase. There were, however, no objective judges in the home to score this behavior, the Ss themselves being the only record keepers.

On the parent questionnaire the Ss subjectively reported (multiple choice items) that they strongly benefited from the program, their children's and their own behavior changing considerably as a function of the program. A total of 100% of the Ss stated that their own behavior in the home environment had changed, and 96% of them said that their child's behavior had been modified in the desired direction.

The Anxiety and Depression scales of the MMPI decreased significantly, but part of this improvement occurred during the waiting period in the Wait group (delayed treatment), thus neutralizing the significant result. There was, however, a larger but nonsignificant decrease in Anxiety and Depression during the treatment period as opposed to the waiting period. The Anxiety and Depression scores on the Lorr-Daston Mood Scale decreased significantly as a function of the treatment, but increased during the follow-up period, the net effect being nonsignificant. This scale of moods was, as anticipated, a very transient measure.

The scores on the Present vs. Ideal Ratings and the Behavior and Achievement Ratings both showed improvement whether or not the Ss had been treated, were in the process of waiting, or were being followed up after treatment. Clearly, on these scales which are ratings of the level of child behavior, the mothers wished to see improvement and checked the items accordingly. They noted improvement when there was no reason to be any. This suggests that subjective rating scales might not be valid measures for outcome research.

There were two other findings that were adjunct to the major hypotheses, but nevertheless important. IQ scores (Henmon-Nelson Test of Mental Ability) showed no systematic relationship with change over the course of treatment for any of the seven independent variables. It was expected that the more intelligent Ss would do better in the program; this did not occur. Also, it was expected that Ss in the small groups ($N = 5$) would do better than the Ss in the large groups ($N = 10$) because of greater opportunity for individual attention. The size of the group, however, was shown to have absolutely no bearing on outcome.

DISCUSSION

The most glaring deficiency in the present design was the lack of an independent means of home observation to determine if the mothers showed any real changes in behavior in the home, and if the children indeed did show improvement. Home observation is an expensive procedure when as many as 30 Ss are treated. The strategy taken in the present study, as a second best effort, was not to measure the child, but use outcome measures of the mother. Thus, the most direct effect of the treatment was whether or not the Ss learned what was taught them. It was found that they did, and that they also knew how to apply what they learned to vignette situations. The Ss, at least intellectually, had skills they did not have before. Whether or not they were able to use their skills is less certain. They stated subjectively that they were able to do as instructed in the home, and showed by daily records of behavior that they were successful in changing behavior. This is good evidence that the Ss were able actually to use what they learned, but not as convincing as objective home observation would have been. For future research, video-tape is recommended to aid the investigators in obtaining reliable home data.

There are very meaningful implications to the findings that intelligence and group size (5 and 10) were not related to outcome. This suggests that the subject matter of simply presented behavior modification information is such that it is accessible to individuals of wide ranges of intelligence, and possibly in large audiences. Psychoanalytic material traditionally has been restricted to the intellectually oriented, and is generally only helpful to individuals over long periods of time. The principles of reinforcement and behavior modification are simple and common sense, and easily adaptable to people who do not necessarily have intellectual values. If this material can be taught to large audiences of low-IQ and/or low-income individuals, the community mental health benefits could be enormous. The Ss in the present study were of a wide range of intelligence, but most were above average, middle class, and educated. It is essential that this research be extended to low-income and nonwhite groups.

One final point should be made to note that attendance at the group meetings was 100% for all Ss. This never has been reported before in parent education literature. There is little doubt that the $50 deposit used as a reinforcer for perfect attendance was accountable for this uniquely excellent showing. It suggests that S's behavior is shaped by reinforcement contingencies as well as anyone else's, and if one wants Ss to behave appropriately, the use of tangible reinforcers is helpful.

REFERENCES

Ayllon, T., and Michael, J. "The psychiatric nurse as a behavioral engineer," *Journal of the Experimental Analysis of Behavior*, 1959, **2**, 323–334.

Becker, W. A longitudinal study of parent-child relationships. Progress report, University of Illinois, 1966.

Brim, O. "Methods of educating parents," in G. Caplan (Ed.), *Prevention of Behavior Disorders in Children*. New York: Basic Books, 1961.

Hawkins, R., Peterson, R., Schweid, E., and Bijou, S. Behavior therapy in the home: Amelioration of problem parent-child relations, with the parent in a therapeutic role. Unpublished manuscript, University of Washington, 1966 (Mimeo).

Hirsch, I., and Breiter, D. The behavioral vignettes. Unpublished manuscript, University of Maryland, 1967 (Mimeo).

Krasner, L., and Ullmann, L. *Research in Behavior Modification.* New York: Holt, Rinehart & Winston, 1965.

Patterson, G. "An application of conditioning techniques to control of a hyperactive child," in L. Ullmann and L. Krasner (Eds.), *Case Studies in Behavior Modification.* New York: Holt, Rinehart & Winston, 1965.

Pumroy, D. A new approach to treating parent-child problems. Paper read at the meeting of the American Psychological Association, New York, September 1965.

Risley, T., and Wolf, M. "Experimental manipulation of autistic behavior and generalization into the home," in R. Ulrich, T. Stachnik, and J. Mabry (Eds.), *Control of Human Behavior.* New York: Scott, Foresman, 1966.

Walder, L., Cohen, S., and Daston, P. Teaching parents and others principles of behavior control for modifying the behavior of children. Progress report to United States Office of Education, 1967.

SECTION 10

SOCIAL BEHAVIOR

The fundamental fact in social behavior is that individuals are attracted to one another. The key importance of this datum has led social psychologists to study it with a view to determining what facilitates or impedes social attraction. A considerable amount of research has shown that perceived similarities are one basis for social attraction. Indeed, the relationship between perceived similarities and attraction has been found to be highly predictable to the point where it can be considered to be a principle or "law." The paper by Donn Byrne, Michael H. Bond, and Michael J. Diamond that begins this section shows how perceived similarities affect perceptions of political candidates. Their research not only confirms the operation of the principle, but also sheds some light on the way in which political choice processes operate.

Social interaction is facilitated through social roles. It is through playing roles and perceiving others in terms of the roles they are playing that we carry our transactions with them. The roles we play also have a decided effect on our personalities, in the sense that they lead us to develop rather predictable patterns of responses. The paper by Richard L. Krebs of Sinai Hospital in Baltimore explores one aspect of male–female role differences. It has been widely observed that girls and women are more trouble-free than boys and men. Boys are more likely to be identified as "behavior problems" in the classroom, and jails house far more men than women. The question thus arises as to whether females are actually more moral or whether they are merely more skillful at avoiding detection. Krebs' findings suggest the latter interpretation, but his is probably not the final word to be said on this controversial subject.

As individuals are drawn together by mutual attraction and form groups, there is a universal tendency for such aggregations to sort their members into status levels, with group members having the most prestige and influence at the top and those who have the least on the bottom. In a democratic society, some of the differences between high, middle, and low status individuals are reduced, but not eliminated altogether, popular belief to the contrary. The third paper, a study by Anthony N. Doob and Alan E. Gross, describes an ingenious technique for measuring the effect that different levels of status have on the observer, who in this instance, is also the

369

victim. Their results show that the response of subjects to frustration depends on who is doing the frustrating—that is, subjects were more likely to express their feelings when the frustrator appeared to have low status than when he seemed to have high status. An interesting secondary result emerged when a comparable group of potential subjects were asked what they would do when frustrated by high and low status individuals. Their responses showed that they expected they would behave the opposite of how subjects had actually behaved. This finding raises the question of whether people can really predict their own social behavior and whether responses to the question "What would you do if . . . ?" can be taken literally.

Is language learned as the result of selective reinforcement of vocal responses, or is it more likely the natural product of man's neuromuscular organization? The first explanation is proposed by Skinner; the second is argued by Lenneberg and Chomsky. Louis Carini of Bennington College put the two theories to the test by observing the language learning of his small son. His conclusions are that Skinnerian theory does not explain enough of what actually occurs when children learn to talk.

The paper by Kerby T. Alvy of the State University of New York at Albany deals with the relationship between language development in children and their ability to solve problems cooperatively. According to Piaget, younger children tend to be primarily concerned with self-expression and less concerned with using language as a way of carrying out social transactions. Alvy's results are consistent with Piaget's observations.

The research by Armand D. Vine of the University of Tennessee and James H. Davis, of the University of Illinois, focuses on the fundamental question of whether problem solving is done more efficiently by groups or by individuals. Their findings support the idea that groups tend to be superior.

The final article consists of a study of intercultural empathy, conducted by the senior editor of this book and Joseph Marrash. The locus of their research was in the Middle East, in Lebanon, and their findings suggest that the ability which an ethnic group possesses for discriminating between American and British personality traits is positively related to the extent to which the group in question has been Westernized.

10.1 Response to Political Candidates as a Function of Attitude Similarity–Dissimilarity

DONN BYRNE, MICHAEL H. BOND, AND MICHAEL J. DIAMOND

The pervasive and powerful effect of the expression of attitude statements on subsequent affective responses toward the individual making the statements is a well-documented phenomenon in the study of interpersonal attraction. Attraction toward a stranger is found to be a positive linear function of the proportion of that stranger's attitudes which are similar to (in agreement with) those of the subject (Byrne, in press; Byrne and Nelson, 1965a). Attitude similarity-dissimilarity affects other types of evaluative responses in addition to attraction. For example, similar strangers are knowledgable about current events, more moral, and better adjusted than dissimilar strangers (Byrne, 1961).

If the stranger in question were a candidate for a political office, there is every reason to expect that the same law of attraction would hold: a linear relationship between candidate–subject similarity of attitudes and attraction toward the candidate. This response should include expressions of affect toward the candidate, probability of voting for the candidate, judgments about the candidate's qualifications, etc.

The investigation of voting behavior has primarily involved field studies on actual elections (Lipset, Lazarsfeld, Barton, and Long, 1954). When attitudinal variables are included in such research, they generally are considered in combination with other determinants such as socioeconomic class, party preference, and the personal appeal of the candidates (e.g., Berelson, Lazarsfeld, and McPhee, 1954; Campbell, Gurin, and Miller, 1954; Campbell and Stokes, 1959; Lazarsfeld, Berelson, and Gaudet, 1948). A somewhat different approach has sought correlations between broad, atti-

Reprinted from *Human Relations*, 1969, **22**, 251–262, by permission of the authors and *Human Relations*.

tude-relevant traits such as authoritarianism political–economic conservatism, and traditional family ideology and response to candidates or specific political issues. The findings are quite consistent in indicating a relationship between a subject's position along such dimensions and his stand on issues or his relative preference for candidates differing in their general liberalism–conservatism (e.g., Adorno, Frenkel-Brunswik, Levinson, and Sanford, 1950; Gump, 1953; Janowitz and Marvick, 1953; Lane, 1955; Milton, 1952; Milton and Waite, 1964; Sanford, 1951; Wrightsman, Radloff, Horton, and Mecherikoff, 1961).

The experimental study of attitudes and voting has been less common. In a preliminary, correlational investigation, Leventhal, Jacobs, and Kudirka (1964) found an association between scores on the F Scale and relative preference for Nixon versus Kennedy. This was followed by an experiment involving considerably greater control of the stimulus conditions. Bogus liberal and conservative candidates, with Republican and Democratic labels counterbalanced, were presented to subjects. Those with high scores on the F Scale tended to vote for the conservative candidate while low scorers tended to vote for the liberal candidate, regardless of party label.

The present investigation was designed to maintain the type of experimental control introduced by Leventhal, et al., and at the same time to move away from broad subject traits toward a more analytical examination of liberal versus conservative orientation on specific issues. The primary goal was an attempt to include voter behavior within the more general theory of interpersonal attraction.

Thus it was hypothesized that when exposed to the views of two political candidates, (a) subjects vote for the candidate with whom they share the greater proportion of similar attitudes, and (b) attraction toward each candidate is a positive linear function of the proportion of that candidate's attitudes which are similar to those of the subject.

A second problem to be considered is the nature of the attitudinal topics which are expected to influence voting and attraction. In studies of attraction between peers, attempts to show differential effects for relatively important and unimportant topics have been consistently unsuccessful (Byrne and Nelson, 1964, 1965b). Instead of the concept of *importance*, George Levinger[1] has suggested that it is the differential *instrumentality* of agreement versus disagreement on a given topic which should affect attraction. Thus, for same-sex friends, attitudes about sexual behavior and about Beatle movies may be equally instrumental to the relationship and hence of equal effect in determining attraction. For opposite-sex friends contemplating marriage, attitudes about sexual behavior may have much greater instrumentality and hence a much greater effect on the relationship than attitudes about movies. In the realm of politics, candidate–subject similarity on liberal–conservative political issues would be expected to have much more effect on response to the candidate than politically irrelevant attitudes such as hobbies or reading interests. Thus, it is hypothesized that (c) candidate–subject similarity on liberal–conservative issues will have a

[1]Personal communication.

greater effect on voting and on attraction than will similarity on issues irrelevant to politics.

METHOD

The subjects consisted of 134 students (97 males 37 females) enrolled in the general psychology course at Stanford University. Early in the quarter, a 56-item attitude scale (Byrne and Nelson, 1964) was administered in order to assess the subjects' own views on a series of topics. Each item is arranged in a six-point format, and the topics cover a wide variety of issues. From this pool of items, six liberal–conservative issues and six politically irrelevant issues were selected for use in the voting experiment.

Several weeks later, the subjects were asked to take part in an investigation of "Research on Voting Behavior." The instructions (adapted from those of Leventhal, et al.) were:

The present study represents an attempt to simulate voting behavior. The major aim of this type of research is to increase our understanding of voters and their reactions to candidates.

It would be helpful if you would imagine yourself living and working in the community in which you eventually expect to live. You must decide between two candidates who are running in a congressional election. Assume that these individuals are roughly equivalent in education, experience, etc.

The views expressed by the two candidates are based on material provided by two actual candidates in the 1966 election. The first six statements are taken from formal speeches while the remaining statements were made on a televised interview program in response to specific questions of the interviewer.

Each subject was given the statements of two candidates, labeled simply A and B. The politically relevant statements were as follows:

CONSERVATIVE CANDIDATE

1. The only sensible way to prevent the outbreak of war is to build a sufficiently powerful military force so that no other nation could risk an attack upon us.

2. Had it not been for this nation's continuing superiority in the number and quality of nuclear weapons, I believe that the free world would by this time have been overrun by the aggressors of World War III.

3. Governments representing both political parties have wisely fought against the admission of the Red Chinese into the United Nations; warlike nations must not be allowed to gain entrance at the point of a gun.

4. One of the most frightening prospects I can imagine is any form of socialized medicine in which the government assumes any influence over medical facilities, and the doctor–patient relationship becomes an impersonal interaction with a civil servant.

5. It has always seemed to me that there is an easy cure for nine-tenths of the so-called poverty problem and that

is a willingness to engage in hard work rather than to lie back and wait for a weekly welfare dole.

6. The most unpleasant aspect of the income tax is its implicit philosophy that financial success is a sin and hence should be penalized by progressively larger tax rates. A sales tax, on the other hand, is tied directly to spending so that all individuals are taxed equally in proportion to their expenditures.

LIBERAL CANDIDATE

1. I think it is almost inevitable that a nation which maintains itself in constant preparation for the possibility of war will, however unwillingly, increase the likelihood of war.

2. One of the tragedies of the cold war period has been the wasted billions spent on the buildup of nuclear armaments because the use of such weapons would mean the end of mankind.

3. It is unthinkable that China, the world's largest nation, is denied admission to the United Nations when that organization represents our best hope of communicating within the family of nations rather than resorting to war.

4. With the progress represented by Medicare, it should be possible to expand its coverage so that every man, woman, and child in this country would be guaranteed medical care throughout his lifetime with all costs paid by tax revenues as with the program in Great Britain.

5. I believe that the time has arrived when it is actually possible to eliminate every aspect of poverty—from inade-

quate housing to underfed children—simply by diverting our limitless resources from bombs and missiles and space ships into a vastly increased welfare program.

6. The most equitable way to provide the necessary funds for expenses at any level of government is the progressive income tax rather than sales taxes. An income tax levies according to ability to pay while a sales tax places the largest proportional tax burden on those least able to afford it.

Each candidate also made six politically irrelevant statements dealing with the fraternity system, Western movies and television programs, science fiction, tipping, strict discipline for children, and gardening. These latter statements took the form, "You could say that my parents exercised strict discipline in raising me, and I sincerely thank them for it." Across subjects, the order of presentation of the liberal and conservative candidates was counterbalanced. Also, the views on the irrelevant issues were varied across candidates so that a specific view on fraternities, for example, was expressed equally often by the liberal and by the conservative.

Two principle dependent variables were the subject's choice of Candidate A or Candidate B when asked to vote and a measure of attraction toward the candidate. The latter consisted of a 13-point scale of feelings labeled "Extremely Negative" on one end, "Extremely Positive" on the other, and "Relatively Indifferent" in the center. This scale was scored from 2 to 14 in order to make the responses comparable to those obtained on the attraction measure used in the previous research in this series (e.g., Byrne and Nelson, 1965a).

Three other measures were included as indices of the success of our experimental manipulation of candidate ideology and of the subjects' perception of the liberal–conservative dimension. They were asked to guess the political party to which each candidate belonged and to rate the relative liberalism or conservatism of each on a 13-point scale. In addition, they were asked to guess each candidate's views on five issues which had not been discussed: escalation versus cessation of bombing in Vietnam, open housing laws, emphasis on rights of suspected criminals versus emphasis on police obtaining confessions, tuition at the University of California, and response to the use of LSD and marijuana.

Subjects also rated each candidate's intelligence, knowledge of current events, and morality. Two open-ended, exploratory questions asked for impressions of the physical appearance of each candidate and the primary determinants of their voting decision.

RESULTS

For the analysis of each of the response variables, the subjects were divided into seven groups on the basis of their responses to the six liberal–conservative issues. Thus, 15 individuals were found to have liberal views on all six issues (6–0), 19 indicated five liberal and one conservative attitude (5–1), 26 responded 4–2, 24 responded 3–3, 23 responded 2–4, 14 responded 1–5, and 13 had conservative views on all six issues (0–6). It should be emphasized that the six attitude items are not conceptualized as a

measure of generalized liberalism–conservatism but simply as a limited attitudinal sample.

Liberalism–Conservatism of Candidates

In guessing the political affiliation of the candidates, all but eight of the subjects assigned the liberal candidate to the Democratic Party and the conservative candidate to the Republican Party.

On the 13-point rating scale of liberalism–conservatism, 2 indicated extreme liberalism, 14 extreme conservatism, and 8 was labeled as neither liberal nor conservative. As may be seen in Table 1, subjects who themselves hold quite diverse attitudes are consistent in their labeling of the two candidates and are also in agreement with the experimental definition of the two political philosophies ($F = 339.72$, $df = 1/129$, $p < .001$).

The dichotomous guesses on the five issues were arbitrarily scored in terms of number of liberal positions assigned to each candidate. Thus, perfect consistency

table 1

Mean Liberal-Conservative Ratings of Liberal and Conservative Candidates by Subjects with Varying Proportions of Liberal and Conservative Attitudes

Subject Group	Liberal Candidate	Conservative Candidate
6–0	3.80	12.00
5–1	3.70	12.30
4–2	5.19	10.81
3–3	5.67	10.71
2–4	5.00	11.30
1–5	4.36	11.00
0–6	4.46	11.46

would yield a guess of five for the liberal and a guess of zero for the conservative. Across the subject groups, the mean guesses ranged from 3.91 to 4.43 for the liberal and .36 to 1.00 for the conservative. Analysis of variance indicated a highly significant difference in guesses about the two candidates ($F = 957.60$, $df = 1/126$, $p < .001$).

All three measures are consistent in suggesting that the experimental manipulation was successful and that subjects respond to liberal and conservative candidates differentially with respect to guessing about their political affiliations, correctly applying the labels of liberal and conservative, and assuming consistency on the candidates' part in responding to other issues.

Voting

Table 2 presents the results of the voting tabulation. It may be seen that relative preference for the two candidates is a function of attitudinal similarity. The biserial correlation between the attitudi-

table 2

Voting Frequencies for Liberal and Conservative Candidates by Subjects with Varying Proportions of Liberal and Conservative Attitudes

Subject Group	Liberal Candidate	Conservative Candidate
6–0	14	1
5–1	14	5
4–2	20	6
3–3	12	12
2–4	7	16
1–5	0	14
0–6	0	13
Total votes	67	67

nal grouping of subjects and candidate choice is .87 ($p < .001$).

Another way of viewing these data is in terms of predictive accuracy. Of the 134 subjects, no prediction could be made for those in the 3–3 group because they are equally similar to each candidate. For the remaining 110 subjects, the similarity hypothesis correctly predicts the voting responses of 83 per cent and leads to an incorrect prediction for 17 per cent. Knowledge of the subject's own political party preference does not increase the accuracy of this prediction. Party preference does, however, allow us to make predictions in the 3–3 group. If we predict that the 3–3 Democrats will vote for the liberal and that the 3–3 Republicans will vote for the conservative, the votes of these individuals correspond 78 per cent to the predictions.

When the politically irrelevant issues are also considered, predictive accuracy drops to 74 per cent. Thus, both hypotheses (a) and (c) are supported.

Attraction

The mean attraction scores toward the two candidates for subjects of varying proportions of similarity are shown in Table 3. The rather obvious interaction between the subjects' own attitudes and attraction toward the two candidates is confirmed by the analysis of variance, summarized in Table 4. The second hypothesis was confirmed.

The relation between subject-candidate similarity and attraction responses was also examined in a correlational analysis. Proportion of similar attitudes on the six issues correlated .58 ($p < .001$) with attraction toward the lib-

table 3

Mean Attraction Responses toward Liberal and Conservative Candidates by Subjects with Varying Proportions of Liberal and Conservative Attitudes

Subject Group	Liberal Candidate	Conservative Candidate	Total
6–0	12.07	4.73	8.40
5–1	9.60	6.95	8.28
4–2	9.37	7.15	8.26
3–3	8.71	7.58	8.15
2–4	8.61	9.26	8.93
1–5	5.00	10.62	7.81
0–6	5.85	11.38	8.62
Total	8.70	8.03	

eral candidate and .58 ($p < .001$) with attraction toward the conservative candidate. Another way of approaching these data is to correlate the subjects' attitudinal position with his *differential* attraction to the two candidates; the resulting coefficient is .70 ($p < .001$). Thus, 49 per cent of the variance of the difference scores in responding to the liberal and the conservative may be accounted for by the subject's own attitudes.

table 4

Summary of Analysis of Variance of Attraction Responses toward Liberal and Conservative Candidates by Subjects with Varying Proportions of Liberal and Conservative Attitudes

Source	df	MS	F
Between			
Between Groups	6	4.65	1.29
Error	128	3.60	
Within			
Trials (Candidates)	1	30.00	3.46
Trials by Groups	6	155.78	17.97*
Error	128	8.67	

*$p < .001$

The effect on attraction of similarity–dissimilarity on the politically irrelevant issues was also determined by means of a correlational analysis. Neither attraction toward the liberal candidate ($r = .12$) nor attraction toward the conservative candidate ($r = .06$) was significantly related to proportion of similar attitudes on the nonpolitical issues. Inclusion of this information along with the liberal–conservative issues actually decreases the relationship between attitude similarity and attraction. That is, proportion of similar attitudes on all 12 issues correlates .46 with attraction toward the liberal and .51 with attraction toward the conservative. Again, the third hypothesis is supported.

Other Responses

On the other three ratings of the candidates, the data were generally consistent with the voting and attraction responses. Subject attitudes were correlated with differential ratings of the two candidates with respect to intelligence ($r = .30, p < .001$), knowledge of current events ($r = .42, p < .001$), and morality ($r = .25, p < .01$). The candidate who shares one's views is apparently perceived quite differently from one who expresses a divergent viewpoint. Analysis of variance corroborated these results and contributed the additional finding that the liberal candidate was rated higher ($p < .01$) on each of these three dimensions than the conservative candidate.

As an exploratory inquiry, the subjects were asked to give their impressions of the physical appearance of each candidate. Their spontaneous replies were categorized into 10 variables such as age, height, etc. Of these, there six significant differences in descriptions of the two candidates, and these responses were independent of the subjects' own attitudes. Specifically, compared to the liberal, the conservative was seen as older ($z = 4.94$, $p < .001$), stronger and more rugged ($z = 4.38$, $p < .001$), larger ($z = 2.60$, $p < .01$), as having neater and more formal clothing ($z = 2.98$, $p < .01$) and as having hair which is shorter ($z = 2.84$, $p < .01$) and lighter in color ($z = 2.32$, $p < .05$). It would appear that there are relatively widely shared stereotypes in this population as to the way that politicians of different political persuasions should look. Descriptions of physical attractiveness, height, baldness, or eyeglasses did not yield significant differences. A few subjects mentioned that a candidate resembled a specific person such as Robert F. Kennedy for the liberal and Ronald Reagan and Barry Goldwater for the conservative.

In response to the general question as to why the particular candidate had been selected, most subjects discussed the importance of the attitudes, often specifying one or two which they saw as crucial. Of the other characteristics ascribed to the candidates, the "rationality" or "reasonableness" or "sanity" of the preferred was the most frequent category; these attributes were assigned with equal frequency to the liberal and to the conservative. There were two characteristics which subjects voting for the liberal candidate stressed more frequently than did those voting for the conservative candidate; the liberal was seen by his supporters as more flexible

($z = 3.16$, $p < .01$) and more humanitarian ($z = 2.67$, $p < .01$) than his opponent.

DISCUSSION

In addition to extending the generality of the similarity–attraction relationship, the present findings suggest the utility of the attraction formulations in the prediction of response to political candidates. The possibility of predicting the voting response of subjects on the basis of subject–candidate attitude similarity is an intriguing one. With the present subjects, predictive accuracy of approximately 80 per cent was attained. It should be noted that the prediction here is not like that of political polls in which individuals are asked for whom they will vote, and then are predicted to behave as they say they will. Here, their voting response is predicted *before* they are even exposed to the candidates, on the basis of the attitudes they hold in relation to the expressed views of the candidates.

Such a relationship could presumably be utilized within this type of experiment to manipulate votes. That is, instead of presenting consistently liberal or consistently conservative views, the ideal candidate for this particular group of "voters" would have ascertained and then expressed the majority view on each issue. On the basis of the subjects' responses to the original attitude scale, the candidate who indicated that he was against the constant preparation for the possibility of war, opposed to the build-up of nuclear armaments, in favor of admitting Red China to the U.N., against socialized medicine, opposed to increased welfare legislation, and in favor of the income tax should easily defeat either of the consistent candidates.

The relevance of the present findings to a non-college population and to a non-laboratory setting is obviously of some interest. In their experimental study, Leventhal, *et al.* (1964) point out that authoritarianism would be expected to affect choice of candidates only in the relatively small and well-educated segment of the population in which a definable ideology is present and only if the candidates are consistent in espousing liberal or conservative ideology. Our approach via attitude similarity assumes that the prediction of voting behavior requires ideological consistency in neither the subjects nor the candidates. What is required is a knowledge of the subjects' views on politically relevant issues and their exposure to the candidate's views on these same issues. It might be noted that in a "real life" setting, a number of forces can act against the voter's contact with and accurate perception of the attitudes of each candidate (e.g., Berelson, *et al.*, 1954) and that non-attitudinal variables must also be considered (e.g., Campbell and Stokes, 1959; Campbell, *et al.*, 1954). As for the uniqueness of the college population in responding to similar and dissimilar attitudes, recent findings indicate that precisely the same attitude–attraction function holds for children, members of the Job Corps, schizophrenics in a state hospital, and alcoholic patients (Byrne, in press; Byrne and Griffitt, 1966). It seems very likely, then, that the present voting data would be replicable with non-college subjects. It is also conceivable, however, that a less sophisticated group would not make as clear a distinction

between politically relevant and irrelevant issues.

It might be added that the subjects in this experiment appeared to be responding in terms of non-laboratory concerns and considerations. When agreements and disagreements about the kinds of issues manipulated here can lead to active and sometimes violent expressions of feeling out in the real world, perhaps it is helpful to insert a subjective note about the affective responses of our subjects. On the open-ended question about the reason for selecting a given candidate, the degree of emotion expressed, appeared to be greatest in the most consistently liberal or consistently conservative groups for whom the subject–candidate differences were greatest. As Berelson, *et al.* (1954) note, such individuals disagree more sharply with the opponent and view him as more of an enemy. A few samples indicate the flavor of these responses:

6–0, *male:* [the liberal] has realistic, practical, and humane answers to vital problems. [the conservative] fosters an individuality that turns members of society in upon themselves, in isolation and fear of change.

6–0, *female:* I think [the conservative] programs will lead to destruction, if not to a war of incalculable harm where his sole indication and system of values is conceived as "might makes right"! I'd rather live peacefully than enforce my morality or my culture or ideas on another human being.

3–3, *male:* I felt that [the liberal] was the "lesser of two evils" since the problem of war is a more crucial problem (more immediate) than the economic problem involved in over-extending the Welfare State. In other words, [the liberal] would probably do *less* immediate damage which would be irreparable.

3-3, *female:* Since I had to make a choice on such limited material, I picked [the liberal] because of his views on the war and the income tax. Frankly, neither one was very exciting.

0-6, *male:* [the liberal] seemed too soft. A middle-of-the-roader who might vacillate while in office. I doubt that [the conservative] would vacillate in office—above all, he's a prideful, strong man. This is what I like to think of our country.

0-6, *female:* The primary determinants were the conservative principles of [the conservative], a step away from socialism and 1984. I am a staunch and rational conservative and proponent of Ayn Rand's philosophy of objectivism where man is an end, not a means. [the liberal's] principles will lead to political, social, and economic animals. I am for free enterprise, what made this country the greatest the world has ever seen in its history. I could destroy any impractical liberal interpretation where morality is carried to an unreal extreme. If we had a Jesus Christ complex and turned the other cheek, the commies would take over. I could talk forever against insipid, spineless left wingers.

The prediction of attraction toward each candidate is surprisingly consistent with previous attitude similarity research. The relationship is best seen in Figure 1. When a straight-line function is fitted to these data by the least squares method, the resulting formula is $Y = 6.11X + 5.30$. A function previously established in attitude-attraction research is $Y = 6.74X + 5.06$ (Byrne and Clore, 1966). The obtained attraction responses in the present investigation do not differ significantly from the responses predicted by the Byrne-Clore function (goodness of fit analysis, $F < 1$). Thus, the present data are predictable from the previously established relationship even though the stranger is a political candidate rather than a peer, the stranger's attitudes are expressed in statement form rather than as items on an attitude scale, the attraction measure is a single 13-point scale rather than two separate scales asking about liking and desirability as a work partner, and the subjects are Stanford undergraduates rather than Texas undergraduates.

REFERENCES

Adorno, T. W., Frenkel-Brunswik, E., Levinson, D. J., and Sanford, R. N. (1950). *The Authoritarian Personality.* New York: Harper.

Berelson, B., Lazarsfeld, P. F., and McPhee, W. N., (1954). *Voting. Chicago:* University of Chicago Press.

Byrne, D. (1961). Interpersonal attraction and attitude similarity," *J. Abnorm. Soc. Psychol.*, **62,** 713–715.

Byrne, D. "Attitudes and attraction," in L. Berkowitz (Ed.), *Advances in Experimental Social Psychology,* Vol. 4., New York Academic Press, in press.

Byrne, D., and Clore, G. L., Jr. (1966). "Predicting interpersonal attraction toward strangers presented in three different stimulus modes," *Psychonomic Science,* **4,** 239–240.

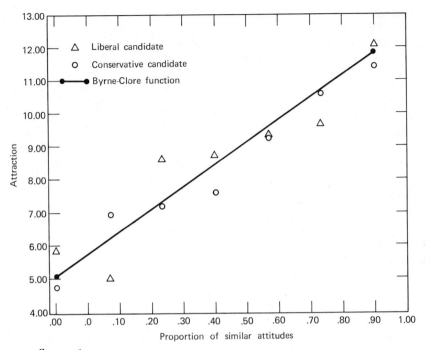

figure 1

Attraction toward political candidates as a function of proportion of similar attitudes.

Byrne, D., and Griffitt, W. (1966). "A developmental investigation of the law of attraction, *J. Pers. Soc. Psychol.*, **4,** 699–702.

Byrne, D., and Nelson, D. (1964). "Attraction as a function of attitude similarity-dissimilarity: the effect of topic importance," *Psychonomic Science*, **1,** 93–94.

Byrne, D., and Nelson, D. (1965). "Attraction as a linear function of proportion of positive reinforcements," *J. Pers. Soc. Psychol.*, **1,** 659–663 (a).

Byrne, D., and Nelson, D. (1965). "The effect of topic importance and attitude similarity-dissimilarity on attraction in a multistranger design," *Psychonomic Science*, **3,** 449–550 (b).

Campbell, A., Gurin, G., and Miller, W. E. (1954). *The Voter Decides.* Evanston, Ill.: Row, Peterson.

Campbell, A., and Stokes, D. E. (1959). "Partisan attitudes and the presidential vote," in E. Burdick and A. J. Brodbeck (Eds.), *American Voting Behavior.* Glencoe, Ill.: The Free Press, 353–371.

Gump, P. V. (1953). "Anti-democratic trends and student reaction to President Truman's dismissal of General McArthur," *J. Soc. Psychol.*, **38,** 131–135.

Janowitz, M., and Marvick, D. (1953). "Authoritarianism and political behavior," *Public Opinion Quarterly*, **17,** 185–201.

Lane, R. E. (1955). "Political personality and electoral choice," *The American Political Science Review*, **49,** 173–190.

Lazarsfeld, P. F., Berelson, B., and Gaudet, H. (1948). *The People's Choice.* New York: Columbia University Press.

Leventhal, H., Jacobs, R. L., and Kudirka,

N. Z. (1964). "Authoritarianism, ideology and political candidate choice," *J. Abnorm. Soc. Psychol.*, **69**, 539–549.

Lipset, S. M., Lazarsfeld, P. F., Barton, A. H., and Linz, J. (1954). "The psychology of voting: an analysis of political behavior," in G. Lindzey (Ed.), *Handbook of Social Psychology.* Vol. II. *Special fields and applications.* Reading, Mass.: Addison-Wesley. 1124–1175.

Milton, O. (1952). "Presidential choice and performance on a scale of authoritarianism," *Amer. Psychol.*, **7**, 597–598.

Milton, O., and Waite, B. (1964). "Presidential preference and traditional family values," *Amer. Psychol.*, **19**, 844–845.

Sanford, F. H. (1951). "Leadership identification and acceptance," in H. Guetzkow (Ed.), *Groups, Leadership, and Men.* Pittsburgh: Carnegie Press, 158–176.

Wrightsman, L. S., Jr., Radloff, R. W., Horton, D. L., and Mecherikoff, M. (1961). "Authoritarian attitudes and presidential voting preferences," *Psychological Reports*, **8**, 43–46.

10.2 Girls—More Moral than Boys or Just Sneakier?

RICHARD L. KREBS

In talking with teachers and reading the education literature (Meyer and Thompson, 1956, Terman and Tyler, 1946) one gets the impression that teachers think that girls are more moral than boys. To check on the existence of this impression and to assess the accuracy of the teachers' perception of girls as more moral than boys, the following research was undertaken.

METHOD

A random sample of sixth grade children was selected from 10 classes in a middle class and a working class school to fit a balanced factorial design with 2 factors, sex and social class. The boys and girls groups at both schools were controlled for IQ. The IQ scores were obtained from school records. While the design called for 132 Ss only 127 Ss were obtained.

(Five working class boys were lost during the study.)

Each S was rated by his teacher on 3 scales of morality previously used by Kohlberg (1958): Trustworthiness, Obedience, and Respect for Others' Rights. These three rating scales were used to measure the teachers' perceptions. While not covering the entire concept of morality they do measure three important aspects of that concept (Kohlberg, 1958).

In order to assess the Ss' actual moral behavior two types of measurements were used. The first type is based on the judgmental approach to morality following the line of research started by Piaget (1948) and expanded by Kohlberg (1958). The second type of measurement of morality is based on behavioral conformity as assessed in experimental situations. This second line of research was started by Hartshorne and May (1928) and has been developed further by such

Reprinted from the *Proceedings of the 76th Annual Convention of the American Psychological Association*, 1968, **3**, 607–608, with permission of the author and the American Psychological Association, Inc.

researchers as Grinder (1961, 1962) and Burton, *et al.* (1961). Each S was given Kohlberg's Moral Judgment Inventory to assess his level of moral judgment. The S's responses to the Inventory were scored on Kohlberg's global scale (1958). To assess the S's behavioral conformity in an experimental situation each child took 3 cheating tests which are adaptions of tests used in previous research by Hartshorne and May (1928–1930) and Grinder (1961). All of the procedures are described in greater detail in a previous paper (Krebs, 1967).

RESULTS

On the scales of Trustworthiness, Obedience and Respect for Others' Rights, teachers rated girls as more moral than boys for both middle class (t values = 10.91, 13.49, and 6.94, respectively, significant beyond .001 level, one-tailed test) and working class groups (t values = 13.58, 5.27, 4.20, all significant beyond .001 level, one-tailed test). However, on the Moral Judgment Inventory girls were not more moral. In fact, middle-class boys were significantly more moral than middle-class girls ($t = 4.54$ significant beyond .001, two-tailed test). There was no significant difference between working class boys and girls on the Moral Judgment Inventory ($t = .40$, not significant).

When boys and girls were compared on the three cheating tests, girls were not consistently more moral than boys for the middle-class group. There was no significant differences between boys and girls in their ability to resist temptation (t values = .26, 1.10, .08, respectively, all not significant). In the working class group, girls did cheat less than boys on 1 of the 3 tests ($t = 5.45$ significant beyond .001, two-tailed test), but not on the other two (t values = .94 and .76, not significant).

DISCUSSION

Teachers do regard girls as more moral than boys. This result is in agreement with an earlier study by Meyer and Thompson (1956) who found that boys receive more disapproval than girls in the classroom, and Hartshorne and May who found that girls have a higher reputation for persistence than boys.

However when moral behavior is assessed by comparing boys and girls on moral judgment and the ability to resist the temptation to cheat, girls are not more moral than boys. Previous research has also generally supported the notion that boys and girls do not differ significantly in their moral behavior. Hartshorne and May (1928–1930) found that in actual persistence girls and boys are essentially equal. Johnson (1943) found no significant difference between boys and girls on cheating tests. Mutterer (1965) and Nelson, Grinder, and Howard (1967) also report no differences between boys and girls on cheating tests. Kohlberg's review of the literature reports few sex-related differences in moral behavior (1963). Evidence suggesting that girls might be more moral than boys in actual behavior comes from the one cheating test in the working class groups in the present study and Hartshorne and May's study (1928–1930) where girls were found to be higher than boys on inhibition.

The weight of evidence suggests that

girls are viewed as more moral than boys but in actual behavior are not more moral. Kohlberg (1963) points out that girls are more conforming to rules and authority than boys are. It appears that the conforming behavior of girls has led their teachers to believe that they are generally more moral than boys. The results of this study and previous research suggests that they have been mistaken.

REFERENCES

Ausubel, D. "Perceived parents' attitudes as determinants of children's ego structure," Child Development, 1954, 25, 173–183.

Burton, R. V., Maccoby, E. E., and Allinsmith, W. "Antecedants of resistance to temptation in four-year-old children," Child Development, 1961, 32, 689–710.

Grinder, R. E. "New techniques for research in children's temptation behavior," Child Development, 1961, 32, 679–688.

Grinder, R. E. "Parental child rearing practices, conscience and resistance to temptation of 6th grade children," Child Development, 1962, 33, 803–820.

Hartshorne, H., and May, M. Studies in the Nature of Character. New York: Macmillan, 1928–1930.

Johnson, L. "Pupil cheating," Education Digest, 1943, 9, 32–34.

Kohlberg, L. The development of modes of moral thinking and choice in the years ten to sixteen. Unpublished doctoral dissertation, University of Chicago, 1958.

Kohlberg, L. "Moral development and identification," in H. Stevenson (Ed.), Child Psychology. Chicago: University of Chicago Press, 1963.

Krebs, R. Some relationships between moral judgment, attention and resistance to temptation. Unpublished doctoral dissertation, University of Chicago, 1967.

Meyer, W., and Thompson, G. "The differences in the distribution of teacher approval and disapproval among sixth grade children," Journal of Educational Psychology, 1956, 47, 385–396.

Mutterer, M. Factors affecting the specificity of preadolescents' behavior in a variety of temptation situations. Unpublished master's thesis, University of Wisconsin, 1965.

Nelson, E., Grinder, R., and Howard J. Resistance to temptation and moral judgment: behavioral correlates of Kohlberg's measure of moral development. Paper presented at the Society for Research in Child Development, New York, March 1967.

Piaget, J. The Moral Judgment of the Child. (Originally published, 1932) Glencoe, Ill.: Free Press, 1948.

Terman, L., and Tyler, L. "Psychological sex differences," in L. Carmichael (Ed.), Manual of Child Psychology. New York: Wiley, 1946.

10.3 Status of Frustrator as an Inhibitor of Horn-Honking Responses

ANTHONY N. DOOB AND ALAN E. GROSS

A. INTRODUCTION

Subjects may consciously attempt to present themselves in a favorable manner, they may cooperate with the experimenter or interviewer, and their reactions may be affected by the measurement process itself. In reviewing a number of such problems, Webb, *et al.* (6, pp. 13–27) point out that some of these sources of contamination can be avoided when field data are collected from people who are unaware that they are subjects participating in an experiment. Although field procedures can reduce demand and reactivity effects, experimental manipulations outside of the laboratory may gain realism at the expense of control. The study reported here is an attempt to investigate unobtrusively some effects of frustration in a naturalistic setting without sacrificing experimental control.

Modern automobile traffic frequently creates situations which closely resemble classical formulations of how frustration is instigated. One such instance occurs when one car blocks another at a signal-controlled intersection. Unlike many traffic frustrations, this situation provides a clearly identifiable frustrator and a fairly typical response for the blocked driver: sounding his horn. Horn honking may function instrumentally to remove the offending driver and emotionally to reduce tension. Both kinds of honks may be considered aggressive, especially if they are intended to make the frustrator uncomfortable by bombarding him with unpleasant stimuli.

One factor that is likely to affect aggressive responses is the status of the frustrator (2, 3). The higher a person's status, the more likely it is he will have power to exercise sanctions, and although it is improbable that a high status driver would seek vengeance against a honker,

Reprinted with slight abridgment from the *Journal of Social Psychology*, 1968, **76**, 213–218, with permission of the authors and The Journal Press.

fear of retaliation may generalize from other situations where aggression against superiors has been punished.

Aggression is not the only kind of social response that may be affected by status. High status may inhibit the initiation of any social response, even a simple informational signal. Although it is difficult in the present study to distinguish informational from aggressive motivation, it is hypothesized that a high status frustrator will generally inhibit horn honking.

B. METHOD

One of two automobiles, a new luxury model or an older car, was driven up to a signal controlled intersection and stopped. The driver was instructed to remain stopped after the signal had changed to green until 15 seconds had elapsed, or until the driver of the car immediately behind honked his horn twice. Subjects were the 82 drivers, 26 women and 56 men, whose progress was blocked by the experimental car. The experiment was run from 10:30 a.m. to 5:30 p.m. on a Sunday, in order to avoid heavy weekday traffic.

1. Status Manipulation

A black 1966 Chrysler Crown Imperial hardtop which had been washed and polished was selected as the high status car.† Two low status cars were

† We have labeled this operation a "status manipulation" because a large expensive car is frequently associated with wealth, power, and other qualities which are commonly regarded as comprising high status. However, it could be argued that Chrysler is potentially inhibiting not because it is a status symbol, but because of some other less plausible attribute (e.g., physical size).

used: a rusty 1954 Ford station wagon and an unobtrusive gray 1961 Rambler sedan. The Rambler was substituted at noon because it was felt that subjects might reasonably attribute the Ford's failure to move to mechanical breakdown. Responses to these two cars did not turn out to be different, and the data for the two low status cars were combined.

2. Location

Six intersections in Palo Alto and Menlo Park, California, were selected according to these criteria: (*a*) a red light sufficiently long to insure that a high proportion of potential subjects would come to a complete stop behind the experimental car before the signal changed to green, (*b*) relatively light traffic so that only one car, the subject's, was likely to pull up behind the experimental car, and (*c*) a narrow street so that it would be difficult for the subject to drive around the car blocking him. Approximately equal numbers of high and low status trials were run at each intersection.

3. Procedure

By timing the signal cycle, the driver of the experimental car usually managed to arrive at the intersection just as the light facing him was turning red. If at least one other car had come to a complete stop behind the experimental car before the signal had turned green, a trial was counted, and when the light changed, an observer started two stop watches and a tape recorder. Observers were usually stationed in a car parked close to the intersection, but when this was not feasible, they were concealed from view in the back seat of the experimental car.

High and low status trials were run simultaneously at different intersections, and the two driver–observer teams switched cars periodically during the day. Drivers wore a plaid sport jacket and white shirt while driving the Chrysler, and an old khaki jacket while driving the older car.

a. Dependent Measures. At the end of each trial, the observer noted whether the subject had honked once, twice, or not at all. Latency of each honk and estimated length of each honk were recorded and later double-checked against tape recordings.

b. Subject Characteristics. Immediately after each trial, the observer took down the year, make, and model of the subject's car. Sex and estimated age of driver, number of passengers, and number of cars behind the experimental car when the signal changed were also recorded.

C. RESULTS AND DISCUSSION

Eight subjects, all men, were eliminated from the analysis for the following reasons: four cars in the low status condition and one in the high status condition went around the experimental car; on one trial the driver of the experimental car left the intersection early; and two cars in the low status condition, instead of honking, hit the back bumper of the experimental car, and the driver did not wish to wait for a honk. This left 38 subjects in the low status condition and 36 in the high status condition.

Although the drivers of the experimental cars usually waited for 15 seconds, two of the lights used in the experiment were green for only 12 seconds;

therefore 12 seconds was used as a cutoff for all data. There were no differences attributable to drivers or intersections.

The clearest way of looking at the results is in terms of the percentage in each condition that honked at least once in 12 seconds. In the low status condition 84 percent of the subjects honked at least once, whereas in the high status condition, only 50 percent of the subjects honked ($\chi^2 = 8.37$, $df = 1$, $p < .01$). Another way of looking at this finding is in terms of the latency of the first honk. When no honks are counted as a latency of 12 seconds, it can be seen in Table 1 that the average latency for the new car was longer for both sexes ($F = 10.71$, $p < .01$).

Thus, it is quite clear that status had an inhibitory effect on honking even once. It could be argued that status would have even greater inhibitory effects on more aggressive honking. Although one honk can be considered a polite way of calling attention to the green light, it is possible that subjects felt that a second honk would be interpreted as aggression.†

Forty-seven percent of the subjects

table 1

Field Experiment (Mean Latency of First Honk in Seconds)

	Sex of Driver	
Frustrator	Male	Female
Low status	6.8 (23)	7.6 (15)
High status	8.5 (25)	10.9 (11)

Note.—Numbers in parentheses indicate the number of subjects.

†Series of honks separated by intervals of less than one second were counted as a single honk.

in the low status condition honked twice at the experimental car, as compared to 19 percent of the subjects in the high status condition ($\chi^2 = 5.26$, $df = 1$, $p < .05$). This difference should be interpreted cautiously because it is confounded with the main result that more people honk generally in the low status condition. Of those who overcame the inhibitions to honk at all, 56 percent in the low status condition and 39 percent in the high status condition honked a second time, a difference which was not significant. First-honk latencies for honkers were about equal for the two conditions. The overall findings are presented in Table 2.

Sex of driver was the only other measure that was a good predictor of honking behavior. In both conditions men tended to honk faster than women ($F = 4.49$, $p < .05$). The interaction of status and sex did not approach significance ($F = 1.17$). These data are consistent with laboratory findings (1) that men tend to aggress more than women.

Most experiments designed to study the effects of frustration have been carried out in the laboratory or the classroom, and many of these have employed written materials (2, 5).

It is undoubtedly much easier to use questionnaires, and if they produce the same results as field experiments, then in the interest of economy, they would have great advantage over naturalistic experiments. However, over 30 years ago, LaPiere warned that reactions to such instruments "may indicate what the responder would actually do when confronted with the situation symbolized in the question, but there is no assurance that it will" (4, p. 236).

table 2

Number of Drivers Honking Zero, One, and Two Times

Frustrator	Honking in 12 seconds		
	Never	Once	Twice
Low status	6	14	18
High status	18	11	7

Note.—Overall $\chi^2 = 11.14$, $p < .01$.

In order to investigate this relationship between actual and predicted behavior, an attempt was made to replicate the present study as a questionnaire experiment. Obviously, the most appropriate sample to use would be one comprised of motorists sampled in the same way that the original drivers were sampled. Because this was not practicable, a questionnaire experiment was administered in a junior college classroom.

Subjects were 57 students in an introductory psychology class. Two forms of the critical item were included as the first of three traffic situations on a one-page questionnaire: "You are stopped at a traffic light behind a black 1966 Chrysler (gray 1961 Rambler). The light turns green and for no apparent reason the driver does not go on. Would you honk at him?" If subjects indicated that they would honk, they were then asked to indicate on a scale from one to 14 seconds how long they would wait before honking. Forms were alternated so that approximately equal numbers of subjects received the Chrysler and Rambler versions. Verbal instructions strongly emphasized that subjects were to answer according to what they actually thought they would do in such a situation. No personal information other than sex, age, and whether or not they were licensed to drive was required.

After the questionnaire had been collected, the class was informed that different kinds of cars had been used for the horn-honking item. The experimenter then asked subjects to raise their hands when they heard the name of the car that appeared in the first item of their questionnaire. All subjects were able to select the correct name from a list of four makes which was read.

One subject (a female in the high status condition) failed to mark the honk latency scale, and another subject in the same condition indicated that she would go around the blocking car. Both of these subjects were eliminated from the analysis, leaving 27 in the high status condition and 28 in the low status condition. The results were analyzed in the same manner as the latency data from the field experiment. Means for each condition broken down by sex are presented in Table 3. Males reported that they thought that they would honk considerably sooner at the Chrysler than at the Rambler, whereas this was slightly reversed for females (interaction of sex and status $F = 4.97, p < .05$). Eleven subjects,

six males in the low status condition and five females in the high status condition indicated that they would not honk within 12 seconds.

It is clear that the behavior reported on the questionnaire is different from the behavior actually observed in the field. The age difference in the samples may account for this disparity. Median estimated age of subjects in the field was 38, compared to a median age of 22 in the classroom. In order to check the possibility that younger males would indeed honk faster at the high status car, the field data were reanalyzed by age. The results for younger males, estimated ages 16 to 30, fit the general pattern of the field results and differed from the results of the classroom experiment. In the field, young males honked sooner at the Rambler than at the Chrysler ($t = 2.74$, $df = 11, p < .02$).

Unfortunately, because these two studies differed in both sample and method, it is impossible to conclude that the differences are due to differences in the method of collecting data. However, it is clear that questionnaire data obtained from this often used population of subjects do not always correspond to what goes on in the real world.

table 3

Questionnaire Experiment (Mean Latency of Honking in Seconds)

Frustrator	Sex of subject	
	Male	Female
Low status	9.1 (18)	8.2 (10)
High status	5.5 (13)	9.2 (14)

Note.—Numbers in parentheses indicate the number of subjects.

REFERENCES

1. Buss, A. H. "Instrumentality of aggression, feedback, and frustration as determinants of physical aggression," *J. of Personal. and Soc. Psychol.*, 1966, **3**, 153–162.

2. Cohen, A. R. "Social norms, arbitrariness of frustration, and status of the agent in the frustration-aggression hypothesis," *J. Abn. and Soc. Psychol.*, 1955, **51**, 222–226.

3. Hokanson, J. E., and Burgess, M. "The

effects of status, type of frustration and aggression on vascular processes," *J. Abn. and Soc. Psychol.,* 1962, **65,** 232–237.

4. LaPiere, R. T. "Attitudes vs. actions," *Social Forces,* 1934, **13,** 230–237.

5. Pastore, N. "The role of arbitrariness in the frustration-aggression hypothesis," *J. Abn. and Soc. Psychol.,* 1952, **47,** 728–731.

6. Webb, E. J., Campbell, D. T., Schwartz, R. D., and Sechrest, L. *Unobtrusive Measures: Nonreactive Research in the Social Sciences.* Chicago, Ill.: Rand McNally, 1966.

10.4 Symbolic Transformations Theorem on Language Learning

LOUIS CARINI

The theorem about learning (Carini, 1967) deduced from the postulates of the theory of symbolic transformatiðns (Carini, 1969) can be applied to the acquisition of language. The theorem (1967) asserts, "that *learning consists in the change from sensory-physiological experience to related or meaningful experiences which are characterized by their ideational or symbolic way of being represented* [p. 5]." Learning then always consists in a movement from sensory experience to experiences which are characterized by being meaningfully represented, and finally by being symbolically represented conceptions which order and integrate experiences and actions. What may begin as a mere sense impression will through learning become meaningful, and will eventually be represented as an idea or concept which can embody a rule or principle which can order sensory and other events. This theorem about learning differs from Skinner's operant conditioning position, and the differences will be demonstrated by comparing the present account of language acquisition with the one espoused by Skinner (1957).

Skinner (1957) says, "A child acquires verbal behavior when relatively unpatterned vocalizations, selectively reinforced, gradually assume forms which produce appropriate consequences in a given verbal community [p. 31]." Lenneberg (1966), however, criticizes operant conditioning explanations of cooing, babbling, and of the increasing articulation of the infant's sound making. He provides evidence that cooing and babbling occur without the benefit of reinforcement, since they occur in deaf children. He also presents evidence that practice in sound making which is required by operant conditioning principles is not necessary for increasing articulateness in the sounds of infants.

Reprinted from the *Proceedings of the 77th Annual Convention of the American Psychological Association*, 1969, **4,** 5–6, with permission of the author and the American Psychological Association, Inc.

Skinner could be said to have explained too much.

As Lenneberg (1966) has also noted, with continued babbling, certain sounds begin to stabilize and are repeated more often than others. When our son was approximately 8 mo. old, we noticed that he was sounding out "toop-toop" whenever he lay on his stomach and rocked up and down as in doing push-ups. The sound was never made without the activity and the activity was never carried out without the sound. Carini[1] said, "The gestures and vocables are embedded in each other, whereas at an earlier point sound patterns and activities occurred together randomly." If the soundings and the activities had occurred separately and now occur together, then these sounding activities must have been learned, for learning consists, at least, in connecting what had previously been unconnected. There is, however, no reason, according to operant conditioning principles, why the infant should learn to connect meaningless sounds with meaningless activities. Skinner has here explained too little.

The sounding out of stabilized phrases is a necessary phase in the acquisition of true words, according to the theorem deduced from the theory of symbolic transformations. The theorem suggests that there will be a learned progression from meaningless sense activities to meaningful ones. Eventually these meaningful actions will become symbolically represented. Certainly, "toop-toop" is by no means a symbolic representation. "Toop-toop" is merely what it is. It is clear, however, that it does

mean the sounding activity, because our sounding "toop-toop" brought forth the sounding activity, brought it forth always, and brought forth nothing else. While one might not want to say that by *mean* we mean that the sounding activity represents something, the fact that the sounding activity can be elicited from him by the sound shows that it is connected to, indeed, welded to and thus means the sounding activity itself. The *learning* consists in connecting random soundings and random activities into a sounding activity which means something implicit to the child.

For Skinner, "toop-toop" should never have occurred, because stabilized babbling terms have no denotative meaning, and thus would never have been reinforced. The operant conditioner waits for a sound resembling a word to appear and then he reinforces that sound by giving a reward. In the case of "toop-toop" the sounding activity appeared in its entirety without any reinforcement from us. When we became aware of it we responded to the sounding activity by saying "toop-toop" back to him. I suppose our saying it could be thought of as constituting reinforcement, but it is preferable not to prejudge the issue by explaining it according to reinforcement, and report what we did do: We responded to the sounding activity by making the sound back at him; to try to determine whether he was reinforced by our response would place us in an inferential position which Skinner abhors. Thus it is that Skinner has explained too little.

If a child can respond to our sound by the sounding activity, he should begin to take on some of the sounds in his

---

[1]Patricia Carini kept notes on her son's sound making and language acquisition.

environment with sounding activities. Carini (see Footnote 1) said, " 'Kit-ten' was used first to refer to the cats, then to some horses in a nearby meadow, then to a farm dog, then to a bull." Though "kit-ten" was the first sounding activity that sounded like one of our words, it could hardly be a denotative word because it referred to not one of the objects to which the word kitten refers. It cannot be a word which represents kittens when it can encompass such diverse animals as a cat, a dog, a bull, or a horse. It must have meant something personal and implicit of his experience of these animals. When I drove the Volkswagen close to the tethered bull, his expression "kit-ten" was impressive! Such sounding activities, for they are expressed with a similar body attitude, are really names (Werner and Kaplan, 1963) which name a personal dynamic experience. Names name individual and personalized emotive experiences, and for the child all of these dynamic creatures brought forth from him the ex-pression "kit-ten" just as the grape is ex-pressed in wine making (Dewey, 1934); the sounding activity "kit-ten" was pressed out of him in the fullness of his experience of these dramatic events.

For Skinner the sounding activity "kit-ten" would have to be a denotative term, because it is a sound that is used in our language to denote young cats and has a publicly agreed upon meaning. According to Carroll's (1964) interpretation of Skinner's position, denotative words occur first and are followed by connotative terms as the many contexts lead the original explicit meaning to be broken down. But a sound which is used in such diverse contexts as cats,

dogs, horses, and bulls, from the beginning, must be, at best, a connotative term rather than a denotative one. The child could not have meant what we mean by kitten when such diverse animals were the occasion of his sounding activity; what he meant must have been whatever dynamic qualities these animals called forth from him. Since denotative terms must mean the same thing to all who participate in the language, "kit-ten" could not have been a denotative word. According to the theorem presented here, denotation would follow connotation, and this sequence is precisely the opposite of what must occur according to operant conditioning. Again Skinner's reinforcement position has explained too little, for the first familiar sounds must only be connotative names; only later will a denotative meaning develop as the child acquires the words which have the specific denotations that all can agree on.

The quality of the sound "kit-ten" had at first a peculiarly wooden or mechanical character. Gradually, however, the mechanical quality began to give way, and at the same time his terms for the cats became much more various: "Kit-Tee!," or "Cattie," for example. There was also a loosening of the sound from the presence of the animals, and at the same time these sounds began to be used only for cats. The sound then finally does denote cats because it is the conventionally used term that he has acquired, and it is used appropriately for that verbal community. Instead of connotation following denotation, denotation follows connotative meanings according to the theorem deduced from the theory of symbolic transformations. Furthermore, the evidence indicates the correctness of that deduction, because the description shows that the child moves from his personalized and implicit terms to more depersonalized and explicit ones. From this point of view the child does have his own implicit and personal experience even before he has a language; language merely expands his original experience and is not something alien to it. The operant conditioning position suggests that the only experience of language that the child has is the explicit verbal behavior placed there by the pedagogy of operant conditioning. Once more Skinner has explained too little, for the richness of meaning attendant upon a developed language is lost according to that account, and, in addition, true denotation could not occur.

The development of the first true word has a longer course than the adherents of operant conditioning suggest. Furthermore, while operant conditioning principles are not able to account for the facts observed as the child develops and learns a language, the same facts are explainable through the theorem deduced from the postulates of the theory of symbolic transformations applied to the acquisition of language.

REFERENCES

Carini, L. "Symbolic transformations theory of learning," *Proceedings of the 75th Annual Convention of the American Psychological Association*, 1967, **2**, 5–6.

Carini, L. "The theory of symbolic transformations," *Acta Psychologica*, 1969, in press.

Carroll, J. B. *Language and Thought*. Englewood Cliffs, N.J.: Prentice-Hall, 1964.

Dewey, J. *Art as Experience*. New York: Minton, Balch, 1934.

Lenneberg, E. "The natural history of language," in F. Smith and G. A. Miller (Eds.), *The Genesis of Language: A Psycholinguistic Approach*. Cambridge, Mass.: MIT Press, 1966.

Skinner, B. F. *Verbal Behavior*. New York: Appleton-Century-Crofts, 1957.

Werner, H., and Kaplan, B. *Symbol Formation: An Organismic-Developmental Approach to Language and the Expression of Thought*. New York: Wiley, 1963.

10.5 Relation of Age to Children's Egocentric and Cooperative Communication

KERBY T. ALVY

A. INTRODUCTION

This study is concerned with two forms of verbal communication, egocentric and cooperative, which are assumed to be functions of the absence and presence of underlying cognitive abilities or operations. The study is based on certain assumptions from Piaget's developmental theory.

Piaget views the child's cognitive development as a continuous process of child–environment interactions which lead to the attainment and elaboration of cognitive operations. He theorizes that a child at an early stage of development will engage in a form of verbal communication that reflects his not having attained the one cognitive operation upon which all socialized speech is based (8, 9). That form of communication is egocentric communication, and the cognitive operation which it lacks is the ability to shift mental perspective in order to con-

sider the hearer's point of view. Egocentric communication may give the impression of being socialized, but it is not because the speaker fails to appreciate that what he sees, thinks, or understands may not be what the hearer sees, thinks, or understands. When the child develops this ability to shift mental perspective, when he becomes able to view a situation or issue from other than his own viewpoint, his verbal communications become potentially cooperative. That is, having attained this basic operation, it is now possible for the child to engage in an exchange of ideas and viewpoints. He now can appreciate that there are other perspectives and he can take these into consideration during a verbal exchange. From this point on, cooperative communication begins to dominate the child's verbal exchanges and egocentric communication diminishes.

The present study seeks to add to the empirical substantiation of these no-

Reprinted with slight abridgment from the *Journal of Genetic Psychology*, 1968, **112**, 275–286, with permission of the author and The Journal Press.

tions by creating a situation that requires one child to assume another's viewpoint in order to cooperate successfully over a commonly shared task. The situation consists of two same-aged children, who are separated by an opaque screen, each having before him identical sets of pictures. The task consists of one child (the listener) having to choose the picture which the other child (the speaker) is describing. The type of verbal exchange which the children engage in should reflect whether or not they have assumed each other's perspective. Specifically, if a speaker uses a description which could refer to two pictures, this ambiguous description would be classified as an egocentric communication because it fails to reflect the speaker's having considered that, from the listener's standpoint, such a description is insufficient to differentiate between the two pictures. This communication is egocentric regardless of whether or not the speaker has actually distinguished the pictures in terms of some differentiating characteristic. The point is that his description fails to reflect an awareness that what is sufficient subjective description may not be sufficient description for an objective presentation of differences, and such a lack of awareness is what one would expect from a child who has not attained the ability to take the hearer's view into consideration. Also, if the speaker persists in using this type of ambiguous description even after he is presented with evidence that his descriptions have been insufficient to allow the listener to differentiate the pictures (evidence derived from either the listener's requesting additional description or by being shown that the listener is choosing the wrong picture), this would be further evidence that he is unable to shift perspective in order to accommodate the listener's problems. Descriptions that refer to only one picture (unambiguous descriptions), or descriptions which could refer to more than one picture but which the speaker changes after receiving evidence that they are insufficient, would be classified as cooperative communications because they presumably reflect the speaker's having shifted perspective in consideration of the listener's problems.

The present study has certain features in common with other laboratory investigations which were explicitly concerned with egocentric and cooperative communications (1, 2, 3). But the present study differs in two important ways. (a) The specific task over which the children are to communicate has not been used previously. (b) The youngest age group in the present study (6 year olds) was not used previously in the other laboratory investigation that dealt with communications between pairs of same aged children. In that study (1), the youngest age group was an 8-year-old group. The other studies (2, 3) investigated communications between different aged children and adults, and communications between different aged children and hypothetical listeners. Thus, the present study differs from other studies in this area mainly in terms of the nature of the task employed and the age and pairings of the subjects utilized.

In addition to the above-mentioned reason, two other considerations support the use of a 6-year-old group. (a) A laboratory study by Glucksburg, Krauss, and Weisberg (5), which was not explicitly concerned with egocentric and cooperative communications, showed that children under five could not complete a task similar to the one used in the current experiment. (*b*) Piaget's field investigation of conversations between same aged children (*8*) led him to hypothesize that, when the content of the communication is of a concrete nature (visually immediate or commonly shared activities), the age at which cooperative communications appears is between 5 and 7.

Since the present study consists of same aged children conversing over a visually immediate and commonly shared activity, it would be expected from Piaget's hypothesis that the 6-year-old children will show some cooperative communications and that the older children will show increasing amounts of cooperative communications. The reverse would be true of egocentric communications: the 6 year olds will show the greatest amount of egocentric communication, and the older children will show decreasing amounts of egocentric communications. Therefore it is predicted that egocentric communications will decrease with age. Also, since egocentric communication implies not having shifted perspective, and since successful completion of the task requires having to shift perspective, it is also predicted that successful completion of the task will vary inversely with the amount of egocentric communications.

B. METHOD

1. Subjects

The Ss were 96 students from Schenectady, New York. There were 16 boys and 16 girls in each of three age groups, 6, 8, and 11. All Ss were assigned partners randomly; the boys were paired with

the same aged boys, the girls with the same aged girls. The mean age for the eight pairs of 6-year-old boys was 6:02 and for the eight pairs of 6-year-old girls, 6:06. The mean age for both the 8-year-old boys and girls was 8:07, and for both the 11-year-old boys and girls the mean age was 11:06.

2. Materials

Two identical sets of nine drawings from a children's book were used (see Figure 1). The drawings were traced from the book, photostatically copied, and pasted on 3" × 4" index cards. These drawings, showing the facial expression of various affective states, were chosen on the basis of the range and nuance of affective expression. The experimentation took place in a room usually used for speech therapy which contained a small table and three small chairs. A $2' \times 2\frac{1}{2}'$ opaque screen was used to separate the Ss during the testing procedure. A portable tape recorder was used to record each session.

3. Procedure

E spoke to the Ss before the experiment began. He told them that they were going to be called out of class two at a time to play a game.

a. Practice Matching Procedure. After a pair of Ss entered the experimental room, E told them they were going to play two games. The E spread a set of nine pictures on the table. E then told Ss that he was going to hand them a picture which was exactly the same as one of the pictures on the table. Ss were instructed to place the picture next to the one on the table that was exactly the

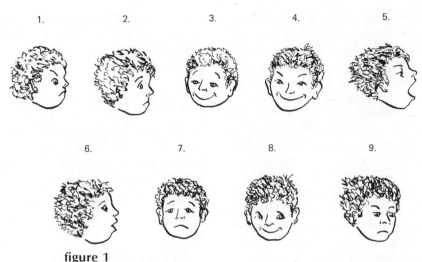

figure 1
Pictures used in practice matching procedure and testing procedure.

same. After S had matched one picture, E handed S another until all nine pictures were matched. After the first S had matched all nine pictures, the other S went through the same matching procedure. If in the course of the matching procedure either of the Ss mismatched a picture and subsequently noticed the mismatch, the S was allowed to correct the error. If the S did not notice the error, E brought it to his attention, allowing the S to correct the error.

b. Testing Procedure. Upon completion of the matching procedure, Ss were told they were going to play another game. They were seated at opposite ends of the small table. E placed a set of nine pictures in front of each S, spreading each set in two parallel rows of five and four pictures. Although each S had the same nine pictures, the pattern of the pictures differed for each S, since E shuffled each set before spreading them in the two rows. E emphasized that one S had the

same nine pictures in front of him as did the other S. E then placed the opaque screen between the Ss, saying that the screen was being used so that neither S could see each other's pictures. The Ss, who were three feet apart, could not see each other but they could see E. The arrangement was such that the Ss and the E formed the angles of a triangle. E turned on the tape recorder which was in full view of the Ss. E spoke to the S on his left (Speaker) and instructed the speaker to pick up one of the pictures (the speaker was allowed to pick up any picture and he was allowed to describe the set of pictures in any order he cared to). The speaker was told to look at the picture, ask himself "what is the boy feeling," then tell the other subject (Listener) what the boy was feeling. Both speaker and listener were informed that, from what the speaker told the listener, the listener had to pick out the picture to which the speaker referred. The listener was informed that, if from what the speaker told him he could not tell which picture was being referred to, he could ask the speaker for additional information to help him decide which picture was being discussed. If in the initial description of the picture the speaker referred to other characteristics than what the boy was experiencing emotionally, he was instructed to refer to affective characteristics. For example, if the speaker originally interpreted "feeling" as a tactile notion (saying, for example, "the boy is feeling a horse") he was told, "Not what the boy may be touching, you're to say what he is feeling." The listener was allowed to ask any type of question that would help him identify the picture being discussed. After the speaker described a picture and the listener made a choice from the pictures before him, they handed their respective pictures to E. E recorded whether a match had occurred and then showed both pictures to the Ss, indicating verbally as well as visually whether a match had occurred. E told Ss to continue playing the game. At least once during a trial, which was defined by an attempted matching of all nine pictures, the E reminded the listener that he could ask questions if he was not being told enough about a picture to allow him to be sure of his choice. After the first trial the Ss were told that they were going to play the same game again. E reshuffled the pictures, spread a set in front of each S, reminded the speaker to tell the listener "what the boy was feeling," and reminded the listener that he could ask questions. The same procedure was followed after the Ss had completed the second trial except that they were informed that this was to be the last time they would play the game. In all, each

pair of Ss went through three trials. At the end of the third trial E asked the Ss not to tell any of their fellow classmates about the games they had played.

C. RESULTS

Table 1 contains a summary of the percentages for the first four dependent measures per age group, sexes combined, and the z scores for comparisons of percentages.

1. Percentage of Total Matched Pictures

To see if the three age groups differed on overall performance on the experimental task, the percentages of total pictures matched on the three trials were computed. With the sexes combined, the percentage of matched pictures for the 6-year-old was 34 per cent, for the 8-year-old group it was 47 per cent, and for the 11-year-old group, 67 per cent. As shown in Table 1, the differences in percentages between the 6 and 8 year olds, and between the 8 and 11 year olds were significant at the .01 level.

In a breakdown according to sex, the percentage of matches for the 6-year-old boys was 37 per cent as compared to 32 per cent for the same aged girls; 50 per cent for the 8-year-old boys as compared to 42 per cent for the same aged girls; and 63 per cent for the 11-year-old boys as compared to 71 per cent for the same aged girls. With a z test statistic, it was shown that these differences between the percentages of the sexes at the same age level were not significant at the .05 level, indicating that sex was not a significant variable underlying the overall differences in performance.

table 1

Percentages for Dependent Measures Per Age Group, and z Scores for Comparisons of Percentages between 6 and 8 Year Olds and between 8 and 11 Year Olds (Sexes Combined)

	Age Group			z scores for Comparisons of Percentages	
Dependent Measure	6	8	11	6 *vs.* 8	8 *vs.* 11
1. Total matched pictures ($N = 432$)[a]	34	47	67	3.9*	6.0*
2. Total speakers using ambiguous descriptions ($N = 48$)[b]	98	77	52	3.1*	3.9*
3. Total speakers not changing ambiguous descriptions ($N = 32$)[c]	91	63	13	2.9*	4.6*
4. Total listeners asking for additional description ($N = 48$)[d]	21	61	73	4.4*	1.1 (n.s.)

*Significant at .01 level.
[a] $N = 432$: 16 (pairs) $\times$ 9 (pictures) $\times$ 3 (trials).
[b] $N = 48$: 16 (speakers) $\times$ 3 (trials).
[c] $N = 32$: 16 (speakers) $\times$ 2 (trials).
[d] $N = 48$: 16 (listeners) $\times$ 3 (trials).

2. Percentage of Total Speakers Using Ambiguous Descriptions

The second measure was designed to get at one of the assumed indicators of egocentric communications, the speaker's use of ambiguous descriptions, descriptions that reflect his not having shifted perspective in order to accommodate the listener's point of view. An ambiguous description was defined as the use of the exact same description to describe two or more pictures on any given trial. A speaker who used the description "feeling mean" to refer to two or more pictures on any given trial would be counted as a speaker who used ambiguous descriptions. The measure employed was the percentage of total speakers, trials combined, using ambiguous descriptions. The percentage of total 6-year-old speakers using ambiguous descriptions was 98 per cent; for the 8-year-old speakers it was 77 per

cent; and for the 11 year olds 52 per cent of the total speakers used ambiguous descriptions. Thus, an inverse relationship exists between the percentage of matched pictures and the percentage of total speakers using ambiguous descriptions. As shown in Table 1, the differences in percentages of total speakers using ambiguous descriptions for the 6 year olds *vs.* the 8 year olds and for the 8 year olds *vs.* the 11 year olds were significant at the .01 level.

3. Percentage of Total Speakers Persisting in the Use of Ambiguous Descriptions

The third measure was designed to get at the other assumed indicator of egocentric communications, the persistence in the use of ambiguous descriptions after receiving information that these descriptions were not leading to matches. Specifically, the percentage of total speakers using ambiguous descriptions on the second and third trial after these exact same ambiguous descriptions had not led to a match on the first and second trial were computed. For example, if the speaker's originally ambiguous description of picture No. 5 on the first trial did not bring about a match, and the speaker used the exact same description to refer to picture No. 5 on the second trial, he would be counted as a speaker who persisted in using ambiguous descriptions. Descriptions were considered ambiguous in terms of the criterion put forth in the last measure. The percentage of total speakers on the second and third trials persisting in the use of ambiguous descriptions was 91 per cent for the 6-year-old group, 63 per cent for the 8 year olds, and for the 11 year olds 13 per cent of the speakers persisted in using ambiguous descriptions. Thus, an inverse relationship exists between percentage of matched pictures and the percentage of total speakers persisting in the use of ambiguous descriptions. As shown in Table 1, the differences in percentages of total speakers persisting in ambiguous descriptions for the 6 year olds *vs.* the 8 year olds and for the 8 year olds *vs.* the 11 year olds were significant at the .01 level.

4. Percentage of Total Listeners Requesting Additional Description

In the previous measures listener behavior was implicitly tapped. An explicit measure of listener behavior is the percentage of total listeners, trials combined, who asked the speakers for additional description. The percentage of total 6-year-old listeners was 21 per cent, for the 8-year-old group it was 61 per cent, and for the 11 year olds it was 73 per cent. Thus, a positive relationship exists between percentage of matched pictures and percentage of listeners asking for additional description. As shown in Table 1, the difference in percentages of total listeners requesting additional description for the 6 year olds *vs.* the 8 year olds was significant at the .01 level, but the difference in percentages for the 8 year olds *vs.* the 11 year olds was not significant.

Although all were encouraged to ask for additional description, only four of the 16 six-year-old listeners asked questions. Of these four, two of them asked questions that were the mere repetitions of the descriptions offered by the speaker. For example, the speaker described a picture as "happy" and the listener asked, "Happy?" "Yes," was the speaker's reply and the listener went ahead and made his choice. Examples of the questions asked by the other two 6-year-old listeners were "Does he have his eyes closed?" "The one with the big mouth open?" and "Would I see the side of his face?" Their 6-year-old counterpart speakers often gave "incorrect" answers to these questions. For example, when one of the listeners asked, "Would I see the side of his face?" referring to a profile shot, the speaker said "Yes" even though the picture to which the speaker was addressing himself was one which showed a front view of the boy's face.

5. Percentage of Total Verbal Exchanges Consisting of More than One Question and One Answer

This measure was designed as a further index of the amount of verbal exchange between the speakers and listeners. The measure was the percentage of total verbal exchanges over any given picture that consisted of more than one question from the listener and more than one answer from the speaker. An example of this type of exchange, which was taken from an exchange between 11 year olds who were discussing picture No. 4, would be as follows: speaker describes the picture as "This boy looks happy"; listener asks, "Is he facing a certain direction?"; speaker answers, "Facing the front direction"; listener asks, "Are his eyes open or closed?"; speaker answers, "Closed, like squinting." The percentage of total 6 year olds engaging in this type of exchange was 20 per cent ($N = 26$), for the 8 year olds 39 per cent ($N = 107$), and for the 11 year olds 48 per cent ($N = 216$). Thus, a positive relationship exists between the percentage of matched pictures and the percentage of total verbal exchanges consisting of more than one question and one answer. With a z test statistic, the difference in percentages of this type of verbal exchange for the 6 year olds $vs.$ the 8 year olds was significant at the .05 level, but the difference in percentages for the 8 year olds $vs.$ the 11 year olds was not significant.

D. DISCUSSION

The results of the present study confirm the predictions that (a) egocentric communications decrease with age and that (b) successful completion of the experimental task, which was a function of the ability to shift mental perspective, varies inversely with the amount of egocentric communications. These results add laboratory confirmation to Piaget's notions concerning the development of coopera-

tive communications between the same aged children. They are also in general agreement with results from other studies (1, 2, 3, 5), which presented different aged children with tasks requiring the ability to shift perspective and which showed a diminution of egocentric communications with age.

Taken as a whole, the results of these studies show that the child's level of cognitive development, as indexed by age or, in the Cowan study (1), by performance on Piagetian tasks, has predictable effects on his interpersonal behaviors which are mediated by language. With the assumption that these results represent a fairly normative estimate of the nature of the interaction between cognitive level and communication skill for the age groups studied, future research devoted to the following three interrelated questions seems most in order. (a) What are the antecedents of the ability to shift perspective and consequently the antecedents of cooperative communication? A first step toward answering this question might be to explore the effects of different child-rearing practices on the rate of attainment of this ability. Would, for example, the various child-rearing practices noted by Harvey, Hunt, and Schroder (6) have differential effects on the rate of attainment? (b) What if anything can be done to accelerate the attainment of the ability to shift mental perspective and thereby accelerate the age at which the child's communications become cooperative? A first step here might be to explore the possibility that the already existing preschool training programs, "Head Start" and nursery school programs, accelerate the attainment of this cognitive ability. (c)

What can be done to improve the efficiency of the older child's cooperative communications? One study has already been devoted to this question. Using pairs of fifth-grade girls, Fry (4) was able to show that training in taking another's viewpoint did improve performance on subsequent tasks that required the ability to shift perspective. But this improvement only held up when the subsequent tasks were similar to the training tasks. The training tasks required succinct and nonredundant messages. When the subsequent task required detailed and extended messages, the trained and nontrained groups did not differ in performance. Though this study is disappointing in the sense that it failed to show that training leads to a more generalized improvement in communication skills, it still leaves unattended the possibility that other less situation-specific training procedures could produce a more generalized and flexible improvement in cooperative communications.

Since the study reported here was concerned with a construct (cognitive shifts of mental perspective) that is inferred from external verbal behavior, only one measure of the children's nonverbal behavior was taken (pictures matched). But other nonverbal behaviors observed by the experimenter suggest that if additional measures are employed the same experimental procedure can yield data that are relevant to other constructs which are not necessarily indicated through external verbal behavior. The following two observations led to this consideration. (a) On the first picture handed to the children during the practice matching procedure, many of them

looked at the picture, then looked down at the nine pictures on the table and quickly matched the picture in their hand with the first one on the table that approximated it. They did not scan the entire set of pictures before making a choice. This sort of behavior was most prevalent with the 6 year olds. (b) During the testing procedure, many of the speakers appeared to be concerned with one picture at a time and not with the task as a whole. These speakers rarely scanned the set of pictures before choosing one to describe. They usually picked up the first picture that came into their field of vision. Once having picked up this picture, they addressed themselves solely to it. It seemed, for all practical purposes, that once they focused on this picture the other pictures no longer existed. Even when they were asked questions which referred to the other pictures, their focus remained on the picture in hand. Again, this sort of behavior was most prominent among the 6 year olds. Indeed, it seemed as if all the 6-year-old speakers oriented themselves toward the task in this way. Two constructs to which these observations are definitely relevant are (a) an impulsive as opposed to an analytic or reflective conceptual style (7) which is indicated by relatively quick responses to stimulus configurations, and (b) Piaget's construct of cognitive egocentrism which is indicated, among other ways, by preferential visual focusing on one or some aspects of a stimulus configuration to the exclusion of the other aspects. Thus, if measures of reaction time and eye movements are taken, the present experimental procedure should yield data relevant to constructs which are not necessarily inferred from external verbal behavior.

E. SUMMARY

This paper was concerned with two forms of verbal communication, egocentric and cooperative, which, according to Piaget, are differentiated in terms of the absence and presence of a specific underlying cognitive operation, the ability to shift mental perspective in order to consider the hearer's point of view. Piaget hypothesizes that egocentric communication decreases and cooperative communication increases with age. The following study, which was designed to further the empirical exploration of these notions within a developmental context, was reported.

Sixteen pairs of 6, 8, and 11 year olds were tested on a verbal communication task where success was assumed to be a function of the ability to take each other's viewpoint. The members of a pair were separated by an opaque screen. Each had before him a set of nine pictures of boys expressing various affective states. The object was for the listener to select the picture being described by the speaker. Each pair was given three trials (a trial consisted of a run-through of all nine pictures). After each individual selection, E held up the pictures so that both children could see whether a match had occurred.

Comparisons of the percentages of matched pictures between 6 and 8, and 8 and 11 year olds resulted in z scores significant beyond the .01 level. Analysis of protocols revealed two major sources

underlying the differences among the groups: decreases in egocentric communications and increases in verbal exchange as a function of age.

These results were interpreted to add laboratory confirmation to Piaget's notions concerning the development of cooperative communications between same aged children, and they were related to results from other studies in the same area. Suggestions for future research concerned with the development of the child's interpersonal verbal behaviors as well as suggestions for using the current experimental procedures to explore constructs which are not inferred from verbal behavior (impulsive conceptual style and cognitive egocentrism) were made.

REFERENCES

1. Cowan, P. A. "Cognitive egocentrism and social interaction," *Amer. Psychol.,* 1966, **21** (7), 623 (Abstract).

2. Feffer, M. H., and Gourevitch, V. "Cognitive aspects of role-taking in children," *J. Personal.,* 1960, **28,** 383–396.

3. Flavell, J. H. "Role-taking and communication skills in children," *Young Child.,* 1966, **21** (3), 164–177.

4. Fry, C. L. The effects of training in communication and role perception on the communicative abilities of children. Unpublished Doctoral dissertation, University of Rochester, Rochester, New York, 1961.

5. Glucksburg, S., Krauss, R. M., and Weisberg, R. "Referential communication in nursery school children," *J. Exper. Child Psychol.,* 1966, **3** (4), 333–342.

6. Harvey, O. J., Hunt, D. E., and Schroder, H. M. *Conceptual Systems and Personality Organization.* New York: Wiley, 1961.

7. Kagan, J., Rosman, B. L., Day, D., Albert, J., and Phelps, W. "Information processing in the child: Significance of analytic attitudes," *Psychol. Monog.*, 1964, **78** (1), Whole No. 578.

8. Piaget, J. *The Language and Thought of the Child.* New York: Harcourt, Brace, 1926.

9. ———. *Comments on Vygotsky's Critical Remarks.* Cambridge, Mass.: M.I.T. Press, 1962.

10.6 Group Problem Solving, Task Divisibility, and Prior Social Organization

ARMAND D. VINE AND JAMES H. DAVIS

For some time, the notion was rather widespread that the greater resources and stimulation afforded by the small group fostered a general problem-solving superiority over the isolated individual. Though not obvious, the group-individual question has turned out to be fairly complicated. Lorge and Solomon (1955) provided an important insight when they, along with others (e.g., Marquart, 1955; Taylor, 1954), questioned the definition of the events in the sample space implied by the Shaw (1932) experiment. The resulting Lorge-Solomon model asserts that grouping neither helps nor hinders solution; a group will solve if it contains at least one solver.

The present experiment was another attempt to find where, if ever, along the work continuum the advantage passes to groups. For example, it is possible that the Davis-Restle (1963) and Olson-Davis (1964) experiments did not permit sufficient division of labor after all; group resources were not used to full potential because the advantages of organized effort beyond general participation were simply not sufficiently self-evident to foster the necessary social investment. Thus, it may be desirable to choose a task allowing a truly substantial division of effort. In the same vein, a work structure imposed upon a face-to-face group might yield the advantage of organization without the suppression of other subtle facets of grouping such as may have taken place in the network situation reported by Davis and Hornseth (in press). In other words, even a rough face-to-face a priori organization might permit short-term groups to turn directly to the business of collective problem solving.

Reprinted from the *Proceedings of the 76th Annual Convention of the American Psychological Association*, 1968, **3**, 411–412, with permission of the authors and the American Psychological Association, Inc.

METHOD

Subjects

Volunteers from introductory psychology classes at Miami University were randomly assigned to the Structured, Unstructured, and Individual conditions. The first two conditions contained 26 four-person, same-sex groups and the latter 26 individuals working alone; all conditions contained equal numbers of males and females.

Apparatus

The three-dimensional problem consisted of three subpuzzles or sets of pieces; the three subpuzzles (hereafter called parts) could be assembled into one large block. Each part was a block of wood approximately $4 \times 4 \times 12$ inches, cut in a wavering line along two dimensions yielding 12 pieces.

The Ss, seated at a table, were observed by E through a one-way mirror. An intercom permitted conversation between E and Ss. The Ss used four toggle switches to signal work progress. Progress signals and interaction data were recorded on an Esterline-Angus event recorder. The E recorded the frequency and duration of utterances by each group member.

Unstructured Condition. Each group was informed that the three subpuzzles could be put together in such a way as eventually to compose a block. Instructions contained only the bare outline of the problem and an encouragement for collective effort.

Structured Condition. Each of three members was designated, at random, to assume responsibility for one of the parts. The fourth member was designated "leader" and was charged with assisting other members or directing effort as he saw fit; he alone could assemble the three parts into the final block. The other members were required to work only at their assigned parts; they could not abandon their subtask in order to work on another's problem.

Individual Condition. Individuals received instructions similar to unstructured groups.

RESULTS

Task

Correctness and solution latency were calculated for each individual subject and each group. All groups solved the problem, but only eight individuals did so. It was not reasonable to arrive at a wrong but acceptable answer, and thus the wrong solutions among individual Ss actually represent *failures to answer* before the alloted time expired. For this reason, mean latencies in just the group conditions were compared in a 2×2 analysis of variance, with sex included as the second factor. There was no significant difference in mean solution time between Structured and Unstructured groups, but the female groups were found on the average to take a significantly longer time to solve than did male groups ($F = 7.99$, $df = 1/48$, $p < .01$). Sex did not interact significantly with structuring.

Grouping efficiency was explored, as in the past, by establishing base-line predictions which took account of the group's potential resources. The Lorge-Solomon Model A, which assumes neither beneficial nor detrimental effects from social interaction, was designed to predict group performance on problems which consist of a single logical step. While the task at hand was clearly not composed of a single event, it was assumed to be so for the purpose of the first analysis. Model B, on the other hand, applies to problems of a multi-phase nature, and Model A is assumed to apply at each part or subproblem. A special case of Model B that considers all parts to be equally probable was used to predict group base-line performance. The discrepancies between group performance and base-line predictions are obvious and large, thereby providing definite evidence for group faciliation of problem solving.

DISCUSSION

Rather surprisingly, the plausible and popular notion that organization per se should benefit performance found no support. Role assignments did "take" in an immediate sense, for the discrepancies in member participation rates were much greater among the Structured than the Unstructured groups. Thus, as suggested elsewhere (Davis and Hornseth, in press), group structure uncorrelated with individual abilities may simply not be very helpful, even though it is sharply defined and apparently functioning.

Of substantially more importance was the finding that grouping, whether Structured or Unstructured, provided a net enhancement of problem solving. It is not uncommon to find that, in direct comparison, a significantly higher proportion of groups solve problems than do individuals. However, this study pro-

vided the first instance, known to us, in which group performance exceeded simple group resources as summarized by models such as those of Lorge and Solomon. Efficient organization of effort (simultaneous action by two or more persons) is, perhaps, the most straightforward explanation. However, recall that Olson and Davis (1964) used a divisible task amenable to organizational facilitation and obtained contrary results (i.e., inhibition of problem solving by groups). Furthermore, when sufficient allowance was made for the pooling of partial solutions (Lorge-Solomon Model B), as properly implied by the divisibility of the problem into three subproblems, group performance was *still* elevated. Needless to say, our inability to organize (structure) groups effectively beforehand hardly increases the appeal of organization as the facilitation mechanism. In particular, observe that the major discrepancy between group data and base lines was due to the fact that the first individual solution occurred so much later than the first group solution. Approximately 75% of all groups had solved before the fastest individual did so.

All in all, the early appearance of group solutions must surely take place in the face of delays due to members becoming acquainted, arranging materials, and generally preparing for work. Yet, group solutions appear quickly relative to individual work. The dilemma resulting from the lack of a gradual group superiority may be resolved by the plausible notion that solution enhancement results from social interaction itself rather than the organized collocation of part problems.

Why should the present experiment offer evidence of that grouping advantage so often proposed, but so rarely if ever found with carefully controlled experiments using the pooling of simple resources arguments such as those advanced by Taylor (1954), Lorge and Solomon (1955), and Restle and Davis (1962) among others? Since no exceptional interpersonal observations of a direct empirical nature are readily at hand, the answer would seem to rest heavily upon task considerations. Recall that the wiggley block problem was chosen because it appeared to require among other things an almost overwhelming effort.

In addition to familiar eureka qualities, the problem initially required the collection of a great deal of information—mainly in the form of attempted fits of puzzle pieces. However, it is with just such a problem that groups would seem, prima facie, to afford the *least* advantage; the coordination of fittings should offer a study in confusion. (Mintz, 1951, has described the kind of disorder to be expected from the social coordination of a physically delicate task.) Surely very little helpful information could be communicated easily about the way curved sticks fit together—at least as compared to arithmetic problems (Olson and Davis, 1964). It would appear that this very reduction of the need for interpersonal verbal communication may have eliminated from consideration many of the liabilities of group problem solution proposed by Maier (1967).

Group members simply may not have communicated with each other as much as do those *S*s working on word puzzles, social decision tasks, etc. The *relative* absence of distracting discussion, either among others or involving oneself, may have permitted task concentration approximating the isolation that some investigators have proposed as offering the better route to efficient group problem-solving performance (e.g., Davis and Restle, 1963). However, reassurance when bored, social expectation surrounding one's effort, etc., may have provided just the right blend to facilitate overall performance in the end.

The faster average problem solving by male groups appears also to reflect a social rather than an intellectual work history phenomenon. Bond and Vinacke (1961) have suggested that female groups tend to concern themselves with the avoidance of potentially disrupting social activity, while male groups tend first to focus upon how the task can best be attacked, dealing with social amenities secondarily.

Although alternative methods are obviously available, the most profitable approach would seem, at present, to be something like that followed in the present investigation, viz., the construction of models predicting definite group products by assuming certain distinct task-social processes. Through the use of such normative or base-line theories, descriptive theory may be approached by successive approximation.

REFERENCES

Bond, J. R., and Vinacke, W. E. "Coalitions in mixed sex triads," *Sociometry*, 1961, **24**, 61–75.

Davis, J. H., and Hornseth, J. P. "Discussion patterns and word problems," *Sociometry*, 1968, in press.

Davis, J. H., and Restle, F. "The analysis

of problems and prediction of group problem solving," *Journal of Abnormal and Social Psychology,* 1963, **66,** 103–116.

Lorge, I., and Solomon, H. "Two models of group behavior in the solution of eureka-type problems," *Psychometrika,* 1955, **20,** 139–148.

Maier, N. R. F. "Assets and liabilities in group problem solving: The need for an integrative function," *Psychological Review,* 1967, **74,** 239–249.

Marquart, D. I. "Group problem solving," *Journal of Social Psychology,* 1955, **41,** 103–113.

Mintz, A. "Nonadaptive group behavior," *Journal of Abnormal and Social Psychology,* 1951, **46,** 150–159.

Olson, P., and Davis, J. H. "Divisible tasks and pooling performance in groups," *Psychological Reports,* 1964, **15,** 511–517.

Restle, F., and Davis, J. H. "Problem solving by individuals and groups," *Psychological Review,* 1962, **69,** 520–536.

Shaw, M. E. "Comparison of individuals and small groups in the rational solution of complex problems," *American Journal of Psychology,* 1932, **44,** 491–504.

Taylor, D. W. "Problem solving by groups," in *Proceedings of the XIV International Congress of Psychology, 1954.* Amsterdam: North Holland Publishing, 1954.

10.7 A Comparative Study of Intercultural Insight and Empathy

HENRY CLAY LINDGREN AND JOSEPH MARRASH

A. INTRODUCTION

Fundamental to success in transactions of all types is the ability to understand and predict the behavior of others. The problems involved in such understanding and prediction are eased considerably when participants in a transaction are members of the same culture who not only share a common language, but also share implicit values, attitudes, and social perceptions. Members of the same culture are also likely to be familiar with the behavioral styles that prevail in, or are characteristic of, their culture, and this knowledge helps reduce the proportion of false predictions, thus making the transactional process more efficient. Within cultural boundaries, there is usually enough similarity between autostereotype (the image one has of oneself) and heterostereotype (the image one has of others) to make communication and mutual understanding possible, and most people learn enough information about the prevailing interpersonal differences among others in their culture in order to construct a variety of heterostereotypes that can be used appropriately in different situations.

Transactions among persons and groups from different cultures do not have these initial advantages of shared similarity and of familiarity. Under such circumstances, information needed to construct new sets of heterostereotypes can be acquired directly through interpersonal contact, or indirectly through hearsay and the mass media of communication. In fact, heterostereotypes acquired indirectly may sometimes be a better basis for intercultural insight than more direct exposure to the behavior of the other, as Gough (5) found in an experiment in which American students attempted to guess the questionnaire responses of Italian subjects before and after they had seen the subjects' per-

Reprinted with slight abridgment from the *Journal of Social Psychology*, 1970, **80**, 135–141, with permission of the authors and The Journal Press.

formance in filmed interviews. There is, of course, a great deal of variation among individuals and groups in the extent to which exposure to information about other cultures is sought and assimilated, and there is also considerable variation with respect to the accuracy of the heterostereotypes into which this information is organized.

The present study addresses itself to the question of variations in heterostereotype accuracy. Specifically, it is concerned with differences in the amount of intercultural insight displayed by certain ethnic groups in the Middle East and the degree to which the groups are reputed to be "oriented to the West." Presumably, the more Western the orientation of a group, the more likely its members are to seek out and expose themselves to information about the peoples of the West.

A Western-oriented group would therefore attempt to develop fairly accurate heterostereotypes of typical members of Western cultures, whereas a group that was not so oriented would be less interested in acquiring information, or would avoid doing so, and as a result would make use of heterostereotypes that would be less valid.

A personality survey conducted by Jamison and Comrey (7) provided the raw material that made the present investigation possible. Jamison and Comrey administered the Comrey Personality Scale to samples of American and British subjects. Responses to the scales were factor analyzed, and differences between the two groups on 52 personality dimensions were computed. The computation of t ratios showed that the two groups differed significantly on a number of these dimensions. Although the differences between the two groups were of the type that many observers have noted in an impressionistic way, the fact that the traits were measured and differences analyzed statistically made the data usable for other types of cross-cultural research, such as the present study.

The traits identified by Jamison and Comrey served as the basis for a 24-item forced-choice questionnaire, constructed by the senior author of this study. Each item consisted of a pair of descriptive statements based on the above-mentioned personality dimensions. One statement in each pair was appropriate to an American dimension, and the other to a British dimension. For example, "Lacks social poise or social presence" was paired with "Tendency to be or feel inadequate." Jamison and Comrey found that Americans tended to score higher than British on the first-named trait, the t ratio of the difference between the two samples being 3.4; whereas British rated higher on the second trait, the t ratio being 6.4. Similarly, "Likes order" (British, t ratio 7.2) was paired with "Submissive, gives in" (American, t ratio 6.4). The 24 pairs of traits constituted the Intercultural Insight Questionnaire, hereafter referred to as ICIQ.

The rationale underlying the questionnaire is that subjects interested in and familiar with British and American people would be more successful in determining which one of each pair of traits is characteristically British and which is characteristically American than subjects less well acquainted with the two peoples and cultures.

The following hypotheses were tested in the present study:

(a) Subjects representing various

ethnic groups will show differences in scores on the ICIQ in terms of the extent to which they are "Western-oriented": that is, in terms of the extent to which they are interested in and favorably disposed to values and mores characteristic of Northern Europe and America. In the Middle East, Armenians are noted especially for Western orientation, and Christian Arabs are reputed to be more favorably oriented to the West than Moslem Arabs. It was therefore predicted that Armenians would score higher on the ICIQ than Christian Arabs, who in turn would be expected to score higher than Moslem Arabs.

(b) Americans will score higher on the ICIQ than members of other cultural groups because (1) as members of one of the cultures concerned they should be better able to recognize traits that are "theirs" and (2) the need to distinguish between one's own cultural group and other cultural groups who share the same language is likely to be stronger than the need that nonspeakers of the language have to make such a distinction. (The same hypothesis could be made with respect to British subjects, but an insufficient number were available for purpose of study.)

(c) Females will score higher than males. From infancy onward girls tend to show a higher degree of social interest than boys and tend to be more interested in social success. The fact that girls get better school marks than boys of the same level of measured achievement may be attributed in part to their greater interest in and mastery of social skills (4). It is quite likely that empathic ability plays an important part in these successes, although research with measures of empathy has shown only a slight superiority for women (2, 8). In any event, the greater interest females show with respect to social relations would suggest that they might do better in a task involving intercultural insight than males would.

(d) Scores on the ICIQ will be positively correlated with scores on a measure of empathy. The assumption here is that the individual who is able, figuratively, to put himself "in the shoes of another" is also the one who will be able to display the intercultural insight needed to identify personality traits associated with one national group or another. Some findings suggesting a possible relationship between intercultural insight and empathy were reported in a study conducted by Aamiry (1), who noted a correlation of .33 between the ICIQ and Elms' Empathic Fantasy Scale (3) for 30 female Jordanian university students. However, the relationship fell just short of the five percent level of confidence.

B. METHOD

Instruments used were the ICIQ and Elms' Empathic Fantasy scale or EFS (3), a set of 10 statements designed to measure tendencies to imagine oneself as a different person, as taking the other person's viewpoint in an argument, and the like, but not merely on grounds of sympathy for the other. To these 10 statements the present researchers added four additional ones, in an attempt to enhance the reliability of the test. The 14 items were interspersed with 10 filler items in order to obscure the intent of the questionnaire and counteract response bias.

The two questionnaires were administered to 317 secondary students in Lebanon: 87 Armenians (39 male, 48 female), 69 Arab Christians (47 male, 22 female), 113 Arab Moslems (63 male, 50 female), and 48 Americans (26 male, 22 female). Apart from a few exceptions, the age range of the samples was 16 to 18 years. All groups were reported by their instructors to be competent enough in English to understand the items on the two tests. However, subjects were encouraged to ask the meaning of any word in the questionnaires that they did not understand. In taking the ICIQ, subjects were asked to identify the description in each pair that was more typically American than British.

C. RESULTS

An analysis of variance of ICIQ scores showed that differences among the four ethnic groups were significant at the .01 level of confidence. (F value of 15.26, with 3 degrees of freedom). Further analysis showed that Arab Moslems ($\overline{X} = 12.4$) did not differ significantly from Arab Christians ($\overline{X} = 12.8$), but that Armenians ($\overline{X} = 14.0$) differed from Americans ($\overline{X} = 15.5$) and Arab Christians at the .01 level of confidence ($t = 2.67$ and 2.75), and from Arab Moslems at the .001 level ($t = 4.18$). American subjects differed from Christian and Moslem Arab groups at the .001 level of confidence ($t = 4.91$ and 6.02). Although female subjects tended to score higher than males, the difference was significant only at the .10 level ($F = 3.68$, with 1 degree of freedom). The ethnic-sex interaction was not significant. Pearson product moment correlations between the ICIQ and

the EFS Scale were an insignificant $-.03$. The corrected split-half reliabilities of the expanded EFS and the ICIQ were .52 and .49 respectively.

D. DISCUSSION

The results support the first hypothesis to the extent that the Armenians, who are reputed to be the most Western-oriented of the Middle East group, score significantly higher on the ICIQ than do either of the Arab groups. Although the Christian Arabs do better than the Moslems, as predicted, the differences were not significant. Furthermore, the mean scores of the two Arab groups are very close to chance.

The second hypothesis is strongly supported by the results. The higher scores made by the American subjects indicate that the ICIQ does have a moderate degree of validity as a measure of culturally differentiated characteristics in the sense that American subjects can discriminate between personality dimensions that are more typically American and those that are more typically British.

The third hypothesis receives only weak support, as is characteristic of comparative studies of empathy among the sexes. However, Hassani and Kadi (6) found, when they administered the ICIQ to 120 English-speaking non-American and non-British secondary school and university students in Lebanon, that the mean score of females on the ICIQ was 14.4, whereas that for males was 12.6, a difference that was significant at the .01 level. Any explanation of the differences between the findings of this study and theirs must be speculative. It might be assumed that the presence in their sample of better educated students (who would be more familiar with English and would have more exposure to appropriate information) might make some difference, if it were not for the fact that the researchers were unable to find any significant difference in ICIQ scores between subjects at the two educational levels.

The fourth hypothesis received no support from the findings. It may be that the interpersonal empathy measured by the EFS is unrelated to cultural insight.

A further examination of Aamiry's (1) findings is in order. She obtained a test-retest reliability of .62 for the original 10 items of the EFS, in contrast to .52 obtained by the present authors for the expanded 14-item form. She also obtained a test-retest reliability of .65 for the ICIQ, in contrast to the .49 obtained in the present study. An explanation of these differences, which may also shed some light on the failure of the present findings to support the fourth hypothesis, is that the graduate students who administered the questionnaires in the present study encountered a number of problems in getting subjects to participate at an optimal level. Questionnaires and objective tests of any type are relatively unknown to the average Middle East student, and he is likely to regard them with some degree of suspicion and apprehensiveness. The forced-choice format of the ICIQ created additional problems. A number of subjects refused to respond to items for which they said they had insufficient information and, in effect, rejected the task. One can only speculate as to the percentage that went

through the motions of cooperating, but either did not understand the nature of the task or did not take it seriously. Aamiry, on the other hand, administered her questionnaires individually to a select group of university students. Her group was undoubtedly more competent in English than were the non-American secondary students in the present study. Either factor—motivation or language competence—would affect the reliability of the questionnaires and could account for the differences in results. The possibility that interpersonal empathy and intercultural insight are positively related is therefore still a viable one, even though the present study does not lend it any support.

In general, the present study provides encouragement for the use of cross-cultural research of questionnaires composed of items found to be associated with the behavioral styles of different cultures. The fact that results were not consistent with reputed differences between Christian and Moslem Arabs may be due to lack of precision in the instrument or to problems in subject motivation, as noted above. On the other hand, it may also be that Christian-Moslem differences in intercultural insight, as far as these groups of subjects were concerned, were actually quite minimal. Although Christian Arabs are generally more likely to study English than Moslem Arabs, and this may indicate a high degree of Western orientation, the fact that these Moslem students had in fact learned English suggests that the differences between the two groups tested were considerably less than would be obtained from a random sample of Arab

Christian and Moslem populations, if it is assumed that suitable tests were available in Arabic to test this difference.

E. SUMMARY

An intercultural insight questionnaire (ICIQ) consisting of 24 pairs of personality descriptions found to be characteristic of Americans and British was administered to American, Armenian, Arab Christian, and Arab Moslem secondary students in Lebanon. Subjects were asked to indicate the trait in each pair that was more characteristic of Americans. Americans scored significantly higher than the other groups, and Armenians scored significantly higher than Arab Christians, and Arab Moslems. Differences between Armenians and Arabs were consistent with the hypothesis that reputed orientation to the Western world (i.e., Northern Europe and America) would be related to intercultural insight as indicated by the ability to discriminate American from British characteristics; however, differences between Arab Christians and Moslems were insignificant and mean scores for these two groups were close to chance. Females scored higher on intercultural empathy than males, but the difference was significant only at the .10 level. Another study (6) that included university, as well as secondary, students in the sample, however, found a significant difference in favor of females. No relationship was found between scores made on the ICIQ and a test of empathy, although a previous exploratory study had found indications that intercultural insight and empathy might be positively related.

REFERENCES

1. Aamiry, A. Relationship between two scales of empathy. Unpublished study, American University of Beirut, Lebanon, 1969.

2. Dymond, R. "Personality and empathy," *J. Consult. Psychol.*, 1950, **14**, 343–350.

3. Elms, A. C. "Influence of fantasy ability on attitude change through role playing," *J. Personal and Soc. Psychol.*, 1966, **4**, 36–43.

4. Garai, J. E., and Scheinfeld, A. "Sex differences in mental and behavioral traits," *Genet. Psychol. Monog.*, 1968, **77**, 169–299.

5. Gough, H. An exploratory cross-cultural study of interpersonal perception. Unpublished paper delivered at a Symposium on Interpersonal Perception, American Psychological Association Convention, San Francisco, California, 1968.

6. Hassani, S., and Kadi, Z. Empathy as a function of sex and education. Unpublished study, American University of Beirut, Lebanon, 1969.

7. Jamison, K., and Comrey, A. L. "Cross-cultural study of British and American personality factors," *Proc., 76th Ann. APA Convention*, 1968, **3**, 167–168.

8. Taft, R. "The ability to judge people," *Psychol. Bull.*, 1955, **52**, 1–24.

SECTION 11

PSYCHOLOGY IN ORGANIZATIONS AND INDUSTRY

Work situations, like other social situations that continue over a period of time, develop certain characteristic patterns that are the result of the kind of expectations that participants have for their job, as well as for other participants. In work situations, the expectations that supervisors and workers have for each other are particularly crucial. The greater power possessed by supervisors means that they have a considerable control over the kind of psychological climate that prevails in the organization. Frank Friedlander and Stuart Greenberg, of Case Western Reserve University, are concerned with the relationship between supervisory attitudes and the performance of what are termed the "hard-core unemployed workers" (HCU)—workers who are largely from minority groups and who have the greatest difficulty in finding and keeping jobs. Friedlander and Greenberg report that the HCU workers and their supervisors have different opinions about the extent to which the psychological climate at work is supportive of and encouraging to the HCU worker, and that those HCU workers who viewed the climate positively were themselves viewed more positively by supervisors and fellow workers. One interesting finding was a *negative* relationship between an HCU worker's reliability (as reflected by promptness in coming to work and low absence record) and the number of weeks he remained employed. In other words, those HCU workers who had the best attendance records were the ones who did not remain employed. The authors suggest that tardiness and absenteeism may be ways of coping with psychological stresses on the job. The HCU worker who does not use these mechanisms evidently finds the situation intolerable and quits.

In the paper by Anastasi and Schaefer included in Section 7 we noted that certain items of a biographical nature were significantly correlated with creativity, and in Section 8 a paper by Barthell and Holmes reported a negative relationship between the level of social activity in high school and later tendencies toward schizophrenia. The article by Heckman, Banas, Lazenby, and Moore in the present section also attempts to identify biographical data that are predictive of future behavior, the criterion in this instance being managerial success. Contrary to popular belief, academic success as reflected by high school and college grades was positively correlated with success.

419

Other relevant and positively correlated variables were leadership, socioeconomic background, parental influence, academic habits, and financial independence.

The paper by Karlene H. Roberts of Stanford University, describes the way in which leadership style changes from the top to the bottom status levels in a large business firm. Attitudes and behavior were for the most part democratic among individuals at the uppermost levels and were most authoritarian among those at the bottom, although some individuals at all levels showed behavior inconsistent with the norms for their status group.

The article by K. D. Kryter of the Stanford Research Institute deals with the problem of aircraft noise. The paper is included here as example of the work of engineering psychologists, a group occupied with the task of adapting machines to man's requirements and need.

The final example of applied psychology to be included in this section consists of a study by George Horsley Smith and Rayme Engel of the effect of what perception psychologists term "background cues" on the judgment of subjects. When the experimenters showed subjects a picture of an automobile with or without the presence of an additional picture of a scantily clad girl, those who were shown the combination picture tended to rate the automobile as more exciting, less safe, and more expensive than did subjects who were shown the automobile alone. An interesting secondary finding is that subjects in the experimental group seemed unaware that their judgment was affected by the presence of the girl's picture.

11.1 Work Climate as Related to the Performance and Retention of Hard-Core Unemployed Workers

FRANK FRIEDLANDER AND STUART GREENBURG

A great deal of emphasis is currently placed upon training the hard-core unemployed (HCU) by providing them with adaptive skills. Adaptive skills are defined as "those which concern the person's relationship to himself and his environment [Brenner, 1968]." This focus proceeds partially on the assumption that training the man to adapt to his job environment is a sufficient method. It places less emphasis upon the exploration of job situational variables, such as the degree to which the job climate in which the HCU is placed is conducive to high work performance, or allows him to implement his adaptive skills. It is possible, for example, that beyond a certain point it is more efficient to attempt to effect change in the job climate rather than to train the HCU to adapt to this climate. This study attempts to explore the climate in which HCU workers are placed and the degree to which this climate is conducive to

performance and retention on the job.

The specific purposes of the research were (a) to compare perceptions by the HCU and his supervisor of the work climate in which the HCU is placed, and (b) to explore the relationships between the performance of the HCU and the nature of his work climate. Further data are also provided on the interrelationship of various criteria of the HCU's work performance. Thus, the primary question to which this study was directed is: In what way and to what extent does job climate effect the performance of the HCU worker?

The sample for this research was composed of 24 matched pairs of the HCU and his respective supervisor in a variety of organizations. The sample was drawn from a larger group (used in a broader longitudinal study) which had the following demographic characteristics: 84% Negro, 7% Puerto Rican,

Reprinted from the *Proceedings of the 77th Annual Convention of the American Psychological Association,* 1969, **4,** 607–608, with permission of the authors and the American Psychological Association, Inc.

7% white; average education was completion of 10th grade; average duration of unemployment prior to job placement was 15 wk.; 23% had prior police records (exclusive of traffic and minor violations); 25% were married; and 70% had no dependents.

JOB CLIMATE

Climate is conceptualized as an interaction of personal factors (personality, needs, values, etc.) and organizational properties (structure, supervisory practices, objectives, etc.). This relationship emphasizes the role of *perception* of organizational properties as an intervening variable (Forehand and von Gilmer, 1964). Central importance is assigned to organizational characteristics only as they are perceived by the employee. Thus, variables such as structure and supervisory practices interact with personality to produce perceptions, and it is only through these perceptions that the relationship between the two may be understood (Likert, 1961).

Of particular concern in this study was the perception by the HCU of the degree to which his work climate was supportive. Preliminary interviews with HCUs indicated that one of the components of the organization climate most relevant to the HCU's retention and performance was the degree to which he perceived the organization climate as supportive. Specifically three aspects of a supportive climate seemed most salient: (*a*) new worker treatment, (*b*) support from peer workers, and (*c*) support from his supervisor.

The specific items which comprised each of the three climate measures are listed below. Response options for each item were on a 5-point multiple choice Likert scale.

1. How are new workers at your plant generally treated? (New Worker Treatment)

> They are usually made to prove themselves (−)
> They are usually given more breaks than others (+)
> They are usually treated like all the others (+)
> They are usually given a hard time (−)

2. What's it like to work where I work? (Support from Peers)

> Each guy has to pretty much take care of himself (−)
> Other workers give you a hand and help you if you don't know how to do something (+)
> Almost everybody gets along well with everybody else (+)
> Most of the workers are hard to get close to (−)
> It's not so smart to make buddies here because people tend to take advantage of you (−)

3. What's it like to work where I work? (Support from Supervisor)

> To get ahead, you have to "brown nose" (−)
> Supervisors would just as soon get rid of you rather than teach you or help you on a job (−)

JOB PERFORMANCE

Three different criteria of the HCU's job performance were obtained: job retention, work effectiveness and work behavior. Job retention was considered relevant since one of the major problems claimed in regard to the employment of the HCU is an unusually short duration on the job. The work-effectiveness criterion was composed of supervisory ratings of four characteristics, each of which was measured by two items: competence (performs his job competently and follows instructions), congeniality (is friendly and agreeable, effort (tries to do his best and works carefully), reliability (shows up each work day, shows up on time). The HCU's supervisor was given the following instructions in this rating: "Compared to other employees doing the same or similar work (or at a similar skill level), how would you rate this employee on each of the following?" The multiple choice format ranged in equal percentile intervals from "top 20%" to "bottom 20%."

The work-behavior criterion was designed to determine the supervisor's general description of the HCU as a person in the work situation. The work behavior criterion was composed of three component characteristics of the HCU as (a) smart (he knows what's going on in life, he does whatever he does well, he knows how to do many things, he is smart); (b) friendly (he is a good friend to people, he is a friendly person); (c) conscientious (he wants to do his best, he does a careful job, he wants to do a good job). A 5-point multiple choice Likert-type scale followed each of these items.

RESULTS

In Table 1, the dramatic differences between the HCU's and his supervisor's perceptions of supportiveness of the immediate work climate is illustrated. Perceptions by the newly employed HCU of the lack of supportiveness provided to new workers is particularly noticeable. In the case of all three climate variables, the difference in perception is at least 2 full scale points (on a 5-point scale), and in all cases the critical ratio of the differences exceeds 8. It is apparent that the HCU perceives his work climate as vastly less supportive than does his supervisor.

Table 2 indicates that HCUs who perceive their climate as supportive also tend to be rated by their supervisor more favorably in terms of work effectiveness

table 1

Comparison of Perceptions of Work Climate Held by the Hard-Core Unemployed and Their Supervisors

Component of Work Climate	Perception of Work Climate Held by		
	HCU	Supervisor	Difference
New worker treatment	1.9	4.0	2.1*
Support from peer workers	2.5	4.5	2.0*
Support from supervisor	2.6	4.9	2.3*

Note.—$N = 24$ matched pairs of workers and their supervisors. HCU = hard-core unemployed.

*$p < .01$.

table 2

Relationships between Perceptions Held by the Hard-Core Unemployed of Their Work Climate and Their Supervisor's Evaluation of Their Work Performance

Perception of His Work Climate by the HCU	Supervisor's Evaluation of HCU's Work Performance						
	Comparative Rating of Work Effectiveness				Perception of HCU's Behavior		
	Compe-tence	Conge-niality	Effort	Relia-bility	Smart	Friendly	Consci-entious
New worker treatment	.49**	.49**	.16	−.03	.43*	.57**	.49**
Support from peer workers	.48**	.55**	.24	−.24	.26	.60**	.40*
Support from supervisor	.61**	.56**	.45*	−.07	.54**	.63**	.58**
Number of weeks worked	−.20	−.12	−.12	−.60**	−.23	−.20	−.13

Note.—$N = 24$. HCU = hard-core unemployed.
 * $p < .05$.
 ** $p < .01$.

and work behavior. Those HUCs who perceive their climate as supportive are consistently rated as more competent and congenial than their fellow workers, and as having the general behavioral characteristics of being smart, friendly, and conscientious. HCUs who perceive their climate as supportive also show some tendency to be rated as exerting their best effort on the job. The only supervisory rating unrelated to work climate appears in the area of worker reliability, where three negative (but nonsignificant) correlations appear.

Perhaps the most interesting finding in Table 2 is that which indicates zero to negative relationships between supervisory ratings of work effectiveness/work behavior and job retention. Those HCUs who are rated as most reliable ("he shows up each day," "he shows up on time") by their supervisors tend to have a relatively short duration on the job. Or conversely, those who remain on the job tend to be rated as less reliable by their supervisor.

DISCUSSION

Two findings from this study might be highlighted since they point toward potentially serious issues in the job performance and retention of the HCU. One of these is the wide gap in perceptions between the HCU and his supervisor concerning the degree to which the work climate is a supportive one. A second issue concerns the lack of any positive relationship between the supervisor's evaluation of the HCU and the HCU's job retention. Of particular concern is the high negative relationship between the HCU's job retention and his reliability as evaluated by his supervisor. His absence and tardiness might be the HCU's avoidance reaction to a job climate he finds very uncomfortable and unsupportive (as indicated in Table 1). Those who are reliable find the situation intolerable after a short period. Others cope with the unfavorable climate by being tardy or absent, but they do remain with the company.

The HCUs were rated higher on competence than reliability. When the HCU is present, his work is comparable to that of other employees; the problem is his absence and lateness, not his competence. Thus, the supervisor and HCU might discuss their differing views of the work climate, focusing on concerns each has about the HCU's unreliability, and the conflicts that reliability creates for the HCU.

REFERENCES

Brenner, M. H. Critical factors in the success of hard-core training programs. Paper read at the Annual Meeting of American Psychological Association, San Francisco, September 1968.

Forehand, G., von Gilmer, B. "Environmental variation in studies of organizational behavior," *Psychological Bulletin,* 1964, **62,** 361–382.

Likert, R. *New Patterns of Management.* New York: McGraw-Hill, 1961.

11.2 Biographical Correlates of Management Success

ROBERT W. HECKMAN,
PAUL A. BANAS,
ROBERT E. LAZENBY, AND
LORETTA M. MOORE

Many studies have been conducted which relate biographical, personality, and mental ability variables to managerial effectiveness. Also, Ghiselli (1968) has recently demonstrated the moderating effects of motivational factors on the relationship between various traits and managerial success. However, much of the previous research in selection and early identification of management potential has ignored the possibility of differential predictor-criterion relationships across functional work areas. Second, few researchers other than Berlew and Hall (1966) have examined the effects of a college graduate's early work experience on his later company success.

The purpose of this concurrent study was to explore the relationship between biographical variables and management success with a special emphasis on examining these relationships for managers in different functions. A second purpose was to examine early work experience factors which might be related to later success and thus useful in structuring a college graduate's early work environment.

METHOD

Sample

The Ss for the present study were college graduates working in a large midwestern manufacturing firm. A stratified random sampling procedure was used with stratification on function, management level, and tenure. The six functions which participated in this study were Industrial Relations ($N = 133$), Manufacturing ($N = 254$), Sales ($N = 207$), Purchasing and Traffic ($N = 110$), Finance ($N = 186$), and Engineering ($N = 221$). Only college graduates hired

Reprinted from the *Proceedings of the 77th Annual Convention of the American Psychological Association,* 1969, **4,** 611–612, with permission of the authors and the American Psychological Association, Inc.

prior to age 31 who had joined the company between 1940 and 1964 were considered for inclusion. The mailed Biographical Inventory Questionnaire (BIQ) was returned by 1329 Ss or 82% of the sample. Nonrespondents and respondents were compared on age, monthly salary, and company experience and no appreciable differences were found. Average age of those responding was 37 yr. with a range of 25–52 years and average tenure was 11 yr. with a range of 3–28 years. Twenty-six percent of these graduates held the master's degree and approximately 1% the PhD. To control for education, those holding the master's or PhD degree were excluded from the analysis for the present study resulting in a sample size of 1111.[1]

Variables

BIQ. A questionnaire containing 161 biographical items hypothesized to be related to management success was mailed to each participant. These items covered academic achievement, participation in extracurricular activities, socioeconomic background, and early work experience factors such as amount of responsibility a person was given and supervision he received. With the exception of a small number of items, response categories, or alternatives, were on a continuum (such as very little—very much or never—very often).

Personnel Records. Tenure, age, education, performance appraisal rating, and respondents' undergraduate institution were obtained from the personnel rec-

ords. A method of assessing college quality developed by Astin (1965) was applied to each manager's undergraduate institution.

Criterion. Monthly salary, corrected for tenure by regression analysis, was the criterion for the present study. Performance appraisal rating, management level, and other measures of progress correlated quite highly with this variable.

Procedure

BIQ items and personnel records data were correlated with the criterion for the total group and for each function separately. Percentage of participants in the high criterion group answering each alternative was compared with that of the low criterion group for the noncontinuous items. Also, respondents were placed into one of nine cells defined by trichotomizing college quality and grade-point average distributions.[2] Percentage of Ss in each cell who were in the high third on the criterion was computed. Finally, two factor analyses of criterion-relevant items were performed by the method of principal components with varimax rotation. The first contained precollege and college background items; the second consisted of early work experience items.

RESULTS

For the total group, over 40% of the items were significantly related to the criterion ($p < .01$). Quality of an individual's undergraduate institution (.33), grades in high school (.30), grades in college (.33),

---

[1] The results of a similar study for the master's and PhD group closely paralleled those of the present sample.

[2] Grades were obtained by self-report, not from college registrars.

scholastic awards in high school (.25), and number of honor societies in college (.27) were among the best predictors.[3] Number of student offices held in college, number of leadership positions held, and ability as an organizer correlated .21, .18, and .20, respectively, with salary progress. Validities in the low teens were found for items measuring socioeconomic background. Seven early work experience items which, in the factor analysis, loaded on a factor named Opportunity to Grow on the Job, had validities ranging from .19 to .34. For these items the respondent assessed such things as his variety of work, autonomy, chance to use initiative, and opportunity to make decisions during his first 2 yr. with the company. Also, those participants who described their first supervisor as participative, receptive to new ideas, and willing to advance subordinates with ability, progressed faster than participants who did not.

The principal differences in predictor-criterion relationships across different functions were as follows: college grades related highest to the criterion for Finance (.41) and Engineering (.37) and lowest for the Manufacturing (.16) and Sales (.16) functions. The items reflecting leadership positions held and belonging to honor societies in college were most highly related to salary progress for Engineering and Sales with validities ranging from .24 to .37. For Industrial Relations and Purchasing and Traffic these items had very low correlations. Variety of work, number of rotational moves, and autonomy during the first 2 yr. of employment were moder-

[3]Numbers in parenthesis are Pearson product-moment correlation coefficients.

ately related to salary progress for Manufacturing, Sales, and Purchasing and Traffic with validities from .16 to .37, but unrelated or weakly associated with salary progress in the other functions. Desire for financial reward was related to the criterion in Sales (.18) and Finance (.10) but not for the other functions.

In examining college quality and college grades, it was found that 64% of those who were from above-average colleges and in the top third of the grade distribution were in the high salary progress group. Only 23% from below-average schools and in the low third of the grade distribution were in this group. Graduates with grades in the top third from below-average colleges have progressed better than individuals with low college grades from above-average schools (48% versus 38% in the high criterion group).

The percentage of respondents in the high and low criterion groups were compared for each alternative of the noncontinuous items. These comparisons indicated that college graduates who apply in person, as compared to those recruited on campus, tended to be in the low salary progress group for all functions, except Engineering. Also, for the Industrial Relations function, liberal arts majors achieved higher salary progress than business majors and for Manufacturing, engineering majors achieved higher salary progress than business majors.

Six factors emerged from the factor analysis of college and precollege criterion relevant items; Leadership Ability, Socioeconomic Background, Scholastic Achievement, Father's Influence, Academic Habits, and Financial Independence. Opportunity to Grow on the Job and Supervision were found to be the underlying dimensions of the early work experience items.

DISCUSSION

In this study significant correlates of salary progress have been isolated which are consistent with research done in other companies. However, it appears that these correlates vary in importance depending on the particular function, which suggests that the efficiency of screening candidates by recruiters or the identification of managerial potential can be enhanced if these correlates are differentially weighted in the decision-making process. Therefore, these findings are being incorporated into a structured interview which will be developed for recruiters. A follow-up study of this interview schedule will be undertaken to determine its effectiveness.

Perhaps the greatest value of this study will be to stimulate further investigations of college graduate utilization. The findings related to early work experience suggest that the kind of environment to which an individual is exposed can enhance or inhibit his subsequent progress. Some questions to be answered are: (*a*) Is one type of environment more consistent with college graduate expectations than another; (*b*) what are the behavioral differences between supervisors who do and do not effectively utilize college graduates; and (*c*) are there specific career patterns that are more desirable than others?

Admittedly, in part due to the inherent weaknesses of a concurrent study, this research must be considered exploratory in nature. One of the biggest limitations is that responses to many of the BIQ items, particularly the early work experience variables, are based on recall of past experiences and may have been affected by progress rather than predictive of it. Second, the criterion is an organizational outcome or reward, and may not reflect actual behavioral dimensions of effective performance. Furthermore, individuals were subgrouped according to company function rather than by an analysis of their work activities.

A more comprehensive study in this area would be longitudinal. New college graduate hires would fill out a biographical inventory. Their early work environment would be rated both by them and their supervisors at 6-mo. intervals. After they had been given time to demonstrate success or lack of success, they would be classified into subgroups based on an objective analysis of their job activities. Following Smith and Kendall's (1963) retranslation technique, behavioral dimensions of success would be developed for each of the homogeneous subgroups. Predictors would be related to behavioral dimensions and interactions of biographical and environmental variables tested. Finally, the relationship between BIQ items, environmental factors, behavioral dimensions and organizational outcomes would be assessed. This complete analysis would be repeated as these Ss progressed to higher management levels, each time using performance in the previous job as a predictor. In this type of analysis dimensions of performance at different levels of management and predictors associated with this performance could be identified. Also, career patterns and manpower planning could be examined in detail.

REFERENCES

Astin, A. *Who Goes Where to College?* Chicago: Science Research Associates, 1965.

Berlew, D. E., and Hall, D. T. "The socialization of managers; The effects of expectations on performance," *Administrative Science Quarterly,* 1966, **11,** 207–223.

Ghiselli, E. A. "Interaction of traits and motivational factors in the determination of the success of managers," *Journal of Applied Psychology,* 1968, **52,** 480–483.

Smith, P. C., and Kendall, L. M. "Retranslation of expectations: An approach to the construction of unambiguous anchors for rating scales," *Journal of Applied Psychology,* 1963, **47,** 149–155.

11.3 Leadership Sift in Organizations

KARLENE H. ROBERTS

For some time, psychologists have been interested in various aspects of leadership. Organizational leadership is afforded particular attention, but with a view to individuals in leadership positions rather than to characterizations of leadership at various levels or in total organizations. No one has asked, for instance, whether an organization can be partially identified by some overall leadership pattern, or whether the kind of leadership observed at an organization's apex sifts to lower management levels. Another unresolved question is how leadership behavior and attitudes professed by leaders mesh. Research has centered on *either* the overt leadership behavior of persons in organizations, *or* their stated behavior (attitudes) about how one should act. Attention has not been directed simultaneously to *both* the overt behavior and the stated attitudes of the *same* set of people in an organization.

The link between attitudes and behavior displayed at different levels within a single organization provides the data for this study of how management styles diffuse through single organizations. Observations were made on the extent to which leadership styles at the summits of organizations were exhibited within the entire management hierarchy. The question of whether management style flows downward through an organization is emphasized.

Models of Organizational Leadership

Early organization theorists developed a position labeled by McGregor (1960), Theory X. These writers posited organizations established on a foundation of rationality and logic, which were impersonal and functioned regardless of the

Reprinted from the *Proceedings of the 76th Annual Convention of the American Psychological Association*, 1968, **3**, 561–562, with permission of the author and the American Psychological Association, Inc.

particular individuals in the structure. Certain assumptions regarding the nature of man underlie this position: work is inherently distasteful to him; he is passive; and he must be rewarded to work, persuaded, and controlled. Principles following from these assumptions were unity of direction, chain of command, and specialization of function.

More recent theorists developed a position labeled, by McGregor, Theory Y. Theory Y states: work is natural to man; people learn to seek responsibility; there is, in the population, a wide distribution of capacity for creativity. Such statements imply an optimal leadership which is democratic.

The flush of enthusiasm for the brand of the organization theory developed by these authors is now waning. Other writers explain that important elements were overlooked, or that on a practical level, management behavior is not adequately represented by either a predominantly Theory X or Theory Y orientation.

Miles (1965) supplemented the X and Y orientations by discussing the form of supervision prevailing in organizations. He distinguished three kinds of managers: the classical, the human relations, and the human resources men. Classical managers believe and behave in an authoritarian manner, while the human relations model requires managers to seek subordinate participation as a means of obtaining cooperation. In contrast, the human resources model views satisfaction as a by-product of effective performance rather than as a factor determining performance. If a manager chooses to disavow the classical position, the human relations approach is easier to accept than the human resources model because it is compatible with the end goal performance requirement.

Classical managers believe and act in accord with Theory X propositions (X attitude, X behavior). Managers who accept Theory X assumptions about people but practice participative management (X attitude, Y behavior) represent the human relations pattern. The human resources supervisors are consistently in line with Theory Y (Y attitudes, Y behavior). A more difficult case is the manager who claims to hold assumptions about people consistent with Theory Y, but whose leadership behavior is extremely authoritarian (Y attitude, X behavior). He may be that new breed of manager who has been heavily exposed to management courses stressing participative processes. He reports that he employs what he thinks is acceptable modern leadership behavior, but he does not believe this approach will work. Alternatively, he may believe in participative management, but his behavior is restricted through fear based on situational constraints. This is the modern paradox.

Focus

Specifically this study asked the following questions, not about individuals, but about organizational hierarchies:

1. What are the relative frequencies of classical human relations, modern paradox, and human resources leadership at the tops of organizations?

2. What is the nature of leadership found at successive levels as one moves down the organization's hierarchy?

3. To what degree is the type of leadership exhibited at the top of the orga-

nization also seen at successively lower levels? That is, to what extent does the leadership at the top sift downward in organizations?

4. Is leadership sift related to organization size?

5. Are certain types of supervisory attitude-behavior combinations characteristic of more effective organizations than other types of leadership?

Empirical investigations of these questions are unavailable. Extrapolation from available findings generally concerned with leadership dimensions addressed here is, at best, extended and tenuous.

METHOD

This was a first attempt to develop a methodology appropriate to the problem at hand.

Attitude and behavior orientations were explored in 6 operating divisions of a large electronics firm. Divisions are located throughout the United States and can be treated in many ways as separate firms. The divisions, with one exception, have 5 management levels, allowing for both attitude and behavior scores at each of 4 levels and attitude scores at Level 5.

Managerial attitude and behavior data were collected from a "Management Decision-Making, Attitude, and Job Satisfaction" questionnaire. Respondents' self-reports on 9 items were combined to yield attitude scores at each managerial level. Behavior scores were calculated from the ratings of managers by their immediate subordinates on 5 Likert-type items.

The organizational summits were assigned attitude and behavior scores by summing the division manager's answers to attitude items and obtaining the mean of his subordinates' ratings on items dealing with his behavior. At lower levels attitude scores were means of individual answers to attitude items at a particular level. Behavior scores were means of subordinates' rating of managers at a particular level.

Two grand means were obtained over all levels in the 6 divisions, one for attitude and one for behavior. Each attitude and behavior level score for each organization was then referred to the appropriate grand mean for identification as X or Y oriented. Scores below the grand mean reflected X-oriented attitudes or behavior, those above the grand mean reflected Y predispositions. The definition of X or Y orientation is, then, a relative one.

Leadership sift is defined as the appearance at successive organizational levels of the leadership style (composed of attitude and behavior) appearing at the organization's apex. High sift organizations are those in which the leadership style manifest at the apex sifts unaltered to the lowest successive management level.

Each of several performance criteria were ranked for all organizations. Separate rankings were combined to yield overall organizational performance scores for each group.

RESULTS

Leadership at the Various Organization Levels. Every possible combination of attitude and behavior exists at the 6 organizational summits, and at every other organizational level. Both attitude and behavior are more likely to be democratic at Levels 1 and 2 than at successively lower levels, until Level 5 is reached.

As one moves down the separate divisions, there is a greater propensity for Theory X than for Theory Y behavior. At Level 1, only 2 of the groups are characterized by authoritarian behavior, while at Level 3, 4 of them are, with 2 also showing attitudes consistent with Theory X. At Level 5, however, attitudes in 4 of the 5 organizations studied reflect Theory Y. Behavior data at this level would be most helpful.

Leadership Sift. In 4 of the divisions leadership style sifts unaltered to Level 3. These are the high sift groups. The styles are not identical for each division. In fact, each shows a different but stable (to Level 3) combination of attitude and behavior. This finding is not easily attributable to chance, and although the evidence should be tested against other possibilities which could produce similar hierarchical patterns, the probability is high that "sift" offers a valid explanation.

Leadership Sift, Organization Size, and Performance. The relationship of leadership sift to either size or performance is tenuous at best. High performance divisions are somewhat more democratic in both attitude and behavior than are low performance groups. Performance and size alone are correlated.

DISCUSSION

Leadership style is certainly one aspect of organizational climate. Its identification within the managerial hierarchy may be a step toward clarifying the essence of organizational structure. This effort is admittedly only a first step carried out in the grossest form. However, it is now possible to identify the 6 divisions according to a more refined concept of supervisory behavior than that of merely indicating what individual managers say they do. The variation of leadership styles within and between organizations has been subjected to a simultaneous cross-sectional photograph, rather than a snapshot. It would be advantageous to take similar pictures over time, thereby gaining an understanding of the relationship between changes in leadership and changes in other organization variables.

Although democratic attitudes and behaviors are seen more frequently at the top of divisions than at successively lower levels, it must not be overlooked that all combinations of attitudes and behaviors exist at all levels. Possibly men at Levels 1 and 2 are less constrained in their leadership style than are *their* subordinate colleagues because they have achieved success.

As one moves progressively down the hierarchies, authoritarian attitudes and behaviors increase. In this sample, Level 3 is composed of young men on their way to the top, and a group for whom Level 3 is, for some reason, the zenith. Both groups may be understandably fearful about their performance, having good reason for conservatism in both attitude and behavior.

Level 4 is a fairly conservative group in both attitude and behavior, and shows some tendency to reflect the style of the next group up. Level 2 mirrors Level 1 in the same way. One can make a case for a mirroring or modeling phenomenon which is overruled only at that point in the organization where situational factors are most salient.

What of Level 5 manifesting such democratic attitudes? Is this a characteristic of young men; is it a result of exposure to the popular management literature; or are organizational constraints fewer here than at the next two higher levels? The present study does not answer such questions. Further research might.

The proposition that leadership style sifts down the management hierarchy is tentatively supported. Further study of this phenomenon is proposed, with an eye to the amount of variance at successively lower levels accounted for by sift, and a better understanding of other artifacts which resemble sift. Although the probability is low that sift occurs in an upward direction, this too should be examined.

A more refined measure of sift might answer several questions. First, under what circumstances is sift functional? Second, what attitude-behavior combination is most often reflected by effective work groups?

Due to lack of research in this area, this study attempted to take several "low definition" photographs of organizational leadership. It is now necessary to sharpen the image of the problem, increasing the specificity with which leadership style can be defined and more sensitively assessing the degree of sift within organizations.

REFERENCES

McGregor, D. *The Human Side of Enterprise.* New York: McGraw-Hill, 1960.

Miles, R. E. "Human relations or human resources?" *Harvard Business Review,* 1965, **43,** 148–156.

11.4 An Example of "Engineering Psychology": The Aircraft Noise Problem

K. D. KRYTER

Engineering psychology is usually defined as the application of psychological research information to the design and/or operation of man-machine systems. It also, of course, involves the doing of the research when that is required, as it often is; but without the application intent, the activity, I believe, does not qualify as "engineering" psychology.

Traditionally, a man-machine system has been taken to be a human operator or operators plus a simple or complex set of electronic or mechanical devices performing some useful function. The purpose of the engineering psychology in this context is, of course, to increase the efficiency and efficacy of a particular man-machine system.

A second, perhaps sometimes secondary, role of engineering psychology has been to provide design criteria or information relative to the protection of the well-being of the operator or user against psychophysiological harm from the machine, even though such harm may not interfere with the ostensible performance of the man-machine system in question. Here we would include design criteria for excessive noise, vibration, light, etc., that could bring annoyance or eventual physiological damage to the operator. This aspect of engineering psychology represents a broadening of responsibility of the engineering psychologist; for example, partial permanent deafness resulting from exposure to the excessive noise made by a piece of machinery may be a handicap to the operator of the machine only when he is *not* operating the machine itself—when he is in the relative quiet of his home or in an office, etc.

The subject of this paper is concerned with a third, even more remote, type of engineering psychology. It has to

Reprinted with slight abridgment from the *American Psychologist*, 1968, **23**, 240–244, with permission of the author and the American Psychological Association, Inc.

do with the fact that machines sometimes have a way of reaching out and affecting people other than the direct operators or users of them; in particular, we will be concerned with the effects upon people of the external sounds from aircraft. The neighborhood noise from ground-based transportation vehicles and heavy industry is, of course, another similar example.

Engineering psychology qualifies for involvement in this problem area merely by broadening, I trust justifiably, our definition of a system to include all the people affected directly through their senses as the result of the operation of the machine part of the system. Extending the definition of man-machine systems this way probably seems reasonable to most of us, but the kinds of research information required for this somewhat "global" man-machine system and the avenues of application of this information are sometimes a bit startling, as I will attempt to show.

THE AIRCRAFT NOISE PROBLEM

Fundamentally, the aircraft noise problem requires two kinds of psychological research information for the man-machine system problem I wish to discuss:

1. Basic behavior or characteristics of the auditory system as a receptor of acoustic energy and
2. The reactions of people to aircraft noise in the environment of, primarily, their homes.

The latter is obviously the true criterion against which we must work and evaluate the results of the basic laboratory-generated information and the re-

sults of any human engineering system design recommendations that might be made. These engineering design recommendations will be:

1. For the design of aircraft engines and the operation of the aircraft to produce the least objectionable kind and amount of sound and/or
2. For the design of the airport-community system so that the sounds and the communities are compatible, i.e., placing the airport away from residential areas or zoning the areas near airports for industrial use only.

But the design recommendations to be made with respect to either, and especially the second, of these parts of the system run head-on into extremely complicated economic, social, legal, and political matters on both a national and international basis. The engineering psychologists who wish or have the opportunity to work on the aircraft noise problem need to consider and, to some extent, understand these practical, real-life parts of the problem if they are to behave and interact sensibly with the people who are responsible for creating and solving the problem.

So before presenting some of the research facts and data that might be used for the "best" engineering of the aircraft noise problem, I will burden you with a few brief comments on the more political-legal aspects of the problem. Most of my comments to follow in this regard apply strictly only to the United States, although the arguments can usually be applied to other countries.

In some countries, such as the United States of America, aviation is a private enterprise and has the right, if not the obligation, to promote its own interests first. If making noise results from these activities, restraints on making noise will be self-imposed by the aviation industry only if the noise hurts aviation business; such restraints may also be government-imposed if it creates a public nuisance, damages health, or destroys the value of property.

Some parts of the aviation industry are making valiant efforts to self-impose noise limits for the benefit of persons on the ground near airports as a matter of good public relations and public responsibility. However, the aviation noise problem has become so acute, and promises to become even worse (Greatrex, 1963), that some government participation in setting and enforcing limitations on aviation noise seems unavoidable at national, if not international, levels. But, regardless of who sets tolerable limits for aircraft noise in a community, a rational reason for setting these limits must be developed.

Three bases for such action have been argued from time to time: that noise (a) is a public nuisance, (b) damages health, and (c) destroys property. Let me remove from consideration the question of "damage to health." I think, although some may disagree with me, that aircraft noise as we know it is not demonstrably dangerous to the health of people in a community near an airport—and I am including not only direct physiological effects but possible indirect effects from loss of sleep, startle, etc. There is no convincing evidence, in my opinion, that significant adverse effects of this sort occur in real life as the result of exposure to aircraft noise per se. Fortunately, man,

at least physiologically, seems to be able to adapt more or less completely to most noises.

The question of "public nuisance" is also a slippery basis for predicting the need for the establishment of aircraft noise limits. In the first place, what bothers some people is acceptable to others; but more importantly, a nuisance can be made legal if it is in the general interest of the public to have the nuisance. Aircraft noise, to a considerable extent, qualifies as legalizable nuisance, inasmuch as aviation has become such an important part of our economy and way of life. Ultimately, this balance between different and conflicting "values" can probably only be settled by application of some form of governmental judgment.

It would seem, however, that damages to property values may provide legal grounds for limiting aircraft noise in communities. (I do not mean to say that in some courts of law and in some legislatures aircraft noise above certain limits will not be considered as hazardous to health and well-being and, therefore, an illegal nuisance. This is certainly a possibility.) In the United States of America and elsewhere it is maintained that neither the government nor any private party can take or destroy property without adequately compensating the owner of the property. Property can, of course, be partly taken or destroyed, and if the presence of aircraft noise at a person's house makes that house less desirable as a house, its value is reduced and the property has been partly "taken" by the presence of the noise, be the noise in the public interest or not. In short, noise may damage or cause a relative decline in the value of a property because it is not acceptable to people trying to live on the property.

THREE CRITERIA FOR ACCEPTABLE AIRCRAFT NOISE

Let me now turn to a discussion of possible criteria of acceptability of aircraft noise in a community. The term "criterion" needs to be defined because it is often misused. By "criterion" I here mean the behavior or response to sound, such as airplane noise, that is deemed to be on the borderline between acceptable and unacceptable. It is not the noise level that produces the behavior that is the criterion, although it is common practice to refer to these just tolerable (according to the criterion) noise conditions as "noise criteria."

In any event, I have recently (Kryter, 1966) had the temerity to describe how, on the basis of existing acoustical, psychological, and sociological data, one could: (a) specify criteria of acceptability of aircraft noise in a community, and (b) specify the noise conditions that would result in behavior that just on the average meets these criteria. Most of the next few paragraphs are taken from the above-referenced article and also were presented at the Inaugural Meeting of the British Acoustical Society on Aircraft Noise (Kryter, 1967).

Criterion 1

A new or novel noise environment that is comparable in basic noisiness to a noise environment known and considered by the average person to be sig-nificantly unacceptable at a residence will likewise be considered significantly un-acceptable at a residence. Obviously, the expressions "average person" and "significantly unacceptable" render this criterion open to interpretation and adjudication. But the approach may have some merit in that it allows persons to evaluate a noise environment that is relatively unknown to them with another with which they are more familiar. Many of the people making decisions about the possible effects of aircraft noise upon people in communities near airports have not been repeatedly exposed to such a noise environment.

Figure 1 suggests that aircraft noise having a perceived noise level (Johnson and Robinson, 1967) in excess of 100 PNdB[1] might be considered by a signifi-

---

[1]So-called perceived noise level in PNdB is presently being used for a basic unit for measuring the sound from aircraft and other sources in terms of its most probable "annoyance" effect on people (Kryter, 1963). A PNdB is found by making certain calculations on octave band or one-third octave band sound pressure level measurements of a sound; the effects on annoyance or the "noisiness" of a sound in terms of pure-tone content (which is an important contributor to the annoyance value of a sound) and duration of a sound can also be evaluated by "corrected" PNdB units.

It might be noted that the information developed for and contained in the PNdB values for a given sound is at least potentially of direct use by the engineer designing aircraft engines, in that the engineer can control the spectrum and frequency loci of pure-tone components and thereby make the engine noise as compatible as possible to the person on the ground under the aircraft. Likewise, engine power settings and other landing and take-off procedures on the aircraft can be specified on the basis of perceived noise levels to reduce community noise in presumably the most effective way possible.

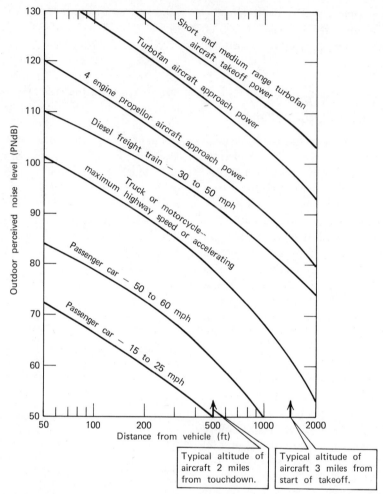

figure 1
Typical levels of intermittent noise produced by vehicles. (An increase of 10 PNdB is usually equivalent to a 100% increase in judged noisiness. See Kryter, 1966.)

cant number of people to be unacceptable in their homes, inasmuch as that is the approximate noise level 50 feet (15m) from trucks or motorcycles at maximum highway speed or in the course of acceleration, or 200 feet from a diesel train going 30 to 50 miles per hour.

These comparisons, to be most meaningful, should include not only peak PNdB levels, but also the number and duration of occurrences. In these respects the exposures to aircraft, truck, motorcycle, and train noise differ greatly, not always in favor of the aircraft noise. Two very similar methods have been developed whereby PNdB values and numbers of daily occurrences of intense sounds are used to depict the total daily noise environment present in a community, as will be described below.

Criterion 2

A noise environment in which vigorous complaints and concerted group action against the noise are made is considered to be an unacceptable noise environment. These are the expected responses from a community when a composite noise rating (CNR) of 100 to 115 is present, see Figure 2. A CNR is calculated, incidentally, according to the following formula: $CNR = PNdB - 12 + 10 \log_{10}N$, where N is number of aircraft flyover events.

Criterion 3

It has been found that in a noise environment having a noise and number index (NNI) of 45 about 50% of the people will report that they are disturbed by the noise in various ways, and that it tends to be rated the worst aspect of a residential environment. Figure 3 illustrates the type of sociological data that substantiates the NNI method of measuring daily exposure to aircraft noise. NNI is calculated as follows; $NNI = PNdB - 80 + 15 \log_{10}N$, where N is number of aircraft flyover events.

In short, it is deduced that a noise, repeated fairly often during each day, having a peak level of 100 PNdB would probably be considered as unacceptable; thus 30 to 40 daily repetitions of an aircraft noise at 100 PNdB would be rated unacceptable by each of three rating methods described above.

SONIC BOOM

Finally, let me make a few remarks about a noise from a proposed commercial aircraft of the future—the so-called sonic boom. This new noise will be a significant problem, it appears, not because it will have any worse effects upon people than the noise from present-day subsonic aircraft near airports—as a matter of fact, research in the United States (Kryter, Johnson, and Young, 1967; Pearsons and Kryter, 1964) and Great Britain (Broadbent and Robinson, 1964; Johnson and Robinson, 1967) indicates that the effects of sonic booms and noise from subsonic jets near airports may actually be roughly comparable—but because the sonic boom will be heard by so many more people and because it may cause some slight amount of structural damage, the overall noise problem could become much worse. For example, it is estimated that transcontinental SST operations over the United States could expose 50,000,000 or so people to 15 or so booms per day. I think that the "absolute" number of bothered people becomes important for two reasons:

1. Practically speaking, there probably is a "critical mass" of people required to exert significant political and social action against a nuisance, and the number of people near present airports appears in many cases to be fewer than this critical size or number.

2. Also practically speaking, whereas it is conceivable that compensation for taking property around airports might be economically feasible, compensation for taking of property in the United States by sonic booms (the property of 50,000,000 people) is hardly conceivable.

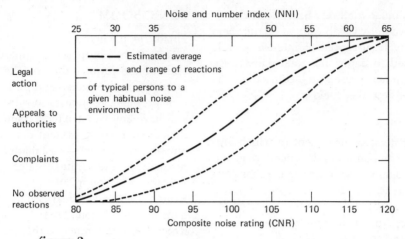

figure 2

General relation between community response to aircraft or other noises and composite noise rating or noise and number index. (See Bolt, Beranek, and Newman, 1964; Wilson, 1963.)

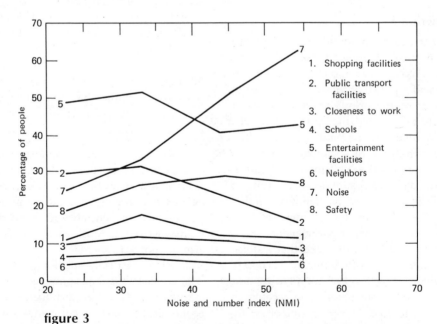

figure 3

Results of interviews in communities within a 10-mile radius of Heathrow Airport, London, showing percentages of people rating their area as a poor, or very poor, place to live for various reasons. (See Wilson, 1963.)

The problem of setting maximum tolerable exposures to sonic booms for communities would perhaps be amenable to solution a priori if some resolution of the question of the acceptability of the noise from subsonic aircraft were forthcoming and if some realistic and convincing estimate could be given as to the political response to complaints of possibly millions of persons, in comparison to the present-day complaints about aircraft noise from but a few tens of thousands near major airports. Indeed, whether the SST will be permitted to operate supersonically when over populated land areas may be largely decided on the basis of research information bearing on these specific points—information which I like to think belongs to the field of engineering psychology, broadly defined.

REFERENCES

Broadbent, D. E., and Robinson, D. W. "Subjective measurements of the relative annoyance of simulated sonic bangs and aircraft noise." *Journal of Sound and Vibration,* 1964, **1**(2), 162.

Greatrex, F. B. "Take-off and landing of the supersonic transport," *Aircraft Engineering,* 1963, August, 1–5.

Johnson, D. R., and Robinson, D. W. "On the subjective evaluation of sonic bangs," *Acustica,* 1967, **18**, 241–258.

Kryter, K. D. Psychological reactions to aircraft noise. *Science,* 1966, **151**, 1346–1355.

Kryter, K. D. Acceptability of aircraft noise. *Journal of Sound and Vibration,* 1967, **5**(2), 364–369.

Kryter, K. D., Johnson, P. J., and Young, J. R. Psychological experiments on sonic booms. Annex B of Sonic Boom Experiments at Edwards Air Force Base, 1967, United States Department of Commerce, Springfield, Va.

Kryter, K. D., and Pearsons, K. S. "Some effects of spectral content and duration on perceived noise level," *Journal of the Acoustical Society of America,* 1963, **35**, 866.

Wilson, A. (Chmn.) *Noise.* (Report of the Committee on the Problem of Noise) London: Her Majesty's Stationary Office, 1963.

Pearsons, K. S., and Kryter, K. D. Laboratory tests of subjective reactions to sonic boom. NASA Report No. CR-187, 1964.

Bolt, Beranek, and Newman Inc. *Land Use Planning Relating to Aircraft Noise.* Washington, D. C.: Federal Aviation Agency, 1964.

11.5 Influence of a Female Model on Perceived Characteristics of an Automobile

GEORGE HORSLEY SMITH AND RAYME ENGEL

An experiment was conducted which shows that certain salient elements in a print advertisement, which are not intrinsic to the product, may nevertheless work at a more or less unconscious level to influence the way consumers feel about the product and the way they rate its objective characteristics. This is not a novel theory, but in practical advertising decisions it is often acted on as a matter of faith or hunch, and usually with unknown consequences, rather than on the basis of carefully controlled experimentation. The present study may suggest the feasibility of conducting inexpensive experiments in which selected stimuli are varied systematically and the effects assessed before spending large sums of money on a campaign in the mass media.

An automobile was selected as the product to be studied, and an attractive female model was the experimental vari-

able. In today's advertising, a young woman is sometimes used to demonstrate features of a car, in which case she serves an explicit selling function; in other cases, she is included more or less decoratively but with, presumably, the implicit function of somehow making the car seem more attractive and worthwhile than if she were not present. This nonintrinsic (implicit) influence of the young female is the one which we chose to study.

The stimulus material consisted of two similar, plastic covered montages, each $13\frac{1}{2}$ in. $\times$ 11 in., with cardboard reinforcement. The experimental montage showed a medium priced two-door hardtop automobile, beige color, with certain changes of detail to render it unidentifiable as to make. This montage included a female model standing in the right foreground with the car behind her. Clipped from *Playboy*, this young redhead

Reprinted from the *Proceedings of the 76th Annual Convention of the American Psychological Association*, 1968, **3**, 681–682, with permission of the authors and the American Psychological Association, Inc.

clad in black lace panties and a simple sleeveless sweater was rated by 15 male observers as attractive in form and erotic in appeal. One hand rested on her hip while the other held a spear—on the theory that this phallic symbol (?) might make her seem more aggressively seductive! She had no obvious function of demonstrating or pointing out features of the car. The control montage contained the identical automobile, without the female. That part of the car concealed by her body in the experimental montage was blocked out by a neutral screen in the control montage.

After 2 waves of pretesting on 60 Ss, the final phase of the research was done on 120 adult respondents obtained through personal interviews in a large upper middle-class housing development in East Brunswick, N.J. in the fall of 1966. Following an ABAB sequence, half the respondents received the experimental treatment and half received the control treatment.

No significant differences were found in the variance of the experimental and the control group on age, sex, income, and number of cars owned. Each group of 60 Ss contained 35 males and 25 females; in each group more than 50% were between 35 and 44 years of age; they were comparable in economic status with the majority reporting between $10,000 and $15,000 annual income.

The 60 respondents in the experimental and the 60 in the control sample were asked to rate the design of the car on a 5-point scale from "Excellent" to "Poor"; to estimate list price with standard equipment; to estimate top speed of the car; and to rate it on seven bipolar concepts: appealing-not appealing, lively-dull, youthful-not youthful, high-horsepower-low-horsepower, safe-unsafe, easy to handle-difficult to handle, wide wheelbase-narrow wheelbase (Osgood, 1957).

Mean scores for the 60 experimental Ss and the 60 control Ss were obtained for each test item; also, separately for the 35 males and 25 females in each group. The significance of the differences between means from independent samples were computed, using a two-tailed test.

Results strongly suggest that inclusion of the female model in the montage influences people's perception of the car in various ways. On items designed to tap the connotative or emotional features of the car, the 60 experimental and the 60 control Ss rated the vehicle very differently. The former saw it as more appealing ($p \leq .01$), more lively ($p \leq .01$), more youthful ($p \leq .01$), and as having a better or more excellent design ($p \leq .01$).

But what about objective characteristics of the unidentified automobile, its assumed cost, and so on? Here too differences show up. The 60 experimental Ss, compared with the 60 controls, are more apt to rate the car as costing an average $340 more ($p \leq .01$), as able to move an average 7.3 mph faster ($p \leq .05$), as less safe ($p \leq .05$), and higher in horsepower ($p \leq .01$). The men but not the women judge the wheelbase to be larger ($p \leq .05$). The car is perhaps seen as harder to handle when the girl is added, but differences are not statistically significant.

In general, the 25 women in the experimental group respond in the same direction as the 35 males. The young female—the "love goddess" in the sociologists' lexicon—perhaps pervasively wields her influence on audiences of the mass media regardless of their own sex.

In supplementary interviews, 23 cooperative men in the experimental group were asked in an informal manner whether they thought the girl in the picture had any influence on their judgments. Twenty-two of these men not only denied this possibility but scarcely acknowledged being aware of the girl in the montage. One admitted that he had noticed the female model and may have been influenced by her presence. Comments from the others include: "I don't let anything but the thing itself influence my judgments. The other is just propaganda." "I never let myself be blinded by advertising; the car itself is what counts." "The car itself. The other is just dressing." "She could influence me, but not as far as the car is concerned." "Girls aren't that important!"

Findings are in line with a body of research which points to the way in which cues of one kind or another can restructure a person's perceptual field without his conscious awareness of what is happening or perhaps with an unacknowledged need to deny what is happening (e.g., Berelson and Steiner, 1964; Smith, 1953).

The present investigation was limited in scope. Generalizations from it to a wide range of products, female types, and interactions of product and female are not justified. But this is just the point. When we undertook this study we frankly did not know how, if at all, the particular "love goddess" would influence imputed price, horsepower, and other attributes of the automobile. Only after extensive pretesting did we begin to formulate fairly firm hypotheses.

Hindsight shows that we were generally right in our guesses about how things would turn out in the final phase of the study.

But in the absence of hindsight based on hard facts, we are left with the simple guess or assumption that the gratuitous inclusion of "attention getters" such as pretty girls, babies and dogs—or living creatures in general—probably does "something" for the advertised product, hopefully something good. Conducting research in advance to pin down what is actually happening in consumers' minds seems like a good idea.

The design we employed was adapted to the requirements of an unsponsored graduate thesis project. With relatively small investments of money and time, it could be modified for use by an advertiser or agency to gauge the effects of features in an advertisement which on hunch seem to have merit, but are not amenable to testing through the usual interviews. It seems perfectly clear from our limited data that we are overly optimistic if we expect rational creatures like consumers to know or admit that a girl or any other irrational feature of an ad influences them to see the product in a different light. This would be tantamount to admitting that they are being brainwashed, which not even politicans can afford to do!

REFERENCES

Berelson, B., and Steiner, G. A. *Human Behavior.* New York: Harcourt, Brace, 1964.

Osgood, C. *The Measurement of Meaning.* Urbana, Ill.: University of Illinois Press, 1957.

Smith, G. H. "Size-distance judgments of human faces," *Journal of General Psychology,* 1953, **49**, 45–64.

SECTION 12

PSYCHOLOGY AND
THE COMMUNITY

In the previous section we presented a number of papers dealing with the application of psychological theory, research findings, and techniques to problems in various types of organizations, mostly business and industrial in nature. In this section we shall include papers dealing with the application of psychology to problems to be encountered in the community. A number of the techniques come under the heading of what has been termed "social intervention."

The first paper is largely descriptive, in the sense that it discusses research that has taken place with respect to the attitudes that American Negroes and whites have toward each other and toward themselves. The discussion is taken from a more extensive review of psychological studies of Negroes and whites conducted by Ralph Mason Dreger of Louisiana State University and Kent S. Miller of Florida State University.

The Operation Headstart Program was initiated during the summer of 1965 in a large-scale attempt to provide remedial experiences (sometimes referred to as "compensatory education") for children from poor homes who had lived in isolation from the main sources of social and intellectual stimulation in the national culture and hence could be considered as culturally or socially "deprived." The participation of psychologists in the program is one example of social intervention. The report by Joyce L. Howard and Walter T. Plant of San Jose State College consists of a study aimed at determining whether the Operation Headstart experience would result in any changes in intelligence test scores. Their findings showed that the average child in the program demonstrated an increase in IQ of four to eight points, depending on the test being used. If IQ increases can be accepted as indications of increases in academic potential, the results of the study suggest that the programs were having some positive effect.

Many of the children from poverty homes come to school ill-prepared for the routines of classroom instruction. They have difficulties in attending to learning tasks, are easily distracted, and often regard teacher permissiveness as an invitation to anarchy. Some are even disturbed by the unfamiliarity of the classroom situation and express their tensions through asocial or antisocial behavior. As a result, many teachers who have to deal with children from poverty homes find that they are spending more time in keeping classrooms under control than they are in teaching the school curriculum. What often happens is that the misbehavior of two or three children leads the teacher to give her attention to them in an attempt to restore order to the classroom. The more attention she pays to misbehavior, the less time she spends on instructional activities that could occupy the attention of the rest of the class. The less time the class as a whole is involved in learning tasks, the more restive and distractible they become. As a result, teachers and students often become locked into a kind of mutually reinforcing behavior pattern, which is characterized by anger, retaliation, and disorder, rather than by interest, involvement, and learning progress.

The report by Robert L. Hamblin and his associates describes an attempt to interrupt the cycle of disorder and punishment through the application of principles drawn from the psychological laboratory. The attention directed by the teacher toward misbehavior, they say, only serves to reinforce disruptive behavior, and order can only be restored if disruptive behavior is ignored and constructive behavior is reinforced. In effect, the teacher places the class on a reinforcement schedule. The results reported by the researchers show a dramatic drop in disruption and an increase in cooperative behavior. The type of experimental treatment reported here has, incidentally, been used successfully in a number of different schools throughout the country.

The fourth paper is not concerned with social intervention but instead examines a phenomenon that has been attracting a great deal of attention in recent years—the tendency of bystanders to ignore the plight of individuals in need of help. Although some writers and critics have blamed this tendency on anomie, a breakdown in social ties, or the "sickness" of society, the experiment conducted by John M. Darley of Princeton and Bibb Latané of Ohio State University suggests that other factors may be operating, such as a tendency for bystanders to respond to the behavior of other bystanders, rather than merely that of the troubled victim.

The paper by Bell, Cleveland, Hanson, and O'Connell deals with responsibility, responsiveness, and social intervention. The problem involves the relationship between the police and members of minority groups, particularly those who are residents of poverty areas in large cities. The police say that the poor do not behave in a socially responsible way; as a consequence, the police feel compelled to give them more attention than they give the relatively more law-abiding middle class. The poor say that their needs and problems are ignored by society as a whole and aggravated by police harassment. The dissatisfaction felt by both sides is expressed through mutual distrust, hostility, and aggressiveness. The psychologists describe a human relations training program attended by both the police and members of the poverty community in Houston in which feelings were aired and views frankly exchanged, a program that was planned to incorporate some of the characteristics of sensitivity training or the encounter group. The program reduced but did not eliminate distrust and hostility altogether. However, it did promote better mutual understanding and seemed to have led both groups to behave more responsibly and responsively to each other.

The recent public interest in ecological problems has been accompanied by the development of a new psychological specialty: environmental psychology. Joachim F. Wohlwill of Clark University was one of the early leaders in this new field to recognize the need for psychologists to become more concerned with the physical environment *per se*, rather than merely with its effects as reflected in stimulus and response. In the course of his paper, Wohlwill develops the theme of the environment as a source of stimulation, drawing on work by Hebb and Berlyne. The inverted-U relationship between stimulus level and performance is a common finding of psychologists who have been working in this field and is one that provides a more generally useful explanation of motivation than the classical drive-reduction hypothesis.

The final paper consists of an address delivered by Kenneth E. Boulding of the University of Colorado at a meeting of the American Association for the Advancement of Science. Boulding deals with some fundamental questions regarding the effect science, and especially behavioral science, is having on the world in which we live.

12.1 Comparative Psychological Studies of Negroes and Whites in the United States: 1959–1965

RALPH MASON DREGER AND KENT S. MILLER

SOCIAL PERCEPTIONS AND ATTITUDES

The decision as to which studies should be discussed under this heading was not an easy one. The marked shifts which have occurred in race relations in the last 5 years and the increased contacts between Negroes and whites have led to a flood of studies which relate to social perception and attitudes. A number of monographs have appeared and in many instances an entire issue of a journal has been devoted to race relations and attitudes. Empirical data lie buried in much of this material but the task of adequately summarizing this broad field is beyond the scope of this paper. In addition, many of the studies involving social perceptions and attitudes are time-bound and of limited pertinence.

We shall attempt to stay within our general guideline of reporting studies in which direct racial comparisons are involved or directly implied, but we shall probably meet with less success than in other sections of this review. Because of the lack of clear boundaries between psychological and sociological literature of this area, and the large number of studies, we have necessarily been selective.

Social Distance

Measures of social distance were obtained from college students in most instances during the review period; the results are inconsistent. Some of this inconsistency can be assumed to be related to the wide range of measures employed and varying circumstances of administration.

Reprinted from the *Psychological Bulletin*, 1968, **70,** No. 3, Part 2 (monograph), with permission of the authors and the American Psychological Association, Inc. The selection reprinted here consists of four pages out of a 58-page monograph.

Triandis and Triandis (1960) reported white students as showing more social distance than Negroes, whereas Fagan and O'Neill (1965) found their Negro subjects expressing more social distance toward a number of ethnic, religious, and political groups than did four white comparison groups. This latter study, a rare replication, revealed that in comparison with a study 10 years earlier, the mean social distance scores decreased for every group except the Negro. The authors offer an explanation that these scores are based in reality in that Negroes have less contact with other ethnic groups with a consequent increase in stereotypy and naiveté.

Additional studies involving college students report Negroes as having more favorable attitudes toward whites than vice versa (Proenza and Strickland, 1965), and, Negroes perceive all other groups (including light-skinned Negroes and mulattoes) as different from self (Derbyshire, 1964).

Residential and personal social distance toward Protestants, Catholics, Jews, and Negroes were measured in 13 different samples of whites in Kansas City (Goldman, Warshay, and Biddle, 1962). The people in all 13 samples preferred residential to personal contact when they were responding to the non-Negro groups, whereas with the Negro they preferred the reverse. The suggestion is made that this general response can be accounted for by a fear of Negro migration into white areas with a consequent, probably irrational fear (cf. Taeuber and Taeuber, 1964) that the neighborhood would deteriorate economically.

Finally, a study by Noel and Pinkney (1964) resulted in the conclusion that the similarities in the correlates of anti-Negro and anti-white prejudice far outweigh the differences. Their study was based on over 2,200 subjects representing "approximate" random samples from four widely spaced American cities, and consequently deserves more attention than the other studies cited in this section.

Modification of Attitudes

With the advent of at least limited desegregation in most sections of the country by 1960, there has been a shift in interest from simply measuring attitudes and behavior to a focus on the circumstances leading to modification of these factors. A wide range of settings and models have been employed, including a children's camp (Yarrow, Campbell, and Yarrow, 1958), school systems (Gottlieb and TenHouten, 1965; Mays, 1963; St. John, 1964; Stinson, 1963; Webster, 1961), interracial housing (Commission on Race and Housing, 1958; Hunt, 1959; Meadow, 1962; Works, 1961), role playing (Webb and Church, 1965), and small group interaction (Burnstein and McRae, 1962; Katz and Cohen, 1962; Mann, 1958).

Most of this research does not fit into any systematic framework and simple generalizations are rare. An exception is the intensive investigation of the relation between prejudice and attitude similarity (Byrne and Andres, 1964; Byrne and McGraw, 1964; Byrne and Wong, 1962; Rokeach and Mezei, 1966; Stein, Hardyck, and Smith, 1965; Triandis, 1961). There is strong evidence that if people of different races interact under conditions favoring the perceptions of belief congruence, then racial attitudes are modifiable.

One of the more significant works to appear during this period is that of Williams (1964). He reported on one phase of the Cornell Studies in Intergroup Relations which involved an intensive study of four cities. The study is a scholarly work containing a mass of empirical data set within a theoretical context. Williams' findings emphasize the complexity of intergroup relations and the significant social and psychological factors involved. The main variables which he finds related to intergroup contact and cooperation or conflict are as follows: status attributes of the individual, cultural values, stereotypes, personality structure, the situation of contact. His surveys clearly indicate that increased interaction of an egalitarian nature lowers the prevalence of ethnic prejudice.

The reader not familiar with recent research in this area could profit from reading Grimshaw's (1964) review of Williams' work, before turning directly to it.

Attitudes, Miscellaneous

In a shotgun fashion, investigators have been concerned with measuring the attitudes of Negroes and whites with respect to nearly every aspect of human behavior. Many of the reports mentioned in this section are timebound, but nevertheless shed some light on current conditions.

Broom and Glenn (1966) used 32 questions asked on national opinion surveys between 1950 and 1960 as a basis for comparing Negro and white differences in attitudes. Although public opinion surveys contain some sampling errors, this report is an excellent example of a relatively inexpensive reworking of earlier data. Negro-white differences were found which could not be due to differences in education or region of residence. In general, Negro-white differences were smaller than differences between Southern and non-Southern whites and between low-education and high-education whites. By age, the response differentiation between Negroes and whites was uneven, suggesting that cultural differences have not diminished much. The greatest differences between the two races were on questions relating to childbearing, domestic, political, and economic issues, and international affairs. The smallest differences were on authoritarianism and personal morality.

The causes of racial friction must seem to investigators to be generally obvious, for there have been few attempts to quantify these causes. Killian and Grigg (1961) tested a modified version of Myrdal's (1944) rank order of discrimination on a group of Jacksonville, Florida, Negroes and whites. The hypothesized inverse relation between the scales of the two groups was not found. Negroes ranked the chance to vote without restriction lower and segregation in public facilities higher than Myrdal postulated. Whites showed more resistance to equal job opportunities than predicted. These attitudes were measured over 5 years ago and some shifts could be expected on the basis of changes which have occurred within that period. Wolfe (1961) and Wolfe and Horn (1962) took a direct approach in attempting to identify the causes of racial friction in some 1,200 Negro and white native Southerners. Subjects were asked a series of questions relating to contact with the other race such as "When were you made the maddest in your life?" Negroes objected to "cursing, chewing out, nicknaming," whereas whites objected to "pilfering, careless work, reneging on debts and promises." No instance of racial friction was reported by 23% of the Negroes and 12% of the whites. The authors imply that there seem to be few grounds for hate between the races, but their methodology was such that serious errors of underreporting were likely.

Gross distortions regarding attitudes of the other race continue to exist among Negroes and whites. For example, in one large scale study only 22% of the whites interviewed recognized that most Negroes favored integration (Matthews and Prothro, 1962).

At least two reports confirm the well-established fact that prejudice and stereotypes are not restricted to any one region of the country or to a single race (Alsop and Quayle, 1963; McDaniel and Babchuk, 1960). Additional findings related to prejudice stem from comparisons of Negroes and Jews in a Northeastern city (Simpson, 1959). Negroes who regularly attended religious services were found to be more highly prejudiced than those who did not, but this same relation was not found among Jewish subjects. Negroes with high-status striving were found to have less prejudice.

Two studies on Florida populations have dealt with the relation between race and alienation and race and anomia. Middleton (1963) asked questions about six different types of alienation (five of which were highly intercorrelated) and found the Negro population scoring significantly higher than the white. Killian and Grigg (1962) cast some doubt on the traditional assumptions concerning the relation between urbanism and anomia. In the urban community, Negroes in general do not differ from whites in anomia, but white-collar Negroes who live in rural areas most frequently display high anomia. Thus it is position in the social structure rather than urban or rural residence that is most likely to be associated with differences in anomia. Somewhat related to the overall issue of alienation is the finding that among a group of adolescents, Negro children were more negatively oriented to society than were Latin or Anglo-American subjects (Pierce-Jones, Reid, and King, 1959).

The marked increase in voter registration among Negroes has led to increased concern with political attitudes within this group. Overviews may be found in some of the general references given earlier in this paper. A general analysis of the role of the Negro voter has been provided by Gosnell and Martin (1963). Erskine (1962) summarized various attitudes as they have been measured by specific polls over a period of years. There is no question about increases in political activity among Negroes. One study of three cities revealed that Negroes of the same social class as whites are more likely to belong to political groups than were the whites (Orum, 1966). There is also no question about the Negro preference for candidates of the Democratic Party (Brink and Harris, 1964; Erskine, 1962; Killian and Grigg, 1964a; Middleton, 1962). With respect to

Negro registration, it has been suggested that political factors are almost as important as socioeconomic ones. Local political organizations, like organizations in general, seem to thrive on opposition (Matthews and Prothro, 1963a, 1963b).

Middleton has been interested not only in the political behavior and alienation of the Negro, but also in his humor (Middleton, 1959; Middleton and Moland, 1959). On the basis of a survey of jokes told on a Negro campus and on a white campus, he found no differences in the extent of joking or in the telling of sexual jokes. To the surprise of no one, Negroes were found to react more favorably than whites to anti-white jokes. But Negroes saw the anti-Negro jokes to be just as funny as did whites. These two studies are typical of a number being reviewed in this section in that they are of some limited interest, but the scope is such that there are no significant generalizations or any general advance in the understanding of racial comparisons or of humor. They are too limited with respect to sample size and design; they stand alone. But for the reader who likes racial jokes, one further reference is given—that of Prange and Vitols (1963).

In contradistinction to the situation obtaining in research on intelligence, it is widely recognized that in ethnic attitude research the race of the experimenter or interviewer is a significant variable. No additional evidence of this fact should be necessary but it continues to accumulate (Athey, Coleman, Reitman, and Tang, 1960; Freedman, 1965; Kraus, 1962; Vaughn, 1964). Surprisingly enough, journal editors continue to accept reports in which this variable was not controlled or even acknowledged.

Additional studies of attitudes directly or indirectly have touched upon consumer motivations (Alexis, 1962; Barban and Grunbaum, 1965; Bullock, 1961a, 1961b; Schwartz, 1963); attitudes toward Communism (Kosa and Nunn, 1964); and attitudes toward Jews (Heller and Pinkney, 1965). Specific differences and similarities by race are reported but they do not fall into easily summarized generalizations.

In closing this section on miscellaneous studies of attitudes, we would like to mention one area in which there has been little change. The authors of social science textbooks continue to present the American Negro in much the same light as they have over the years. Marcus (1961) found no improvement in comparing the texts of 1960 with those of 1949. A few attempts are being made to incorporate into textbooks present and past realities in respect to the importance of the Negro tenth of the United States population. McGraw-Hill, for example, is publishing its *Skyline Series*, "A program which reflects the cultural realities of our times," a reading series. Although we have heard that some school systems are calling for history texts which give a more accurate picture of the Negro's place in American history, at present our impression from cursory examination of texts is that neither Negro nor white children would ever know of the truly significant part Negroes have played in our history (cf. e.g., Kaiser, 1962, for recent trends in Negro historiography). School children continue to receive a picture of America as an all-white nation.

The material reviewed in the preceding sections clearly suggests that there are reliable differences in perceptions and attitudes of Negroes and whites. But evidence continues to mount which indicates that much of the variance is due to factors such as place of residence, education, position in the social structure, and belief congruence. And, in many instances, similarities far outweigh differences—for example, with respect to anti-Negro and anti-white prejudice.

There is still a need for simple quantification of attitudes because of the stereotypes and lack of information one race has regarding another. This need is illustrated by the finding cited above that in one sample only 22% of the whites realized that most Negroes favor integration. But it is good to note that studies are currently being directed beyond mere quantification to a look at the conditions under which perception changes. Also, there has been an increased emphasis upon theoretical issues, a recognition that a number of variables must be looked at simultaneously, and a willingness to study the perception and attitudes of groups other than students. On the negative side, the journals continue to publish studies which are time-bound and of quite limited generalizability. Methodological errors such as failure to control for the effect of the race of the interviewer still appear.

REFERENCES

Alexis, M. "Some Negro-white differences in consumption," *American Journal of Economics and Sociology,* 1962, **21,** 11–28.

Alsop, S., and Quayle, O. "What northerners really think of Negroes," *Saturday Evening Post,* 1963, **236**(Sept. 7), 17–21.

Athey, K. R., Coleman, J. E., Reitman, A. P., and Tang, J. "Two experiments showing the effect of the interviewer's racial background on response to questionnaires concerning racial issues." *Journal of Applied Psychology,* 1960, **44,** 224–246.

Barban, A. M., and Grunbaum, G. "A factor analytic study of Negro and white responses to advertising stimuli," *Journal of Applied Psychology,* 1965, **49,** 274–280.

Brink, W., and Harris, L. *The Negro Revolution in America.* New York: Simon & Schuster, 1964.

Broom, L., and Glenn, N. D. "Negro-white differences-in reported attitudes and behavior," *Sociology and Social Research,* 1966, **50,** 187–200.

Bullock, H. A. "Consumer motivations in black and white: Part I." *Harvard Business Review,* 1961, **39,** 89–104 (a).

Bullock, H. A. "Consumer motivations in black and white: Part II." *Harvard Business Review,* 1961, **39,** 110–124 (b).

Burnstein, E., and McRae, A. V. "Some effects of shared threat and prejudice in racially mixed groups, " *Journal of Abnormal and Social Psychology,* 1962, **64,** 257–263.

Byrne, D., and Andres, D. "Prejudice and interpersonal expectancies," *Journal of Negro Education,* 1964, **33,** 441–445.

Byrne, D., and McGraw, C. "Interpersonal attraction toward Negroes," *Human Relations,* 1964, **17,** 201–213.

Byrne, D., and Wong, T. J. "Racial prejudice, inter-personal attraction, and assumed dissimilarity of attitudes," *Journal of Abnormal and Social Psychology,* 1962, **64,** 246–253.

Commission on Race and Housing. *Where Shall We Live?* Berkeley: University of California Press, 1958.

Derbyshire, R. L. "Social distance and identity conflict in Negro college students," *Sociology and Social Research,* 1964, **48,** 301–314.

Erskine, H. G. "The Polls: Race relations," *Public Opinion Quarterly,* 1962, **26,** 137–148.

Fagan, J., and O'Neill, M. "A comparison of social distance scores among college-student samples," *Journal of Social Psychology,* 1965, **66,** 281–290.

Freedman, P. I. "Race as a factor in persuasion," *American Journal of Orthopsychiatry,* 1965, **35,** 268.

Goldman, M., Warshay, L. H., and Biddle, E. H. "Residential and personal social distance toward Negroes and non-Negroes," *Psychological Reports,* 1962, **10,** 421–422.

Gosnell, H. F., and Martin, R. E. "The Negro as voter and office holder," *Journal of Negro Education,* 1963, **32,** 415–425.

Gottlieb, D., and TenHouten, W. D. "Racial composition and the social system of three high schools," *Journal of Marriage and the Family,* 1965, **27,** 204–212.

Grimshaw, A. D. "Research on intergroup relations and conflict: A review," *Journal of Conflict Resolution,* 1964, **8,** 492–504.

Heller, C. S., and Pinkney, A. "The attitudes of Negroes toward Jews," *Social Forces,* 1965, **43,** 364–369.

Hunt, C. L. "Negro-white perceptions of interracial housing," *Journal of Social Issues,* 1959, **15,** 24–29.

Kaiser, E. "Trends in American Negro historiology," *Journal of Negro Education,* 1962, **31,** 468–479.

Katz, I., and Cohen, M. "The effects of training Negroes upon cooperative problem solving in biracial teams," *Journal of Abnormal and Social Psychology,* 1962, **64,** 319–325.

Killian, L. M., and Grigg, C. M. "Rank orders of discrimination of Negroes and whites in a southern city," *Social Forces,* 1961, **39,** 235–239.

Killian, L. M., and Grigg, C. M. "Negro perceptions of organizational effectiveness." *Social Problems,* 1964, **11,** 380–388 (a).

Kosa, J., and Nunn, C. Z. "Race, deprivation, and attitude," *Phylon,* 1964, **25,** 337–346.

Kraus, S. "Modifying prejudice: Attitude change as a function of the race of the communicator," *Audiovisual Communications Review,* 1962, **10,** 14–22.

Malzberg, B. *The Mental Health of the Negro.*

Albany, New York: Research Foundation for Mental Hygiene, Inc., 1963.

Mann, J. H. "The influence of racial prejudice on sociometric choices and perceptions," *Sociomery,* 1958, **21,** 150–158.

Marcus, L. *The Treatment of Minorities in Secondary School Textbooks,* New York: Anti-Defamation League of B'nai B'rith, 1961.

Matthews, D. R., and Prothro, J. W. "Southern racial attitudes: Conflict, awareness, and political change," *Annals of the American Academy of Political and Social Science,* 1962, **344,** 108–121.

Matthews, D. R., and Prothro, J. W. "Social and economic factors and Negro voter registration in the south," *American Political Science Review,* 1963, **57,** 24–44 (a).

Matthews, D. R., and Prothro, J. W. "Political factors and Negro voter registration in the south," *American Political Science Review,* 1963, **57,** 355–367 (b).

Maurer, A. "Not science—expediency," *Perspectives in Biology and Medicine,* 1962, **5,** 259–262.

Mays, N. "Behavioral expectations of Negro and white teachers on recently desegregated public school faculties," *Journal of Negro Education,* 1963, **32,** 218–266.

McDaniel, P. A., and Babchuk, N. "Negro conceptions of white people in a northeastern city," *Phylon,* 1960, **21,** 7–19.

Meadow, K. P. "Negro white differences among newcomers to a transitional urban area," *Journal of Intergroup Relations,* 1962, **3,** 320–330.

Middleton, R. "Negro and white reactions to racial humor," *Sociometry,* 1959, **22,** 175–183.

Middleton, R. "The civil rights issue and presidential voting among southern Negroes and whites," *Social Forces,* 1962, **40,** 209–215.

Middleton, R. "Alienation, race and education," *American Sociological Review,* 1963, **28,** 973–977.

Middleton, R., and Moland, J. "Humor in Negro and white subcultures: A study of jokes among university students," *American Sociological Review,* 1959, **23**, 61–69.

Myrdal, G. *An American Dilemma: The Negro Problem and Modern Democracy.* New York: Harper, 1944.

Noel, D. L., and Pinkney, A. "Correlates of prejudice: Some racial differences and similarities," *American Journal of Sociology,* 1964, **69**, 609–622.

Orum, A. M. "A reappraisal of the social and political participation of Negroes," *American Journal of Sociology,* 1966, **72**, 32–46.

Pierce-Jones, J., and King, F. J. "Perceptual differences between Negro and white adolescents of similar symbolic brightness," *Perceptual and Motor Skills,* 1960, **11**, 191–194.

Pierce-Jones, J., Reid, J. B., and King, F. J. "Adolescent racial and ethnic group differences in social attitudes and adjustment," *Psychological Reports,* 1959, **5**, 549–552.

Prange, A. J., Jr., and Vitols, M. M. "Cultural aspects of the relatively low incidence of depression in southern Negroes," *International Journal of Social Psychiatry,* 1962, **8**, 104–112.

Proenza, L., and Strickland, B. R. "A study of prejudice in Negro and white college students," *Journal of Social Psychology,* 1965, **67**, 273–281.

Rokeach, M., and Mezei, L. "Race and shared belief as factors in social choice," *Science,* 1966, **151**, 167–172.

St. John, N. H. "De facto segregation and interracial association in high school," *Sociology of Education,* 1964, **37**, 326–344.

Schwartz, J. "Men's clothing and the Negro," *Phylon,* 1963, **24**, 224–231.

Simpson, R. L. "Negro-Jewish prejudice: Authoritarianism and some social variables as correlates," *Social Problems,* 1959, **7**, 138–146.

Stein, D. D., Hardyck, J. A., and Smith, M. B. "Race and belief: An open and shut case," *Journal of Personality and Social Psychology,* 1965, **1**, 281–289.

Stinson, H. N. The effects of desegregation on adjustment and values of Negro and white students. Unpublished doctoral dissertation, George Peabody College for Teachers, 1963.

Taeuber, K. E., and Taeuber, A. F. "The Negro as an immigrant group: Recent trends in racial and ethnic segregation in Chicago," *American Journal of Sociology,* 1964, **69**, 374–382.

Triandis, H. C. "A note on Rokeach's theory of prejudice," *Journal of Abnormal and Social Psychology,* 1961, **62**, 184–186.

Triandis, H. C., and Triandis, L. M. "Race, social class, religion, and nationality as determinants of social distress," *Journal of Abnormal and Social Psychology,* 1960, **61**, 110–118.

Vaughn, G. M. "The effect of the ethnic grouping of the experimenter upon children's responses to tests of an ethnic nature," *British Journal of Social and Clinical Psychology,* 1964, **3**, 66–70.

Webb, S. C., and Church, J. C. "The effect of role taking on the judgment of attitudes," *Journal of Social Psychology,* 1965, **65**, 279–292.

Webster, S. W. "The influence of interracial contact on social acceptance in a newly integrated school," *Journal of Educational Psychology,* 1961, **52**, 292–296.

Williams, R. M., Jr. *Strangers Next Door.* Englewood Cliffs, N. J.: Prentice-Hall, 1964.

Wolfe, J. B. "Incidents of friction between Negroes and whites in southeastern U.S.A.," *Mankind Quarterly,* 1961, **2**, 122–127.

Wolfe, J. B., and Horn, P. "Racial friction in the deep south," *Journal of Psychology,* 1962, **54**, 139–152.

Works, E. "The prejudice-interaction hypothesis from the point of view of the Negro minority group," *American Journal of Sociology,* 1961, **67**, 47–52.

Yarrow, M. R., Campbell, J. D., and Yarrow, L. J. "Acquisition of new norms: A study of racial desegregation," *Journal of Social Issues,* 1958, **14**, 8–28.

12.2 Psychometric Evaluation of an Operation Headstart Program

JOYCE L. HOWARD AND WALTER T. PLANT

A. INTRODUCTION

In 1940, a volume of research investigators was published (16) which dealt with the effects of nursery school attendance upon changes in intelligence test scores. Many of these investigations seem to have been provoked by the controversial research reported by Wellman (15).

More recent investigations of the effects of preschool education have had as a focus what is done in the preschool situation and to whom, rather than the earlier focus upon preschool attendance *per se.* The intent of the recent research appears to be the study of preschool activities presumed to be related to subsequent school performance expectations, and with specific intellectual functions for specific groups of children with demonstrated deficiencies.

Not uncommonly, recent experi-

mental or trial preschool programs have focused upon language development with children shown to be deficient in language usage (5, 12). Several programs have recently emphasized language development and general perceptual development with low socioeconomic racial-minority-group children (2, 6, 9, 10). The point is that contemporary research has focused upon organized and programmed treatment programs for lower socioeconomic subjects rather than upon whether or not subjects had or did not have some type of preschool educational experience. Even though the foci of investigations of effects of preschool educational experience have changed, the short-term criterion measures used to evaluate programs have remained essentially the same. Many of the 1940 studies reported in Whipple (16) involved the use of individual intelligence test data to evaluate preschool effects. Studies in the

Reprinted with slight abridgment from the *Journal of Genetic Psychology,* 1967, **111,** 281–288, with permission of the authors and The Journal Press.

1960's also employed the same type of measures (1, 9).

It is presumed that the continued use of individual intelligence tests as evaluative devices is due to the repeated finding that scores from these measures correlate higher with indices of educational performance than with any other nontest validation criteria.

The preschool program of this study was a part of project Operation Headstart of Summer 1965. Over 500,000 children across the country participated in the Operation Headstart program that first summer of this massive federally sponsored preschool program for children with presumed learning deficiencies.

The primary problem of the current study was to determine if a short-time, enriched preschool program (Operation Headstart) improved the likelihood of school success as predicted from an increase in individual intelligence test scores for treated subjects.

B. PROCEDURE

The program with which this study is concerned was carried out at the Mayfair School in San Jose, California. The Mayfair School attendance area is primarily composed of families whose children are those for whom the national Operation Headstart program was established. The attendance area is composed mainly of Mexican American families, and has been described as blighted (4) and as a Western ghetto (13).

1. Selection of Operation Headstart Ss

The children who participated in the Mayfair Operation Headstart program were those who had been preregistered for the Fall 1965 kindergarten classes at the Mayfair School. In order to qualify for inclusion into the program, two criteria had to be met: (a) the annual income of the child's family could not exceed $3,000.00, and (b) the child's parents had to agree to remain in town all summer, thereby enabling their child to attend the program on a daily basis. The first 45 children on the preregistration list who met the selection criteria were formed into three classes with 15 children in each. Since one child was taken out of the program a few days after it began, only 44 children were tested at the beginning of the eight-week program. Eleven of these moved away from the school attendance area, and 33 subjects were retested with the same instruments 90 to 120 days later while in kindergarten. The participants in the program who stayed in the area and were enrolled in kindergarten at Mayfair School in September 1965 were considered the experimental subjects and will hereafter be referred to as Operation Headstart subjects or OHS.

2. Selection of Comparison Ss

Ideally, a sample of children meeting the same selection criteria as were met by the OHS, but not in any preschool program should have been selected and tested both before and after the Operation Headstart program. However, this was impossible due to the hurried implementation of the program both locally and nationally for this first year. Therefore, it was necessary to select an *ad hoc* matched comparison group. Before any test data had been tabulated, the selection of the matched comparison group was made by the second author from information accumulated for the entire kindergarten at the beginning of the school year. Subjects were matched with the OHS on four factors: (*a*) sex, (*b*) chronological age within 60 days, (*c*) parental occupational level as categorized by the Hollingshead and Redlich (*11*) system, and (*d*) parental ethnic-racial origin. The comparison *S*s participated in the testing program of the entire kindergarten of the Mayfair School at the same time the OHS were tested in the same kindergarten classes. Hereafter, the matched comparison group will be designated MCG.

3. The Program and Teachers

As in the regular school program, the teachers for the Mayfair School Operation Headstart program were qualified and experienced professionals. All three teachers had taught in primary grades in the area, and were familiar with behavior patterns of the group participating in the program. In preparation for teaching in the program, all three teachers attended a week-long training and orientation program. This training consisted of lectures regarding the cultural background, educational deficiencies, and behavior patterns of their future pupils; class demonstrations; and the making of teaching aids.

There was very little emphasis placed upon preparing the OHS for school *per se* as most of their activities were self-directed and not organized. The only group or planned activities were song and story times, and selected field trips.

4. Psychological Tests Used

All of the children participating in the Operation Headstart program at Mayfair School were given three individual tests near the beginning of the project sessions. The tests were the *Stanford-Binet, LM* (*14*), the *Peabody Picture Vocabulary Test: Form A* (*7*), and the *Pictorial Test of Intelligence* (*8*). The first administration of the test to the OHS in July 1965 is called Testing Session I (TS I). In October and November of 1965— Testing Session II (TS II)—the same tests were administered to each child in the kindergarten classes at Mayfair School. In addition, from December 1965 to January 1966, a new test was also given to each kindergarten student. The new scale used in Testing Session III (TS III) was comprised of a verbal half and a performance half and was still in the process of national standardization. The test author, name, and distributor are unidentified by agreement with all parties concerned, and the test will herein be called the EX test.

All testing was accomplished without examiners' knowing which children had been in Operation Headstart and which children had not. One team of examiners did the initial testing (TS I), and a second team the "in kindergarten" testing (TS II and TS III).

5. Comparisons Made and Statistical Procedures Used

There were two sets of analyses conducted. One measure of the short-term effects of the OH program was to determine whether there were mean gains on the three individual intelligence tests for the 33 OHS over the 90 to 120 days. Such comparisons were made for TS I *vs.* TS II.

A second measure of the short-term effects of the OH program was to compare the "in kindergarten" test performance of the OH group with that of subjects like the OHS who had not had the OH experience. Four such comparisons were made.

The correlated *t* test procedure was used for both sets of analyses. This statistical procedure was considered appropriate because for the test-retest comparisons the scores on the two occasions were obtained from the same individuals and, for the latter comparisons, the Ss of the two groups were individually matched.

C. RESULTS

1. TS I *vs.* TS II Analyses

As indicated, *t* tests of the significance of the difference between correlated means were computed for the TS I–TS II analyses for the OH sample. The results of these analyses are found in Table 1.

As is easily seen, all three test-retest analyses yielded statistically significant mean gains beyond the .01 level. The greatest gains occurred for the PPVT and the PTI tests. The mean gain on the PPVT is particularly noteworthy because it was larger than the average of the two standard deviations for TS I and TS II.

2. Matched-Pair Analyses

The correlated *t* test comparisons for the matched-pair analyses are found in Table 2.

Careful inspection of the data in Table 2 yields several relevant observations. Of primary interest is the fact that the means for the OHS are numerically higher than those for their matched pairs. Three of the five comparisons reached acceptable levels of statistical significance.

D. DISCUSSION

The mean intelligence test scores of the OHS were significantly higher after participating in the Operation Headstart program and attending kindergarten for six weeks than they were at the beginning of the program. These comparisons seem to indicate that there was some positive effect of the OH program upon the intelligence test scores of the participants. Also, at Testing Session II and Testing Session III, three out of five comparisons were statistically significant,

table 1

SB-LM, PPVT, and PTI Three-Month Test-Retest Comparisons for Operation Headstart Subjects ($N = 33$)

Test	Mean TS I	Sigma TS I	Mean TS II	Sigma TS II	*r* TS I-TS II	Mean diff. TS I-TS II	*t*
SB-LM IQ	91.16	14.08	94.91	12.92	.88	3.75	3.18**
PPVT IQ	76.44	17.59	94.72	14.22	.60	18.28	7.13**
PTI IQ	85.58	13.11	93.58	12.61	.74	8.00	4.35**

** Sig. beyond .01 level.

Note.—SB-LM = Stanford-Binet, LM; PPVT = Peabody Picture Vocabulary Test; PT I = Pictorial Test of Intelligence; TS I = Testing Session I; TS II = Testing Session II.

table 2

SB-LM, PPVT, PTI, and EX-Test Comparisons for Operation Headstart and Matched-Pair
Subjects ($N = 33$)

Test	OH Subjects		MCG Subjects		r OHS-MCG	Mean diff. OHS-MCG	t
	Mean	Sigma	Mean	Sigma			
			TS II				
SB-LM IQ	94.97	12.97	91.06	11.43	.26	3.91	1.17
PPVT IQ	94.55	14.32	86.91	15.79	.03	7.64	2.02*
PTI IQ	93.84	13.00	87.50	14.76	.07	6.34	1.89*
			TS III				
EX Verb. X	65.50	16.81	58.63	22.12	.05	6.88	1.43
EX Perf. X	31.81	10.62	23.84	9.52	.09	7.97	3.03**

*Sig. beyond .05 level.
**Sig. beyond .01 level.
Note.—SB-LM = Stanford-Binet, LM; PPVT = Peabody Picture Vocabulary Test; PT I = Pictorial
Test of Intelligence; OHS = Operation Headstart subjects; MCG = Matched Comparison Group; EX =
new unpublished test; TS II = Testing Session II; and TS III = Testing Session III.

and all five favored the OHS over their matched "in kindergarten" pairs. Again, these comparisons seem to indicate a positive effect of the OH program.

It is of interest to note these apparent short-term positive advantages for the OHS and to remember that there was little formal planning of the OH activities. Other investigations wherein extensive planning of activities and programming of these activities occurred have also yielded positive results with the same or similar short-term criterion measures (1, 2, 3, 5, 9). It would seem that the major evaluation task for investigators is to determine which set of arrangements yields the most positive results over a short period of time and, more importantly, which yield the most enduring positive results for the treated subjects.

E. SUMMARY

This study was a psychometric evaluation of an Operation Headstart program during the summer of 1965 at the Mayfair School in San Jose, California. Due to the late local and national implementation of Operation Headstart in its first summer, little formal planning and programming of summer preschool activities was possible. The OHS were left somewhat to their own resources; the activities with the exception of story and music times and selected field trips were largely self-directed.

Prior to and during the first few days of the OH program, in Testing Session I (TS I), all of the participants were administered the *Stanford-Binet, LM* test, the *Peabody Picture Vocabulary Test,* and the *Pictorial Test of Intelligence.* In order that it might be determined whether the program had affected the participants' intelligence test scores, the same battery was administered in October and November 1965—Testing Session II (TS II)—to the entire kindergarten at the Mayfair School wherein the OHS were students. In addition, in December 1965 and January 1966—Testing Session III (TS III)—a new and unpublished individual intelligence test with a verbal and performance part herein called the EX test was administered to all kindergarten *S*s at the Mayfair School.

The experimental group (OHS) was composed of 33 preschool subjects who not only attended the Operation Headstart program at Mayfair School, but also attended kindergarten there. A matched comparison group (MCG) also attended kindergarten at Mayfair School, but the members had not been in any preschool program including the Operation Headstart program. The groups of matched pairs were matched on sex, age, parental occupational level, and their racial-ethnic origin.

Through the use of *t* tests for the significance of the difference between correlated means it was found that (*a*) the intelligence test means for the OHS were significantly higher for TS II than for TS I, and (*b*) the intelligence test means for the OHS were all higher than for the MCG, and three of the five were statistically significantly higher.

Both sets of analyses seemed to indicate a positive effect for the OH program. Because the OH program under observation was largely unplanned and unprogrammed, it was suggested that future investigations will need to be designed in such a way as to determine which set of preschool arrangements will yield the most positive results of a short-term and long-term nature.

REFERENCES

1. Ametjian, A. The effects of a preschool program upon the intellectual development and social competency of lower-class children. Unpublished Doctoral dissertation, Stanford University, Stanford, California, 1965.

2. Boger, H. "An experimental study of the effect of perceptual training on group IQ test scores of elementary pupils in rural ungraded schools," *J. Educ. Res.*, 1952, **46**, 43–53.

3. Brazziel, W. F., and Terrell, M. "An experiment in the development of readiness in a culturally disadvantaged group of first-grade children," *J. Negro Educ.*, 1962, **31**, 4–7.

4. Clark, M. *Health in the Mexican-American Culture.* Berkeley: Univ. Calif. Press, 1959.

5. Dawe, H. C. "A study of the effect of an educational program upon language development and related mental functions in young children," *J. Exper. Educ.*, 1942, **11**, 200–209.

6. Deutsch, M. "The role of social class in language development and cognition," *Amer. J. Orthopsychiat.*, 1965, **35**, 78–88.

7. Dunn, L. M. Peabody Picture Vocabulary Test: Manual. Minneapolis: Amer. Guid. Services, 1959.

8. French, J. L. Pictorial Test of Intelligence: Manual. Boston: Houghton Mifflin, 1964.

9. Gray, S. W., and Klaus, R. A. "An experimental preschool program for culturally deprived children," *Child Devel.*, 1965, **36**, 887–898.

10. Gray, S. W., Klaus, R. A., Miller, J. O., and Forrester, B. J. *The Early Training Project: A Handbook of Aims and Activities.* Nashville, Tenn.: Geo. Peabody Coll. for Teachers, 1965.

11. Hollingshead, A. B., and Redlich, F. C. *Social Class and Mental Illness.* N.Y.: Wiley, 1958.

12. Peters, C. C., and McElwee, A. R. "Improving functioning intelligence by analytical

training in a nursery school," *Elem. Sch. J.,* 1944, **45,** 213–219.

13. Plant, W. T. Effects of preschool stimulation upon subsequent school performance among the culturally disadvantaged. Project 3102, Contract No. OE-6-10-118, Cooperative Research Branch, U.S. Office of Education, San Jose State College, San Jose, California, 1965–1970.

14. Terman, L. M., and Merrill, M. A. *Stanford-Binet Intelligence Scale: Manual for the Third Revision Form LM.* Boston: Houghton Mifflin Co., 1960.

15. Wellman, B. L. "The effect of preschool attendance upon the IQ," *J. Exper. Educ.,* 1932, **1,** 48–69.

16. Whipple, G. M., Ed. *Intelligence: Its Nature and Nurture* (39th Yearbook, Nat. Soc. for Study Educ., Part II). Chicago: Univ. Chicago Press, 1940.

12.3 Changing the Game from "Get the Teacher" to "Learn"

ROBERT L. HAMBLIN,
DAVID BUCKHOLDT,
DONALD BUSHELL,
DESMOND ELLIS, AND
DANIEL FERRITOR

Almost any educator of experience will assure you that it is next to impossible—and often actually impossible—to teach normal classroom subjects to children who have extreme behavior problems, or who are "too young." Yet at four experimental classrooms of the Central Midwestern Regional Educational Laboratories (CEMREL), we have been bringing about striking changes in the behavior and learning progress of just such children.

In the 18 months of using new exchange systems and working with different types of problem children, we have seen these results:

1. Extraordinarily aggressive boys, who had not previously responded to therapy, have been tamed.

2. Two-year-olds have learned to read about as fast and as well as their 5-year-old classmates.

3. Four ghetto children, too shy, too withdrawn to talk, have become better than average talkers.

4. Several autistic children, who were either mute or could only parrot sounds, have developed functional speech, have lost their bizarre and disruptive behavior patterns, and their relationships with parents and other children have improved. All of these children are on the road to normality.

Our system is deceptively simple. Superficially, in fact, it may not even seem new—though, in detail, it has never been tried in precisely this form in the classroom before. In essence, we simply

Reprinted from *Trans-Action*, 1969, 6(3), 20–31, by permission of the editors of *Trans-Action*. Copyright © 1969 by *Trans-Action Magazine*, New Brunswick, New Jersey. The portion reprinted here consists of the first six pages of the twelve-page article.

reinforce "good" behavior and nonpunitively discourage "bad" behavior. We structure a social exchange so that as the child progresses, we reinforce this behavior—give him something that he values, something that shows our approval. Therefore, he becomes strongly motivated to continue his progress. To terminate bizarre, disruptive or explosive patterns, we stop whatever has been reinforcing that undesirable behavior—actions or attention that teachers or parents have unwittingly been giving him in exchange, often in the belief that they were punishing and thus discouraging him. Study after study has shown that whenever a child persists in behaving badly, some adult has, perhaps inadvertently, been rewarding him for it.

"Socialization" is the term that sociologists use to describe the process of transforming babies—who can do little but cry, eat, and sleep—into adults who can communicate and function rather effectively in their society. Socialization varies from culture to culture, and, while it is going on all around us, we are seldom aware of it. But when normal socialization breaks down, "problems" occur—autism, nonverbal or hyperaggressive behavior, retardation, delinquency, crime, and so on.

The authors, after years of often interesting but by and large frustrating research, realized that the more common theories of child development (Freudian, neo-Freudian, the developmental theories of Gesell and Piaget, and a number of others) simply do not satisfactorily explain the socialization process in children. Consequently in desperation we began to move toward the learning theories and then toward the related exchange theories of social structure. Since then, working with problem children, our view has gradually been amplified and refined. Each experimental classroom has given us a different looking glass. In each we can see the child in different conditions, and can alter the conditions which hinder his socialization into a civilized, productive adult capable of happiness.

By the time they become students, most children love to play with one another, to do art work, to cut and paste, to play with Playdoh, to climb and swing on the playground, and so on. Most pre-schools also serve juice and cookie snacks, and some have television sets or movies. There is, consequently, no dearth of prizes for us to reward the children for good behavior. The problem is not in finding reinforcers, but in managing them.

THE BASIC SYSTEM: TOKEN EXCHANGE

One of the simpler and most effective ways, we found, was to develop a token-exchange system. The tokens we use are plastic discs that children can earn. A child who completes his arithmetic or reading may earn a dozen tokens, given one by one as he proceeds through the lessons. And at the end of the lesson period comes the reward.

Often it is a movie. The price varies. For four tokens, a student can watch while sitting on the floor; for eight, he gets a chair; for 12, he can watch while sitting on the table. Perhaps the view is better from the table—anyway, the children almost always buy it if they have enough tokens. But if they dawdled so much that they earned fewer than four, they are "timed out" into the hall while the others see the movie. Throughout the morning, therefore, the children earn, then spend, then earn, then spend.

This token-exchange system is very powerful. It can create beneficial changes in a child's behavior, his emotional reactions, and ultimately even his approach to life. But it is not easy to set up, nor simple to maintain.

At the beginning the tokens are meaningless to the children; so to make them meaningful, we pair them with M&M candies, or something similar. As the child engages in the desired behavior (or a reasonable facsimile), the teacher gives him a "Thank you," an M&M, and a token. At first the children are motivated by the M&Ms and have to be urged to hold on to the tokens; but then they find that the tokens can be used to buy admission to the movie, Playdoh, or other good things. The teacher tells them the price and asks them to count out the tokens. Increasingly, the teacher "forgets" the M&Ms. In two or three days the children get no candy, just the approval and the tokens. By then, they have learned.

There are problems in maintaining a token exchange. Children become disinterested in certain reinforcers if they are used too frequently, and therefore in the tokens that buy them. For instance, young children will work very hard to save up tokens to play with Playdoh once a week; if they are offered Playdoh every day, the charm quickly fades. Some activities—snacks, movies, walks outdoors—are powerful enough to be used every day.

As noted, the children we worked with had different behavior problems, reflecting various kinds of breakdowns in the socialization process. Each experiment we conducted concentrated on a particular type of maladjustment or a particular group of maladjusted children to see how a properly structured exchange system might help them. Let us look at each experiment, to see how each problem was affected.

AGGRESSION

Unfortunately, our world reinforces and rewards aggressive behavior. Some cultures and some families are open and brazen about it—they systematically and consciously teach their young that it is desirable, and even virtuous, to attack certain other individuals or groups. The child who can beat up the other kids on the playground is sometimes respected by his peers, and perhaps by his parents; the soldier achieves glory in combat. The status, the booty, or the bargaining advantages that come to the aggressor can become reinforcement to continue and escalate his aggressions.

In more civilized cultures the young are taught not to use aggression, and we try to substitute less harmful patterns. But even so, aggression is sometimes reinforced unintentionally—and the consequences, predictably, are the same as if the teaching were deliberate.

In the long run civilized cultures are not kind to hyperaggressive children. A recent survey in England, for instance, found that the great majority of teachers felt that aggressive behavior by students disturbed more classrooms than anything else and caused the most anxiety among teachers. At least partly as a result, the dropout rates for the hyperaggressives was $2\frac{1}{2}$ times as great as for "normals," and disproportionate numbers of hyper-aggressives turned up in mental clinics.

The traditional treatment for aggressive juveniles is punishment—often harsh punishment. This is not only of dubious moral value, but generally it does not work.

We took seriously—perhaps for the first time—the theory that aggression is a type of exchange behavior. Boys become aggressive because they get something for it; they continue to be aggressive because the rewards are continuing. To change an aggressive pattern in our experimental class at Washington University, therefore, we had to restructure appropriately the exchange system in which the boys were involved.

As subjects we (Ellis and Hamblin) found five extraordinarily aggressive 4-year-old boys, all referred to us by local psychiatrists and social workers who had been able to do very little with them. Next, we hired a trained teacher. We told her about the boys and the general nature of the experiment—then gave her her head. That is, she was allowed to use her previous training during the first period—and this would provide a baseline comparison with what followed after. We hoped she would act like the "typical teacher." We suspect that she did.

LET'S PLAY "GET THE TEACHER"

The teacher was, variously, a strict disciplinarian, wise counselor, clever arbitrator, and sweet peacemaker. Each role failed miserably. After the eighth day, the average of the children was 150 sequences of aggression per day! Here is what a mere four minutes of those sequences were like:

Mike, John, and Dan are seated together playing with pieces of Playdoh. Barry, some distance from the others, is seated and also is playing with Playdoh. The children, except Barry, are talking about what they are making. Time is 9:10 A.M. Miss Sally, the teacher, turns toward the children and says, "It's time for a lesson. Put your Playdoh away." Mike says, "Not me." John says, "Not me." Dan says, "Not me." Miss Sally moves toward Mike. Mike throws some Playdoh in Miss Sally's face. Miss Sally jerks back, then moves forward rapidly and snatches Playdoh from Mike. Puts Playdoh in her pocket. Mike screams for Playdoh, says he wants to play with it. Mike moves toward Miss Sally and attempts to snatch the Playdoh from Miss Sally's pocket. Miss Sally pushes him away. Mike kicks Miss Sally on the leg. Kicks her again, and demands the return of his Playdoh. Kicks Miss Sally again. Picks up a small steel chair and throws it at Miss Sally. Miss Sally jumps out of the way. Mike picks up another chair and throws it more violently. Miss Sally cannot move in time. Chair strikes her foot. Miss Sally pushes Mike down on the floor. Mike starts up. Pulls over one chair. Now another, another. Stops a moment. Miss Sally is picking up chairs, Mike looks at Miss Sally. Miss Sally moves toward Mike. Mike runs away.

John wants his Playdoh. Miss Sally says "No." He joins Mike in pulling over chairs and attempts to grab Playdoh from Miss Sally's pocket. Miss Sally pushes him away roughly. John is screaming that he wants to play with his Playdoh. Moves toward phonograph. Pulls it off the table; lets it crash onto the floor. Mike has his coat on. Says he is going home. Miss Sally asks Dan to bolt the door. Dan gets to the door at the same time as Mike. Mike hits Dan in the face. Dan's nose is bleeding. Miss Sally walks over to Dan, turns to the others, and says that she is taking Dan to the washroom and that while she is away, they may play with the Playdoh. Returns Playdoh from pocket to Mike and John. Time: 9:14 A.M.

Wild? Very. These were barbarous little boys who enjoyed battle. Miss Sally did her best but they were just more clever than she, and they *always* won. Whether Miss Sally wanted to or not, they could always drag her into the fray, and just go at it harder and harder until she capitulated. She was finally driven to their level, trading a kick for a kick and a spit in the face for a spit in the face.

What Miss Sally did not realize is that she had inadvertantly structured an exchange where she consistently reinforced aggression. First, as noted, whenever she fought with them, she *always lost.* Second, more subtly, she reinforced their aggressive pattern by giving it serious attention—by looking, talking, scolding, cajoling, becoming angry, even striking back. These boys were playing a teasing

game called "Get the Teacher." The more she showed that she was bothered by their behavior, the better they liked it, and the further they went.

These interpretations may seem far-fetched, but they are borne out dramatically by what happened later. On the twelfth day we changed the conditions, beginning with B1 (see Figure 1). First, we set up the usual token exchange to reinforce cooperative behavior. This was to develop or strengthen behavior that would replace aggression. Any strong pattern of behavior serves some function for the individual, so the first step in getting rid of a strong, disruptive pattern is substituting another one that is more useful and causes fewer problems. Not only therapy, but simple humanity dictates this.

First, the teacher had to be instructed in how *not to reinforce* aggression. Contrary to all her experience, she was asked to turn her back on the aggressor, and at the same time to reinforce others' cooperation with tokens. Once we were able to coach her and give her immediate feedback over a wireless-communication system, she structured the exchanges almost perfectly. The data in Figures 1 and 2 show the crucial changes: a gradual increase in cooperation—from about 56 to about 115 sequences per day, and a corresponding decrease in aggression from 150 to about 60 sequences!

These results should have been satisfactory, but we were new at this kind of experimentation, and nervous. We wanted to reduce the frequency of aggression to a "normal" level, to about 15 sequences a day. So we restructured the exchange system and thus launched A2.

In A2, we simply made sure that

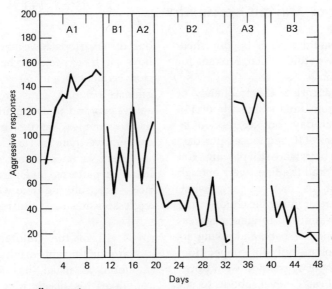

figure 1

Frequency of aggressive sequences by days for five 4-year-old boys. In A1, A2, and A3 the teacher attempted to punish aggression but inadvertently reinforced it. In B1, B2, and B3 she turned her back or otherwise ignored aggression and thus did not reinforce it.

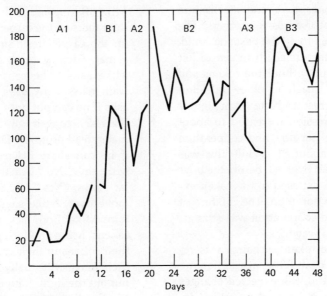

figure 2

Frequency of cooperative sequences. In A1, A2, and A3 the teacher structured a weak approval exchange for cooperation and a disapproval exchange for noncooperation. In B1, B2, and B3, she structured a token exchange for cooperation.

aggression would always be punished. The teacher was told to *charge* tokens for any aggression.

To our surprise, the frequency of cooperation remained stable, about 115 sequences per day; but aggression *increased* to about 110 sequences per day! Evidently the boys were still playing "Get the Teacher," and the fines were enough reinforcement to increase aggression.

So, instead of fining the children, the teacher was again told to ignore aggression by turning her back and giving attention and tokens only for cooperation. The frequency of aggression went down to a near "normal" level, about 16 sequences per day (B2), and cooperation increased to about 140 sequences.

Then, as originally planned, the conditions were again reversed. The boys were given enough tokens at the beginning of the morning to buy their usual supply of movies, toys, and snacks, and these were not used as reinforcers. The teacher was told to do the best she could. She was not instructed to return to her old pattern, but without the tokens and without our coaching she did—and with the same results. Note A3 in Figures 1 and 2. Aggression increased to about 120 sequences per day, and cooperation decreased to about 90. While this was an improvement over A1, before the boys had ever been exposed to the token exchange, it was not good. The mixture of aggression and cooperation was strange, even weird, to watch.

When the token exchange was restructured (B3) and the aggression no longer reinforced, the expected changes recurred—with a bang. Aggression decreased to seven sequences on the last day, and cooperation rose to about 181 sequences. In "normal" nursery schools,

our observations have shown that five boys can be expected to have 15 aggression sequences and 60 cooperation sequences per day. Thus, from extremely aggressive and uncooperative, our boys had become less aggressive and far more cooperative than "normal" boys.

Here is an example of their new behavior patterns, taken from a rest period—precisely the time when the most aggressive acts had occurred in the past:

All of the children are sitting around the table drinking their milk; John, as usual, has finished first. Takes his plastic mug and returns it to the table. Miss Martha, the assistant teacher, gives him a token. John goes to cupboard, takes out his mat, spreads it out by the blackboard, and lies down. Miss Martha gives him a token. Meanwhile, Mike, Barry, and Jack have spread their mats on the carpet. Dan is lying on the carpet itself since he hasn't a mat. Each of them gets a token. Mike asks if he can sleep by the wall. Miss Sally says "Yes." John asks if he can put out the light. Miss Sally says to wait until Barry has his mat spread properly. Dan asks Mike if he can share his mat with him. Mike says "No." Dan then asks Jack. Jack says, "Yes," but before he can move over, Mike says "Yes." Dan joins Mike. Both Jack and Mike get tokens. Mike and Jack get up to put their tokens in their cans. Return to their mats. Miss Sally asks John to put out the light. John does so. Miss Martha gives him a token. All quiet now. Four minutes later—all quiet. Quiet still, three minutes later. Time: 10:23 A.M. Rest period ends.

⊀The hyperaggressive boys actually had, and were, double problems; they were not only extremely disruptive, but they were also washouts as students. Before the token system (A1), they paid attention to their teacher only about 8 percent of the lesson time (see Figure 3). The teacher's system of scolding the youngsters for inattention and taking their attention for granted with faint approval, if any, did not work at all. To the pupils, the "Get the Teacher" game was much more satisfying.

After the token exchange was started, in B1, B2, B3, and B4, it took a long, long time before there was any appreciable effect. The teacher was being trained from scratch, and our methods were, then, not very good. However, after we set up a wireless-communication system that allowed us to coach the teacher from behind a one-way mirror and to give her immediate feedback, the children's attention began to increase. Toward the end of B3, it leveled off at about 75 percent—from 8 percent! After the token exchange was taken out during A2, attention went down to level off at 23 percent; put back in at B4, it shot back up to a plateau of about 93 percent. Like a roller coaster: 8 percent without, to 75 with, to 23 without, to 93 with.

NORMAL CHILDREN

These results occurred with chronic, apparently hopeless hyperaggressive boys. Would token exchange also help "nor-

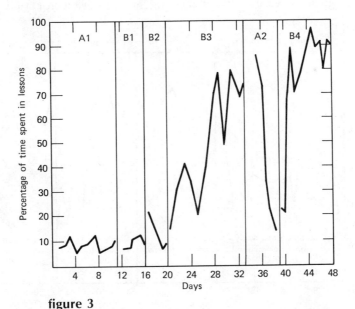

figure 3

Percentage of scheduled time spent in lessons by days for five hyperaggressive boys. In A1 and A2, teacher structured approval exchange for attendance, disapproval for nonattendance. In B1 and B2, a token exchange for attendance was structured, but not effectively until B2 and B4.

mal," relatively bright upper-middle-class children? Sixteen youngsters of that description—nine boys and seven girls, ranging from 2 years 9 months to 4 years 9 months—were put through an experimental series by Bushell, Hamblin, and Denis Stoddard in an experimental pre-school at Webster College. All had about a month's earlier experience with the token-exchange system. The results are shown in Figure 4.

STUDY IN 15-MINUTE PERIODS

At first, the study hour was broken up into 15-minute periods, alternating between the work that received tokens, and the play or reward that the tokens could be used for. Probably because the children were already familiar with token exchange, no great increase in learning

took place. On the 22nd day, we decided to try to increase the learning period, perhaps for the whole hour. In A2 (Figure 4), note that the time spent in studying went up rapidly and dramatically—almost doubling—from 27 to level off at 42 minutes.

During B, the token exchange was taken out completely. The teachers still gave encouragement and prepared interesting lessons as before. The rewards—the nature walks, snacks, movies, and so on—were retained. But, as in a usual classroom, they were given to the children free instead of being sold. The children continued at about the same rate as before for a few days. But after a week, attention dropped off slowly, then sharply. On the last day it was down to about 15 minutes—one-third the level of the end of the token period.

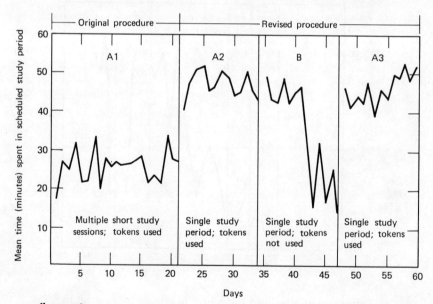

figure 4

Sixteen upper-middle-class pre-schoolers. In A1, A2, and A3 the token exchange was used; in B, only approval.

In A3, the token exchange was reinstituted. In only three days, attention snapped back from an average of 15 minutes to 45 minutes. However, by the end of A3, the students paid attention an average of 50 of the available 60 minutes.

A comparison of the record of these normals with the record of the hyperaggressive boys is interesting. The increase in attention brought by the token exchange, from about 15 minutes to 50, is approximately threefold for the normal children; but for the hyperaggressive boys—who are disobedient and easily distracted—it is about eleven-fold, from 8 percent to 93 percent of the time. The increase was not only greater, but the absolute level achieved was higher. This indicates strongly, therefore, that the more problematic the child, the greater may be the effect of token exchange on his behavior.

The high rates of attention were not due to the fact that each teacher had fewer children to work with. Individualized lessons were not enough. Without the token exchange, even three teachers could not hold the interest of 16 children 2 to 4 years old—at least not in reading, writing, and arithmetic.

Praise and approval were not enough as rewards. The teachers, throughout the experiment, used praise and approval to encourage attention; they patted heads and said things like "Good," "You're doing fine," and "Keep it up"; yet, in B, when the token exchange was removed, this attention nevertheless ultimately declined by two-thirds. Social approval is important, but not nearly so powerful as material reinforcers.

Finally, it is obvious that if the reinforcers (movies, snacks, toys, or whatever) do not seem directly connected to the work, they will not sustain a high level of study. To be effective with young children, rewards must occur in a structured exchange in which they are given promptly as recompense and thus are directly connected to the work performed.

12.4 Bystander Intervention in Emergencies: A Diffusion of Responsibility

JOHN M. DARLEY AND BIBB LATANÉ

Several years ago, a young woman was stabbed to death in the middle of a street in a residential section of New York City. Although such murders are not entirely routine, the incident received little public attention until several weeks later when the New York Times disclosed another side to the case: at least 38 witnesses had observed the attack—and none had even attempted to intervene. Although the attacker took more than half an hour to kill Kitty Genovese, not one of the 38 people who watched from the safety of their own apartments came out to assist her. Not one even lifted the telephone to call the police (Rosenthal, 1964).

Preachers, professors, and news commentators sought the reasons for such apparently conscienceless and inhumane lack of intervention. Their conclusions ranged from "moral decay," to "dehumanization produced by the urban environment," to "alienation," "anomie,"

and "existential despair." An analysis of the situation, however, suggests that factors other than apathy and indifference were involved.

A person witnessing an emergency situation, particularly such a frightening and dangerous one as a stabbing, is in conflict. There are obvious humanitarian norms about helping the victim, but there are also rational and irrational fears about what might happen to a person who does intervene (Milgram and Hollander, 1964). "I didn't want to get involved," is a familiar comment, and behind it lies fears of physical harm, public embarrassment, involvement with police procedures, lost work days and jobs, and other unknown dangers.

In certain circumstances, the norms favoring intervention may be weakened, leading bystanders to resolve the conflict in the direction of nonintervention. One of these circumstances may be the pres-

Reprinted with slight abridgment from the *Journal of Personality and Social Psychology,* 1968, **8**, 377–383, with permission of the authors and the American Psychological Association, Inc.

ence of other onlookers. For example, in the case above, each observer, by seeing lights and figures in other apartment house windows, knew that others were also watching. However, there was no way to tell how the other observers were reacting. These two facts provide several reasons why any individual may have delayed or failed to help. The responsibility for helping was diffused among the observers; there was also diffusion of any potential blame for not taking action; and finally, it was possible that somebody, unperceived, had already initiated helping action.

When only one bystander is present in an emergency, if help is to come, it must come from him. Although he may choose to ignore it (out of concern for his personal safety, or desires "not to get involved"), any pressure to intervene focuses uniquely on him. When there are several observers present, however, the pressures to intervene do not focus on any one of the observers; instead the responsibility for intervention is shared among all the onlookers and is not unique to any one. As a result, no one helps.

A second possibility is that potential blame may be diffused. However much we may wish to think that an individual's moral behavior is divorced from considerations of personal punishment or reward, there is both theory and evidence to the contrary (Aronfreed, 1964; Miller and Dollard, 1941, Whiting and Child, 1953). It is perfectly reasonable to assume that, under circumstances of group responsibility for a punishable act, the punishment or blame that accrues to any one individual is often slight or nonexistent.

Finally, if others are known to be present, but their behavior cannot be closely observed, any one bystander can assume that one of the other observers is already taking action to end the emergency. Therefore, his own intervention would be only redundant—perhaps harmfully or confusingly so. Thus, given the presence of other onlookers whose behavior cannot be observed, any given bystander can rationalize his own inaction by convincing himself that "somebody else must be doing something."

These considerations lead to the hypothesis that the more bystanders to an emergency, the less likely, or the more slowly, any one bystander will intervene to provide aid. To test this proposition it would be necessary to create a situation in which a realistic "emergency" could plausibly occur. Each subject should also be blocked from communicating with others to prevent his getting information about their behavior during the emergency. Finally, the experimental situation should allow for the assessment of the speed and frequency of the subjects' reaction to the emergency. The experiment reported below attempted to fulfill these conditions.

PROCEDURE

Overview. A college student arrived in the laboratory and was ushered into an individual room from which a communication system would enable him to talk to the other participants. It was explained to him that he was to take part in a discussion about personal problems associated with college life and that the discussion would be held over the intercom system, rather than face-to-face, in order to avoid embarrassment by preserving the anonymity of the subjects. During the course of the discussion, one of the other subjects underwent what appeared to be a very serious nervous seizure similar to epilepsy. During the fit it was impossible for the subject to talk to the other discussants or to find out what, if anything, they were doing about the emergency. The dependent variable was the speed with which the subjects reported the emergency to the experimenter. The major independent variable was the number of people the subject thought to be in the discussion group.

Subjects. Fifty-nine female and thirteen male students in introductory psychology courses at New York University were contacted to take part in an unspecified experiment as part of a class requirement.

Method. Upon arriving for the experiment, the subject found himself in a long corridor with doors opening off it to several small rooms. An experimental assistant met him, took him to one of the rooms, and seated him at a table. After filling out a background information form, the subject was given a pair of headphones with an attached microphone and was told to listen for instructions.

Over the intercom, the experimenter explained that he was interested in learning about the kinds of personal problems faced by normal college students in a high pressure, urban environment. He said that to avoid possible embarrassment about discussing personal problems with strangers several precautions had been taken. First, sub-

jects would remain anonymous, which was why they had been placed in individual rooms rather than face-to-face. (The actual reason for this was to allow tape recorder simulation of the other subjects and the emergency.) Second, since the discussion might be inhibited by the presence of outside listeners, the experimenter would not listen to the initial discussion, but would get the subject's reactions later, by questionnaire. (The real purpose of this was to remove the obviously responsible experimenter from the scene of the emergency.)

The subjects were told that since the experimenter was not present, it was necessary to impose some organization. Each person would talk in turn, presenting his problems to the group. Next, each person in turn would comment on what the others had said, and finally, there would be a free discussion. A mechanical switching device would regulate this discussion sequence and each subject's microphone would be on for about 2 minutes. While any microphone was on, all other microphones would be off. Only one subject, therefore, could be heard over the network at any given time. The subjects were thus led to realize when they later heard the seizure that only the victim's microphone was on and that there was no way of determining what any of the other witnesses were doing, nor of discussing the event and its possible solution with the others. When these instructions had been given, the discussion began.

In the discussion, the future victim spoke first, saying that he found it difficult to get adjusted to New York City and to his studies. Very hesitantly, and with obvious embarrassment, he mentioned that he was prone to seizures, particularly when studying hard or taking exams. The other people, including the real subject, took their turns and discussed similar problems (minus, of course, the proneness to seizures). The naive subject talked last in the series, after the last prerecorded voice was played.[1]

When it was again the victim's turn to talk, he made a few relatively calm comments, and then, growing increasingly louder and incoherent, he continued:

I-er-um-I think I-I need-er-if-if could-er-er-somebody er-er-er-er-er-er-er give me a little-er-give me a little help here because-er-I-er-I'm-er-er-h-h-having a-a-a real problem-er-right now and I-er-if somebody could help me out it would-it would-er-er s-s-sure be-sure be good . . . because-er-there-er-er-a cause I-er-I-uh-I've got a-a one of the-er-sei-----er-er-things coming on and-and-and I could really-er-use some help so if somebody would-er-give me a little h-help-uh-er-er-er-er-er c-could somebody-er-er-help-er-uh-uh-uh(choking sounds) . . . . I'm gonna die-er-er-I'm . . . gonna die-er-help-er-er-seizure-er-[chokes, then quiet].

The experimenter began timing the speed of the real subject's response at the beginning of the victim's speech. Informed judges listening to the tape have

[1] To test whether the order in which the subjects spoke in the first discussion round significantly affected the subjects' speed of report, the order in which the subjects spoke was varied (in the six-person group). This had no significant or noticeable effect on the speed of the subjects' reports.

estimated that the victim's increasingly louder and more disconnected ramblings clearly represented a breakdown about 70 seconds after the signal for the victim's second speech. The victim's speech was abruptly cut off 125 second after this signal, which could be interpreted by the subject as indicating that the time allotted for that speaker had elapsed and the switching circuits had switched away from him. Times reported in the results are measured from the start of the fit.

Group Size Variable. The major independent variable of the study was the number of other people that the subject believed also heard the fit. By the assistant's comments before the experiment, and also by the number of voices heard to speak in the first round of the group discussion, the subject was led to believe that the discussion group was one of three sizes: either a two-person group (consisting of a person who would later have a fit and the real subject), a three-person group (consisting of the victim, the real subject, and one confederate voice), or a six-person group (consisting of the victim, the real subject, and four confederate voices). All the confederates' voices were tape-recorded.

Variations in Group Composition. Varying the kind as well as the number of bystanders present at an emergency should also vary the amount of responsibility felt by any single bystander. To test this, several variations of the three-person group were run. In one three-person condition, the taped bystander voice was that of a female, in another a male, and in the third a male who said that he was a premedical student who occasionally worked in the emergency wards at Bellevue hospital.

In the above conditions, the subjects were female college students. In a final condition males drawn from the same introductory psychology subject pool were tested in a three-person female-bystander condition.

Time to Help. The major dependent variable was the time elapsed from the start of the victim's fit until the subject left her experimental cubicle. When the subject left her room, she saw the experimental assistant seated at the end of the hall, and invariably went to the assistant. If 6 minutes elapsed without the subject having emerged from her room, the experiment was terminated.

As soon as the subject reported the emergency, or after 6 minutes had elapsed, the experimental assistant disclosed the true nature of the experiment, and dealt with any emotions aroused in the subject. Finally the subject filled out a questionnaire concerning her thoughts and feelings during the emergency, and completed scales of Machiavellianism, anomie, and authoritarianism (Christie, 1964), a social desirability scale (Crowne and Marlowe, 1964), a social respon-

sibility scale (Daniels and Berkowitz, 1964), and reported vital statistics and socioeconomic data.

RESULTS

Plausibility of Manipulation

Judging by the subjects' nervousness when they reported the fit to the experimenter, by their surprise when they discovered that the fit was simulated, and by comments they made during the fit (when they thought their microphones were off), one can conclude that almost all of the subjects perceived the fit as real. There were two exceptions in different experimental conditions, and the data for these subjects were dropped from the analysis.

Effect of Group Size on Helping

The number of bystanders that the subject perceived to be present had a major effect on the likelihood with which she would report the emergency (Table 1). Eighty-five percent of the subjects who thought they alone knew of the victim's plight reported the seizure before the victim was cut off, only 31% of

table 1
Effects of Groups Size on Likelihood and Speed of Response

Group Size	N	% Responding by End of Fit	Time in Sec.	Speed Score
2 (S and victim)	13	85	52	.87
3 (S, victim, and 1 other)	26	62	93	.72
6 (S, victim, and 4 others)	13	31	166	.51

Note.—p value of differences: $\chi^2 = 7.91$, $p < .02$; $F = 8.09$, $p < .01$, for speed scores.

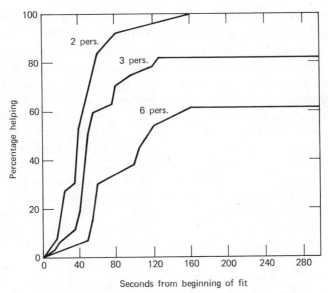

figure 1

Cumulative distributions of helping responses.

those who thought four other bystanders were present did so.

Every one of the subjects in the two-person groups, but only 62% of the subjects in the six-person groups, ever reported the emergency. The cumulative distributions of response times for groups of different perceived size (Figure 1) indicates that, by any point in time, more subjects from the two-person groups had responded than from the three-person groups, and more from the three-person groups than from the six-person groups.

Ninety-five percent of all the subjects who ever responded did so within the first half of the time available to them. No subject who had not reported within 3 minutes after the fit ever did so. The shapes of these distributions suggest that had the experiment been allowed to run for a considerably longer

time, few additional subjects would have responded.

Speed of Response

To achieve a more detailed analysis of the results, each subject's time score was transformed into a "speed" score by taking the reciprocal of the response time in seconds and multiplying by 100. The effect of this transformation was to de-emphasize differences between longer time scores, thus reducing the contribution to the results of the arbitrary 6-minute limit on scores. A high speed score indicates a fast response.

An analysis of variance indicates that the effect of group size is highly significant ($p < .01$). Duncan multiple-range tests indicate that all but the two- and three-person groups differ significantly from one another ($p < .05$).

Victim's Likelihood of Being Helped

An individual subject is less likely to respond if he thinks that others are present. But what of the victim? Is the inhibition of the response of each individual strong enough to counteract the fact that with five onlookers there are five times as many people available to help? From the data of this experiment, it is possible mathematically to create hypothetical groups with one, two, or five observers.[2] The calculations indicate that the victim is about equally likely to get help from one bystander as from two. The victim is considerably more likely to have gotten help from one or two observers than from five during the first minute of the fit. For instance, by 45 seconds after the start of the fit, the victim's chances of having been helped by the single bystanders were about 50%, compared to none in the five observer condition. After the first minute, the likelihood of getting help from at least one person is high in all three conditions.

[2]The formula for the probability that at least one person will help by a given time is $1 - (1 - P)N$ where n is the number of observers and P is the probability of a single individual (who thinks he is one of n observers) helping by that time.

Effect of Group Composition on Helping the Victim

Several variations of the three-person group were run. In one pair of variations, the female subject thought the other bystander was either male or female; in another, she thought the other bystander was a premedical student who worked in an emergency ward at Bellevue hospital. As Table 2 shows, the variations in sex and medical competence of the other bystander had no important or detectable affect on speed of response. Subjects responded equally frequently and fast whether the other bystander was female, male, or medically experienced.

Sex of the Subject and Speed of Response

Coping with emergencies is often thought to be the duty of males, especially when females are present, but there was no evidence that this was the case in this study. Male subjects responded to the emergency with almost exactly the same speed as did females (Table 2).

Reasons for Intervention or Nonintervention

After the debriefing at the end of the experiment each subject was given a

table 2

Effects of Group Composition on Likelihood and Speed of Response[a]

Group Composition	N	% Responding by End of Fit	Time in Sec.	Speed Score
Female S, male other	13	62	94	74
Female S, female other	13	62	92	71
Female S, male medic other	5	100	60	77
Male S, female other	13	69	110	68

[a]Three-person group, male victim.

15-item checklist and asked to check those thoughts which had "crossed your mind when you heard Subject 1 calling for help." Whatever the condition, each subject checked very few thoughts, and there were no significant differences in number or kind of thoughts in the different experimental groups. The only thoughts checked by more than a few subjects were "I didn't know what to do" (18 out of 65 subjects), "I thought it must be some sort of fake" (20 out of 65), and "I didn't know exactly what was happening" (26 out of 65).

It is possible that subjects were ashamed to report socially undesirable rationalizations, or, since the subjects checked the list *after* the true nature of the experiment had been explained to them, their memories might have been blurred. It is our impression, however, that most subjects checked few reasons because they had few coherent thoughts during the fit.

We asked all subjects whether the presence or absence of other bystanders had entered their minds during the time that they were hearing the fit. Subjects in the three- and six-person groups reported that they were aware that other people were present, but they felt that this made no difference to their own behavior.

Individual Difference Correlates of Speed of Report

The correlations between speed of report and various individual differences on the personality and background measures were obtained by normalizing the distribution of report speeds within each experimental condition and pooling these scores across all conditions ($n = $ 62–65). Personality measures showed no important or significant correlations with speed of reporting the emergency. In fact, only one of the 16 individual difference measures, the size of the community in which the subject grew up, correlated ($r = -.26$, $p < .05$) with the speed of helping.

DISCUSSION

Subjects, whether or not they intervened, believed the fit to be genuine and serious. "My God, he's having a fit," many subjects said to themselves (and were overheard via their microphones) at the onset of the fit. Others gasped or simply said "Oh." Several of the male subjects swore. One subject said to herself, "It's just my kind of luck, something has to happen to me!" Several subjects spoke aloud of their confusion about what course of action to take, "Oh God, what should I do?"

When those subjects who intervened stepped out of their rooms, they found the experimental assistant down the hall. With some uncertainty, but without panic, they reported the situation. "Hey, I think Number 1 is very sick. He's having a fit or something." After ostensibly checking on the situation, the experimenter returned to report that "everything is under control." The subjects accepted these assurances with obvious relief.

Subjects who failed to report the emergency showed few signs of the apathy and indifference thought to characterize "unresponsive bystanders." When the experimenter entered her room to terminate the situation, the subject often asked if the victim was "all right." "Is he being taken care of?" "He's all right isn't he?" Many of these subjects showed physical signs of nervousness; they often had trembling hands and sweating palms. If anything, they seemed more emotionally aroused than did the subjects who reported the emergency.

Why, then, didn't they respond? It is our impression that nonintervening subjects had not decided *not* to respond. Rather they were still in a state of indecision and conflict concerning whether to respond or not. The emotional behavior of these nonresponding subjects was a sign of their continuing conflict, a conflict that other subjects resolved by responding.

The fit created a conflict situation of the avoidance-avoidance type. On the one hand, subjects worried about the guilt and shame they would feel if they did not help the person in distress. On the other hand, they were concerned not to make fools of themselves by overreacting, not to ruin the ongoing experiment by leaving their intercom, and not to destroy the anonymous nature of the situation which the experimenter had earlier stressed as important. For subjects in the two-person condition, the obvious distress of the victim and his need for help were so important that their conflict was easily resolved. For the subjects who knew there were other bystanders present, the cost of not helping was reduced and the conflict they were in more acute. Caught between the two negative alternatives of letting the victim continue to suffer or the costs of rushing in to help, the nonresponding bystanders vacillated between them rather than choosing not to respond. This distinction may be aca-

demic for the victim, since he got no help in either case, but it is an extremely important one for arriving at an understanding of the causes of bystanders' failures to help.

Although the subjects experienced stress and conflict during the experiment, their general reactions to it were highly positive. On a questionnaire administered after the experimenter had discussed the nature and purpose of the experiment, every single subject found the experiment either "interesting" or "very interesting" and was willing to participate in similar experiments in the future. All subjects felt they understood what the experiment was about and indicated that they thought the deceptions were necessary and justified. All but one felt they were better informed about the nature of psychological research in general.

Male subjects reported the emergency no faster than did females. These results (or lack of them) seem to conflict with the Berkowitz, Klanderman, and Harris (1964) finding that males tend to assume more responsibility and take more initiative than females in giving help to dependent others. Also, females reacted equally fast when the other bystander was another female, a male, or even a person practiced in dealing with medical emergencies. The ineffectiveness of these manipulations of group composition cannot be explained by general insensitivity of the speed measure, since the group-size variable had a marked effect on report speed.

It might be helpful in understanding this lack of difference to distinguish two general classes of intervention in emergency situations: direct and reportorial. Direct intervention (breaking up a fight, extinguishing a fire, swimming out to save a drowner) often requires skill, knowledge, or physical power. It may involve danger. American cultural norms and Berkowitz's results seem to suggest that males are more responsible than females for this kind of direct intervention.

A second way of dealing with an emergency is to report it to someone qualified to handle it, such as the police. For this kind of intervention, there seem to be no norms requiring male action. In the present study, subjects clearly intended to report the emergency rather than take direct action. For such indirect intervention, sex or medical competence does not appear to affect one's qualifications or responsibilities. Anybody, male or female, medically trained or not, can find the experimenter.

In this study, no subject was able to tell how the other subjects reacted to the fit. (Indeed, there were no other subjects actually present.) The effects of group size on speed of helping, therefore, are due simply to the perceived presence of others rather than to the influence of their actions. This means that the experimental situation is unlike emergencies, such as a fire, in which bystanders interact with each other. It is, however, similar to emergencies, such as the Genovese murder, in which spectators knew others were also watching but were prevented by walls between them from communication that might have counteracted the diffusion of responsibility.

The present results create serious difficulties for one class of commonly given explanations for the failure of bystanders to intervene in actual emergencies, those involving apathy or indifference. These explanations generally assert that people who fail to intervene are somehow different in kind from the rest of us, that they are "alienated by industrialization," "dehumanized by urbanization," "depersonalized by living in the cold society," or "psychopaths." These explanations serve a dual function for people who adopt them. First, they explain (if only in a nominal way) the puzzling and frightening problem of why people watch others die. Second, they give individuals reason to deny that they too might fail to help in a similar situation.

The results of this experiment seem to indicate that such personality variables may not be as important as these explanations suggest. Alienation, Machiavellianism, acceptance of social responsibility, need for approval, and authoritarianism are often cited in these explanations. Yet they did not predict the speed or likelihood of help. In sharp contrast, the perceived number of bystanders did. The explanation of bystander "apathy" may lie more in the bystander's response to other observers than in presumed personality deficiencies of "apathetic" individuals. Although this realization may force us to face the guilt-provoking possibility that we too might fail to intervene, it also suggests that individuals are not, of necessity, "noninterveners" because of their personalities. If people understand the situational forces that can make them hesitate to intervene, they may better overcome them.

SUMMARY

Ss overheard an epileptic seizure. They believed either that they alone heard the emergency, or that 1 or 4 unseen others were also present. As predicted the presence of other bystanders reduced the individual's feelings of personal responsibility and lowered his speed of reporting ($p < .01$). In groups of size 3, males reported no faster than females, and females reported no slower when the 1 other bystander was a male rather than a female. In general, personality and background measures were not predictive of helping. Bystander inaction in real-life emergencies is often explained by "apathy," "alienation," and "anomie." This experiment suggests that the explanation may lie more in the bystander's response to other observers than in his indifference to the victim.

REFERENCES

Aronfreed, J. "The origin of self-criticism." *Psychological Review,* 1964, **71,** 193–219.

Berkowitz, L., Klanderman, S., and Harris, R. "Effects of experimenter awareness and sex of subject on reactions to dependency relationships," *Sociometry,* 1964, **27,** 327–329.

Christie, R. "The prevalence of machiavellian orientations." Paper presented at the meeting of the American Psychological Association, Los Angeles, 1964.

Crowne, D., and Marlowe, D. *The Approval Motive.* New York: Wiley, 1964.

Daniels, L., and Berkowitz, L. "Liking and response to dependency relationships." *Human Relations,* 1963, **16,** 141–148.

Milgram, S., and Hollander, P. "Murder they heard," *Nation,* 1964, **198,** 602–604.

Miller, N., and Dollard, J. *Social Learning and Imitation.* New Haven: Yale University Press, 1941.

Rosenthal, A. M. *Thirty-eight Witnesses.* New York: McGraw-Hill, 1964.

Whiting, J. W. M., and Child, I. *Child Training and Personality.* New Haven: Yale University Press, 1953.

12.5 Small Group Dialogue and Discussion: An Approach to Police-Community Relationships

ROBERT L. BELL, SIDNEY E. CLEVELAND, PHILIP G. HANSON, AND WALTER E. O'CONNELL

INTRODUCTION AND BACKGROUND TO THE PROBLEM

There seems to be general agreement that the most pressing domestic problem confronting the country is that of rising urban tension. To a large degree urban tension, "The Urban Crisis," means increased friction between the city police force and segments of the black community. Resentments and frustrations nursed for years by the previously complacent black community find a target in the urban police force. Since, for many members of minority groups, the police represent the status quo and all that is feared and hated in white society, it is the police officer who becomes the object of hostility whether deserved or not by his actual behavior. The President's Riot Commission report by the National Advisory Commission on Civil Disorders found that "almost invariably the incident that ignites disorder arises from police action."[1] Usually, the police action giving rise to the outbreak of violence is in itself routine and innocuous, but for the black community it may symbolize a long history of injustice and legitimate grievances.

Until May 1967, Houston, Texas, the

[1] U. S. Riot Commission, Report of the National Advisory Commission on Civil Disorders, (Kerner Commission), N.Y., Bantam Books, 1968.

Reprinted by special permission of the authors and the *Journal of Criminal Law, Criminology and Police Science*, (Northwestern School of Law), © 1969, Volume 60, No. 2, pp. 242–246.

nation's sixth largest city, had enjoyed relative calm as far as any widespread racial disturbance was concerned. Although numerous incidents involving blacks and the police pointed to rising tensions, no overt violence had erupted. But on May 16–17, 1967, four hours of gunfire occurred between the police and students at Texas Southern University, a predominantly Negro institution in Houston. One officer was killed by a bullet of undetermined origin. Student rooms and belongings were ransacked by the police, ostensibly in search of hidden weapons.

This incident alerted the city administration to the fact that a racial crisis was at hand. Many feared another Watts or Detroit. A study by Justice,[2] a psychologist, and an assistant to the mayor for race relations, found that Negro antagonism toward the police had increased significantly over the pre-TSU riot period. A team of interviewers had studied attitudes of 1798 Negroes from 22 different neighborhoods, concerning jobs, wages, the police, etc., prior to the TSU outbreak. Following the TSU incident the study was repeated in the same neighborhoods to assess attitudinal change. Results of these surveys indicated a significant rise in hostile feelings toward the police following the outbreak of violence.

The results of these surveys were influential in persuading the city administration that some type of educational or advisory program was needed to reduce existing tensions within the city. Originally the city advisors had in mind

a lecture series on community relations to be presented to the police.

However a lecture series seemed inappropriate and ineffective since it provided no opportunity for badly needed exchange between the police and community. Instead, a small group interaction program involving police and community members seemed more promising, since such a program would provide full opportunity for exchange of attitudes between officers and the participating community. Dr. Melvin P. Sikes,[3] then a clinical psychologist on the staff at the Houston VA Hospital, was asked to organize such a program.

Human Relations Training for Police and Community. The model employed to serve as a structural and procedural guideline in devising the police-community program was that provided by the Houston VA Hospital Human Relations Training Laboratory.[4] This Laboratory also supplied the police-community program with a majority of the professional group leaders with experience in human relations training.

The Houston VA Human Relations Training Laboratory applies the concepts and techniques of "T" group theory and sensitivity training to the problems of psychiatric patients. Departing from the traditional psychiatric treatment emphasis on the medical model, the Laboratory stresses a learning approach in the acquisition of new techniques to solve

[2]Justice, B., Detection of Potential Community Violence. Dissemination document-Grant 207 (5.044) Office of Law Enforcement Assistance, U.S. Department of Justice, Washington, D.C., 1968.

[3]Sikes, M. P. and Cleveland, S. E., "Human relations training for police and community," *American Psychologist,* 1968, **23**, 766–769.
[4]Hanson, P. G., Rothaus, P., Johnson, D. L., and Lyle, F. A. "Autonomous groups in human relations training for psychiatric patients," *Journal of Applied Behavioral Science,* **2**, 305–323 (1966).

problems in living. Human relations training techniques have also been applied to the successful resolution of conflict between union and management groups, in community interracial strife, and in industry to cope with departmental friction. Accordingly, it was felt that the human relations approach would be suitable for dealing with police-community relationships.

Program Design and Format. A series of human relations training laboratories were devised, each lasting six weeks with about 200 police officers and an equal number of community members attending. The officers and citizens meet for three hours once a week over the six-week period. Approximately 40 officers and community members are scheduled for a three-hour session each of the five work days. These officers and citizens are further divided into three smaller groups meeting concurrently. The program will continue until the entire police force of approximately 1400 men has been involved.

Meetings are held in the neighborhood community centers and at the Police Academy. An effort is made to recruit a cross-section of the community but especially representatives of minority and poverty groups and dissidents. Most of the officers attend in uniform but outside their regular tour of duty and receive extra salary from the city for their 18 hours of participation. Police are required to attend, but community participation is, of course, voluntary. Doctoral level psychologists with experience in human relations training and group therapy serve as group leaders. Financial support is entirely from private and local sources.

Fees for the psychologists' professional services and funds for incidental expenses supporting the program are met through voluntary contributions from Houston business and industry. The cost for one six-week session is approximately $20,000 with half this amount going to police salaries.

The major goals of the program are to promote a cooperative relationship between the community and police and to effect greater mutual respect and harmony. In order to achieve these ends the group sessions are structured so as to have the police and community first examine the damaging stereotypes they have of each other; second, to consider the extent to which these stereotypes affect their attitudes, perceptions and behaviors toward each other; third, to look at the ways in which each group reinforces these stereotypes in the eyes of the other; and fourth, to develop a cooperative, problem-solving attitude directed toward resolving differences and reducing conflict to a level where both groups can work together constructively.

In the initial session police and community first meet separately to develop images of their own group and the other group. This strategy was taken from an exercise used successfully by Blake, Mouton, and Sloma[5] in resolving conflict in a union-management situation. Police are asked to develop a list of statements as to how they see themselves and a second list of their view of the community. Community members do likewise. The groups are then brought

[5] Blake, R. R., Mouton, Jane S., and Sloma, R. L. "The union-management intergroup laboratory: Strategy for resolving intergroup conflict," *The Journal of Applied Behavioral Science*, Vol. 1, #1, 1965.

together and these images compared and discussed. Subsequent sessions are devoted to correction of distortions identified in these lists, diagnosis of specific areas of disagreement, identification of key issues and sources of friction and, finally, devising methods for conflict resolution.

The resulting self and other images developed by the police and community groups are far too numerous to be listed. However, a summary of some of the more salient images serves to present the flavor of this aspect of the sessions.

Police Self-Image. As officers we are ethical, honest, physically clean and neat in appearance, dedicated to our job, with a strong sense of duty. Some officers are prejudiced, but they are in the minority, and officers are aware of their prejudice and lean over backwards to be fair. We are a close knit, suspicious group, distrustful of outsiders. We put on a professional front; hard, calloused, and indifferent, but underneath we have feelings. We treat others as nicely as they will let us. We are clannish, ostracized by the community, used as scapegoats, and under scrutiny even when off duty trying to enjoy ourselves. We are the blue minority.

Police Image of Community. Basically the public is cooperative and law-abiding, but uninformed about the duties, procedures, and responsibility of the police officer. The upper class, the rich, support the police, but feel immune to the law and use their money and influence to avoid police action against themselves and their children. The middle class support the police and are more civic-minded than upper or lower classes.

The major share of police contact with the middle class is through traffic violations. The lower class has the most frequent contact with the police and usually are uncooperative as witnesses or in reporting crime. They have a different sense of values, live only for today and do not plan for tomorrow. As police officers we see the Houston Negro in two groups, (1) Negro—industrious, productive, moral, law-abiding, and not prone to violence; (2) "nigger"—lazy, immoral, dishonest, unreliable, and prone to violence.

Community Self-Image. We lack knowledge about proper police procedures and do not know our rights, obligations, and duties in regard to the law. There is a lack of communication among social, geographical, racial, and economic segments of the community. We do not involve ourselves in civic affairs as we should, and we have a guilty conscience about the little crimes (traffic violations) we get away with, but are resentful when caught. We relate to the police as authority figures, and we feel uncomfortable around them. The black community feels itself second class in relation to the police. The majority of the community is law-abiding, hard working, pays taxes, is honest and reliable.

Community Image of Police. Some police abuse their authority, act as judge, jury, and prosecutor, and assume a person is guilty until proven innocent. They are too often psychologically and physically abusive, name-calling, handle people rough, and discriminate against blacks in applying the law. Police are cold and mechanical in performance of their duties. We expect them to be perfect, to make no mistakes and to set the standard for behavior. The police see the world only through their squad car windshield and are walled off from the community. Our initial reaction when we see an officer is "blue."

PROGRAM EVALUATION

In an attempt to determine to what extent this community action program was achieving its stated goal of increased mutual respect and harmony between police and citizens, a number of procedures were followed.

Police and community participants were asked to complete a questionnaire at the close of their final session, inquiring about their reaction to the program. Results from about 800 police and 600 citizens completing the program indicate enthusiastic acceptance by the participating community and grudging to moderately good acceptance by the police. For example, 93 percent of the community rate the program either Good, Very Good, or Excellent, only seven percent rating it Poor. For the police, 85 percent rate it between Good and Excellent with 15 percent rating it Poor. However, where 18 percent of the community rate it Excellent, only four percent of the police do so. Moreover, 65 percent of the community say that as a result of the program their feelings about the police are more positive, 31 percent unchanged, and 4 percent more negative. For the police, 37 percent reflect a more positive community attitude, 61 percent report no change, and 2 percent more negative.

For the community the most frequently expressed reaction to the pro-

gram is increased recognition and appreciation of the police officer as an individual and a human being rather than a member of an undifferentiated group, "the blue minority." Citizens most often comment on their tendency to dehumanize the police and see them as unfeeling, authoritarian robots, rather than real people who sometimes make honest mistakes, get angry, or behave unwisely.

For their part the police most often record a sense of gratification that as a result of the program the community gains some appreciation of the policeman's role, what he can do and cannot do. The police seem surprised as to how misinformed the public is regarding police procedures and limits of authority.

Later evaluation of the program included administration of a questionnaire especially designed to assess attitudes about the poor, minority groups and the community at large.[6] As might be expected, the police and black community differ widely on social issues involving poverty and minority groups as measured by this questionnaire, with the police scoring at the high prejudice end of the scale. However, participation in this program serves to attenuate to a significant degree the extreme attitudes held by the police. There is one exception to this latter statement in that one police group *increased* their prejudice scores following participation in the program. However, these officers were tested the week following the fracas between Chi-

---

[6] This questionnaire is called the Community Attitude Survey (CAS). It contains 38 items requiring response to each statement on a six point continuum from strongly agree to strongly disagree. The scale yields a General Prejudice score and four sub-scores touching on special aspects of community relations.

cago police and demonstrators at the Democratic National Convention when feelings were running high among the police about the issue of "law and order."

Problems Inherent in a Community Action Program. This police-community program did not proceed evenly or without problems. Consistent community participation has been a major problem. Although recruitment of the community was effected through announcements by the news media, social clubs, churches, and even door-to-door solicitation, citizen cooperation often failed to materialize. Inconsistent community participation disrupted the continuity of group discussions. Many citizens turned out for the initial session, largely to express grievances and blow-off steam. Having accomplished this, they often did not return for subsequent sessions.

Extremist groups from the community attended, often for other than constructive purposes. For example, an organized group of black militants descended on one meeting and engaged the police in a heated recitation of complaints and verbal abuse. However, when the group leader finally called a halt to the harassment and suggested the group now consider possible constructive solutions to these complaints, the militants abruptly departed. These hit-and-run tactics employed by some community participants were especially difficult to control.

Extreme right-wing white political group members came apparently only to maintain the status quo, "Support their local police" and take copious notes for the purpose of publishing slanted and captious articles about the program. For example, a local newspaper with strong right-wing political bias published an article describing the "brain washing" techniques, self-criticism and confessional approaches used by the "Communist Revolution" and left the reader with the impression that this police-community program was similar in goals and procedure.

Some of the police were not sympathetic either to the goals or substance of the program and attempted to sabotage the program where possible, by refusing to participate in the group discussions or by adopting a hostile and belligerent stance. Both the police and community tended to be suspicious of the program and its "real" intent and purpose.

Retention of effective group leaders for the program proved difficult. Leaders for a program such as this need personal attributes that would tax the resources of an Eagle Scout, including having poise and maturity, being experienced and skillful in handling difficult groups, intuitive, inventive, and resourceful. A third of the group leaders were, themselves, minority group members, and these leaders appeared to enjoy a decided advantage in working with both the police and community. But attrition among group leaders was high. Many reasons were given for resigning from the program, chief among them being the emotionally exhausting strain of the sessions and lack of visible reward from either police or community in the form of recognition as to the positive contribution made by the program. The repetitious and monotonous character of the sessions was another frequently mentioned detraction. Each six-week session carried a deadly encore of issues already dealt with in preceding laboratories. It was difficult for group leaders to build up interest in still another round of self-righteous accusations by the community and massive denials by the police. Some group leaders withdrew because they could not take the hostility expressed within their group, hostility they assumed to be directed at them personally. These leaders failed to recognize that the hostility, whether expressed by police or community, was not a personal attack on them, but rather for what the leader represented as an agent of change. Experienced leaders were able to interpret this phenomenon to the group and focus their attention on their own resistance to change.

SUMMARY

Has the exposure of 1400 police officers and a corresponding number of community members been worth the time, money, and effort expended? One can point to the fact that there has been no further rioting and neither the asssassination of Martin Luther King, Jr., or Robert F. Kennedy was followed by racial incidents. Houston police characterize 1968 as a "cool" summer in contrast to 1967. Another encouraging sign is that the Mayor's office reports a 70 percent drop in citizen complaints about police behavior for the seven-month period following inception of the program.[7] Also, there are other suggestions of improvements in police-community relations: a white police officer organizes his own group of blacks and whites for continuing discussions in his home; officers stop their squad cars to talk with black people in their neighborhood for no other reason than to meet them.

Despite setbacks in the program and the sometimes contrary results of individual laboratories, the consensus of the participating staff, the city administrators, and the business patrons providing financial support has been cautiously affirmative in proclaiming the program a success. No claim is made that 18 hours of discussion will sweep away years of rancor and distrust. But it is a necessary beginning.

[7] *Op cit.* 2.

12.6 The Physical Environment: A Problem for a Psychology of Stimulation

JOACHIM F. WOHWILL

INTRODUCTION

As a psychologist this writer has been struck by a curious paradox. Psychologists never tire to point out the importance of stimulus factors as a determinant of behavior, and of the role of environmental influences in behavior. Yet, as a group they have had relatively little to say on the important problems relating to man's response to his physical environment. . . . It may be instructive to examine briefly . . . some of the likely reasons for this seeming lack of attention given to these problems by psychologists; our primary aim, however, is to point more positively to some recent developments in the experimental psychology of motivation which appear to have interesting implications for the study of the impact of the physical environment on behavior and for approaches to environmental design.

That child psychologists, personality psychologists, and social psychologists with an environmentalist bias should have neglected the role of the physical environment in behavior is readily understandable. For the most part they have been interested in the interpersonal, social, and cultural aspects of the environment, in line with the prevalent drive theory of motivation, built on the concepts of appetitive and aversive reinforcement, which has featured much of their thinking. According to this conception, it is *people* who administer rewards and punishments; the natural and artificial surroundings in which people live thus have little power to influence behavior. Not surprisingly, this has been less true of those working outside of a stimulus-response reinforcement model, notably within a field-theoretical framework. Yet even here, where the vocabulary of boundaries, barriers and field

Reprinted with slight abridgment from the *Journal of Social Issues*, 1966, **22**(4), 29–38, with permission of the author and The Society for the Psychological Study of Social Issues, a division of the American Psychological Association.

forces might seem to favor attention to variables of the physical environment, primary interest has remained in the analysis of interpersonal interaction, social encounters, and the like.

Turning now to the side of experimental psychology, ever since the appearance in 1949 of Hebb's influential *The Organization of Behavior*, the role of sensory stimulation from the environment, not only for the normal development of perceptual and cognitive functions but for motivational processes as well, has become of increasing concern. Yet, starting from the premise that stimulation is good, indeed essential for the development and maintenance of normal behavior, most of the efforts of workers in this area have been devoted to demonstrating the deleterious effects of drastic reductions in level of stimulation, whether as a short-term condition with human adults (cf. the work on "sensory deprivation," [9]) or as a more prolonged condition of the early experience of animals (e.g., *10*, 1961). Where attempts have been made to enhance the behavioral effectiveness of animals, e.g., their problem-solving ability, by providing for "enriched" stimulus environments, the research has typically started from a straightforward "the more, the better" assumption. The success of such efforts is not surprising, if one bears in mind the impoverished level of stimulation provided by the typical laboratory environment used as the base of comparison for most of these studies, but its relevance to the living conditions under which modern man operates is doubtful.

A recent extension of this stimulus-enrichment approach to the study of "imprinting" in newly hatched chicks, that is, the development of the following response to the mother, is particularly instructive in revealing the psychologists' conception of an optimal set of stimulus conditions. The authors describe the treatment to which the experimental animals were subjected immediately after hatching as follows:

> The complex environment . . . consisted of a black-walled enclosure with random stripes and blotches of white paint. Above was a bank of six 200-W light bulbs which flashed on and off at 1-sec. intervals. Two metronomes produced a constant ticking. A radio, tuned to a local AM station, played constantly at high volume. Every 30 min. *E* stroked each chick's back with a foam rubber brush and with a whisk broom for 15 sec., rang a bicycle bell for 2 min., and gave a gentle puff of air from an air compressor (5, p. 654).

Let it be recorded that this treatment apparently worked wonders on the imprinting response of these chicks, which developed both earlier and much stronger than for chicks who started life amidst more humdrum environmental conditions. Yet this positive result will not be altogether reassuring to some who may see in the treatment described above only a slight caricature of the frenetic bombardment from stimuli of all kinds encountered in certain urban environments. After all, newborn chicks, even of the Vantress Broiler variety used in this study, are not to be equated to human beings, and the imprinting response hardly constitutes a valid model of human behavior and adjustment. Such doubting Thomases could derive support for their skepticism, moreover, by pointing to the case of the typical "culturally deprived" child from the slums, who is apt to grow up under just such conditions of overstimulation, without great profit to his general intellectual development or emotional well being.

A whole host of questions arise at this point: Is there a particular level of stimulation conducive to optimal development? Does patterned stimulation differ in its effects on development from unpatterned (e.g., noise)? Above all, what is the role of meaning (as invested in language and in object stimuli) in modulating the effects of stimulation on development, and what conditions promote the sifting out of meaningful from meaningless stimuli by the child? Though some research with animals has been carried out relative to the first of these questions, the others have remained virtually untouched, so that in the aggregate the evidence available thus far is probably of limited significance for an understanding of the effects of the stimulus conditions characterizing our typical physical environments on the development of the individual.

Once we turn away from the study of the effects of stimulus experience on development, however, we find a considerable body of recent work that is of direct relevance for us, dealing with the stimulus correlates of the arousal of human attention and with human activity involving the seeking out of stimulation. Psychologists have come to recognize what persons in the amusement and recreation industries—to say nothing of observant parents—have known all along: that a large part of the everyday activity of the human (or of the animal, for that matter) has as its aim not to *reduce* unpleasant tensions, e.g., from the hunger or sex drives, but rather to heighten the

level of incoming stimulation, by voluntary exposure to stimulus objects or situations that are novel, incongruous, surprising or complex. Man, it seems, is ever curious, ever eager to explore, and unlike the proverbial cat, appears generally to thrive on such activity.

This is not the place to review the extensive literature in this area, dealing with the motivational and arousal properties of stimulation, or to enter into a discussion of the complex theoretical issues raised by this work (cf. *1, 3, 4, 12*). Let us rather examine its possible relevance to problems of man's response to his physical environment, and some of the questions raised by an attempt to apply such notions to this problem area. We will confine ourselves to a discussion, necessarily oversimplified, of three main questions.

DIMENSIONS OF STIMULATION

What are the chief dimensions of stimulation that are of concern to the student of environmental psychology? Those most frequently discussed by psychologists include simple intensity, novelty, complexity, and temporal change or variation; to these we may add surprisingness and incongruity, which have been more specifically emphasized by Berlyne (*1*). If only in an illustrative sense, all of these can be shown to touch on important aspects of our physical environment. To start with intensity, questions of level of noise and illumination have been of concern to industrial designers, architects and planners for some time, although outside of an industrial context there has been little systematic research on the effects of different levels of auditory or visual intensity on behavior. The importance of *novelty* is well known to observers of that favorite pastime, sightseeing, a facet of behavior which can play an important role in questions of urban design (e.g., the role of San Francisco's cable-cars), as well as in the administration of our natural recreation areas. *Complexity* of stimulation may well be a major factor in differential evaluation of urban, suburban and rural environments, as it is in the response to more particular features of our environment, e.g., samples of modern architecture or highway layouts. *Variation* in the stimulus imput enters into diverse problems in environmental design that in one way or another have concerned the need to reduce boredom or monotony, from the subtle variations in design introduced into the construction of housing a la Leavittown to the layout of highways, e.g., the avoidance of long, straight stretches.[1]

Surprisingness and *incongruity* are likewise of interest to us, notably in architecture and landscape design. As an example, the pleasing effect of surprise in the exploration of a building complex is nicely brought out by Nairn (*8*, p. 33 ff) in his perceptive analysis of the layout of the entrance to the Wellesley College campus. The same author lays a good deal of stress on the role of incongruity, though mainly in a negative sense, i.e.,

[1] Other ways in which the variable of temporal change, as well as of complexity of the stimulus input affect our perception of and locomotion within our geographical environment are brought out succinctly in the paper following this one, by A. E. Parr ["Psychological effects of urbanology," *J. Soc. Issues*, 1966, **22**(4), 39–45]. Many of the points made in that paper are quite apposite to the kind of analysis of the stimulus properties of our environment being presented here.

by bringing out the jarring effect of the juxtaposition of different structures lacking in any relationship to one another. Whether some degree of incongruity may nevertheless serve a positive function (in the sense of heightening our attention, if not necessarily our affective evaluation of a scene) must remain an unanswered question at this time. (We may note, in any event, that some degree of incongruity in our environment is inevitable, if only because architectural styles change—cf. the contemporary look of the area around Harvard Square.)

While it may thus be easy to illustrate the relevance of these "collative" variables (as Berlyne calls them) to our response to the physical environment, systematic research in this area will have to come to grips with the problems of operational definition and measurement of these variables, in situations not permitting their control or manipulation by the investigator. Even in the laboratory air-tight definitions allowing for consistent differentiation of the effects of novelty from surprise, on the one hand, or temporal variation on the other are difficult to formulate. Similarly the measurement of novelty (particularly in the long-term sense) and of complexity poses considerable problems. All of these are of course greatly magnified when dealing with ready-made stimuli taken from the actual physical environment, such as landscapes, or urban scenes. In such a situation it may be necessary to compromise to a certain extent with scientific rigor, but this is no reason to shy away from research in such real-life settings. If it is impossible to manipulate variables independently, their relative contributions can generally still be assessed through techniques of statistical control and multivariate analysis.

A more critical problem is that of the measurement of these variables, in the absence of systematic, controlled manipulation. Here we will have to resort to indirect methods based on ratings or other subjective scaling methods. It is worth noting in this connection, that a recent study (7) utilizing judges' ratings to assess complexity of landscapes, still showed consistent relationships between this variable and the relative interest (i.e., fixation times) of these stimuli. More recent developments in the area of stimulus scaling techniques (11), some of which allow for the construction of a metric scale even with purely subjective judgments, lessen the need for independent, objective measures of the physical stimulus.

THE CONCEPT OF AN OPTIMAL LEVEL OF STIMULATION

A number of psychologists working in this area have advanced an optimal-level hypothesis, postulating an inverted-U shaped relationship between magnitude of stimulation along the dimensions considered above and the arousal value of, interest in or preference for a given stimulus. Except for variables representing continua of stimulus intensity, systematic evidence on this point is actually fairly meager.[2] Nevertheless the concept

deserves our consideration, in view of its patent relevance to man's response to the wide range of stimulation encountered in the physical environment. It ties in directly, furthermore, with Helson's Adaptation-level theory, which represents a much more general framework for the study of the most diverse responses to any stimuli varying along some assumed dimension (cf. 6 and Figure 1). In a nutshell, this theory maintains that for any specified dimension of stimulus variation the individual establishes an AL (adaptation-level) which determines his judgmental or evaluative response to a given stimulus located on that dimension. In particular, with reference to an evaluative response, the principle is that deviations from the AL in either direction are evaluated positively within a certain range, while beyond these boundaries they are experienced as unpleasant. Thus we obtain a function such as the following:

Let us try to apply this hypothesis to a person's choice of a vacation spot. To this end, let us conceive of a hybrid dimension of "closeness to civilization," which probably represents a composite of such variables as intensity, complexity, temporal variation and novelty. Take a person living in a small eastern city, so that his AL may be assumed to be somewhere in the middle of our dimension. Where will he go for his vacation? He may either be drawn to the kaleidoscopic attractions of a big metropolis like New York, or, alternatively, to the restful vistas of Vermont or the Cape Cod seashore. However, in accordance with the notion that beyond a certain range marked discrepancies from the AL are no longer experienced as pleasant or desirable, we may hypothesize that, in the first

[2] As Fiske and Maddi (3, p. 9) note, most of their book is concerned with understimulation, rather than overstimulation, which they identify with stress. But in view of the emphasis given in their own formulation to the concept of an optimal level of activation, their readiness to dismiss the problem of overstimulation as unimportant is difficult to understand.

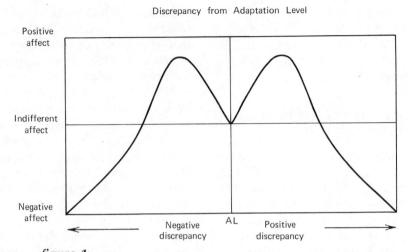

figure 1

Changes in affective response to stimuli as a function of extent of deviation from adaptation level (after Helson, 1964).

case, our vacationer will tend to avoid or be repelled by places representing the more extreme levels of stimulation to be found in the big city (e.g., Times Square at New Years Eve; the subway during rush hour).[3] If, on the other hand, he chooses the open country, he is apt to

[3] Though this proposition might seem to lack surface plausibility, it derives some limited support from the results of a pilot study carried out by two Clark undergraduates, Kenneth Holm and Harlan Sherwin, who interviewed tourists at Penn. Station to obtain their reactions to New York City. Of those who lived in suburban districts, one-third expressed some degree of positive reaction to the New York subways, whereas less than 10% of those residing in either small-town or country areas or in a metropolitan area gave any positive responses. It is also interesting to note that, in another sample of suburbanites, only 40% picked the crowds and noise as the aspects they disliked most about New York City, whereas 80% of the country-, small-town- or city-dwellers chose these aspects. (The suburbanites responded almost as frequently to the *dirt* of the city.)

want a motel room with TV, or to stick to the more populated resort areas.

This would seem to represent a plausible research hypothesis, though there are bound to be exceptions from this norm, e.g., hardy souls preferring a more nearly total isolation from civilization, or on the contrary a more intensive immersion in the stimulation offered by the big city. If so, this would show that not only the AL itself, but the degree of departure from it that would be experienced as pleasurable may vary considerably from one person to the next. This would admittedly make life more complex for the researcher investigating these problems, but would not pose any insuperable difficulties, provided independent measures of these parameters were available. It may also be noted that our model implies that such wilderness-fanciers would be least likely to come from a big metropolitan area; conversely, among those most strongly attracted to the excitement of the bustling metropolis, we should expect to find the visitor from a small town relatively underrepresented.

THE QUESTION OF LONG-TERM ADAPTATION EFFECTS

The concept of adaptation-level itself brings up a further question: What are the long-range effects of exposure to a given environment featured by a particular level of intensity, complexity, incongruity, etc., of stimulation? (In the very nature of the case, if the environment remains constant, novelty and surprisingness effectively cease to be relevant variables.) According to AL theory, the individual's AL will be shifted to a value corresponding more nearly to that environment.[4] This is of course no more than an expression of the fact of adaptation. The question arises, however, whether in spite of the individual's capacity to adapt to an astonishingly wide range of environmental conditions, such prolonged exposure to stimulus environments falling near the extreme of the complexity or intensity dimension, for instance, may not leave its mark nevertheless. That is, it is possible that the arousal value or the subjective evaluation of the stimulus environment by the individual may become assimilated to some

[4] It should be noted that for environmental settings characterized by either very low or very high levels of stimulation, the AL should be expected to fall considerably short of this extreme value, since the effects of exposure to a given environment on the AL are superimposed on factors of a more intrinsic sort, relating to the individual's assumed needs for a certain modal level of stimulation lying within some intermediate range.

normal range, and his behavior become effectively adapted to it; yet more subtle long-term effects on behavior may nevertheless occur. For instance, a commuter subjected morning and evening to rush-hour traffic conditions on the New York subways may come to experience them as no more arousing than would his wife taking a quiet, uncrowded bus ride through suburban streets (though his evaluation of the experience is apt to remain rather more negative). He may even develop the knack of reading and assimilating "all the news that's fit to print," unawares of the din and shoving around him. Yet the cumulative effect of the exposure of these conditions may still leave a residue detectable in his behavior, which might take the form of heightened arousal thresholds, lessened frustration tolerance, or the like, representing the price being paid for this surface adaptation. Or take the child growing up among a steady backdrop of high-intensity TV signals, rattling subway trains and yells from neighbors: he may well adapt to these conditions of noise, but perhaps only by shutting out from awareness much of the input—notably speech—to which in fact he needs to become sensitized for his optimal development.

Admittedly we are operating largely on hunches in our estimates of such long-term behavioral effects of exposure to particular levels of stimulation, but their possible reality can hardly be discounted, especially in view of the considerable evidence in this respect uncovered at the physiological level (cf. 2). There are, furthermore, undoubtedly large individual differences in tolerance of or adaptability to extreme levels of stimulation, . . . [and] much migration behavior may be interpretable as an individual's response to his experienced level of stress emanating from the physical as well as the social environment.

CONCLUSION

In closing, we may express the hope that ultimately attention to questions such as these will lead to the creation of a science of environmental esthetics as a branch of psychology concerned with man's effective response to the qualitative and quantitative features of the world of natural and man-made stimuli surrounding him. Esthetics, to be sure, has not been a particularly flourishing branch of psychology in the past, no more than it has, until recently, represented an area of concern in our social, political, and economic life. But it is perhaps not an entirely fortuitous coincidence that the attention which leaders in our public life have most recently been giving to the beautification of our artificial environment, as well as to the preservation of natural beauty, comes at the very time that the "new look" in the field of motivation is bringing psychologists ever closer to the realm of esthetics. (It is significant that the two books which are the primary sources with respect to this "new look," i.e., Berlyne (1); Fiske and Maddi (3), both include a chapter on esthetics.) The time would thus seem most auspicious for experimental psychologists to take their place alongside their colleagues in social psychology, so-

ciology, geography, architecture, planning, etc., in a broadside attack on the problems facing us in improving the quality of our environment.

REFERENCES

1. Berlyne, D. E. *Conflict, Arousal and Curiosity.* New York: McGraw-Hill, 1960.
2. Dubos, P. *Man Adapting.* New Haven: Yale Univer. Press, 1965.
3. Fiske, D. W. and S. R. Maddi, Eds., *Functions of Varied Experience.* Homewood, Ill.: Dorsey Press, 1961.
4. Fowler, H. *Curiosity and Exploratory Behavior.* New York: Macmillan, 1965.
5. Haywood, H. C., and D. W. Zimmerman. "Effects of early environmental complexity on the following response in chicks," *Percept. Mot. Skills,* 1964, **18,** 653–658.
6. Helson, H. *Adaptation-Level Theory.* New York: Harper-Row, 1964.
7. Leckart, B. T. and P. Bakan. "Complexity judgments of photographs and looking time," *Percept. Mot. Skills,* 1965, **21,** 16–18.
8. Nairn, I. *The American Landscape,* New York: Random House, 1965.
9. Solomon, P., et al. Eds. *Sensory Deprivation.* Cambridge: Harvard Univer. Press, 1961.
10. Thompson, R. W. and T. Schaefer, Jr. "Early environmental stimulation," in *Functions of Varied Experience,* D. W. Fiske and S. R. Maddi, Eds. Homewood, Ill.: Dorsey Press, 1961, 81–105.
11. Torgerson, W. S. *Theory and Methods of Scaling.* New York: Wiley and Sons, 1958.
12. White, R. W. "Motivation reconsidered: the concept of competence," in *Functions of Varied Experience.* D W. Fiske and S. R. Maddi, Eds. Homewood, Ill.: Dorsey Press, 1961, 278–325.

12.7 Dare We Take the Social Sciences Seriously?

KENNETH E. BOULDING

The title of this paper is a rhetorical question, designed to arouse specific expectations in the hearer. It is not couched in the language of science, but the language of oratory. It is indeed as inappropriate to this august gathering as a chorus girl at the first Thanksgiving dinner. I chose it deliberately, however, because it illustrates in its very form and style the problem with which I wish to struggle.

Science is one subculture among many in our society. That is a statement in the rhetoric of science itself. The concept of a subculture is a concept of the social sciences, not of the world of literature and oratory. I would find it hard to preach a fiery sermon or make a rousing political speech addressed to a subculture. It is an ugly word and in some sense an ugly concept. It involves what might

be called a Copernican stance on the part of man, standing off from his own activities and his own society and observing them in Olympian detachment. I once happened to be with a group of anthropologists at a conference on the fourth of July. In the evening the fireworks were beginning to go off in the local park and one of them said, "Let's go down and see the tribal rites." The implications of this remark are profound. The anthropologist stands apart even from his own culture. The ordinary citizen probably never thinks of the fourth of July celebrations as tribal rites, any more than a tribe thinks of tribal rites as tribal rites. The citizen is unselfconscious about his national holidays and his national allegiance. The social scientist begins to see these as special cases of general principles. He participates in

Reprinted from the *American Behavioral Scientist*, 1967, **10**(10), 12–16, and from the *American Psychologist*, 1967, **22**, 879–887, with permission of the author and the editors of the *American Behavioral Scientist*. Copyright 1967 by Sage Publications, Inc.

his own society as a participant-observer and so inevitably begins to have values different from a participant.

All the sciences are themselves a part of the system which they study. All scientists are participant-observers in their own systems. In the physical sciences, and to a somewhat lesser extent in the biological sciences, it is possible for a time to maintain the myth of non-participation, and to suppose that the scientist simply studies an empirical world which is not affected by the fact that he is studying it; even in the physical sciences, however, this myth has had to be abandoned, in the justly famous Heisenberg principle. Increasingly the scientist is creating the universe which he studies. Physicists are producing particles unknown in nature. Chemists have produced elements unknown in nature and innumerable new compounds. The biologist produces new hybrids, new genetic arrangements and may shortly begin to intervene in genetic evolution on a massive scale. Our knowledge of ecology is likely to change the whole ecological system of the earth.

Social sciences are dominated by the fact that the social scientist and the knowledge which he creates are themselves integral parts of the system which is being studied. Hence the system changes as it is studied and because it is studied. There can be no myth of an unchanging universe with the scientist acquiring abstract knowledge about it. Economists are no longer interested in merely observing and predicting the course of the business cycle, they are interested in controlling it, even in abolishing it. The development of polls and sample surveys has profoundly changed the political system and the way in which political decisions are made. Anthropologists unquestionably have contributed substantially to the downfall of empire by revealing the cultural and artistic achievements of so-called primitive peoples. Aesthetically, indeed, in the twentieth century one might almost say that Africa has defeated Greece, and for the first time in human history, as a result of the spread of communication, a world style is emerging. The peace researchers are aiming not merely to understand the international system but to transform it through the explicit understanding of it, as economists have transformed the economy.

If science is a subculture it must have a value system. What characterizes and distinguishes one subculture from another is its value system, that is, a set of legitimated preferences. A subculture consists of a set of people having something in common. They may have certain physical characteristics in common. They may have certain technologies in common. Each person in the set may have a common body of knowledge and skill. There may be a common language, a common vocabulary, and certain common life experiences. All men, however, or nearly all, have two legs, reproduce with approximately the same technology, communicate with each other through some sort of language, have a common age pattern from birth to babyhood, childhood, adolescence, adulthood, old age and death, and grow up in some kind of a kinship structure. What differentiates the cultures and subcultures of mankind is uncommon knowledge,

knowledge which is common to the members of the subculture but which is not common to the rest of mankind, and uncommon values, that is, sets of preferences which members of the subculture have in common which differ from those outside it. Americans like raw power, masculinity, democratic institutions, coffee, hot dogs, and French fries, whereas the Japanese like ceremony, technical skill, green tea, and raw fish.

Every subculture, furthermore, has an ethic, that is to say, a value system for evaluating and legitimating preference systems. It is the possession of a common ethic more than any other characteristic which differentiates one culture from another and even one subculture from another. It is not enough that throughout the subculture there should be a wide preference, shall we say, for beef as over against ham. To a considerable extent, what creates the common preference is an ethic, that is, preference for preference systems in which beef is preferred to ham, and a feeling that those preference systems in which ham is preferred to beef are not themselves to be preferred. When there is an ethic there is a strong tendency for the preferences of different individuals to converge. Whether there is a dynamics of convergence which itself produces the ethic or whether the ethic produces the convergence we need not now inquire.

A scientific subculture is like all others in that its constituent members share certain preferences and likewise an ethic. Again, whether the ethic came first and created the preferences, or whether the preferences, by converging, came to be common and so implied an ethic, is hard to determine. Probably both proc-

esses have been at work. Thus, in its European origins the scientific subculture can well be regarded as a mutation from reformed (and counterreformed) Christian culture, and one which took over many of the ethical preferences of the culture out of which it grew. Without denying the debt of modern science to the Greeks, to Islam, to the Chinese, and to the Jews, and without implying any ethnocentric superiority, for the random element in these processes is strong, the fact remains that it did not grow up as a separate subculture producing a self-sustaining expansion of knowledge either in Athens or in Baghdad, or in Peking or in the medieval ghettoes. Its founding fathers, Galileo, Copernicus, Kepler, Newton, Boyle, and so on, were products of a predominantly Christian culture and themselves for the most part accepted an ethic which was derived from it. More than that, it was Christian culture in its more puritan aspects, a culture in which Luther had challenged successfully traditional outward authority and in which innumerable writers hymned the praises of veracity, simplicity, purity, and the testing of truth in experience. This may be one key to the mystery of why science originated in Europe and not in China, which is still a major mystery of history.

Thus it can be argued that the ethic of the scientific subculture in considerable measure originated outside it. Just as Christianity as a cultural phylum may properly be regarded as a mutation out of Judaism, with some hybrid qualities, but inheriting the ethical system out of which it grew, so science can be regarded as a mutation out of Christianity, again inheriting in part the ethic of its parental matrix. Once a subculture gets under way, of course, it differentiates itself as a social species from its surroundings and it begins to develop ethical systems of its own. Science is no exception to this rule. The idea that the scientific culture is exempt from ethical principles is one which will not stand up to a moment of examination. These ethical principles, however, are fairly simple. There is, in the first place, a high preference for veracity. The only really unforgivable sin of the scientist is deliberate deception and the publication of false results. The career of any scientist who has destroyed his credibility in this way is virtually over.

Along with the preference for veracity goes also a strong preference for truth. These are not the same things. Veracity is the absence of deceit and truth is the absence of error. There is a profound epistemological difference between these two phenomena. The deceiver usually knows that he is deceiving, although there is, of course, the phenomenon of self-deception. The man whose image of the world is in error obviously does not know this, for if he knew it he would not hold this particular view. The testing of error, therefore, is a much more difficult problem than the testing of deceit, and most of the aspects of the technology of science are methods that we might almost call the rituals for the detection of error. Error is detected by the falsification of predictions. This involves the comparison of two images. An inference of the future derived from the basic image of the world which is to be tested is then compared with an image of how the future turned out once it had become past. If there is no disappointment, that is, if the two images

coincide, no error is detected, so the failure to detect error does not necessarily imply that no error exists. If the two images do not coincide, that is, if there is disappointment, then error of some kind is detected. The error might be, of course, in either of the two images and a large part of the technology of science is devoted to insuring that the error is not in the image of the past. This is done by refinement of instrumentation, careful recording, quantitative measurements and so on. There must also be defences against error in inference, that is, in the way in which the image of the future is derived from the basic image of the world. If both these sources of error have been eliminated and there is still disappointment, the scientist is forced to revise his basic model or theory. It has been by this means fundamentally that science has progressed.

It should be pointed out, however, that the method by which the scientific subculture discovers error is not different in essence from the method by which error is detected in the folk culture, that is, in the ordinary business of life. We find our way to a meeting by folk knowledge, not by scientific knowledge. We had an image of where it was in our minds, we had an image of the future in which a meeting was happening, and if we had gone to the wrong place, or the right place at the wrong time, error would very soon have been revealed. It is by this kind of elimination of error that we find our way around town, that we find our way around in our personal relationships, and even how we learn to drive or to ski. The thing which differentiates science from folk culture is not the method of eliminating error, but the complexity of the systems which are imagined, the refinement of the expectations and the refinement of the records by which disappointment is tested.

The social sciences differ from the natural, even the biological sciences, in that there is a good deal of quite accurate folk knowledge about the system which they study, that is, the social system. Our folk knowledge of physical or biological systems is accurate as far as it goes. In finding our way around town there is no necessity to know that the earth is a sphere, and the flat earth, which is the folk image, is quite adequate. Similarly, it is folk knowledge which enables us to procreate children without any necessity for knowing about the details of fertilization and mitosis. In these areas, however, the scientific subculture is sharply differentiated from the folk culture. If we want to navigate a satellite or produce a new drug or a new hybrid, or even explode a nuclear weapon, we do not call in the old wives. In social systems the old wives, or at least their husbands, are called in all the time. Creating a peaceful world, abolishing slums, solving the race problem, or overcoming crime and so on, are not regarded as suitable subjects for scientific technology but are regarded as fields where a pure heart and a little commonsense will do all that is really necessary. Either we have no really explicit concept of social systems at all, or we regard knowledge about social systems as something which can be achieved in the ordinary business of life. In the case of simple social systems, this is true. In the case of complex systems, unfortunately, it is totally false, and many of our failures and difficulties arise from this fact. We have very little concept of

what might be called social astronautics. Social astronauts who have to operate the complex social systems are sent into social space with what is the equivalent of the image of a flat earth.

There is a certain implication in the title of this paper that we do not take the social sciences seriously. This seems like rather a brash assertion when we reflect, for instance, that economics has a good claim to be the second oldest of the sciences (after physics), having reached its fundamental theoretical formulation in 1776 at the hands of Adam Smith at a time when chemistry was still floundering in the phlogiston theory, biology and geology had not gone beyond taxonomy, the theory of evolution was 100 years off, and sociology, psychology, and anthropology as separate sciences were hardly thought of. Economics, furthermore, has had a substantial impact on economic policy, not all of which has been necessarily good, but in which one can detect a continual increase in the sophistication with which the economy is guided. The English Poor-Law of 1834 may have been unnecessary and a false deduction under the circumstances of the time from what were essentially sound principles. The record of free trade is fairly impressive even if it is somewhat ambiguous, and the Keynesian economics has undoubtedly scored resounding victories. One has only to compare the miserable failure of the 20 years after the First World War with the at least moderate success of the 20 years after the Second World War to see what difference a more sophisticated approach to economics and to economic policy has been able to make.

Judged by their impact on society,

the other social sciences do not look so good. The record of industrial psychology, for instance, is not one in which one can put unbounded confidence. It has been naïve about the more subtle aspects of the social system; it is not altogether exempt from the accusation of having corrupted its principles for the sake of its masters (Baritz, 1960). Even here there has been a learning process at work, and the surprises and the disappointments, such as the "Hawthorne effects," have at least detected a certain amount of error and contributed to an overall learning process. Clinical psychology and psychiatry likewise can only be counted as minor successes. There is not much evidence that recovery from mental illness is markedly affected by any kinds of treatment. Psychoanalysis, whatever its virtues, is much too expensive to deal with the mass problem. Our knowledge of the learning and maturation processes in the human being is still extremely primitive. It is quite possible, for instance, that child-rearing practices based on Watsonian behavioral psychology may have actually done a great deal of damage both to individuals and to the society. The alternative methods of Dr. Spock are much more agreeable, but again we really know very little about their overall impact. All the experimentation with animals, important as it is, has not thrown much light on the complexities of the learning process when it involves the use of language and symbols. One may certainly be permitted to doubt whether all the rat psychology of the last 50 years has contributed anything toward the improvement of social policy even in the field of education. This of course is not to say it should not have

been done. In exploring the tree of knowledge every promising limb should be followed at least to the point where its end is clearly in sight. One cannot help the impression, however, that in this matter we have not found the main trunk and that until we do so we will continue to be frustrated.

In even hinting that we do not take the social sciences seriously I have no intention of belittling the large mass of important work which has gone on in them and which continues to go on which has already produced a major impact, as I have suggested in a recent essay (Boulding, 1966). Nevertheless, there are legitimate causes for dissatisfaction, both with the organization of the social sciences, with the amount of work which goes into them, with the quality at least of some of its work, and by the absence of an adequate vision of the future.

The disciplinary and departmental organization of the social sciences at the moment has unquestionably arisen in response to need. There is nothing intrinsically wrong with specialization; it is, indeed, a necessity. The days of the Renaissance man are over and no one could be expected to cover even a small part of the field of the social sciences. Nonetheless, there are good reasons for raising the question as to whether the existing types of specialization and especially the existing departmental structure is not now a handicap rather than a convenience. One reason for raising this question is that the social sciences are not really separated from each other by different levels of systems in their subject matter. Crystallography is separated from physiology by a very sharp difference in the level of the systems which are being studied, even though there no doubt may be fruitful interaction between them. Sociology, economics, political science, and anthropology, however, are not distinguished by any great difference in the level of the systems which constitute their subject matter. In a real sense, they are all studying the same thing, that is, the total social system. The only real distinction of systems levels seems to be the difference between small systems and large. The social psychologist and the psychologist, for instance, are concerned more with the study of small systems, the sociologist and the economist more with the study of larger systems. Even this distinction, however, cuts across the existing fields and departments.

There is, of course, a difference between the disciplines in the social sciences in what might be called the focus of abstraction. The basic abstraction of economics is the phenomenon of exchange, and economics could well be defined as the study of how society is organized through exchange and how commodities and other exchangeables are produced and consumed. In dividing up the study of particular social institutions those tend to go to economics which operate mainly in an exchange environment, such as banks, corporations, businesses, and the exchange aspects of the household as a spending unit. The political scientist focuses on the abstraction of the threat, more or less legitimated. He studies how society is organized through threats, legitimated by political institutions. In apportioning for study particular institutions and organizations the political scientist tends to concentrate on organizations which have

the tax power, and which can obtain revenue by a legitimated threat system. Of these, of course, the national state is the chief, and so the study of the international system as the interaction of national states likewise usually falls in political science. Sociology has a less clear focus of abstraction, but in practice there is a tendency for it to concentrate around those aspects, institutions, and organizations of the social system which are concerned primarily with what I call the integrative system, that aspect of society which deals with status, identity, legitimation, loyalty, love, and their opposites, in which society is organized through the common recognition of status and community. In dividing up the institutions among the disciplines, sociology tends to get things like the family, the church, philanthropic and welfare organizations, informal groups, and so on, which are primarily institutions of the integrative system. Sociologists themselves will probably dispute this characterization, arguing that they deal mainly with the social and organizational structure of all social institutions. In some sense, however, each science can study any particular object from the point of view of its focus of abstraction.

The status of psychology in the social sciences is somewhat confused. It is a loose collection of largely unrelated disciplines, ranging from physiology of behavior on the one hand to clinical psychology and psychiatry on the other. Its relation to the other social sciences is rather like that of physics to chemistry. The person is in some sense an "atom" of the social system, and psychology has the task both of describing the input-output relationships of the person as a black box, but also perhaps of opening the lid of the box to some extent and increasing knowledge about the system which is inside. Social psychology is more clearly a social science. Its basic abstraction is that of role rather than of the person, the role being thought of as a node in a system of inputs from other roles and outputs to other roles. The role occupant does not even have to be a person, it may be a machine or an animal, though roles which are occupied by persons have centrality in the social system which other roles do not.

Anthropology is the aristocrat of the social sciences and somewhat aloof from the others. Traditionally it has studied small societies in their totality which has meant in practice for the most part the study of primitive societies. Its methods are looser, it has less theory, in some ways it stands closer to the humanities than to the social sciences, and acts as a bridge between the two. It has some ambition to study complex total societies. Here, however, it runs into a difficulty that it does not have a methodology complex enough to deal with the complexities of advanced societies.

We should not leave this very brief survey without noting the place of history, geography, and linguistics, and perhaps the field of communications, all of which also stand a little uneasily between the social sciences and the humanities, and perhaps in consequence are undergoing certain transformations. The business of history is to build up an image of the past by the study of the deposits of the past. In a broad sense it straddles all the sciences, as it reaches back into cosmology, palaeontology, archeology, and so on into the history of literate societies. Geography likewise straddles all the sciences, as it studies the relations in space through geomorphology, through plant and animal ecology, through human ecology. Communications science is again a growing field with one foot in art and literature on the one side and coming through linguistics, semantics, into the physiology of speech and hearing. Running like a horizontal line through the whole spectrum we have philosophy, general systems, epistemology, ethics, and so on, which stand on a somewhat different systems level from the particular disciplines.

When one looks at the disciplines in terms of their subject matter it is clear that physiology, for instance, is a study in a very different kind of system from economics, but it is not clear that economics is studying a very different kind of system from sociology or even from political science. One does not have to jump from this proposition to the conclusion that departments of economics, sociology, and political science, and so on, should be abolished, and their respective professional associations merged. Nevertheless, the question must be asked whether the existing structure does not at many points seriously hinder the study of the social system as a totality, and whether it does not operate to prevent the development of that general social theory which the nature of the system itself would seem to require.

It is when we look at the overall information collection processing apparatus of the social sciences, and the theory-testing procedures which depend on this apparatus, that we find the greatest source of dissatisfaction. The situation is best, perhaps, in economics, where in the last 30 years or so we have developed a system of economic statistics and carefully collected sample data, which is at least adequate for gross purposes, such as economic stablilization. Even here, when we come to such problems as the impacts of changing technology of the economy we find that the overall data are very poor indeed and we have to rely on what is essentially journalism or interesting stories about fancy machines. We also do not know enough about the distribution of income or about the impact on distribution of overall government policies at all levels. Compared with the information systems of the other social sciences, however, these are relatively minor defects. A recent work (Bauer, 1966) has spelled out in considerable detail the deficiencies of our present information system, even on the national level.

At the international level the situation is much worse. The information collection and processing apparatus of the international system is not only inadequate, it is corrupt; it is not merely a zero, it is a minus. It is an enormous apparatus designed, in fact, to produce misinformation and to prevent feedback from inadequate images of the world so that the whole organization of the international system becomes organizationally schizophrenic, that is, the existing images of the world are confirmed no matter what happens. Information is collected without any precautions about sampling, it is processed by a system which has strong value filters which tend to filter out anything which challenges the prevailing image of the world. The one possible exception to this gloomy picture is the information apparatus of the United Nations and the related agencies, where at least the representatives of national states are exposed to each other's points of view, and where an international secretariat collects and processes information with at least a world bias. The United Nations, however, is a pitifully small organization, and though we get a lot out of it for what we put in, what we put in is so little that it cannot achieve major changes in the system. It is not surprising, therefore, that the international system is by far the most costly and the most dangerous element in the whole world social system. It costs about $150 billion a year and it produces a positive probability of almost total disaster.

One can cite many examples of policies of government in which the failure to recognize that what was involved was essentially a social system has led if not to disaster at least to gross inefficiency. Flood control is a famous example where the attempt to treat floods as a purely engineering and physical problem instead of as a parameter in the social system has led to what may be disastrous interference with the whole ecological system of the river basins and has built into the system positive probabilities of very large-scale disasters. Floods are not a problem of a river but are indeed part of its normal way of life. They are a problem only to people and the absurd attempt to "conquer" the rivers is likely to lead to increasing disasters as people build on flood plains which cannot be protected from a hundred-year flood.

One could extend the list substantially of areas of social policy where we have made serious mistakes because we have neglected the social systems aspects of the problem, and treat social systems as if they were physical systems. Urban renewal has been thought of in primarily physical terms, and as a result has broken up communities and may easily have worsened the problem of poverty. Road building has been done largely in terms of cement, not in terms of people. Agricultural policy has been designed in terms of commodities, and while its by-products have been favorable, from the point of view of technical development, it has done very little, again, to solve the problem of agricultural poverty. Even welfare policies, like social security, though they are obviously a part of the social system, have not been designed with any overall concepts of the dynamics of society in view, but are designed rather as measures to relieve immediate problems rather than to develop a long-range program of social change. The critics of society, unfortunately, do not seem to be much better informed than its defenders. They have romantic notions about revolutions or about how to change the existing power structure. They tend to preach and lament rather than to develop accurate and testable images of social dynamic processes. It is not surprising that under these circumstances social reform has so often proved disappointing. The prohibition movement is perhaps the most striking example of a large grass roots movement for social reform which failed of its objective and perhaps even made the problem worse than before because of its naïveté about social change. Whether the current reform movements are really much better

only the future will show. They may be luckier than the prohibitionists, but one wonders if they are really more sophisticated.

I have suggested elsewhere almost as a kind of fantasy to illustrate the magnitude of the problem that if we made a study of the "sociosphere," that is, the total sphere of the world social system, with the same degree of seriousness with which we study the atmosphere we would need a world network of social data stations analogous to the network of weather stations. These social data stations would be engaged in a constant collection of data from their local areas by carefully sampled statistically significant methods and would transmit this data to a central agency for processing in the form of maps, indices, distributions, and other statistical images. The need for this is particularly great in the international system. It is great also however in many aspects of social policy. The information processing capability of the modern computer opens up a whole new epistemological field. It is by no means absurd to suppose for instance, that all the records of the human race might be codified in a single computer and then searched to reveal hitherto unsuspected patterns. What we are looking for in all the sciences is repeatable patterns. We can think of the social system as if it were a four-dimensional structure, three dimensions of space and one of time, a structure which may have strong random elements in it but in which also nonrandom patterns can be perceived. In a structure of such complexity, however, the pattern requires complex images, complex inferences, complex predictions, and complex instruments of perception if predictions are to be compared with reality. At the moment neither our theoretical structures, nor our inferences, nor our predictions, nor our perceptual apparatus and instrumentation in the social sciences are in any way adequate to measure up to the complexity of the social system. In this sense we do not take the social sciences seriously. We are using salt spoons to clear away snow drifts and reading glasses to study the structure of molecules. It is not surprising that up to now our results have been ambiguous.

We are still left with two further questions: One, could we take the social sciences seriously, and two, should we do so. I would answer both these questions with a cautious affirmative. There certainly seems to be no reason why our theoretical structure, our inferences, and our perceptual apparatus should prove intractable to improvement, if we set our best minds on the problem and if we were prepared to devote economic resources to the kind of instrumentation which, say, the nuclear physicist now demands. The network of social data stations which I suggested above would probably not cost more than a billion dollars a year and the return for this investment might be enormous in terms of disasters avoided, stable peace established, and development fostered. By and large, the social sciences have not been ambitious enough to want to study the sociosphere as a totality. They have been content with the kind of professional advancement which comes from the adequate processing of small pieces of information. They have not had the larger

vision of the study of the sociosphere as a totality. Economists have perhaps come closest to this but they are handicapped by the limitations of their own abstraction, and as a result have been unable to deal satisfactorily even with such problems as the process of world development.

That we could develop much more realistic images of the sociosphere can hardly be denied. The question whether we should develop such images or how far we should develop them is not so easily answered. We cannot assume in any of the sciences that the development of more realistic and complex images of the world leaves the human value structure unchanged. Our image of value and our image of fact are symbiotic. They are part of a single knowledge structure and it is naïve in the extreme to suppose that they are independent. The view that science or any other knowledge process is simply the servant of existing folk values is doomed to disappointment. Science is corrosive of all values which are based exclusively on simple epistemological processes. The natural sciences have created an image of the world in which ghosts, witches, and things that go bump in the night are so little valued that they have withered and died in the human imagination. Biology has created a world in which the folk ideas of racial purity can no longer survive. Similarly, the social sciences are creating a world in which national loyalty and the national state can no longer be taken for granted as sacred institutions, in which religion has to change profoundly its views on the nature of man and of sin, in which family loyalty and affection becomes a much more self-conscious and less simple-minded affair, and in which, indeed, all ethical systems are profoundly desacralized. There is a deep and seemingly unresolvable conflict between the ethic of science on the one hand, and the ethic of the American Legion, the United States Department of Defense, the Communist Party, the John Birch Society, the Jesuits, and the Jehovah's Witnesses on the other hand. One method by which these conflicts have been resolved in practice has been the remarkable human capacity for holding two incompatible images in the head at the same time. Up to a point these incompatibilities are even creative. It is hard, however, for an astrophysicist to be a Jehovah's Witness or for a biologist to be a racist, and it may become hard for a social scientist to be a good Russian Communist or even a 100% American liberal without strong mental reservations.

The real problem of the impact of the social sciences on the folk culture or even on the literary culture that is dominant in the international system, is that it operates in the same system as that of the folk or literary culture in which it is imbedded. Social science presents much more of a challenge and a problem to the politician than do the physical or biological sciences. In the case of the latter it is possible to maintain the fiction that the scientist should be on tap but not on top. The scientist, in other words, gives power but not values. He is merely a servant of values which are derived from other parts of the social system. In the case of the social sciences this myth is harder to maintain. It is not without reason that southern senators and the

patriotic societies distrust the social scientist, for at this point there may be deep conflict between the values which are created and sustained by folk images of the world and the values which both create the social sciences and are fostered by them. It is true, I think, of all scientists that when they become the servants of power they lose an essential element of the ethic of science itself. Here lies the fundamental dilemma. The power structure pays for the sciences, and if the sciences are to survive in any society they must find a niche in the power structure, either purchasing power or political power. How, however, do we find a niche in the power structure which does not confine or corrupt its occupant? The classical answer to this problem has been the concept of the university, a niche, as it were, specially designed to protect its occupants against the very power structure which has created it. In earlier days the church or the monastery provided such a niche. Whether niches like this can be created within the structure of government itself is one of the unsolved problems of our day. The National Science Foundation, the National Institutes of Health certainly represent an attempt to find an answer to this problem. Whether we should institutionalize the social sciences still further within this framework and create, say, a National Social Science Foundation, as is proposed (Carter, 1966), is a problem which troubles the judgment and consciences of a great many who are concerned. The cloud of the "Camelot" fiasco hangs heavily over the relations between Government and the social sciences, and foreshadows all too clearly the possible shape of things to come. It could well be that the kind of knowledge which would result from taking the social sciences seriously would turn out to be more threatening to traditional values and institutions even than the H bomb and bacteriological weapons. The folk knowledge itself, however, will be quite incapable of dealing with this problem, simply because it would itself represent a social system of enormous complexity. It looks therefore as if only the social sciences themselves could solve the problems which they themselves might create, which looks suspiciously like the principle that another little drink will cure drunkenness. Until we have drunk deeper of this particular spring, however, the dangers of a little learning may be all too apparent.

REFERENCES

Baritz, L. *The Servants of Power.* Middletown: Wesleyan University Press, 1960.

Bauer, R. A. (Ed.) *Social Indicators.* Cambridge: Massachusetts Institute of Technology Press, 1966.

Boulding, K. E. *The Impact of the Social Sciences.* New Brunswick: Rutgers University Press, 1966.

Carter, L. J. "Social sciences, where do they fit in the politics of science?" *Science,* 1966, **154,** 488.

INDEX

515